AF655962

A FIRST COURSE
ON
OPERATIONS RESEARCH
AND
INFORMATION THEORY

For Engineering, Computer Science, Economics, Management, Statistics, Applied Mathematics, MCA courses. Also useful for MSc, MA, IAS (Main Examination) and other competitive examinations. Furthermore, contents of the first few chapters are included in BSc (Honours) Mathematics syllabus of almost every Indian university

A FIRST COURSE ON OPERATIONS RESEARCH AND INFORMATION THEORY

Dr Sanat Kumar Mazumder

Professor
Department of Mathematics
Bengal Engineering and Science Univesity, Shibpur
Howrah 711 103 (WB)

New Central Book Agency (P) Ltd

LONDON
HYDERABAD ERNAKULAM BHUBANESWAR
NEW DELHI KOLKATA PUNE GUWAHATI

REGD OFFICE
8/1 Chintamoni Das Lane, Kolkata 700 009, India
email: ncbapvtltd@eth.net

OVERSEAS
NCBA (UK) Ltd, 149 Park Avenue North, Northampton, NN3 2HY, UK
email: ncbauk@yahoo.com

EXPORT
NCBA Exports Pvt. Ltd, 212 Shahpur Jat, New Delhi 110 049
email: ncbaexports@ncbapvtltd.com

BRANCHES

212 Shahpur Jat
New Delhi 110 049
email: ncbadel@ncbapvtltd.com

House No. 3-1-315, 1st Floor
Nimboliadda, Kachiguda, **Hyderabad** 500 027
email: ncbahydb@ncbapvtltd.com

Shop Nos. 3 & 4, Vinayak Towers
681/B Budhwar Peth, Appa Balwant Chowk
Pune 411 002
email: ncbapune@ncbapvtltd.com

GSS Shopping Complex, 1st Floor
Opposite College Post Office, Convent Road
Ernakulam 682 035
email: ncbaernk@ncbapvtltd.com

Shop No. 15, Bharati Towers, Ground Floor
Forest Park, **Bhubaneswar** 751 001
email: ncbabub@ncbapvtltd.com

Radhamayee Complex (Second Floor)
Opp. SBI, Panbazar, Jaswanta Road
Guwahati 781 001
email: ncbaguwahati@ncbapvtltd.com

A FIRST COURSE ON OPERATIONS RESEARCH AND INFORMATION THEORY • Dr Sanat Kumar Mazumder

© Copyright reserved by the Author

Publication, Distribution, and Promotion Rights reserved by the Publisher

All rights reserved. No part of the text in general, and the figures, diagrams, page layout, and cover design in particular, may be reproduced or transmitted in any form or by any means—electronic, mechanical, photocopying, recording, or by any information storage and retrieval system—without the prior written permission of the Publisher

First Published: September 2013

PUBLISHER AND TYPESETTER
New Central Book Agency (P) Ltd
8/1 Chintamoni Das Lane, Kolkata 700 009

PRINTER
New Central Book Agency (P) Ltd
Web-Offset Division, Dhulagarh, Sankrail, Howrah

COVER DESIGNER
Soumen Paul

TECHNICAL EDITOR
Dipan Roy

PROJECT SUPERVISOR
Abhijit Sen

PROJECT TEAM
Prodip Baidya, Pradip Biswas, and Prabhat Jas

ISBN 978 81 7381 884 4

Price ₹ 325.00

Dedicated to

My Beloved Parents

Contents

Preface

OPERATIONS RESEARCH is a subject which deals with the application of optimisation techniques to complex problems arising in direction and management of men, materials, equipments and money in industry, business, and government to achieve maximum productivity.

The text attempts to provide both theoretical and computational aspects of the subject as well as a number of practical applications. It begins with an overview of operations research followed by fourteen chapters covering every possible aspect of operations research — linear programming, transportation, assignment, travelling salesman and sequencing problems, advanced topics in LP model, sensitivity analysis, integer programming, distance based network techniques, inventory control, queueing theory, project management, decision and game theory, replacement analysis, product scheduling, parametric linear programming, dynamic programming and, finally, a brief introduction to information theory.

In preparing this book, special efforts have been made to make sure that the text is self-contained and that suitable numerical examples and graphical illustrations are provided to aid the readers in understanding the concepts and methods discussed in the treatise. Besides, each chapter contains many exercises, which include (1) simple numerical problems to reinforce the material discussed in the text, (2) problems introducing new material related to that developed in the text and also some exercises for advanced students, (3) multiple choice questions (MCQ) for different competitive examinations.

Any suggestion for the improvement of the book is highly solicited.

My heartfelt acknowledgement goes to the eminent scholar Dr Murari Mitra, Professor and Head of the Department of Mathematics, Bengal Engineering and Science University, Shibpur, and to all faculties and non-teaching staff of the Department of Mathematics, BESU, Shibpur.

I take this opportunity to express my sincere reverence to my parents, parents-in-law for their affection and advice. I also tender my heartfelt compliment to my wife Mrs Suparna Mazumder for her unqualified support and constant inspiration.

In preparing the manuscript, I have consulted a number of standard books on the subject. To all the authors of those books — both Indian and foreign — I express my sincere gratitude.

Gurupurnima
22nd July 2013

Dr Sanat Kumar Mazumder

Overview of Operations Research

The roots of operations research can be traced back many decades, when early attempts were made to apply a scientific approach in the management of organisations. However, the beginning of the activity — called *operations research* — has generally been attributed to the military services early in World War II. Because of the war effect, there was an urgent need to allocate scarce resources to various military operations and to the activities within each operation in an effective manner. Therefore, the British and then the American military management called upon a large number of scientists to apply a scientific approach to dealing with this and other strategic and tactical problems. In effect they were asked to do research on operations. These teams of scientists were the first operations research teams. Their efforts allegedly were instrumental in winning the Air Battle of Britain, the Island Campaign in the Pacific, the Battle of the North Atlantic, and so on.

Spurred on by the apparent success of operations research in the military, the industry gradually became interested in this new field. As the industrial boom following the war was running its course, the problems caused by the increasing complexity and specialisation in organisations were again coming to the forefront. It was becoming apparent to a growing number of people — including business consultants who had served on or with the operations research teams during the war — that these were basically the same problems, but in different contexts than that had been faced by the military. In this way operations research began to creep into industry, business, and civil government.

At least two other factors that played a key role in the rapid growth of operations research during this period can be identified. One was the substantial progress that was made early in improving the techniques available to operations research. After the war, many of the scientists who had participated in operations research teams or who had heard about this work were motivated to pursue research relevant to the field — as a benefit important advancements in the state of the art resulted. A prime example is the simplex method for solving linear programming problems, developed by George Dantzig in 1947. Many of the standard tools of operations research, e.g., linear programming, queueing theory, and inventory theory, were relatively well-developed before the end of the 1950s. In addition to this rapid advancement in the theory of operations research, a second factor that gave great impetus to the growth of the field was the onslaught of the computer revolution. A large amount of computations usually was required to deal most effectively with the complex problems typically considered by operations research. Doing this manually would often be out of the question. Therefore, the development of computers, with their ability to perform mathematical calculations thousands or even millions of times faster than that of a human being, was a tremendous boon to operations research.

As its name implies, operations research involves *research on operations.* This says something about both the approach and the area of applications of the field. Thus, operations research is applied to problems that concern how to conduct and coordinate the operations or activities within an organisation. The nature of the organisation is essentially immaterial, and, in fact, operations research has been applied extensively in business, industry, civil government and agencies, hospitals, so forth.

Therefore, in a particular sense, operations research involves creative scientific research into the fundamental properties of operations. However, there is more to it than this. Specifically, operations research is also concerned with the practical management of the organisation. Thus, to be successful, it must also provide positive understandable conclusions to the decision-maker(s) when they are needed. An additional characteristic that was mentioned in passing is that operations research attempts to find the best or optimal solution to the problem under consideration. Rather than being content with merely improving the status quo, the goal is to identify the best possible course of action. Although it must be interpreted carefully, this *search for optimality* is a very important theme in operations research.

In short, operations research is concerned with optimal decision-making in — and modelling of — deterministic and probabilistic systems that originate from real life. These applications — which occur in government, business, engineering, economics, and the natural and social sciences — are largely characterised by the need to allocate limited resources. In these situations, considerable insight can be obtained from scientific analysis, which is one that is provided by operations research.

The contribution of the operations research approach stems primarily from:

(i) The structuring of the real life situation into a mathematical model and abstracting the essential elements so that a solution relevant to the decision-maker's objective can be sought. This involves looking at the problems in the context of the entire system.

(ii) Exploring the structure of such solutions and developing systematic procedures for obtaining them.

(iii) Developing a solution — including the mathematical theory, if necessary — that yields an optimal value of the system measure of desirability.

Because of the great impact of operations research, professional societies have devoted to this field and related activities have been founded in a number of countries throughout the world. Operations research also has had considerable impact in the colleges and universities. Today most of the major universities in every country offer courses in this field, and many of them offer advanced degrees either in or with specialisation in operations research.

Chapter 1

Relevant Mathematical Background

1.1 MATRICES AND DETERMINANTS

1.1.1 Definition

Given: $m \times n$ real numbers, we arrange them in the form of a rectangular array of m rows and n columns, thus

$$A = \begin{pmatrix} a_{11} & a_{12} & \dots & a_{1n} \\ a_{21} & a_{22} & \dots & a_{2n} \\ \vdots & & & \\ a_{m1} & a_{m2} & \dots & a_{mn} \end{pmatrix} = \left(a_{ij}\right)_{m\times n} \quad \begin{matrix} i = 1,2,\dots,m \\ j = 1,2,\dots,n \end{matrix}$$

Such an array subject to rules of operation defined below is called a *real matrix* of order $m \times n$.

1.1.2 Operations on Matrices

(a) Equality of two matrices — Two matrices A and B are said to be equal, if and only if they have the same order and their corresponding elements are equal.

If $A = \left(a_{ij}\right)_{m\times n}$ and $B = \left(b_{ij}\right)_{m\times n}$, then $A = B$, if and only if $a_{ij} = b_{ij}$ for all i and j.

(b) We can easily verify that —

(i) for any matrix $A, A = A$ (Reflexive property)

(ii) if $A = B$, then $B = A$ (Symmetric property)

(iii) if $A = B$ and $B = C$, then $A = C$ (Transitive property)

Therefore, *equality of matrices* is an *Equivalence relation.*

(c) Addition of matrices — Two matrices are said to be conformable for matrix addition only when they are of the same order, the sum is also a matrix of same order obtained by adding corresponding elements.

AFCOORAIT—1

(i) If $A=(a_{ij})_{m\times n}$, $B=(a_{ij})_{m\times n}$, then $C=A+B=(c_{ij})_{m\times n}$, where $c_{ij}=a_{ij}+b_{ij}$.

(ii) If A, B, C are conformable for addition, then

$A+B=B+A$ (Commutative Law)

$A+(B+C)=(A+B)+C$ (Associative Law)

(d) Subtraction of two matrices — If A and B are two matrices of same order, then the difference $A-B$ is a matrix of same order whose elements are obtained by subtracting the elements of B from the corresponding elements of A.

if $A=(a_{ij})_{m\times n}$, $B=(b_{ij})_{m\times n}$, $D=A-B=(d_{ij})_{m\times n}$, where $d_{ij}=a_{ij}-b_{ij}$.

(e) Multiplication of a matrix by a Scalar — To multiply a matrix A by a scalar λ is just to multiply every element of A by λ. If $A=(a_{ij})_{m\times n}$ and λ is a scalar, then $\lambda A=(T_{ij})_{m\times n}$, where $T_{ij}=\lambda a_{ij}$. The three basic properties are

(i) $(\lambda+\mu)A=\lambda A+\mu A$ (Distributive property)

(ii) $\lambda(A+B)=\lambda A+\lambda B$ (Distributive property)

(iii) $\lambda(\mu A)=(\lambda\mu)A$ (Associative property)

(f) Multiplication of two matrices — Two matrices A and B are said to be comfortable for the product AB if the number of columns in A is equal to number of rows in B. Symbolically, if

$$A=(a_{ij})_{m\times n}\quad B=(b_{jk})_{n\times p},\text{ then } AB=(c_{ik})_{m\times p},$$

where $\sum_{j=1}^{n} a_{ij}b_{jk}=c_{ik}$ (called *inner product*).

Example: $$\begin{pmatrix}0&1&2&3\\3&2&1&0\end{pmatrix}_{2\times4}\begin{pmatrix}0&3\\1&2\\2&1\\3&0\end{pmatrix}_{4\times2}=\begin{pmatrix}14&4\\4&14\end{pmatrix}_{2\times2}$$

In matrix multiplication

(i) The rule $AB=BA$ does not hold good in general.

(ii) From $AB=0$ we should not always conclude that $A=0$ or, $B=0$.

(iii) From $AB=AC$ or, $BA=CA$ we cannot, in general, conclude that $B=C$, even if $A\neq 0$.

(iv) The multiplication of matrices is associative, i.e., let $A=(a_{ij})_{m\times n}$, $B=(b_{jk})_{n\times p}$, $C=(c_{kr})_{p\times q}$, then associative law states $(AB)C=A(BC)$.

(v) Matrix multiplication is distributive w.r.t. addition; let $A=(a_{ij})_{m\times n}$, $B=(b_{jk})_{n\times p}$, $C=(c_{jk})_{n\times p}$, then distributive law states: $A(B+C)=AB+AC$.

1.1.3 The Transpose of a Matrix

(a) The matrix A^T of order $n\times m$ obtained by interchanging rows and columns in a matrix A of order $m\times n$ is called the *transpose of A*.

(b) If A^T and B^T are the transpose of the matrices A and B respectively and if λ is a scalar, then the following relations hold good.

(i) $(A^T)^T=A$ (ii) $(\lambda A)^T=\lambda A^T$ (iii) $(A+B)^T=A^T+B^T$ (iv) $(AB)^T=B^TA^T$ (NOT A^TB^T)

Example: $A = \begin{pmatrix} 1 & -1 & 2 \\ 2 & 1 & 0 \end{pmatrix}$ and $B \begin{pmatrix} 1 & 3 \\ 2 & 0 \\ -1 & 1 \end{pmatrix}$.

Then $AB = \begin{pmatrix} -3 & 5 \\ 4 & 6 \end{pmatrix}$, $(AB)^T = \begin{pmatrix} -3 & 4 \\ 5 & 6 \end{pmatrix}$, $A^T = \begin{pmatrix} 1 & 2 \\ -1 & 1 \\ 2 & 0 \end{pmatrix}$ and $B^T = \begin{pmatrix} 1 & 2 & -1 \\ 3 & 0 & 1 \end{pmatrix}$.

$$\therefore\ B^T A^T = \begin{pmatrix} -3 & 4 \\ 5 & 6 \end{pmatrix}.$$

It is verified that: $(AB)^T = B^T A^T$. [CP 2004]

1.1.4 Special Types of Matrices

Given a square matrix of order $n \times n$,

$$A = (a_{ij})_{n\times n} = \begin{pmatrix} a_{11} & a_{12} & \dots & a_{1n} \\ a_{21} & a_{22} & \dots & a_{2n} \\ \vdots & & & \\ a_{n1} & a_{n2} & \dots & a_{nn} \end{pmatrix}.$$

(i) The square matrix A is said to be a *Diagonal matrix* if $a_{ij} = 0$ for all $i \neq j$ and is denoted by D. Therefore, D is of the form

$$D = \begin{pmatrix} a_{11} & 0 & \dots & 0 \\ 0 & a_{22} & \dots & 0 \\ \vdots & & & \\ 0 & 0 & \dots & a_{nn} \end{pmatrix}.$$

(ii) A square matrix A is said to be a *Scalar matrix* if each element of main diagonal equals a scalar α and all other elements are zero, that is, $a_{ij} = \alpha\ \forall\ i = j$
$= 0\ \forall\ i \neq j$

$$S = \begin{pmatrix} \alpha & 0 & 0 & \dots & 0 \\ 0 & \alpha & 0 & \dots & 0 \\ \vdots & & & & \\ 0 & 0 & 0 & \dots & \alpha \end{pmatrix}.$$

(iii) A square matrix A is called an *Identity matrix* or *Unit matrix* if $a_{ij} = 1\ \forall\ i = j$
$= 0\ \forall\ i \neq j$
and is usually denoted by I when the order need not be emphasised.

$$I = \begin{pmatrix} 1 & 0 & 0 & \dots & 0 \\ 0 & 1 & 0 & \dots & 0 \\ \vdots & & & & \\ 0 & 0 & 0 & \dots & 1 \end{pmatrix}.$$

(iv) A matrix (of any order) is called a *Null matrix* if all the elements are zero. We use a capital letter O to denote a null matrix.

$$O=\begin{pmatrix}0&0\\0&0\end{pmatrix},\ O=\begin{pmatrix}0&0\\0&0\\0&0\end{pmatrix},\ O=\begin{pmatrix}0&0&0\\0&0&0\\0&0&0\end{pmatrix}$$

are null matrices of order $2\times2, 3\times2, 3\times3$ respectively.

(v) A square matrix $A=\left(a_{ij}\right)_{n\times n}$ are called *Upper triangular* and *Lower triangular* matrices according as $a_{ij}=0$ for $i>j$ and $i<j$.

For examples: $\begin{pmatrix}2&4&6\\0&3&5\\0&0&9\end{pmatrix}$ and $\begin{pmatrix}5&0&0\\6&2&0\\3&4&1\end{pmatrix}$ are upper and lower triangular matrices of order 3×3.

(vi) Given a square matrix A of order n, we define $A^2=A\cdot A, A^3=A^2\cdot A, A^4=A^3\cdot A$ and so on, we may write for convenience, $A^0=I$. If $\lambda_0,\lambda_1,\ldots,\lambda_n$ are scalars we may form the matrix expression:

$$\lambda_0 I+\lambda_1 A+\lambda_2 A^2+\cdots+\lambda_n A^n\ (\lambda_n\neq 0)$$

We call this expression a polynomial in the square matrix A of degree n.

Example: *If* $A=\begin{pmatrix}1&2\\-3&0\end{pmatrix}$, *what is the matrix corresponding to the polynomial* $A^2+3A+5I$?

Solution: Here, $A^2=A\cdot A=\begin{pmatrix}-5&2\\-3&-6\end{pmatrix}$.

$$\therefore\ A^2+3A+5I=\begin{pmatrix}-5&2\\-3&-6\end{pmatrix}+\begin{pmatrix}3&6\\-9&0\end{pmatrix}+\begin{pmatrix}5&0\\0&5\end{pmatrix}=\begin{pmatrix}3&8\\-12&-1\end{pmatrix}.$$

(vii) Symmetric and Skew-symmetric Matrices — A square matrix $A=\left(a_{ij}\right)_{n\times n}$ is called *symmetric* if $A^T=A$, i.e., if $a_{ij}=a_{ji}$ for all i and j. On the other hand, A is called *skew-symmetric* if $A^T=-A$, i.e., if $a_{ij}=-a_{ji}$. In a skew-symmetric matrix the elements of main diagonal are all zero since $a_{ii}=-a_{ii}$ or $a_{ii}=0$.

$\begin{pmatrix}a&h&g\\h&b&f\\g&f&c\end{pmatrix},\begin{pmatrix}0&1&2\\1&2&8\\2&8&4\end{pmatrix}$ are symmetric matrices.

$\begin{pmatrix}0&a&b&c\\-a&0&d&e\\-b&-d&0&f\\-c&-e&-f&0\end{pmatrix}\begin{pmatrix}0&a&b\\-a&0&c\\-b&-c&0\end{pmatrix}$ are skew-symmetric matrices.

(a) If A is a skew-symmetric matrix, then A^2 is symmetric.

(b) For any matrix A, the matrices A^TA and AA^T are both symmetric.

(c) A square matrix A can be expressed in a unique way as a sum of a symmetric matrix $P=\frac{1}{2}\left(A+A^T\right)$ and a skew-symmetric matrix $Q=\frac{1}{2}\left(A-A^T\right)$.

1.1.5 Determinants

Let $A = \begin{pmatrix} a_{11} & a_{12} & a_{13} \\ a_{21} & a_{22} & a_{23} \\ a_{31} & a_{32} & a_{33} \end{pmatrix}$ be a square matrix of order three. The determinant of the matrix A

$$= \det A = \begin{vmatrix} a_{11} & a_{12} & a_{13} \\ a_{21} & a_{22} & a_{23} \\ a_{31} & a_{32} & a_{33} \end{vmatrix}$$

$$= a_{11}(a_{22}a_{33} - a_{32}a_{23}) - a_{21}(a_{12}a_{33} - a_{32}a_{13}) + a_{31}(a_{12}a_{23} - a_{22}a_{13})$$

$$= a_{11}\begin{vmatrix} a_{22} & a_{23} \\ a_{32} & a_{33} \end{vmatrix} - a_{21}\begin{vmatrix} a_{12} & a_{13} \\ a_{32} & a_{33} \end{vmatrix} + a_{31}\begin{vmatrix} a_{12} & a_{13} \\ a_{22} & a_{23} \end{vmatrix}$$

[Expansion in terms of the elements of first column]

Similarly, one can rearrange this expansion, grouping it by elements of first row. The following scheme may be helpful for the readers to decide the signs during the expansion in terms of the elements of any row or column $\begin{vmatrix} + & - & + \\ - & + & - \\ + & - & + \end{vmatrix}$.

(a) *Properties*:

(i) The value of a determinant of any order is unaltered if rows and columns are interchanged.

(ii) The interchange of adjacent rows or columns does not alter the numerical value of the determinant but only its sign is changed.

(iii) If any two rows or columns of a determinant of third order are identical the value of the determinant is zero.

(iv) If all the elements of one row or of one column are multiplied by the same constant, the value of the determinant is multiplied by that constant.

(v) If one row or column of a determinant be expressed as a linear combination of the remaining rows or columns, then value of the determinant is zero.

(b) *Minors and Cofactors*: Let $D = \begin{vmatrix} a_{11} & a_{12} & a_{13} \\ a_{21} & a_{22} & a_{23} \\ a_{31} & a_{32} & a_{33} \end{vmatrix} = |a_{ij}|$ be a determinant of third order. By *minor of an element a_{ij} of D* denoted by M_{ij} we mean a second order determinant obtained by deleting from D, the row and column in which that element occurs.

For examples: $M_{21} = \text{minor of } a_{21} = \begin{vmatrix} a_{12} & a_{13} \\ a_{32} & a_{33} \end{vmatrix}$

$M_{32} = \text{minor of } a_{32} = \begin{vmatrix} a_{11} & a_{13} \\ a_{21} & a_{23} \end{vmatrix}$, etc.

When the minor of an element a_{ij} of a determinant is taken with a definite sign, we call such a *signed minor* as the *cofactor of that element* and denoted by A_{ij}.

Therefore, $A_{ij} = \text{cofactor of } a_{ij} \text{ in } D = (-1)^{i+j} M_{ij}$.

e.g., $A_{21} = \text{cofactor of } a_{21} \text{ in } D = (-1)^{2+1} M_{21} = -\begin{vmatrix} a_{12} & a_{13} \\ a_{32} & a_{33} \end{vmatrix}$

$A_{33} = \text{cofactor of } a_{33} \text{ in } D = (-1)^{3+3} M_{33} = +\begin{vmatrix} a_{11} & a_{12} \\ a_{21} & a_{22} \end{vmatrix}$, etc.

(i) If we expand the determinant in terms of element using corresponding cofactor, then we have

$$\sum_{k=1}^{3} a_{ik}A_{jk} = \begin{cases} D & \text{if } i = j \\ 0 & \text{if } i \neq j. \end{cases}$$

(ii) A determinant remains unaltered under an operation of the form $C_i \longrightarrow C_i + \alpha C_j + \beta C_k, j, k \neq i$, called *column operation* or an operation of the form $R_i \longrightarrow R_i + \alpha R_j + \beta R_k, j, k \neq i$, called *Row operation* but remember that column and row operations do not take place simultaneously.

Example: $\begin{vmatrix} 1 & 1 & 1 \\ \alpha & \beta & \gamma \\ \beta\gamma & \gamma\alpha & \alpha\beta \end{vmatrix} = \begin{vmatrix} 1 & 1-1 & 1-1 \\ \alpha & \beta-\alpha & \gamma-\alpha \\ \beta\gamma & \gamma\alpha-\beta\gamma & \alpha\beta-\beta\gamma \end{vmatrix} \left\langle \begin{matrix} C_2 \to C_2 - C_1 \\ C_3 \to C_3 - C_1 \end{matrix} \right\rangle$

$$= (\beta-\alpha)(\gamma-\alpha) \begin{vmatrix} 1 & 0 & 0 \\ \alpha & 1 & 1 \\ \beta\gamma & -\gamma & -\beta \end{vmatrix}$$

$$= (\beta-\alpha)(\gamma-\alpha)(\gamma-\beta) \ \langle \text{Expand along first row} \rangle$$

(c) *Product of two determinants:*

The product of two determinants is also a determinant of same order.

(i) Row-by-Row multiplication Rule: The elements in the ith row and jth column is obtained by multiplying the elements of ith row by corresponding elements of jth row and, then add.

Let $D_1 = \begin{vmatrix} a_1 & b_1 & c_1 \\ a_2 & b_2 & c_2 \\ a_3 & b_3 & c_3 \end{vmatrix}$, $D_2 = \begin{vmatrix} a_1' & b_1' & c_1' \\ a_2' & b_2' & c_2' \\ a_3' & b_3' & c_3' \end{vmatrix}$.

$$\therefore D_1D_2 = \begin{vmatrix} a_1a_1' + b_1b_1' + c_1c_1' & a_1a_2' + b_1b_2' + c_1c_2' & a_1a_3' + b_1b_3' + c_1c_3' \\ a_2a_1' + b_2b_1' + c_2c_1' & a_2a_2' + b_2b_2' + c_2c_2' & a_2a_3' + b_2b_3' + c_2c_3' \\ a_3a_1' + b_3b_1' + c_3c_1' & a_3a_2' + b_3b_2' + c_3c_2' & a_3a_3' + b_3b_3' + c_3c_3' \end{vmatrix}.$$

(ii) Similarly, we can apply *Row-by-Column multiplication rule* to find the product D_1D_2. Here multiply the elements of ith row with corresponding elements of jth column and add to find the element in the ith row and the jth column of D_1D_2.

(d) *Adjugate and Reciprocal determinants:*

Let $\Delta = \begin{vmatrix} a_{11} & a_{12} & a_{13} \\ a_{21} & a_{22} & a_{23} \\ a_{31} & a_{32} & a_{33} \end{vmatrix} = |a_{ij}|$, $\Delta' = \begin{vmatrix} A_{11} & A_{12} & A_{13} \\ A_{21} & A_{22} & A_{23} \\ A_{31} & A_{32} & A_{33} \end{vmatrix} = |A_{ij}|$.

where A_{ij} is the cofactor of a_{ij} in Δ for all i and j. The determinant Δ' is called the *adjugate* or *adjoint* of Δ.

If $\Delta \neq 0$, then the determinant $\Delta^* = \begin{vmatrix} \frac{A_{11}}{\Delta} & \frac{A_{12}}{\Delta} & \frac{A_{13}}{\Delta} \\ \frac{A_{21}}{\Delta} & \frac{A_{22}}{\Delta} & \frac{A_{23}}{\Delta} \\ \frac{A_{31}}{\Delta} & \frac{A_{32}}{\Delta} & \frac{A_{33}}{\Delta} \end{vmatrix} = \frac{|A_{ij}|}{\Delta^3} = \frac{\Delta'}{\Delta^3}$ is called the *reciprocal* or *inverse* determinant of Δ.

(i) $\Delta\Delta' = \begin{vmatrix} a_{11} & a_{12} & a_{13} \\ a_{21} & a_{22} & a_{23} \\ a_{31} & a_{32} & a_{33} \end{vmatrix} \begin{vmatrix} A_{11} & A_{12} & A_{13} \\ A_{21} & A_{22} & A_{23} \\ A_{31} & A_{32} & A_{33} \end{vmatrix} = \Delta^3. \quad \therefore \Delta' = \Delta^2.$

(ii) $\Delta^* = \frac{\Delta'}{\Delta^3} = \frac{\Delta^2}{\Delta^3} = \frac{1}{\Delta}$, where $\Delta \neq 0$.

(e) *Symmetric and Skew-Symmetric determinants:*

A determinant is *symmetric* when its elements remain same after transposition. A third order symmetric determinant has the form $\begin{vmatrix} a & h & g \\ h & b & f \\ g & f & c \end{vmatrix}$. Note that in a symmetric determinant a pair of elements equidistant from the main diagonal are equal both in magnitude and in sign. But if the determinant be such that a pair of elements equidistant from main diagonal are equal in magnitude but opposite in sign, we call such a determinant a *skew-symmetric* determinant. A third order skew-symmetric determinant has the form $\begin{vmatrix} 0 & h & f \\ -h & 0 & f \\ -g & -f & 0 \end{vmatrix}$.

(i) A skew-symmetric determinant of odd order is always zero but of any even odder is a perfect square.

(ii) The adjugate of a symmetric determinant is itself a symmetric determinant.

(iii) In a skew-symmetric determinant diagonal elements must all be zeros.

(f) *Solution of Linear equations: Cramer's Rule*:

Let $a_{11}x_1 + a_{12}x_2 + a_{13}x_3 = b_1$

$a_{21}x_1 + a_{22}x_2 + a_{23}x_3 = b_2$

$a_{31}x_1 + a_{32}x_2 + a_{33}x_3 = b_3$

be a system of three linear equations in three unknown x_1, x_2, x_3.

$D = |a_{ij}| = \begin{vmatrix} a_{11} & a_{12} & a_{13} \\ a_{21} & a_{22} & a_{23} \\ a_{31} & a_{32} & a_{33} \end{vmatrix} \neq 0$ be the determinant of the coefficients.

Then *Cramer's Rule* states:

$$\frac{x_1}{D_{x_1}} = \frac{x_2}{D_{x_2}} = \frac{x_3}{D_{x_3}} = \frac{1}{D},$$

where D_{x_i} $(i = 1, 2, 3)$ is the determinant obtained from D by replacing the elements of the x_ith column by the elements b_1, b_2, b_3, i.e., the column of constants $\begin{pmatrix} b_1 \\ b_2 \\ b_3 \end{pmatrix}$.

(i) The system of equations is *consistent* if $D \neq 0$ and that there is one and only one solution of the system.

(ii) If $D = 0$, the system may or may not be consistent.
If $D = 0$ and at least one of $D_{x_1}, D_{x_2}, D_{x_3} \neq 0$, then the system is certainly inconsistent but if $D = 0$ and $D_{x_1} = D_{x_2} = D_{x_3} = 0$, then the system may or may not be consistent. We require the concept of rank of a matrix for further investigation and shall discuss later.

(iii) If in the system all the right-hand side constants are zero we call the system a set of *homogeneous linear equations.* Such a set is always satisfied by $x_1 = x_2 = x_3 = 0$ called a *trivial solution.* Now solution other than the trivial solution can exist if $D = 0$ but we cannot definitely say this, unless we investigate further.

1.1.6 Inverse of a Square Matrix

If A and B be two square matrices of order n such that $AB = BA = I$, then B is called the *inverse* of A and we write $B = A^{-1}$. One may also say that A is an inverse of B and write $A = B^{-1}$. Thus, $AA^{-1} = A^{-1}A = I, BB^{-1} = B^{-1}B = I$.

Now every square matrix has an inverse. Only non-singular square matrices have inverses (i.e., only those square matrices whose determinant $\neq 0$ have inverses).

If an inverse of A exists, then this is unique. We shall never get more than one inverse of a given square matrix A.

Important Properties

(i) If A^{-1} exists, then $\left(A^{-1}\right)^{-1} = A$.

(ii) If A^{-1} exists, then $\left(A^{T}\right)^{-1} = \left(A^{-1}\right)^{T}$.

(iii) If A^{-1}, B^{-1} exist, where A and B are both square matrices of same order, then $(AB)^{-1} = B^{-1}A^{-1}$.
Extension of this property is that for non-singular matrices (square) $A_1, A_2, \ldots, A_k$ of same order

$$(A_1A_2\ldots A_k)^{-1} = A_k^{-1}A_{k-1}^{-1}\ldots A_2^{-1}A_1^{-1}.$$

(iv) Let $A\left(a_{ij}\right)_{n\times n}$ be a square matrix of order n. A_{ij} denote the cofactor of a_{ij} in determinant A. We construct a matrix of the cofactors of the elements of A and then transpose it. Such a matrix is called *Adjoint of A.*

$$\operatorname{Adj} A = \left(A_{ji}\right)_{n\times n}$$

An important relation between A and its Adjoin A is

$$A \cdot \operatorname{Adj} A = \operatorname{Adj} A \cdot A = \det A \cdot I.$$

A square matrix A has an inverse, if and only if $\det A \neq 0$ and is computed by the formula:

$$A^{-1} = \frac{\operatorname{Adj} A}{\det A} : \det A \neq 0.$$

Example: $A = \begin{pmatrix} 3 & 2 & 1 \\ 1 & 1 & 1 \\ 5 & 1 & -1 \end{pmatrix}$. [CU(H) 1992]

$$\det A = 2 \neq 0.$$

$$\operatorname{Adj} A = \begin{pmatrix} \begin{vmatrix} 1 & 1 \\ 1 & -1 \end{vmatrix} & -\begin{vmatrix} 2 & 1 \\ 1 & -1 \end{vmatrix} & \begin{vmatrix} 2 & 1 \\ 1 & 1 \end{vmatrix} \\ -\begin{vmatrix} 1 & 1 \\ 5 & -1 \end{vmatrix} & \begin{vmatrix} 3 & 1 \\ 5 & -1 \end{vmatrix} & -\begin{vmatrix} 3 & 1 \\ 1 & 1 \end{vmatrix} \\ \begin{vmatrix} 1 & 1 \\ 5 & 1 \end{vmatrix} & -\begin{vmatrix} 3 & 2 \\ 5 & 1 \end{vmatrix} & \begin{vmatrix} 3 & 2 \\ 1 & 1 \end{vmatrix} \end{pmatrix} = \begin{pmatrix} -2 & 3 & 1 \\ 6 & -8 & -2 \\ -4 & 7 & 1 \end{pmatrix}$$

$$A^{-1} = \frac{1}{2}\begin{pmatrix} -2 & 3 & 1 \\ 6 & -8 & -2 \\ -4 & 7 & 1 \end{pmatrix} = \begin{pmatrix} -1 & 3/2 & 1/2 \\ 3 & -4 & -1 \\ -2 & 7/2 & 1/2 \end{pmatrix}.$$

1.1.7 Rank of a Matrix

From a matrix A if we retain any r rows and any r columns and delete all other rows or columns, then we get a square sub-matrix of order r. Its determinant is called a *minor of order r*.

A matrix A is said to be of rank r, if and only if A has at least one minor of order $r \neq 0$ while all minors of order more than $r = 0$.

(a) Determination of rank by considering minors:

Example 1: $A = \begin{pmatrix} 1 & 2 & 3 \\ 2 & 3 & 4 \\ 3 & 5 & 7 \end{pmatrix}$

$\det A = 0$, since $\begin{vmatrix} 1 & 2 \\ 2 & 3 \end{vmatrix} \neq 0$. Therefore, rank of $A = 2$.

Example 2: $A = \begin{pmatrix} 6 & 1 & 3 & 8 \\ 4 & 2 & 6 & -1 \\ 10 & 3 & 9 & 7 \\ 16 & 4 & 12 & 15 \end{pmatrix}$

We have $\det A = \begin{vmatrix} 6 & 1 & 3 & 7 \\ 4 & 2 & 6 & -1 \\ 6 & 1 & 3 & 8 \\ 6 & 1 & 3 & 8 \end{vmatrix} \quad (R_3' = R_3 - R_2,\ R_4' = R_4 - R_3)$

$= 0$ (R_3', R_4' are identical).

Consider minor of order 3: $\begin{vmatrix} 6 & 1 & 3 \\ 4 & 2 & 6 \\ 10 & 3 & 9 \end{vmatrix} = 0$. All the minors of order 3 are zero that can be shown in a similar way. Now since $\begin{vmatrix} 6 & 1 \\ 4 & 2 \end{vmatrix} \neq 0$, the rank of the matrix is 2.

(b) Determination of rank by elementary transformation:

The method (a) is laborious if the matrix is of order more than three. So we introduce some simplified method.

The following operations called *elementary transformation*, on a matrix do not change its order or its rank.

Rule 1. The interchange of the ith and jth rows, denoted by R_{ij} and that of ith and jth columns by C_{ij}.

Rule 2. $R_i(\lambda)$ or $C_j(\lambda)$ denotes the multiplication of every element of the ith row or jth column by a non-zero scalar λ.

Rule 3. The addition to the elements of ith row of λ times the corresponding elements of the jth row denoted by $R_{ij}(\lambda)$. A similar meaning of the symbol $C_{ij}(\lambda)$.

(i) The Normal or Canonical form:

Every matrix A of rank $r > 0$ can be put in any one of the forms:

$$I_r, \quad \begin{pmatrix} I_r & 0 \\ 0 & 0 \end{pmatrix}, \quad (I_r \quad 0), \quad \begin{pmatrix} I_r \\ 0 \end{pmatrix}$$

by means of elementary transformations. Such form of A is called the *normal* or *canonical form* of A. The rank of matrix, when reduced to normal form, is the order of the unit matrix.

Example: $A = \begin{pmatrix} 0 & 0 & 1 & 2 & 1 \\ 1 & 3 & 1 & 0 & 3 \\ 2 & 6 & 4 & 2 & 8 \\ 3 & 9 & 4 & 2 & 10 \end{pmatrix}$ [CU(H) 1985]

$$\xrightarrow{R_{12}} \begin{pmatrix} 1 & 3 & 1 & 0 & 3 \\ 0 & 0 & 1 & 2 & 1 \\ 2 & 6 & 4 & 2 & 8 \\ 3 & 9 & 4 & 2 & 10 \end{pmatrix} \xrightarrow[R_{41}(-3)]{R_{31}(-2)} \begin{pmatrix} 1 & 3 & 1 & 0 & 3 \\ 0 & 0 & 1 & 2 & 1 \\ 0 & 0 & 2 & 2 & 2 \\ 0 & 0 & 1 & 2 & 1 \end{pmatrix}$$

$$\xrightarrow[R_{32}(-2),\ R_{42}(-1)]{R_{12}(-1)} \begin{pmatrix} 1 & 3 & 0 & -2 & 2 \\ 0 & 0 & 1 & 2 & 1 \\ 0 & 0 & 0 & -2 & 0 \\ 0 & 0 & 0 & 0 & 0 \end{pmatrix} \xrightarrow{R_3(-1/2)} \begin{pmatrix} 1 & 3 & 0 & -2 & 2 \\ 0 & 0 & 1 & 2 & 1 \\ 0 & 0 & 0 & 1 & 0 \\ 0 & 0 & 0 & 0 & 0 \end{pmatrix}$$

$$\xrightarrow[R_{23}(-2)]{R_{13}(2)} \begin{pmatrix} 1 & 3 & 0 & 0 & 2 \\ 0 & 0 & 1 & 0 & 0 \\ 0 & 0 & 0 & 1 & 0 \\ 0 & 0 & 0 & 0 & 0 \end{pmatrix} \xrightarrow[C_{51}(-2)]{C_{21}(-3)} \begin{pmatrix} 1 & 0 & 0 & 0 & 0 \\ 0 & 0 & 1 & 0 & 1 \\ 0 & 0 & 0 & 1 & 0 \\ 0 & 0 & 0 & 0 & 0 \end{pmatrix}$$

$$\xrightarrow{C_{53}(-1)} \begin{pmatrix} 1 & 0 & 0 & 0 & 0 \\ 0 & 0 & 1 & 0 & 0 \\ 0 & 0 & 0 & 1 & 0 \\ 0 & 0 & 0 & 0 & 0 \end{pmatrix} \xrightarrow{C_{23}} \begin{pmatrix} 1 & 0 & 0 & 0 & 0 \\ 0 & 1 & 0 & 0 & 0 \\ 0 & 0 & 0 & 1 & 0 \\ 0 & 0 & 0 & 0 & 0 \end{pmatrix}$$

$$\xrightarrow{C_{34}} \begin{pmatrix} \begin{bmatrix} 1 & 0 & 0 \\ 0 & 1 & 0 \\ 0 & 0 & 1 \end{bmatrix} & \begin{bmatrix} 0 & 0 \\ 0 & 0 \\ 0 & 0 \end{bmatrix} \\ \begin{bmatrix} 0 & 0 & 0 \end{bmatrix} & \begin{bmatrix} 0 & 0 \end{bmatrix} \end{pmatrix} = \begin{pmatrix} I_3 & 0 \\ 0 & 0 \end{pmatrix}.$$

A is the fully reduced normal form and the rank of A = order of identity matrix = 3.

(ii) Echelon form of a matrix:

A matrix A is said to be a *Echelon form* if

(a) Every row of A which has all its entries zero occurs below every row which has a non-zero entry.

(b) The first non-zero entry in each non-zero row is equal to 1.

(c) The number of zeros before the first non-zero element in a row is less than the number of such zeros in the next row.

The rank of a matrix in *Echelon form* is equal to the number of *non-zero* rows of the matrix.

Example: $A = \begin{pmatrix} 0 & 1 & -3 & -1 \\ 1 & 0 & 1 & 1 \\ 3 & 1 & 0 & 2 \\ 1 & 1 & -2 & 0 \end{pmatrix}$

$$\xrightarrow{R_{12}} \begin{pmatrix} 1 & 0 & 1 & 1 \\ 0 & 1 & -3 & -1 \\ 3 & 1 & 0 & 2 \\ 1 & 1 & -2 & 0 \end{pmatrix} \xrightarrow[R_{41}(-1)]{R_{31}(-3)} \begin{pmatrix} 1 & 0 & 1 & 1 \\ 0 & 1 & -3 & -1 \\ 0 & 1 & -3 & -1 \\ 0 & 1 & -3 & -1 \end{pmatrix} \xrightarrow[R_{42}(-1)]{R_{32}(-1)} \begin{pmatrix} 1 & 0 & 1 & 1 \\ 0 & 1 & -3 & -1 \\ 0 & 0 & 0 & 0 \\ 0 & 0 & 0 & 0 \end{pmatrix}$$

which is the row-reduced echelon matrix of A. Since there are two non-zero rows the rank of A is 2.

1.1.8 Consistency and Solution of System of Linear Equations

Consider a system of m linear equations in n unknown

$$\begin{aligned} a_{11}x_1 + a_{12}x_2 + \ldots + a_{1n}x_n &= b_1 \\ a_{21}x_1 + a_{22}x_2 + \ldots + a_{2n}x_n &= b_2 \\ &\vdots \\ a_{m1}x_1 + a_{m2}x_2 + \ldots + a_{mn}x_n &= b_m \end{aligned} \qquad (S)$$

If the right side constant (b's) are all zero, then the system is called *homogeneous system;* otherwise the system is *non-homogeneous.*

The matrix form of (S) is

$$AX = B \ldots (S_1)$$

where $A = \begin{pmatrix} a_{11} & a_{12} & \dots & a_{1n} \\ a_{21} & a_{22} & \dots & a_{2n} \\ \vdots & & & \\ a_{m1} & a_{m2} & \dots & a_{mn} \end{pmatrix}$ called *Coefficient matrix.*

$$X = \begin{pmatrix} x_1 \\ x_2 \\ \vdots \\ x_n \end{pmatrix} \quad B = \begin{pmatrix} b_1 \\ b_2 \\ \vdots \\ b_n \end{pmatrix}$$

$A_B = \begin{pmatrix} a_{11} & a_{12} & \dots & a_{1n} & b_1 \\ a_{21} & a_{22} & \dots & a_{2n} & b_2 \\ \vdots & & & & \\ a_{m1} & a_{m2} & \dots & a_{mn} & b_m \end{pmatrix}$ called *Augmented matrix.*

(a) Non-homogeneous system:
If rank of $A \neq$ rank of A_B, the equations are *inconsistent* and they have *no solution.*
If rank of $A =$ rank of $A_B =$ no. of unknowns, then the equations are *consistent* and they have a *unique solution.*
If rank of $A =$ rank of $A_B \neq$ no. of unknowns, then the equations are *consistent* but they have an *infinite number of solutions.*
Let the common rank of A and A_B be k if $k < m$, then the elementary row transformation will eliminate $(m-k)$ of the equations and the m given equations will be replaced by an equivalent system of k equations. From these k equations, we can express the values of k of the unknowns in terms of the remaining $(n-k)$ unknowns and we can give any arbitrary values to these unknowns. The following cases may arise:
Case (i) if $k = n$, then $n - k = 0$, no variables will be assigned an arbitrary value and the solution will be unique
Case (ii) if $k < n$, then $n - k > 0$, arbitrary values will be assigned to $(n-k)$ variables and hence, we get an infinite number of solutions
Case (iii) if $k \leq m \leq n$ and $n - k > 0$, then also arbitrary values will be given to $(n-k)$ variables and the system will have an infinite number of solutions
Case (iv) if $m > n$, then the system is consistent, if $k \leq n$. For equality the solution is unique, otherwise, there will be an infinite number of solutions

(b) Homogeneous system: For homogeneous the system (S_1) can be written as $AX = 0$. Now the rank of A is same as rank of A_B and as such the set of homogeneous equations is always *consistent.* In fact, $x_1 = x_2 = \cdots = x_n = 0$ is always a solution of the homogeneous system. This solution is called *Trivial solution.*

(i) A necessary and sufficient condition that a system of m homogeneous linear equations in n unknowns $(m \leq n)$ $AX = 0$ having *non-trivial* solutions is that the coefficient matrix A has a rank less than the number of unknowns. In case $m > n$, the coefficient matrix A has a rank $< n$ and the system has non-trivial solutions. If $m = n$, then the condition for existence of non-trivial solution is that the coefficient matrix A must be singular [$\det A = 0$ and rank $(A) < n$].

(ii) For the system $AX = 0 (m \le n)$ if the rank of A is k_1, then k_1 of the unknowns can be expressed as a linear functions of the remaining $(n - k_1)$ unknowns. Giving arbitrary values to these $(n - k_1)$ unknowns, we get an infinite number of solutions.

Example:

$$\begin{aligned} x + \quad y + z &= 0 \\ 2x - \quad y - 3z &= 0 \\ 3x - \quad 5y + 4z &= 0 \\ x + 17y + 4z &= 0 \end{aligned}$$

[VU 1986; CU(P) 1996]

Here, $A = \begin{pmatrix} 1 & 1 & 1 \\ 2 & -1 & -3 \\ 3 & -5 & 4 \\ 1 & 17 & 4 \end{pmatrix}$

$$A \xrightarrow[R_{31}(-3),\ R_{41}(-1)]{R_{21}(-1)} \begin{pmatrix} 1 & 1 & 1 \\ 0 & -3 & -5 \\ 0 & -8 & 1 \\ 0 & 16 & 3 \end{pmatrix} \xrightarrow[R_3(3)]{R_4(3)} \begin{pmatrix} 1 & 1 & 1 \\ 0 & -3 & -5 \\ 0 & -24 & 3 \\ 0 & 48 & 9 \end{pmatrix}$$

$$\xrightarrow[R_{42}(16)]{R_{32}(-8)} \begin{pmatrix} 1 & 1 & 1 \\ 0 & -3 & -5 \\ 0 & 0 & 43 \\ 0 & 0 & -71 \end{pmatrix} \xrightarrow[R_{43}(\frac{71}{43})]{R_{21}(-1)} \begin{pmatrix} 1 & 1 & 1 \\ 0 & -3 & -5 \\ 0 & 0 & 43 \\ 0 & 0 & 0 \end{pmatrix}$$

Rank of $A = 3 =$ the number of unknowns. Hence, the only solution is $x = 0,\ y = 0,\ z = 0$.

1.1.9 Partitioned Matrices

A matrix divided into sub-matrices by horizontal and/or vertical lines is called a *partitioned matrix.*

Given a matrix $A = \begin{pmatrix} a_{11} & a_{12} & a_{13} & a_{14} \\ a_{21} & a_{22} & a_{23} & a_{24} \\ a_{31} & a_{32} & a_{33} & a_{34} \end{pmatrix}$.

Let $A_{11} = \begin{pmatrix} a_{11} & a_{12} & a_{13} & a_{14} \\ a_{21} & a_{22} & a_{23} & a_{24} \end{pmatrix}$ $\quad A_{21} = \begin{pmatrix} a_{31} & a_{32} & a_{33} & a_{34} \end{pmatrix}$.

$B_{11} = \begin{pmatrix} a_{11} & a_{12} & a_{13} \\ a_{21} & a_{22} & a_{23} \\ a_{31} & a_{32} & a_{33} \end{pmatrix}$ $\quad B_{12} = \begin{pmatrix} a_{14} \\ a_{24} \\ a_{34} \end{pmatrix}$.

Then two among the many possible ways of partitioning A are given by $\begin{pmatrix} A_{11} \\ A_{21} \end{pmatrix}$ $\quad (B_{11} \quad B_{12})$ and so on.

(a) The rule for addition of partitioned matrices is the same as the rule for addition of ordinary matrices, if sub-matrices in corresponding positions be conformable for addition. Similarly, multiplication of partitioned matrices obeys the same formal law as established for ordinary matrices.

If $A = \begin{pmatrix} A_{11} & A_{12} \\ A_{21} & A_{22} \end{pmatrix}$ $\quad B = \begin{pmatrix} B_{11} & B_{12} \\ B_{21} & B_{22} \end{pmatrix}$

$A+B=\begin{pmatrix} A_{11}+B_{11} & A_{12}+B_{12} \\ A_{21}+B_{21} & A_{22}+B_{22} \end{pmatrix}$ provided that A_{ij} and corresponding B_{ij} are conformable for matrix addition.

$AB=\begin{pmatrix} A_{11}B_{11}+A_{12}B_{21} & A_{11}B_{12}+A_{12}B_{22} \\ A_{21}B_{11}+A_{22}B_{21} & A_{21}B_{12}+A_{22}B_{22} \end{pmatrix}$ provided that all the products $A_{ip}B_{pj}$ can be formed.

(b) Inversion of a matrix by partitioning: Here, we have to see how the inverse of an nth order non-singular partitioned matrix can be computed.

Let $M=\begin{pmatrix} a & b \\ c & d \end{pmatrix}$, where a, b, c, d are submatrices of order $l\times l$, $l\times m$, $m\times l$ and $m\times m$ respectively.

Let M^{-1} exists and $M^{-1}=\begin{pmatrix} A & B \\ C & D \end{pmatrix}$, where A, B, C, D are matrices of same order as that of a, b, c, d respectively.

Since $MM^{-1}=I \Rightarrow \begin{pmatrix} a & b \\ c & d \end{pmatrix}\begin{pmatrix} A & B \\ C & D \end{pmatrix}=\begin{pmatrix} I_l & 0 \\ 0 & I_m \end{pmatrix}$, where I_l and I_m are identity matrices of order $l\times l$ and $m\times m$.

Now, we have $aA+bC=I_l$.

$$aB+bD=0$$
$$cA+dC=0$$
$$cB+dD=I_m.$$

If d has an inverse d^{-1}, then we get after minor simplification

$$A=(a-bd^{-1}c)^{-1}, \quad B=-Abd^{-1},$$
$$C=-d^{-1}cA, \quad D=d^{-1}-d^{-1}cB.$$

$$\therefore\ M^{-1}=\begin{pmatrix} (a-bd^{-1}c)^{-1} & -Abd^{-1} \\ (-d^{-1}cA) & d^{-1}-d^{-1}cB \end{pmatrix}$$

For example: If $M=\begin{pmatrix} I & Q \\ 0 & R \end{pmatrix}$, then $M^{-1}=\begin{pmatrix} I & -QR^{-1} \\ 0 & R^{-1} \end{pmatrix}$.

1.2 VECTOR SPACES

1.2.1 Definitions and Examples

Let $\{F,+,\bullet\}$ be a field. The elements of F will be called *scalars*. Let V be a non-empty set whose elements will be called *vectors*. Then V be a vector space over the field F if the following axioms hold:

(I) *Addition axioms*: A binary operation $\oplus$, called *vector addition*, is defined in V and under this operation, V is an abelian group.

(i) V is closed under $\oplus$, $\forall\, \boldsymbol{\alpha},\boldsymbol{\beta}\in V$, $\boldsymbol{\alpha}\oplus\boldsymbol{\beta}\in V$.

(ii) Vector addition is associative, $\forall\, \boldsymbol{\alpha},\boldsymbol{\beta},\boldsymbol{\gamma}\in V$ $\boldsymbol{\alpha}\oplus(\boldsymbol{\beta}\oplus\boldsymbol{\gamma})=(\boldsymbol{\alpha}\oplus\boldsymbol{\beta})\oplus\boldsymbol{\gamma}$.

(iii) $\exists$ an element $\boldsymbol{O}\in V$ such that $\forall\, \boldsymbol{\alpha}\in V$

$$\boldsymbol{\alpha}\oplus\boldsymbol{O}=\boldsymbol{O}\oplus\boldsymbol{\alpha}=\boldsymbol{\alpha}$$

$\boldsymbol{O}$ is called *null vector*.

(iv) $\forall \boldsymbol{\alpha} \in V\ \exists$ a vector $(-\boldsymbol{\alpha}) \in V$ such that $\boldsymbol{\alpha} \oplus (-\boldsymbol{\alpha}) = (-\boldsymbol{\alpha}) \oplus \boldsymbol{\alpha} = \boldsymbol{O}$.
The element $(-\boldsymbol{\alpha}) \in V$ is called the *additive inverse* of $\boldsymbol{\alpha}$.

(v) $\forall\ \boldsymbol{\alpha}, \boldsymbol{\beta} \in V, \boldsymbol{\alpha} \oplus \boldsymbol{\beta} = \boldsymbol{\beta} \oplus \boldsymbol{\alpha}$, Commutative Law follows.

(II) *Scalar Multiplication axioms*: Another binary operation, called scalar multiplication, is defined for each scalar $\lambda \in F$ and any vector $\boldsymbol{\alpha} \in V$ there corresponds a unique vector $\lambda\boldsymbol{\alpha} \in V$. This scalar multiplication obeys the following axioms.

(M1) V is closed under scalar multiplication.

(M2) $\forall\ \lambda \in F$ and $\boldsymbol{\alpha}, \boldsymbol{\beta} \in V, \lambda(\boldsymbol{\alpha} \oplus \boldsymbol{\beta}) = \lambda\boldsymbol{\alpha} \oplus \lambda\boldsymbol{\beta}$.

(M3) $\forall\ \lambda, \mu \in F$ and $\boldsymbol{\alpha} \in V, (\lambda + \mu)\boldsymbol{\alpha} = \lambda\boldsymbol{\alpha} \oplus \mu\boldsymbol{\beta}$.

(M4) $\forall\ \lambda, \mu \in F$ and $\boldsymbol{\alpha} \in V, (\lambda\mu)\boldsymbol{\alpha} = \lambda(\mu\boldsymbol{\alpha})$.

(M5) $1\boldsymbol{\alpha} = \boldsymbol{\alpha}\ \forall\ \boldsymbol{\alpha} \in V$ and 1 is the multiplicative identity of the field F.

The vector space V over the field F is usually denoted by $V(F)$. But if F is understood from the context we may say V is a vector space. Again, if F is a field of real numbers R, then V is a *real vector space.* Similarly, if F is the field of complex numbers we speak of complex vector space.

Examples:

(i) V is the set of all $m \times m$ matrices with their elements as real numbers and F is the real field R. Then $V(R)$ is a real vector space.

(ii) The set of all polynomials over any field F is a vector space.

(iii) The set S of all real valued continuous functions defined on $[a, b]$ is a vector space over the field of real numbers.

1.2.2 Linear Combination, Linearly Dependent and Linearly Independent Set of Vectors

Definition 1 (Linear combination). *Let $V(F)$ be a vector space. If $\boldsymbol{x}_1, \boldsymbol{x}_2, \ldots, \boldsymbol{x}_k \in V(F)$, then the expression*

$$\sum_{i=1}^{k} \lambda_i \boldsymbol{x}_i = \lambda_1 \boldsymbol{x}_1 + \lambda_2 \boldsymbol{x}_2 + \cdots + \lambda_k \boldsymbol{x}_k,$$

where $\lambda_1, \lambda_2, \ldots, \lambda_k \in F$ is called a linear combination of the set of vectors $\{\boldsymbol{x}_1, \boldsymbol{x}_2, \ldots, \boldsymbol{x}_k\}$.

Definition 2 (Linearly dependent). *Let V be a vector space over a field F. The set $S_k = \{\boldsymbol{x}_1, \boldsymbol{x}_2, \ldots, \boldsymbol{x}_k\}$ of V is said to be linearly dependent if there exist scalars $\lambda_1, \lambda_2, \ldots, \lambda_k \in F$ not all of them zero, some of them may be zero such that*

$$\sum_{i=1}^{k} \lambda_i \boldsymbol{x}_i = 0.$$

Definition 3 (Linearly independent). *Let V be a vector space over a field F. The set $S_k = \{\boldsymbol{x}_1, \boldsymbol{x}_2, \ldots, \boldsymbol{x}_k\}$ of V is said to be linearly independent if every linear combination of these k vectors is a null vector, only when each scalar coefficient is zero, i.e., $\lambda_1 \boldsymbol{x}_1 + \lambda_2 \boldsymbol{x}_2 + \cdots + \lambda_k \boldsymbol{x}_k = 0 \Rightarrow \lambda_i = 0$ for all $i = 1, 2, \ldots, k$.*

Remark. An infinite set of vectors of $V(F)$ is *linearly independent* if its every finite subset is linearly independent, otherwise it is *linearly dependent.*

Example 1.2.1. *Express $\boldsymbol{x} = (-1, 2, 4)$ as a linear combination of $\boldsymbol{x}_1 = (-1, 2, 0)$, $\boldsymbol{x}_2 = (0, -1, 1)$, $\boldsymbol{x}_3 = (3, -4, 2)$ of $V_3(R)$ or R^3.*

Solution: Let $(-1,2,4)=\lambda_1(-1,2,0)+\lambda_2(0,-1,1)+\lambda_3(3,-4,2)$.

Therefore,
$$\begin{aligned} -\lambda_1 \quad\quad + 3\lambda_3 &= -1 \\ 2\lambda_1 - \lambda_2 - 4\lambda_3 &= 2 \\ 0\lambda_1 + \lambda_2 + 2\lambda_3 &= 4 \end{aligned}$$

Solving, we get $\lambda_1 = 4$, $\lambda_2 = 2$, $\lambda_3 = 1$.

$\therefore (-1,2,4)=4(-1,2,0)+2(0,-1,1)+1(3,-4,2)$.

Example 1.2.2. *Prove that the subset* $\{(1,2,0),(0,3,1),(-1,0,1)\}$ *of* R^3 *is linearly independent, whereas the subset* $\{(1,2,1),(3,1,5),(3,-4,7)\}$ *of* R^3 *is linearly dependent.*

Solution: (i) $\lambda_1(1,2,0)+\lambda_2(0,3,1)+\lambda_3(-1,0,1)=(0,0,0)$

$$\Rightarrow \begin{aligned} \lambda_1 + 0\lambda_2 - \lambda_3 &= 0 \\ 2\lambda_1 + 3\lambda_2 + 0\lambda_3 &= 0 \\ 0\lambda_1 + \lambda_2 + \lambda_3 &= 0 \end{aligned}$$

Coefficient matrix $A_1 = \begin{pmatrix} 1 & 0 & -1 \\ 2 & 3 & 0 \\ 0 & 1 & 1 \end{pmatrix}$.

$$\therefore \det(A_1) = 1 \neq 0.$$

Rank of the matrix = 3 = Number of unknowns and, therefore, $\lambda_1 = \lambda_2 = \lambda_3 = 0$ has unique solution and the given subset is linearly independent.

(ii) $\lambda_1(1,2,1)+\lambda_2(3,1,5)+\lambda_3(3,-4,7)=(0,0,0)$

$$\Rightarrow \begin{aligned} \lambda_1 + 3\lambda_2 + 3\lambda_3 &= 0 \\ 2\lambda_1 + \lambda_2 - 0\lambda_3 &= 0 \\ \lambda_1 + 5\lambda_2 + 7\lambda_3 &= 0 \end{aligned}$$

Coefficient matrix $A_2 = \begin{pmatrix} 1 & 3 & 3 \\ 2 & 1 & -4 \\ 1 & 5 & 7 \end{pmatrix}$.

$\therefore \det(A_2) = 0$ but $\begin{vmatrix} 1 & 3 \\ 2 & 1 \end{vmatrix} \neq 0$. Rank of $A_2 = 2$ which is less than number of unknowns. Hence, the above homogeneous system will have a non-zero solution (For example, $\lambda_1 = 3, \lambda_3 = -2, \lambda_3 = 1$). Hence, the given subset is linearly dependent.

Example 1.2.3. *Show that in the vector space* $F(x)$ *of polynomials over the real field the set of vectors* $\{1, x, x - x^2\}$ *is linearly independent.*

Solution: The null vector in $F(x)$ is the *zero polynomial*

$$\lambda_1 \cdot 1 + \lambda_2 x + \lambda_3 \left(x - x^2\right) = 0 \text{ (zero polynomial)}$$
$$\Rightarrow \lambda_1 + (\lambda_2 + \lambda_3)\, x + (-\lambda_3)\, x^2 = 0 + 0x + 0x^2$$
$$\Rightarrow \lambda_1 = 0, \quad \lambda_2 + \lambda_3 = 0, \quad -\lambda_3 = 0$$
$$\Rightarrow \lambda_1 = \lambda_2 = \lambda_3 = 0.$$

$\therefore \{1, x, x - x^2\}$ is linearly independent.

Example 1.2.4. *If $\boldsymbol{\alpha}, \boldsymbol{\beta}, \boldsymbol{\gamma}$ are linearly independent vectors in $V_n(R)$ or R^n, then prove that $\boldsymbol{\alpha}+\boldsymbol{\beta}, \boldsymbol{\alpha}-2\boldsymbol{\beta}, \boldsymbol{\alpha}-2\boldsymbol{\beta}+\boldsymbol{\gamma}$ are also linearly independent in R^n.*

Solution: $\lambda_1(\boldsymbol{\alpha}+\boldsymbol{\beta})+\lambda_2(\boldsymbol{\alpha}-2\boldsymbol{\beta})+\lambda_3(\boldsymbol{\alpha}-2\boldsymbol{\beta}+\boldsymbol{\gamma})=\mathbf{0}$

$\Rightarrow (\lambda_1+\lambda_2+\lambda_3)\boldsymbol{\alpha}+(\lambda_1-2\lambda_2-2\lambda_3)\boldsymbol{\beta}+\lambda_3\boldsymbol{\gamma}=\mathbf{0}$

Since $\boldsymbol{\alpha}, \boldsymbol{\beta}, \boldsymbol{\gamma}$ are linearly independent, we must have

$$\begin{aligned} \lambda_1 + \lambda_2 + \lambda_3 &= 0 \\ \lambda_1 - 2\lambda_2 - 2\lambda_3 &= 0 \\ \lambda_3 &= 0. \end{aligned}$$

$$\text{Coefficient matrix: } A = \begin{pmatrix} 1 & 1 & 1 \\ 1 & -2 & -2 \\ 0 & 0 & 1 \end{pmatrix}.$$

$\therefore \det(A) = -3 \neq 0$. Rank of $A = 3 =$ no. of unknowns $\lambda_1 = \lambda_2 = \lambda_3 = 0$ has the only solution and hence the vectors are linearly independent in R^3.

Remarks.

1. Any subset of a linearly independent set of vectors of $V(F)$ is linearly independent.
2. In a vector space $V(F)$ any set of vectors which contains the null vector $\boldsymbol{O}$ is linearly dependent.
3. Any superset of a given set of linearly dependent vectors is linearly dependent.

1.2.3 Linear Span, Basis and Dimension of a Vector Space

Definition (Linear span). Let $V(F)$ be a vector space and S be any non-empty subset of V. Then the linear span of S usually denoted by $\mathcal{L}(S)$, we mean the set of all linear combinations of finite sets of elements of S.

Therefore, $\mathcal{L}(S) = \{\lambda_1\boldsymbol{x}_1 + \lambda_2\boldsymbol{x}_2 + \cdots + \lambda_n\boldsymbol{x}_n : (\boldsymbol{x}_1, \boldsymbol{x}_2, \ldots, \boldsymbol{x}_n)$ is any arbitrary finite subset of S and $(\lambda_1, \lambda_2, \ldots, \lambda_n)$ is any n arbitrary finite subset of $F\}$.

Definition (Basis). A subset S of a vector space $V(F)$ is said to form a basis, if

(i) S contains vectors which are linearly independent.
(ii) S generates $V(F)$, i.e., $\mathcal{L}(S) = V$ or $\forall\ \boldsymbol{\alpha} \in V$ is a linear combination of a finite number of elements of S.

Example 1.2.5. *In the real vector space $V_n(R)$ or R^n there are n unit vectors*

$$\begin{aligned} \boldsymbol{e}_1 &= (1,0,0,\ldots,0) \\ \boldsymbol{e}_2 &= (0,1,0,\ldots,0) \\ &\vdots \\ \boldsymbol{e}_n &= (0,0,0,\ldots,1) \end{aligned}$$

We now prove that they form a basis in R^n.

Proof. $\lambda_1\boldsymbol{e}_1+\lambda_2\boldsymbol{e}_2+\cdots+\lambda_n\boldsymbol{e}_n=\mathbf{0}$

$\Rightarrow \lambda_1(1,0,\ldots,0)+\lambda_2(0,1,\ldots,0)+\lambda_n(0,0,\ldots,1)=(0,0,\ldots,0)$

$\Rightarrow (\lambda_1,\lambda_2,\ldots,\lambda_n)=(0,0,\ldots,0)$

$\Rightarrow \lambda_i=0$ for all $i=1,2,\ldots,n$

$\therefore$ the set $B_n = \{e_i | i = 1, 2, \ldots, n\}$ of unit vectors of $V_n(R)$ or R^n are linearly independent.

Again, any vector $(\alpha_1, \alpha_2, \ldots, \alpha_n)$ of R^n is a linear combination of the elements of B_n

$$(\alpha_1, \alpha_2, \ldots, \alpha_n) = \alpha_1 \boldsymbol{e}_1 + \alpha_2 \boldsymbol{e}_2 + \cdots + \alpha_n \boldsymbol{e}_n.$$

Therefore, $R^n \subseteq \mathscr{L}(B_n)$ and obviously $\mathscr{L}(B_n) \subseteq R^n$.

Thus, $\mathscr{L}(B_n) = R^n$.

Hence, B_n is a basis. Such a basis is known as *Standard basis* of R^n.

In R^2 standard basis $B_2 = \{e_1 = (1,0), e_2 = (0,1)\}$

In R^3 standard basis $B_3 = \{e_1 = (1,0,0), e_2 = (0,1,0), e_3 = (0,0,1)\}$.

Definition (Dimension of vector space). The number of elements in any basis set of a finite dimensional vector space $V(F)$ is called the *dimension* of the vector space and is denoted by dim V.

$V_n(F)$ is n-dimensional, if its basis contains n elements. For example, the vector space R^3 is of dimension 3 as $B_3 = \{(1,0,0), (0,1,0), (0,0,1)\}$ is basis of R^3.

Example 1.2.6. *Show that the set S of vectors* $(1,0,0)$, $(0,2,1)$, $(1,1,0)$ *form a basis of real vector space* R^3.

[CU(H) 1995]

Solution: $\lambda_1(1,0,0) + \lambda_2(0,2,1) + \lambda_3(1,1,0) = (0,0,0)$.

$$\Rightarrow \lambda_1 + \lambda_3 = 0$$
$$2\lambda_2 + \lambda_3 = 0$$
$$\lambda_2 = 0.$$

Coefficient matrix $A = \begin{pmatrix} 1 & 0 & 1 \\ 0 & 2 & 1 \\ 0 & 1 & 0 \end{pmatrix}$.

$$\therefore \det(A) = -1 \neq 0.$$

Rank of the matrix $A = 3 =$ number of unknowns. Therefore, $\lambda_1 = \lambda_2 = \lambda_3 = 0$, the only solution of the system of homogeneous equations. Hence, S is linearly independent.

Now, let $(\alpha_1, \alpha_2, \alpha_3) \in R^3$ any vector can be expressed as a linear combination of three vectors of S

$$(\alpha_1, \alpha_2, \alpha_3) = \lambda_1'(1,0,0) + \lambda_2'(0,2,1) + \lambda_3'(1,1,0)$$

$$\Rightarrow \lambda_1' + \lambda_3' = \alpha_1 \qquad \Rightarrow \lambda_1' = \alpha_1 - \alpha_2 + 2\alpha_3$$
$$2\lambda_1' + \lambda_3' = \alpha_2 \qquad \lambda_2' = \alpha_3$$
$$\lambda_2' = \alpha_3 \qquad \lambda_3' = \alpha_2 - 2\alpha_3$$

Thus, S is linearly independent and any vector of R^3 can be expressed as a linear combination of three vectors of S. Hence, S is a basis of R^3.

Example 1.2.7. *Show that the set* $S = \{(1,0,0), (1,1,0), (1,1,1), (0,1,0)\}$ *span the vector space* R^3 *but is not a basis set.*

[CU(H) 1983; VU 1996]

Solution: We know that $\mathscr{L}(S) \subseteq R^3$. (1)

Let $(\alpha_1, \alpha_2, \alpha_3)$ be any element of R^3,

$$(\alpha_1, \alpha_2, \alpha_3) \in \mathscr{L}(S).$$

If we can find $\lambda_1, \lambda_2, \lambda_3, \lambda_4$ such that

$$(\alpha_1,\alpha_2,\alpha_3) = \lambda_1(1,0,0)+\lambda_2(1,1,0)+\lambda_3(1,1,1)+\lambda_4(0,1,0)$$
$$=(\lambda_1+\lambda_2+\lambda_3, \lambda_2+\lambda_3+\lambda_4, \lambda_3),\text{ hence,}$$

$$\begin{aligned} \lambda_1+\lambda_2+\lambda_3 &= \alpha_1 & \Rightarrow \lambda_1 &= \alpha_1-\alpha_2+\lambda_4 \\ \lambda_2+\lambda_3+\lambda_4 &= \alpha_2 & \lambda_2 &= \alpha_2-\alpha_3-\lambda_4 \\ \lambda_3 &= \alpha_3 & \lambda_3 &= \alpha_3. \end{aligned}$$

If we take $\lambda_4 = 0$ (particular) we see that $(\alpha_1,\alpha_2,\alpha_3) = (\alpha_1-\alpha_2)(1,0,0)+(\alpha_2-\alpha_3)(1,1,0)+\alpha_3(1,1,1)+0(0,1,0)$ which shows that $(\alpha_1,\alpha_2,\alpha_3)\in \mathscr{L}(S)$ and hence, $R^3 \subseteq \mathscr{L}(S)$. (2)

From (1) and (2), $\mathscr{L}(S) = R^3$, so that S spans the vector space R^3.

Again, the following relation of *linear dependence* shows that S is not a basis of the vector space R^3.

Example 1.2.8. *Determine k so that the vectors* $(1,-1,2)$, $(0,k,3)$ *and* $(-1,2,3)$ *are linearly dependent.*

[CP 1997]

Solution: $\lambda_1(1,-1,2)+\lambda_2(0,k,3)+\lambda_3(-1,2,3) = (0,0,0)$

$$\begin{aligned} \Rightarrow \lambda_1 + 0\lambda_2 - \lambda_3 &= 0 \\ -\lambda_1 + k\lambda_2 + 2\lambda_3 &= 0 \\ 2\lambda_1 + 3\lambda_2 + 3\lambda_3 &= 0. \end{aligned}$$

$$\text{Coefficient matrix } A = \begin{pmatrix} 1 & 0 & -1 \\ -1 & k & 2 \\ 2 & 3 & 3 \end{pmatrix}.$$

If $\det(A) = 0$, then the set of homogeneous equations has non-trivial solution and the set of vectors will then be linearly dependent.

Now $\det(A) = 5k-3 = 0 \Rightarrow k = 3/5$.

Example 1.2.9. *Let V be a real vector space with* $\{\boldsymbol{\alpha},\boldsymbol{\beta},\boldsymbol{\gamma}\}$ *as a basis. Prove that the set* $\{\boldsymbol{\alpha}+\boldsymbol{\beta}+\boldsymbol{\gamma}, \boldsymbol{\beta}+\boldsymbol{\gamma}, \boldsymbol{\gamma}\}$ *is also a basis of V.*

Solution: Let $\boldsymbol{\alpha}_1 = \boldsymbol{\alpha}+\boldsymbol{\beta}+\boldsymbol{\gamma}$

$$\boldsymbol{\alpha}_2 = \boldsymbol{\beta}+\boldsymbol{\gamma}$$
$$\boldsymbol{\alpha}_3 = \boldsymbol{\gamma}$$

$$\lambda_1\boldsymbol{\alpha}_1+\lambda_2\boldsymbol{\alpha}_2+\lambda_3\boldsymbol{\alpha}_3 = \mathbf{0}$$
$$\Rightarrow \lambda_1\boldsymbol{\alpha}+(\lambda_2+\lambda_1)\boldsymbol{\beta}+(\lambda_1+\lambda_2+\lambda_3)\boldsymbol{\gamma} = \mathbf{0}$$
$$\Rightarrow \lambda_1 = 0, \quad \lambda_1+\lambda_2 = 0, \quad \lambda_1+\lambda_2+\lambda_3 = 0,$$

since $\boldsymbol{\alpha},\boldsymbol{\beta},\boldsymbol{\gamma}$ is linearly independent.

$\therefore \lambda_1 = 0, \lambda_2 = 0, \lambda_3 = 0$ and this proves that $\{\boldsymbol{\alpha}_1,\boldsymbol{\alpha}_2,\boldsymbol{\alpha}_3\}$ is linearly independent.

V is a vector space of dimension 3 and $\{\boldsymbol{\alpha}_1,\boldsymbol{\alpha}_2,\boldsymbol{\alpha}_3\}$ is linearly independent set containing 3 vectors of V. Therefore, $\{\boldsymbol{\alpha}_1,\boldsymbol{\alpha}_2,\boldsymbol{\alpha}_3\}$ is a basis for V.

Important Remarks

1. *Replacement Theorem*: If $\{\boldsymbol{\alpha}_1,\boldsymbol{\alpha}_2,\ldots,\boldsymbol{\alpha}_n\}$ be a basis of vector space V over a field F and a vector $\boldsymbol{\beta} \neq \mathbf{0} \in V$ is expressed as $\boldsymbol{\beta} = \sum_{i=1}^{n} \lambda_i\boldsymbol{\alpha}_i, \lambda_i \in F$ with one of the coefficient λ_k (for some $i = k$) associated with $\boldsymbol{\alpha}_k$ not zero, then we can form a new basis by replacing $\boldsymbol{\alpha}_k$ by $\boldsymbol{\beta}$ so that the new basis will be $\{\boldsymbol{\alpha}_1,\boldsymbol{\alpha}_2,\ldots,\boldsymbol{\alpha}_j,\boldsymbol{\beta},\boldsymbol{\alpha}_{j+1},\ldots,\boldsymbol{\alpha}_n\}$.

2. If a set S of n vectors of a finite dimensional vector space $V(F)$ of dim $V = n$ generates $V(F)$, then S is a basis of V.
3. If $V(F)$ be a finite dimensional vector space of dimension n, then any set of n linearly independent vectors in V forms a basis of V.

1.2.4 Basic Solution, Degenerate Basic Solution and Basic feasible Solution

Definition (Basic solution). Given a system of m simultaneous linear equations in n unknowns in matrix form $AX = \boldsymbol{b}$, where

$$A = \begin{pmatrix} a_{11} & a_{12} & \dots & a_{1n} \\ a_{21} & a_{22} & \dots & a_{2n} \\ \vdots & & & \\ a_{m1} & a_{m2} & \dots & a_{mn} \end{pmatrix}, \quad \boldsymbol{X} = \begin{pmatrix} x_1 \\ x_2 \\ \vdots \\ x_n \end{pmatrix}, \quad \boldsymbol{b} = \begin{pmatrix} b_1 \\ b_2 \\ \vdots \\ b_m \end{pmatrix}.$$

Suppose, rank $(A) = m$ and B be any $m \times m$ sub-matrix formed by m linearly independent columns of A. Then as solution obtained by setting $(n - m)$ variables not associated with B equal to zero and solving the resulting system

$$B\boldsymbol{X}_B = \boldsymbol{b}$$
$$\text{or } \boldsymbol{X}_B = B^{-1}\boldsymbol{b}$$

is called a *Basic solution* to the given system of equations. The m variables which are associated with B are called *Basic Variables.* The $m \times m$ non-singular sub-matrix B of A is called as *Basis Matrix* and the columns of B as *Basic Vectors.* The variables which are not associated with B are called *non-basic variables.*

Example 1.2.10. *Find all the basic solutions of the system of equations*

$$2x_1 + x_2 + 4x_3 = 11$$
$$3x_1 + x_2 + 5x_3 = 14$$

[KU(MSc) 1992; CU(P) 1996]

Solution: Matrix form of equations: $AX = \boldsymbol{b}$, where

$$A = \begin{pmatrix} 2 & 1 & 4 \\ 3 & 1 & 5 \end{pmatrix}, \quad \boldsymbol{X} = \begin{pmatrix} x_1 \\ x_2 \\ x_3 \end{pmatrix}, \quad \boldsymbol{b} = \begin{pmatrix} 11 \\ 14 \end{pmatrix}.$$

Rank $(A) = 2$. Therefore, the maximum number of independent columns of A is 2. Possible sub-matrices consisting of independent columns of A are

$$B_1 = \begin{pmatrix} 2 & 1 \\ 3 & 1 \end{pmatrix}, \quad B_2 = \begin{pmatrix} 1 & 4 \\ 1 & 5 \end{pmatrix}, \quad B_3 = \begin{pmatrix} 2 & 4 \\ 3 & 5 \end{pmatrix}.$$

(B_1, B_2, B_3) are the basis matrices of the system of equations.

Corresponding to B_1, basic variables x_1, x_2 and non-basic variable x_3.

Corresponding to B_2, basic variables x_2, x_3 and non-basic variable x_1.

Corresponding to B_3, basic variables x_1, x_3 and non-basic variable x_2.

Let $\boldsymbol{X}_{B_1}=\begin{pmatrix}x_1\\x_2\end{pmatrix}$, $\boldsymbol{X}_{B_2}=\begin{pmatrix}x_2\\x_3\end{pmatrix}$, $\boldsymbol{X}_{B_3}=\begin{pmatrix}x_1\\x_3\end{pmatrix}$.

Basic solution associated to $B_1: B_1\boldsymbol{X}_{B_1}=\boldsymbol{b}\Rightarrow \boldsymbol{X}_{B_1}=B_1^{-1}\boldsymbol{b}\Rightarrow \boldsymbol{X}_{B_1}=\begin{pmatrix}2&1\\3&1\end{pmatrix}^{-1}\begin{pmatrix}11\\14\end{pmatrix}$

$$\Rightarrow \boldsymbol{X}_{B_1}=\begin{pmatrix}-1&1\\3&-2\end{pmatrix}\begin{pmatrix}11\\14\end{pmatrix}\Rightarrow \boldsymbol{X}_{B_1}=\begin{pmatrix}3\\5\end{pmatrix}.$$

Similarly, $X_{B_2}=\begin{pmatrix}-1\\3\end{pmatrix}$ and $X_{B_3}=\begin{pmatrix}1/2\\5/2\end{pmatrix}$.

Thus, all the basic solutions of the system of equations are $(3,5,0^*)^T$, $(0^*,-1,3)^T$ and $(1/2,0^*,5/2)^T$, where 0^* solution corresponds to non-basic variable.

Example 1.2.11. *Find all the basic solutions of the system of equations*

$$2x_1+3x_2-x_3+4x_4=8$$
$$x_1-2x_2+6x_3-7x_4=-3.$$

[JU(MSc) 1981]

Solution: Matrix form of the system $AX=\boldsymbol{b}$, where

$$A=\begin{pmatrix}2&3&-1&4\\1&-2&6&-7\end{pmatrix},\quad \boldsymbol{X}=\begin{pmatrix}x_1\\x_2\\x_3\\x_4\end{pmatrix},\quad \boldsymbol{b}=\begin{pmatrix}8\\-3\end{pmatrix}.$$

Rank $(A)=2$. Possible sub-matrices consisting of linearly independent columns of A are

$$B_1=\begin{pmatrix}2&3\\1&-2\end{pmatrix},\quad B_2=\begin{pmatrix}2&-1\\1&6\end{pmatrix},\quad B_3=\begin{pmatrix}2&4\\1&-7\end{pmatrix},$$

$$B_4=\begin{pmatrix}3&-1\\-2&6\end{pmatrix},\quad B_5=\begin{pmatrix}3&4\\-2&-7\end{pmatrix},\quad B_6=\begin{pmatrix}-1&4\\6&-7\end{pmatrix},$$

$$\boldsymbol{X}_{B_1}=\begin{pmatrix}x_1\\x_2\end{pmatrix},\quad \boldsymbol{X}_{B_2}=\begin{pmatrix}x_1\\x_3\end{pmatrix},\quad \boldsymbol{X}_{B_3}=\begin{pmatrix}x_1\\x_4\end{pmatrix},$$

$$\boldsymbol{X}_{B_4}=\begin{pmatrix}x_2\\x_3\end{pmatrix},\quad \boldsymbol{X}_{B_5}=\begin{pmatrix}x_2\\x_4\end{pmatrix},\quad \boldsymbol{X}_{B_6}=\begin{pmatrix}x_3\\x_4\end{pmatrix}.$$

The basic solution corresponding to basis matrix B_1 is obtained by setting non-basic variables $x_3=0$, $x_4=0$ and solving the resulting system

$$B_1\boldsymbol{X}_{B_1}=\boldsymbol{b}\Rightarrow \boldsymbol{X}_{B_1}=B_1^{-1}\boldsymbol{b}\Rightarrow \boldsymbol{X}_{B_1}=\begin{pmatrix}2&3\\1&-2\end{pmatrix}\begin{pmatrix}8\\-3\end{pmatrix}\Rightarrow \boldsymbol{X}_{B_1}=\begin{pmatrix}1\\2\end{pmatrix}.$$

$$\text{Similarly, } \boldsymbol{X}_{B_2} = \begin{pmatrix} \frac{45}{13} \\ -\frac{14}{13} \end{pmatrix}, \quad \boldsymbol{X}_{B_3} = \begin{pmatrix} \frac{22}{9} \\ \frac{7}{9} \end{pmatrix}, \quad \boldsymbol{X}_{B_4} = \begin{pmatrix} \frac{45}{16} \\ \frac{7}{16} \end{pmatrix},$$

$$\boldsymbol{X}_{B_5} = \begin{pmatrix} \frac{44}{13} \\ -\frac{7}{13} \end{pmatrix}, \quad \boldsymbol{X}_{B_6} = \begin{pmatrix} \frac{44}{17} \\ \frac{45}{17} \end{pmatrix}.$$

Thus, all the basic solutions of the system of equations are

$$(1, \; 2, \; 0^*, \; 0^*)^T; \quad \left(\frac{45}{13}, \; 0^*, \; -\frac{14}{13}, \; 0^*\right)^T; \quad \left(\frac{22}{9}, \; 0^*, \; 0^*, \; \frac{7}{9}\right)^T;$$

$$\left(0^*, \; \frac{45}{16}, \; \frac{7}{16}, \; 0^*\right)^T; \quad \left(0^*, \; \frac{44}{13}, \; 0^*, \; -\frac{7}{13}\right)^T; \quad \left(0^*, \; 0^*, \; \frac{44}{17}, \; \frac{45}{17}\right)^T.$$

Notes.

1. The basic solutions are finite in number. The possible number of basic solutions in a system of m equations in n unknowns will be the same as the number of combinations of n things taken m at a time and is

$$^nC_m = \frac{n!}{m!\,(n-m)!}.$$

2. We can partition the matrices A and $\boldsymbol{X}$ as $A = (B, \; R)$ and $\boldsymbol{X} = [\boldsymbol{X}_B \;\; \boldsymbol{X}_R]$, where B is an $m \times m$ non-singular matrix and R is an $m \times (n-m)$ matrix.

$$\boldsymbol{X}_B = (x_1, x_2, \ldots, x_m)^T, \qquad \boldsymbol{X}_R = (x_{m+1}, x_{m+2}, \ldots, x_n)^T.$$

Then the equation $A\boldsymbol{X} = \boldsymbol{b}$ can be written as $A\boldsymbol{X} = B\boldsymbol{X}_B + R\boldsymbol{X}_R = \boldsymbol{b}$.
Now setting $\boldsymbol{X}_R = \boldsymbol{0}$, we have $\boldsymbol{X}_B = B^{-1}\boldsymbol{b}$.

Definition (Degenerate basic solution). A basic solution to the system of equations $A\boldsymbol{X} = \boldsymbol{b}$ is called *degenerate* if one or more of the basic variables vanish.

In Ex. 1.2.10, none of the basic solutions is a degenerate basic solution as well as in Ex. 1.2.11 none is degenerate basic solutions. All the solutions obtained in the above examples are non-degenerate basic solutions where not a single basic variable vanishes.

Definition (Basic feasible solution). A basic solution to the system of equations $A\boldsymbol{X} = \boldsymbol{b}$ is said to be a *basic feasible solution* if all the values of basic variables are non-negative. If any basic variable has negative value the corresponding basic solution is called a *non-basic feasible* solution.

In Ex. 1.2.10, $(3, 5, 0^*)^T$, $\left(\frac{1}{2}, 0^*, \frac{5}{2}\right)^T$ are basic feasible solution, whereas $(0^*, -1, 3)^T$ is not a basic feasible solution.

In Ex. 1.2.11, the basic feasible solutions are $(1, 2, 0^*, 0^*)^T$, $\left(\frac{22}{9}, 0^*, 0^*, \frac{7}{9}\right)^T$, $\left(0^*, \frac{45}{16}, \frac{7}{16}, 0^*\right)$, $\left(0^*, 0^*, \frac{44}{17}, \frac{45}{17}\right)^T$, the rest are the non-basic feasible solutions.

Example 1.2.12. *Find the degenerate basic feasible solution, if any, of the following system of equations*

$$A\boldsymbol{X} = \boldsymbol{b}, \text{ where } A = \begin{pmatrix} 2 & 1 & -1 \\ 3 & 2 & 1 \end{pmatrix}, \quad \boldsymbol{X} = \begin{pmatrix} x_1 \\ x_2 \\ x_3 \end{pmatrix}, \quad \boldsymbol{b} = \begin{pmatrix} 2 \\ 3 \end{pmatrix}.$$

Solution: Maximum number of basic solutions $= {}^3C_2 = 3$.

Rank $(A) = 2$. Possible basis matrix consisting of 2 linearly independent columns of A are

$$B_1 = \begin{pmatrix} 2 & 1 \\ 3 & 2 \end{pmatrix}, \qquad B_2 = \begin{pmatrix} 1 & -1 \\ 2 & 1 \end{pmatrix}, \qquad B_3 = \begin{pmatrix} 2 & -1 \\ 3 & 1 \end{pmatrix},$$

$$\boldsymbol{X}_{B_1} = \begin{pmatrix} x_1 \\ x_2 \end{pmatrix}, \qquad \boldsymbol{X}_{B_2} = \begin{pmatrix} x_2 \\ x_3 \end{pmatrix}, \qquad \boldsymbol{X}_{B_3} = \begin{pmatrix} x_1 \\ x_3 \end{pmatrix}.$$

Basic solution corresponding to B_1: $\boldsymbol{X}_{B_1} = \begin{pmatrix} 2 & 1 \\ 3 & 2 \end{pmatrix}^{-1} \begin{pmatrix} 2 \\ 3 \end{pmatrix} = \begin{pmatrix} 1 \\ 0 \end{pmatrix}, \quad x_3 = 0.$

Basic solution corresponding to B_2: $\boldsymbol{X}_{B_2} = \begin{pmatrix} 1 & -1 \\ 2 & 1 \end{pmatrix}^{-1} \begin{pmatrix} 2 \\ 3 \end{pmatrix} = \begin{pmatrix} 5/3 \\ -1/3 \end{pmatrix}, \quad x_1 = 0.$

Basic solution corresponding to B_3: $\boldsymbol{X}_{B_3} = \begin{pmatrix} 2 & -1 \\ 3 & 1 \end{pmatrix}^{-1} \begin{pmatrix} 2 \\ 3 \end{pmatrix} = \begin{pmatrix} 1 \\ 0 \end{pmatrix}, \quad x_2 = 0.$

All basic solutions of the system are: $(1,0,0^*)^T$, $\left(0^*, \frac{5}{3}, -\frac{1}{3}\right)^T$, $(1,0^*,0)^T$.

According to the definitions given above the basic solutions $(1,0,0^*)^T$ and $(1,0^*,0)^T$ are degenerate basic feasible solutions but $\left(0^*, \frac{5}{3}, -\frac{1}{3}\right)^T$ is a non-degenerate and not a basic feasible solution.

1.2.5 Convex Sets in R^n

The main objective of this section is to introduce the fundamental concept of convex sets, describe some properties of these sets and derive the basic results for convex sets.

Definition (Line). Let $\boldsymbol{x}^1, \boldsymbol{x}^2 \in R^n$. The line through $\boldsymbol{x}^1$ and $\boldsymbol{x}^2$ is defined as the set

$$\{\boldsymbol{x} \mid \boldsymbol{x} = (1-\lambda)\boldsymbol{x}^1 + \lambda \boldsymbol{x}^2,\ \lambda \in \mathbb{R} \text{ (real number)}\}$$

or equivalently

$$\{\boldsymbol{x} \mid \boldsymbol{x} = p_1\boldsymbol{x}^1 + p_2\boldsymbol{x}^2,\ p_1, p_2 \in \mathbb{R},\ p_1 + p_2 = 1\}.$$

Definition (Line Segments). Let $\boldsymbol{x}^1, \boldsymbol{x}^2 \in R^n$, we define the following line segments joining $\boldsymbol{x}^1$ and $\boldsymbol{x}^2$.

(i) Closed line segment $[\boldsymbol{x}^1, \boldsymbol{x}^2] = \{\boldsymbol{x} \mid \boldsymbol{x} = (1-\lambda)\boldsymbol{x}^1 + \lambda\boldsymbol{x}^2,\ 0 \le \lambda \le 1\}$

(ii) Open line segment $(\boldsymbol{x}^1, \boldsymbol{x}^2) = \{\boldsymbol{x} \mid \boldsymbol{x} = (1-\lambda)\boldsymbol{x}^1 + \lambda\boldsymbol{x}^2,\ 0 < \lambda < 1\}$

(iii) Closed open line segment $[\boldsymbol{x}^1, \boldsymbol{x}^2) = \{\boldsymbol{x} \mid \boldsymbol{x} = (1-\lambda)\boldsymbol{x}^1 + \lambda\boldsymbol{x}^2,\ 0 \le \lambda < 1\}$

(iv) Open closed line segment $(\boldsymbol{x}^1, \boldsymbol{x}^2] = \{\boldsymbol{x} \mid \boldsymbol{x} = (1-\lambda)\boldsymbol{x}^1 + \lambda\boldsymbol{x}^2,\ 0 < \lambda \le 1\}$.

Definition (Convex Set). A set $\Gamma \subset R^n$ is a *convex set* if the closed line segment joining every two points of Γ is in Γ. Mathematically, $\Gamma \subset R^n$ is convex set, if

$$\left.\begin{array}{l} \boldsymbol{x}^1, \boldsymbol{x}^2 \in \Gamma \subset R^n \\ \lambda \in \mathbb{R},\ 0 \le \lambda \le 1 \end{array}\right\} \Longrightarrow [\boldsymbol{x}^1, \boldsymbol{x}^2] \in \Gamma \Longrightarrow (1-\lambda)\boldsymbol{x}^1 + \lambda\boldsymbol{x}^2 \in \Gamma.$$

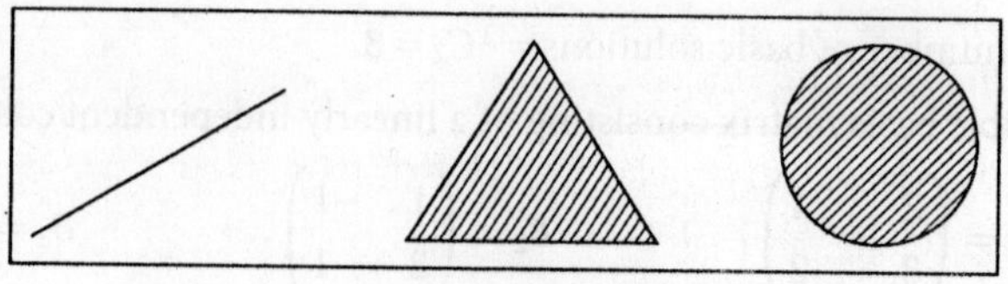

Convex Sets

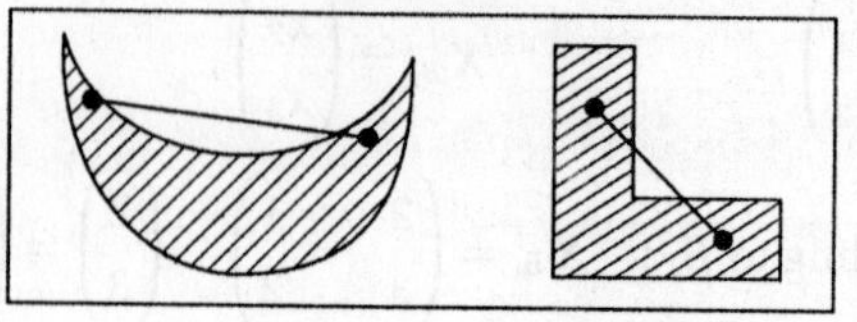

Non-convex Sets

Example 1.2.13. *Show that* $\Gamma = \{(x_1, x_2) | x_1 + 2x_2 = 5\} \subset R^2$ *is a convex set.*

Solution: Let $\boldsymbol{u} = (u_1, u_2)$, $\boldsymbol{v} = (v_1, v_2) \in \Gamma$.

Then line segment joining $\boldsymbol{u}$ and $\boldsymbol{v}$ is given by $\lambda\boldsymbol{u} + (1-\lambda)\boldsymbol{v} = \boldsymbol{w}$, $0 \le \lambda \le 1$.

$$\boldsymbol{w} = \{\lambda u_1 + (1-\lambda)v_1, \lambda u_2 + (1-\lambda)v_2\} = \{u_1', v_1'\}.$$

$$\begin{aligned} \text{Now } \boldsymbol{u}_1' + 2\boldsymbol{v}_1' &= \lambda u_1 + (1-\lambda)v_1 + 2\lambda u_2 + 2(1-\lambda)v_2 \\ &= \lambda(u_1 + 2u_2) + (1-\lambda)(v_1 + 2v_2) \\ &= 5\lambda + (1-\lambda)5 \\ &= 5 \quad [\because u_1 + 2u_2 = 5, v_1 + 2v_2 = 5] \end{aligned}$$

Therefore, the line segment joining $\boldsymbol{u}, \boldsymbol{v} \in \Gamma$. Hence, Γ is a convex set.

Example 1.2.14. *Show that* $S = \{(x_1, x_2) | 3x_1^2 + 2x_2^2 \le 6\} \subset R^2$ *is a convex set.*

Solution: Let $\boldsymbol{u}, \boldsymbol{v} \in S$, $\boldsymbol{u} = (u_1, u_2)$, $\boldsymbol{v} = (v_1, v_2)$.

The closed segment joining $\boldsymbol{u}$ and $\boldsymbol{v}$ is the set $\{\boldsymbol{w} | \boldsymbol{w} = \lambda\boldsymbol{u} + (1+\lambda)\boldsymbol{v},\ 0 \le \lambda \le 1\}$.

Let $\boldsymbol{w} = (w_1, w_2)$ so that $w_1 = \lambda u_1 + (1-\lambda)v_1$

$$w_2 = \lambda u_2 + (1-\lambda)v_2$$

$$\begin{aligned} \text{Now } 3w_1^2 + 2w_2^2 &= \lambda^2(3u_1^2 + 2u_2^2) + (1-\lambda)^2[3v_1^2 + 2v_2^2] + 2\lambda(1-\lambda)[3u_1v_1 + 2u_2v_2] \\ &\le 6\lambda^2 + (1-\lambda)^2 \cdot 6 + 12\lambda(1-\lambda). \end{aligned}$$

$$\therefore 3w_1^2 + 2w_2^2 \le 6 \left[\because 3u_1v_1 + 2u_2v_2 \le \sqrt{\left(\sqrt{3}u_1\right)^2 + \left(\sqrt{2}u_2\right)^2}\sqrt{\left(\sqrt{3}v_1\right)^2 + \left(\sqrt{2}v_2\right)^2}\right]$$

$\therefore \boldsymbol{w} = (w_1, w_2)$ is in S and hence, S is a convex set.

Definition (Half Spaces and Hyperplane). Let $\boldsymbol{c} \in R^n$ and $\boldsymbol{c} \neq \boldsymbol{0}$ and $\alpha \in \mathbb{R}$. Then the sets

$$U^- = \{\boldsymbol{x} | \boldsymbol{x} \in R^n,\ \boldsymbol{cx} < \alpha\}$$

$$\text{and } U^+ = \{\boldsymbol{x} | \boldsymbol{x} \in R^n,\ \boldsymbol{cx} > \alpha\}$$

are called *open half spaces* and the sets

$$V^- = \{\boldsymbol{x} | \boldsymbol{x} \in R^n,\ \boldsymbol{cx} \le \alpha\}$$

$$\text{and } V^+ = \{\boldsymbol{x} | \boldsymbol{x} \in R^n,\ \boldsymbol{cx} \ge \alpha\}$$

are *called closed half spaces* and the set

$$H_n = \{x \mid x \in R^n,\ cx = \alpha\}$$

is called the *Hyperplane* in R^n.

If $\alpha = 0$, $cx = 0$, then the hyperplane passes through the origin. If $\alpha \neq 0$, x^1 and x^2 be two distinct points on the hyperplane, then $c\,(x^1 - x^2) = 0$. Thus, c is orthogonal to any vector $(x^1 - x^2)$ on the hyperplane.

Definition (Vertex). Let Γ be a convex set in R^n, each $x \in \Gamma$ for which there exist no two distinct $x^1, x^2 \in \Gamma$ different from x such that $x \in [x^1, x^2]$ is called a *vertex* of Γ or an *extreme* point of Γ.

1. A convex set $\Gamma \subset R^n$ may have no vertices. For examples, the plane $\{x \mid x \in R^n,\ cx = \alpha\}$, An open ball $B_\delta(\bar{x}) = [x \mid \|x - \bar{x}\| < \delta]$ have no vertices.
2. Example of a finite number of vertices is $\Lambda = \{x \mid x \in R^n,\ x \geq 0,\ ex = 1\}$, where e is an n-vector of ones and has n vertices $e^i, = 1, 2, \ldots, n$, where $e^i_j = \begin{cases} 1, & \text{if } i = j \\ 0, & \text{if } i \neq j. \end{cases}$
3. Example of an infinite number of vertices is closed ball $B_\delta(\bar{x}) = \{x \mid x \in R^n,\ \|x - \bar{x}\| = \delta\}$ has an infinite number of vertices.

Some Important Results

Result 1. *A hyperplane is a convex set.*

Proof. Let $H_n = \{x \mid x \in R^n,\ cx = \alpha,\ \alpha \in \mathbb{R}\}$ be a hyperplane in R^n.

Let $x^1, x^2 \in H_n$, then $cx^1 = \alpha, cx^2 = \alpha$.

Now $x^3 = \lambda x^1 + (1 - \lambda)\, x^2$ a closed line segment joining x^1, x^2.

Then
$$\begin{aligned} cx^3 &= c\,[\lambda x^1 + (1-\lambda) x^2] \\ &= \lambda c x^1 + (1-\lambda) c x^2 \\ &= \lambda \alpha + (1-\lambda)\alpha \\ &= \alpha. \end{aligned}$$

$x^3 \in H_n$. Hence, H_n is a convex set.

Result 2. *If $(\Gamma_i)_{i \in I}$ is a family (finite or infinite) of convex sets in R^n, then their intersection $\bigcap_{i \in I} \Gamma_i$ is a convex set.*

Proof. Let $x^1, x^2 \in \bigcap_{i \in I} \Gamma_i$ and $0 \leq \lambda \leq 1$, then for each $i \in I$, $x^1, x^2 \in \Gamma_i$ and since Γ_i is convex, $(1 - \lambda) x^1 + \lambda x^2 \in \Gamma_i$. Hence, the theorem.

Result 3. *A set $\Gamma \subset R^n$ is convex if and only if for each integer $m \geq 1$, every convex combination of any m points of Γ is in Γ. Equivalently a necessary and sufficient condition for the sets Γ to be convex is that for each integer $m \geq 1$.*

$$\left.\begin{aligned} & x^1, x^2, \ldots, x^m \in \Gamma \\ & p_1, p_2, \ldots, p_m \geq 0 \\ & \sum_{i=1}^{m} p_i = 1 \end{aligned}\right\} \Rightarrow p_1 x^1 + p_2 x^2 + \cdots + p_m x^m \in \Gamma$$

Proof. A point $\boldsymbol{b} \in R^n$ is said to be a *convex combination* of vectors $\boldsymbol{a}^1, \boldsymbol{a}^2, \ldots, \boldsymbol{a}^m \in R^n$ if there exists m real numbers $p_1, p_2, \ldots, p_m$ such that

$$\boldsymbol{b} = p_1\boldsymbol{a}^1 + p_2\boldsymbol{a}^2 + \cdots + p_m\boldsymbol{a}^m, \quad p_1, p_2, \ldots, p_m \geq 0, \quad \sum_{i=1}^{m} p_i = 1.$$

The sufficiency of this result is trivial. If $m = 2$, then Γ is convex by definition of convex set.

The necessity of this result will be shown by mathematical induction. For $m = 1$, it holds trivially, for $m = 2$ it holds as a consequence of the definition of convex set. Assume that result holds for particular m and will now show that it also holds for $(m+1)$.

Let $\boldsymbol{x}^1, \boldsymbol{x}^2, \ldots, \boldsymbol{x}_m, \boldsymbol{x}^{m+1} \in \Gamma$

$$p_1, p_2, \ldots, p_m, p_{m+1} \geq 0 \quad \text{and} \quad \sum_{i=1}^{m+1} p_i = 1.$$

If $p_{m+1} = 0$, then $p_1\boldsymbol{x}^1 + p_2\boldsymbol{x}^2 + \cdots + p_m\boldsymbol{x}^m \in \Gamma$ as it holds for m

If $p_{m+1} = 1$, then $p_1\boldsymbol{x}^1 + p_2\boldsymbol{x}^2 + \cdots + p_{m+1}\boldsymbol{x}^{m+1} = \boldsymbol{x}^{m+1} \in \Gamma$

If $0 < p_{m+1} < 1$,

$$\sum_{i=1}^{m+1} p_i x^i = \sum_{i=1}^{m} p_i \left[\frac{p_1}{\sum p_i} x^1 + \cdots + \frac{p_m}{\sum p_i} x^m \right] + p_{m+1} x^{m+1}$$

A point in Γ since the result holds for m

A point in Γ because the result holds for $m = 2$

Hence, the result.

Result 4. *The sum* $\Gamma + \Lambda$ *of two convex sets* Γ *and* Λ *in* R^n *is a convex set.*

Proof. Let $\Gamma, \Lambda \subset R^n$. Their sum is defined by

$$\Gamma + \Lambda = \{\boldsymbol{z} \mid \boldsymbol{z} = \boldsymbol{x} + \boldsymbol{y},\ \boldsymbol{x} \in \Gamma,\ \boldsymbol{y} \in \Lambda\}.$$

Now, let $\boldsymbol{z}^1, \boldsymbol{z}^2 \in \Gamma + \Lambda$, then $\boldsymbol{z}^1 = \boldsymbol{x}^1 + \boldsymbol{y}^1$, $\boldsymbol{z}^2 = \boldsymbol{x}^2 + \boldsymbol{y}^2$, where $\boldsymbol{x}^1, \boldsymbol{x}^2 \in \Gamma$ and $\boldsymbol{y}^1, \boldsymbol{y}^2 \in \Lambda$.

For $0 \leq \lambda \leq 1$,

$$(1-\lambda) z^1 + \lambda z^2 = \left[(1-\lambda) x^1 + \lambda x^2\right] + \left[(1-\lambda) y^1 + \lambda y^2\right]$$

→ A point in Γ ← by convexity of Γ → A point in Λ ← by convexity of Λ

Hence, $\Gamma + \Lambda$ is a convex set.

Definition (Polytope and Polyhedron). A set in R^n which is the intersection of a finite number of closed half spaces in R^n is called a *polytope.* If a polytope is bounded, i.e., for each $\boldsymbol{x}^*$ in the polytope $\|\boldsymbol{x}^*\| \leq \delta$ for some fixed $\delta \in \mathbb{R}$ it is called a *polyhedron.*

Definition (Convex Hull). Let $\Gamma \subset R^n$. The *convex hull* on Γ, usually denoted by $[\Gamma]$ is the intersection of all convex sets in R^n containing Γ.

Result 5. *The convex hull* $[\Gamma]$ *of a set* $\Gamma \subset R^n$ *is equal to the set of all convex combinations of points of* Γ.

Proof. Let $\Lambda = \left\{ \boldsymbol{x} \mid \boldsymbol{x} = \sum_{i=1}^{k} p_i \boldsymbol{a}^i,\ p_i \in \mathbb{R},\ \boldsymbol{a}^i \in \Gamma,\ \sum_{i=1}^{k} p_i = 1,\ p_i \geq 0,\ k \geq 1 \right\}$

If $\boldsymbol{x}^1, \boldsymbol{x}^2 \in \Lambda$, then $\boldsymbol{x}^1 = \sum_{i=1}^{k} p_i \boldsymbol{a}^i, \quad p_i \in \mathbb{R}, \quad \boldsymbol{a}^i \in \Gamma, \quad p_i \geq 0, \quad \sum_{i=1}^{k} p_i = 1$

$$\boldsymbol{x}^2 = \sum_{i=1}^{m} q_i \boldsymbol{b}^i, \quad q_i \in \mathbb{R}, \quad \boldsymbol{b}^i \in \Gamma, \quad q_i \geq 0, \quad \sum_{i=1}^{m} q_i = 1.$$

For $0 \leq \lambda \leq 1$, $\lambda \boldsymbol{x}^1 + (1-\lambda)x^2 = \lambda \sum_{i=1}^{k} p_i \boldsymbol{a}^i + (1-\lambda) \sum_{i=1}^{m} q_i \boldsymbol{b}^i$

$$\lambda p_i \geq 0,\ (1-\lambda) q_i \geq 0,\ \sum_{i=1}^{k} \lambda p_i + \sum_{i=1}^{m} (1-\lambda) q_i = 1.$$

Thus, $\lambda \boldsymbol{x}^1 + (1-\lambda)\boldsymbol{x}^2 \in \Lambda$ and Λ is convex. It is also clear that $\Gamma \subset \Lambda$. Since Γ is convex, then $[\Gamma] \subset \Lambda$. We also have the convex set $[\Gamma]$ containing Γ must also contains all convex combination of the points of Γ. Hence, $\Lambda \subset [\Gamma]$ and, therefore, $\Lambda = [\Gamma]$.

Result 6. *The set of all convex combinations of a finite number of points is a convex set.*

Proof. Let $S = \left\{ \boldsymbol{x} \mid \boldsymbol{x} = \sum_{i=1}^{m} \lambda_i \boldsymbol{x}_i,\ \lambda_i \geq 0,\ \sum_{i=1}^{m} \lambda_i = 1 \right\}$.

To prove S is a convex set, take two points $\boldsymbol{x}', \boldsymbol{x}'' \in S$ and consider the closed line segment of $\boldsymbol{x}', \boldsymbol{x}''$ as $\boldsymbol{x}^* = \lambda \boldsymbol{x}' + (1-\lambda)\boldsymbol{x}'', 0 \leq \lambda \leq 1$.

Since $\boldsymbol{x}', \boldsymbol{x}'' \in S$, $\boldsymbol{x}' = \sum_{i=1}^{m} \lambda_i' \boldsymbol{x}_i, \quad \lambda_i' \geq 0, \quad \sum_{i=1}^{m} \lambda_i' = 1$

$$\boldsymbol{x}'' = \sum_{i=1}^{m} \lambda_i'' \boldsymbol{x}_i, \quad \lambda_i'' \geq 0, \quad \sum_{i=1}^{m} \lambda_i'' = 1$$

$$\boldsymbol{x}^* = \lambda \sum_{i=1}^{m} \lambda_i' \boldsymbol{x}_i + (1-\lambda) \sum_{i=1}^{m} \lambda_i'' \boldsymbol{x}_i = \sum_{i=1}^{m} \lambda_i^* \boldsymbol{x}_i, \text{ where } \lambda_i^* = \lambda \lambda_i' + (1-\lambda)\lambda_i''.$$

Since $0 \leq \lambda < 1, 1-\lambda \geq 0, \lambda \geq 0, \lambda_i' \geq 0, \lambda_i'' \geq 0$ imply that $\lambda_i^* \geq 0$ and also

$$\sum_{i=1}^{m} \lambda_i^* = \lambda \sum_{i=1}^{m} \lambda_1' + (1-\lambda) \sum_{i=1}^{m} \lambda_1'' = 1.$$

$\therefore$ S is a convex set as $\boldsymbol{x}^* \in S$ and $\boldsymbol{x}^*$ is arbitrary.

1.2.6 Convex and Concave Functions

In this section we briefly introduce convex and concave functions defined on subset of R^n. These two functions are extremely important in different mathematical programming because they are among the few functions for which sufficient optimality criteria can be given, and they are the only functions for which necessary optimality conditions can be given without linearisation.

Definition (Convex function). A function θ defined on a set $\Gamma \subset R^n$ is said to be *convex* at $\boldsymbol{x}^1 \in \Gamma$, if

$$\left.\begin{array}{c} \boldsymbol{x}^2 \in \Gamma \\ 0 \le \lambda \le 1 \\ (1-\lambda)\boldsymbol{x}^1 + \lambda \boldsymbol{x}^2 \in \Gamma \end{array}\right\} \Rightarrow (1-\lambda)\theta\left(\boldsymbol{x}^1\right) + \lambda\theta\left(\boldsymbol{x}^2\right) \ge \theta\left[(1-\lambda)\,\boldsymbol{x}^1 + \lambda \boldsymbol{x}^2\right]$$

θ is said to be convex on Γ, if it is convex at each $\boldsymbol{x} \in \Gamma$.

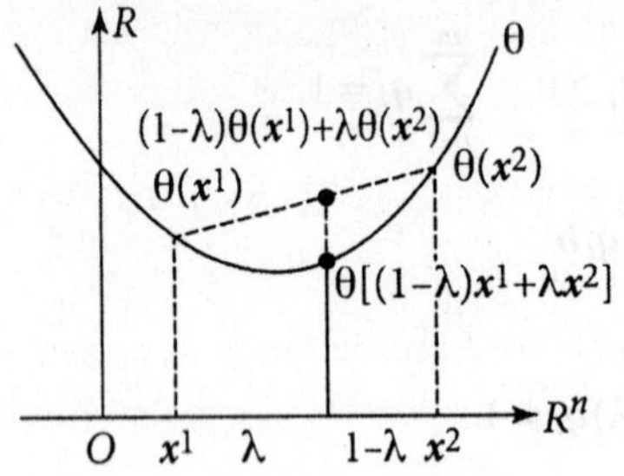

Fig. 1 Convex function θ on R^n

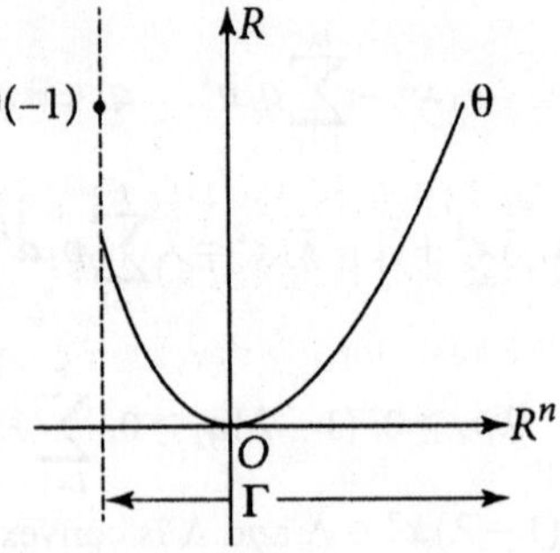

Fig. 2 Convex function θ on $\Gamma[-1,\infty)$

Definition (Concave function). A function θ defined on a set $\Gamma \subset R^n$ is said to be *concave* at $\boldsymbol{x}^1 \in \Gamma$, if

$$\left.\begin{array}{c} \boldsymbol{x}^2 \in \Gamma \\ 0 \le \lambda \le 1 \\ (1-\lambda)\boldsymbol{x}^1 + \lambda \boldsymbol{x}^2 \in \Gamma \end{array}\right\} \Rightarrow (1-\lambda)\theta\left(\boldsymbol{x}^1\right) + \lambda\theta\left(\boldsymbol{x}^2\right) \le \theta\left[(1-\lambda)\,\boldsymbol{x}^1 + \lambda \boldsymbol{x}^2\right]$$

θ is said to be concave on Γ, if it is concave at each $\boldsymbol{x} \in \Gamma$.

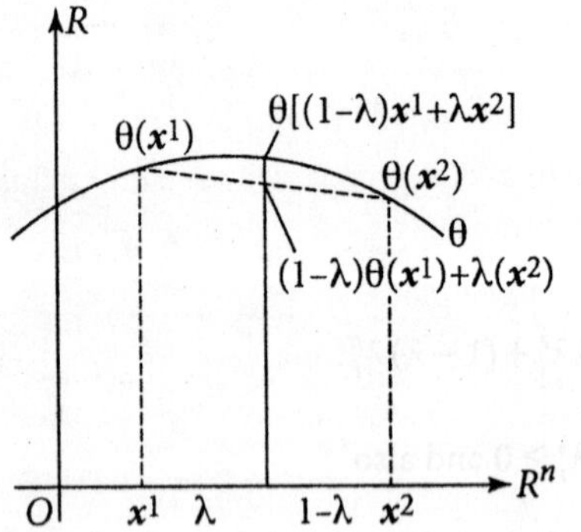

Fig. 3 Concave function θ on R^n

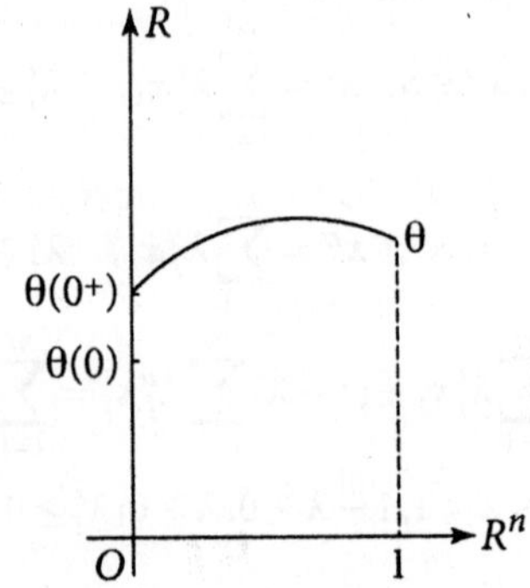

Fig. 4 Concave function θ on $\Gamma[0,1]$

Obviously, θ is concave at $\boldsymbol{x} \in \Gamma$, if and only if $-\theta$ is convex at $\boldsymbol{x} \in \Gamma$. Hence, results obtained for convex functions can be changed into results for concave functions by appropriate multiplication by (-1) and vice versa.

Important Result

Let $f = (f_1, f_2, \ldots, f_m)$ be an m dimensional vector function defined on $\Gamma \subset R^n$. If f is convex at $\boldsymbol{x}^1 \in \Gamma$, then each non-negative linear combination of its components f_i

$$\theta(\boldsymbol{x}) = pf(\boldsymbol{x}),\ p \ge 0 \text{ is convex at } \boldsymbol{x}^1.$$

Proof. Let $\boldsymbol{x} \in \Gamma, 0 \leq \lambda \leq 1$ and let $(1-\lambda)\boldsymbol{x}^1 + \lambda \boldsymbol{x} \in \Gamma$, then

$$\begin{aligned}\theta\left[(1-\lambda)\boldsymbol{x}^1+\lambda\boldsymbol{x}\right] &= pf\left[(1-\lambda)\boldsymbol{x}^1+\lambda\boldsymbol{x}\right]\\ &\leq p\left[(1-\lambda)f\left(\boldsymbol{x}^1\right)+\lambda f(\boldsymbol{x})\right] \ \left[\text{by convexity of } f \text{ at } \boldsymbol{x}^1 \text{ and } p \geq 0\right]\\ &= (1-\lambda)pf\left(\boldsymbol{x}^1\right)+\lambda pf(\boldsymbol{x})\\ &= (1-\lambda)\theta\left(\boldsymbol{x}^1\right)+\lambda\theta(\boldsymbol{x}).\end{aligned}$$

Hence, $\theta(\boldsymbol{x})$ is convex at $\boldsymbol{x}^1$.

1.3 REVIEW OF PROBABILITY DISTRIBUTIONS, STOCHASTIC PROCESS AND THE z-TRANSFORM

This section is the basis for the development of all the probabilistic decision models presented in the different chapters. The material in this section is designed to provide you with a basic and fundamental understanding of these topics.

1.3.1 Random Variables and Probability Distribution

If corresponding to every point $\cup$ of the event space S, we have by a given rule, a real value of $X = X(\cup)$, i.e., X is a real valued function defined on S, then X is called a *random variable* (r.v.). The set of all values which X takes up will be called the *spectrum* of the r.v.

For examples: (i) Let the random experiment consist in throwing a die and X denote the number on the turned up face of the die. Then X is an r.v., the spectrum consists of six points $\{1,2,3,4,5,6\}$.

(ii) The number of telephone calls during a fixed interval of time is an r.v., the spectrum of which is the set of all non-negative integers $0,1,2,\ldots$

An r.v. may be *discrete* or *continuous*. A discrete variable takes on specific values at discrete points on the real line, and a continuous variable assumes any value over a continuous range of the real line. The two r.v.'s mentioned above are of discrete type. But in the component failure model, the r.v. is continuous.

Associated with the r.v. x is a function $f(x)$ that can be used to assign probability measure to this r.v. This function is called *probability density function* (pdf). If x is a continuous r.v. on the range $(-\infty, +\infty)$, its pdf $f(x)$ must satisfy $f(x) \geq 0: -\infty < x \leq \infty$.

$$\int_{-\infty}^{\infty} f(x)\,dx = 1.$$

Similarly, if x is a discrete r.v., its *probability mass function* (pmf) $p(x)$, which defines the probability that x assumes a given value, must satisfy $p(x) \geq 0 \ \forall \ x$.

$$\sum_{\text{all } x} p(x) = 1.$$

Example 1.3.1. *To illustrative the properties of* pdf, *consider*

$$f(x) = \begin{cases} kx(1-x), & 0 < x < 1 \\ 0, & \text{elsewhere} \end{cases}$$

For $f(x)$ to be a pdf, the condition $\int_{-\infty}^{\infty} f(x)\,dx = 1$ must be satisfied.

$$\int_0^1 kx(1-x)\,dx = 1 \Rightarrow k\int_0^1 (x-x^2)\,dx = 1 \Rightarrow \frac{k}{6} = 1 \Rightarrow k = 6.$$

Since $k > 0$, it follows that $f(x) \geq 0$.

Similarly, for the die-rolling experiment, the associated probabilities of the discrete r.v.'s are given by

x	1	2	3	4	5	6
$p(x)$	1/6	1/6	1/6	1/6	1/6	1/6

which satisfy the conditions of a pmf.

Another useful probability measure is the *cumulative density function* (cdf). Let $F(x)$ represent the cdf for continuous r.v. $x, -\infty < x < \infty$. For any real number a, $F(a)$ defines the probability that $x \leq a$,

$$F(a) = P\{x \leq a\} = P\{-\infty < x \leq a\} = \int_{-\infty}^{a} f(x)\,dx.$$

Now, for $b > a$, the event $-\infty < x \leq a$ and $a < x \leq b$ are mutually exclusive, and

$$(-\infty < x \leq a) + (a < x \leq b) = (-\infty < x \leq b)$$
$$\Rightarrow P(-\infty < x \leq a) + P(a < x \leq b) = P(-\infty < x \leq b)$$
$$\Rightarrow P(a < x \leq b) = P(-\infty < x \leq b) - P(-\infty < x \leq a)$$
$$\Rightarrow \int_a^b f(x)\,dx = \int_{-\infty}^{b} f(x)\,dx - \int_{-\infty}^{a} f(x)\,dx = F(b) - F(a).$$

The given probability equals the area under $f(x)$ enclosed in the range $a < x \leq b$.

Since $P(a < x \leq b) = F(b) - F(a) = \int_a^b \frac{d}{dx} F(x)\,dx$

or, $P(a < x \leq b) = \int_a^b f(x)\,dx.$

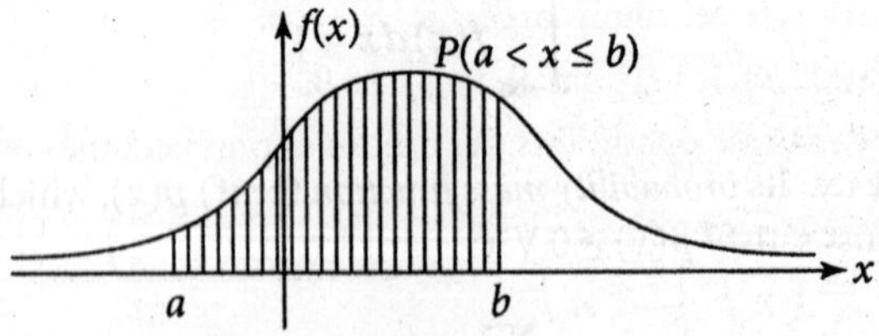

Fig. 5

Therefore,

$$f(x) = \frac{d}{dx} F(x).$$

Thus, the probability law of r.v. x is in general defined completely by either $f(x)$ or $F(x)$. The curve $y = f(x)$ is called the *density curve*, which gives a useful graphical representation in the continuous case.

Similar definitions can be made for the cdf in the discrete case by substituting $p(x)$ for $f(x)$ in all the properties above. This will require changing integration to summation and differentiation is replaced by differences.

1.3.2 Discrete Probability Distributions

I. Binomial Distribution

An r.v. x which takes two values 0 and 1 with probabilities $P(x=0)=q$ and $P(x=1)=p$, $p+q=1$ is called *Bernoulli variate* and is said to have a *Bernoulli distribution.*

Consider n independent Bernoulli trials, n is finite, in which the probability of success S, i.e., $P(x=S)=p$ and probability of failure F, i.e., $P(x=F)=q=1-p$ in each trial.

The probability of k successes and consequently $(n-k)$ failures in n independent trials is given by $p^k q^{n-k}$. Now k successes in n trials can occur in ${}^nC_k$ different ways and the probability of each of these ways is $p^k q^{n-k}$, the addition law of probability gives

$$P(x=k)={}^nC_k p^k q^{n-k}, \quad k=0,1,2,\ldots,n.$$

This is the *binomial distribution* with parameters n and p. It is a *discrete distribution* and satisfies the conditions for pmf, $P(x=k)\geq 0 \;\forall\; k=0,1,2,\ldots,n$.

$$\sum_{k=0}^{n} P(x=k)=\sum_{k=0}^{n} {}^nC_k p^k q^{n-k}=(q+p)^n=1.$$

Another important distribution that occurs from Bernoulli independent trials is *negative binomial* distribution. Let j and l represent the number of trials and a fixed number of successes respectively. The negative binomial pmf is given by

$$P(x=j)={}^{j-1}C_{l-1}p^l q^{j-l}, \quad j=l,l+1,l+2,\ldots$$

In particular, when $l=1$, it is a *geometric distribution*

$$P(x=j)=pq^{j-1}, \quad j=1,2,3,\ldots$$

II. Poisson Distribution

Suppose that in the binomial distribution

(i) n, the number of trials, is indefinitely large, i.e., $n\to\infty$.

(ii) p, the probability of success, is very small, i.e., $p\to 0$.

(iii) $np=\lambda>0$, then under these conditions the binomial pmf becomes:

$$P(x=k)={}^nC_k\left(\frac{\lambda}{n}\right)^k\left(1-\frac{\lambda}{n}\right)^{n-k}=\frac{1\cdot\left(1-\frac{1}{n}\right)\left(1-\frac{2}{n}\right)\ldots\left(1-\frac{k-1}{n}\right)}{k!}\cdot\frac{\lambda^k\left(1-\frac{\lambda}{n}\right)^n}{\left(1-\frac{\lambda}{n}\right)^k}.$$

Now as $n\to\infty$,

$$P(x=k)=\frac{\lambda^k e^{-\lambda}}{k!}, \quad k=0,1,2,\ldots$$

which is the *Poisson distribution.* Thus, if n is large and p small such that $\lambda=np>0$, the *Poisson distribution* approximates the *binomial.* A typical application of Poisson distribution occurs in analysing waiting line problems (chapter of Queueing Models).

Example 1.3.2. *A radioactive source emits on the average 2.5 particles per second. Calculate the probability that 3 or more particles will be emitted in an interval of 4 seconds.*

Solution: Here, $\lambda = 2.5$ so that the number of particles emitted in an interval of 4 seconds is Poisson distributed with parameter $\lambda = 10$. Hence, the required probability is

$$P(x \geq 3) = 1 - P(x=0) - P(x=1) - P(x=2) - P(x=3) = 1 - \sum_{k=0}^{3} \frac{e^{-10}10^k}{k!}.$$

1.3.3 Continuous Probability Distributions

I. Normal Distribution

This is defined by

$$f(x) = \frac{1}{\sqrt{2\pi}\sigma} e^{-\frac{(x-\mu)^2}{2\sigma^2}}, \quad -\infty < x < \infty$$

where $\mu, \sigma > 0$ being the parameters of the normal distribution.

$$\text{We have} \int_{-\infty}^{\infty} f(x)\,dx = \frac{1}{\sqrt{2\pi}\sigma} \int_{-\infty}^{\infty} e^{-\frac{(x-\mu)^2}{2\sigma^2}} dx = \frac{1}{\sqrt{\pi}} \int_{-\infty}^{\infty} e^{-z^2} dz$$

$$= \frac{2}{\sqrt{\pi}} \int_{0}^{\infty} e^{-z^2} = \frac{1}{\sqrt{\pi}} \int_{0}^{\infty} e^{-t} t^{-1/2} dt \frac{\Gamma\left(\frac{1}{2}\right)}{\sqrt{\pi}} = 1.$$

The cdf of normal distribution is defined by

$$F(x) = \int_{-\infty}^{x} \frac{1}{\sqrt{2\pi}\sigma} e^{-\frac{(y-\mu)^2}{2\sigma^2}} dy.$$

Typical pdf and cdf of normal distribution are shown in the following figures.

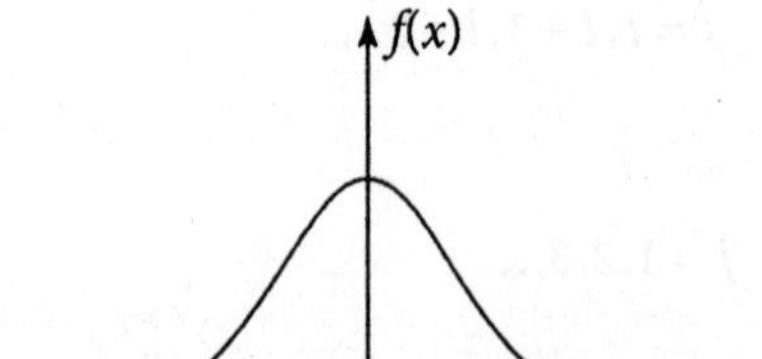

Fig. 6

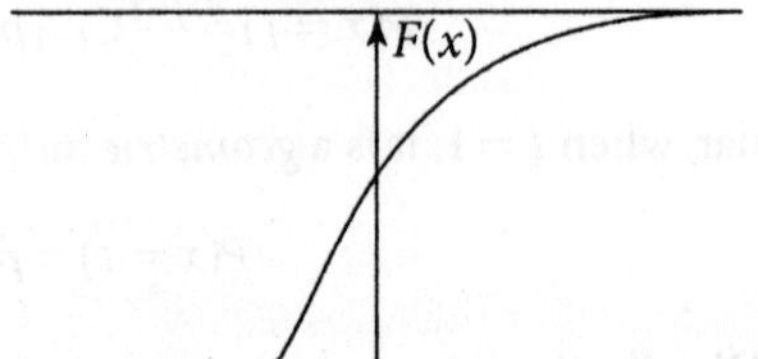

Fig. 7

The expression for the cdf $F(x)$ cannot be evaluated in a closed form suitable for computation. For this reason, normal tables that give the values of $F(x)$ of a function of x are available. These tables are based on the following *Standard normal* pdf

$$\phi(z) = \frac{1}{\sqrt{2\pi}} e^{-z^2/2}, \quad -\infty < z < \infty$$

with $\mu = 0$ and $\sigma = 1$. The corresponding cdf is given by

$$\Phi(z) = \frac{1}{\sqrt{2\pi}} \int_{-\infty}^{z} e^{-y^2/2} dy.$$

This is obtained from regular form by making the substitution $z = \frac{x-\mu}{\sigma}$.

II. Exponential Distribution

An important distribution often encountered in waiting-line or Queueing theory is the *exponential distribution.* A continuous r.v. x assumes non-negative values is said to have an exponential distribution with parameter $\mu > 0$ if its pdf is given by

$$f(x) = \begin{cases} \mu e^{-\mu x}, & x > 0 \\ 0, & \text{otherwise.} \end{cases}$$

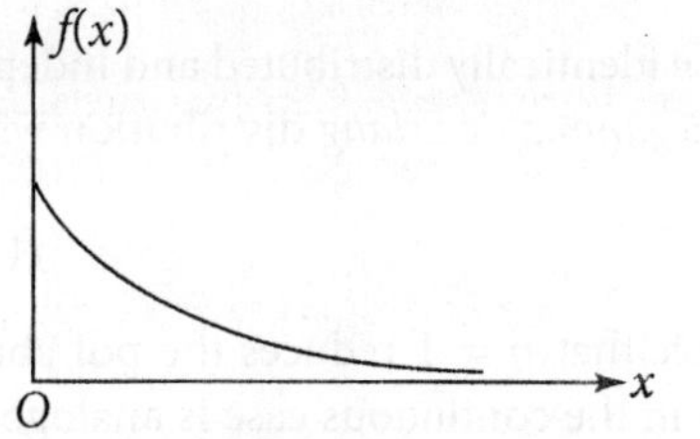

Fig. 8

The distribution is illustrated in Fig. 8.

Two useful important properties of exponential distribution are:

(i) If $x_1, x_2, \ldots, x_n$ are independent r.v.'s having an exponential distribution with parameter $\mu_i (i = 1, 2, \ldots, n)$, then $z = \min(x_1, x_2, \ldots, x_n)$ has exponential distribution with parameter $\sum_{i=1}^{n} \mu_i$.

(ii) If $x_i (i = 1, 2, \ldots, n)$ are identically distributed, following exponential distribution with parameter μ, then $z = \min(x_1, x_2, \ldots, x_n)$ has exponentially distributed with parameter $n\mu$.

III. Rectangular Distribution

An r.v. x is said to have a continuous *rectangular* (*or uniform*) distribution over an interval (a, b) if its pdf is given by

$$f(x) = \begin{cases} \dfrac{1}{b-a}, & a < x < b \\ 0, & \text{otherwise.} \end{cases}$$

a and b are the two parameters and the distribution is rectangular, since the curve $f(x)$ describes a rectangle over the x-axis and between the ordinates $x = a$ and $x = b$. The cdf is given by

$$f(x) = \begin{cases} 0, & -\infty < x < a \\ \dfrac{x-a}{b-a}, & a < x < b \\ 1, & b < x < \infty. \end{cases}$$

Since $F(x)$ is not continuous at $x = a$ and $x = b$, it is not differentiable there. Thus,

$$\frac{d}{dx} F(x) = \frac{1}{b-a} \neq 0$$

exists everywhere except at the points $x = a$ and $x = b$. The graphs of $f(x)$ and $F(x)$ are given below:

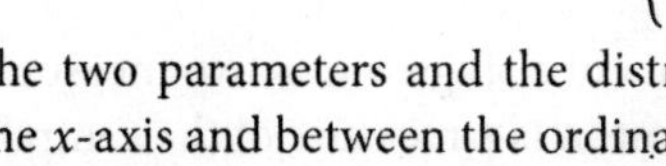

Fig. 9

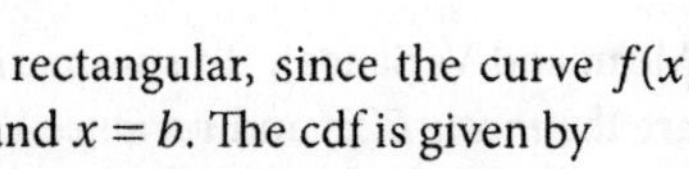

Fig. 10

IV. Gamma Distribution

Given n identically distributed and independent exponential r.v.'s, the distribution of the sum of these r.v.'s yields a *gamma* or *Erlang* distribution with its pdf given by

$$f(x)=\frac{\mu(\mu x)^{n-1}e^{-\mu x}}{(n-1)!}, \quad x>0.$$

Notice that $n = 1$ reduces the pdf above to the exponential density function. The exponential distribution in the continuous case is analogous to the geometric in discrete case. In a similar way the gamma distribution (sum of exponential r.v.'s) is analogous to the negative binomial (sum of geometric r.v.'s).

1.3.4 Expectation, Mean and Variance

Definition (Expectation). Let x be an r.v. and define $\sigma(x)$ as any function of x. Define $E\{\sigma(x)\}$ as the expected value of $\sigma(x)$ w.r.t. the probability distribution of x. Then

$$E\{\sigma(x)\}=\begin{cases}\displaystyle\int_{-\infty}^{\infty}\sigma(x)f(x)\,dx, & x \text{ continuous}\\ \displaystyle\sum_{\text{all } x}\sigma(x)p(x), & x \text{ discrete.}\end{cases}$$

The basic definition of expectation shows that if $\sigma(x)=b$ (any constant), then

$$E\{\sigma(x)\}=E(b)=b.$$

If $\sigma(x)=b\pm h(x)$, then

$$E\{\sigma(x)\}=E\{b\pm h(x)\}=b\pm E\{h(x)\}.$$

Definition (Mean and Variance). In summarising the data of a single r.v. x, two measures are commonly used. These are the *mean* $E(x)$ and *variance* Var(x). The mean is a measure of the central tendency of the distribution and the variance is the measure of dispersion of the distribution around its mean.

$$\text{Thus, } E(x)=\begin{cases}\displaystyle\int_{-\infty}^{\infty}xf(x)\,dx=\int_{-\infty}^{\infty}x\,dF(x), & x \text{ continuous}\\ \displaystyle\sum_{\text{all } x}xp(x), & x \text{ discrete.}\end{cases}$$

If $x=b_1x_1+b_2x_2+\cdots+b_nx_n$, where b_i is a constant and x_i is an r.v., $i=1,2,\ldots,n$, then

$$E(x)=\sum_{i=1}^{n}b_iE(x_i).$$

E can be considered as a *linear operator* in this case. The assumption of *independence* is not required in this case.

But if $x=x_1x_2\ldots x_n$,

$$E(x)=E(x_1)E(x_2)\ldots E(x_n)=\prod_{i=1}^{n}E(x_i)$$

provided $x_1, x_2,\ldots, x_n$ are independent.

The *variance* of a distribution is obtained by substituting $\sigma(x)=[x-E(x)]^2$ in the expectation formula.

$$\text{Thus, } \operatorname{Var}(x) = E[x - E(x)]^2$$
$$= E\left[x^2 - 2xE(x) + \{E(x)\}^2\right]$$
$$= E(x^2) - 2E(x)E(x) + \{E(x)\}^2$$
$$= E(x^2) - \{E(x)\}^2.$$

1.3.5 Stochastic Process

A *stochastic process* $X = \{X(t),\ t \in T \text{(index set)}\}$ is a collection of r.v.'s. For each $t \in T$, $X(t)$ is an r.v. The state $X(t)$ at time t actually represents the outcomes of the process at that time. If the index set T is enumerable then the corresponding stochastic process is called *discrete time stochastic process.* Again, if the index set is continuous the process is called *continuous time stochastic process.*

Consider a discrete time stochastic process $\{X_n : n = 0, 1, 2, \ldots\}$. If $X_n = i$, then the process is said to be in state i at time t. Suppose that whenever the process in state i there is a fixed probability p_{ij} that the state will be in the next state, i.e., suppose that

$$P(X_{n+1} = j | X_n = i, X_{n-1} = i_{n-1}, X_{n-2}, \ldots X_0 = i_0)$$
$$= P(X_{n+1} = j | X_n = i) \text{ for all possible } i_0, i_1, i_2, \ldots, i_{n-1}, i \text{ and } j, n \geq 0$$
$$= p_{ij}.$$

Such a stochastic process is called a *Markov chain.* Therefore, for a Markov chain the conditional probability of any future state X_{n+1} given that past states $X_0, X_1, X_2, \ldots, X_{n-1}$ and the present state X_n is independent of past states and depends only on present state. This is called the *Markovian property.*

p_{ij} is called the *transition probability* or is also referred to as the *one step transition probability.*

The transition probabilities can be more conveniently arranged in a matrix form as follows:

$$P = \left(p_{ij}\right) = \begin{pmatrix} p_{00} & p_{01} & \cdots & p_{0k} & \cdots \\ p_{10} & p_{11} & \cdots & p_{1k} & \cdots \\ p_{20} & p_{21} & \cdots & p_{2k} & \cdots \\ \vdots & \vdots & \cdots & \vdots & \cdots \end{pmatrix}$$

P is called *unit step transition matrix* or *stochastic matrix* because all the transition probabilities p_{ij} are fixed and independent of time. The probabilities p_{ij} must satisfy the conditions

$$\sum_j p_{ij} = 1 \text{ for all } i$$

$$p_{ij} \geq 0 \text{ for all } i.$$

$$\text{Now define } p_{ij}^{(0)} = \delta_{ij} = \begin{cases} 1 & \text{for } i = j \\ 0 & \text{for } i \neq j \end{cases}$$
$$p_{ij}^{(1)} = p_{ij} = P(X_{n+1} = j / X_0 = i)$$
$$p_{ij}^{(n)} = P(X_n = j \,|\, X_0 = i)$$
$$\therefore\ p_{ij}^{(n+1)} = P(X_{n+1} = j \,|\, X_n = k)$$
$$= \sum_k P(X_{n+1} = j \,|\, X_n = k)\, P(X_n = k \,|\, X_0 = i)$$
$$= \sum_k p_{ik}^{(n)} p_{kj} = \sum_k p_{ik} p_{kj}^{(n)} \text{ by similar argument.}$$

Therefore, in general:

$$p_{ij}^{(m+n)} = \sum_k p_{ik}^{(m)} p_{kj}^{(n)} \tag{1.3.5a}$$

and corresponding matrix form: $P^{(2)} = \left(p_{ij}^{(2)}\right) = \sum_k p_{ik}^{(1)} p_{kj}^{(1)} = P \cdot P = P^2$

$$P^{(3)} = \left(p_{ij}^{(3)}\right) = \sum_k p_{ik}^{(2)} p_{kj}^{(1)} = P^2 \cdot P = P^3$$

so that in general, we get $P^{(n)} = P^n$,

$$P^{(m+n)} = P^m \cdot P^n = P^{m+n}. \tag{1.3.5b}$$

Eqs (1.3.5a) reflects the fact that the first m steps lead the system from state i to some intermediate state k and the last n steps from state k to state j. These equations are known as *Chapman-Kolmogorov equations.*

One usually thinks a Markov chain as describing the transitional behaviour of a system over equally spaced interval of time. Situations exist, however, where the time spacings are dependent on the characteristics of the system and hence, may not be equal. This case is referred to as *imbedded Markov chains.*

A Markov chain is said to be *irreducible* if every state j can be reached from every other state i after a finite number of transitions; that is, for $i \neq j$, $p_{ij}^{(n)} > 0$ for $1 \leq n < \infty$.

An important definition in Markov chain analysis is the *first return time.* Given that the system is initially at state j, it may return to state j, for the first time at the nth step, $n \geq 1$. The number of steps before the system return to state j is called the first return time. Let $f_{jj}^{(n)}$ denote the probability that the first return to state j occurs at the nth step. Then given the transition matrix $P = \left(p_{ij}\right)$ an expression for $f_{jj}^{(n)}$ can be determined as follows:

$$p_{jj} = f_{jj}^{(1)}$$

$$p_{jj}^{(2)} = f_{jj}^{(2)} + f_{jj}^{(1)} p_{jj}$$

$$\Rightarrow f_{jj}^{(2)} = p_{jj}^{(2)} - f_{jj}^{(1)} p_{jj}.$$

By induction it can be proved that

$$f_{jj}^{(n)} = p_{jj}^{(n)} - \sum_{m=1}^{n-1} f_{jj}^{(m)} p_{jj}^{(n-m)}.$$

The probability of at least one returns to state j is

$$f_{jj} = \sum_{n=1}^{\infty} f_{jj}^{(n)}.$$

If $f_{jj} = 1$, the system is certain to return to j.

Define $\mu_{jj} =$ Mean return $= \sum_{n=1}^{\infty} n f_{jj}^{(n)}$. If $f_{jj} < 1$, it is not certain that the system will return to state j.

Hence, the states of a Markov chain can be classified based on the definition of first return times as follows:

(i) A state is *transient,* if $f_{jj} < 1$.

(ii) A state is *recurrent,* if $f_{jj} = 1$.

(iii) A state is *periodic* with period t, if $p_{jj}^{(n)} = 0$ whenever n is not divisible by t.

(iv) A recurrent state is *ergodic,* if it is a periodic, i.e., an *irreducible* Markov chain is *ergodic,* if all its states are *ergodic.*

1.3.6 The z-Transform

An important transformation function used with non-negative discrete r.v.'s is the z-transforms. Let v be a discrete r.v. defined over a set of non-negative integers, and let $p(v)$ be its pmf. Then the z-transform of $p(v)$ defined by

$$z\left(p_v\right)=z(p(v))=P(z)=\sum_{v=0}^{\infty} p_v z^v$$

where z is determined such that $z(p(v))$ converges. Since $\sum_{v=1}^{\infty} p_v=1$, $z(p(v))$ will always be convergent for $-1<z<1$ so that the z-transform for a given pmf is unique.

Let $p^{(v)}(z)=\frac{d^v}{dz^v}P(z)$, then the following *properties* can be established:

(i) $P(0)=p_0$

(ii) $P(1)=\sum_{v=0}^{\infty} p_v=1$

(iii) $P^{(v)}(0)=v!\,p_v$ $\qquad P(z)=p_0+p_1 z+p_2 z^2+p_3 z^3+\ldots$

$$P^{(1)}(z)=p_1+2p_2 z+3p_3 z^2+\ldots$$
$$P^{(1)}(0)=p_1 1!$$

Again, $P^{(2)}(z)=2p_2+6p_3 z+\ldots$

$P^{(2)}(0)=2p_2=p_2 2!$

In general, $P^{(v)}(0)=p_v v!$.

(iv) We have $P^{(1)}(1)=\sum_{v=1}^{\infty} v p_v=E(v)$

$$P^{(2)}(1)=\sum_{v=2}^{\infty} v(v-1)\,p_v=\sum_{v=2}^{\infty} v^2 p_v-\sum_{v=2}^{\infty} v p_v=E\left(v^2\right)-E(v)$$

$$\operatorname{Var}(v)=E\left(v^2\right)-\{E(v)\}^2=P^{(2)}(1)+P^{(1)}(1)-\{P^{(1)}(1)\}^2$$

(v) $z\left(p_{v-1}\right)=\sum_{v=0}^{\infty} p_{v-1} z^v=z\sum_{k=0}^{\infty} p_k z^k=zP(z)$

(vi) $z\left(p_{v+1}\right)=\sum_{v=0}^{\infty} p_{v+1} z^v=\frac{1}{z}\left(\sum_{k=0}^{\infty} p_k z^k-p_0\right)=\frac{1}{z}\left[P(z)-p_0\right]$

(vii) For general non-negative sequences of r.v.'s having pmf's $p(v)$ and $q(v)$

$$z\left(p_v+q_v\right)=\sum_{v=0}^{\infty}\left(p_v+q_v\right) z^v=P(z)+Q(z)$$

(viii) $z\left(bp_v\right)=\sum_{v=0}^{\infty} bp_v z^v=bP(z)$, where b is constant

(ix) Let $\mu_v=q_v * p_v=q_0 p_v+q_1 p_{v-1}+\cdots+q_{v-1} p_1+q_v p_0$. Therefore, z-transform of the convolution

$$\begin{aligned} z(\mu_\nu) = \sum_{\nu=0}^{\infty} \mu_\nu z^\nu &= q_0p_0 + (q_0p_1 + q_1p_0)\, z + (q_0p_2 + q_1p_1 + q_2p_0)\, z^2 + \ldots \\ &= q_0\left(p_0 + p_1z + p_2z^2 + \ldots\right) + q_1z\left(p_0 + p_1z + p_2z^2 + \ldots\right) + \ldots \\ &= \left(q_0 + q_1z + q_2z^2 + \ldots\right)\left(p_0 + p_1z_1 + p_2z^2 + \ldots\right) \\ &= z(q_\nu)\, z(p_\nu) = Q(z)P(z). \end{aligned}$$

Thus, the z-transform of the convolution of two pmf's is the product of their z-transform.

Example 1.3.3. *z-transform of Poisson distribution with parameter λ*

$$p_\nu = \frac{e^{-\lambda}\lambda^\nu}{\nu!} : \nu = 0, 1, 2, \ldots$$

$$z(p_\nu) = \sum_{\nu=0}^{\infty} \frac{e^{-\lambda}\cdot\lambda^\nu}{\nu!} z^\nu = \frac{e^{-\lambda}}{e^{-\lambda z}} \sum_{\nu=0}^{\infty} \frac{(\lambda z)^\nu e^{-\nu z}}{\nu!} = e^{\lambda(z-1)}.$$

$$\therefore\ E(\nu) = P^{(1)}(1) = \lambda e^{\lambda(z-1)}\Big|_{z=1} = \lambda \text{ and } P^{(2)}(1) = \lambda^2 e^{\lambda(z-1)}\Big|_{z=1} = \lambda^2.$$

$$\operatorname{Var}(\nu) = P^{(2)}(1) + P^{(1)}(1) - \left[P^{(1)}(1)\right]^2 = \lambda^2 + \lambda - \lambda^2 = \lambda.$$

1.4 EXERCISE 1

1. (a) Find all real x for which the rank of the matrix is less than 4:

(i) $\begin{pmatrix} x & 1 & 1 & 1 \\ 1 & x & 1 & 1 \\ 1 & 1 & x & 1 \\ 1 & 1 & 1 & x \end{pmatrix}$ [CU(H) 1986] (ii) $\begin{pmatrix} 1+x & 2 & 3 & 4 \\ 1 & 2+x & 3 & 4 \\ 1 & 2 & 3+x & 4 \\ 1 & 2 & 3 & 4+x \end{pmatrix}$.

(b) Prove that the points (x_1, y_1), (x_2, y_2) and (x_3, y_3) are collinear, if and only if the rank of matrix $\begin{pmatrix} x_1 & y_1 & 1 \\ x_2 & y_2 & 1 \\ x_3 & y_3 & 1 \end{pmatrix}$ be less than 3.

(c) Reduce the matrix $A = \begin{pmatrix} 0 & 1 & -3 & -1 \\ 1 & 0 & 1 & 1 \\ 3 & 1 & 0 & 2 \\ 1 & 1 & -2 & 0 \end{pmatrix}$ to row-reduced echelon form and show that its rank is 2.

(d) Show by reducing the matrices to normal forms that the rank of the matrix

(i) $\begin{pmatrix} 1 & 2 & 0 & -1 \\ 3 & 4 & 1 & 2 \\ -2 & 3 & 2 & 5 \end{pmatrix}$ is 3 (ii) $\begin{pmatrix} 0 & 1 & -3 & -1 \\ 1 & 0 & 1 & 1 \\ 3 & 1 & 2 & 2 \\ 1 & 1 & -2 & 0 \end{pmatrix}$ is 3.

(e) If from a square matrix A of order n and rank ρ, a square sub-matrix B consisting of m rows of A be selected, then show that $\mu \geq \rho + m - n$, where μ, the rank of B. [JNU 1992]

(f) Consider the system of non-homogeneous equations:
$$\begin{aligned} x + ay + za &= 1 \\ ax + y + 2az &= -4 \\ ax - ay + 4z &= 2. \end{aligned}$$

Show that

(i) the equations are consistent and has only one solution, when $a \neq -1, a \neq 2$.
(ii) when $a = -1$, the equations have an infinite number of solution.
(iii) when $a = 2$, the system is inconsistent. [CU(H) 1984; NBU(H) 1994]

(g) Choose λ so that rank of $\begin{pmatrix} \lambda & 2 & -2 \\ 4 & 2\lambda & 01 \\ 6 & 6 & \lambda \end{pmatrix} = \text{rank of} \begin{pmatrix} \lambda & 2 & -2 & 1 \\ 1 & 2\lambda & -1 & 3 \\ 6 & 6 & \lambda & -1 \end{pmatrix}$. [BESU (Engg) 2006]

(h) A non-zero matrix A is *nilpotent* of order $k \geq 2$, if $A^k = 0$ and $A^{k-1} \neq 0$. Hence, $(I - A)^{-1} = I + A + A^2 + \cdots + A^{k-1}$. Show that the matrix $A = \begin{pmatrix} 1 & 1 & 3 \\ 5 & 2 & 6 \\ -2 & -1 & -3 \end{pmatrix}$ is nilpotent of order 3 and, hence, deduce that $A^{-1} = \begin{pmatrix} 0 & 1 & -1 \\ -5 & -1 & -6 \\ 2 & 1 & 4 \end{pmatrix}$. [BESU (Engg) 2003]

2. (a) In $R^3, \boldsymbol{\alpha} = (4,3,5), \boldsymbol{\beta} = (0,1,3), \boldsymbol{\gamma} = (2,1,1), \boldsymbol{\delta} = (4,2,2)$.
Examine if (i) $\boldsymbol{\alpha}$ is a linear combination of $\boldsymbol{\beta}$ and $\boldsymbol{\gamma}$ (ii) $\boldsymbol{\beta}$ is a linear combination of $\boldsymbol{\gamma}$ and $\boldsymbol{\delta}$.

(b) In $R^3, \boldsymbol{a}_1 = (1,1,2), \boldsymbol{a}_2 = (0,2,1), \boldsymbol{a}_3 = (2,2,4)$, determine whether

(i) $\boldsymbol{a}_1$ is a linear combination of $\boldsymbol{a}_2, \boldsymbol{a}_3$
(ii) $\boldsymbol{a}_2$ is a linear combination of $\boldsymbol{a}_3, \boldsymbol{a}_1$
(iii) $\boldsymbol{a}_3$ is a linear combination of $\boldsymbol{a}_1, \boldsymbol{a}_2$.

(c) Let $\boldsymbol{\alpha}_1 = (1,2,0)$, $\boldsymbol{\alpha}_2 = (3,-1,1)$, $\boldsymbol{\alpha}_3 = (4,1,1)$; show that the set $S = \{\boldsymbol{\alpha}_1, \boldsymbol{\alpha}_2, \boldsymbol{\alpha}_3\}$ is linearly dependent.

(d) Show that the set of vectors $S = \{(1,2,4), (1,0,0), (0,1,0), (0,0,1)\}$ is linearly dependent in R^3, but the set $T = \{(1,2,0), (0,3,1), (-1,0,1)\}$ is linearly independent.

(e) In the vector space R^3 let $\boldsymbol{a}_1 = (1,2,1)$, $\boldsymbol{a}_2 = (3,1,5)$, $\boldsymbol{a}_3 = (3,-4,7)$. Show that the subspace spanned by $S = \{\boldsymbol{a}_1, \boldsymbol{a}_2\}$ and $T = \{\boldsymbol{a}_1, \boldsymbol{a}_2, \boldsymbol{a}_3\}$ are the same, that is $\mathscr{L}(T) = \mathscr{L}(S)$.

(f) Show that the vectors $\boldsymbol{\alpha} = (1,2,4), \boldsymbol{\beta} = (2,-1,3), \boldsymbol{\gamma} = (0,1,2), \boldsymbol{\delta} = (-3,7,2)$ are linearly dependent and the relation between them is $-9\boldsymbol{\alpha} + 12\boldsymbol{\beta} + 5\boldsymbol{\delta} - 5\boldsymbol{\gamma} = 0$.

(g) Determine whether the following vectors are linearly dependent or independent.

(i) $\{(2,2,8), (1,0,4), (1,2,4)\}$ in R^3
(ii) $\{(3,0,2), (7,0,9), (4,1,2)\}$ in R^3
(iii) $\{(1,2,3), (4,-1,2), (3,1,-2)$ in R^3
(iv) $\{(1,1,2,4), (2,-1,-5,2), (1,-1,-4,0), (2,1,1,6)\}$ in R^4.

(h) Select a basis, if any such exists, of R^3 from the set $\{\boldsymbol{a}_1, \boldsymbol{a}_2, \boldsymbol{a}_3, \boldsymbol{a}_4\}$, where $\boldsymbol{a}_1 = (1,-3,2)$, $\boldsymbol{a}_2 = (2,4,1)$, $\boldsymbol{a}_3 = (3,1,3)$, $\boldsymbol{a}_4 = (1,1,1)$. [CU(H) 1992; VU 1996]

(i) Show that the vectors

(i) {(2,1,0), (1,1,0), (4,2,0)} form a basis of R^3

(ii) {(1,1,2), (1,2,5), (5,3,4)} do not form a basis of R^3

(iii) {(2,1,4), (1,−1,2), (3,1,−2)} from a basis of R^3.

3. (a) If $\{\alpha_1, \alpha_2, \alpha_3\}$ be a basis of a real vector space V and $\beta_1 = \alpha_1 + \alpha_2$, $\beta_2 = 2\alpha_1 + 3\alpha_2 + 4\alpha_3$, $\beta_3 = \alpha_1 + 2\alpha_2 + 3\alpha_3$, prove that $\{\beta_1, \beta_2, \beta_3\}$ is also a basis of V. [CU(H) 1994]

(b) Let V be a real vector space with a basis $\{\alpha_1, \alpha_2, \ldots, \alpha_n\}$. Examine if $\{\alpha_1 + \alpha_2, \alpha_2 + \alpha_3, \ldots, \alpha_n + \alpha_1\}$ is also a basis of V.

(c) If $\{\alpha_1, \alpha_2, \ldots, \alpha_n\}$ be a basis of a vector V over a field F and $\omega = \{\omega_1, \omega_2, \ldots, \omega_n\}$ be any set of $(n+1)$ vectors in V, prove that ω is linearly dependent in V.

4. (a) Find a basis for R^3 containing the set of vectors given below:

(i) {(2,4,2), (3,6,2)} (ii) {(1,1,2), (3,5,2)}. [CP 2003]

(b) Show that the vectors $\alpha = (1,0,-1)$, $\beta = (1,2,1)$, $\gamma = (0,-3,2)$ form a basis of R^3. Express each of the standard basis vectors: (1,0,0), (0,1,0), (0,0,1) as a linear combination of α, β, γ.

(c) Let $V(R) = P_n$ be the vector space of polynomials in t over the field of real numbers of degree $\leq n$, show that the set $S = \{1, t, t^2, \ldots, t^n\}$ is a basis of V. [MCA(Ent) 1991]

5. (a) Obtain all the basic solutions to the following system of linear equation

$$x_1 + 2x_2 + x_3 = 4$$
$$2x_1 + x_2 + 5x_3 = 5.$$

(b) Find all the basic feasible solutions of the following problem:

$$2x_1 + 3x_2 + x_3 + x_4 = 8$$
$$x_1 - 2x_2 + 6x_3 - 7x_4 = -3$$

and choose the one which maximise $z = 2x_1 + 3x_2 + 4x_3 + 7x_4$. [JNU(MSc) 1994]

(c) Show that the following system of linear equations has two degenerate basic feasible solutions and the non-degenerate basic solution is not feasible:

$$3x_1 + x_2 - x_3 = 3$$
$$2x_1 - x_2 + x_3 = 2.$$

(d) Show that although $(2,3,2)^T$ is a feasible solution to the system of equations

$$x_1 + x_2 + 2x_3 = 9$$
$$3x_1 + 2x_2 + 5x_3 = 22$$
$$x_1, \quad x_2, \quad x_3 \geq 0,$$

it is not a basic solution. How many basic solutions this system may have? Find all the basic feasible solutions of the system.

6. (a) Show that all three of the basic solutions of the system

$$x_1 + 2x_2 + 3x_3 = 6$$
$$2x_1 + x_2 + 4x_3 = 4$$

exists and they are $\left(0^*, \frac{12}{5}, \frac{2}{5}\right)^T$, $(-6, 0^*, 4)^T$ and $\left(\frac{2}{3}, \frac{8}{3}, 0^*\right)^T$. [KU 1982]

(b) If $\boldsymbol{\alpha}_1 = \begin{pmatrix} 3 \\ 4 \end{pmatrix}, \boldsymbol{\alpha}_2 = \begin{pmatrix} -1 \\ 2 \end{pmatrix}, \boldsymbol{\alpha}_3 = \begin{pmatrix} 1 \\ 4 \end{pmatrix}$ and $\boldsymbol{b} = \begin{pmatrix} 1 \\ 4 \end{pmatrix}$, then determine whether all possible basic solutions exist for the following set of equations: $[\boldsymbol{\alpha}_1, \boldsymbol{\alpha}_2, \boldsymbol{\alpha}_3]\,\boldsymbol{x} = \boldsymbol{b}$. [JU(MSc) 1998]

(c) Find all the basic feasible solutions of the equations

$$\begin{aligned} 2x_1 + 6x_2 + 2x_3 + x_4 &= 3 \\ 6x_1 + 4x_2 + 4x_3 + 6x_4 &= 2. \\ x_1,\ x_2,\ x_3,\ x_4 &\geq 0. \end{aligned}$$

Show that all the basic solutions are degenerate.

7. (a) If x_1, x_2 be real, show that the set given by

(i) $S_1 = \{(x_1, x_2) \mid x_1 + x_2 \leq 50,\ x_1 + 2x_2 \leq 80, 2x_1 + x_2 \geq 0,\ x_1, x_2 \geq 0\}$ is a convex set.
(ii) $S_2 = \{(x_1, x_2) \mid x_1, x_2 \leq 1, x_1 x_2 \geq 0\}$ is not a convex set.
(iii) $S_3 = \left\{(x_1, x_2) \mid x_2^2 \geq 4x_1\right\}$ is not a convex set.
(iv) $S_4 = \left\{(x_1, x_2) \mid x_2 - 3 \geq -x_1^2,\ x_1, x_2 \geq 0\right\}$ is a convex set.

(b) Find the extreme points, if any, of the following sets:

(i) $A = \{(x, y) \mid x^2 + y^2 \leq 25\}$.
(ii) $B = \{(x_1, x_2) \mid |x_1| \leq 1, |x_2| \leq 1\}$
(iii) $C = \left\{(x_1, x_2) \mid x_1^2 + x_2^2 \leq 1,\ x_1, x_2 \geq 0\right\}$.

8. (a) Express the point $(0.4, 0.6)$ as a convex combination of the four extreme points of the convex set defined by the rectangle and its interior whose vertices are $(0,0)$, $(1,0)$, $(1,1)$, $(0,1)$.

(b) Give examples of (i) Convex hull in R^2 (ii) Convex hull in R^3 (iii) Convex polyhedron in R^2.

9. (a) Find the homogeneous linear system whose solution space is exactly the same as the subspace of R^3 spanned by the vectors $\{(-1, 1, 3), (1, 2, -1)\}$.

(b) For what values of a, does the vector $(a^2, -3a, -2)$ belong to the span of the set

$$S = \{(1,2,3), (1,1,1), (0,1,2)\}?$$

(c) Do the polynomials $t^2 + 2t + 1, t^2 - t + 2, t^3 + 2, -t^3 + t^2 - 5t + 2$ span $\mathscr{P}_3$, vector space of all polynomials of degree ≤ 3?

10. Let $S = \{V_1, V_2, \ldots, V_n\}$ be a set of vectors in a vector space. Show that S is linearly dependent if and only if one of the vectors in S is a linear combination of all other vectors.

11. (a) Given an r.v. j which assumes the values $k, k+1, k+2, \ldots$, where k is a positive integer, show that

$$P(x = j) = {}^{j-1}C_{k-1} p^k (1-p)^{k-k}, \quad 0 < p < 1$$

is a proper probability mass function.

(b) An r.v. t has the following cdf:

$$F(t) = \begin{cases} 1 - e^{-2t}, & t \geq 0 \\ 0, & t < 0. \end{cases}$$

Find (i) The corresponding pdf, (ii) $P[t < 5 \text{ or } t > 10]$, (iii) $P[3 < t < 5 \text{ and } 6 < t < 7]$.

12. Let $x_1, x_2, \ldots, x_n$ be independent and identical exponential r.v.'s with mean $1/\mu$. Define m such that $x_1+x_2+\cdots+x_m \le t \le x_1+x_2+\cdots+x_{m+1}$.
Show that m is Poisson with mean μt.

13. Consider the following pmf of a discrete r.v. x that represent the monthly demand of a certain item

x	0	1	2	3
$p(x)$	0.1	0.2	0.3	0.4

If the monthly demand are independent and identical, find the pmf for a 2-month demand.

14. (a) Classify the following Markov chain and find the stationary distribution: $\begin{pmatrix} \frac{1}{4} & \frac{1}{4} & \frac{1}{2} \\ \frac{1}{4} & \frac{3}{4} & 0 \\ \frac{1}{2} & 0 & \frac{1}{2} \end{pmatrix}$.

(b) Find the z-transform of binomial distribution with parameters (n, p). From this determine its mean and variance.

ANSWERS

1. (a) (i) $1, -3$ (ii) $0, -10$.
(g) $\lambda = -1$.
2. (a) (i) $\alpha = \beta + 2\gamma$ (ii) $\beta \ne c\gamma + d\delta$.
(b) (i) Yes (ii) No (iii) Yes.
(g) (i) l.d. (ii) l.i. (iii) l.i. (iv) l.i.
(h) (a_1, a_2, a_3) cannot form a basis but (a_1, a_2, a_4) can.
5. (a) $(2,1,0^*)^T, (5,0^*,-1)^T, \left(0^* \frac{5}{3}, \frac{2}{3}\right)^T$.
(b) $(1,2,0^*,0^*)^T, \left(\frac{22}{9}, 0^*, 0^*, \frac{7}{9}\right)^T, \left(0^*, \frac{45}{16}, \frac{7}{16}, 0^*\right)^T, \left(0^*, 0^*, \frac{44}{17}, \frac{45}{17}\right)$.
(d) $3, (4,5,0^*)^T, (0^*,1,4)^T$.
7. (b) (i) Every point on the circumference of circle.
(ii) $(1,1), (-1,1), (1,-1), (-1,-1)$.
(iii) $(0,1), (0,0), (1,0)$ and all points on the circular boundary.
8. (a) $\frac{1}{5}(0,0)+\frac{1}{5}(1,0)+\frac{1}{5}(1,1)+\frac{2}{5}(0,1)$.
9. (a) $y_1+x_1-x_2=0, y_2-x_1+2x_2=0, y_3-3x_1+x_2=0$.
(b) $a=1$.
(c) No.
11. (b) (i) $f(t)=2e^{-2t}, t\ge 0$, (ii) $1-e^{-10}+e^{-20}$.
13. $(0.01, 0.04, 0.1, 0.2, 0.25, 0.24, 0.16)$.
14. (a) $p_1 = p_2 = p_3 = \frac{1}{3}$.

Chapter 2

General Linear Programming Models

2.1 THE LP MODEL AND RESOURCE ALLOCATION

2.1.1 Introduction

LP is a resource allocation model that seeks the best allocation of limited sources to a number of competing activities. LP has been applied with considerable success to a multitude of practical problems. From economic stand point LP seeks the best allocation to limited resources to specific economic activities.

It was in 1947 that George Dantzig and his associates found out a technique for solving military planning problems while they were working on a project for US Air Force. This technique consisted of representing the various activities of an organisation as an LP model and arriving at the optimal solution by minimising a linear objective function. Afterwards, Dantzig suggested this approach for solving industrial, management problems.

2.1.2 Definition: General LP Problem

We write the mathematical structure of general LP model as follows:

Optimise $Z = c_1x_1 + c_2x_2 + \cdots + c_nx_n$

$$\text{subject to } a_{11}x_1 + a_{12}x_2 + \ldots + a_{1n}x_n \ (\leq = \geq) b_1$$
$$a_{21}x_1 + a_{22}x_2 + \ldots + a_{2n}x_n \ (\leq = \geq) b_2$$
$$\vdots$$
$$a_{m1}x_1 + a_{m2}x_2 + \ldots + a_{mn}x_n \ (\leq = \geq) b_m$$
$$x_1, x_2, \ldots, x_n \geq 0$$

There are n activities whose levels (unknown values) are represented by $x_1, x_2, \ldots, x_n$ called the *decision variables.* There are also m resources whose availabilities are given by $b_1, b_2, \ldots, b_m$. Each unit of activity j consumes an amount a_{ij} of resources i. This means that the quantity

$$\sum_{j=1}^{n} a_{ij}x_j$$

represents the total usage by all n activities of resources i and known as *constraints.*

The objective function

$$\sum_{j=1}^{n} c_j x_j$$

represents the measure of the contributions of different activities. In the maximisation case c_j represents the profit per unit of activity j, whereas in the case of minimisation c_j represents the cost per unit.

In addition the physical properties of the situation require that the decision variables are non-negative. There may be real situation where the variables are unrestricted in sign. These variables are somehow converted to non-negative restrictions.

Note that the worth of an activity cannot be judged in terms of objective coefficients c_j only; the activity's consumption of the available resources is also an important factor. Because all the activities of the model are competing for limited resources, the relative contribution of an activity w.r.t. the other activity depends on both its objective coefficient c_j and its consumption of resources a_{ij}.

A set of values of the decision variables $x_1, x_2, \ldots, x_n$, which satisfies the set of constraints and the non-negativity restrictions, is called a *feasible solution.* Out of several feasible solutions which in addition optimise (maximise or minimise) the objective function, is called *optimal solution.*

2.1.3 Compact Form of Representation of LP Model

Form 1: Using summation notation

$$\text{Optimise } Z = \sum_{j=1}^{n} c_j x_j$$

$$\text{subject to } \sum_{j=1}^{n} a_{ij}x_j \ (\leq = \geq) b_i, \quad i = 1, 2, \ldots, m$$
$$x_j \geq 0, \quad j = 1, 2, \ldots, n$$

Form 2: Matrix form of LP model

Optimise $Z = \boldsymbol{cx}$

subject to $A\boldsymbol{x} \ (\leq = \geq) \boldsymbol{b}$

$\boldsymbol{x} \geq \boldsymbol{0}$

where $A = (a_{ij})_{m\times n}$, $x = \begin{pmatrix} x_1 \\ x_2 \\ \vdots \\ x_n \end{pmatrix}_{n\times 1}$, $c = (c_1, c_2, \ldots, c_n)_{1\times n}$,

$b = \begin{pmatrix} b_1 \\ b_2 \\ \vdots \\ b_n \end{pmatrix}_{m\times 1}$, $0 = (0, 0, \ldots, 0)_{1\times n}$.

Remark (Objective function). Optimise $Z = cx$ as also the constraints $Ax(\leq = \geq)b$ with equality sign represent *hyperplanes*. The constraints with $\leq$ or $\geq$ types of inequalities are the *closed half spaces* in the *n*-dimensional *Euclidean space.*

2.1.4 Formulation of LP Models

The formulation of mathematical model can be initiated by answering the following three questions:

1. What does the model seek to determine? In other words, what are variables (unknowns) of the problem?
2. What constraints must be imposed on the variables to satisfy the limitations of the modelled system?
3. What is the objective that needs to be achieved in order to determine the optimum (best) solution from among all the feasible values of the variables?

Example 2.1.1 (Product-mix problem). *The ABC company produces three different items. The production process utilises three operations. Figure below shows the sequence of producing items* 1, 2 *and* 3. *Item* 2 *does not pass through operation* 2 *and item* 3 *goes through operations* 1 *and* 2 *only. The processing times per unit of each item are shown in the respective boxes. Since the same operations are used in the company's other production activities, the daily usages of operations* 1, 2 *and* 3 *by all three items are limited to* 430, 460 *and* 420 *minutes, respectively.*

A market study shows that the expected per unit profits for items 1, 2 and 3 are ₹ 3, ₹ 2 and ₹ 5. Formulate this product-mix problem in an LP model.

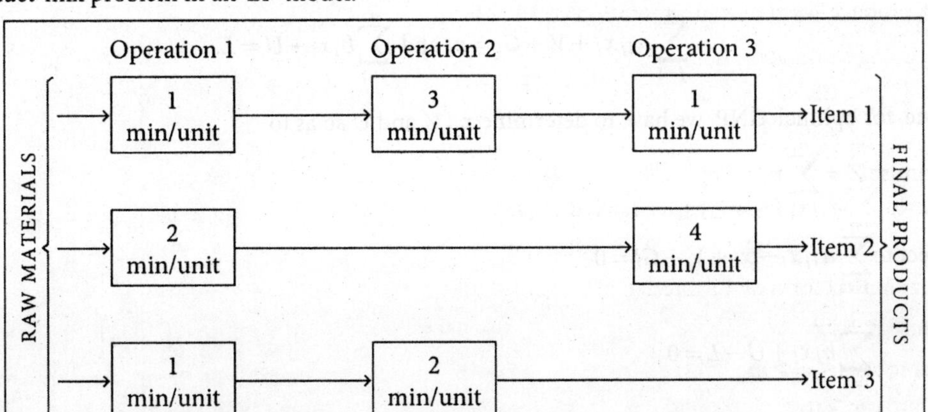

Mathematical Formulation

Let x_1 = number of units of item 1

x_2 = number of units of item 2

x_3 = number of units of item 3

that is, x_j number of items, where $j = 1,2,3$. The model is formulated in terms of x_j as:

Maximise $Z = 3x_1 + 2x_2 + 5x_3$ (daily profit)

subject to operation 1: $x_1 + 2x_2 + x_3 \leq 430$ [limits on daily

operation 2: $3x_1 + \quad + 2x_3 \leq 460$ usages of operations]

operation 3: $x_1 + 4x_2 \quad \leq 420$

$x_j \geq 0, j = 1,2,3$ (non-negativity).

Example 2.1.2 (Input-Output Model in Economics). *This is a classical model to maximise a country's gross national product (GNP). Suppose that a country has n industries employing a labour force of L with unemployment level of U. Let the fraction of the output sale of the ith industry to the jth industry be a_{ij} that to the government demand by G_i with unsold inventory V_i employing b_i amount of labour per unit of goods of the ith industry. The above data is presented in the following table:*

Output \ *Input*		*To Industry* 1	2	…	n	*Unsold inventory*	*Govt. Dem.*	*Total*
From Industry	1	a_{11}	a_{12}	…	a_{1n}	V_1	G_1	x_1
	2	a_{21}	a_{22}	…	a_{2n}	V_2	G_2	x_2
	⋮	⋮	⋮	⋮	⋮	⋮	⋮	⋮
	n	a_{n1}	a_{n2}	…	a_{nn}	V_n	G_n	x_n
Labour		b_1	b_2	…	b_n	U		L

where x_i is the total output of the ith industry with average price p_i for a unit of output. Pose this input-output problem as an LP model.

Solution: The constraints on x_i are obviously

$$\sum_{j=1}^{n} a_{ij}x_j + V_i + G_i = x_i \text{ and } \sum_{j=1}^{n} b_i x_i + U = L.$$

Hence, for optimal GNP, we have to determine x_i, V_i and U so as to

Maximise $Z = \sum_{i=1}^{n} p_i x_i$

subject to $\sum_{j=1}^{n} a_{ij}x_j - x_i + V_i + G_i = 0$

$$\sum_{j=1}^{n} b_i x_i + U - L = 0$$

$$x_i, V_i, U \geq 0.$$

Example 2.1.3 (Advertising media selection problem). *An advertising company wishes to plan its advertising strategy in three different media — Television, Radio and Magazines. The purpose of advertising is to reach as large a number of potential customers as possible. Following data have been obtained from market survey.* [IAS 1995]

	Television	*Radio*	*Magazine* I	*Magazine* II
Cost of an adv. unit	₹ 30,000	₹ 20,000	₹ 15,000	₹ 10,000
No. of potential customers reached per unit	₹ 2,00,000	₹ 6,00,000	₹ 1,50,000	₹ 1,00,000
No. of female customers reached per unit	₹ 1,50,000	₹ 4,00,000	₹ 70,000	₹ 50,000

The company wants to spend not more than ₹ 4,50,000 *on advertising. Following are the further requirements that must be met:*

(i) *at least one million exposures take place among female customers*
(ii) *advertising on magazines be limited to* ₹ 1,50,000
(iii) *at least* 3 *advertising units be bought on magazine* I *and* 2 *units on magazine* II
(iv) *the number of advertising units on television and radio should each be between* 5 *and* 10.

With these information formulate an LP *model for the problem.*

Solution: Let $x_T, x_R, x_{M_1}, x_{M_2}$ denote the number of advertising units to be bought on television, radio, magazine I and magazine II respectively.

The *objective* is to maximise the total number of potential customers reached,

i.e., Maximise $Z = 10^5\left(2x_T + 6x_R + 1.5x_{M_1} + x_{M_2}\right)$.

Subject to the *constraints are:*

On the advertising budget: $30000x_T + 20000x_R + 15000x_{M_1} + 10000x_{M_2} \le 450,000$
or, $30x_T + 20x_R + 15x_{M_1} + 10x_{M_2} \le 450$

On number of female customers reached by the advertising campaign: $150000x_T + 400000x_R + 70000x_{M_1} + 50000x_{M_2} \ge 10^6$
or, $15x_T + 40x_R + 7x_{M_1} + 5x_{M_2} \ge 100$

On expenses on magazines advertising: $15000x_{M_1} + 10000x_{M_2} \le 150000$
or, $15x_{M_1} + 10x_{M_2} \le 150$

On number of units on magazines: $x_{M_1} \ge 3,\ x_{M_2} \ge 2$

On number of units on television: $5 \le x_T \le 10$

On number of units of radio: $5 \le x_R \le 10$

Universal *constraints*: $x_T, x_R, x_{M_1}, x_{M_2} \ge 0.$

Example 2.1.4 (Bank loan model). *Suppose,* RBI *is in the process of devising a new policy of giving loans to four sectors: Commercial, Personal, Home and Car to an individual. The total capital is* C (in ₹) *and the bank estimates that it can charge at rates* r_1, r_2, r_3, r_4 *respectively in the four sectors. From previous experience the bank knows that the probability of recoverable bad debts in the four sectors will be* p_1, p_2, p_3, p_4 *which are usually small fractions. For viability of the policy the bank sets at least* 40% *of the total capital for commercial loans and to encourage housing sector it sets that the home loans must be at least* 50% *of the personal and car loans. On bad debts the bank's policy is that the total must not exceed* 5% *of the total loans given. The bank's ultimate aim to find the optimal investments* I_1, I_2, I_3, I_4 *in the four sectors. Using the above data formulate the problem as an* LP *model.* [MBA(CU) 2001]

Solution: *Formulation.* The *objective function Z* is given by

$$Z = \sum_{j=1}^{4} r_j\left(1-p_j\right)I_j - \sum_{j=1}^{4} p_j I_j = \sum_{j=1}^{4}\left[r_j - p_j\left(1+r_j\right)\right]I_j.$$

The LP *model* becomes

$$\text{Maximise } Z = \sum_{j=1}^{4}\left[r_j - p_j\left(1+r_j\right)\right]I_j$$

$$\text{subject to } \sum_{j=1}^{4} I_j \le C$$

$$I_1 \ge 0.4C$$

$$I_3 \ge 0.5(I_2 + I_4)$$

$$\sum_{j=1}^{4} p_j I_j \le 0.05 \sum_{j=1}^{4} I_j$$

$$I_j \ge 0, \quad j = 1,2,3,4.$$

Example 2.1.5 (Investment problem). *A Mutual fund company has ₹ 20 lakh available for investment in government bonds, blue-chip stock, speculative stocks and short-term deposits. The annual expected demand and risk factor a region below.*

Type of investment	*Annual expected return*	*Risk factor*
Government bonds	14%	12
Blue-chip stock	19%	24
Speculative stocks	23%	48
Short-term deposits	12%	6

Mutual fund is required to keep at least ₹ 2 lakh in short-term deposits and not to exceed average risk factor of 42. Speculative stock must be at most 20% of the total amount invested. How should Mutual fund invest so as to maximise its total expected annual return? Formulate this as a LP *model.*

Solution: *Formulation.* Let x_1, x_2, x_3, x_4 denote the amount of funds to be invested in government bonds, blue-chip stocks, speculative stocks and short-term deposits respectively.

Since the Mutual Fund Company has ₹ 20 lakh available investment: $x_1 + x_2 + x_3 + x_4 \leq 2000000$

Also Mutual Fund is required to keep at least ₹ 2 lakh in short-term deposits: $x_4 \geq 200000$

Since the average risk factor for Mutual Fund Company should not exceed 42: $\frac{12x_1+24x_2+48x_3+6x_4}{x_1+x_2+x_3+x_4} \leq 42$

or, $30x_1 + 18x_2 - 6x_3 + 36x_4 \geq 0$

Further, speculative stocks must be at most 20% of the total amount invested, therefore: $x_3 \leq 0.20(x_1 + x_2 + x_3 + x_4)$

or, $0.2x_1 + 0.2x_2 - 0.8x_3 + 0.2x_4 \geq 0$

Finally, since the objective function is to maximise the total expected: Maximise $Z = 0.14x_1 + 0.19x_2 + 0.23x_3 + 0.12x_4$

Thus, the required LP *model* for Mutual Fund Company is

$$\begin{aligned}
&\text{Maximise } Z = 0.14x_1 + 0.19x_2 + 0.23x_3 + 0.12x_4\\
&\text{subject to } x_1 + x_2 + x_3 + x_4 \leq 2 \times 10^6\\
&\qquad x_4 \geq 2 \times 10^6\\
&\qquad 30x_1 + 18x_2 - 6x_3 + 36x_4 \geq 0\\
&\qquad 0.2x_1 + 0.2x_2 - 0.8x_3 + 0.2x_4 \geq 0\\
&\qquad x_1, x_2, x_3, x_4 \geq 0.
\end{aligned}$$

Example 2.1.6 (Flight scheduling problem). *The Air India, which operates out of a Dum Dum Airport terminal has 8 aircrafts of Type I, 15 of Type II and 12 of Type III available for today's flights. The tonnage capacities (in thousand of tons) are 4.5 for Type I, 7 for Type II and 4 for Type III.*

The Air India dispatches its planes to cities Bangaluru and Chennai. Tonnage requirements are 20 at Bangaluru and 30 at Chennai; excess tonnage capacity supplied to a city has no value. A plane can fly once only during the day.

The cost of sending a plane from the terminal to each city is given below:

	Type I	*Type II*	*Type III*
Bangaluru	23	5	1.4
Chennai	58	10	3.9

Formulate the LP model to minimise the air transportation cost.

Solution: *Formulation.* Let $x_{B_1}, x_{B_2}, x_{B_3}$ and $x_{C_1}, x_{C_2}, x_{C_3}$ denote the number of planes of Types I, II and III to be dispatched to cities Bangaluru and Chennai respectively.

Cost function Z is given by $Z = 23x_{B_1} + 5x_{B_2} + 1.4x_{B_3} + 58x_{C_1} + 10x_{C_2} + 3.9x_{C_3}$. On the basis of the information given the LP model to minimise the air transportation cost Z is as follows:

$$\begin{aligned}
&\text{Minimise } Z = 23x_{B_1} + 5x_{B_2} + 1.4x_{B_3} + 58x_{C_1} + 10x_{C_2} + 3.9x_{C_3}\\
&\text{subject to } x_{B_1} + x_{C_1} \leq 8\\
&\qquad x_{B_2} + x_{C_2} \leq 15\\
&\qquad x_{B_3} + x_{C_3} \leq 12
\end{aligned}$$

$$4.5x_{B_1} + 7x_{B_2} + 4x_{B_3} = 20$$
$$4.5x_{C_1} + 7x_{C_2} + 4x_{C_3} = 30$$
$$x_{B_i}, x_{C_i} \geq 0, \quad i = 1,2,3.$$

Example 2.1.7. *In all the previous examples, the constraints represents permanent relationships; that is, the left and right sides of each constraint are related by one of three relationships* $\leq, =,$ *or* $\geq$. *Practical situations exist, however, where it may be advantageous to violate a constraint, possibly at the expenses of incurring a penalty. For example, a company entertaining a number of business ventures usually operates under limited capital restrictions, but may elect to exceed that limit by borrowing additional money. The penalty incurred in this case is the cost of borrowed money (interest). Naturally, a loan can be justified on an economic basis only if the new business ventures are profitable. This type of modelling is sometimes referred to as* GOAL PROGRAMMING, *since the model automatically adjusts the level of certain resources to satisfy the goal of the decision-maker.*

Solution: Let us now formulate a *goal programming model*, which is a special type of LP *model* by considering the following example:

Two product P I and P II are manufactured by passing sequentially through two different machines M I and M II. The time available for two products on each machine is limited to 8 hours daily but may be exceeded by up to 4 hours on an overtime basis. Each overtime hour will cost an additional ₹ 5. The production rates for the two products together with their profits per unit are summarised below.

	Production rate (Units/hr)	
Machine	P I	P II
M I	5	6
M II	4	8
Profit per unit	₹ 6	₹ 4

It is required to determine the production level for each product that will maximise the net profit.

Mathematical Formulation

In this model it is required to determine the *number of units of each product* (variables) that maximises *net profit* (objective) provided that the *maximum allowance machine hours are exceeded only on an overtime basis* (constraints).

x_j = number of units project j, $j = 1,2$.

In absence of overtime option: $\dfrac{x_1}{5} + \dfrac{x_2}{6} \leq 8 \quad (\text{M I})$

$$\frac{x_1}{4} + \frac{x_2}{8} \leq 8 \quad (\text{M II})$$

To include the overtime option: $\dfrac{x_1}{5} + \dfrac{x_2}{6} - y_1 \leq 8$

$$\frac{x_1}{4} + \frac{x_2}{8} - y_2 \leq 8$$

where $y_j (j = 1,2)$ are variables unrestricted in sign due to the following reasons:

If $y_j < 0$, the 8 hour limit on the capacity of the machine is not exceeded and no overtime is needed.

If $y_j > 0$, the used machine hours will exceed the daily limit and y_j will then represent overtime hours.

We have accounted for the overtime option by letting'y_j unrestricted values.

Next, we need to limit the daily use of overtime to 4 hours and also to include the cost of overtime in the objective function. Since $y_j > 0$ only when overtime is used, the constraints $y_j \leq 4$, $j = 1,2$ which will provide the restriction on overtime.

Our goal is to maximise the net profit that equals the total profit from the two products less the additional cost of overtime

Overtime cost = (cost/hr) × (overtime hrs) = $5\{\max(0, y_j)\}$

where $\max(0, y_j) = 0 : y_j < 0$ yields zero overtime cost.

Hence, the *complete model* can be written as

$$\text{Maximise } Z = 6x_1 + 4x_2 - 5\{\max(0, y_1) + \max(0, y_2)\}$$

$$\begin{aligned}
\text{subject to } \quad \frac{x_1}{5} + \frac{x_2}{6} - y_1 \qquad &= 8 \\
\frac{x_1}{4} + \frac{x_2}{8} \qquad - y_2 &= 8 \\
y_1 \qquad &\leq 4 \\
y_2 &\leq 4 \\
x_1, x_2 \geq 0, \; y_1, y_2 &\text{ unrestricted in sign.}
\end{aligned}$$

To convert the model to LP *model:*

Let $\sigma_j = \max\{0, y_j\}$ which is equivalent to $\sigma_j \geq y_j$ and $\sigma_j \geq 0$ because the negative coefficient of σ_j in the objective function will force it to assume the smallest possible non-negative value zero or y_j. Thus, LP *model* ultimately takes the form:

$$\text{Maximise } Z = 6x_1 + 4x_2 - 5(\sigma + \sigma_2)$$

$$\begin{aligned}
\text{subject to } \quad \frac{x_1}{5} + \frac{x_2}{6} - y_1 \qquad &= 8 \\
\frac{x_1}{4} + \frac{x_2}{8} \qquad - y_2 &= 8 \\
y_1 \qquad - \sigma_1 &\leq 0 \\
y_2 \qquad - \sigma_2 &\leq 0 \\
y_1 \qquad &\leq 4 \\
y_2 &\leq 4. \\
x_1, x_2, \sigma_1, \sigma_2 \geq 0, \text{ but } y_1, y_2 &\text{ unrestricted in sign.}
\end{aligned}$$

2.1.5 Graphical Solution of LP Model

The LP model can be solved graphically when it has only two variables. For models with three or more variables, the graphical method is either impractical or impossible. There are two methods in the solution of an LP model by graphical approach.

Method 1. Search approach method:

Step 1: Plot a graph representing all the constraints of the problem and identify the solution space which satisfies all the constraints simultaneously. The non-negativity restrictions confine all the feasible values to the first quadrant. The solution space (feasible region) may be bounded or unbounded. Compute the coordinates of all the corner points of the feasible region.

Step 2: Find the value of the objective function at each corner (extreme) point. Finally, select the extreme point that optimises (maximises or minimises) the value of the objective function, which gives the required *optimum feasible solution.*

Method 2. ISO-*profit or* ISO-*cost approach*

First step is same as method 1.

Step 2: We choose a convenient profit (or cost) and draw iso-profit (iso-cost) line so that it falls within the feasible region. Move this iso-profit (iso-cost) line parallel to itself farther (closer) from (to) the origin. Identify the optimum solution as the coordinates of that point on the feasible region touched by the highest possible iso-profit line (or lower possible iso-cost line) which gives the required *optimum feasible solution*.

Example 2.1.8. *Make a graphical representation of the set of constraints in the following* LPP.

$$\text{Maximise } Z = 4x_1 + 3x_2$$
$$\text{subject to } \quad x_1 + x_2 \leq 50$$
$$x_1 + 2x_2 \leq 80$$
$$2x_1 + x_2 \geq 20$$
$$x_1, x_2 \geq 0$$

Find the extreme points of the feasible region and obtain the optimal solution of the problem.

Solution: [CU 1992; VU 1994]

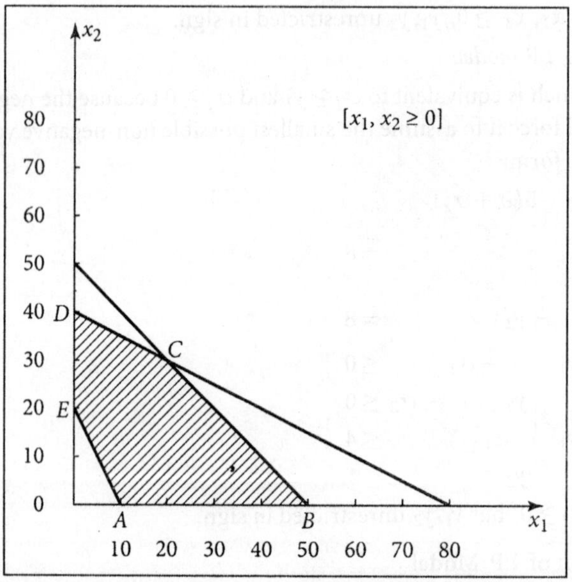

$ABCDE$ is the feasible region satisfying all the constraints simultaneously.

Coordinates of extreme points are: $A(10,0)$, $B(50,0)$, $C(20,30)$ (point of intersection of lines $x_1 + x_2 = 50$ and $x_1 + 2x_2 = 80$) $D(0,40)$, $E(0,20)$.

Values of objective function at the extreme points are: $z_A = 40$, $z_B = 200$, $z_C = 170$, $z_D = 120$, $z_E = 60$.

The maximum value is 200 and it occurs at the extreme point $B(50,0)$. Hence, by *Method* 1 the optimal solution is given by $\left\langle x_1^* = 50,\ x_{20}^* = 0,\ Z_{\max} = 200 \right\rangle$.

Example 2.1.9. *A farm is engaged in breeding pigs. The pigs are fed on various products grown on the farm. In view of the need to ensure certain nutrient constituents* N_1, N_2, N_3, *it is necessary to buy two additional products* P_1 *and* P_2. *One unit of* P_1 *contains* 36 *units of* N_1, 3 *units of* N_2 *and* 20 *units of* N_3. *One unit of product* P_2 *contains* 6 *units of* N_1, 12 *units of* N_2 *and* 10 *units of* N_3. *The minimum requirement of* N_1, N_2

and N_3 is 108 units, 36 units and 100 units respectively. Product P_1 costs ₹ 20 per unit and P_2 costs ₹ 40 per unit.

Formulate this Diet Problem as an LP *model and solve it graphically.* [CU(H) 2006]

Solution: *Formulation.* On the basis of the information, the appropriate mathematical formulation of the LP model is:

Minimise $Z = 20x_1 + 40x_2$

subject to $36x_1 + 6x_2 \geq 108$

$3x_1 + 12x_2 \geq 36$

$20x_1 + 10x_2 \geq 100$

$x_1, x_2 \geq 0.$

Graphical Solution

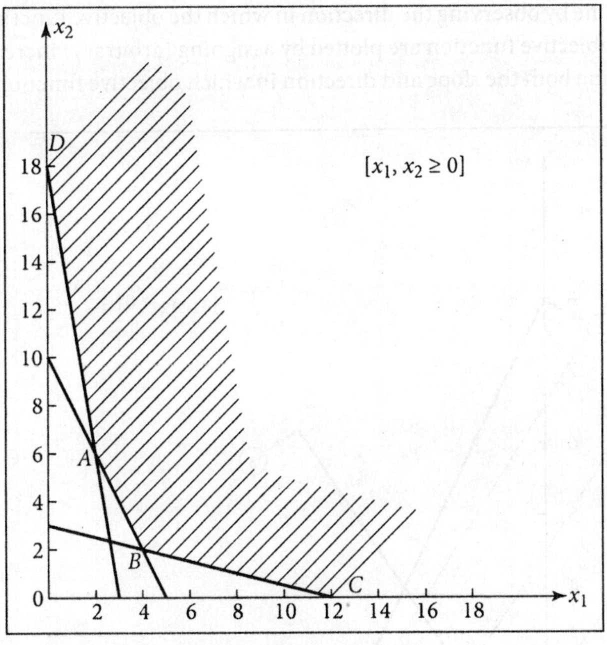

$ABCD$ are the four extreme points of the unbounded feasible region satisfying all the constraints simultaneously.

Coordinates of extreme points in the shaded region:

$A(2,6)$ (Point of intersection of $36x_1 + 6x_2 = 108$ and $20x_1 + 10x_2 = 100$)

$B(4,2)$ (Point of intersection of $3x_1 + 12x_2 = 36$ and $20x_1 + 10x_2 = 100$)

$C(12,0)$

$D(0,18)$

Values of the objective function at extreme points: $z_A = 280$, $z_B = 160$, $z_C = 240$, $z_D = 720$.

Since the problem is a minimisation problem, the optimum solution admits at any one corner in the finite region of unbounded feasible space. Here minimum occurs at the point $B(4,2)$. Therefore, the required optimum solution is $\langle x_1^* = 4, x_2^* = 2, Z_{\min} = 160 \rangle$.

Remark. For maximisation LP model such an unbounded feasible region does not attain any optimal solution.

Example 2.1.10. *Solve graphically the following* LPP.

Maximise $Z = 3x_1 + 2x_2$

subject to $x_1 + 2x_2 \leq 6$ (1)

$2x_1 + x_2 \leq 8$ (2)

$-x_1 + x_2 \leq 1$ (3)

$2x_2 \leq 2$ (4)

$x_1, x_2 \leq 0.$

Solution: Use *Method* 2.

$OABCDE$ solution space satisfying all constraints simultaneously. Each point within or on the boundary represents a feasible point. Although there is an infinity of feasible points in the solution space, the optimum solution can be determine by observing the direction in which the objective function increases. The parallel lines representing the objective function are plotted by assigning (arbitrary) increasing values to $Z = 3x_1 + 2x_2$ in order to determine both the slope and direction in which objective function increases. We use $Z = 6$ and $Z = 9$.

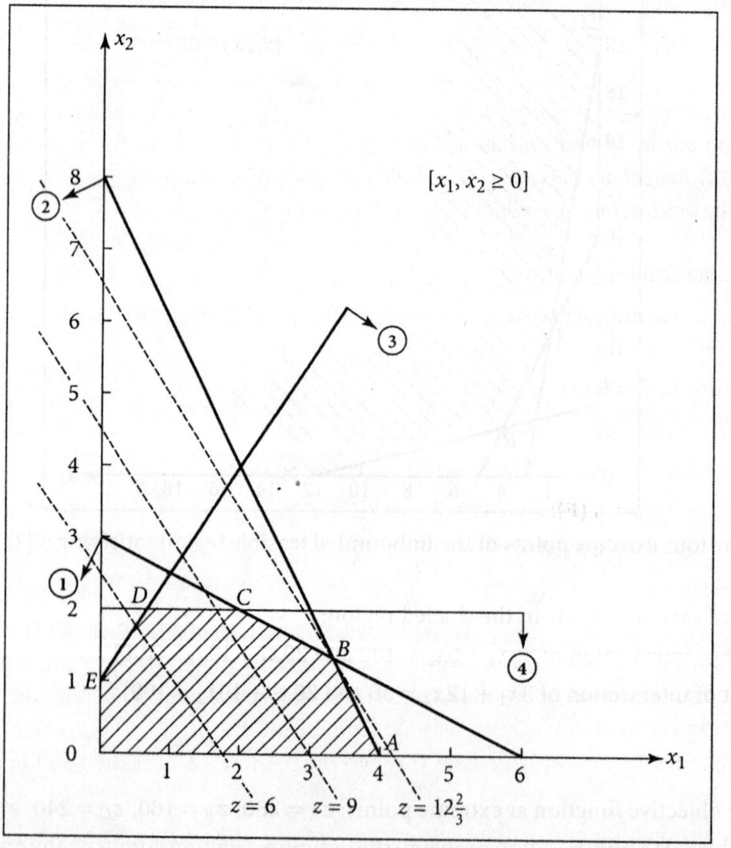

Finally, to find the optimum solution, we move the profit line *uphill* to the point where any further increase of profit would render an infeasible solution. Figure shows that the optimum solution occurs at point

B, the point of intersection of (1) and (2) given by

$$x_1 + 2x_2 - 6 = 0$$
$$2x_1 + x_2 - 6 = 0$$

$$\frac{x_1}{-16+6} = \frac{x_2}{-12+8} = \frac{1}{1-4}$$

$$(x_1, x_2) = \left(3\tfrac{1}{3}, 1\tfrac{1}{3}\right)$$

Required optimum solution is $\left\langle x_1^* = 3\frac{1}{3},\ x_2^* = 1\frac{1}{3},\ Z_{\max} = 12\frac{2}{3}\right\rangle$.

Example 2.1.11. *A company has two bottling plants, one located at Kolkata and the other at North Bengal. Each plant produces three drinks — Whisky, Beer and Fruit juices — named W, B and F respectively. The number of bottles produced per day are as follows:*

	Plant at	
	Kolkata	*North Bengal*
Whiskey (W)	1500	1500
Beer (B)	3000	1000
Fruit Juices (F)	2000	5000

A market survey indicates that during hot summer month, April, there will be a demand of 20,000 bottles of Whisky. 40,000 bottles of beer and 44,000 bottles of fruit juices. The operating costs per day for plants at Kolkata and North Bengal are 600 and 400 monetary units. For how many days each plant be run in April so as to minimise the production cost, while still meeting the market demand?

Solution: Mathematical formulation.

Let x_1, x_2 denote the number of days in April for which the bottling plants at Kolkata and North Bengal must be run. Then as per the information given the LP model is

objective: Minimise $Z = 600x_1 + 400x_2$

subject to: For Whisky (W): $1500x_1 + 1500x_2 \geq 20{,}000$ (1)

For Beer (B): $3000x_1 + 1000x_2 \geq 40{,}000$ (2)

For Fruit juices (F): $2000x_1 + 5000x_2 \geq 44{,}000$. (3)

Non-negative restrictions: $x_1, x_2 \geq 0$.

Graphical Solution

The objective function, when $Z = 0$, gives the equation $600x_1 + 400x_2 = 0$ which is shown by the line L_1 passing through origin. As Z increases from zero, the line L_1 moves to the right, parallel to itself. Since we are interested in minimising Z we gradually increase the value of Z till the line passes through the nearest corner of the shaded unbounded feasible region from the origin. This gives the minimum value of Z corresponding to the line L_2 which passes through the point $C(12, 4)$ as the point of intersection of lines (2) and (3).

Therefore, the production cost will be minimum if plants at Kolkata and North Bengal are run for 12 days and 4 days respectively giving the minimum production cost as $600 \times 12 + 400 \times 4 = 8800$ monetary units.

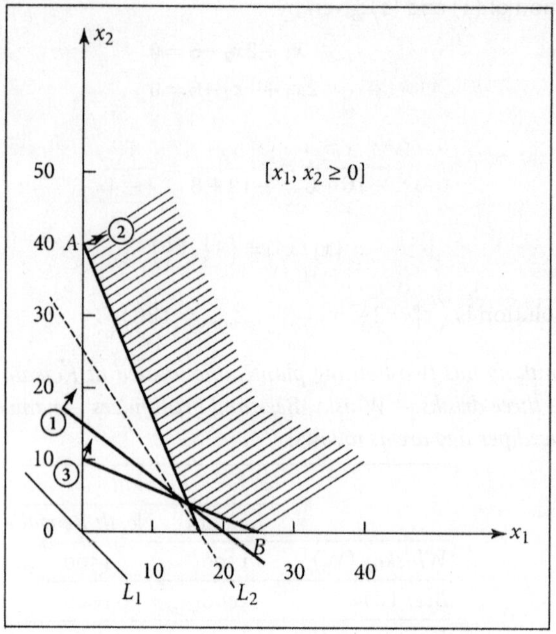

2.2 SLACK VARIABLES, SURPLUS VARIABLES, UNRESTRICTED VARIABLES AND STANDARD FORM OF AN LP MODEL

2.2.1 Slack Variables

Let the constraints of a general LP model be

$$a_{11}x_1 + a_{12}x_2 + \ldots + a_{1n}x_n \leq b_1$$
$$a_{21}x_1 + a_{22}x_2 + \ldots + a_{2n}x_n \leq b_2$$
$$\vdots$$
$$a_{r1}x_1 + a_{r2}x_2 + \ldots + a_{rn}x_n \leq b_r$$

$$\text{i.e., } \sum_{j=1}^{n} a_{ij}x_j \leq b_i, \ i = 1,2,\ldots,r$$

Then the non-negative variables $x_{n+1}, x_{n+2}, \ldots, x_{n+r} \geq 0$ which transformed '$\leq$' inequality into an equality by adding to the left, called *slack variables* so that

$$a_{11}x_1 + a_{12}x_2 + \ldots + a_{1n}x_n + x_{n+1} = b_1$$
$$a_{21}x_1 + a_{22}x_2 + \ldots + a_{2n}x_n + x_{n+2} = b_2$$
$$\vdots$$
$$a_{r1}x_1 + a_{r2}x_2 + \ldots + a_{rn}x_n + x_{n+r} = b_r$$

$$\text{i.e., } \sum_{j=1}^{n} a_{ij}x_j + x_{n+i} = b_i, \ i = 1,2,\ldots,r$$

$$\text{or, } x_{n+i} = b_i - \sum_{j=1}^{n} a_{ij}x_j, \ i = 1,2,\ldots,r$$

or, Slack = Requirements−Production.

2.2.2 Surplus Variables

Suppose, another set of constraints of a general LP model is

$$a_{r+11}x_1 + a_{r+12}x_2 + \cdots + a_{r+1n}x_n \geq b_{r+1}$$
$$a_{r+21}x_1 + a_{r+22}x_2 + \cdots + a_{r+2n}x_n \geq b_{r+2}$$
$$\vdots$$
$$a_{l1}x_1 + \quad a_{l2}x_2 + \quad \cdots + a_{ln}x_n \geq b_l$$
$$\text{i.e., } \sum_{j=1}^{n} a_{ij}x_j \geq b_i, \; i = r+1, r+2, \ldots, l.$$

Then the non-negative variables $x_{n+r+1}, x_{n+r+2}, \ldots, x_{n+l} \geq 0$ which transformed '≥' inequality into an equality by subtracting from the left, called *Surplus Variables* so that

$$\begin{aligned}
&a_{r+11}x_1 + a_{r+12}x_2 + \ldots + a_{r+1n}x_n - \quad x_{n+r+1} && = b_{r+1}\\
&a_{r+21}x_1 + a_{r+22}x_2 + \ldots + a_{r+2n}x_n \qquad - x_{n+r+2} && = b_{r+2}\\
&\vdots\\
&a_{l1}x_1 + \quad a_{l2}x_2 + \ldots + \quad a_{ln}x_n \qquad\qquad - x_{n+l} && = b_l
\end{aligned}$$

$$\text{i.e., } \sum_{j=1}^{n} a_{ij}x_j - x_{n+i} \geq b_i, \; i = r+1, r+2, \ldots, l$$

$$\text{or, } x_{n+i} = \sum_{j=1}^{n} a_{ij}x_j - b_i, \; i = r+1, r+2, \ldots, l$$

or, Surplus = Production−Requirements.

2.2.3 Unrestricted Variables

A variable which may be positive, negative or zero is called an *unrestricted variable.* Since in an LP model every variable is non-negative in nature by physical situation of the model, we can easily convert an unrestricted variable in sign variable to the difference of two non-negative variables.

Thus, an unrestricted variable x_j can be written as $x_j = x_j' - x_j''$, where $x_j', x_j'' \geq 0$.

For example, we can write $-7 = (+2) - (+9)$.

Note that $x_j >=< 0$ according as $x_j' >=< x_j''$.

2.2.4 Standard Form of LP Model

Consider the following LP model consisting of r-constraints with '≤' types, $(l - r)$ constraints with '≥' types inequalities and $(m - l)$ constraints with equality so that the total numbers of constraints of the model are m.

$$\text{Optimise (Maximise or Minimise) } Z = \sum_{j=1}^{n} c_j x_j$$

$$\text{subject to } \sum_{j=1}^{n} a_{ij}x_j \le b_i,\ i=1,2,\ldots,r$$

$$\sum_{j=1}^{n} a_{ij}x_j \ge b_i,\ i=r+1,r+2,\ldots,l$$

$$\sum_{j=1}^{n} a_{ij}x_j = b_i,\ i=l+1,l+2,\ldots,m$$

$$x_j \ge 0,\ i=1,2,\ldots,n$$

Introducing slack and surplus variables to the inequality constraints and taking costs equal to zero in the objective function corresponding to slack and surplus variables, we write the above LP model into a form which we shall call the *Standard (Sometimes Canonical) form* of an LP model.

$$\text{Optimise (Maximise or Minimise) } Z=\sum_{j=1}^{n} c_jx_j+\sum_{i=1}^{r} 0\cdot x_{n+1}+\sum_{l=r+1}^{l} 0\cdot x_{n+i}$$

$$\text{subject to } \sum_{j=1}^{n} a_{ij}x_j + x_{n+i} = b_i,\ i=1,2,\ldots,r$$

$$\sum_{j=1}^{n} a_{ij}x_j - x_{n+i} = b_i,\ i=r+1,r+2,\ldots,l$$

$$\sum_{j=1}^{n} a_{ij}x_j \qquad = b_i,\ i=l+1,l+2,\ldots,m$$

$$x_j \ge 0,\ j=1,2,\ldots,n$$

are called *decision variables* $x_{n+i} \ge 0$ for $i=1,2,\ldots,r$ are *slack variables* and for $i=r+1,\ r+2,\ldots,l$ are *surplus variables.*

Remark. Every maximisation/minimisation LP model as well as the inequality constraints $\le$ or $\ge$ can be converted into minimisation/maximisation model and corresponding inequalities $\ge$ or $\le$ by appropriate adjustment.

Example 2.2.1. *Reduce the following problem in its standard form:*

$$\text{Maximise } Z=2x_1+x_2-6x_3-x_4$$

$$\begin{aligned}\text{subject to } 3x_1 \qquad\qquad\qquad + x_4 &\le 25\\ x_1+x_2+x_3+x_4 &= 20\\ 4x_1 \qquad +6x_3 \qquad &\ge 5\\ 2\le 2x_1 \qquad +3x_3+2x_4 &\le 30\\ x_1,x_2,x_3,x_4 &\ge 0.\end{aligned}$$

[CU(P) 2005; KU 2002]

Solution: *Standard form:*

$$\text{Maximise } Z=(2x_1+x_2-6x_3-x_4)+(0x_5+0x_6)+(0x_7+0x_8)$$

$$\begin{aligned}
\text{subject to } 3x_1 \quad\quad\quad\quad + x_4 + x_5 &= 25\\
2x_1 + 3x_3 + 2x_4 \quad\quad + x_6 &= 30\\
4x_1 + 6x_3 \quad\quad\quad\quad - x_7 &= 5\\
2x_1 + 3x_3 + 2x_4 \quad\quad\quad\quad - x_8 &= 20\\
x_1 + x_2 + x_3 + x_4 &= 20\\
x_1, x_2, x_3, x_4 &\geq 0 \text{ decision variables}\\
x_5, x_6 &\geq 0 \text{ slack variables}\\
x_7, x_8 &\geq 0 \text{ surplus variables.}
\end{aligned}$$

Example 2.2.2. *Reduce the following minimisation problem to a maximisation problem in its standard form:*

$$\begin{aligned}
\textit{Minimise } W &= 3w_1 - 2w_2 + 4w_3\\
\textit{subject to } w_1 - w_2 + 3w_3 &\geq 1\\
-2w_1 - 3w_2 + 5w_3 &\leq 3\\
4w_1 + 2w_2 &\geq 2\\
w_1, w_2, w_3 &\geq 0.
\end{aligned}$$

Solution: *Standard maximisation form:*

$$\begin{aligned}
\text{Maximise } W^* &= (-3w_1 + 2w_2 - 4w_3) + 0w_4 + 0w_5 + 0w_6\\
\text{subject to } w_1 - w_2 + 3w_3 - w_4 &= 1\\
-2w_1 - 3w_2 + 5w_3 + \quad + w_5 + &= 3\\
4w_1 + 2w_2 + \quad\quad - w_6 &= 2\\
w_1, w_2, w_3 &\geq 0 \text{ decision variables}\\
w_4, w_6 &\geq 0 \text{ surplus variables}\\
w_5 &\geq 0 \text{ slack variables.}
\end{aligned}$$

Example 2.2.3. *Put the following* LP *model in a standard maximisation form:*

$$\begin{aligned}
\textit{Minimise } Z &= 3x_1 - 4x_2 + 7x_3\\
\textit{subject to } x_1 + x_2 + 7x_3 &\leq 50\\
x_1 + 9x_2 - 5x_3 &\leq 40\\
5x_1 + 3x_2 &\leq 20\\
|3x_2 + 4x_3| &\leq 100\\
x_1, x_2 &\geq 0, \ x_3 \textit{ is unrestricted in sign.}
\end{aligned}$$

[CU(H) 1993; VU 2001]

Solution: *Standard maximisation form:*

$$\begin{aligned}
\text{Maximise } Z^* &= -3x_1 + 4x_2 - 7\left(x_3' - x_3''\right) + 0x_4 + 0x_5 + 0x_6 + 0x_7 + 0x_8\\
\text{subject to } x_1 + x_2 + 7\left(x_3' - x_3''\right) + x_4 &= 50\\
x_1 + 9x_2 - 5\left(x_3' - x_3''\right) - x_5 &= 40\\
5x_1 + 3x_2 - x_6 &= 20\\
3x_2 + 4\left(x_3' - x_3''\right) + x_7 &= 100\\
-3x_2 - 4\left(x_3' - x_3''\right) + x_8 &= 100
\end{aligned}$$

where $x_3 = x_3' - x_3''$ and $x_1, x_2, x_3', x_3'' \geq 0$ decision variables

$x_4, x_7, x_8 \geq 0$ slack variables

$x_5, x_6 \geq 0$ surplus variables.

2.3 SOME IMPORTANT ANALYTICAL RESULTS

Consider the following standard LP model

$$\begin{aligned} &\text{Maximise } Z = \boldsymbol{cx} \\ &\text{subject to } A\boldsymbol{x} = \boldsymbol{b} \\ &\boldsymbol{x} \geq \boldsymbol{0} \end{aligned} \tag{2.3a}$$

where $\boldsymbol{c}, \boldsymbol{x}$ are n-component vectors, $\boldsymbol{b}$ is an m component vector and $A = (a_{ij})_{m \times n}$, $i = 1, 2, \ldots, m;\ j = 1, 2, \ldots, n$.

Result 3.1 If Ω be the set of all feasible solution of $A\boldsymbol{x} = \boldsymbol{b}, \boldsymbol{x} \geq 0$ and if $\boldsymbol{x}^* \in \Omega$ maximises the objective function $Z = \boldsymbol{cx}$, then $\boldsymbol{x}^*$ also minimises $Z^* = (-\boldsymbol{c})\boldsymbol{x}$ over Ω.

Proof. Let $\boldsymbol{x} \neq \boldsymbol{x}^*$ be any other feasible solution in Ω. Then since $\boldsymbol{x}^*$ maximises $Z = \boldsymbol{cx}$

$$\begin{aligned} \boldsymbol{cx}^* &\geq \boldsymbol{cx}, \quad \forall\, \boldsymbol{x} \in \Omega \\ \text{or,} \quad -\boldsymbol{cx}^* &\leq -\boldsymbol{cx}, \quad \forall\, \boldsymbol{x} \in \Omega \\ \text{or,} \quad (-\boldsymbol{c})\boldsymbol{x}^* &\leq (-\boldsymbol{c})\boldsymbol{x}, \quad \forall\, \boldsymbol{x} \in \Omega \end{aligned}$$

which indicates that $\boldsymbol{x}^*$ minimises the objective function $Z^* = (-\boldsymbol{c})\boldsymbol{x}, \forall\, \boldsymbol{x} \in \Omega$.

Hence, a solution which minimises $Z^* = (-\boldsymbol{c})\boldsymbol{x}$ also maximises the objective function $Z = \boldsymbol{cx}$.

Result 3.2 The set of all feasible solutions of LP problem is a convex set.

Proof. Let the constraints of the problem are $A\boldsymbol{x} = \boldsymbol{b}, \boldsymbol{x} \geq \boldsymbol{0}$.

Ω be the set of feasible solutions and $\boldsymbol{x}_1, \boldsymbol{x}_2 \in \Omega$, then

$$A\boldsymbol{x}_1 = \boldsymbol{b},\ A\boldsymbol{x}_2 = \boldsymbol{b},\ \boldsymbol{x}_1, \boldsymbol{x}_2 \geq \boldsymbol{0}. \tag{2.3b}$$

Let $\boldsymbol{x}^*$ be the convex combination of $\boldsymbol{x}_1$ and $\boldsymbol{x}_2$, then

$$\boldsymbol{x}^* = \lambda \boldsymbol{x}_1 + (1-\lambda)\boldsymbol{x}_2 : \lambda \in [0, 1].$$

$$\begin{aligned} \text{Now } A\boldsymbol{x}^* &= A[\lambda \boldsymbol{x}_1 + (1-\lambda)\boldsymbol{x}_2] = \lambda A\boldsymbol{x}_1 + (1-\lambda)A\boldsymbol{x}_2 \\ &= \lambda \boldsymbol{b} + (1-\lambda)\boldsymbol{b} \text{ [using (2.3b)]} \\ &= \boldsymbol{b}. \end{aligned}$$

Also, $\boldsymbol{x}^* = \lambda \boldsymbol{x}_1 + (1-\lambda)\boldsymbol{x}_2 \geq 0\ [\boldsymbol{x}_1, \boldsymbol{x}_2 \geq \boldsymbol{0}, \lambda \boldsymbol{x}_1, (1-\lambda)\boldsymbol{x}_2 \geq \boldsymbol{0}]$.

Therefore, $\boldsymbol{x}^*$ is a feasible solution and $\boldsymbol{x}^* \in \Omega$.

Hence, the set Ω is a convex set.

Result 3.3 The objective function of LP model assumes its optimal value at an extreme point of the convex set of feasible solutions.

Proof. Consider the maximisation problem (2.3a) and assume: (i) finite number of extreme points are $\boldsymbol{x}_1, \boldsymbol{x}_2, \ldots, \boldsymbol{x}_n$, (ii) set of all feasible solutions is strictly bounded.

Let $\boldsymbol{x}_0$ be the optimal solution of (2.3a). If $\boldsymbol{x}_0$ be an extreme point, then the result is automatically proved. Suppose, $\boldsymbol{x}_0$ is not an extreme point while it gives the optimal value of objective function as Z_0, where

$$Z_0 = \text{maximum value} = \boldsymbol{cx}_0. \tag{2.3c}$$

$\boldsymbol{x}_0$ can be expressed as a convex combination of $\boldsymbol{x}_1, \boldsymbol{x}_2, \ldots, \boldsymbol{x}_k$ as it is not an extreme point.

$$\boldsymbol{x}_0 = \sum_{i=1}^{k} \mu_i \boldsymbol{x}_i : \mu_i \geq 0, \sum_{i=1}^{k} \mu_i = 1. \tag{2.3d}$$

From (2.3c),

$$Z_0 = \boldsymbol{c}\boldsymbol{x}_0 = \boldsymbol{c}\sum_{i=1}^{k} \mu_i \boldsymbol{x}_i = \sum_{i=1}^{k} \mu_i \boldsymbol{c}\boldsymbol{x}_i. \tag{2.3e}$$

If $\boldsymbol{c}\boldsymbol{x}^* = \max_i \{\boldsymbol{c}\boldsymbol{x}_i\}$, where $\boldsymbol{x}^*$ is an extreme point, then from (2.3e),

$$Z_0 \leq \sum_{i=1}^{k} \mu_i \boldsymbol{c}\boldsymbol{x}^* = \boldsymbol{c}\boldsymbol{x}^* \sum_{i=1}^{k} \mu_i = \boldsymbol{c}\boldsymbol{x}^* \text{ [by (2.3d)]} \tag{2.3f}$$

Let $Z^* = \boldsymbol{c}\boldsymbol{x}^*$, then $Z^* \geq Z_0$ which was assumed to be the maximum value of objective function.

Hence, $Z^* = Z_0$ shows that there must be an extreme point $\boldsymbol{x}^*$, where the objective function will take on its maximum value.

Remarks.

1. An equivalent statement of the above result: The objective function has its optimal value at an extreme point of the convex polyhedron generated by the set of feasible solutions of the LPP (since the set of all convex combinations of a finite number of points is the convex polyhedron generated by these points).
2. A minimisation LP model will have similar proof.

Result 3.4 If the objective function assumes its optimal value at more than one extreme point, then every convex combination of these extreme points also gives the optimal value of the objective function.

Proof. Let the objective function assume its optimal value Z_0 at extreme points $\boldsymbol{x}_1, \boldsymbol{x}_2, \ldots, \boldsymbol{x}_k$ of the convex set of feasible solution Ω. Then $Z_0 = \boldsymbol{c}\boldsymbol{x}_1 = \boldsymbol{c}\boldsymbol{x}_2 = \cdots = \boldsymbol{c}\boldsymbol{x}_k$.

$$\boldsymbol{x}^* = \sum_{i=1}^{k} \mu_i \boldsymbol{x}_i : \mu_i \geq 0, \sum_{i=1}^{k} \mu_i = 1$$

be the convex combination of $\{\boldsymbol{x}_1, \boldsymbol{x}_2, \ldots, \boldsymbol{x}_k\}$.

Then $\boldsymbol{c}\boldsymbol{x}^* = \boldsymbol{c}\sum_{i=1}^{k} \mu_i x_i = \mu_1 \boldsymbol{c}\boldsymbol{x}_1 + \mu_2 \boldsymbol{c}\boldsymbol{x}_2 + \cdots + \mu_k \boldsymbol{c}\boldsymbol{x}_k$

$$= \mu_1 Z_0 + \mu_2 Z_0 + \cdots + \mu_k Z_0 = Z_0 \sum_{i=1}^{k} \mu_i = Z_0.$$

Hence the theorem. This result shows that either the optimal solution is unique or infinite in numbers.

2.4 SIMPLEX METHOD

2.4.1 Fundamental Theorem of LP Model

If the LP model attains an optimal solution, then the optimal solution will coincide with at least one basic feasible solution (BFS) of the problem.

Proof. Let $\boldsymbol{x}_0$ is an optimal solution of LP model (2.3a), Assume that the first k components of $\boldsymbol{x}_0$ are non-zero and remaining $(n-k)$ components of $\boldsymbol{x}_0$ are zero, so that

$$\boldsymbol{x}_0 = (x_1, x_2, \ldots, x_k, 0, 0, \ldots, 0)^T.$$

Now $A\boldsymbol{x_0}=\boldsymbol{b}$ gives

$$\sum_{j=1}^{k} a_{ij}x_j = b_i, \quad i=1,2,\ldots,m.$$

Again, if $A=(\boldsymbol{\alpha_1},\boldsymbol{\alpha_2},\ldots,\boldsymbol{\alpha_k},\boldsymbol{\alpha_{k+1}}\ldots\boldsymbol{\alpha_n})$, where $\alpha_j=(a_{1j},a_{2j},\ldots,a_{mj})$, $j=1,2,\ldots,n$, then

$$\boldsymbol{\alpha_1 x_1 + \alpha_2 x_2 + \cdots + \alpha_k x_k = b}. \tag{2.4a}$$

Also

$$Z_0 = Z_{\max} = \sum_{j=1}^{k} c_j x_j. \tag{2.4b}$$

Case 1. If $\boldsymbol{\alpha_1},\boldsymbol{\alpha_2},\ldots,\boldsymbol{\alpha_k}$ corresponding to non-zero components of $\boldsymbol{x_0}$ be linearly independent, then $\boldsymbol{x_0}$ is a BFS by definition. Hence, the theorem holds.

Case 2. If $k=m$, then BFS will be non-degenerate and if $k<m$, then it will form a degenerate BFS with $(m-k)$ of the basic variables equal to zero.

Case 3. If $\boldsymbol{\alpha_1},\boldsymbol{\alpha_2},\ldots,\boldsymbol{\alpha_k}$ are linearly dependent then there exists scalars $\mu_j, j=1,2,\ldots,k$ of which at least one of the μ_j's is non-zero and

$$\sum_{j=1}^{k} \mu_j \boldsymbol{\alpha_j} = \boldsymbol{0}. \tag{2.4c}$$

Let

$$\tau = \max_{1\le j\le k}\left\{\frac{\mu_j}{x_j}\right\}. \tag{2.4d}$$

$\tau>0$ as $x_j>0\ \forall\ j=1,2,\ldots,k$ and at least one μ_j is positive. Using (2.4a) and (2.4c),

$$\left(x_1-\frac{\mu_1}{\tau}\right)\boldsymbol{\alpha_1}+\left(x_2-\frac{\mu_2}{\tau}\right)\boldsymbol{\alpha_2}+\cdots+\left(x_k-\frac{\mu_k}{\tau}\right)\boldsymbol{\alpha_k}=\boldsymbol{b}.$$

Therefore,

$$\boldsymbol{x_1^*}=\left(\left(x_1-\frac{\mu_1}{\tau}\right),\left(x_2-\frac{\mu_2}{\tau}\right),\ldots,\left(x_k-\frac{\mu_k}{\tau}\right)\right)^T \tag{2.4e}$$

is a solution of $A\boldsymbol{x}=\boldsymbol{b}$.

From (2.4d), $\tau \ge \dfrac{\mu_j}{x_j}$

or, $\left(x_j-\dfrac{\mu_j}{\tau}\right)\ge 0 \quad \forall\ j=1,2,\ldots,k$

or, $\boldsymbol{x_1^*}\ge 0$

or, $\boldsymbol{x_1^*}$ is a feasible solution of $A\boldsymbol{x}=\boldsymbol{b}, \boldsymbol{x}\ge\boldsymbol{0}$.

Again, from (2.4d), $x_j-\dfrac{\mu_j}{\tau}=0$ for at least one value of j.

Now,

$$Z^*=\boldsymbol{c}\boldsymbol{x_1^*}=\sum_{j=1}^{k}c_j\left(x_j-\frac{\mu_j}{\tau}\right)=\sum_{j=1}^{k}c_jx_j-\frac{1}{\tau}\sum_{j=1}^{k}c_j\mu_j=Z_0-\frac{1}{\tau}\sum_{j=1}^{k}c_j\mu_j. \tag{2.4f}$$

If we can show that

$$\sum_{j=1}^{k} c_j \mu_j = 0,$$

then $Z^* = Z_0$, which will prove $\boldsymbol{x}_1^*$ is an optimal solution.

If possible, let

$$\sum_{j=1}^{k} c_j \mu_j \neq 0$$

and we find a suitable real number λ such that

$$\lambda \sum_{j=1}^{k} c_j \mu_j > 0 \text{ or, } \sum_{j=1}^{k} c_j \left(\lambda \mu_j\right) > 0 \text{ or, } \sum_{j=1}^{k} c_j \left(x_j + \lambda \mu_j\right) > \sum_{j=1}^{k} c_j x_j = Z_0 \tag{2.4g}$$

From (2.4a) and (2.4c),

$$\sum_{j=1}^{k} \left(x_j + \lambda \mu_j\right) \boldsymbol{a}_j = \boldsymbol{b}$$

so that

$$\left(\left(x_1 + \lambda \mu_1\right), \left(x_2 + \lambda \mu_2\right), \ldots, \left(x_k + \lambda \mu_k\right), 0, 0, \ldots, 0\right)^T \tag{2.4h}$$

is also a solution of $A\boldsymbol{x} = \boldsymbol{b}$.

Now choose λ such that $x_j + \lambda \mu_j \geq 0$ or, $\lambda \geq -\left(\dfrac{x_j}{\mu_j}\right)$, if $\mu_j > 0$

$$\leq -\left(\frac{x_j}{\mu_j}\right), \text{ if } \mu_j < 0.$$

If we take λ in a manner such that

$$\max_j \left\{ -\frac{x_j}{\mu_j} \middle| \mu_j > 0 \right\} \leq \lambda \leq \min_j \left\{ -\frac{x_j}{\mu_j} \middle| \mu_j < 0 \right\}$$

then we observe from (2.4g) the feasible solution gives a greater value of the objective function than Z_0 which contradicts our assumption that Z_0 is the optimal value and thus

$$\sum_{j=1}^{k} c_j \mu_j = 0.$$

Hence, $\boldsymbol{x}_1^*$ is also an optimal solution.

Remark. This theorem tells us that to optimise the objective function, we shall have to find all BFS of the system of equations as given by the constraints of LP model and then to check which of these BFS will optimise the objective function. This has been already illustrated in the solution of an LP model by *graphical approach.*

2.4.2 Reduction of a Feasible Solution to a Basic Feasible Solution

If an LP model has a feasible solution (FS), then it also has a basic feasible solution (BFS).

Proof. Consider the LP model (2.3a) and let $\rho(A) = m$. Since there does exist a feasible solution, we must have $\rho(A, b) = \rho(A)$ and $m < n$.

Let $\boldsymbol{x} = (x_1, x_2, \ldots, x_n)$ be a feasible solution so that $x_j \geq 0$ for all j. To be precise, suppose $\boldsymbol{x}$ has k positive components and remaining $(n-k)$ components be zero. Then

$$\boldsymbol{a}_1 x_1 + \boldsymbol{a}_2 x_2 + \cdots + \boldsymbol{a}_k x_k = \boldsymbol{b},$$

where $\boldsymbol{a}_1, \boldsymbol{a}_2, \ldots, \boldsymbol{a}_k$ are the first k columns of A.

Case 1. If $k < m$, then $\{\boldsymbol{a}_1, \boldsymbol{a}_2, \ldots, \boldsymbol{a}_k\}$ can be extended to $\{\boldsymbol{a}_1, \boldsymbol{a}_2, \ldots, \boldsymbol{a}_k, \boldsymbol{a}_{k+1}, \ldots, \boldsymbol{a}_m\}$ to form a basis for column of A

$$\boldsymbol{a}_1 x_1 + \boldsymbol{a}_2 x_2 + \cdots + \boldsymbol{a}_m x_m = \boldsymbol{b},$$

where $x_j = 0$ for $j = k+1, k+2, \ldots, m$.

So a degenerate BFS with $(m-k)$ of the basic variables zero.

Case 2. If $k = m$, the given solution is a non-degenerate BFS with $x_1, x_2, \ldots, x_k$ as the basic variables.

Case 3. If $k > m$, $\{\boldsymbol{a}_1, \boldsymbol{a}_2, \ldots, \boldsymbol{a}_k\}$ is linearly dependent. Let $(\mu_1, \mu_2, \ldots, \mu_k)$ be a set of constants (not all zero) such that

$$\sum_{j=1}^{k} \mu_j \boldsymbol{a}_j = \boldsymbol{0}$$

for any r, let $\mu_r \neq 0$, then

$$\boldsymbol{a}_r = -\sum_{\substack{j \neq r \\ j=1}}^{k} \frac{\mu_j}{\mu_r} \boldsymbol{a}_j \text{ or, } \sum_{\substack{j \neq r \\ j=1}}^{k} \left(x_j - x_r \frac{\mu_j}{\mu_r} \right) \boldsymbol{a}_j = \boldsymbol{b}.$$

We have a solution with not more than $(k-1)$ non-zero components. To ensure that these are positive, we shall choose $\boldsymbol{a}_r$ in such way that

$$x_j - x_r \frac{\mu_j}{\mu_r} \geq 0, \ \forall\, j \neq r.$$

This requires that either $\mu_j = 0$ or, $\dfrac{x_j}{\mu_j} \geq \dfrac{x_r}{\mu_r}$, if $\mu_j > 0$

$$\leq \frac{x_r}{\mu_r}, \text{ if } \mu_j < 0.$$

Now, if we select

$$\frac{x_r}{\mu_r} = \min_j \left\{ \frac{x_j}{\mu_j} \middle| \mu_j > 0 \right\}$$

then for each of $(k-1)$ variables

$$x_j - x_r \frac{\mu_j}{\mu_r}$$

is non-negative and so, we have a feasible solution with not more than $(k-1)$ non-zero components.

Conclusion. Consider this new feasible solution with not more than $(k-1)$ non-zero components. If corresponding set of $(k-1)$ columns of A is linearly independent, case 1/2 applies and we arrives at a BFS If this set again linearly dependent, we may repeat the process to arrive at a feasible solution with not more than $(k-2)$ non-zero components. With this argument ultimately, we get a FS. With associated set of columns of A linearly independent, Case 1 then applies and we do get a basic feasible solution.

Example 2.4.1. *Let $x_1 = 2$, $x_2 = 4$ and $x_3 = 1$ be a feasible solution* (FS) *to the system of equations*

$$\begin{aligned} 2x_1 - \ x_2 + 2x_3 &= 2 \\ x_1 + 4x_2 \qquad &= 18. \end{aligned}$$

Reduce the given FS to a BFS. [CU(H) 2009; KU(H) 2002]

Solution: $A\boldsymbol{x} = \boldsymbol{b}$ gives $A = \begin{pmatrix} 2 & -1 & 2 \\ 1 & 4 & 0 \end{pmatrix}$, $\boldsymbol{x} = \begin{pmatrix} x_1 \\ x_2 \\ x_3 \end{pmatrix}$, $\boldsymbol{b} = \begin{pmatrix} 2 \\ 18 \end{pmatrix}$.

$\rho(A) =$ rank A = 2, there are two linearly independent columns of A.

$\therefore\ \mu_1\boldsymbol{\alpha}_1 + \mu_2\boldsymbol{\alpha}_2 + \mu_3\boldsymbol{\alpha}_3 = \boldsymbol{0}$, where μ_1, μ_2 and μ_3 are scalars — not all zero. Let $\mu_3 = -1$, then $\alpha_3 = \mu_1\boldsymbol{\alpha}_1 + \mu_2\boldsymbol{\alpha}_2$ or, $2 = 2\mu_1 - \mu_2$ and $0 = \mu_1 + 4\mu_2$ or, $\mu_1 = 8/9, \mu_2 = -2/9$.

Now

$$\frac{x_r}{\mu_r} = \min_j\left\{\frac{x_j}{\mu_j}\middle|\mu_j > 0\right\} = \frac{2}{8/9} = \frac{9}{4} = \frac{x_1}{\mu_1}.$$

This indicates that $\boldsymbol{\alpha}_1$ can be removed. Hence, the new solution with not more than two non-zero variables is given by

$$x_1^* = 2 - \frac{9}{4} \times \frac{8}{9} = 0 \quad x_2^* = 4 - \frac{9}{4} \times \left(-\frac{2}{9}\right) = \frac{9}{2} \quad x_3^* = 1 - \frac{9}{4} \times (-1) = \frac{13}{4}.$$

A basic feasible solution is: $x_2^* = \frac{9}{2}$, $x_3^* = \frac{13}{4}$ with $x_1^* = 0$ (non-basic).

Example 2.4.2. $x_1 = 1, x_2 = 1, x_3 = 1$ *and* $x_4 = 0$ *is a feasible solution of the system of equations*

$$\begin{aligned} x_1 + 2x_2 + 4x_3 + \ x_4 &= 7 \\ 2x_1 - \ x_2 + 3x_3 - 2x_4 &= 4. \end{aligned}$$

Reduce the FS to two different BFS. [JNU (Comp. Sc) 1990]

Solution: Given: $(1,1,1,0)$ is a FS but not basic. We can write the given equations as

$$x_1\boldsymbol{\alpha}_1 + x_2\boldsymbol{\alpha}_2 + x_3\boldsymbol{\alpha}_3 + x_4\boldsymbol{\alpha}_4 = \boldsymbol{b}$$

where $\boldsymbol{\alpha}_1 = \begin{pmatrix} 1 \\ 2 \end{pmatrix}$, $\boldsymbol{\alpha}_2 = \begin{pmatrix} 2 \\ -1 \end{pmatrix}$, $\boldsymbol{\alpha}_3 = \begin{pmatrix} 4 \\ 3 \end{pmatrix}$, $\boldsymbol{\alpha}_4 = \begin{pmatrix} 1 \\ -2 \end{pmatrix}$, $\boldsymbol{b} = \begin{pmatrix} 7 \\ 4 \end{pmatrix}$.

For the given FS $(1,1,1,0)$

$$\boldsymbol{\alpha}_1 + \boldsymbol{\alpha}_2 + \boldsymbol{\alpha}_3 = \boldsymbol{b}.$$

The solution being non-basic, the vectors $\boldsymbol{\alpha}_1, \boldsymbol{\alpha}_2, \boldsymbol{\alpha}_3$ are linearly dependent, and we assume

$$\mu_1\boldsymbol{\alpha}_1 + \mu_2\boldsymbol{\alpha}_2 + \mu_3\boldsymbol{\alpha}_3 = \boldsymbol{0}.$$

where at least one of μ_1, μ_2, μ_3 is not zero.

Now

$$\mu_1\begin{pmatrix}1\\2\end{pmatrix}+\mu_2\begin{pmatrix}2\\-1\end{pmatrix}+\mu_3\begin{pmatrix}4\\3\end{pmatrix}=\begin{pmatrix}0\\0\end{pmatrix}$$

$$\text{or, } \mu_1 + 2\mu_2 + 4\mu_3 = 0$$

$$2\mu_1 + (-1)\mu_2 + 3\mu_3 = 0$$

$$\text{or, } \frac{\mu_1}{2} = \frac{\mu_2}{1} = \frac{\mu_3}{-1} = k(\neq 0).$$

Assuming $k = 1, \mu_1 = 2, \mu_2 = 1, \mu_3 = -1$.

$\therefore\ 2\boldsymbol{\alpha}_1 + \boldsymbol{\alpha}_2 - \boldsymbol{\alpha}_3 = \mathbf{0}.$

Now

$$\min_j\left\{\frac{x_j}{\mu_j}\middle|\mu_j>0\right\}=\frac{x_r}{\mu_r}\text{ or, }\frac{x_r}{\mu_r}=\left\{\frac{1}{2},\frac{1}{1}\right\}=\frac{1}{2}=\frac{x_1}{\mu_1}.$$

Hence, $\boldsymbol{\alpha}_1$ is to be eliminated.

Eliminating $\boldsymbol{\alpha}_1$ from $\boldsymbol{\alpha}_1 + \boldsymbol{\alpha}_2 + \boldsymbol{\alpha}_3 = \boldsymbol{b}$ and $2\boldsymbol{\alpha}_1 + \boldsymbol{\alpha}_2 - \boldsymbol{\alpha}_3 = \mathbf{0}$, we get

$$\tfrac{1}{2}\boldsymbol{\alpha}_2 + \tfrac{3}{2}\boldsymbol{\alpha}_3 = \boldsymbol{b}.$$

Thus, a basic feasible solution is $\left(0, \frac{1}{2}, \frac{3}{2}, 0\right)$, since $\boldsymbol{\alpha}_2$ and $\boldsymbol{\alpha}_3$ are linearly independent.

Again, the other criterion is for $\mu_j < 0$. Here, $\mu_3 < 0$. Hence, $\boldsymbol{\alpha}_3$ is to be removed, and

$$\boldsymbol{\alpha}_1 + \boldsymbol{\alpha}_2 + \boldsymbol{\alpha}_3 = \boldsymbol{b}$$

$$\text{and } 2\boldsymbol{\alpha}_1 + \boldsymbol{\alpha}_2 - \boldsymbol{\alpha}_3 = \mathbf{0}$$

gives $3\boldsymbol{\alpha}_1 + 2\boldsymbol{\alpha}_2 = \boldsymbol{b}$ showing that $(3, 2, 0, 0)$ is another BFS.

Remark. As we know the maximum number of BFS of the system will be ${}^4C_2 = 6$, we shall be able to get them by different selections of the removing vectors.

2.5 SOME NECESSARY DEFINITIONS AND NOTATIONS

We are now in a position to develop some iterâtive processes for solving LP model. One such process is *simplex method.* Before explaining this method we shall introduce a few definitions and notations to be used in our further discussions in connection with the iterative processes.

After introducing the slack and the surplus variables, let the LP model in its standard form as

$$\text{Maximise } Z = \boldsymbol{c}\boldsymbol{x}$$

$$\text{subject to } A\boldsymbol{x} = \boldsymbol{b} \qquad (2.5a)$$

$$\boldsymbol{x} \geq \mathbf{0}$$

where $\boldsymbol{x} = \left[\boldsymbol{x}_{\text{decision}}, \boldsymbol{x}_{\text{slack}}, \boldsymbol{x}_{\text{surplus}}\right] = \boldsymbol{x}_{\text{Legitimate}} \geq 0.$

Let B be an $m \times m$ non-singular sub-matrix consisting of m linearly independent columns of $A = \left(a_{ij}\right)_{m\times n}$. B is called the *basis matrix.*

The *basic variables* corresponding to the basis matrix B be denoted by

$$\boldsymbol{x}_B = \left(x_{B_1}, x_{B_2}, \ldots, x_{B_m}\right).$$

The system of equations $Ax = \boldsymbol{b}$ reduces to

$$B\boldsymbol{x_B} = \boldsymbol{b}$$
$$\text{or, } \boldsymbol{x_B} = B^{-1}\boldsymbol{b} = \frac{\text{Adj } B}{|B|}\boldsymbol{b},$$

since B is a non-singular square matrix.

The variables which are not associated with $\boldsymbol{x_B}$ are called *non-basic variables.*

2.5.1 Associated Cost Vector

Let $\boldsymbol{x_B}$ be a basic feasible solution of LP model (2.5a). Then the vector $\boldsymbol{c_B} = (c_{B_1}, c_{B_2}, \ldots, c_{B_m})$, where c_{B_i}, $i = 1, 2, \ldots, m$, are components of c associated with the basic variables is called *cost vector* associated with the basic feasible solution $\boldsymbol{x_B}$.

The value of the objective function for the basic feasible solution $\boldsymbol{x_B}$ and corresponding associated cost vector $\boldsymbol{c_B}$ is given by $Z = \boldsymbol{c_B x_B}$.

2.5.2 Optimal Basic Feasible Solution

A basic feasible solution $\boldsymbol{x_B^*}$ is called an *optimal basic feasible* solution of (2.5a), if

$$Z^* = \boldsymbol{c_B^* x_B^*} \geq Z = \boldsymbol{c_B x_B},$$

where $Z = \boldsymbol{c_B x_B}$ is the value of the objective function for any other basic feasible solution of the problem.

2.5.3 Net Evaluation

Let $A = (a_{ij})_{m\times n} = (\boldsymbol{a_1}, \boldsymbol{a_2}, \ldots, \boldsymbol{a_j}, \ldots, \boldsymbol{a_n})$
and $B = (\boldsymbol{\beta_1}, \boldsymbol{\beta_2}, \ldots, \boldsymbol{\beta_m})$.

Any column $\boldsymbol{a_j}$ of A may be expressed as a linear combination of $\boldsymbol{\beta_1}, \boldsymbol{\beta_2}, \ldots, \boldsymbol{\beta_m}$

$$\boldsymbol{a_j} = \sum_{i=1}^{m} y_{ij}\boldsymbol{\beta_i} = B\boldsymbol{y_j},$$

where

$$\boldsymbol{y_j} = (y_{1j}, y_{2j}, \ldots, y_{mj}) = B^{-1}\boldsymbol{a_j}. \tag{2.5b}$$

Now we introduce a new quantity z_j defined by

$$z_j = \boldsymbol{c_B y_j} = y_{1j}c_{B_1} + y_{2j}c_{B_2} + \cdots + y_{mj}c_{B_m} = \sum_{i=1}^{m} y_{ij}c_{B_i}.$$

Then

$$z_j - c_j = \sum_{i=1}^{m} y_{ij}c_{B_i} - c_j$$

is called the *Net-evaluation.*

2.5.4 Replacement of a Basis Vector

Suppose, an LPP have basic feasible solution, if we drop one of the basis vector and introduce a non-basis vector in the basis set, then the new solution is also a basic feasible solution.

Let $\boldsymbol{x_B}$ be a BFS of (2.5a), then

$$B\boldsymbol{x_B} = \boldsymbol{b}, \quad \boldsymbol{x_B} \geq 0. \tag{2.5c}$$

$$\boldsymbol{\alpha}_j = y_{1j}\boldsymbol{\beta}_1 + y_{2j}\boldsymbol{\beta}_2 + \cdots + y_{mj}\boldsymbol{\beta}_m = B\boldsymbol{y}_j.$$

For $y_{rj} \neq 0$ we can write,

$$\boldsymbol{\beta}_r = \frac{\boldsymbol{\alpha}_j}{y_{rj}} - \sum_{i=1}^{m} \frac{y_{ij}}{y_{rj}} \boldsymbol{\beta}_i.$$

From (2.5c),

$$\boldsymbol{b} = \sum_{i=1}^{m} x_{B_i}\boldsymbol{\beta}_i + x_{B_r}\left[\frac{\boldsymbol{\alpha}_j}{y_{rj}} - \sum_{i=1}^{m}\frac{y_{ij}}{y_{rj}}\boldsymbol{\beta}_i\right] = \sum_{i=1}^{m}\left[x_{B_i} - x_{B_r}\frac{y_{ij}}{y_{rj}}\right]\boldsymbol{\beta}_i + x_{B_r}\frac{\boldsymbol{\alpha}_j}{y_{rj}}.$$

Obviously,

$$\hat{x}_{B_i} = x_{B_i} - x_{B_r}\frac{y_{ij}}{y_{rj}} \ \forall\ i = 1,2,\ldots,m \text{ and } i \neq r$$

$$\text{and } \hat{x}_{B_r} = \frac{x_{B_r}}{y_{rj}}. \tag{2.5d}$$

Case 1. If $x_{B_r} = 0$, the new set of basic variables are non-negative, since the existence of basic feasible solution $\boldsymbol{x_B}$.

Case 2. If $x_{B_r} \neq 0$, then we must have $y_{rj} > 0$.

Therefore,

$$\frac{x_{B_i}}{y_{ij}} \geq \frac{x_{B_r}}{y_{rj}} : y_{ij} > 0 \text{ and } i \neq r$$

$$\leq \frac{x_{B_r}}{y_{rj}} : y_{ij} < 0 \text{ and } i \neq r.$$

Select

$$\frac{x_{B_r}}{y_{rj}} = \min_i \left\{ \frac{x_{B_i}}{y_{ij}} \middle| y_{ij} > 0,\ i \neq r \right\} \tag{2.5e}$$

then new set of basic variable is non-negative and hence $\hat{\boldsymbol{x}}_{\boldsymbol{B}}$ is feasible.

2.5.5 Improvement of a Basic Feasible Solution

Let $\boldsymbol{x_B}$ be a basic feasible solution to LP model (2.5a) and $\hat{\boldsymbol{x}}_{\boldsymbol{B}}$ be another basic solution obtained by admitting a non-basic column vector $\boldsymbol{\alpha}_j$ in the basis, for which the net evaluation $z_j - c_j < 0$. Then $\hat{\boldsymbol{x}}_{\boldsymbol{B}}$ is an improved basic feasible solution to the problem.

To proof the above statement let $\hat{\boldsymbol{\alpha}}_j$ be the column vector introduced in the basis, such that $z_j - c_j < 0$. Let $\boldsymbol{\beta}_r$ be the vector removed from basis and $\hat{\boldsymbol{x}}_{\boldsymbol{B}}$, the new basic feasible solution. From (2.5d),

$$\hat{x}_{B_i} = x_{B_i} - x_{Br}\frac{y_{ij}}{y_{rj}} : i = 1,2,\ldots,m,\ i \neq r \tag{2.5f}$$

$$\hat{x}_{Br} = \frac{x_{Br}}{y_{rj}}$$

$$\begin{aligned}\hat{z} &= \sum_{i=1}^{m} \hat{c}_{B_i}\hat{x}_{B_i} = \sum_{i=1}^{m} c_{B_i}\left(x_{B_i} - x_{Br}\frac{y_{ij}}{y_{rj}}\right) + \hat{c}_{Br}\frac{x_{Br}}{y_{rj}} \\ &= \sum_{i=1}^{m} c_{B_i}\left(x_{B_i} - x_{Br}\frac{y_{ij}}{y_{rj}}\right) + c_j\frac{x_{Br}}{y_{rj}} \quad [\because \hat{c}_{Br} = c_j] \\ &= z^* - \left(z_j - c_j\right)\frac{x_{Br}}{y_{rj}} \qquad (2.5g) \\ &> z^*, \text{ since } \frac{x_{Br}}{y_{rj}} > 0.\end{aligned}$$

Hence, new basic feasible solution $\hat{\boldsymbol{x}}_{\boldsymbol{B}}$ give an improved value of the objective function.

Remarks.

1. If $z_j - c_j = 0$ for at least one j for which $y_{ij} > 0$, then another basic feasible solution is found to give an unchanged value of the objective function.
2. If the feasible solution happens to be a degenerate, then an increase in the value of z^* depends on x_{Br}/y_{rj}. In any case, $z_j - c_j < 0$ implies $\hat{z}$ can never be less than z^*.

2.5.6 Important Observations

From (2.5d),

$$\hat{z} > z^*, \text{ if } z_j - c_j < 0 \text{ for } \frac{x_{Br}}{y_{rj}} \geq 0.$$

Hence, if the problem be that of maximising, then we shall select that $\boldsymbol{a}_j$ for $\boldsymbol{\beta}_r$ which will make $\frac{x_{Br}}{y_{rj}}(z_j - c_j)$ minimum most negative or in fact will make $(z_j - c_j)$ minimum most negative in order to minimise the computation involved.

We shall determine the vector $\boldsymbol{a}_k$ to enters the basis according to rule

$$z_k - c_k = \min_j \{z_j - c_j \mid z_j - c_j < 0\}.$$

The vector which is deleted from basis is called *departing* or *leaving* vector and is determined by using the criterion

$$\frac{x_{Br}}{y_{rj}} = \min_i \left\{ \frac{x_{B_i}}{y_{ij}} \,\middle|\, y_{ij} > 0 \right\}.$$

2.6 SOME USEFUL THEOREMS

Theorem 1 (Unbounded solution). *Let there exist a basic feasible solution to a given* LPP. *If for at least one j, $y_{ij} \leq 0$ $(i = 1, 2, \ldots, m)$ and $z_j - c_j < 0$, then there does not exists any optimum solution to this problem.*

Proof. Consider the problem (2.5a) and a basic feasible solution $\boldsymbol{x_B}$ so that

$$B\boldsymbol{x}_B = b, \quad \boldsymbol{x_B} \geq \boldsymbol{0} \quad \text{and} \quad z^* = \boldsymbol{c_B x_B} = \sum_{i=1}^{m} c_{B_i} x_{B_i}$$

Now

$$\boldsymbol{b} = B\boldsymbol{x_B} + v\boldsymbol{a}_j - v\boldsymbol{a}_j, \text{ where } \boldsymbol{a}_j \in A \text{ and } v \text{ is a scalar}$$

$$= \sum_{i=1}^{m} x_{B_i}\boldsymbol{\beta}_i + v\boldsymbol{a}_j - v\sum_{i=1}^{m} y_{ij}\boldsymbol{\beta}_i = \sum_{i=1}^{m} (x_{B_i} - v y_{ij})\boldsymbol{\beta}_i + v\boldsymbol{a}_j. \tag{2.6a}$$

If $v > 0$, then $(x_{B_i} - v y_{ij}) \geq 0$ provided $y_{ij} \leq 0$ which shows that there exists a feasible solution whose components may be positive. But in general, it may not be a basic solution.

Again,

$$\hat{z} = \sum_{i=1}^{m} c_{B_i}(x_{B_i} - v y_{ij}) + v c_j = \sum_{i=1}^{m} c_{B_i} x_{B_i} - v(z_j - c_j) \quad \left[\because \sum_{i=1}^{m} c_{B_i} y_{ij} = z_j\right]$$

$$= z^* - v(z_j - c_j). \tag{2.6b}$$

Note that $v > 0$, $z_j - c_j < 0$ imply $z \to -\infty$ as $v \to +\infty$ as hence there is no limit to the optimum value of the objective function and thus there exists an unbounded solution to the problem.

Remarks.

1. If $y_{ij} < 0$ for at least one j for which $z_j - c_j = 0$, then $\hat{z} = z^*$.
2. If $y_{ij} < 0$ for at least one j for which $z_j - c_j > 0$, then there exists a feasible solution to the problem.

Theorem 2 (Optimality conditions). *A necessary and sufficient condition for a basic feasible solution to an LPP to be an optimum (maximum/minimum) is that* $z_j - c_j \geq 0$ (≤ 0) *for all j for which* $\boldsymbol{a}_j \notin B$.

Proof. Let us prove theorem for maximisation LPP (for minimisation problem the proof is exactly similar).
Step 1 (Necessary condition). It follows immediately from discussion (2.5.5) and theorem 1 above that the condition is absolutely necessary.
Step 2 (Sufficient condition). Assume the existence of basic feasible solution x_B and corresponding cost vector $\boldsymbol{c}_B$.

Then $B\boldsymbol{x}_B = \boldsymbol{b}$, $\boldsymbol{x}_B \geq \boldsymbol{0}$ and $z^* = \boldsymbol{c}_B\boldsymbol{x}_B$.
For all j for which $\boldsymbol{a}_j \notin \boldsymbol{B}$ we are given $z_j - c_j \geq 0$.
Let $\boldsymbol{a}_j = \beta_j$ for all such j for which $\boldsymbol{a}_j \in B$.
Then $\boldsymbol{y}_j = \boldsymbol{B}^{-1}\boldsymbol{\beta}_j = \boldsymbol{e}_j$ (the unit vector) and $z_j - c_j = \boldsymbol{c}_B\boldsymbol{y}_j - c_j = \boldsymbol{c}_B\,\boldsymbol{e}_j - c_j = 0$.
Thus, $z_j - c_j \geq 0\ \forall\ j$, where $\boldsymbol{a}_j \in A$.
Now, let $\boldsymbol{x}$ be a feasible solution. Then

$$\sum_{j=1}^{n}\left(z_j - c_j\right)x_j \geq 0 \text{ or, } \sum_{j=1}^{n} z_j x_j \geq \sum_{j=1}^{n} c_j x_j \text{ or, } \sum_{j=1}^{n} \boldsymbol{c}_B\boldsymbol{y}_j x_j \geq \sum_{j=1}^{n} c_j x_j \quad \left[\because\ z_j = \boldsymbol{c}_B\boldsymbol{y}_j\right]$$

$$\text{or, } \sum_{i=1}^{m} c_{B_i}\sum_{j=1}^{n} y_{ij}x_j \geq \sum_{j=1}^{n} c_j x_j \text{or, } \sum_{i=1}^{m} c_{B_i}x_{B_i} \geq \sum_{j=1}^{n} c_j x_j \quad \left[\because\ x_{B_i} = \textstyle\sum_{j=1}^{n} y_{ij}x_j, i = 1, 2, \ldots, m\right]$$

$$\text{or, } \boldsymbol{c}_B\boldsymbol{x}_B \geq \boldsymbol{c}\boldsymbol{x} \text{ or, } z^* \geq z,$$

where z is the value of the objective function for the feasible solution $\boldsymbol{x}$. Hence, z^* is an optimum for that basic feasible solutions for which $z_j - c_j > 0$ for all j such that $\boldsymbol{a}_j \notin B$.

Theorem 3. *Any convex combination of p different optimum solutions to an* LP *model is again an optimum solution to the model.*

Proof. Let $\boldsymbol{x}_1, \boldsymbol{x}_2, \ldots, \boldsymbol{x}_p$ be p different optimum solution to the LP model (2.5a) and Z^* be the optimum value of objective function Z.

Obviously, $A\boldsymbol{x}_1 = A\boldsymbol{x}_2 = \cdots = A\boldsymbol{x}_p = \boldsymbol{b}$

$\boldsymbol{c}\boldsymbol{x}_1 = \boldsymbol{c}\boldsymbol{x}_2 = \cdots = \boldsymbol{c}\boldsymbol{x}_p = Z^*$

$\boldsymbol{x}_1, \boldsymbol{x}_2, \ldots, \boldsymbol{x}_p \geq \boldsymbol{0}$

Let

$$\hat{\boldsymbol{x}} = \sum_{i=1}^{p} \lambda_i \boldsymbol{x}_i, \quad \lambda_i \geq 0\ \forall\ i, \quad \sum_{i=1}^{p} \lambda_i = 1$$

be a convex combination of $\boldsymbol{x}_1, \boldsymbol{x}_2, \ldots, \boldsymbol{x}_p$. Then

$$A\hat{\boldsymbol{x}} = A\left(\sum_{i=1}^{p} \lambda_i \boldsymbol{x}_i\right) = \sum_{i=1}^{p} \lambda_i A\boldsymbol{x}_i = \sum_{i=1}^{p} \lambda_i \boldsymbol{b} = \boldsymbol{b}\sum_{i=1}^{p} \lambda_i = \boldsymbol{b}.$$

Further, since $\boldsymbol{x}_i \geq \mathbf{0}$, $\lambda_i \geq 0\ \forall\ i = 1,2,\ldots,p$, therefore, every component of $\hat{\boldsymbol{x}}$ be non-negative. Thus, $\hat{\boldsymbol{x}}$ is a feasible solution to the LP model.

Again,

$$\boldsymbol{c}\hat{\boldsymbol{x}} = \boldsymbol{c}\left(\sum_{i=1}^{p} \lambda_i \boldsymbol{x}_i\right) = \sum_{i=1}^{p} \lambda_i \boldsymbol{c}\boldsymbol{x}_i = \sum_{i=1}^{p} \lambda_i Z^* = Z^* \sum_{i=1}^{p} \lambda_i = Z^*.$$

Hence, a *convex combination* of p different optimum solutions to an LP model is also an optimum solution of the model.

2.7 ALTERNATIVE OPTIMA OF AN LP MODEL

If in an LPP the optimum solution which will optimise the objective function be not unique, then we say that there are *alternative optima*. The alternative optima, if exist, may be basic or non-basic. We discuss the cases below:

Case 1. Let $z_j - c_j = 0$ for some non-basis vector $\boldsymbol{a}_j$ and $y_{ij} > 0$ for at least one $i = r$ (say). Then the vector $\boldsymbol{\beta}_r$ in B is replaced by $\boldsymbol{a}_j$ and we immediately get a new BFS. If Z_{new} be the value of the objective function with this new BFS and Z_B, the corresponding value for old BFS $\boldsymbol{x}_B$, then we already know from (2.5g)

$$Z_{\text{new}} = Z_B - \frac{x_{Br}}{y_{rj}}\left(z_j - c_j\right) = Z_B \quad \left[\because\ z_j - c_j = 0 \text{ for non-basis vector}\right]$$

Thus, *if there be an optimum* BFS *to an* LPP *and if $z_j - c_j = 0$ for some non-basis vector and $y_{ij} > 0$ for at least one i, then there exists an alternative optimal solution.*

Case 2. Assume the existence of an optimal BFS $\boldsymbol{x}_B$ and for $\boldsymbol{a}_j$ not in the basis $z_j - c_j = 0$ and $y_{ij} \leq 0$, $i = 1,2,\ldots,m$.

From (2.6a) and (2.6b),

$$\sum_{i=1}^{m}\left(x_{B_i} - \nu y_{ij}\right)\boldsymbol{\beta}_i + \nu \boldsymbol{a}_j = \boldsymbol{b} : \nu > 0,\ y_{ij} \leq 0,\ i = 1,2,\ldots,m$$

which can have $(m+1)$ non-zero positive variables.

$$Z_{\text{new}} = Z_B - \nu\left(z_j - c_j\right) = Z_B \quad \left[\because\ z_j - c_j = 0\right]$$

Thus, *if there be an optimum* BFS *to an* LPP *and if $z_j - c_j = 0$ for some non-basic vector and $y_{ij} \leq 0$ for all $i = 1,2,\ldots,m$, then there will exist an alternative non-basic optimal solution.*

Case 3.

(i) If $\boldsymbol{x}_B$ be a non-degenerate BFS and $z_j - c_j > 0$ for all non-basic vectors, then there will be *non-alternative optima* because in this situation the value of the objective function will decrease.

(ii) But if $\boldsymbol{x}_B$ be a degenerate BFS giving the optimum value z_B and $z_j - c_j > 0$ for non-basic $\boldsymbol{a}_j$ and if $x_{Br} = 0$ while $y_{rj} > 0$, then we have to delete $\boldsymbol{\beta}_r$ from the basis matrix because $\frac{x_{Br}}{y_{rj}} = 0$ (a minimum). From (2.5g),

$$Z_{\text{new}} = Z_B - \frac{x_{Br}}{y_{rj}}\left(z_j - c_j\right) = Z_B \quad \left[\because\ \frac{x_{Br}}{y_{rj}} = 0\right]$$

under these circumstances, we get an alternative optima which is basic.

2.8 SIMPLEX ALGORITHM

The followings are the computational procedure to be followed for the solution of maximisation LP model by simplex method.

Step 1. If any of the components of availability vector $\boldsymbol{b}=(b_1,b_2,\ldots,b_m)^T$ be negative, multiply the corresponding constraint by (-1) and adjust the direction of inequality accordingly. (For example, $2x_1+3x_2+5x_3 \geq -3$ should be written as $-2x_1-3x_2-5x_3 \leq 3$).

Step 2. Add slack and surplus variables to the constraints according to their requirement and put the problem in its standard form.

Step 3. Construct the simplex table by choosing the initial BFS $\boldsymbol{x_B}=\boldsymbol{B}^{-1}\boldsymbol{b}$ in the following form:

		c_j	c_1	c_2	$\cdots$	c_j	$\cdots$	c_n
c_{B1}	y_1	x_{B1}	y_{11}	y_{12}	$\cdots$	y_{1j}	$\cdots$	y_{1n}
c_{B2}	y_2	x_{B2}	y_{21}	y_{22}	$\cdots$	y_{2j}	$\cdots$	y_{2n}
$\vdots$	$\vdots$	$\vdots$	$\vdots$	$\vdots$	$\cdots$	$\vdots$	$\cdots$	$\vdots$
c_{Br}	y_r	x_{Br}	y_{r1}	y_{r2}	$\cdots$	y_{rj}	$\cdots$	y_{rn}
$\vdots$	$\vdots$	$\vdots$	$\vdots$	$\vdots$	$\cdots$	$\vdots$	$\cdots$	$\vdots$
c_{Bm}	y_m	x_{Bm}	y_{m1}	y_{m2}	$\cdots$	y_{mj}	$\cdots$	y_{mn}
		z_j-c_j	z_1-c_1	z_2-c_2	$\cdots$	z_j-c_j	$\cdots$	z_n-c_n

Step 4. Calculate net evaluation

$$z_j-c_j=\boldsymbol{c_B}\boldsymbol{y_j}-c_j=\sum_{i=1}^{m}c_{B_i}y_{ij}-c_j$$

and test the following.

(i) if $z_j-c_j \geq 0 \; \forall \; j=1,2,\ldots,n$, then the solution $\boldsymbol{x_B}$ is optimum and the process stops here.

(ii) if $z_j-c_j<0$ for at least one j, then we move on to the next step.

Step 5. Choose the most negative z_j-c_j if more than one are negative. Suppose, for some $j=k$ (particular) z_k-c_k is most negative, then the vector $\boldsymbol{y_k}$ will be the *entering* (↑) *vector* in the new basis.

Now to find the departing vector which departs from current basis we compute

$$\min_i\left\{\frac{x_{B_i}}{y_{ik}}\middle| y_{ik}>0\right\}$$

called *minimum ratio* (MR).

Let minimum occurs for some $i=r$ (particular), then $\boldsymbol{y}_r$(→) have to be removed from the basis. The leading common element which lies in the rth row and kth column y_{rk} is called *key element* (or sometimes called *pivot element*).

Step 6. Construct the new simplex table where we drop $\boldsymbol{y}_r$ from the basis and introduce $\boldsymbol{y_k}$ in place of it. Divide the key-row by key-element. The other rows of the new tableau are then computed by transformation rule given by

$$\hat{y}_{ir}=y_{ij}-\frac{y_{ik}\times y_{rj}}{y_{rk}} \quad : \quad i\neq r$$

$$=\frac{y_{rj}}{y_{rk}} \quad : \quad i=r. \tag{2.8a}$$

Step 7. GO BACK to *Step 4* as long as $z_j - c_j \geq 0$ for all $j = 1, 2, \ldots, n$, where the *algorithm* terminates and give us the desired optimal solution of LP model.

Flow chart:

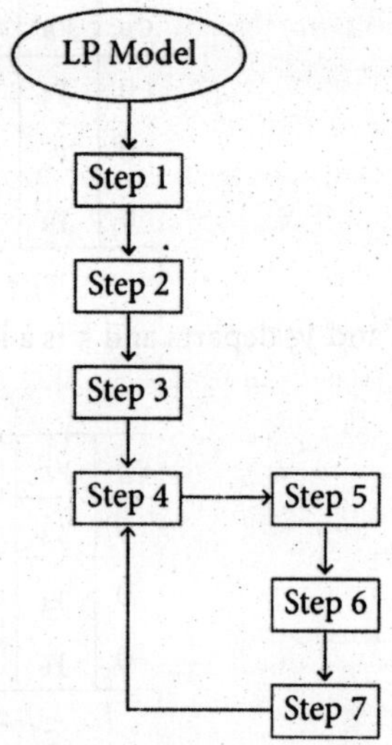

Remark. For minimisation LP model either convert the model into maximisation form or *Step 4*, *Step 7* maintain the reverse inequality, and conditions are changed accordingly.

Example 2.8.1. *Solve the following problem by simplex method.*

$$\begin{aligned} &\textit{Maximise } Z = 3x_1 + 2x_2 + x_3 \\ &\textit{subject to} \quad 3x_1 + 4x_2 + 3x_3 \leq 42 \\ &\qquad\qquad\quad 5x_1 \qquad\quad + 3x_3 \leq 45 \\ &\qquad\qquad\quad 3x_1 + 6x_2 + 2x_3 \leq 41 \\ &\qquad\qquad\qquad\qquad x_1, x_2, x_3 \leq 0. \end{aligned}$$

[CU 1982]

Solution: *Standard maximisation form:*

$$\text{Maximise } Z = 3x_1 + 2x_2 + x_3 + 0x_4 + 0x_5 + 0x_6$$

$$\begin{aligned} \text{subject to} \quad 3x_1 + 4x_2 + 3x_3 + x_4 \qquad\qquad &= 42 \\ 5x_1 \qquad\quad + 3x_3 \qquad + x_5 \qquad &= 45 \\ 3x_1 + 6x_2 + 2x_3 \qquad\qquad + x_6 &= 41 \\ x_1, x_2, x_3 &\leq 0 \\ x_4, x_5, x_6 &\leq 0, \text{ slack variables.} \end{aligned}$$

Since $\begin{pmatrix} 1 \\ 0 \\ 0 \end{pmatrix}, \begin{pmatrix} 0 \\ 1 \\ 0 \end{pmatrix}$ and $\begin{pmatrix} 0 \\ 0 \\ 1 \end{pmatrix}$ are linearly independent columns of A and as we know that unit vector always form a standard basis. Therefore, we take $B = \begin{pmatrix} 1 & 0 & 0 \\ 0 & 1 & 0 \\ 0 & 0 & 1 \end{pmatrix}$ as the initial basis sub-matrix of A and initial básic variable $x_B = (x_4 \quad x_5 \quad x_6)^T$ with initial basic feasible solution as

$$\boldsymbol{B x_B = b} \text{ or, } \boldsymbol{x_B = B^{-1} b} = \begin{pmatrix} 1 & 0 & 0 \\ 0 & 1 & 0 \\ 0 & 0 & 1 \end{pmatrix} \begin{pmatrix} 42 \\ 45 \\ 41 \end{pmatrix} = \begin{pmatrix} 42 \\ 45 \\ 41 \end{pmatrix}.$$

To check whether the initial basic feasible solution is an optimum solution we start the simplex iteration as follows:

(T 1)

		c_j	3	2	1	0	0	0	
c_B	y_B	x_B	y_1	y_2	y_3	y_4	y_5	y_6	MR
0	y_4	42	3	4	3	1	0	0	$\frac{42}{3}$
0	y_5	45	⑤	0	3	0	1	0	$\frac{45}{5}$ →
0	y_6	41	3	6	2	0	0	1	$\frac{41}{3}$
		$z_j - c_j$	$-3\uparrow$	-2	-1	0	0	0	

y_1 enters and y_5 departs and 5 is a key element.

(T 2)

		c_j	3	2	1	0	0	0	
c_B	y_B	x_B	y_1	y_2	y_3	y_4	y_5	y_6	MR
0	y_4	15	0	4	$\frac{6}{5}$	1	$-\frac{3}{5}$	0	$\frac{15}{4}$
0	y_1	9	1	0	$\frac{3}{5}$	0	$\frac{1}{5}$	0	X
0	y_6	14	0	⑥	$\frac{1}{5}$	0	$-\frac{3}{5}$	1	$\frac{14}{6}$ →
		$z_j - c_j$	0	$-2\uparrow$	$\frac{4}{5}$	0	$\frac{3}{5}$	0	

y_2 enters and y_6 departs and 6 is the key element.

(T 2) is obtained from (T 1): First we fill up the key row by dividing each element of that row by key element. The remaining elements will then be determined by using the rule stated in (2.8a) [For example, $42 - \frac{45\times3}{5} = 15$, $41 - \frac{45\times3}{5} = 14$, etc.]

(T 3)

		c_j	3	2	1	0	0	0
c_B	y_B	x_B	y_1	y_2	y_3	y_4	y_5	y_6
0	y_4	$\frac{17}{3}$	0	0	$\frac{16}{15}$	1	$-\frac{1}{5}$	$-\frac{2}{3}$
3	y_1	$\frac{3}{2}$	1	0	$\frac{3}{5}$	0	$\frac{1}{5}$	0
2	y_2	$\frac{7}{3}$	0	1	$\frac{1}{30}$	0	$-\frac{1}{10}$	$\frac{1}{6}$
		$z_j - c_j$	0	0	$\frac{13}{15}$	0	$\frac{2}{5}$	$\frac{1}{3}$

(T 3) indicates that the solution is optimal as $z_j - c_j \geq 0$ for all j. The optimal solution is also unique as for all non-basic $z_j - c_j > 0$ and $z_j - c_j = 0$ for all basic vectors. Hence, the required optimal solution is

$$\left\langle x_1^* = \tfrac{3}{2},\quad x_2^* = \tfrac{7}{3},\quad x_3^* = 0,\quad Z_{\max} = \tfrac{55}{6} \right\rangle.$$

Example 2.8.2. *The following incomplete tableau represents the second stage in the solution of an LPP by the simplex method. All the variables corresponding to zero coefficients of the objective function are slack variables. Determine the unknowns a, b, c, d, e (The notations have their usual meanings).*

[CU(H) 1980; All India NET 2010]

		c_j	1	c	d	3	-1	0	0	0
c_B	y_B	x_B	y_1	y_2	y_3	y_4	y_5	y_6	y_7	y_8
0	y_6	9	13	0	1	-1	9	1	0	3
0	y_7	4	-2	0	0	4	1	0	1	1
a	y_2	2	b	1	0	-1	1	0	0	1
		$z_j - c_j$	15	0	2	e	5	0	0	4

Solution: We have $(0\times 3+0\times 1+a\times 1)-0=4$ or, $a=\ 4$

$(0\times 13+0\times -2+4\times b)-1=15$ or, $b=\ 4$

$(0\times 0+0\times 0+4\times 1)-c=0$ or, $c=\ 4$

$(0\times 1+0\times 0+4\times 0)-d=2$ or, $d=-2$

$(0\times -1+0\times 4+4\times -1)-3=e$ or, $e=-7$.

Example 2.8.3. *Show by solving the following LPP by simplex method that the problem has an unbounded solution.*

$$\begin{aligned}
&\textit{Maximise } Z=107x_1+x_2+2x_3\\
&\textit{subject to } 14x_1+x_2-6x_3+3x_4=7\\
&\quad 16x_1+x_2-6x_3 \le 5\\
&\quad 3x_1-x_2-x_3 \le 0\\
&\quad x_1,x_2,x_3,x_4 \ge 0.
\end{aligned}$$

Solution: *Standard form:*

$$\begin{aligned}
&\text{Minimise } Z=107x_1+x_2+2x_3+0x_4+0x_5+0x_6\\
&\text{subject to } \tfrac{14}{3}x_1+\tfrac{1}{3}x_2-2x_3+x_4 = \tfrac{7}{3}\\
&\quad 16x_1+x_2-6x_3+x_5=5\\
&\quad 3x_1-x_2-x_3+x_6=0\\
&\quad x_1,x_2,x_3,x_4 \ge 0\\
&\quad x_5,x_6 \ge 0, \text{ slack variables.}
\end{aligned}$$

Note that in writing the standard form we reduce the number of slack variables. We cannot add any variable in the first constraint as this constraint gives the column $\begin{pmatrix}1\\0\\0\end{pmatrix}$ of the initial basis by dividing throughout the coefficient of x_4 of that constraint. One should be careful about this before starting simplex iteration.

(T 1)

c_B	y_B	x_B (c_j)	107	1	2	0	0	0	
			y_1	y_2	y_3	y_4	y_5	y_6	MR
0	y_4	$\frac{7}{3}$	$\frac{14}{3}$	$\frac{1}{3}$	-2	1	0	0	$\frac{1}{2}$
0	y_5	5	16	1	-6	0	1	0	$\frac{5}{16}$
0	y_6	0	(3)	-1	-1	0	0	1	0 →
		z_j-c_j	-107↑	-1	-2	0	0	0	

Introduce y_1 and drop y_6. 3 is the key element.

(T 2)

c_B	y_B	x_B (c_j)	107	1	2	0	0	0
			y_1	y_2	y_3	y_4	y_5	y_6
0	y_4	$\frac{7}{3}$	0	$\frac{17}{9}$	$-\frac{4}{9}$	1	0	$-\frac{14}{9}$
0	y_5	5	0	$\frac{19}{3}$	$-\frac{2}{3}$	0	1	$-\frac{16}{3}$
0	y_1	0	1	$-\frac{1}{3}$	$-\frac{1}{3}$	0	1	$\frac{1}{3}$
		z_j-c_j	0	$-\frac{110}{3}$	$-\frac{113}{3}$	0	0	$\frac{107}{3}$

(T 2) shows that $z_3 - c_3 = -\frac{113}{3}$ being the most negative one. The column vector y_3 will not enters the basis since y_{i3} are non-positive. This is a clear indication that the problem has an unbounded solution (following from Theorem 1).

2.9 ARTIFICIAL VARIABLES AND CHARNES' BIG-M (OR PENALTY) METHOD

We know that to start with a simplex iteration we need the initial basic feasible solution. If all the constraints of the problem involve $\leq$ type inequalities, then we are to introduce *slack variable* to each of these inequalities to convert them into equations. The coefficient of these slack variables will provide the initial basis matrix. But if the constraints involve $\leq, =$ and $\geq$ types, no such identity matrix is obtained.

For example: Constraints:

$$\begin{aligned} 5x_1 + 2x_2 &\leq 5 \\ 2x_1 - x_2 &\geq 1 \\ 6x_1 + 2x_2 &\leq 9 \end{aligned}$$

Equation form:

$$\begin{aligned} 5x_1 + 2x_2 + x_3 \quad &= 5 \\ 2x_1 - x_2 \quad - x_4 &= 1 \\ 6x_1 + 2x_2 \quad &= 9 \end{aligned} \tag{2.9a}$$

Coefficient matrix: $A = \begin{pmatrix} 5 & 2 & 1 & 0 \\ 2 & -1 & 0 & -1 \\ 6 & 2 & 0 & 0 \end{pmatrix}$.

To get rid of these difficulties for finding the initial BFS to start simplex iteration, we take the help of some other variables which are known as *artificial variables.* Introducing these artificial variables, one with each of the constraints with $\geq$ and $=$ type (if necessary), we get equation in their simple forms and at the same time, we get initial BFS to start simplex iteration.

The vector of the coefficient matrix associated with artificial variables are called *artificial vectors.* These artificial vectors themselves or along with vectors associated with the slack variable or sometimes with decision variables will provide an identity matrix.

From (2.9a), *Standard form of constraints:*

$$\begin{aligned} 5x_1 + 2x_2 + x_3 \qquad\qquad &= 5 \\ 2x_1 - x_2 \quad - x_4 + x_{a_1} \quad &= 5 \\ 6x_1 + 2x_2 \qquad\qquad + x_{a_2} &= 9 \\ x_3 &\geq 0, \text{ slack variable} \\ x_{a_1}, x_{a_2} &\geq 0, \text{ artificial variables.} \end{aligned}$$

Coefficient matrix: $A = \left(\begin{matrix} 5 \\ 2 \\ 6 \end{matrix} \quad \begin{matrix} 2 \\ -1 \\ 2 \end{matrix} \quad \begin{bmatrix} 1 \\ 0 \\ 0 \end{bmatrix} \quad \begin{matrix} 0 \\ -1 \\ 0 \end{matrix} \quad \begin{bmatrix} 0 \\ 1 \\ 0 \end{bmatrix} \quad \begin{bmatrix} 0 \\ 0 \\ 1 \end{bmatrix} \right)$.

Note that the introduction of artificial variables is just a useful tactics to get an initial BFS but in practice the artificial variables has no real physical significance and as such our ultimate aim will be to remove these artificial variables from the solution at the earliest.

The removal of artificial variables from the basis is carried out by usual simplex method. A large negative price $(-M)$ is assigned to each of the artificial variable in a maximisation LP model and positive price (M) in a minimisation model where M is a very large number, no matter however large.

This idea of assigning a large price for artificial variable was introduced by A. Charnes and hence it is known as *Charnes' Big-M (or Penalty) method.*

Example 2.9.1. *Solve by Charnes' Big-M method the following* LPP:

Maximise $Z = x_1 + 2x_2 + 3x_3 - x_4$

$$\begin{aligned} \textit{subject to} \quad x_1 + 2x_2 + 3x_3 &= 15 \\ 2x_1 + x_2 + 5x_3 &= 20 \\ x_1 + 2x_2 + x_3 + x_4 &= 10 \\ x_1, x_2, x_3, x_4 &\geq 0. \end{aligned}$$

[CU(H) 1984; JU 1979; BESU(Engg) 2006]

Solution: *Standard form:*

Maximise $Z = x_1 + 2x_2 + 3x_3 - x_4 - Mx_{a_1} - Mx_{a_2}$

$$\begin{aligned} \text{subject to} \quad x_1 + 2x_2 + 3x_3 \quad + x_{a_1} \phantom{+x_{a_2}} &= 15 \\ 2x_1 + x_2 + 5x_3 \quad + x_{a_2} &= 20 \\ x_1 + 2x_2 + x_3 + x_4 &= 10 \\ x_1, x_2, x_3, x_4 &\geq 0 \\ x_{a_1}, x_{a_2} &\geq 0, \text{ artificial variables.} \end{aligned}$$

Note that the decision variable $x_4 \geq 0$ will provide a column $\begin{pmatrix} 0 \\ 0 \\ 1 \end{pmatrix}$ of initial basis matrix and that will reduce the addition of number of artificial variable. (The reader should be careful about this important observation before starting simplex iteration).

(T 1)

		c_j	1	2	3	-1	$-M$	$-M$	
c_B	y_B	x_B	y_1	y_2	y_3	y_4	y_{a_1}	y_{a_2}	MR
$-M$	y_{a_1}	15	1	2	3	0	1	0	$\frac{15}{3}$
$-M$	y_{a_2}	20	2	1	(5)	0	0	1	$\frac{20}{5}$ →
-1	y_4	10	1	2	1	1	0	0	$\frac{10}{1}$
		$z_j - c_j$	$-3M-2$	$-3M-4$	$-8M-4$↑	0	0	0	

Introduce $\mathbf{y_3}$, drop $\mathbf{y_{a_2}}$, 5 is the key element.

Remarks.

1. While examining the largeness of the terms like $(pM+q)$ obtained in the row of $(z_j - c_j)$ only term containing M counts. If pM for two terms be tied, then q term can be used to break the tie.
2. Although the introduction of the artificial variables is a necessity as we mentioned earlier, our first aim will be to eliminate it from the basis at the first iteration or at some subsequent iteration. By simplex method we do so and as soon as the artificial variable is deleted from the basis we forget about it. Hence, in the next tableau we drop the departing artificial variable and omit all the entries corresponding to it.

(T 2)

		c_j	1	2	3	−1	$-M$	
c_B	y_B	x_B	y_1	y_2	y_3	y_4	y_{a_1}	MR
$-M$	y_{a_1}	3	$-\frac{1}{5}$	$\boxed{\frac{7}{5}}$	0	0	1	$\frac{15}{7}$ →
3	y_3	4	$\frac{2}{5}$	$\frac{1}{5}$	1	0	0	20
−1	y_4	6	$\frac{3}{5}$	$\frac{9}{5}$	0	1	0	$\frac{30}{9}$
		$z_j - c_j$	$\frac{M}{5} - \frac{2}{5}$	$-\frac{7}{5}M - \frac{16}{5}\uparrow$	0	0	0	

(T 3)

		c_j	1	2	3	−1	
c_B	y_B	x_B	y_1	y_2	y_3	y_4	MR
2	y_2	$\frac{15}{7}$	$-\frac{1}{7}$	1	0	0	—
3	y_3	$\frac{25}{7}$	$\frac{3}{7}$	0	1	0	$\frac{25}{3}$
−1	y_4	$\frac{15}{7}$	$\boxed{\frac{6}{7}}$	0	0	1	$\frac{15}{6}$ →
		$z_j - c_j$	$-\frac{6}{7}\uparrow$	0	0	0	

Introduce y_1, drop $y_4 \cdot \frac{6}{7}$ is the key element.

(T 4)

		c_j	1	2	3	−1
c_B	y_B	x_B	y_1	y_2	y_3	y_4
2	y_2	$\frac{5}{2}$	0	1	0	$\frac{1}{6}$
3	y_3	$\frac{5}{2}$	0	0	1	$-\frac{1}{2}$
1	y_1	$\frac{5}{2}$	1	0	0	$\frac{7}{6}$
		$z_j - c_j$	0	0	0	1

(T 4) shows all $z_j - c_j \geq 0$ for all j. The optimal solution is

$$\left\langle x_1^* = \tfrac{5}{2}, \quad x_2^* = \tfrac{5}{2}, \quad x_3^* = \tfrac{5}{2}, \quad x_3^* = 0, \quad Z_{\max} = 15 \right\rangle$$

Example 2.9.2. *Show that the following* LPP *has no feasible solution:*

Maximise $Z = x_1 + 4x_2 + 3x_3$

subject to $2x_1 - x_2 + 5x_3 = 40$

$x_1 + 2x_2 - 3x_3 \geq 22$

$3x_1 + x_2 + 2x_3 = 30$

$x_1, x_2, x_3 \geq 0.$

Solution: *Standard form:*

Maximise $Z = x_1 + 4x_2 + 3x_3 + 0x_4 - Mx_{a_1} - Mx_{a_2} - Mx_{a_3}$

subject to $2x_1 - x_2 + 5x_3 + x_{a_1} = 40$

$x_1 + 2x_2 - 3x_3 + x_{a_2} = 22$

$3x_1 + x_2 + 2x_3 + x_{a_3} = 30$

$x_1, x_2, x_3 \geq 0$

$x_4 \geq 0$ surplus variable

$x_{a_1}, x_{a_2}, x_{a_3} \geq 0$ artificial variables.

(T 1)

		c_j	1	2	3	-1	$-M$	$-M$	$-M$	
c_B	y_B	x_B	y_1	y_2	y_3	y_4	y_{a_1}	y_{a_2}	y_{a_3}	MR
$-M$	y_{a_1}	40	2	-1	1	0	1	0	0	$\frac{40}{2}$
$-M$	y_{a_2}	22	1	2	-3	-1	0	1	0	$\frac{22}{1}$
$-M$	y_{a_3}	30	③	1	2	0	0	0	1	$\frac{30}{3}$ →
		$z_j - c_j$	$-6M-1$↑	$-2M-4$	-3	M	0	0	0	

Introduce $\mathbf{y_1}$, drop $\mathbf{y_{a_3}}$. 3 is the key element.

(T 2)

		c_j	1	4	3	0	$-M$	$-M$	
c_B	y_B	x_B	y_1	y_2	y_3	y_4	y_{a_1}	y_{a_2}	MR
$-M$	y_{a_1}	20	0	$-\frac{5}{3}$	$-\frac{1}{3}$	0	1	0	X
$-M$	y_{a_2}	12	0	$\boxed{\frac{5}{3}}$	$-\frac{11}{3}$	-1	0	1	$\frac{36}{5}$ →
1	y_1	10	1	$\frac{1}{3}$	$\frac{2}{3}$	0	0	0	30
		$z_j - c_j$	0	$-\frac{11}{3}$↑	$4M-\frac{7}{3}$	M	0	0	

Introduce $\mathbf{y_2}$, drop $\mathbf{y_{a_2}}$. $\frac{5}{3}$ is the key element.

(T 3)

		c_j	1	4	3	0	$-M$
c_B	y_B	x_B	y_1	y_2	y_3	y_4	y_{a_1}
$-M$	y_{a_1}	32	0	0	-4	-1	1
4	y_2	$\frac{32}{5}$	0	1	$-\frac{11}{5}$	$-\frac{3}{5}$	0
1	y_1	$\frac{38}{5}$	1	0	$\frac{21}{15}$	$\frac{1}{5}$	0
		$z_j - c_j$	0	0	$4M-\frac{156}{5}$	$M-\frac{11}{5}$	0

In (T 3) the coefficient of M in each $z_j - c_j$ is non-negative and an artificial vector appears in the basis, not at the zero level but at a positive level. This shows that the given LPP does not possess any feasible solution.

Example 2.9.3. *Given an* LPP.

Maximise $Z = 6x_1 + 4x_2$

subject to $2x_1 + 3x_2 \leq 30$

$3x_1 + 2x_2 \leq 24$

$x_1 + x_2 \geq 3$

$x_1, x_2 \leq 0.$

Use Big-M method to show that the optimum solution is not unique and the two possible alternative optimal solutions are (i) $x_1^* = 8, x_2^* = 0$ *(ii)* $x_1^* = \frac{12}{5}, x_2^* = \frac{42}{5}$ *with* $Z_{\max} = 48$. [IAS 1993]

Solution: *Standard form* to start simplex iterations:

Maximise $Z = 6x_1 + 4x_2 + 0x_3 + 0x_4 + 0x_5 - Mx_{a_1}$

$$\text{subject to } 2x_1 + 3x_2 + x_3 = 30$$
$$3x_1 + 2x_2 + x_4 = 24$$
$$x_1 + x_2 + x_5 + x_{a_1} = 3$$
$$x_1, x_2 \geq 0;\ x_3, x_4 \geq 0, \text{ slack variables}$$
$$x_5 \geq 0, \text{ surplus variable and}$$
$$x_{a_1} \geq 0, \text{ artificial variable.}$$

(T 1)

		c_j	6	4	0	0	0	$-M$	
c_B	y_B	x_B	y_1	y_2	y_3	y_4	y_5	y_{a_1}	MR
0	y_3	20	2	3	1	0	0	0	$\frac{30}{2}$
0	y_4	24	3	2	0	1	0	0	$\frac{24}{3}$
$-M$	y_{a_1}	3	(1)	1	0	0	-1	1	$\frac{3}{1}$ →
		$z_j - c_j$	$-M-6$↑	$-M-4$	0	0	M	0	

y_1 enters, y_{a_1} departs. 1 is the key element.

(T 2)

		c_j	6	4	0	0	0	
c_B	y_B	x_B	y_1	y_2	y_3	y_4	y_5	MR
0	y_3	24	0	1	1	0	2	$\frac{24}{2}$
0	y_4	15	0	-1	0	1	(3)	$\frac{15}{3}$ →
6	y_1	3	1	1	0	0	-1	X
		$z_j - c_j$	0	2	0	0	-6↑	0

y_5 enters, y_4 departs. 3 is the key element.

(T 3)

		c_j	6	4	0	0	0
c_B	y_B	x_B	y_1	y_2	y_3	y_4	y_5
0	y_3	14	0	$\frac{5}{3}$	1	$-\frac{2}{3}$	0
0	y_5	5	0	$-\frac{1}{3}$	0	$\frac{1}{3}$	1
6	y_1	8	1	$\frac{2}{3}$	0	$\frac{1}{3}$	0
		$z_j - c_j$	0	0	0	2	0

Since all $z_j - c_j \geq 0$, an optimum solution has been reached. The optimum basic feasible solution is

$$\langle x_1^* = 8,\quad x_2^* = 0,\quad Z_{\max} = 48 \rangle$$

An important observation: (Existence of *alternative optima*). From optimum table (T 3), $z_2 - c_2$ for the non-basic variable x_2 is zero. According to the discussion made earlier this is a clear indication that the *current solution is not unique.* We can bring y_2 into the basis in place of y_3 or y_5. The resulting new basic solutions will also be an optimum solution.

For example: Introducing $\mathbf{y}_2$ and dropping $\mathbf{y}_3$, the alternative optimum table is:

(T 4)

		c_j	6	4	0	0	0
c_B	y_B	x_B	y_1	y_2	y_3	y_4	y_5
0	y_2	$\frac{42}{5}$	0	1	$\frac{3}{5}$	$-\frac{2}{5}$	0
0	y_5	$\frac{39}{5}$	0	0	$\frac{1}{5}$	$\frac{1}{5}$	1
6	y_1	$\frac{12}{5}$	1	0	$-\frac{2}{5}$	$\frac{3}{5}$	0
		$z_j - c_j$	0	0	0	2	0

Therefore, an alternative optimum basic feasible solution of the problem is

$$\left\langle x_1^* = \tfrac{12}{5},\quad x_2^* = \tfrac{42}{5},\quad Z_{\max} = 48\right\rangle.$$

Example 2.9.4. *An incomplete tableau of an* LPP *by simplex method is given below (intermediate stage).*

		c_j	-4	-2	0	0	0	$-M$
c_B	y_B	x_B	y_1	y_2	y_3	y_4	y_5	y_{a_1}
-4	y_1	$\frac{24}{5}$			$-\frac{2}{5}$	0	$\frac{1}{5}$	
$-M$	y_{a_1}	$\frac{18}{5}$			$\frac{1}{5}$	-1	$\frac{2}{5}$	
-2	y_2	$\frac{63}{5}$						
		$z_j - c_j$	0	0	$-\frac{M}{5}+\frac{6}{5}$	M	$-\frac{2M}{5}+\frac{2}{5}$	0

(i) *Complete the table,* (ii) *Find the entering and departing vectors,* (iii) *Show that the unique optimal solution of the problem is* $x_1^* = 3$, $x_2^* = 18$. [Visva-Bharati 1984]

Solution:

$$\text{(i) } \mathbf{y}_1 = \begin{pmatrix}1\\0\\0\end{pmatrix},\quad \mathbf{y}_2 = \begin{pmatrix}0\\0\\1\end{pmatrix},\quad \mathbf{y}_3 = \begin{pmatrix}-\frac{2}{5}\\ \frac{1}{5}\\ \frac{1}{5}\end{pmatrix} \quad \left[\begin{aligned} &\because \frac{8}{5} - \frac{M}{5} - 2x - 0 = -\frac{M}{5} + \frac{6}{5} \\ &x = \frac{1}{5}\end{aligned}\right],$$

$$\mathbf{y}_4 = \begin{pmatrix}0\\-1\\0\end{pmatrix} \quad \left[\begin{aligned} &\because 0 + M - 2a - 0 = M \\ &a = 0\end{aligned}\right],\quad \mathbf{y}_5 = \begin{pmatrix}\frac{1}{5}\\ \frac{2}{5}\\ -\frac{3}{5}\end{pmatrix} \quad \left[\begin{aligned} &\because -\frac{4}{5} - \frac{2M}{5} - 2c - 0 = -\frac{2M}{5} + \frac{2}{5} \\ &c = -\frac{3}{5}\end{aligned}\right],$$

$$\mathbf{y}_{a_1} = \begin{pmatrix}0\\1\\0\end{pmatrix}.$$

The complete form of the given incomplete table is:

		c_j	-4	-2	0	0	0	$-M$	
c_B	y_B	x_B	y_1	y_2	y_3	y_4	y_5	y_{a_1}	MR
-4	y_1	$\frac{24}{5}$	1	0	$-\frac{2}{5}$	0	$\frac{1}{5}$	0	24
$-M$	y_{a_1}	$\frac{18}{5}$	0	0	$\frac{1}{5}$	-1	$\boxed{\frac{2}{5}}$	1	9 →
-2	y_2	$\frac{63}{5}$	0	1	$\frac{1}{5}$	0	$-\frac{3}{5}$	0	X
		$z_j - c_j$	0	0	$-\frac{M}{5}+\frac{6}{5}$	M	$-\frac{2M}{5}+\frac{2}{5}$ ↑	0	

(ii) y_5 entering and y_{a_1} departing vectors.

(iii) The next table is:

		c_j	-4	-2	0	0	0
c_B	y_B	x_B	y_1	y_2	y_3	y_4	y_5
-4	y_1	3	1	0	$-\frac{1}{2}$	$\frac{1}{2}$	0
0	y_5	9	0	0	$\frac{1}{2}$	$-\frac{5}{2}$	1
-2	y_2	18	0	1	$\frac{1}{2}$	$-\frac{3}{2}$	0
		$z_j - c_j$	0	0	1	1	0

All $z_j - c_j \geq 0$ and the optimum table indicates that the optimum solution $x_1^* = 3$, $x_2^* = 18$ is a unique solution.

2.10 TWO-PHASE SIMPLEX METHOD FOR SOLUTION OF LP MODEL

The *two-phase* method for the solution of an LP model are separated into two distinct phases. In *Phase* 1, we first derive all the artificial variables at zero level and in *Phase* 2, we actually optimise the objective function starting with a basic feasible solution which either contains no artificial variable or there appears some artificial variable at zero level. We critically explain the method below:

Phase 1. Consider the maximisation LP model. In *Phase* 1, we construct a new objective function

$$Z_{\text{new}} = 0x_1 + 0x_2 + \cdots + 0x_n - 1\cdot x_{a_1} - 1\cdot x_{a_2} - \cdots - 1\cdot x_{am}$$

where (-1) is the price of each of the m artificial variables $\boldsymbol{x}_{\text{art}} = (x_{a_1}, x_{a_2}, \ldots, x_{a_n})$ and 0-price has been assigned to each of legitimate variables $\boldsymbol{x}_{\text{leg}} = \left(\boldsymbol{x}_{\text{decision}}, \boldsymbol{x}_{\text{slack}}, \boldsymbol{x}_{\text{surplus}}\right) = (x_1, x_2, \ldots, x_n)$.

According to our construction of Z_{new} it is clear that

$$\text{maximum } Z_{\text{new}} = 0, \text{ if all artificial variables are at zero level}$$
$$< 0, \text{ if at least one artificial variable is at positive level.}$$

Therefore, if in *Phase* 1 we use *simplex method* to maximise Z_{new} subject to the constraints given in LP model, then we may face any one of the following three situations:

(i) max $Z_{\text{new}} = 0$, i.e., all the artificial variables may disappear from the basis and we get a BFS.

(ii) max $Z_{\text{new}} = 0$, but one or more artificial variables appear in the basis at zero level and also, we get a BFS.

(iii) max $Z_{\text{new}} < 0$, because one or more artificial variables appear in the basis at the positive level. The optimality condition being satisfied, the original LP model has no feasible solution.

Thus, if the iteration in *Phase* 1 ends in either (i) or (ii) only, we go to *Phase* 2 for the optimal solution of the original LP model.

Phase 2. We assign the actual price to each of the legitimate variables and a price zero to any of the artificial variable present in the last iteration of *Phase* 1 at zero level. The first table in *Phase* 2 is almost identical with the last table of *Phase* 1, the only difference being the row of $(z_j - c_j)$ and this is because of the fact that new prices have been entered in the table.

This should be noted that when max $Z_{\text{new}} = 0$ and one or more artificial variables appear in the basis at zero level we would no longer have a BFS and we must take care so that these artificial variables may never become positive in any subsequent iteration of *Phase* 2.

The problem of maximising new objective function subject to the constraints of the original model will be called *auxiliary* LP *model*. Hence, in *two-phase* simplex method we solve auxiliary LPP in *Phase* 1.

Example 2.10.1. *Use two-phase simplex method to solve:*

Maximise $Z = 5x_1 + 8x_2$

subject to $3x_1 + 2x_2 \geq 3$

$x_1 + 4x_2 \geq 4$

$x_1 + x_2 \leq 5$

$x_1, x_2 \geq 0.$ **[VU 1986]**

Solution: Standard maximisation form by introducing non-negative slack, surplus and artificial variables.

Maximise $Z = 5x_1 + 8x_2 + 0x_3 + 0x_4 + 0x_5$

$$\begin{aligned} \text{subject to } 3x_1 + 2x_2 - x_3 \qquad\quad + x_{a_1} \quad &= 3 \\ x_1 + 4x_2 \qquad - x_4 \qquad + x_{a_2} &= 4 \\ x_1 + x_2 \qquad\quad + x_5 \qquad &= 5 \\ x_1, x_2, x_3, x_4, x_5, x_{a_1}, x_{a_2} &\geq 0. \end{aligned} \tag{2.10a}$$

Phase 1. Solution of auxiliary LPP by constructing

Maximise $Z_{\text{new}} = 0x_1 + 0x_2 + 0x_3 + 0x_4 + 0x_5 - x_{a_1} - x_{a_2}$

subject to the set of constraints (2.10a).

(T 1)

		c_j	0	0	0	0	0	−1	−1	
c_B	y_B	x_B	y_1	y_2	y_3	y_4	y_5	y_{a_1}	y_{a_2}	MR
−1	y_{a_1}	3	3	2	−1	0	0	1	0	$\frac{3}{2}$
−1	y_{a_2}	4	1	(4)	0	−1	0	0	1	$\frac{4}{4}$ →
0	y_5	5	1	1	0	0	1	0	0	$\frac{5}{1}$
		$z_j - c_j$	−4	−6↑	1	1	0	0	0	

Introduce y_2, drop y_{a_2}. 4 is the key element.

(T 2)

		c_j	0	0	0	0	0	−1	
c_B	y_B	x_B	y_1	y_2	y_3	y_4	y_5	y_{a_1}	MR
−1	y_{a_1}	1	$\boxed{\frac{5}{2}}$	0	−1	$\frac{1}{2}$	0	1	$\frac{2}{5}$ →
0	y_2	1	$\frac{1}{4}$	1	0	$-\frac{1}{4}$	0	0	4
0	y_5	4	$\frac{3}{4}$	0	0	$\frac{1}{4}$	1	0	$\frac{16}{3}$
		$z_j - c_j$	$-\frac{5}{2}$ ↑	0	1	$-\frac{1}{2}$	0	0	

Introduce y_1, y_{a_1} drop. $\frac{5}{2}$ is the key element.

(T 3)

		c_j	0	0	0	0	0
c_B	y_B	x_B	y_1	y_2	y_3	y_4	y_5
−1	y_{a_1}	$\frac{2}{5}$	1	0	$-\frac{2}{5}$	$\frac{1}{5}$	0
0	y_2	$\frac{9}{10}$	1	0	$\frac{1}{10}$	$-\frac{3}{10}$	0
0	y_5	$\frac{37}{10}$	0	0	$\frac{3}{10}$	$\frac{1}{10}$	1
		$z_j - c_j$	0	0	0	0	0

Since all $z_j - c_j \geq 0$, the current basic feasible solution is optimal and no artificial variable appears in the optimum basis, so we proceed to *Phase* 2.

Phase 2. Here the objective function

Maximise $Z = 5x_1 + 8x_2 + 0x_3 + 0x_4 + 0x_5$.

The last basis of *Phase* 1 (T 3) will be the starting basis of *Phase* 2 and the optimum table T 3 of *Phase* 1 will serve as initial table of *Phase* 2 with a change only in the row of $(z_j - c_j)$ and column of C_B due to the change of the objective row (c_j).

(T 4)

		c_j	5	8	0	0	0	
c_B	y_B	x_B	y_1	y_2	y_3	y_4	y_5	MR
5	y_1	$\frac{2}{5}$	1	0	$-\frac{2}{5}$	$\boxed{\frac{1}{5}}$	0	2 →
8	y_2	$\frac{9}{10}$	0	1	$\frac{1}{10}$	$\frac{3}{10}$	0	X
0	y_5	$\frac{37}{10}$	0	0	$\frac{3}{10}$	$\frac{1}{10}$	1	37
		$z_j - c_j$	0	0	$-\frac{6}{5}$	$-\frac{7}{5}$ ↑	0	

y_4 enters and y_1 leaves the basis. $\frac{1}{5}$ is the key element.

(T 5)

		c_j	5	8	0	0	0	
c_B	y_B	x_B	y_1	y_2	y_3	y_4	y_5	MR
0	y_4	2	5	0	−2	1	0	X
8	y_2	$\frac{3}{2}$	$\frac{3}{2}$	1	$-\frac{1}{2}$	0	0	X
0	y_5	$\frac{7}{2}$	$-\frac{1}{2}$	0	$\boxed{\frac{1}{2}}$	0	1	7 →
		$z_j - c_j$	7	0	−4 ↑	0	0	

y_3 enters and y_5 leaves the basis. $\frac{1}{2}$ is the key element.

(T 6)

		c_j	5	8	0	0	0
c_B	y_B	x_B	y_1	y_2	y_3	y_4	y_5
0	y_4	16	3	0	0	1	4
8	y_2	5	1	1	0	0	1
0	y_3	7	−1	0	1	0	2
		$z_j - c_j$	3	0	0	0	8

Since all $z_j - c_j \geq 0$, the current basic feasible solution is optimal. The optimal solution is

$$\langle x_1^* = 0, \quad x_2^* = 5, \quad Z_{\max} = 40 \rangle.$$

Example 2.10.2. *The following incomplete table represents the second stage of the auxiliary* LPP *in* Phase 1 *of a maximising* LP *model when solved by two-phase simplex method.*

		c_j	0	0	0	0	x
c_B	y_B	x_B	y_1	y_2	y_3	y_4	y_{a_1}
0	y_3	1	2	1	1	0	0
y	y_{a_1}	6	1	4	0	t	1
		$z_j - c_j$	z	−4	0	1	0

(i) *Determine the unknowns x, y, z and t and complete the table.*

(ii) *Find the entering and departing vectors and also the key element.*

(iii) *Show that the original* LP *model does not possess any feasible solution.* [NET Exam 1998]

Solution: (i) Since for *Phase* 1 we construct the new objective function as maximise $Z_{\text{new}} = 0x_1 + 0x_2 + 0x_4 - x_{a_1}$. Therefore, value of $x = -1$ and $y = -1$ also.

Now $2 \times 0 + 1 \times (-1) - 0 = z$ implies $z = -1$. Also, $0 \times 0 + t \times (-1) - 0 = 1$ implies $t = -1$.

$\therefore\ x = -1, y = -1, z = -1, t = -1.$

The complete table is

		c_j	0	0	0	0	−1	
c_B	y_B	x_B	y_1	y_2	y_3	y_4	y_{a_1}	MR
0	y_3	1	2	(1)	1	0	0	1 →
−1	y_{a_1}	6	1	4	0	−1	1	$\frac{6}{4}$
		$z_j - c_j$	−1	−4 ↑	0	1	0	

(ii) $\boldsymbol{y_2}$ entering and $\boldsymbol{y_3}$ departing vectors. 1 is the key element. The next iteration is given below:

		c_j	0	0	0	0	−1
c_B	y_B	x_B	y_1	y_2	y_3	y_4	y_{a_1}
0	y_2	1	2	1	1	0	0
−1	y_{a_1}	2	−7	0	−4	−1	1
		$z_j - c_j$	7	0	4	1	0

(iii) Since all $z_j - c_j \geq 0$, an optimum basic feasible solution to the auxiliary LPP has been reached. But max $Z_{\text{new}} = -2 < 0$ and an artificial vector y_{a_1} appears in the optimum basis at the positive level. Therefore, the original LP model does not possess any feasible solution according to two-phase simplex method.

Example 2.10.3. *Solve by two-phase simplex method the following* LPP.

Maximise $Z = 2x_1 + x_2 + x_3$

subject to $4x_1 + 6x_2 + 3x_3 \leq 8$

$3x_1 - 6x_2 - 4x_3 \leq 1$

$2x_1 + 3x_2 - 5x_3 \geq 4$

$x_1, x_2, x_3 \leq 0.$ [CU(H) 1984]

Solution: Standard maximisation form by introducing non-negative slack, surplus and artificial variables.

Maximise $Z = 2x_1 + x_2 + x_3 + 0x_4 + 0x_5 + 0x_6$

$$\begin{aligned} \text{subject to } 4x_1 + 6x_2 + 3x_3 + x_4 &= 8 \\ 3x_1 - 6x_2 - 4x_3 + x_5 &= 1 \\ 2x_1 + 3x_2 - 5x_3 + x_6 + x_{a_1} &= 4 \end{aligned} \tag{2.10b}$$

$x_1, x_2, x_3 \geq 0,\ x_4, x_5 \geq 0$, slack variables

$x_6 \geq 0$, surplus variable

$x_{a_1} \geq 0$, artificial variable.

Phase 1. Solution of *auxiliary* LPP by constructing new objective function.

Maximise $Z_{\max} = 0x_1 + 0x_2 + 0x_3 + 0x_4 + 0x_5 + 0x_6 - x_{a_1}$

subject to the set of constraints given in (2.10b).

(T 1)

		c_j	0	0	0	0	0	0	−1	
c_B	y_B	x_B	y_1	y_2	y_3	y_4	y_5	y_6	y_{a_1}	MR
0	y_4	8	4	(6)	3	1	0	0	0	$\frac{8}{6}$ →
0	y_5	1	3	−6	−4	0	1	0	0	X
−1	y_{a_1}	4	2	3	−5	0	0	−1	1	$\frac{4}{3}$
		$z_j - c_j$	−2	−3↑	5	0	0	1	0	

Introduce y_2, drop y_4. 6 is the key element.

(T 2)

		c_j	0	0	0	0	0	0	−1
c_B	y_B	x_B	y_1	y_2	y_3	y_4	y_5	y_6	y_{a_1}
0	y_2	$\frac{4}{3}$	$\frac{2}{3}$	1	$\frac{1}{2}$	$\frac{1}{6}$	0	0	0
0	y_5	9	7	0	−1	1	1	0	0
−1	y_{a_1}	0	0	0	$-\frac{13}{2}$	$-\frac{1}{2}$	0	−1	1
		$z_j - c_j$	0	0	$\frac{13}{2}$	$\frac{1}{2}$	0	1	0

All $z_j - c_j \geq 0$, maximum $Z_{\text{new}} = 0$, one artificial vector y_{a_1} appear in the optimum basis of auxiliary LPP at zero level. Therefore, we start *Phase 2* by taking the original objective function.

Phase 2. *Objective function:*

Maximise $Z = 2x_1 + x_2 + x_3 + 0x_4 + 0x_5 + 0x_6 + 0x_{a_1}$.

The last basis of *Phase* 1 will be the starting basis of *Phase* 2 and optimum table of *Phase* 1 will serve as initial table of *Phase* 2 with a change in objective row c_j as well as net evaluation row $z_j - c_j$.

(T 3)

		c_j	2	1	1	0	0	0	0	
c_B	y_B	x_B	y_1	y_2	y_3	y_4	y_5	y_6	y_{a_1}	MR
1	y_2	$\frac{4}{3}$	$\frac{2}{3}$	1	$\frac{1}{2}$	$\frac{1}{6}$	0	0	0	2
0	y_5	9	(7)	0	-1	1	1	0	0	$\frac{9}{7}$ →
0	y_{a_1}	0	0	0	$-\frac{13}{2}$	$-\frac{1}{2}$	0	-1	1	X
		$z_j - c_j$	$-\frac{4}{3}$↑	0	$-\frac{1}{2}$	$\frac{1}{6}$	0	0	0	

Introduce y_1, drop y_5. 7 is the key element.

(T 4)

		c_j	2	1	1	0	0	0	0
c_B	y_B	x_B	y_1	y_2	y_3	y_4	y_5	y_6	y_{a_1}
1	y_2	$\frac{10}{21}$	0	1	$\frac{25}{42}$	$\frac{1}{14}$	$-\frac{2}{21}$	0	0
2	y_1	$\frac{9}{7}$	1	0	$-\frac{1}{7}$	$\frac{1}{7}$	$\frac{1}{7}$	0	0
0	y_{a_1}	0	0	0	$-\frac{13}{2}$	$-\frac{1}{2}$	0	-1	1
		$z_j - c_j$	0	0	$\frac{1}{7}$	$\frac{5}{4}$	$\frac{4}{21}$	0	0

All $z_j - c_j \geq 0$, still an artificial vector y_{a_1} appears in the optimal basis in *Phase* 2 at zero level. This has a clear indication that the artificial variable has no contribution to the optimum solution of the original problem. The optimum solution is given by

$$x_1^* = \frac{9}{7}, \quad x_2^* = \frac{10}{21}, \quad x_3^* = 0, \quad Z_{\max} = \frac{64}{21}.$$

2.11 EXERCISE 2

1. A production planar in a soft drink plant has two bottling machines A and B. A is designed for 8-ounce bottles and B for 16-ounce bottles. However, each can be used on both types with some loss of efficiency. The following data is available

Machine	8-ounce bottles	16-ounce bottles
A	100/min	40/min
B	60/min	75/min

The machine can be run 8 hours per day, 5 days per week, profit on 8-ounce bottle is 15 paise and on 16-ounce bottle is 25 paise. Weekly production of the drink cannot exceed 300,000 ounces and the market can absorb 25,000 of 8-ounce bottles and 7000 of 16-ounce bottles per week. The planner wishes to maximise his profit. Formulate this as an LP model.

2. A firm produces an alloy having the following specifications (i) Specific gravity ≤ 0.98, (ii) Chromium $\geq 8\%$, (iii) Melting point $\geq 450\,^{\circ}$C.

Raw materials A, B, C having the properties in the table below can be used to make the alloy.

Property	Properties of raw materials		
	A	B	C
Specific gravity	0.92	0.97	1.04
Chromium	7%	13%	16%
Melting point	440 °C	490 °C	480 °C

Costs of various raw materials per unit ton are: ₹ 90 for A, ₹ 280 for B and ₹ 40 for C. The objective is to find the proportions in which A, B, C be used to obtain an alloy of desired properties in which the cost of raw materials is minimum. Formulate this *blending problem* as an LP model.

3. A firm manufactures two products A and B on which the profits earned per unit are ₹ 3 and ₹ 4 respectively. Each product is processed on two machines M_1 and M_2. Product A requires one minute of processing time on M_1 and two minutes on M_2 while processing of product B requires one minute on M_1 and one minute on M_2. M_1 is not available for more than 7 hours 30 minutes while M_2 is available for 10 hours during any working day. Find the number of units of products A and B need to be manufactured to get maximum profit. Formulate this as an LP model and solve by *graphical method*.

4. Using graphical method, show that the LPP

   Maximise $Z = 2x_1 + 3x_2$

   subject to $x_1 - x_2 \leq 2$

   $x_1 + x_2 \leq 4$

   $x_1, x_2 \geq 0$

   has an unbounded solution.

5. A firm manufactures three products A, B and C. The profits per unit product are ₹ 3, ₹ 2 and ₹ 4 respectively. The firm has two machines and the required processing time in minutes for each machine on each product is given below.

Macines	Products		
	A	B	C
X	4	3	5
Y	2	2	4

Machines X and Y have 2000 and 1500 machine-minutes respectively. The firm must manufacture 100 A's, 200 B's and 50 C's but not more than 150 A's. Set up an LP model to maximise the profit.

[IIM(Kol) 1996; Roorke(M Tech) 1977]

6. The manager of an oil refinery has to decide upon the optimal mix of two possible blending processes of which the inputs and outputs per production run are as follows:

Process	Input		Output	
	Crude A	Crude B	Gas X	Gas Y
1	5	3	5	8
2	2	4	5	4

The maximum amount available of Crudes A and B are 200 units and 150 units respectively. Market requirements show that at least 100 units of gas X and 80 units of gas Y must be produced. The profit per production run from process 1 and process 2 are ₹ 3 and ₹ 4 respectively. Formulate the problem as an LPP.

[MBA(CU) 2000; M Tech(JU) 2004]

7. The financial secretary of a firm wants to invest a sum of ₹ 10,000 so as to maximise its yield. He has the following alternatives:

Investment type	A_1	A_2	B_1	B_2	C_1	C_2
Yield	3%	2.5%	3.5%	4%	5%	4.5%

It is the firm's policy that at least 40% of the whole amount be invested in units of type A and not more than 35% in any of the other two types. Make a model for the investment plan if the whole of ₹ 10,000 is to be invested. [IIT(M Tech) 2001, ISI(OR) 1993]

8. A firm is engaged in breeding pigs. The pigs are fed on various products grown on the farm. Because of the need to ensure certain nutrient constituents, it is necessary to buy additionally one or two products, which we shall call A and B. The nutrient constituents (vitamins and proteins) in each unit of the products are given below:

Nutrients	Nutrient contents in the products A	B	Minimum amount of Nutrients
1	36	6	108
2	3	12	36
3	20	20	100

Product A costs ₹ 20 per unit and product B costs ₹ 40 per unit. Formulate the LP model for products A and B to be purchased at the lowest possible costs so as to provide the pigs with nutrients not less than given in the table. [MBA(DU) 1973; CU(H) 2005]

9. A security dealer recommends two types of investments A and B to his client. Investment A returns 6% and B 8%. The client has almost ₹ 100,000 to invest. The client wants total annual return to be at least ₹ 7000 and at least 2/5th of the amount to be invested in investment B. The security dealer gets 5% of the income from investment A and 4% of the income from investment B. Construct mathematical model for the problem to maximise the total fee of the security dealer.

[JNU(Com Sc) 1979; MBA(CU) 1998]

10. Write the constraints associated with the solution space shown in the figure below:

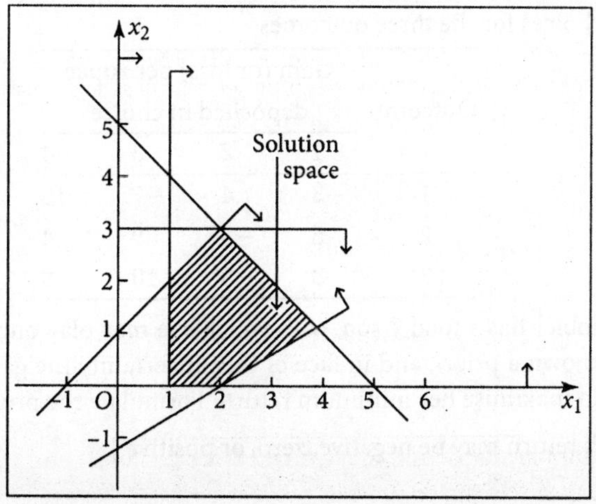

Hence, determine the optimum solution assuming that the objective function is (i) Minimise $Z = 2x_1 + 6x_2$ (ii) Maximise $W = -3x_1 + 4x_2$.

11. Consider the following problem.

Maximise $Z = 3x_1 + 2x_2$

subject to $2x_1 + x_2 \leq 2$

$3x_1 + 4x_2 \leq 12$

$x_1, x_2 \geq 0.$

Show graphically that the problem has no *feasible extreme* points. What can one conclude concerning the solution to the problem?

12. A manufacturer produces three models I, II and III of a certain product. He uses two types of raw materials A and B of which 4000 and 6000 units are available, respectively. The raw material requirements per unit of the three models are given below:

Raw materials	Requirement per unit I	II	III
A	2	3	5
B	4	2	7

The labour time for each unit of model I is twice that of model II and three times that of model III. The entire labour force of the factory can produce the equivalent of 1500 units of model I. A market survey indicates that the minimum demand for the three models is 200, 200 and 150 units, respectively. However, the ratios of the number of units produced must be equal to 3 : 2 : 5. Assume that the profit per unit of models I, II and III is ₹ 30, ₹ 20 and ₹ 50, respectively. Formulate the problem as an LP model to determine the number of units of each product that will maximise profit.

[MBA(CU) 1984; JU (M Sc) 1998]

13. A gambler plays a game that requires dividing her money among four different choices. The game has three outcomes. The following table gives the corresponding gain (or loss) per rupee deposited in each of the four choices for the three outcomes.

Outcome	Gain (or loss) per rupee deposited in choice 1	2	3	4
1	−3	4	−7	15
2	5	−3	9	4
3	3	−9	10	−8

Assume that the gambler has a total ₹ 500, with which she may play only once. The exact outcome of the game is not known a priori, and in face of this uncertainty the gambler decides to make the allocation that would maximise her minimum return. Formulate the problem as an LP model.

[**Note.** The gambler's return may be negative, zero, or positive.]

[IAS (Main) 1986]

14. Make a graphical representation of the set of constraints of the following LPP. Find the extreme points of the feasible region. Finally, solve the problems graphically.

(i) Maximise $Z = 2x_1 + x_2$
subject to $x_1 + x_2 \geq 5$
$2x_1 + 3x_2 \leq 20$
$4x_1 + 3x_2 \leq 25$
$x_1, x_2 \geq 0.$
[BU(H) 1983; BESU(Engg) 2001]

(ii) Maximise $Z = 20x_1 + 10x_2$
subject to $x_1 + 2x_2 \leq 40$
$3x_1 + x_2 \geq 30$
$4x_1 + 3x_2 \geq 60$
$x_1, x_2 \geq 0.$ [BU(P) 1986]

(iii) Maximise $Z = 4x_1 + 3x_2$
subject to $2x_1 + x_2 \leq 1000$
$x_1 + x_2 \leq 800$
$0 \leq x_1 \leq 400$
$0 \leq x_2 \leq 700.$ [BU(P) 1986]

15. Show that the LPP
Maximise $Z = 6x_1 + 10x_2$
subject to $3x_1 + 5x_2 \leq 10$
$5x_1 + 3x_2 \leq 15$
$x_1, x_2 \geq 0$
has infinite number of optimal solution. [KU(H) 1981]

16. (a) Let $x_1 = 2$, $x_2 = 4$ and $x_3 = 1$ be a feasible solution to the system of equations

$$2x_1 - x_2 + 2x_3 = 2$$
$$x_1 + 4x_2 = 18.$$

Reduce the given feasible solution to a basic feasible solution.

(b) If $x_1 = 2$, $x_2 = 3$, $x_3 = 1$ is a feasible solution of the LPP
Maximise $Z = x_1 + 2x_2 + 4x_3$
subject to $2x_1 + x_2 + 4x_3 = 11$
$3x_1 + x_2 + 5x_3 = 14$
$x_1, x_2, x_3 \geq 0.$
Find a basic feasible solution of the problem. [CU(H) 1980; BESU(Engg) 2005]

(c) Reduce the feasible solution $x_1 = 2$, $x_2 = 1$, $x_3 = 1$ to the system of equations

$$x_1 + 4x_2 - x_3 = 5$$
$$2x_1 + 3x_2 + x_3 = 8$$

to a basic feasible solution. [VU(H) 1985]

(d) $x_1 = 1$, $x_2 = 2$, $x_3 = 1$, $x_4 = 0$ is a feasible solution of the set of equations

$$11x_1 + 2x_2 - 9x_3 + 4x_4 = 6$$
$$15x_1 + 3x_2 - 12x_3 + 5x_4 = 9.$$

Find out the basic feasible solutions and prove that one of them is non-degenerate and other is degenerate.

(e) Given the linear system: $2x_1 - x_2 + 2x_3 = 10$
$x_1 + 4x_2 = 18$
and non-negativity restriction $x_1, x_2, x_3 \geq 0$ obtain a basic feasible solution starting from the feasible solution $x_1 = 2$, $x_2 = 4$, $x_3 = 5$. [CU(H) 1982]

17. Express the following LPP in the standard *matrix form.*

Maximise $Z = 4x_1 + 2x_2 + 6x_3$

subject to $2x_1 - 3x_2 + 2x_3 \geq 6$

$3x_1 + 4x_2 = 8$

$6x_1 - 4x_2 + x_3 \leq 0$

$x_1, x_2, x_3 \geq 0.$

18. Express the following LPP in the standard form .

Maximise $Z = 3x_1 + 2x_2 + 5x_3$

subject to $2x_1 - 3x_2 \leq 3$

$x_1 + 2x_2 + 3x_3 \geq 5$

$3x_1 + 2x_3 \leq 2$

$x_1, x_2 \geq 0$ and x_3 unrestricted in sign.

19. Convert the following LPP to the standard form

Maximise $Z = 2x_1 + 3x_2 + 5x_3$

subject to $x_1 + x_2 - x_3 \geq -5$

$-6x_1 + 7x_2 - 9x_3 \leq 4$

$x_1 + x_2 + 4x_3 = 10$

$x_1, x_2 \geq 0$, x_3 unrestricted. [BESU(Engg) 2000]

20. Consider the following problem:

Maximise $Z = 2x_1 - 4x_2 + 5x_3 - 6x_4$

subject to $x_1 + 4x_2 - 2x_3 + 8x_4 \leq 2$

$-x_1 + 2x_2 + 3x_3 + 4x_4 \leq 1$

$x_1, x_2, x_3, x_4 \geq 0.$

Determine: (i) The maximum number of possible basic solutions, (ii) The feasible extreme points, (iii) The optimal basic feasible solution.

21. Transform the following LPP into the form where all the constraints are of equality type.

Maximise $Z = 2x_1 + x_2 - 6x_3 - x_4$

subject to $3x_1 + 8x_4 \leq 25$

$x_1 + x_2 + x_3 + x_4 = 20$

$4x_1 + 6x_3 \leq 5$

$2 \leq 2x_1 + 3x_3 + 2x_4 \leq 30$

$x_k \geq 0, \ k = 1, 2, 3, 4$ [CU(H) 1980; BESU(Engg) 2000]

22. Put the following LPP in a standard *maximisation form.*

Minimise $Z = 3x_1 - 4x_2 + 7x_3$

subject to $x_1 + x_2 + 7x_3 \leq 50$

$x_1 + 9x_2 - 5x_3 \geq 40$

$5x_1 + 3x_2 = 20$

$|3x_2 + 4x_3| \leq 100$

$x_1, x_2 \geq 0$, x_3 unrestricted. [JNU(Com Sc) 2002]

23. (a) Determine the optimum solution of the following LPP by enumerating all the basic solutions

Maximise $Z = 2x_1 - 4x_2 + 5x_3 - 6x_4$

subject to $x_1 + 4x_2 - 2x_3 + 8x_4 \leq 2$

$-x_1 + 2x_2 + 3x_3 + 4x_4 \leq 1$

$x_1, x_2, x_3, x_4 \geq 0.$ [MBA(IGNOU) 2001]

(b) Compute all the basic feasible solutions to the LPP.

Maximise $Z = 2x_1 + 3x_2 + 4x_3 + 7x_4$

subject to $2x_1 + 3x_2 - x_3 + 4x_4 \leq 8$

$x_1 - 2x_2 + 6x_3 - 7x_4 = -3$

$x_1, x_2, x_3, x_4 \geq 0$

and choose that one which maximises Z. [Roorkee (BE) 1991; CU(H) 1993; BESU(Engg) 2006]

24. Solve the following LPP by *simplex method:*

(i) Minimise $Z = x_1 - 3x_2 + 2x_3$

subject to $3x_1 - x_2 + 2x_3 \leq 7$

$-2x_1 - 4x_2 \leq 12$

$-4x_1 + 3x_2 + 8x_3 \leq 10$

$x_1, x_2, x_3 \geq 0.$ [MBA(IGNOU) 2006; JU(MSc) 1972]

(ii) Maximise $Z = 3x_1 + 2x_2 + 5x_3$

subject to $x_1 + 2x_2 + x_3 \leq 430$

$3x_1 + 2x_3 \leq 460$

$x_1 + 4x_2 \leq 420$

$x_1, x_2, x_3 \geq 0.$ [MBA(IGNOU) 2006; JU(MSc) 1972]

(iii) Minimise $Z = x_1 + 2x_2$

subject to $-x_1 + 2x_2 \leq 8$

$x_1 + 2x_2 \leq 12$

$x_1 - 2x_2 \leq 3$

$x_1, x_2 \geq 0.$

Obtain an alternative optimal basic feasible solution, if it exists.

(iv) Minimise $Z = 3x_1 + x_2 + 3x_3$

subject to $2x_1 + x_2 + x_3 \leq 2$

$x_1 + 2x_2 + 3x_3 \leq 5$

$2x_1 + 2x_2 + x_3 \leq 6$

$x_1, x_2, x_3 \geq 0.$ [BU(H Maths) 1982]

(v) Minimise $Z = 4x_1 + x_2 + 4x_3 + 5x_4$

subject to $-4x_1 + 6x_2 + 5x_3 - 4x_4 \leq 20$

$3x_1 - 2x_2 + 4x_3 + x_4 \leq 10$

$8x_1 - 3x_2 + 3x_3 + 2x_4 \leq 20$

$x_k \geq 0, k = 1, 2, 3, 4.$

(vi) Minimise $Z = x_1 + 2x_2 + 3x_2$

subject to $x_1 + 2x_2 + 3x_3 \leq 10$

$x_1 + x_2 \leq 5$

$x_1 \leq 1$

$x_1, x_2, x_3 \geq 0.$

Find at least two alternative optimal basic feasible solutions of the problem.

25. Consider the problem:

Maximise $X = 3x_1 + x_2$

subject to $x_1 + 2x_2 \leq 5$

$x_1 + x_2 - x_3 \leq 2$

$7x_1 + 3x_2 - 5x_3 \leq 20$

$x_1, x_2, x_3 \geq 0.$

Show that the optimal solution is degenerate and that there exist alternative solutions.

26. Use Charnes' Big-M method to solve the following LPP:

(i) Minimise $Z = 4x_1 + 8x_2 + 3x_3$

subject to $x_1 + x_2 \geq 2$

$2x_1 + x_3 \geq 5$

$x_1, x_2, x_3 \geq 0.$

[CU(H Maths) 1990; BESU(Engg) 2009]

(ii) Maximise $Z = 2x_1 + x_2 + 3x_3$

subject to $x_1 + x_2 + 2x_3 \leq 5$

$3x_1 + 3x_2 + 4x_3 = 12$

$x_1, x_2, x_3 \geq 0.$

[JU(MSc) 1992]

(iii) Minimise $Z = 2x_1 - 3x_2$

subject to $-x_1 + x_2 \geq -2$

$5x_1 + 4x_2 \geq 46$

$7x_1 + 2x_2 \geq 32$

$x_1, x_2 \geq 0.$

[CU(H Maths) 1987; BESU(Engg) 2010]

(iv) Minimise $Z = 6x_1 + 4x_2$

subject to $2x_1 + 3x_2 \leq 30$

$3x_1 + 2x_2 \leq 24$

$x_1 + x_2 \geq 3$

$x_1, x_2 \geq 0.$

Show that the solution is not unique.

[CU(H Maths) 1990; BESU(Engg) 2009]

27. Consider the problem:

Minimise $Z = 3x_1 + 2x_2 + 3x_3$

subject to $2x_1 + x_2 + x_3 \leq 2$

$3x_1 + 4x_2 + 2x_3 \geq 8$

$x_1, x_2, x_3 \geq 0.$

By using the M-technique show that the optimal solution can include an artificial basic variable at the zero level. Hence, conclude that a feasible solution exists.

28. Solve the following LPP by Big-M method:

(i) Minimise $Z = x_1 + 2x_2 + 3x_3 - x_4$

subject to $x_1 + 2x_2 + 3x_3 = 15$

$2x_1 + x_2 + 5x_3 = 20$

$x_1 + 2x_2 + x_3 + x_4 = 10$

$x_1, x_2, x_3, x_4 \geq 0.$

[IAS (Main) 1995; IIT Kanpur (MTech) 1992]

(ii) Minimise $Z = 60x_1 + 80x_2$

subject to $x_1 \leq 400$

$x_2 \leq 200$

$x_1 + x_2 = 500$

$x_1, x_2 \geq 0.$

[MBA(CU) 1997; VU(BSc H) 1998]

(iii) Minimise $Z = 6x_1 - 3x_2 + 2x_3$
subject to $2x_1 + x_2 + x_3 \leq 16$
$3x_1 + 2x_2 + x_3 \leq 18$
$x_1 - 2x_3 \geq 8$
$x_1, x_2, x_3 \geq 0.$ [IAS (Main) 1995; IIT Kanpur (MTech) 1992]

29. Consider the problem:
Maximise $Z = x_1 + 5x_2 + 3x_3$
subject to $x_1 + 2x_2 + x_3 = 3$
$2x_1 - x_2 = 4$
$x_1, x_2, x_3 \geq 0.$
Let x_A be an artificial variable in the second constraint equation. Solve the problem by using x_3 and x_A for a starting basic solution.

30. Solve the following LPP, using *two-phases* of the simplex method:

(i) Minimise $Z = x_1 + x_2$
subject to $2x_1 + x_2 \geq 4$
$x_1 + 7x_2 \geq 7$
$x_1, x_2 \geq 0.$
[DU (BSc) 1991, WBUT (MCA) 2002]

(ii) Minimise $Z = 2x_1 + x_2$
subject to $5x_1 + 10x_2 - x_3 = 8$
$x_1 + x_2 + x_4 = 7$
$x_1, x_2, x_3, x_4 \geq 0.$

(iii) Minimise $Z = \frac{15}{2}x_1 - 3x_2$
subject to $3x_1 - x_2 - x_3 \geq 3$
$x_1 - x_2 + x_3 \geq 2$
$x_1, x_2, x_3 \geq 0.$
[Roorkee MSc(Maths) 2004]

(iv) Minimise $Z = 5x_1 - 2x_2 + 3x_3$
subject to $2x_1 + 2x_2 - x_3 \geq 2$
$3x_1 - 4x_2 \leq 3$
$x_2 + 3x_3 \leq 5$
$x_1, x_2, x_3 \geq 0.$
[KU(H) 1982]

(v) Minimise $Z = 2x_1 - x_2 + 2x_3$
subject to $x_1 + x_2 - 3x_3 \geq 8$
$4x_1 - x_2 + x_3 \geq 2$
$2x_1 + 3x_2 - x_3 \geq 4$
$x_1, x_2, x_3 \geq 0.$
[CU(H) 1982]

(vi) Minimise $Z = x_1 - 2x_2 - 3x_3$
subject to $-2x_1 + x_2 + 3x_3 = 2$
$2x_1 + 3x_2 + 4x_3 = 1$
$x_1, x_2, x_3 \geq 0.$
[Meerut U. MSc (Maths) 1991]

31. (i) A small scale industrialist produces four types of machines M_1, M_2, M_3, and M_4 made of steel and brass. The amount of steel and brass required for each machine and the number of man-weeks of labour required to manufacture and assemble one unit of each machine are as follows:

	M_1	M_2	M_3	M_4	Availability
Steel	6	5	3	2	100 kg
Brass	3	4	9	2	75 kg
Man-weeks	1	2	1	2	20

The labour is restricted to 20 man-weeks, steel is restricted to 100 kg per week and brass to 75 kg per week. The industrialist's profit on each unit of M_1, M_2, M_3 and M_4 is ₹ 6, ₹ 4, ₹ 7 and ₹ 5 respectively. How many of each type of machine should be produced to maximise his profit and how much is his profit?

(ii) Show how the following inequality in absolute form can be replaced by two regular inequalities

$$\left|\sum_{j=1}^{n} a_{ij}x_j\right| < b_i,\ b_i > 0.$$

Also show how the following objective function can be linearised.

$$\text{Minimise } Z = \max\left\{\left|\sum_{j=1}^{n} c_{1j}x_j\right|, \left|\sum_{j=1}^{n} c_{2j}x_j\right|, \ldots, \left|\sum_{j=1}^{n} c_{mj}x_j\right|\right\}.$$

32. Solve the following LPP

(i) Minimise $Z = 4x_1 + 2x_2$

subject to $3x_1 + x_2 \geq 27$

$-x_1 - x_2 \leq 21$

$x_1 + 2x_2 \geq 30$

x_1 and x_2 are unrestricted in sign. [IAS (Main) 1975; ICWA (Final) 1992]

(ii) Minimise $Z = 2x_1 + 5x_2$

subject to $x_1 + 2x_2 \leq 8$

$x_1 \leq 4$

$0 \leq x_2 \leq 3$

x_1 is unrestricted in sign.

ANSWERS

1. Maximise $Z = 0.15x_1 + 0.25x_2$

subject to $2x_1 + 5x_2 \leq 480000$

$5x_1 + 4x_2 \leq 720000$

$8x_1 + 16x_2 \leq 300000$

$0 \leq x_1 \leq 25000$

$0 \leq x_2 = 7000$.

2. Minimise $Z = 90x_1 + 280x_2 + 40x_3$

subject to $0.92x_1 + 0.97x_2 + 1.04x_3 \geq 0.98$

$7x_1 + 13x_2 + 16x_3 \geq 8$

$440x_1 + 490x_2 + 480x_3 \geq 450$

$x_1 + x_2 + x_3 = 100$

$x_1, x_2, x_3 \geq 0$.

3. $x_A = 0, x_B = 450, Z_{\max} = 1800$

5. Maximise $Z = 3x_A + 2x_B + 2x_C$

subject to $4x_A + 3x_B + 5x_C \leq 2000$

$2x_A + 3x_B + 4x_C \leq 1500$

$100 \leq x_A \leq 150,\ x_B \geq 200,\ x_C \geq 50 = 50.$

6. Maximise $Z = 3x_1 + 4x_2$

subject to
$$\begin{aligned} 5x_1 + 4x_2 &\le 200 \\ 3x_1 + 5x_2 &\le 150 \\ 5x_1 + 4x_2 &\ge 100 \\ 8x_1 + 4x_2 &\ge 80 \\ x_1, x_2 &\ge 0. \end{aligned}$$

7. Maximise $Z = 0.03x_{A_1} + 0.025x_{A_2} + 0.035x_{B_1} + 0.04x_{B_2} + 0.05x_{C_1} + 0.045x_{C_2}$

subject to
$$\begin{aligned} x_{A_1} + x_{A_2} + x_{B_1} + x_{B_2} + x_{C_1} + x_{C_2} &= 10000 \\ x_{A_1} + x_{A_2} &\ge 4000 \\ x_{B_1} + x_{B_2} &\le 3500 \\ x_{C_1} + x_{C_2} &\le 3500 \\ x_{A_1}, x_{A_2}, x_{B_1}, x_{B_2}, x_{C_1}, x_{C_2} &\ge 0. \end{aligned}$$

8. Maximise $Z = 20x_A + 40x_B$

subject to
$$\begin{aligned} 36x_A + 6x_B &\ge 108 \\ 3x_A + 12x_B &\ge 36 \\ 20x_A + 10x_B &\ge 100 \\ x_A, x_B &\ge 0. \end{aligned}$$

9. Maximise $Z = 0.06 \times 0.05x_1 + 0.08 \times 0.04x_2$

subject to
$$\begin{aligned} x_1 + x_2 &\le 100000 \\ 0.06x_1 + 0.08x_2 &\ge 7000 \\ x_2 &\ge 0.4(x_1 + x_2) \\ x_1, x_2 &\ge 0. \end{aligned}$$

10. Constraints are:
$$\begin{aligned} x_1 + x_2 &\le 5 \\ x_1 - 2x_2 &\le 2 \\ x_1 &\ge 1 \\ -x_1 + x_2 &\le 1 \\ x_1, x_2 &\ge 0. \end{aligned}$$

(i) Optimum solution: $x_1^* = 1, x_2^* = 0, Z_{\min} = 2.$

(ii) Optimum solution: $x_1^* = 2, x_2^* = 3, W_{\max} = 6.$

12. Maximise $Z = 30x_1 + 20x_2 + 50x_3$

subject to
$$\begin{aligned} 2x_1 + 3x_2 + 5x_3 &\le 4000 \\ 4x_1 + 2x_2 + 7x_3 &\le 6000 \\ x_1 + \tfrac{1}{2}x_2 + \tfrac{1}{3}x_3 &\le 1500 \\ \tfrac{1}{3}x_1 = \tfrac{1}{2}x_2 &= \tfrac{1}{5}x_3 \\ x_1 &\ge 200 \\ x_2 &\ge 200 \\ x_3 &\ge 150. \end{aligned}$$

13. Maximise $Z = 6x_1 + 4x_2 - 5\left(y_1'' + y_2''\right)$

subject to
$$\frac{x_1}{5} + \frac{x_2}{6} + y_1' - y_1'' = 8$$
$$\frac{x_1}{4} + \frac{x_2}{8} + y_2' - y_2'' = 8$$
$$y_1'' \leq 4$$
$$y_2'' \leq 4$$
$$x_1, x_2, y_1', y_1'', y_2', y_2'' \geq 0.$$

14. (i) $(5,0), \left(\frac{25}{4},0\right), \left(\frac{5}{2},5\right), \left(0,\frac{20}{3}\right), (0,5)$, $x_1^* = \frac{25}{4}$, $x_2^* = 0$, $Z_{\max} = \frac{25}{2}$.

(ii) $(15,0), (40,0), (4,18), (6,12)$, $x_1^* = 6$, $x_2^* = 12$, $Z_{\min} = 240$.

(iii) $(0,0), (400,0), (400,200), (200,600), (100,700), (0,700)$, $x_1^* = 200$, $x_2^* = 600$, $Z_{\max} = 2600$.

16. (a) $x_2 = \frac{9}{2}$, $x_3 = \frac{13}{4}$ with $x_1 = 0$ (non-basic).

(b) $x_1 = \frac{1}{2}$, $x_3 = \frac{5}{2}$ with $x_2 = 0$ (non-basic).

(c) $x_1 = \frac{17}{5}$, $x_2 = \frac{2}{5}$ with $x_3 = 0$ (non-basic).

$x_2 = \frac{13}{7}$, $x_3 = \frac{17}{7}$ with $x_1 = 0$ (non-basic).

(d) $x_1 = 3$, $x_3 = 3$, $x_4 = 0$ with $x_2 = 0$ (non-basic).

$x_2 = 3$, $x_3 = 0$, $x_4 = 0$ with $x_1 = 0$ (non-basic).

(e) $x_1 = 0$, $x_2 = \frac{9}{2}$, $x_3 = \frac{29}{4}$.

17. *Matrix form*: Maximise $Z = \boldsymbol{cx}$

subject to $A\boldsymbol{x} = \boldsymbol{b}$

$\boldsymbol{x} \geq \boldsymbol{0}$

where $x = (x_1, x_2, x_3, x_4, x_5)^T$

$c = (4, 2, 6, 0, 0)$

$b = (6, 8, 10)^T$

$$A = \begin{pmatrix} 2 & 3 & 2 & -1 & 0 \\ 3 & 4 & 0 & 0 & 0 \\ 6 & -4 & 1 & 0 & 1 \end{pmatrix}.$$

18. *Standard form*: Maximise $Z = 3x_1 + 2x_2 + 5x_3' - 5x_3'' + 0s_1 + 0s_2 + 0s_3$

subject to
$$\begin{aligned} 2x_1 - 3x_2 \qquad\qquad\qquad + s_1 \qquad\qquad &= 3 \\ x_1 + 2x_2 + 3x_3' - 3x_3'' \qquad - s_2 \qquad &= 5 \\ 3x_1 \qquad + 2x_3' - 2x_3'' \qquad\qquad + s_3 &= 2 \end{aligned}$$
$$x_1,\ x_2,\ x_3 = x_3' - x_3'' \geq 0,\ x_3',\ x_3'';\ s_1, s_2,\ x_3 \geq 0.$$

19. *Standard form*: Maximise $Z = 2x_1 + 3x_2 + 5x_3' - 5x_3'' + 0x_4 + 0x_5$

subject to
$$\begin{aligned} -x_1 - x_2 + x_3' - x_3'' + x_4 \qquad &= 3 \\ -6x_1 + 7x_2 - 9x_3' + 9x_3'' \qquad + x_5 &= 4 \\ x_1 + x_2 + 4x_3' - 4x_3'' \qquad\qquad &= 10 \end{aligned}$$
$$x_1,\ x_2,\ x_3',\ x_3'',\ x_4,\ x_5 \geq 0.$$

20. (i) 16.

(ii) $(8,0,3,0,0,0)$; $(2,0,0,0,0,3)$; $\left(0,0,\frac{1}{3},0,\frac{8}{3},0\right)$, $(0,0,0,0,2,1)$; $\left(0,\frac{1}{2},0,0,0,0\right)$; $\left(0,0,0,\frac{1}{4},0,0\right)$.
(iii) $(8,0,3,0,0,0)$, $Z_{\max}=31$.

21. *Standard form*: Maximise $Z=2x_1+x_2-6x_3-x_4+0x_5+0x_6+0x_7+0x_8$

$$\begin{aligned}
\text{subject to } 3x_1 \qquad\qquad + x_4 + x_5 &= 25\\
x_1 + x_2 + x_3 + x_4 &= 20\\
4x_1 + 6x_3 - x_6 &= 5\\
2x_1 + 3x_3 + 2x_4 - x_7 &= 2\\
2x_1 + 3x_3 + 2x_4 + x_8 &= 30\\
x_k \ge 0,\ k=1,2,\ldots,8.
\end{aligned}$$

22. *Standard form* (maximisation form)

Maximise $\hat{Z}=(-z)=-3x_1+4x_2-7\left(x_3'-x_3''\right)+0x_4+0x_5+0x_6+0x_7+0x_8+0x_9$

$$\begin{aligned}
\text{subject to } x_1+x_2+7\left(x_3'-x_3''\right)+x_4 &= 50\\
x_1+9x_2-5\left(x_3'-x_3''\right) - x_5 &= 40\\
5x_1+3x_2 + x_6 &= 20\\
5x_1+3x_2 - x_7 &= 20\\
3x_2+4\left(x_3'-x_3''\right) + x_8 &= 100\\
-3x_2-4\left(x_3'-x_3''\right) + x_9 &= 100\\
x_k \ge 0,\ k=1,\ 2,\ 4,\ 5,\ 6,\ 7,\ 8,\ 9,\ x_3',\ x_3'' \ge 0.
\end{aligned}$$

23. (a) $x_1=8, x_2=0, x_3=3, x_4=0, Z_{\max}=31$.
(b) $(1,2,0,0)$, $\left(\frac{22}{9},0,0,\frac{7}{9}\right)$, $\left(0,\frac{45}{16},\frac{7}{16},0\right)$, $\left(0,0,\frac{44}{17},\frac{45}{17}\right)$, $x_1^*=0, x_2^*=0, x_3^*=\frac{44}{17}, x_4^*=\frac{45}{17}, Z_{\max}=\frac{491}{17}$.

24. (i) $x_1^*=4, x_2^*=5, x_3^*=0, Z_{\min}=-11$.
(ii) $x_1^*=0, x_2^*=100, x_3^*=230, Z_{\max}=1350$.
(iii) $x_1^*=\frac{15}{2}, x_2^*=\frac{9}{4}, Z_{\max}=12; x_1^*=2, x_2^*=5, Z_{\max}=12$.
(iv) $x_1^*=\frac{1}{5}, x_2^*=0, x_3^*=\frac{8}{5}, Z_{\max}=\frac{27}{5}$.
(v) There is an unbounded solution to the given LPP.
(vi) $x_1^*=0, x_2^*=0, x_3^*=\frac{10}{3}, Z_{\max}=10$.
Alternative: $x_1^*=0, x_2^*=5, x_3^*=0, Z_{\max}=10; x_1^*=0, x_2^*=4, x_3^*=\frac{1}{3}, Z_{\max}=10$.

26. (i) $x_1^*=\frac{5}{2}, x_2^*=0, x_3^*=0, Z_{\min}=10$.
(ii) $x_1^*=3, x_2^*=2, x_3^*=0, Z_{\max}=8$.
(iii) $x_1^*=4, x_2^*=2, Z_{\max}=2$.
(iv) $x_1^*=8, x_2^*=0, Z_{\max}=48$.
Alternative solution: $x_1^*=\frac{12}{5}, x_2^*=\frac{42}{5}, Z_{\max}=48$.

28. (i) $x_1^*=x_2^*=x_3^*=\frac{5}{2}, x_4^*=0, Z_{\max}=15$.
(ii) $x_1^*=300, x_2^*=200, Z_{\min}=34000$.
(iii) $x_1^*=\frac{2}{3}, x_2^*=8, x_3^*=0, Z_{\max}=-20$.

29. $x_1^*=2, x_2^*=0, x_3^*=1, Z_{\max}=5$.

30. (i) $x_1^* = \frac{21}{13}, x_2^* = \frac{10}{13}, Z_{\max} = \frac{31}{13}$.

(ii) $x_1^* = 0, x_2^* = \frac{4}{5}, x_3^* = 0, x_4^* = \frac{1}{5}, Z_{\min} = \frac{4}{5}$.

(iii) $x_1^* = \frac{5}{4}, x_2^* = 0, x_3^* = \frac{3}{4}, Z_{\min} = \frac{75}{8}$.

(iv) $x_1^* = \frac{23}{3}, x_2^* = 5, x_3^* = 0, Z_{\max} = \frac{85}{3}$.

(v) The given problem has an unbounded solution.

(vi) The given problem has an infeasible solution.

(vii) $M_1^* = 15, M_2^* = 0, M_3^* = \frac{10}{3}, M_4^* = 0, Z_{\max} = \frac{340}{3}$.

32. (i) $x_1^* = \frac{24}{5}, x_2^* = \frac{63}{5}, Z_{\min} = \frac{222}{5}$.

(ii) $x_1^* = 2, x_2^* = 3, Z_{\max} = 19$.

Chapter 3

Duality and Dual-Simplex Method

3.1 INTRODUCTION

For every LPP there is associated another LPP in such a manner that the two problems have interesting relations with each other. The original problem is called the *primal* and the associated problem is referred to as the *dual.* The relations between two problems provide us with new tools which can be used to develop simplex-like algorithms achieve computational efficiency. It is true that, an additional constraint requires more computational effort than an additional variable. Thus, if the primal problem should have a large number of constraints and relatively few variables, its dual problem would probably require less computational labour since the numbers of variables and constraints are interchanged in the two problems.

Definition 1. *Primal problem*

$$\begin{aligned} &\text{Maximise } Z = \boldsymbol{c}^T\boldsymbol{x} \\ &\text{subject to } A\boldsymbol{x} \leq \boldsymbol{b} \\ &\qquad \boldsymbol{x} \geq \boldsymbol{0} \end{aligned} \tag{3.1a}$$

where $A = \left(a_{ij}\right)_{m\times n}$, $\boldsymbol{x} = (x_1, x_2, \ldots, x_n)^T$, $\boldsymbol{c} = (c_1, c_2, \ldots, c_n)^T$ are n-component vectors and $\boldsymbol{b} = (b_1, b_2, \ldots, b_m)^T$ is m component vector. The LPP (3.1a) is taken as the *primal problem* whose associated dual LPP is defined as *dual problem.*

Definition 2. *Dual problem*

$$\begin{aligned} &\text{Maximise } W = \boldsymbol{b}^T \boldsymbol{v} \\ &\text{subject to} A^T \boldsymbol{v} \geq \boldsymbol{c} \\ &\qquad \boldsymbol{v} \geq \boldsymbol{0} \end{aligned} \tag{3.1b}$$

where $\boldsymbol{v} = (v_1, v_2, \ldots, v_m)^T$ is m component vector called *dual variables.*

The primal problem has m constraints, whereas the dual problem has n constraints. The former has n variables called *primal variables* while the latter has m variables called *dual variables.* It is a matter of indifference whether the original problem looks like (3.1a) or (3.1b). Now as any LPP can be recast into the form (3.1a), hence, every LPP has a dual problem and, therefore, we conclude an important result: *Dual of the dual problem is the primal problem.*

3.2 PRIMAL AND DUAL PROBLEMS

In the primal problem (3.1a) we view the components of $\boldsymbol{x}$ as n products manufactured out of m resources, supplying up $b_1, b_2, \ldots, b_m$ units. With the current market prices $c_1, c_2, \ldots, c_n$ of $x_1, x_2, \ldots, x_n$, the manufacturer maximises the sales with available resources.

In the dual scenario (3.1b), the manufacturer negotiates the unit purchasing *shadow prices* also known as *Marginal prices* $v_1, v_2, \ldots, v_m$ from the m resources with the objective of minimising the total purchasing price $\boldsymbol{b}^T\boldsymbol{v}$. Since, the marketing prices $c_1, c_2, \ldots, c_n$ of the n products and the *product-resource conversion ratios* $a_{11}, a_{12}, \ldots$ are open information in a market, the manufacturer knows that a supplier would certainly charge him as much as possible, so that $A^T\boldsymbol{v} \geq \boldsymbol{c}$, that is,

$$\sum_{i=1}^{m} a_{ij} v_i \geq c_j \quad (j = 1, 2, \ldots, n).$$

Example 3.2.1. *Obtain the dual problem of the following* LPP *and verify that the dual of the dual problem is the primal problem.*

$$\begin{aligned} &\textit{Maximise } Z = x_1 - x_2 + 3x_3 \\ &\textit{subject to } x_1 + x_2 + x_3 \leq 10 \\ &\qquad 2x_1 - x_3 \leq 2 \\ &\qquad 2x_1 - 2x_2 + 3x_3 \leq 6 \\ &\qquad x_1, x_2, x_3 \geq 0. \end{aligned}$$

[CU(P) 1996; BU(H) 2001]

Solution: The primal problem is stated as

$$\begin{aligned} &\text{Maximise } Z = \boldsymbol{c}^T \boldsymbol{x} \\ &\text{subject to } A\boldsymbol{x} \leq \boldsymbol{b} \\ &\qquad \boldsymbol{x} \geq \boldsymbol{0} \end{aligned}$$

where $\boldsymbol{c} = (1, -1, 3)^T$, $\boldsymbol{b} = (10, 2, 6)^T$, $\boldsymbol{x} = (x_1, x_2, x_3)^T$, $A = \begin{pmatrix} 1 & 1 & 1 \\ 2 & 0 & -1 \\ 2 & -2 & 3 \end{pmatrix}$.

The dual of this primal is:

Minimise $W = \boldsymbol{b}^T \boldsymbol{v}$

subject to $A^T \boldsymbol{v} \geq \boldsymbol{c}$

$\boldsymbol{v} \geq \mathbf{0}.$

The dual problem is therefore

Minimise $W = 10v_1 + 2v_2 + 6v_3$

subject to
$$\begin{aligned} v_1 + 2v_2 + 2v_3 &\geq 1 \\ v_1 \qquad - 2v_3 &\geq -1 \\ v_1 - v_2 + 3v_3 &\geq 3 \\ v_1,\ v_2,\ v_3 &\geq 0. \end{aligned}$$

Now taking this as the primal problem, its dual problem is:

Maximise $\tilde{Z} = y_1 - y_2 + 3y_3$

subject to
$$\begin{aligned} y_1 + y_2 + y_3 &\leq 10 \\ 2y_1 \qquad - y_3 &\leq 2 \\ 2y_1 - 2y_2 + 3y_3 &\leq 6 \\ y_1,\ y_2,\ y_3 &\geq 0 \end{aligned}$$

which is the same as the given problem and hence it is verified that the dual of the dual is the primal.

Example 3.2.2. *Obtain the dual of the following* LPP.

Maximise $Z = x_1 + 3x_2 + 5x_3 + 4x_4 + 9x_5$

subject to
$$\begin{aligned} 3x_1 + 2x_2 + 4x_3 + x_4 + 5x_5 &= 15 \\ x_1 + 2x_2 + x_3 + 5x_4 + 5x_5 &= 13 \\ 2x_3 + 6x_4 + 3x_5 &= 6 \\ x_1,\ x_2,\ x_3,\ x_4,\ x_5 &\geq 0. \end{aligned}$$

Solution: To put the problem in a standard primal form, we first write constraints as in equations with $\leq$ types

Maximise $Z = x_1 + 3x_2 + 5x_3 + 4x_4 + 9x_5$

subject to
$$\begin{aligned} 3x_1 + 2x_2 + 4x_3 + x_4 + 5x_5 &\leq 15 \\ -3x_1 - 2x_2 - 4x_3 - x_4 - 5x_5 &\leq -15 \\ x_1 + 2x_2 + x_3 + 5x_4 + 5x_5 &\leq 13 \\ -x_1 - 2x_2 - x_3 - 5x_4 - 5x_5 &\leq -13 \\ -2x_3 - 6x_4 - 3x_5 &\leq -6 \\ x_j \geq 0,\ j &= 1,2,\ldots,5. \end{aligned}$$

Following the same procedure as Ex. 3.3.1 the dual problem is:

Minimise $W = 15v_1 - 15v_2 + 13v_3 - 13v_4 - 6v_5$

subject to
$$\begin{aligned} 3v_1 - 3v_2 + v_3 - v_4 \qquad &\geq 1 \\ 2v_1 - 2v_2 + 2v_3 - 2v_4 \qquad &\geq 3 \\ 4v_1 - 4v_2 + v_3 - v_4 - 2v_5 &\geq 5 \\ v_1 - v_2 + 5v_3 - 5v_4 - 6v_5 &\geq 4 \\ 5v_1 - 5v_2 + 5v_3 - 5v_4 - 3v_5 &\geq 9 \\ v_i \geq 0,\ i &= 1,2,\ldots,5. \end{aligned}$$

The above dual problem can be rewritten as below:

$$\begin{aligned}
&\text{Minimise } \tilde{W} = 15y_1 + 13y_2 - 6y_3 \\
&\text{subject to } 3y_1 + y_2 \geq 1 \\
&\qquad 2y_1 + 2y_2 \geq 3 \\
&\qquad 4y_1 + y_2 - 2y_3 \geq 5 \\
&\qquad y_1 + 5y_2 - 6y_3 \geq 4 \\
&\qquad 5y_1 + 5y_2 - 3y_3 \geq 9.
\end{aligned}$$

$y_1 = v_1 - v_2$, $y_2 = v_3 - v_4$ are unrestricted in sign but $y_3 = v_5 \geq 0$.

Example 3.2.3. *Obtain the dual of the following primal.*

$$\begin{aligned}
&\textit{Maximise } Z = -x_1 - x_2 - x_3 \\
&\textit{subject to } x_1 - 3x_2 + 4x_3 \leq 5 \\
&\qquad -x_1 + 3x_2 - 4x_3 \leq -5 \\
&\qquad x_1 - 2x_2 \leq 3 \\
&\qquad -2x_2 + x_3 \leq -4 \\
&\qquad x_1,\ x_2 \geq 0,\ x_3 \textit{ is unrestricted.}
\end{aligned}$$

[JU 2010; BESU(Engg) 2011]

Solution: Since x_3 is unrestricted, take $x_3 = x_4 - x_5$, where $x_4,\ x_5 \geq 0$ and rewrite the problem as below:

$$\begin{aligned}
&\text{Maximise } Z = -x_1 - x_2 - x_4 + x_5 \\
&\text{subject to } x_1 - 3x_2 + 4x_4 - 4x_5 \leq 5 \\
&\qquad -x_1 + 3x_2 - 4x_4 + 4x_5 \leq -5 \\
&\qquad x_1 - 2x_2 \leq 3 \\
&\qquad -2x_2 + x_4 - x_5 \leq -4 \\
&\qquad x_1,\ x_2,\ x_4,\ x_5 \geq 0.
\end{aligned}$$

The dual problem is given by:

$$\begin{aligned}
&\text{Minimise } W = 5v_1 - 5v_2 + 3v_3 - 4v_4 \\
&\text{subject to } v_1 - v_2 + v_3 \leq -1 \\
&\qquad -3v_1 + 3v_2 - 2v_3 - 2v_4 \leq -1 \\
&\qquad 4v_1 - 4v_2 + v_4 \leq -1 \\
&\qquad -4v_1 + 4v_2 - v_4 \leq 1 \\
&\qquad v_1,\ v_2,\ v_3,\ v_4 \geq 0.
\end{aligned}$$

The above dual is rewritten as:

$$\begin{aligned}
&\text{Maximise } \tilde{W} = 5y_1 - 3y_2 + 4y_3 \\
&\text{subject to } y_1 - y_2 \leq 1 \\
&\qquad -3y_1 + 2y_2 + 2y_3 \leq 1 \\
&\qquad 4y_1 - y_3 \leq 1 \\
&\qquad -4y_1 + y_3 \leq -1.
\end{aligned}$$

$y_1 = v_2 - v_1$ is unrestricted in sign, $v_3 = y_2 \geq 0$, $v_4 = y_3 \geq 0$.

Note that the last two constraints can be written as a single constraint: $4y_1 - y_2 = 1$.

Remark. It is observed from the above examples:

(i) If any of the constraints in the *primal problem* be a perfect equality, then the corresponding *dual variable* is unrestricted in sign.

(ii) If any variable of the *primal problem* be unrestricted in sign, then the corresponding constraint of the *dual problem* will be an equality.

3.3 SOME IMPORTANT THEOREMS OF DUALITY

Theorem 1 (Weak-duality theorem). *If $\boldsymbol{x}$ be any feasible solution to the primal problem and $\boldsymbol{v}$ be any feasible solution to the associated dual problem, then $\boldsymbol{c}^T\boldsymbol{x} \le \boldsymbol{b}^T\boldsymbol{v}$.*

Proof. Since $\boldsymbol{x}$ is the feasible solution to primal problem (3.1a), we have $A\boldsymbol{x} \le \boldsymbol{b}$ (3.4a)

$$\boldsymbol{x} \ge \boldsymbol{0}.$$

Again, $\boldsymbol{v}$ is the feasible solution to its associated dual problem (3.1b), $A^T\boldsymbol{v} \le \boldsymbol{c}$ (3.4b)

$$\boldsymbol{v} \ge \boldsymbol{0}.$$

Premultiplying (3.4a) by $\boldsymbol{v}^T$: $\boldsymbol{v}^T A\boldsymbol{x} \le \boldsymbol{v}^T\boldsymbol{b}$ (3.4c)

$$\Rightarrow \boldsymbol{v}^T A\boldsymbol{x} \ge \boldsymbol{b}^T\boldsymbol{v}.$$

Premultiplying (3.4b) by $\boldsymbol{x}^T$: $\boldsymbol{x}^T A^T\boldsymbol{v} \le \boldsymbol{x}^T\boldsymbol{c}$ (3.4d)

$$\Rightarrow \boldsymbol{v}^T A\boldsymbol{x} \ge \boldsymbol{c}^T\boldsymbol{x}.$$

From (3.4c) and (3.4d), $\boldsymbol{c}^T\boldsymbol{x} \le \boldsymbol{b}^T\boldsymbol{v}$

$$\therefore Z \le W.$$

Primal objective function $\le$ dual objective function.

Theorem 2 (Strong-duality theorem). *If $\boldsymbol{x}^*$ is a feasible solution to the primal problem and $\boldsymbol{v}^*$ is a feasible solution to its associated dual problem under condition $\boldsymbol{c}^T\boldsymbol{x}^* = \boldsymbol{b}^T\boldsymbol{v}^*$, then $\boldsymbol{x}^*$ and $\boldsymbol{v}^*$ are respectively the optimal solution of their problems.*

Proof. Given: $\boldsymbol{c}^T\boldsymbol{x}^* = \boldsymbol{b}^T\boldsymbol{v}^*$. (3.4e)

Now for any feasible solution $\boldsymbol{x}$ of primal problem (3.1a) and any feasible solution $\boldsymbol{v}^*$ of dual problem (3.1b), we have from *Theorem* 1,

$$\boldsymbol{c}^T\boldsymbol{x} \le \boldsymbol{b}^T\boldsymbol{v}^*. \tag{3.4f}$$

Using (3.4e),

$$\boldsymbol{c}^T\boldsymbol{x} \le \boldsymbol{c}^T\boldsymbol{x}^*. \tag{3.4g}$$

(3.4g) indicates that $\boldsymbol{x}^*$ is an optimal solution to the primal.

Similarly, for any feasible solution $\boldsymbol{x}^*$ of primal problem (3.1a) and any feasible solution $\boldsymbol{v}$ of dual problem (3.1b),

$$\boldsymbol{c}^T\boldsymbol{x}^* \le \boldsymbol{b}^T\boldsymbol{v}. \tag{3.4h}$$

Using (3.4e),

$$\boldsymbol{b}^T\boldsymbol{v}^* \le \boldsymbol{b}^T\boldsymbol{v}. \tag{3.4i}$$

(3.4i) shows that $\boldsymbol{v}^*$ is the optimal solution of dual.

Theorem 3. *If the primal problem has an unbounded objective function, then the dual problem has no feasible solution.*

Proof. If possible, let primal problem (3.1a) has an unbounded objective function and the corresponding dual problem (3.2b) has a finite optimal solution. But since the dual of the dual is the primal and if the primal has an optimal feasible solution, then so has its dual, the primal problem must have a finite optimal solution. But this contradicts our assumption. Hence, the dual has no finite optimal solution, if the primal be unbounded.

Theorem 4. *If the dual problem has no feasible solution and the primal problem has a feasible solution, then the primal objective function is unbounded.*

Proof. Suppose that the dual problem does not admit of any feasible solution but the primal problem does. Now any feasible solution $\hat{\boldsymbol{x}}$ to the primal will make the objective function equal to $\boldsymbol{c}^T\hat{\boldsymbol{x}}$. This $\hat{\boldsymbol{x}}$ cannot be the optimal solution to the primal; because, if it were then, by the *strong-duality theorem*, a feasible solution to the dual problem would have to exist. But this contradicts our assumption. Thus, the primal can have no optimal solution. So the primal will have the objective function unbounded as no feasible solution to the primal can be optimal.

Theorem 5. *For any pair of optimal solutions to a primal and its associated dual problems:*

(i) *For each $j = 1,2,\ldots,n$, the product of the jth primal variable and jth dual surplus variable is zero.*

(ii) *For each $i = 1,2,\ldots,m$, the product of the ith dual variable and ith primal slack variable is also zero.*

Proof. If we add slack variables to the primal problem (3.1a) the equivalent form of the primal problem is:

Maximise $Z = \boldsymbol{c}^T\boldsymbol{x}$

subject to $A\boldsymbol{x} + \boldsymbol{x}_s = \boldsymbol{b}$ (3.4j)

$\boldsymbol{x}, \boldsymbol{x}_s \geq \boldsymbol{0}.$

Similarly, equivalent form of dual problem by introducing surplus variables is:

Minimise $W = \boldsymbol{b}^T\boldsymbol{v}$

subject to $A^T\boldsymbol{v} - \boldsymbol{v}_s = \boldsymbol{c}$ (3.4k)

$\boldsymbol{v}, \boldsymbol{v}_s \geq \boldsymbol{0}.$

Premultiplying (3.4j) by $\boldsymbol{v}^T$: $\boldsymbol{v}^T A\boldsymbol{x} + \boldsymbol{v}^T\boldsymbol{x}_s = \boldsymbol{v}^T\boldsymbol{b}$

$$\Rightarrow \boldsymbol{x}^T A^T\boldsymbol{v} + \boldsymbol{x}_s^T\boldsymbol{v} = \boldsymbol{b}^T\boldsymbol{v}. \tag{3.4l}$$

Premultiplying (3.4k) by $\boldsymbol{x}^T$: $\boldsymbol{x}^T A^T\boldsymbol{v} - \boldsymbol{x}^T\boldsymbol{v}_s = \boldsymbol{x}^T\boldsymbol{c}$

$$\Rightarrow \boldsymbol{x}^T A^T\boldsymbol{v} - \boldsymbol{x}^T\boldsymbol{v}_s = \boldsymbol{c}^T\boldsymbol{x}. \tag{3.4m}$$

Eqs (3.4l) and (3.4m) are valid for any feasible solutions $(\boldsymbol{x}, \boldsymbol{x}_s)$ and $(\boldsymbol{v}, \boldsymbol{v}_s)$. Let us assume that problems (3.4j) and (3.4k) are the primal and associated dual problems and they have the optimal solutions $(\boldsymbol{x}^*, \boldsymbol{x}_s^*)$, $(\boldsymbol{v}^*, \boldsymbol{v}_s^*)$ respectively.

Recalling that the cost coefficients corresponding to slack and surplus variables are zero and for the optimal solution,

$$\boldsymbol{c}^T\boldsymbol{x}^* = \boldsymbol{b}^T\boldsymbol{v}^*. \tag{3.4n}$$

We have from (3.4l) and (3.4m),

$$\boldsymbol{x}^{*T} A^T\boldsymbol{v}^* + \boldsymbol{x}_s^{*T}\boldsymbol{v}^* = \boldsymbol{b}^T\boldsymbol{v}^* \tag{3.4o}$$

$$\boldsymbol{x}^{*T} A^T\boldsymbol{v}^* - \boldsymbol{x}^{*T}\boldsymbol{v}_s^* = \boldsymbol{c}^T\boldsymbol{x}^*. \tag{3.4p}$$

(3.4o)–(3.4p) and using (3.4n),

$$x_s^{*T} v^* + x^{*T} v_s^* = 0. \tag{3.4q}$$

Since $x, v, x_s, v_s \geq 0$, we get from (3.4q),

$$\begin{aligned} v_i x_{si} &= 0 \ \forall \ i = 1,2,\ldots,m \\ x_j v_{sj} &= 0 \ \forall \ j = 1,2,\ldots,n \end{aligned} \tag{3.4r}$$

which will prove the required theorem. The results (3.4q) and (3.4r) are known as *Complementary Slackness Conditions.*

Theorem 6. *If* $(\hat{x}, \hat{x}_s)$, $(\hat{v}, \hat{v}_s)$ *are the feasible solutions to the primal and associated dual problems under conditions where complementary slackness holds, then* $(\hat{x}, \hat{x}_s)$, $(\hat{v}, \hat{v}_s)$ *are also the optimal solutions to their respective problems.*

Proof. Since complementary slackness holds: $\hat{v}^T \hat{x}_s + \hat{x}^T \hat{v}_s = 0$

$$\Rightarrow \hat{v}^T \hat{x}_s = -\hat{x}^T \hat{v}_s.$$

Adding both sides $\hat{v}^T A\hat{x}$: $\hat{v}^T A\hat{x} + \hat{v}^T \hat{x}_s = \hat{v}^T A\hat{x} - \hat{x}^T \hat{v}_s$

$$\begin{aligned} &\Rightarrow \hat{v}^T (A\hat{x} + \hat{x}_s) = \hat{x}^T (A^T \hat{v} - \hat{v}_s) \\ &\Rightarrow \hat{v}^T b = \hat{x}^T c \ [\because A\hat{x} + \hat{x}_s = b, A^T \hat{v} - \hat{v}_s = c] \\ &\Rightarrow b^T \hat{v} = c^T \hat{x}. \end{aligned} \tag{3.4s}$$

In view of *Theorem* 2, the eq. (3.4s) shows that $(\hat{x}, \hat{x}_s)$ and $(\hat{v}, \hat{v}_s)$ are optimal solutions of primal and dual problems respectively.

Remark. If the primal problem does not admit of any feasible solution, but the dual problem does, then there will exist no finite optimal to the dual problem.

3.4 PRIMAL-DUAL METHOD

The optimal solution to the dual problem (Primal problem) is obtained by reading off the optimal table of the Primal problem (Dual problem) with the use of the following useful rules.

Suppose that an optimal solution to the dual (Primal) problem has been obtained by the application of either *Simplex method* or *Big-M method* or *Two-phase method.*

Rule 1. If the primal (dual) variables be related to a slack and/or surplus variables in the dual (primal) problem, then its optimal solution is directly read off from the net evaluation row of the optimal dual (primal) simplex table as the net evaluation corresponding to this slack and/or (surplus) variables.

Rule 2. If the primal (dual) variable be related to an artificial variable in the dual (primal) problem, then its optimal solution is directly read off from the net evaluation row of the optimal dual (primal) simplex table from the net evaluation relating to artificial variable after putting the penalty cost M equal to zero and accordingly change the sign.

Rule 3. If either of primal (dual) problem has *unbounded solution,* then other will have *no feasible solution.*

Example 3.4.1. *From the optimal table of the following primal problem, find the optimal solution to the associated dual problem.*

Maximise $Z = 30x_1 + 23x_2 + 29x_3$

subject to $6x_1 + 5x_2 + 3x_3 \leq 26$

$4x_1 + 2x_2 + 5x_3 \leq 7$

$x_1, x_2, x_3 \geq 0.$

Solution: *Standard form of primal:*

Maximise $Z = 30x_1 + 23x_2 + 29x_3 + 0x_{s_1} + 0x_{s_2}$

subject to $6x_1 + 5x_2 + 3x_3 + x_{s_1} = 26$

$4x_1 + 2x_2 + 5x_3 + x_{s_2} = 7$

$x_1, x_2 \geq 0, x_{s_1}, x_{s_2} \geq 0$, slack variables.

(T 1)

	c_j		30	23	29	0	0	
c_B	x_B	b	y_1	y_2	y_3	y_{s_1}	y_{s_2}	MR
0	y_{s_1}	26	6	5	3	1	0	$\frac{26}{6}$
0	y_{s_2}	7	$(4)^*$	2	5	0	1	$\frac{7}{4}$ →
	$z_j - c_j$		$-30\uparrow$	-23	-29	0	0	

(T 2)

	c_j		30	23	29	0	0	
c_B	x_B	b	y_1	y_2	y_3	y_{s_1}	y_{s_2}	MR
0	y_{s_1}	$\frac{31}{2}$	0	2	$-\frac{9}{2}$	1	$-\frac{3}{2}$	$\frac{31}{4}$
30	y_1	$\frac{7}{4}$	1	$\left(\frac{1}{2}\right)^*$	$\frac{5}{4}$	0	$\frac{1}{4}$	$\frac{1}{4}$ →
	$z_j - c_j$		0	$-8\uparrow$	$\frac{17}{2}$	0	$\frac{15}{2}$	

(T 3)

	c_j		30	23	29	0	0
c_B	x_B	b	y_1	y_2	y_3	y_{s_1}	y_{s_2}
0	y_{s_1}	$\frac{17}{2}$	-4	0	$-\frac{19}{2}$	1	$-\frac{5}{2}$
23	y_2	$\frac{7}{2}$	2	1	$\frac{5}{2}$	0	$\frac{1}{2}$
	$z_j - c_j$		16	0	$\frac{57}{2}$	0	$\frac{23}{2}$

(i) Since all $z_j - c_j \geq 0 \;\forall\; j$, an optimal solution of the primal problem has been reached and is given by

$$x_1^* = 0,\; x_2^* = \tfrac{7}{2},\; Z_{\max} = \tfrac{161}{2}.$$

(ii) To read the solution of the associated dual problem from optimal table (T 3) of primal problem we apply *Rule* 1 and observe that the net evaluation row $\left(z_j - c_j\right)$ of optimal table corresponding to slack variables y_{s_1} and y_{s_2} are 0 and $\frac{23}{2}$ respectively.

Hence, the optimal solution of the associated dual problem will be

$$v_1^* = 0,\; v_2^* = \tfrac{23}{2},\; W_{\min} = 26 \times 0 + 7 \times \tfrac{23}{2} = \tfrac{161}{2}.$$

Example 3.4.2. *Solve the dual of the following primal problem and from the optimal table of dual problem obtain the optimal solution of primal problem.*

Maximise $f(x_1, x_2) = 2x_1 + 3x_2$

subject to $-x_1 + 2x_2 \leq 4$

$x_1 + x_2 \leq 6$

$x_1 + 3x_2 \leq 9$

$x_1, x_2 \leq 0.$

Solution: Associated dual problem:

Minimise $W(v_1, v_2, v_3) = 4v_1 + 6v_2 + 9v_3$

subject to $-v_1 + v_2 + v_3 \geq 2$

$2v_1 + v_2 + 3v_3 \geq 3$

$v_1, v_2, v_3 \geq 0.$

Standard form of dual problem:

Maximise $W^*(v_1, v_2, v_3) = -4v_1 - 6v_2 - 9v_3 - Mv_{a1} - Mv_{a2}$

subject to $-v_1 + v_2 + v_3 - v_{s_1} + v_{a1} = 2$

$2v_1 + v_2 + 3v_3 - v_{s_2} + v_{a2} = 3$

$v_1, v_2, v_3 \geq 0,\ v_{s_1}, v_{s_2} \geq 0$ surplus variables

$v_{a1}, v_{a2} \geq 0$ artificial variables.

(T 1)

		c_j	-4	-6	-9	0	0	$-M$	$-M$	
c_B	v_B	b	y_1	y_2	y_3	y_{s_1}	y_{s_2}	y_{a_1}	y_{a_2}	MR
$-M$	y_{a_1}	2	-1	1	1	-1	0	1	0	$\frac{2}{1}$
$-M$	y_{a_2}	3	2	1	$\boxed{3}^*$	0	-1	0	1	$\frac{2}{3} \rightarrow$
		$z_j - c_j$	$-M+4$	$-2M+6$	$-4M+9\uparrow$	M	M	0	0	

(T 2)

		c_j	-4	-6	-9	0	0	$-M$	$-M$	
c_B	v_B	b	y_1	y_2	y_3	y_{s_1}	y_{s_2}	y_{a_1}	y_{a_2}	MR
$-M$	y_{a_1}	1	$-\frac{5}{2}$	$\boxed{\frac{2}{3}}$	0	-1	$\frac{1}{3}$	1	$-\frac{1}{3}$	$\frac{3}{2} \rightarrow$
-9	y_3	1	$\frac{2}{3}$	$\frac{1}{3}$	1	0	$-\frac{1}{3}$	0	$\frac{1}{3}$	3
		$z_j - c_j$	$\frac{5}{3}M - 2$	$-\frac{2}{3}M + 3\uparrow$	0	M	$-\frac{1}{3}M + 3$	0	$\frac{4}{3}M - 3$	

(T 3)

		c_j	-4	-6	-9	0	0	$-M$	$-M$
c_B	v_B	b	y_1	y_2	y_3	y_{s_1}	y_{s_2}	y_{a_1}	y_{a_2}
-6	y_2	$\frac{3}{2}$	$-\frac{5}{2}$	1	0	$-\frac{3}{2}$	$\frac{1}{2}$	$\frac{3}{2}$	$-\frac{1}{2}$
-9	y_3	$\frac{1}{2}$	$\frac{3}{2}$	0	1	$\frac{1}{2}$	$-\frac{1}{2}$	$-\frac{1}{2}$	$\frac{1}{2}$
		$z_j - c_j$	$\frac{11}{2}$	0	0	$\frac{9}{2}$	$\frac{3}{2}$	$M - \frac{9}{2}$	$M - \frac{3}{2}$

(i) Optimal solution of the dual problem:

$$v_1^* = 0,\ v_2^* = \frac{3}{2},\ v_3^* = \frac{1}{2},\ W_{\min} = \frac{27}{2}.$$

(ii) Using *Rule* 2 optimal solution of primal problem is obtained from the row of $z_j - c_j$ in the optimal table (T 3) of dual after putting the penalty cost $M = 0$ and changing the sign of artificial variables y_{a_1} and y_{a_2}.

$\therefore$ optimal solution of primal problem:

$$x_1^* = \tfrac{9}{2},\ x_2^* = \tfrac{3}{2},\ f_{\max} = \tfrac{27}{2}.$$

Example 3.4.3. *Solve the* LPP.

Maximise $Z = x_1 - 2x_2$

subject to $x_1 + 2x_2 \geq 1$

$-x_1 + x_2 \leq 1$

$x_1, x_2 \geq 0.$

Show that it has unbounded solution. What can you say about the nature of the solution of its dual?

Solution: *Standard form* of LPP.

Maximise $Z = x_1 - 2x_2 + 0x_3 + 0x_4 - Mx_{a_1}$

subject to $x_1 + 2x_2 - x_3 \qquad + x_{a_1} = 1$

$-x_1 + x_2 \qquad + x_4 \qquad = 1$

$x_1, x_2 \geq 0,\ x_3 \geq 0,$ surplus variable

$x_4 \geq 0,$ slack variable

$x_{a_1} \geq 0,$ artificial variable.

(T 1)

		c_j	1	-2	0	0	$-M$	
c_B	x_B	b	y_1	y_2	y_3	y_4	y_{a_1}	MR
$-M$	y_{a_1}	1	1	⓶	-1	0	1	$\frac{1}{2}$ →
0	y_4	1	-1	1	0	1	0	1
		$z_j - c_j$	$-M-1$	$-2M+2$↑	M	0	0	

(T 2)

		c_j	1	-2	0	0	$-M$	
c_B	x_B	b	y_1	y_2	y_3	y_4	y_{a_1}	MR
-2	y_2	$\frac{1}{2}$	($\frac{1}{2}$)	1	$-\frac{1}{2}$	0	$\frac{1}{2}$	1 →
0	y_4	$\frac{1}{2}$	$-\frac{3}{2}$	0	$\frac{1}{2}$	1	$-\frac{1}{2}$	X
		$z_j - c_j$	-2↑	0	1	0	$M-1$	

(T 3)

		c_j	1	-2	0	0	$-M$
c_B	x_B	b	y_1	y_2	y_3	y_4	y_{a_1}
1	y_1	1	1	2	-1	0	1
0	y_4	2	0	3	-1	1	-2
		$z_j - c_j$	0	4	-1↑	0	$M+1$

Thus, we see that in the final table (T 3) $(z_3 - c_3)$ is most negative, being (-1). Hence, y_3 will enter the basis. But $y_{13} < 0$, $y_{23} < 0$. Hence, the given problem has unbounded solution. Therefore, we arrive at the conclusion by *Rule* 3 that the dual problem will have no feasible solution.

Example 3.4.4. *A company makes three products X, Y and Z out of three raw materials A, B and C. The number of units of raw materials required to produce one unit of the product is as given in the following table:*

	X	*Y*	*Z*
A	1	2	1
B	2	1	4
C	2	5	1

The unit profit contribution of the products X, Y and Z are ₹ 40, ₹ 25 and ₹ 50 respectively. The number of units of raw materials available are 36, 60 and 45 respectively.

(i) *Determine the product-mix that will maximise the total profit.*

(ii) *From the optimal simplex table, write the optimal solution to its associated dual problem. Also give the economic interpretation.* [IAS(Main) 1988]

Solution: (i) Let the company produce x_1, x_2 and x_3 units of products X, Y and Z respectively. Then the mathematical formulation of the problem is:

Maximise $P = 40x_1 + 25x_2 + 50x_3$

$$\text{subject to } \begin{aligned} x_1 + 2x_2 + x_3 &\le 36 \\ 2x_1 + x_2 + 4x_3 &\le 60 \\ 2x_1 + 5x_2 + x_3 &\le 45 \\ x_1, x_2, x_3 &\ge 0. \end{aligned}$$

Standard form.

Maximise $P = 40x_1 + 25x_2 + 50x_3 + 0x_{s_1} + 0x_{s_2} + 0x_{s_3}$

$$\text{subject to } \begin{aligned} x_1 + 2x_2 + x_3 + x_{s_1} &= 36 \\ 2x_1 + x_2 + 4x_3 + x_{s_2} &= 60 \\ 2x_1 + 5x_2 + x_3 + x_{s_3} &= 45 \end{aligned}$$

$x_1, x_2, x_3 \ge 0$, $x_{s_1}, x_{s_2}, x_{s_3} \ge 0$, slack variables.

(T 1)

		c_j	40	25	50	0	0	0	
c_B	x_B	b	y_1	y_2	y_3	y_{s_1}	y_{s_2}	y_{s_3}	MR
0	y_{s_1}	36	1	2	1	1	0	0	$\frac{36}{1}$
0	y_{s_2}	60	2	1	(4)	0	1	0	$\frac{60}{4}$ →
0	y_{s_3}	45	2	5	1	0	0	1	$\frac{45}{1}$
		$z_j - c_j$	−40	−25	−50↑	0	0	0	

(T 2)

		c_j	40	25	50	0	0	0	
c_B	x_B	b	y_1	y_2	y_3	y_{s_1}	y_{s_2}	y_{s_3}	MR
0	y_{s_1}	21	$\frac{1}{2}$	$\frac{7}{4}$	0	1	$-\frac{1}{4}$	0	42
50	y_3	15	$\frac{1}{2}$	$\frac{1}{4}$	1	0	$\frac{1}{4}$	0	30
0	y_{s_3}	30	$\boxed{\frac{3}{2}}$	$\frac{19}{4}$	0	0	$-\frac{1}{4}$	1	20 →
	$z_j - c_j$		$-15\uparrow$	$-\frac{25}{2}$	0	0	$\frac{25}{2}$	0	

(T 3)

		c_j	40	25	50	0	0	0
c_B	x_B	b	y_1	y_2	y_3	y_{s_1}	y_{s_2}	y_{s_3}
0	y_{s_1}	11	0	$\frac{1}{6}$	0	1	$-\frac{1}{6}$	$-\frac{1}{3}$
50	y_3	5	0	$-\frac{4}{3}$	1	0	$\frac{1}{3}$	$-\frac{1}{3}$
40	y_1	20	1	$\frac{19}{6}$	0	0	$-\frac{1}{6}$	$\frac{2}{3}$
		$z_j - c_j$	0	35	0	0	10	10

(i) Optimal solution to the given primal problem:

$$x_1^* = 20,\ x_2^* = 0,\ x_3^* = 5,\ P_{\text{max}} = ₹1050.$$

(ii) From the optimal table (T 3) of the primal problem the optimal solution of associated dual problem is

$$v_1^* = 0,\ v_2^* = 10,\ v_3^* = 10,\ C_{\text{min}} = ₹1050.$$

Economic Interpretation

Suppose, the company wants to sell the three raw materials A, B and C instead of using them for making products X, Y and Z and thereby selling the products earns a profit of ₹ 1050. Let the selling price were ₹ v_1, ₹ v_2 and ₹ v_3 per unit of raw materials A, B and C respectively. Then the cost to the purchaser of all the three raw materials will be ₹ $(36v_1 + 60v_2 + 45v_3)$. Of course, the purchaser will like to set the selling prices of A, B and C so that the total cost is minimum. So the objective function will be to minimise $36v_1 + 60v_2 + 45v_3$.

Table (T 3) indicates that the marginal values of raw materials A, B and C are ₹ 0, ₹ 10 and ₹ 10 per unit respectively, the company will get the same contribution of ₹ 1050 which the company is going to get if the company uses these resources for producing products X, Y and Z and then sells them.

3.5 DUAL-SIMPLEX METHOD

We already showed that at any primal iteration $(z_j - c_j)$, the objective equation coefficient of x_j equals the difference between the left and right sides of the associated dual constraint. In the case of maximisation, the primal iteration is not optimal, $z_j - c_j < 0$ for at least one variable. Only at the optimum we have $z_j - c_j \geq 0$ for all j.

Looking at this condition from duality stand point, we have

$$z_j - c_j = \sum_{i=1}^{m} a_{ij} y_i - c_j.$$

Thus, when $z_j - c_j < 0$,

$$\sum_{i=1}^{m} a_{ij} y_i < c_j$$

which means that the dual is infeasible when the primal is non-optimal. On the other hand, when $z_j - c_j \geq 0$,

$$\sum_{i=1}^{m} a_{ij} y_i \geq c_j$$

which means that the dual becomes feasible when the primal reaches optimality.

The above method suggests a new solution method for linear programs, which starts infeasibility but optimal. The new method, called the *dual-simplex,* will then maintain optimality and the successive iteration will work to clear the infeasibility. When feasibility is reached, the process terminates since the solution is both feasible and optimal. This type of problem is encountered in certain LP models; but more importantly, it is used directly in carrying out post-optimality of LP models, as we shall show in the subsequent chapter. The method is equally applicable in integer programming, parametric programming as well as some non-LPP.

3.5.1 Mathematical Illustration

Consider the primal and its associated dual problem as defined by (3.1a) and (3.1b) respectively. Suppose, for primal problem the current basis matrix is B and a basic solution is $\boldsymbol{x_B} = B^{-1}\boldsymbol{b}$ with all $z_j - c_j \geq 0$ but one or more basic variables $x_{Br} < 0$.

As our ultimate aim is to obtain a non-negative basic solution, we wish to select one of the negative x_{Br} to be driven to zero and consequently be removed from the basis.

The transformation formula giving the new value of z, when one basic variable is removed and a non-basic variable is introduced in place of it as

$$\hat{z} = z - \frac{x_{Br}}{y_{rk}}(z_k - c_k), \tag{3.6a}$$

where non-basic x_k replaces x_{Br}. In order to maintain $\hat{z} - z \geq 0$, we must choose an entering variable x_k, only if $y_{rk} < 0$ which in fact makes $\hat{z} - z \geq 0$, since $z_k - c_k \geq 0$.

Let $x_{Br} < 0$ for some r. Then we select that x_{Br} to leave from the basis corresponding to the most negative one. In order to select the entering variable we recall the standard simplex method in which the transformation formula for net evaluation is

$$\hat{z}_j - \hat{c}_j = \left(z_j - c_j\right) - \frac{y_{rj}}{y_{rk}}(z_k - c_k). \tag{3.6b}$$

Since we require $y_{rk} < 0$ and as $z_k - c_k \geq 0$, therefore, for any non-basic variable x_k for which $y_{rj} < 0$, we can ensure $\hat{z}_j - \hat{c}_j \geq 0$.

From (3.6b),

$$z_j - c_j \geq \frac{y_{rj}}{y_{rk}}(z_k - c_k) \Rightarrow \frac{z_j - c_j}{y_{rj}} \leq \frac{z_k - c_k}{y_{rk}} : y_{rj} < 0.$$

Hence, if x_{Br} is selected to leave the basis, then the variable x_k enters the basis, if

$$\frac{z_k - c_k}{y_{rk}} = \theta_k = \max_j \left\{ \frac{z_j - c_j}{y_{rj}} : y_{rj} < 0 \right\} \tag{3.6c}$$

when no such $y_{rj} < 0$, then there exists no feasible solution.

Thus, *dual-simplex method* is very similar to the standard simplex method. Dual-simplex method works towards feasibility, by maintaining optimality of problem while simplex method moves towards optimality by maintaining the feasibility condition.

3.5.2 Dual-Simplex Algorithm

The followings are the computational procedures to be followed in *dual-simplex method.*

Step 1. Convert the minimisation LPP into maximisation LPP if the original problem is given in minimisation form. Next convert '$\geq$' type of inequalities representing the constraints of the problem, if any, into those of '$\leq$' type of inequalities.

Step 2. Introduce slack variables in the constraints of the problem and obtain an initial basic feasible solution. Put this solution in the starting *dual-simplex table.*

Step 3. Test the nature of $(z_j - c_j)$ for all j in the starting table:

(i) If all $(z_j - c_j)$ and x_{B_i} are non-negative for all i and j, then an optimality of the solution has been reached.

(ii) If $z_j - c_j \geq 0$ for all j and at least one $x_{B_i} < 0$ for some i, then GO TO *Step* 4.

(iii) If at least one $z_j - c_j < 0$ for some j and at the same time at least one $x_{B_i} < 0$ for some i, then this method is not applicable for that particular problem.

Step 4. Select the most negative x_{B_i} (if more than one $x_{B_i} < 0$); let for some $i = k$, x_{B_k} is most negative, then the corresponding basic variable $\mathbf{y_k}$ leaves the basis.

Step 5. Now test the nature of y_{kj}, $j = 1, 2, \ldots, n$.

(i) If all $y_{kj} \geq 0$, then there exists no feasible solution to the problem.

(ii) If at least one $y_{kj} < 0$ for some j, compute the *replacement ratio*

$$\theta_j = \left\{ \frac{z_j - c_j}{y_{kj}} : y_{kj} < 0 \right\}, \quad j = 1, 2, \ldots, n$$

and select the maximum of these ratios. Suppose, for some particular $j = r$,

$$\frac{z_r - c_r}{y_{kr}} = \theta_r = \max \left\{ \frac{z_j - c_j}{y_{kj}} \middle| y_{kj} < 0 \right\}.$$

Then the non-basic variable $\mathbf{y_r}$ enters the basis which replaces the position of leaving basic variable $\mathbf{y_k}$.

Step 6. Check the new iterated dual-simplex table for optimality. Repeat the procedure until an optimal solution has been reached or there is any indication of the non-existence of the feasible solution of the given problem.

3.6 PROBLEMS

Example 3.6.1. *Use dual-simplex method to solve the* LPP.

Maximise $Z = -x_1 - 2x_2$

subject to $2x_1 + x_2 \geq 4$

$x_1 + 7x_2 \geq 7$

$x_1, x_2 \geq 0.$

Solution: Standard form for starting dual-simplex iteration.

Maximise $Z = -x_1 - 2x_2 + 0x_3 + 0x_4$

subject to $-2x_1 - x_2 + x_3 = -4$

$-x_1 - 7x_2 + x_4 = -7$

$x_1, x_2 \geq 0,\ x_3, x_4 \geq 0$, slack variables.

(T 1)

		c_j	-1	-2	0	0	
c_B	x_B	b	y_1	y_2	y_3	y_4	
0	y_3	-4	-2	-1	1	0	
0	y_4	-7	-1	(-7)	0	1	$\rightarrow$
		$z_j - c_j$	1	$2\uparrow$	0	0	

All $z_j - c_j \geq 0$, $x_{B_k} = \min\{-4, -7\} = -7$, y_4 leaves the basis

$$\theta_r = \max\left\{\frac{z_j - c_j}{y_{kj}}\bigg| y_{kj} < 0\right\} = \max\left\{\frac{1}{-1}, \frac{2}{-7}\right\}$$

$= -\frac{2}{7}$, y_2 enters the basis.

(T 2)

		c_j	-1	-2	0	0	
c_B	x_B	b	y_1	y_2	y_3	y_4	
0	y_3	-3	$\left(-\frac{13}{7}\right)$	0	1	$-\frac{1}{7}$	$\rightarrow$
-2	y_2	1	$\frac{1}{7}$	1	0	$-\frac{1}{7}$	
		$z_j - c_j$	$\frac{5}{7}\uparrow$	0	0	$\frac{2}{7}$	

All $z_j - c_j \geq 0$, only negative x_{B_k} is -3, y_3 leaves the basis

$$\theta_r = \max\left\{\frac{5/7}{-13/7}, \frac{2/7}{-1/7}\right\} = \max\left\{-\frac{5}{13}, -2\right\}$$

$= -\frac{5}{13}$, y_1 enters the basis.

(T 3)

		c_j	-1	-2	0	0
c_B	x_B	b	y_1	y_2	y_3	y_4
-1	y_1	$\frac{21}{13}$	1	0	$-\frac{7}{13}$	$\frac{1}{13}$
-2	y_2	$\frac{10}{13}$	0	1	$\frac{1}{13}$	$-\frac{14}{91}$
		$z_j - c_j$	0	0	$\frac{5}{3}$	$\frac{3}{13}$

All $z_j - c_j \geq 0$ and $x_{B_i} \geq 0$. An optimal solution has been reached and is given by

$$\left\langle x_1^* = \tfrac{21}{13},\ x_2^* = \tfrac{10}{13},\ Z_{\max} = -\tfrac{41}{13}\right\rangle$$

Example 3.6.2. *Use dual-simplex method to solve the* LPP.

Minimise $Z = 3x_1 + 6x_2 + x_3$

subject to $x_1 + x_2 + x_3 \geq 6$

$x_1 - 5x_2 - x_3 \geq 4$

$x_1 + 5x_2 + x_3 \geq 24$

$x_1, x_2, x_3 \geq 0.$

Solution: *Standard form for starting dual-simplex iteration:*

Maximise $\hat{Z} = -3x_1 - 6x_2 - x_3 + 0x_4 + 0x_5 + 0x_6$

subject to $-x_1 - x_2 - x_3 + x_4 = -6$

$-x_1 + 5x_2 + x_3 + x_5 = -4$

$-x_1 - 5x_2 - x_3 + x_6 = -24$

$x_1, x_2, x_3 \geq 0,\ x_4, x_5, x_6 \geq 0$ are slack variables.

(T 1)

		c_j	−3	−6	−1	0	0	0	
c_B	x_b	b	y_1	y_2	y_3	y_4	y_5	y_6	
0	y_4	−6	−1	−1	−1	1	0	0	
0	y_5	−4	−1	5	1	0	1	0	
0	y_6	−24	−1	−5	[−1]	0	0	1	→
		$z_j - c_j$	3	6	1↑	0	0	0	

All $z_j - c_j \geq 0$, $x_{B_k} = \min\{-6, -4, -24\} = -24$, y_6 leaves the basis.

$$\theta_r = \max\left\{\frac{3}{-1}, \frac{6}{-5}, \frac{1}{-1}\right\} = 1,\ y_3 \text{ enters the basis.}$$

(T 2)

		c_j	−3	−6	−1	0	0	0	
c_B	x_b	b	y_1	y_2	y_3	y_4	y_5	y_6	
0	x_4	18	0	4	0	1	0	−1	
0	y_5	−28	[−2]	0	0	0	1	1	→
−1	y_3	24	1	5	1	0	0	−1	
		$z_j - c_j$	2↑	1	0	0	0	1	

All $z_j - c_j \geq 0$. (T 2) indicates clearly y_5 leaves the basis and y_1 replaces it.

(T 3)

		c_j	−3	−6	−1	0	0	0
c_B	x_b	b	y_1	y_2	y_3	y_4	y_5	y_6
0	y_4	18	0	4	0	1	0	−1
−3	y_1	14	1	0	0	0	$-\frac{1}{2}$	$-\frac{1}{2}$
−1	y_3	10	0	5	1	0	$\frac{1}{2}$	$-\frac{1}{2}$
		$z_j - c_j$	0	1	0	0	1	2

All $z_j - c_j \geq 0$ and $x_{B_i} \geq 0$. An optimal feasible solution has been reached and is given by

$$\langle x_1^* = 14,\ x_2^* = 0,\ x_3^* = 10,\ Z_{\min} = 52 \rangle$$

3.7 EXERCISE 3

1. Write down the *dual* of the following LPP.

(a) Maximise $Z = 6x_1 - 3x_2$
subject to
$$3x_1 + 2x_2 \leq 25$$
$$x_1 + 2x_2 \leq 16$$
$$x_1 \geq 4$$
$$x_2 \geq 3$$
$$x_1, x_2 \geq 0.$$
[KU(H) 1999]

(b) Maximise $Z = x_1 + x_2 + x_3$
subject to
$$x_1 - 3x_2 + 4x_3 = 5$$
$$x_1 - 2x_2 \leq 3$$
$$2x_2 - x_3 \geq 4$$
$x_1, x_2 \geq 0$, x_3 is unrestricted in sign.
[CU(H) 1988]

(c) Minimise $W = 7v_1 + 4v_2$
subject to
$$v_1 + v_2 \geq 2$$
$$4v_1 - 3v_2 \geq 3$$
$$2v_1 + v_2 \geq -1$$
$v_1 \geq 0$, v_2 unrestricted.
[KU(H) 2008]

(d) Minimise $Z = 6x_1 + 3x_2$
subject to
$$6x_1 - 3x_2 + x_3 \geq 2$$
$$3x_1 + 4x_2 + x_3 \geq 5$$
$$x_1, x_2, x_3 \geq 0.$$

(e) Maximise $Z = x_1 + x_2$
subject to
$$2x_1 + x_2 = 5$$
$$3x_1 - x_2 = 6$$
x_1, x_2 unrestricted.

(f) Maximise $Z = 7x_1 + 3x_2 + 8x_3$
subject to
$$8x_1 + 2x_2 + x_3 \geq 3$$
$$3x_1 + 6x_2 + 4x_3 \geq 4$$
$$4x_1 + x_2 + 5x_3 \geq 1$$
$$x_1 + 5x_2 + 2x_3 \geq 7$$
$$x_1, x_2, x_3 \geq 0.$$
[DU(H) 1974, CU(P) 2005]

(g) Maximise $Z = x_1 + 4x_2 + 3x_3$
subject to
$$2x_1 + 3x_2 - 5x_3 \leq 2$$
$$3x_1 - x_2 + 6x_3 \geq 1$$
$$x_1 + x_2 + x_3 = 4$$
$x_1, x_2 \geq 0$,
x_3 unrestricted.

(h) Maximise $Z = x_1 - x_2 + 3x_3 + 2x_4$
subject to
$$x_1 + x_2 \geq 1$$
$$x_1 - 3x_2 - x_3 \leq 7$$
$$x_1 + x_3 - 3x_4 = -2$$
$x_1, x_2 \geq 0$,
x_2, x_3 are unrestricted in sign. [CU(H) 1982]

(i) Maximise $Z = 20x_1 + 40x_2$
subject to
$$2x_1 + 20x_2 \geq 40$$
$$20x_1 + 3x_2 \geq 20$$
$$4x_1 + 15x_2 \geq 30$$
$$x_1, x_2 \geq 0.$$

2. Solve the following problem by considering its dual.

Minimise $Z = 5x_1 + 6x_2 + 3x_3$

subject to
$$\begin{aligned} 5x_1 + 5x_2 + 3x_3 &\geq 50 \\ x_1 - x_2 + x_3 &\geq 20 \\ 7x_1 + 6x_2 - 9x_3 &\geq 30 \\ 5x_1 + 5x_2 + 5x_3 &\geq 35 \\ 2x_1 + 4x_2 - 15x_3 &\geq 10 \\ 12x_1 + 10x_2 &\geq 90 \\ x_2 - 10x_3 &\geq 20 \\ x_1, x_2, x_3 &\geq 0. \end{aligned}$$

Compare the number of constraints in the two problems.

3. (a) Given that an LPP has an unbounded solution, why is it that its dual must necessarily be infeasible?

(b) Consider the problem: Maximise $Z = 8x_1 + 6x_2$

subject to
$$\begin{aligned} x_1 - x_2 &\leq \tfrac{3}{5} \\ x_1 - x_2 &\geq 2 \\ x_1, x_2 &\geq 0. \end{aligned}$$

Show that both the primal and the dual problems have no feasible space.

(c) Show that the solution of the following LPP is unbounded by showing that the dual is infeasible and the primal is feasible.

Minimise $W = w_1 - 5w_2 + 6w_3$

subject to
$$\begin{aligned} 2w_1 + 4w_3 &\geq 50 \\ w_1 + 2w_2 &\geq 30 \\ w_3 &\geq 10 \end{aligned}$$

w_1, w_2, w_3 unrestricted. [IAS(Main) 1997]

4. Use *duality* to find the optimal solution, if any, of the following LPP.

(a) Minimise $Z = 15x_1 + 10x_2$

subject to
$$\begin{aligned} 3x_1 + 5x_2 &\geq 5 \\ 5x_1 + 2x_2 &\geq 3 \\ x_1, x_2 &\geq 0. \end{aligned}$$

[CU(MSc) 1976; BESU(Engg) 2010]

(b) Maximise $Z = 3x_1 + 4x_2$

subject to
$$\begin{aligned} x_1 - x_2 &\leq 1 \\ x_1 + x_2 &\geq 4 \\ x_1 - 3x_2 &\leq 3 \\ x_1, x_2 &\geq 0. \end{aligned}$$

[CU(H) 2001]

(c) Maximise $Z = 2x_1 + x_2$

subject to
$$\begin{aligned} x_1 + 2x_2 &\leq 10 \\ x_1 + x_2 &\leq 6 \\ x_1 - x_2 &\leq 2 \\ x_1 - 2x_2 &\leq 1 \\ x_1, x_2 &\geq 0. \end{aligned}$$

(d) Minimise $Z = 4x_1 + 2x_2 + 3x_3$

subject to
$$\begin{aligned} 2x_1 + 4x_3 &\geq 5 \\ 2x_1 + 3x_2 + x_3 &\geq 4 \\ x_1, x_2, x_3 &\geq 0. \end{aligned}$$

5. Apply simplex method to solve the LPP.
Maximise $Z = 30x_1 + 23x_2 + 9x_3$
subject to $6x_1 + 5x_2 + 3x_3 \leq 26$
$4x_1 + 2x_2 + 5x_3 \leq 7$
$x_1, x_2, x_3 \geq 0.$
Also read the solution to the dual from the optimal table of primal.

6. Consider the problem: Maximise $Z = 2x_2 - 5x_3$
subject to $x_1 + x_3 \geq 2$
$2x_1 + x_2 + 6x_3 \leq 6$
$x_1 - x_2 + 3x_3 = 0$
$x_1, x_2, x_3 \geq 0.$
(i) Write its dual.
(ii) Solve the primal and then find the solution of dual.

7. By drawing the constraints of both the following primal problem and its dual, show that each of these problems has no feasible solution.
Maximise $Z = 3x_1 + 4x_2$
subject to $x_1 - x_2 \leq -1$
$-x_1 + x_2 \leq 0$
$x_1, x_2 \geq 0.$ [CU(H) 1988, 2005; BESU(Engg) 2011]

8. Show that the following LPP
Maximise $Z = x_1 - 2x_2$
subject to $x_1 + 2x_2 \geq 1$
$-x_1 + x_2 \leq 1$
$x_1, x_2 \geq 0$
has an unbounded solution. Hence, discuss the nature of the primal problem. [CU(H) 1986, 1988]

9. Use duality to solve the LPP.
Minimise $Z = 10x_1 + 2x_2$
subject to $x_1 + 2x_2 + 2x_3 \geq 1$
$x_1 - 2x_2 \geq -1$
$x_1 - x_2 + 3x_3 \geq 3$
$x_1, x_2, x_3 \geq 0.$

10. Solving the dual problem, discuss the nature of the following primal problem. Determine the exact nature of the problem by using graphical method to the primal problem.
Maximise $Z = 3x_1 + 4x_2$
subject to $x_1 - x_2 \leq 1$
$x_1 + x_2 \geq 4$
$x_1 - 3x_2 \leq 3$
$x_1, x_2 \geq 0.$ [CU(H) 1987]

11. Solve the following problems by the *dual-simplex method*:

(a) Minimise $Z = 2x_1 + 3x_2$

subject to $2x_1 + 3x_2 \leq 30$

$x_1 + 2x_2 \geq 10$

$x_1, x_2 \geq 0.$

(b) Minimise $Z = 5x_1 + 6x_2$

subject to $x_1 + x_2 \geq 2$

$4x_1 + x_2 \geq 4$

$x_1, x_2 \geq 0.$

(c) Maximise $Z = -2x_1 - x_2$

subject to $3x_1 + x_2 \geq 3$

$4x_1 + 3x_2 \geq 6$

$x_1 + 2x_2 \geq 3$

$x_1, x_2 \geq 0.$

[JNU(Com Sc) 1999, Meerut(MSc Maths) 2004]

(d) Minimise $Z = 6x_1 + 7x_2 + 3x_3 + 5x_4$

subject to $5x_1 + 6x_2 - 3x_3 + 4x_4 \geq 12$

$x_2 + 5x_3 - 6x_4 \geq 10$

$2x_1 + 5x_2 + x_3 + x_4 \geq 8$

$x_1, x_2, x_3, x_4 \geq 0.$

[BESU(Engg) 2012]

(e) Minimise $Z = 3x_1 + 2x_2 + x_3 + x_4$

subject to $2x_1 + 4x_2 + 5x_3 + x_4 \geq 10$

$3x_1 - x_2 + 7x_3 - 2x_4 \geq 2$

$5x_1 + 2x_2 + x_3 + 6x_4 \geq 15$

$x_1, x_2, x_3, x_4 \geq 0.$

(f) Minimise $Z = x_1 + 3x_2 + 2x_3$

subject to $4x_1 - 5x_2 + 7x_3 \leq 8$

$2x_1 - 4x_2 + 2x_3 \geq 2$

$x_1 - 3x_2 + 2x_3 \leq 2$

$x_1, x_2, x_3 \geq 0.$

[BU(H) 2005]

(g) Minimise $Z = 110x_1 + 150x_2 + 122x_3$

subject to $20x_1 + 12x_2 + 14x_3 \geq 17.6$

$10x_1 + 18x_2 + 22x_3 \geq 14.8$

$x_1, x_2, x_3 \geq 0.$

[KU(MSc Maths) 1984; BESU(Engg) 2013]

(h) Maximise $Z = -3x_1 - 2x_2$

subject to $x_1 + x_2 \geq 1$

$x_1 + x_2 \leq 7$

$x_1 + 2x_2 \geq 10$

$x_2 \leq 3$

$x_1, x_2 \geq 0.$

[BU(H) 2001, 2003, 2006]

(i) Minimise $Z = x_1 + x_2$

subject to $2x_1 + x_2 \geq 2$

$-x_1 - x_2 \geq 1$

$x_1, x_2 \geq 0.$

[CU(MSc Appl) 1984]

(j) Maximise $Z = -2x_1 - 3x_2 - x_3$

subject to $2x_1 + x_2 + 2x_3 \geq 3$

$3x_1 + 2x_2 + x_3 \geq 4$

$x_1, x_2, x_3 \geq 0.$

[CU(MSc Appl) 1980]

ANSWERS

1. (a) Minimise $W = 25v_1 + 16v_2 - 4v_3 - 3v_4$

subject to $3v_1 + v_2 - v_3 \geq 6$

$2v_1 + 2v_2 - v_4 \geq -3$

$v_1, v_2, v_3, v_4 \geq 0.$

(b) Maximise $W = 5v_1 - 3v_2 + 4v_3$

subject to $v_1 - v_2 \leq 1$

$-3v_1 + 2v_2 + 2v_3 \leq 1$

v_1 unrestricted in sign

$v_2, v_3 \geq 0.$

(c) Maximise $Z = 2x_1 + 3x_2 - x_3$

subject to $x_1 + 4x_2 + 2x_3 \leq 7$

$x_1 - 3x_2 + x_3 = 4$

$x_1, x_2, x_3 \geq 0.$

(d) Maximise $W = 2v_1 + 5v_2$

subject to $6v_1 + 3v_2 \leq 6$

$-3v_1 + 4v_2 \leq 3$

$v_1 + v_2 \leq 0$

$v_1, v_2 \geq 0.$

(e) Minimise $W = 5v_1 + 6v_2$
subject to $2v_1 + 3v_2 = 1$
$v_1 - v_2 = 1$
v_1, v_2 unrestricted.

(f) Maximise $W = 3v_1 + 4v_2 + v_3 + 7v_4$
subject to $8v_1 + 3v_2 + 4v_3 + v_4 \leq 7$
$2v_1 + 6v_2 + v_3 + 5v_4 \leq 3$
$v_1 + 4v_2 + 5v_3 + 2v_4 \leq 8$
$v_1, v_2, v_3, v_4 \geq 0.$

(g) Minimise $W = 2v_1 - v_2 + 4v_3$
subject to $2v_1 - 3v_2 + v_3 \geq 1$
$3v_1 + v_2 + v_3 \geq 4$
$-5v_1 - 6v_2 + v_3 = 3$
$v_1, v_2 \geq 0,$
v_3 is unrestricted.

(h) Minimise $W = v_1 + 7v_2 - 2v_3$
subject to $-v_1 + v_2 + v_3 \geq 1$
$v_1 + 3v_2 = 1$
$-v_2 + v_3 = 3$
$3v_3 \leq -2$
$v_1, v_2 \geq 0,$
v_3 unrestricted.

(i) Maximise $Y = 40y_1 + 20y_2 + 30y_3$
subject to $2y_1 + 20y_2 + 4y_3 \leq 20$
$20y_1 + 3y_2 + 15y_3 \leq 40$
$y_1, y_2, y_3 \geq 0.$

2. Solve the dual in three iterations. The primal optimal solution is $x_1^* = 0, x_2^* = 20, x_3^* = 0, Z_{\min} = 120$.

4. (a) $x_1^* = \frac{5}{19}, x_2^* = \frac{16}{19}, Z_{\min} = \frac{235}{19}$.

(b) The dual has no feasible solution. Hence, the primal has either unbounded solution or no feasible solution.

(c) $x_1^* = 4, x_2^* = 2, Z_{\max} = -10$.

(d) $x_1^* = 0, x_2^* = \frac{11}{12}, x_3^* = \frac{5}{4}, Z_{\min} = \frac{67}{12}$.

5. Solution of primal: $x_1^* = 0, x_2^* = \frac{7}{2}, x_3^* = 0, Z_{\max} = \frac{161}{2}$.
Solution of dual: $v_1^* = 0, v_2^* = \frac{23}{2}, W_{\min} = \frac{161}{2}$.

9. $x_1^* = \frac{3}{5}, x_2^* = 0, x_3^* = \frac{4}{5}, Z_{\min} = 6$.

10. The primal has no feasible solution or unbounded solution.

11. (a) $x_1^* = 0, x_2^* = 5, Z_{\min} = 15$.

(b) $x_1^* = 2, x_2^* = 0, Z_{\min} = 10$.

(c) $x_1^* = \frac{3}{5}, x_2^* = \frac{6}{5}, Z_{\max} = -\frac{12}{5}$.

(d) $x_1^* = 0, x_2^* = \frac{30}{11}, x_3^* = \frac{16}{11}, x_4^* = 0, Z_{\min} = \frac{258}{11}$.

(e) $x_1^* = \frac{65}{23}, x_2^* = 0, x_3^* = \frac{20}{23}, x_4^* = 0, Z_{\min} = \frac{215}{23}$.

(f) $x_1^* = 1, x_2^* = x_3^* = 0, Z_{\min} = 1$.

(g) $x_1^* = 0.6, x_2^* = 0, x_3^* = 0.4, Z_{\min} = 114.8$.

(h) $x_1^* = 4, x_2^* = 3, Z_{\max} = -18$.

(i) The given problem has no feasible solution.

(j) $x_1^* = \frac{5}{4}, x_2^* = 0, x_3^* = \frac{1}{4}, Z_{\max} = -\frac{11}{4}$.

Chapter 4

Sensitivity Analysis

4.1 INTRODUCTION

The LP solution always provides us with dynamic information. A static optimum solution will become obsolete as soon as the conditions under which the model is constructed change. Sensitivity analysis is concerned with studying possible changes in the available optimum solution as a result of making changes in the original model.

Suppose, after obtaining an optimum solution of a certain LP model an error has been detected which may be due to some wrong value used for requirement coefficient or due to an extra addition of a decision variable, etc. There are two alternatives to correct this error.

(i) Again, solve the problem by correcting the missing data.

(ii) To find an efficient procedure to obtain the optimum solution of the corrected LP model so that the computational labour will be minimum.

The main objective of the present chapter is to discuss some methods by which one has just to perform certain additional computations after obtaining current optimum solution, in order to obtain the optimum solution to the new post-optimal problem.

The variations in an LP model, which are studied by sensitivity analysis in this chapter include:

1. Changes in the cost vector ***c***.
2. Changes in the requirement vector ***b***.
3. Addition or deletion of some variables to or from original LP model.
4. Addition or deletion of some linear constraints so that the original structure changes in LP model.

While dealing with these changes, one important objective is to find the maximum or minimum extent to which a parameter or a set of parameters can change so that the current optimum solution remains optimal. In other words, the objective is to determine how sensitive is the optimum solution to the changes in these parameters.

4.2 CHANGES IN THE COST VECTOR

Consider an LPP.

Maximise $Z = c_1x_1 + c_2x_2 + \cdots + c_kx_k + \cdots + c_nx_n = \boldsymbol{cx}$

subject to $A\boldsymbol{x} = \boldsymbol{b}$

$\boldsymbol{x} \geq \boldsymbol{0}$

where $A = \left(a_{ij}\right)_{m\times n}$, $\boldsymbol{b} = (b_1, b_2, \ldots, b_m)^T$, $\boldsymbol{c} = (c_1, c_2, \ldots, c_n)$ and $\boldsymbol{x} = (x_1, x_2, \ldots, x_n)^T$. (4.2a)

Assume that an optimum basic feasible solution $\boldsymbol{x_B}$ having basis matrix B has already been obtained for the problem (4.2a).

We now want to change the cost vector $\boldsymbol{c}$ of the problem (4.2a) and replace it by a new cost vector $\boldsymbol{c}^*$ so that the new problem takes the form

Maximise $Z^* = \boldsymbol{c}^*\boldsymbol{x}$

subject to $A\boldsymbol{x} = \boldsymbol{b}$ (4.2b)

$\boldsymbol{x} \geq \boldsymbol{0}$.

Let $\boldsymbol{c}^* = \left(c_1^*, c_2^*, \ldots, c_k^*, \ldots, c_n^*\right) = (c_1 + \delta c_1, \ldots, c_2 + \delta c_2, \ldots, c_k + \delta c_k, \ldots, c_n + \delta c_n)$.

That is, $c_k^* = c_k + \delta c_k \ \forall\ k = 1, 2, \ldots, n$.

Clearly, such a change in any cost component which is not associated with some basic variable, does not alter the value of the objective function in the optimal solution, but if the cost component is associated with optimum basic solution $\boldsymbol{x_B}$, then any changes in $\boldsymbol{c}$ may produce some change in the optimal solution of the problem, because in that case $z_k - c_k = \boldsymbol{c_B y_k} - c_k \ \forall\ k = 1, 2, \ldots, n$.

Therefore, there are two possibilities of changes occur in the cost vector.

Case 1. c_k is not in the optimum basis $\boldsymbol{c_B}$.

Case 2. c_k is in the optimum basis $\boldsymbol{c_B}$.

Case 1. $c_k \notin \boldsymbol{c_B}$, the net evaluation corresponding to the kth coefficient is given by

$$\begin{aligned} z_k^* - c_k^* &= z_k - (c_k + \delta c_k),\ \text{here } z_k^* = z_k \text{ as } c_k \notin \boldsymbol{c_B} \\ &= (z_k - c_k) - \delta c_k. \end{aligned}$$

Hence, the current optimal solution of the new problem (4.2b) remains optimum, if

$$\begin{aligned} & z_k^* - c_k^* \geq 0 \\ \text{or, } & (z_k - c_k) - \delta c_k \geq 0 \\ \text{or, } & \delta c_k \leq (z_k - c_k) \\ \text{or, } & \boxed{-\infty < \delta c_k \leq (z_k - c_k),\ k = 1, 2, \ldots, n} \end{aligned} \tag{4.2c}$$

Case 2. $c_k \in \boldsymbol{c_B}$, we know that $z_j - c_j = \boldsymbol{c_B y_j} - c_j = \sum_{i=1}^{m} c_{B_i} y_{ij} - c_j$, $j = 1, 2, \ldots, n$. (4.2d)

For new problem (4.2b), for $j \neq k$,

$$z_j^* - c_j^* = \sum_{\substack{i=1 \\ i \neq k}}^{m} c_{B_i} y_{ij} + (c_k + \delta c_k)\, y_{kj} - c_j = \sum_{i=1}^{m} c_{B_i} y_{ij} - c_{B_k} y_{kj} + (c_k + \delta c_k) y_{kj} - c_j$$

$$= \left(\sum_{i=1}^{m} c_{B_i} y_{ij} - c_j \right) + \delta c_k y_{kj} \;\; [\because\, c_{B_k} = c_k]$$

$$= \left(z_j - c_j\right) + \delta c_k y_{kj} \text{ [using (4.2d)].}$$

Hence, the new solution remains optimum, if $z_j^* - c_j^* = z_j - c_j + \delta c_k y_{kj} \geq 0 \;\forall\; j \neq k$

$$\text{or, } \delta c_k \geq -\frac{z_j - c_j}{y_{kj}}, \text{ if } y_{kj} > 0$$

$$\leq -\frac{z_j - c_j}{y_{kj}}, \text{ if } y_{kj} < 0.$$

$$\boxed{\therefore \max\left\{ -\frac{z_j - c_j}{y_{kj}} \,\middle|\, y_{kj} > 0 \right\} \leq \delta c_k \leq \min\left\{ -\frac{z_j - c_j}{y_{ky}} \,\middle|\, y_{kj} < 0 \right\}} \quad (4.2e)$$

Note that if $j = k, z_j^* - c_j^* = 0$ as x_k, in that case, represents as a basic variable.

Expressions (4.2c) and (4.2d) indicate the ranges of discrete changes of the cost-coefficients, in other words, maximum and minimum sensitivities of cost coefficients of post-optimal LPP.

4.3 CHANGES IN THE REQUIREMENT VECTOR

Consider the LPP (4.2a) and assume the existence of an optimum basic feasible solution $\boldsymbol{x}_B = B^{-1}\boldsymbol{b}$ of the problem (4.2a) where B is the optimum basis matrix.

Now we want to substitute a new requirement vector $\boldsymbol{b}^*$ in place of $\boldsymbol{b}$ and solve the following new problem:

Maximise $\hat{Z} = \boldsymbol{cx}$

subject to $A\boldsymbol{x} = \boldsymbol{b}^*$ (4.3a)

$\boldsymbol{x} \geq \boldsymbol{0}$

$$\text{Let } \boldsymbol{b}^* = \begin{pmatrix} b_1 + \delta b_1 \\ b_2 + \delta b_2 \\ \vdots \\ b_k + \delta b_k \\ \vdots \\ b_m + \delta b_m \end{pmatrix} \text{ so that } b_k^* = b_k + \delta b_k \;\forall\; k = 1, 2, \ldots, m$$

$$= \begin{pmatrix} b_1^* \\ b_2^* \\ \vdots \\ b_k^* \\ \vdots \\ b_m^* \end{pmatrix}_{m \times 1}$$

If x_B^* be the basic feasible solution of the new posed problem (4.3a), then

$$x_B^* = B^{-1}b^* = B^{-1}b + B^{-1}(\delta b_1, \delta b_2, \ldots, \delta b_k, \ldots, \delta b_m) = x_B + \sum_{k=1}^{m} (\delta b_k)\beta_k, \tag{4.3b}$$

where β_k is the kth column of B^{-1}.

Note that B is the current basis matrix. Since no other changes are made in new problem (4.3a), therefore, the current basic variables $(x_{B1}, x_{B2}, \ldots, x_{Bm})$ continue to constitute a set of basic variable in the new problem (4.3a).

Hence, when only one component of b, say b_k, is changed to $b_k + \delta b_k$ for $k = 1, 2, \ldots, m$, then the ith basic variable x_{B_i} of the new problem (4.3a) by using (4.3b) is given by

$$x_{B_i}^* = x_{B_i} + b_{ik}\delta b_k, \tag{4.3c}$$

where b_{ik} is the (i, k)th element of B^{-1}.

Now in order to maintaining the feasibility of the basic solution of the new problem we must have

$$\begin{aligned} x_{B_i}^* \geq 0 &\Rightarrow x_{B_i} + b_{ik}\delta b_k \geq 0 \\ &\Rightarrow \delta b_k \geq -\frac{x_{B_i}}{b_{ik}}, \text{ if } b_{ik} > 0 \\ &\quad\quad\;\; \leq -\frac{x_{B_i}}{b_{ik}}, \text{ if } b_{ik} < 0. \end{aligned}$$

Thus, the range for discrete changes of δb_k in b_k for $k = 1, 2, \ldots, m$ which maintain the condition of feasibility of the new problem (4.3a) is given by

$$\boxed{\max\left\{-\frac{x_{B_i}}{b_{ik}}\middle| b_{ik} > 0\right\} \leq \delta b_k \leq \min\left\{-\frac{x_{B_i}}{b_{ik}}\middle| b_{ik} < 0\right\}} \tag{4.3d}$$

Again, since $z_j - c_j = c_B y_j - c_j$ and $y_j = B^{-1}y$ remains unchanged as the above expressions are independent of b, therefore, any changes in b will not violate the condition of optimality $z_j - c_j \geq 0$ for $j = 1, 2, \ldots, n$ of the new post-optimal problem (4.3a).

Example 4.3.1. *Maximise* $Z = -x_1 + 3x_2 - 2x_3$

subject to
$$\begin{aligned} 3x_1 - x_2 + x_3 &\leq 7 \\ -2x_1 + 4x_2 \quad &\leq 12 \\ -4x_1 + 3x_2 + 8x_3 &\leq 10 \\ x_1, x_2, x_3 &\geq 0. \end{aligned}$$

If we solve the above problem by simplex method then obtain the following starting table and optimum table (the intermediate tables are left to the reader). [BESU(MSc) 2005, CU(MSc) 1992]

Starting *Table* (T 1)

		c_j	-1	3	-2	0	0	0	
C_B	B	x_B	y_1	y_2	y_3	y_4	y_5	y_6	MR
0	y_4	7	3	-1	2	1	0	0	X
0	y_5	12	-2	4	0	0	1	0	$\frac{12}{4} \longrightarrow$
0	y_6	10	-4	3	8	0	0	1	$\frac{10}{3}$
		$z_j - c_j$	1	$-3\uparrow$	2	0	0	0	

Optimum *Table* (T 2)

		c_j	-1	3	-2	0	0	0
C_B	B	x_B	y_1	y_2	y_3	y_4	y_5	y_6
-1	y_1	4	1	0	$\frac{4}{5}$	$\frac{3}{5}$	$\frac{1}{10}$	0
3	y_2	5	0	1	$\frac{2}{5}$	$\frac{1}{5}$	$\frac{3}{10}$	0
0	y_6	11	0	0	10	1	$-\frac{1}{2}$	1
		$z_j - c_j$	0	0	$\frac{12}{5}$	0	$\frac{4}{5}$	0

Discussions

(1) The optimum solution of Ex. 4.3.1 is given by $x_1^* = 4,\ x_2^* = 5,\ x_3^* = 0,\ Z_{\max} = 11.$

(2) Ranges for discrete changes of cost-coefficients.

Here, $\boldsymbol{c} = (c_1, c_2, c_3, c_4, c_5, c_6)$ and $\boldsymbol{c_B} = (c_1, c_2, c_6)$.

Since c_4, c_5, c_6 are the cost-coefficients corresponding to the slack variables, so we are not interested about their changes.

(i) $c_3 \notin \boldsymbol{c_B}$, using $-\infty < \delta c_k \le z_k - c_k \ \forall\ c_k \notin \boldsymbol{c_B}$.

We have $-\infty < \delta c_3 \le \dfrac{12}{3} \Rightarrow -\infty < c_3 + \delta c_3 \le -2 + \dfrac{12}{5} \Rightarrow -\infty < c_3^* \le \dfrac{2}{5}.$

(ii) $c_1, c_2 \in \boldsymbol{c_B}$, using: $\max\left\{-\dfrac{z_j - c_j}{y_{kj}} \middle| y_{kj} > 0\right\} \le \delta c_k \le \min\left\{-\dfrac{z_j - c_j}{y_{kj}} \middle| y_{kj} < 0\right\}.$

We have $\max\left\{-\dfrac{12/5}{4/5}, -\dfrac{4/5}{1/10}, -\dfrac{0}{3/5}\right\} \le \delta c_1 < \infty \Rightarrow 0 \le \delta c_1 < \infty \Rightarrow -1 \le c_1^* \le \infty.$

Again, $\max\left\{-\dfrac{12/5}{2/5}, -\dfrac{0}{3/5}, -\dfrac{4/5}{3/10}\right\} \le \delta c_2 < \infty \Rightarrow 0 \le \delta c_2 \le \infty \Rightarrow 3 \le c_2^* < \infty.$

(iii) If we take for new problem $c_2^* = 2$ instead of 3, then $z_2^* - c_2^* = 0,\ z_1^* - c_1^* = 0,\ z_3^* - c_3^* = 2,\ z_4^* - c_4^* = -\frac{1}{5} < 0,\ z_5^* - c_5^* = \frac{1}{2},\ z_6^* - c_6^* = 0$, so that the current optimal solution is no longer optimal. To find the post-optimal solution we use the last optimum table and perform the additional computation as follows:

(T 3)

		c_j	−1	3	−2	0	0	0	
C_B	B	x_B	y_1	y_2	y_3	y_4	y_5	y_6	MR
−1	y_1	4	1	0	$\frac{4}{5}$	$\boxed{\frac{3}{5}}$	$\frac{1}{10}$	0	$\frac{20}{3}$ →
2	y_2	5	0	1	$\frac{2}{5}$	$\frac{1}{5}$	$\frac{3}{10}$	0	25
0	y_6	11	0	0	1	1	$-\frac{1}{2}$	1	11
	$z_j - c_j$		0	0	2	$-\frac{1}{5}$ ↑	$\frac{1}{2}$	0	

(T 4)

		c_j	−1	2	−2	0	0	0
C_B	B	x_B	y_1	y_2	y_3	y_4	y_5	y_6
0	y_4	$\frac{20}{3}$	$\frac{5}{2}$	0	$\frac{4}{3}$	1	$\frac{1}{6}$	0
2	y_2	$\frac{11}{3}$	$-\frac{1}{3}$	1	$\frac{2}{5}$	0	$\frac{4}{5}$	0
0	y_6	$\frac{13}{3}$	$-\frac{5}{3}$	0	$\frac{13}{3}$	0	$-\frac{2}{3}$	1
	$z_j - c_j$		$\frac{1}{3}$	0	$\frac{34}{15}$	0	$\frac{8}{15}$	0

$z_j - c_j \geq 0 \; \forall \; j$. Hence, an optimal solution of the new problem after changing the coefficient c_2 of original problem which does not belong to the range of discrete changes gives $x_1^* = 0$, $x_2^* = \frac{11}{3}$, $x_3^* = 0$, $Z_{\max} = \frac{22}{3}$.

(3) Range for discrete change of requirement coefficients.

From the optimum table (T 2),

$$\boldsymbol{x_B} = \begin{pmatrix} x_1 \\ x_2 \\ x_6 \end{pmatrix} = \begin{pmatrix} 4 \\ 5 \\ 11 \end{pmatrix}, \qquad \boldsymbol{b} = \begin{pmatrix} 7 \\ 12 \\ 10 \end{pmatrix}, \qquad B^{-1} = \begin{pmatrix} 3/5 & 1/10 & 0 \\ 1/5 & 3/10 & 0 \\ 1 & -1/2 & 1 \end{pmatrix}.$$

Using: $\max\left\{-\frac{x_{B_i}}{b_{ik}}\middle| b_{ik} > 0\right\} \leq \delta b_k \leq \min\left\{-\frac{x_{B_i}}{b_{ik}}\middle| b_{ik} < 0\right\}$.

$$\max\left\{-\frac{4}{3/5}, -\frac{5}{1/5}, -\frac{11}{1}\right\} \leq \delta b_1 < \infty \Rightarrow -\frac{20}{3} \leq \delta b_1 < \infty \Rightarrow 7 - \frac{20}{3} \leq b_1^* < \infty \Rightarrow \frac{1}{3} \leq b_1^* < \infty.$$

$$\max\left\{-\frac{4}{1/10}, -\frac{5}{3/10}\right\} \leq \delta b_2 \leq \min\left\{-\frac{11}{-1/2}\right\} \Rightarrow -\frac{50}{3} \leq \delta b_2 \leq 22 \Rightarrow 12 - \frac{50}{3} \leq b_2^* \leq 12 + 22$$
$$\Rightarrow -\frac{14}{3} \leq b_2^* \leq 34.$$

$$-11 \leq \delta b_3 \leq \infty \Rightarrow 10 - 11 \leq b_3^* \leq \infty \Rightarrow -1 \leq b_3^* \leq \infty.$$

If we replace $b_2^* = 35$ instead of 12 in the original problem (which does not belong to the range of discrete change $-\frac{14}{3} \leq b_2^* \leq 34$ by post-optimal analysis), then

$$\boldsymbol{x_B^*} = B^{-1}\boldsymbol{b^*} \Rightarrow \begin{pmatrix} x_1 \\ x_2 \\ x_3 \end{pmatrix} = \begin{pmatrix} 3/5 & 1/10 & 0 \\ 1/5 & 3/10 & 0 \\ 1 & -1/2 & 1 \end{pmatrix} \begin{pmatrix} 7 \\ 35 \\ 10 \end{pmatrix} = \begin{pmatrix} 77/10 \\ 119/10 \\ -1/2 \end{pmatrix},$$

which shows that the current optimal feasible solution of original problem is no longer feasible for the new problem. Therefore, to find the optimal feasible solution of new problem we take the optimum table (T 2) of original problem by only changing the column of $\boldsymbol{x_B}$ and row of $z_j - c_j$ accordingly and use *dual-simplex* method for additional computation in the following manner.

(T 5)

		c_j	-1	3	-2	0	0	0	
C_B	B	x_B	y_1	y_2	y_3	y_4	y_5	y_6	MR
-1	y_1	$\frac{77}{10}$	1	0	$\frac{4}{5}$	$\frac{3}{5}$	$\frac{1}{10}$	0	X
3	y_2	$\frac{119}{10}$	0	1	$\frac{2}{5}$	$\frac{1}{5}$	$\frac{3}{10}$	0	X
0	y_6	$-\frac{1}{2}$	0	0	10	1	$-\frac{1}{2}$	1	$-\frac{8}{5} \rightarrow$
		$z_j - c_j$	0	0	$\frac{12}{5}$	0	$\frac{4}{5}\uparrow$	0	

(T 6)

		c_j	-1	3	-2	0	0	0
C_B	B	x_B	y_1	y_2	y_3	y_4	y_5	y_6
-1	y_1	$\frac{38}{5}$	1	0	$\frac{14}{5}$	$\frac{16}{25}$	0	$\frac{1}{5}$
3	y_2	$\frac{61}{5}$	0	1	$\frac{32}{5}$	$\frac{4}{5}$	0	$\frac{3}{5}$
0	y_5	1	0	0	-20	-2	1	0
		$z_j - c_j$	0	0	$\frac{92}{5}$	$\frac{44}{25}$	0	$\frac{8}{5}$

The required optimal feasible solution of post-optimal problem by changing the coefficient b_2^* is given by $x_1^* = \frac{38}{5}$, $x_2^* = \frac{61}{5}$, $x_3^* = 0$, $Z_{\max} = 29$.

Example 4.3.2. *Find the limits of variations δc_1, δc_2, δc_3, δc_4, δc_5, δc_6 respectively for a certain LPP whose optimal table is given below, so that the optimal solution remains optimal.*

[BESU(MSc) 2004, JNU(Com Sc) 1998]

		c_j	-1	-1	3	0	-3	0
C_B	B	x_B	y_1	y_2	y_3	y_4	y_5	y_6
-1	y_2	5	$\frac{2}{5}$	1	0	$\frac{1}{10}$	$\frac{4}{5}$	0
3	y_3	6	$\frac{1}{5}$	0	1	$\frac{3}{10}$	$\frac{2}{5}$	0
0	y_6	8	1	0	0	$-\frac{1}{2}$	10	1
		$z_j - c_j$	$\frac{6}{5}$	0	0	$\frac{4}{5}$	$\frac{17}{5}$	0

Discussions

(i) The optimal solution is: $x_1^* = 0$, $x_2^* = 5$, $x_3^* = 6$, $x_4^* = 0$, $x_5^* = 0$, $x_6^* = 8$, $Z_{\max} = 13$.

(ii) $\boldsymbol{c} = (c_1, c_2, c_3, c_4, c_5, c_6)$, $\boldsymbol{c_B} = (c_2, c_3, c_6)$.

As c_1, c_4, $c_5 \notin \boldsymbol{c_B}$, the permissible limits of the variations δc_1, δc_4, δc_5 for which the current optimal. solution remains optimal are given by

$$-\infty < \delta c_1 \le z_1 - c_1 \Rightarrow -\infty < \delta c_1 \le 6/5$$
$$-\infty < \delta c_4 \le z_4 - c_4 \Rightarrow -\infty < \delta c_4 \le 4/5$$
$$-\infty < \delta c_5 \le z_5 - c_5 \Rightarrow -\infty < \delta c_5 \le 17/5.$$

Again, since $c_2, c_3, c_6 \in c_B$, the permissible limits of variation of $\delta c_2, \delta c_3, \delta c_6$ are given by

$$\min\left\{-\frac{z_j - c_j}{y_{2j}}\middle| y_{2j} < 0\right\} \ge \delta c_2 \ge \max\left\{-\frac{z_j - c_j}{y_{2j}}\middle| y_{2j} > 0\right\}$$
$$\Rightarrow \infty \ge \delta c_2 \ge \max\left\{\frac{-6/5}{2/5}, \frac{-4/5}{1/10}, \frac{-17/5}{4/5}\right\}$$
$$\Rightarrow -3 \le \delta c_2 < \infty \text{ [as no } y_{2j} < 0].$$

Similarly, $\max\left\{\frac{-6/5}{1/5}, \frac{-4/5}{3/10}, \frac{-17/5}{2/5}\right\} \le \delta c_3 \le \infty \Rightarrow -\frac{8}{3} \le \delta c_3 < \infty$

and $\max\left\{\frac{-6/5}{1}, \frac{-17/5}{10}\right\} \le \delta c_6 \le \min\left\{\frac{-4/5}{-1/2}\right\} \Rightarrow -\frac{6}{5} \le \delta c_6 \le \frac{8}{5}.$

Note that the variations $\delta c_2, \delta c_3, \delta c_6$ given above will not violate the optimality of the current optimal solution.

Example 4.3.3. *For the following LPP find the limits of variations of requirement coefficients for which the present optimal feasible solution remains feasible and optimal.*

Maximise $Z = 3x_1 + 4x_2 + x_3 + 7x_4$

subject to $8x_1 + 3x_2 + 4x_3 + x_4 \le 7$

$2x_1 + 6x_2 + x_3 + 5x_4 \le 3$

$x_1 + 4x_2 + 5x_3 + 2x_4 \le 8$

$x_1, x_2, x_3, x_4 \ge 0.$

Solution: *Standard form:* Maximise $Z = 3x_1 + 4x_2 + x_3 + 7x_4 + 0x_5 + 0x_6 + 0x_7$

subject to $8x_1 + 3x_2 + 4x_3 + x_4 + x_5 = 7$

$2x_1 + 6x_2 + x_3 + 5x_4 + x_6 = 3$

$x_1 + 4x_2 + 5x_3 + 2x_4 + x_7 = 8$

$x_j \ge 0,\ j = 1, 2, 3, 4;$ decision variables

$j = 5, 6, 7;$ slack variables.

The initial and optimal tables obtained by solving the LPP using simplex method are given below (the intermediate tables are left to the reader).

Initial table:

		c_j	3	4	1	7	0	0	0	
c_B	B	x_B	y_1	y_2	y_3	y_4	y_5	y_6	y_7	MR
0	y_5	7	8	3	4	1	1	0	0	$\frac{7}{1}$
0	y_6	3	2	6	1	(5)	0	1	0	$\frac{3}{5}\rightarrow$
0	y_7	8	1	4	5	2	0	0	1	$\frac{8}{2}$
		$z_j - c_j$	−3	−4	−1	−7↑	0	0	0	

Optimal table:

		c_j	3	4	1	7	0	0	0
c_B	B	x_B	y_1	y_2	y_3	y_4	y_5	y_6	y_7
3	y_1	$\frac{16}{19}$	1	$\frac{9}{38}$	$\frac{1}{2}$	0	$\frac{5}{38}$	$-\frac{1}{38}$	0
7	y_4	$\frac{5}{19}$	0	$\frac{21}{19}$	0	1	$-\frac{1}{19}$	$\frac{8}{38}$	0
0	7_7	$\frac{126}{19}$	0	$\frac{59}{38}$	$\frac{9}{2}$	0	$-\frac{1}{38}$	$\frac{15}{38}$	1
		$z_j - c_j$	0	$\frac{169}{38}$	$\frac{1}{2}$	0	$\frac{1}{38}$	$\frac{53}{38}$	0

Discussions

1. From optimal table we observe that all $z_j - c_j \geq 0$ as well as $x_B \geq 0$ so that optimality as well as feasibility conditions are satisfied. Therefore, required solution is $x_1^* = \frac{16}{19}$, $x_2^* = 0$, $x_3^* = 0$, $x_4^* = \frac{5}{19}$, $Z_{\max} = \frac{930}{19}$.

2. Here, $x_B = \begin{pmatrix} x_1 \\ x_4 \\ x_7 \end{pmatrix} = \begin{pmatrix} \frac{16}{19} \\ \frac{5}{19} \\ \frac{126}{19} \end{pmatrix}$, $b = \begin{pmatrix} 7 \\ 3 \\ 8 \end{pmatrix}$, $B^{-1} = \begin{pmatrix} \frac{5}{38} & -\frac{1}{38} & 0 \\ -\frac{1}{19} & \frac{8}{38} & 0 \\ -\frac{1}{38} & -\frac{15}{38} & 1 \end{pmatrix}$.

The limits of variations of the requirement coefficients $\delta b_1, \delta b_2, \delta b_3$ are given by

$$\max\left\{\frac{-16/19}{5/38}\right\} \leq \delta b_1 \leq \min\left\{\frac{-5/19}{-1/19}, \frac{-126/19}{-1/38}\right\} \Rightarrow -\frac{32}{5} \leq \delta b_1 \leq 5$$

$$\max\left\{\frac{-5/19}{8/38}\right\} \leq \delta b_2 \leq \min\left\{\frac{-16/19}{-1/38}, \frac{-126/19}{-15/38}\right\} \Rightarrow -\frac{5}{4} \leq \delta b_2 \leq \frac{84}{5}$$

$$-\frac{126}{19} \leq \delta b_3 \leq \infty.$$

The above variations δb_1, δb_2, δb_3 will not violate the condition of feasibility of the current solution. As $(z_j - c_j)$ is independent of requirement coefficients the optimality condition remains optimal for any variation of the requirement coefficient.

4.4 STRUCTURAL CHANGES IN LP MODEL

Consider the following LP model.

$$\text{Maximise } Z = c_1x_1 + c_2x_2 + \cdots + c_qx_q + \cdots + c_nx_n$$

$$\begin{aligned} \text{subject to } \; & a_{11}x_1 + a_{12}x_2 + \ldots + a_{1n}x_n = b_1 \\ & a_{21}x_1 + a_{22}x_2 + \ldots + a_{2n}x_n = b_2 \\ & \vdots \qquad\qquad\qquad \vdots \qquad \vdots \\ & a_{m1}x_1 + a_{m2}x_2 + \ldots + a_{mn}x_n = b_m \\ & x_1, x_2, \ldots, x_n \geq 0. \end{aligned} \tag{4.4a}$$

By applying the appropriate method, an optimum basic feasible solution x_B with B as basis matrix of model (4.4a) has been obtained.

(A) Addition of a Variable

We want to study the effect on the current optimal solution by post-optimal addition of a new non-negative variable $x_{n+1} \geq 0$ with activity column a_{n+1} and cost coefficient c_{n+1} to the model (4.4a).

Clearly, it is necessary to compute only

$$z_{n+1} - c_{n+1} = \boldsymbol{c_B y_{n+1}} - c_{n+1} \text{ and } \boldsymbol{y_{n+1}} = B^{-1}\boldsymbol{a_{n+1}}, \tag{4.4b}$$

where B is the current optimum basis and $\boldsymbol{c_B}$ is the associated cost vector.

Now two cases are possible:

(i) $z_{n+1} - c_{n+1} \geq 0$, then the current optimum basic feasible solution $\boldsymbol{x_B}$ remains optimum for the post-optimal problem.

(ii) $z_{n+1} - c_{n+1} < 0$, then $\boldsymbol{x_B}$ may further be improved by introducing $\boldsymbol{y_{n+1}}$ into the basis and then apply usual simplex method.

(B) Deletion of a Variable

Let a variable x_q be deleted from LP model (4.4a). The effect of this deletion on the optimality of the current optimum feasible solution $\boldsymbol{x_B}$ need to check the following two cases:

(i) $x_q \notin x_B$, then the deletion of x_q has no contribution towards the current optimal feasible solution $\boldsymbol{x_B}$ so that the solution remains optimal for the new problem.

(ii) $x_q \in \boldsymbol{x_B}$. In this case we solve the post-optimal problem by the following approach:
Assign a cost $(-M)$ to x_q and then apply the standard simplex method, taking the modified current optimum table as the starting table to reach a new optimum solution.

(C) Addition of a Constraint

Originally there are m constrains in the model (4.4a). Let one more constraint be added post-optimally to the given model

$$a_{m+11}x_1 + a_{m+12}x_2 + \cdots + a_{m+1n}x_n = b_{m+1}. \tag{4.4c}$$

Let us now study the effect of this addition on the optimality of the current optimum basic feasible solution $\boldsymbol{x_B}$ of the problem.

Case 1. If $\boldsymbol{x_B}$ satisfies the new constraint (4.4c), then $\boldsymbol{x_B}$ remains optimum for the new problem which follows from the fact that the extra constraint (4.4c) cannot enlarge the feasible region. Hence, $\boldsymbol{x_B}$ remains optimum for the new problem.

Case 2. If $\boldsymbol{x_B}$ does not satisfy the new constraints (4.4c), then we have to search for other optimum solution.

For simplicity let us write the $(m+1)$ constraints in the form

$$\begin{aligned} A\boldsymbol{x} &= \boldsymbol{b} \\ \boldsymbol{ax} + x_s &= b_{m+1} \\ \boldsymbol{x}, x_s &\geq \boldsymbol{0}, \end{aligned} \tag{4.4d}$$

where $\boldsymbol{x}^T \in R^n$, $\boldsymbol{b} \in R^m$, $A = \left(a_{ij}\right)_{m\times n}$, $\boldsymbol{a} = (a_{m+11}, a_{m+12}, \ldots, a_{m+1n})$.

Let $\boldsymbol{x}^*_{\boldsymbol{B}} = \begin{pmatrix} x_B \\ x_s \end{pmatrix}$ be a feasible solution to the new problem.

This can be proved easily by collecting the activity columns corresponding to $x_{B1}, x_{B2}, \ldots, x_{Bm}, x_s$ into an $(m+1)\times(m+1)$ matrix

$$B^* = \begin{pmatrix} B & 0 \\ \boldsymbol{u} & 1 \end{pmatrix}, \tag{4.4e}$$

where $u = (a_{m+11}, a_{m+12}, \ldots, a_{m+1m})$, a_{m+1i} being the ith component of u, that is, when $x_{B_i} = x_i$, $u_i = a_{m+1i}$.

It can be shown that $(B^*)^{-1} = \begin{pmatrix} B^{-1} & 0 \\ -u\,B^{-1} & 1 \end{pmatrix}$. (4.4f)

Now using this inverse of the new basis, we can compute all the values required to fill in the simplex table for the new model. The values of the basic variables are given by

$$x_B^* = \begin{pmatrix} x_B \\ x_s \end{pmatrix} = (B^*)^{-1} b^* = \begin{pmatrix} B^{-1} & 0 \\ -u\,B^{-1} & 1 \end{pmatrix} \begin{pmatrix} b \\ b_{m+1} \end{pmatrix} = \begin{pmatrix} B^{-1} b \\ b_{m+1} - u\,B^{-1} b \end{pmatrix} = \begin{pmatrix} x_B \\ b_{m+1} - u x_B \end{pmatrix}. \quad (4.4g)$$

Again, for new model each column of activity matrix is $a_j^* = \begin{pmatrix} a_j & a_{m+1j} \end{pmatrix}$.

$$y_j^* = (B^*)^{-1} a_j^* = \begin{pmatrix} B^{-1} & 0 \\ -u\,B^{-1} & 1 \end{pmatrix} \begin{pmatrix} a_j \\ a_{m+1j} \end{pmatrix} = \begin{pmatrix} B^{-1} a_j \\ a_{m+1j} - u y_j \end{pmatrix} \quad (4.4h)$$

Optimality conditions: $z_j^* - c_j^* = z_j^* - c_j$ (as no change in cost coefficient)

$$= c_B^* y_j^* - c_j = (c_B \;\; 0) \begin{pmatrix} y_j \\ a_{m+1j} - u y_j \end{pmatrix} - c_j$$

$$= c_B y_j - c_j = z_j - c_j \text{ (which is same as before).}$$

Conclusion. We see that none of the entries in the optimum simplex table of the original LP model used be changed. It is necessary only to add a new row for the $(m+1)$th basic variable x_j whose value and y_j components are given by (4.4g) and (4.4h) respectively. The new post-optimal problem can then be solved by *dual-simplex* method.

Example 4.4.1. *Considering* Ex. 4.3.3, *write here the standard form of the problem, initial and optimum table only.*

Maximise $Z = 3x_1 + 4x_2 + x_3 + 7x_4 + 0x_5 + 0x_6 + 0x_7$

subject to $8x_1 + 3x_2 + 4x_3 + x_4 + x_5 = 7$

$2x_1 + 6x_2 + x_3 + 5x_4 + x_6 = 3$

$x_1 + 4x_2 + 5x_3 + 2x_4 + x_7 = 8.$

$x_j \geq 0$, $j = 1, 2, 3, 4$; decision variables

$j = 5, 6, 7$; slack variables.

Initial table:

		c_j	3	4	1	7	0	0	0	
c_B	B	x_B	y_1	y_2	y_3	y_4	y_5	y_6	y_7	MR
0	y_5	7	8	3	4	1	1	0	0	$\frac{7}{1}$
0	y_6	3	2	6	1	5	0	1	0	$\frac{3}{5}$ →
0	y_7	8	1	4	5	2	0	0	1	4
		$z_j - c_j$	−3	−4	−1	−7↑	0	0	0	

Optimum table:

	c_j		3	4	1	7	0	0	0
c_B	B	x_B	y_1	y_2	y_3	y_4	y_5	y_6	y_7
3	y_1	$\frac{16}{19}$	1	$\frac{9}{38}$	$\frac{1}{2}$	0	$\frac{5}{38}$	$-\frac{1}{38}$	0
7	y_4	$\frac{5}{19}$	0	$\frac{21}{19}$	0	1	$-\frac{1}{9}$	$\frac{8}{38}$	0
0	y_7	$\frac{126}{19}$	0	$\frac{59}{38}$	$\frac{9}{2}$	0	$-\frac{1}{38}$	$-\frac{15}{38}$	1
	$z_j - c_j$		0	$\frac{169}{38}$	$\frac{1}{2}$	0	$\frac{1}{38}$	$\frac{53}{38}$	0

Discussions

(1) We now discuss the effect on adding a new variable $x_8 \geq 0$ to the problem. Given that coefficient of x_8 in the constraint of the problem is (2,7,3) and the cost component is 5.

$$\boldsymbol{x_B} = \begin{pmatrix} x_1 \\ x_4 \\ x_7 \end{pmatrix} = \begin{pmatrix} \dfrac{16}{19} \\ \dfrac{5}{19} \\ \dfrac{126}{19} \end{pmatrix}, \quad \boldsymbol{c_B} = (3 \quad 7 \quad 0), \quad B^{-1} = \begin{pmatrix} \dfrac{5}{38} & -\dfrac{1}{38} & 0 \\ -\dfrac{1}{19} & \dfrac{8}{38} & 0 \\ -\dfrac{1}{38} & -\dfrac{15}{38} & 1 \end{pmatrix}$$

$$\boldsymbol{a_8} = \begin{pmatrix} 2 \\ 7 \\ 3 \end{pmatrix}, \quad \boldsymbol{y_8} = B^{-1}\boldsymbol{a_8} = \begin{pmatrix} \dfrac{5}{38} & -\dfrac{1}{38} & 0 \\ -\dfrac{1}{19} & \dfrac{8}{38} & 0 \\ -\dfrac{1}{38} & -\dfrac{15}{38} & 1 \end{pmatrix} \begin{pmatrix} 2 \\ 7 \\ 3 \end{pmatrix} = \begin{pmatrix} \dfrac{3}{28} \\ \dfrac{26}{19} \\ \dfrac{7}{38} \end{pmatrix}$$

$$z_8 - c_8 = (3 \quad 7 \quad 0) \begin{pmatrix} \dfrac{3}{28} \\ \dfrac{26}{19} \\ \dfrac{7}{38} \end{pmatrix} - 5 = \frac{183}{38} > 0.$$

Since $z_8 - c_8 > 0$, the optimal feasible solution of the current problem $\boldsymbol{x_B}$ remains optimal so that the post-optimal addition of new variable $x_8 \geq 0$ does not affect the original problem.

In particular, if $c_8 = 12$ instead of $c_8 = 5$, then

$$z_8 - c_8 = -\frac{83}{38} < 0.$$

Therefore, the current optimal solution is no longer optimum by post-optimal addition of a new variable $x_8 \geq 0$. To find the new optimum solution we proceed as follows:

		c_j	3	4	1	7	0	0	0	12	
c_B	B	x_B	y_1	y_2	y_3	y_4	y_5	y_6	y_7	y_8	MR
3	y_1	$\frac{16}{19}$	1	$\frac{9}{38}$	$\frac{1}{2}$	0	$\frac{5}{38}$	$-\frac{1}{38}$	0	$\frac{3}{38}$	$\frac{32}{3}$
7	y_4	$\frac{5}{19}$	0	$\frac{21}{19}$	0	1	$-\frac{1}{19}$	$\frac{4}{19}$	0	$\frac{26}{19}$	$\frac{5}{26}$ →
0	y_7	$\frac{126}{19}$	0	$\frac{59}{38}$	$\frac{9}{2}$	0	$-\frac{1}{38}$	$-\frac{15}{38}$	1	$\frac{7}{38}$	$\frac{252}{7}$
		$z_j - c_j$	0	$\frac{126}{38}$	$\frac{1}{2}$	0	$\frac{1}{38}$	$\frac{53}{38}$	0	$-\frac{83}{38}$ ↑	

y_8 will be the entering vector which replace y_4 in the current basis. By simplex transformation we shall move towards the required optimum solution (The remaining calculation is left for the reader).

(2) Let the variable $x_4 \in \boldsymbol{x_B}$ be deleted from the original LPP. Since the variable deleted is a basic variable it will change the current optimum basic feasible solution. To find the new optimum solution we assign a cost $(-M)$ to x_4, where M is a very large number no matter, however, large. We take the optimum simplex table of the original problem as the initial table for the new problem with only one change in the cost coefficient of x_4 so that the row of $(z_j - c_j)$ in the table changes accordingly.

		c_j	3	4	1	$-M$	0	0	0	
c_B	B	x_B	y_1	y_2	y_3	y_4	y_5	y_6	y_7	MR
3	y_1	$\frac{16}{19}$	1	$\frac{9}{38}$	$\frac{1}{2}$	0	$\frac{5}{38}$	$-\frac{1}{38}$	0	$\frac{32}{9}$
$-M$	y_4	$\frac{5}{19}$	0	$\frac{21}{19}$	0	1	$-\frac{1}{19}$	$\frac{8}{38}$	0	$\frac{5}{21}$ →
0	y_7	$\frac{126}{19}$	0	$\frac{59}{38}$	$\frac{9}{2}$	0	$-\frac{1}{38}$	$-\frac{15}{38}$	1	$\frac{252}{59}$
		$z_j - c_j$	0	$-\frac{21M}{19} - \frac{125}{38}$ ↑	$\frac{1}{2}$	0	$\frac{M}{19} + \frac{15}{38}$	$-\frac{8M}{38} - \frac{3}{8}$	0	

		c_j	3	4	1	0	0	0
c_B	B	x_B	y_1	y_2	y_3	y_4	y_5	y_6
3	y_1	$\frac{209}{266}$	1	0	$\frac{1}{2}$	$\frac{1}{7}$	$-\frac{1}{14}$	0
4	y_2	$\frac{5}{21}$	0	1	0	$-\frac{1}{21}$	$\frac{4}{21}$	0
0	y_7	$\frac{13997}{798}$	0	0	$\frac{9}{2}$	$\frac{1}{21}$	$-\frac{187}{266}$	1
		$z_j - c_j$	0	0	$\frac{1}{2}$	$\frac{5}{21}$	$\frac{23}{42}$	0

Hence, we observe that after deletion of a basic variable the post-optimal problem gives another optimum solution by applying some minor additional computation without solving the problem once again.

Required optimum solution is: $x_1^* = \frac{209}{266}, x_2^* = \frac{5}{21}, x_3^* = 0, Z_{\max} = \frac{139}{42}$.

(3) Here we add a new constraint $2x_1 + 3x_2 + x_3 + 5x_4 \le 4$ and check whether the post-optimal addition of the constraint produce any change in the optimum solution $\boldsymbol{x_B}$ of the original problem.

$$\boldsymbol{x_B} = \begin{pmatrix} \frac{16}{19} \\ \frac{5}{19} \\ \frac{126}{19} \end{pmatrix} = \begin{pmatrix} x_1 \\ x_4 \\ x_7 \end{pmatrix}, \quad B = \begin{pmatrix} 1 & 0 & 0 \\ 0 & 1 & 0 \\ 0 & 0 & 1 \end{pmatrix}.$$

After the addition of new constraint — the new basis matrix is given by [using (4.4e)]

$$B^* = \begin{pmatrix} B & 0 \\ u & 1 \end{pmatrix} = \begin{pmatrix} I_3 & 0 \\ u & 1 \end{pmatrix}, \text{ where } u = \begin{pmatrix} 2 \\ 5 \\ 0 \end{pmatrix}.$$

Adding slack variable $x_8 \geq 0$ in the constraint, we get

$$2x_1 + 3x_2 + x_3 + 5x_4 + 0x_5 + 0x_6 + 0x_7 + x_8 = 4.$$

The optimum solution of new post-optimal problem is given by [using (4.4g)]

$$\boldsymbol{x}_B^* = \begin{pmatrix} \boldsymbol{x}_B \\ 4 - u\boldsymbol{x}_B \end{pmatrix} = \begin{pmatrix} \frac{16}{19} \\ \frac{5}{19} \\ \frac{126}{19} \\ 1 \end{pmatrix} \left[\text{as } 4 - (2 \quad 5 \quad 0) \begin{pmatrix} \frac{16}{19} \\ \frac{5}{19} \\ \frac{126}{19} \end{pmatrix} = 1 \right],$$

which shows that $\boldsymbol{x}_B^* > 0$ and solution is feasible. Since the post-optimal addition of a constraint does not alter the condition of optimality, therefore, the current optimal feasible solution remains optimal for the new problem.

But if we take the constraint as $2x_1 + 3x_2 + x_3 + 5x_4 \leq 2$, in that case

$$\boldsymbol{x}_B^* = \begin{pmatrix} \frac{16}{19} \\ \frac{5}{19} \\ \frac{126}{19} \\ -1 \end{pmatrix}.$$

This indicates $\boldsymbol{x}_B^*$ is not feasible. So we search for the feasible solution. To do this we use *dual-simplex* method. We take the optimum table of the original problem with an addition of a row due to new constraint. The new row will be calculated using the eq. (4.4h).

		c_j	3	4	1	7	0	0	0	0
c_B	B	x_B	y_1	y_2	y_3	y_4	y_5	y_6	y_7	y_8
3	y_1	$\frac{16}{19}$	1	$\frac{9}{38}$	$\frac{1}{2}$	0	$\frac{5}{38}$	$-\frac{1}{38}$	0	0
7	y_4	$\frac{5}{19}$	0	$\frac{21}{19}$	0	1	$-\frac{1}{19}$	$\frac{8}{38}$	0	0
0	y_7	$\frac{126}{19}$	0	$\frac{59}{38}$	$\frac{9}{2}$	0	$-\frac{1}{38}$	$-\frac{15}{38}$	1	0
0	y_8	-1	0	-3	0	0	0	-1	0	1 $\rightarrow$
		$z_j - c_j$	0	$\frac{169}{38}$	$\frac{1}{2}$	0	$\frac{1}{38}$	$\frac{53}{38}\uparrow$	0	0

$$\left[\because (-2 \quad -5 \quad 0)\begin{pmatrix}1\\0\\0\end{pmatrix}+2=0, \quad (-2 \quad -5 \quad 0)\begin{pmatrix}\frac{9}{38}\\ \frac{21}{19}\\ \frac{59}{38}\end{pmatrix}+3=-3, \text{ etc.}\right]$$

		c_j	3	4	1	7	0	0	0	0
c_B	B	x_B	y_1	y_2	y_3	y_4	y_5	y_6	y_7	y_8
3	y_1	$\frac{33}{38}$	1	$\frac{12}{38}$	$\frac{1}{2}$	0	$\frac{5}{38}$	0	0	$-\frac{1}{38}$
7	y_4	$\frac{2}{38}$	0	$\frac{9}{19}$	0	1	$-\frac{1}{19}$	0	0	$\frac{4}{19}$
0	y_7	$\frac{267}{38}$	0	$\frac{47}{19}$	$\frac{9}{2}$	0	$-\frac{1}{38}$	0	1	$-\frac{15}{38}$
0	y_8	1	0	3	0	0	0	1	0	-1
		$z_j - c_j$	0	$\frac{10}{3}$	$\frac{1}{2}$	0	$\frac{1}{38}$	0	0	$\frac{53}{8}$

Since all $x_B > 0$ and $z_j - c_j \geq 0$ an optimal feasible solution of the new problem has been reached. The required solution is given by $x_1^* = \frac{33}{38}$, $x_2^* = 0$, $x_3 = 0$, $x_4^* = \frac{2}{38}$, $Z_{\max} = \frac{113}{38}$.

Example 4.4.2. *The optimum simplex table for a maximisation problem is given below.*

		c_j	5	12	5	0	$-M$
c_B	B	x_B	y_1	y_2	y_3	y_4	y_5
12	y_2	$\frac{8}{5}$	0	1	$\frac{1}{5}$	$\frac{2}{5}$	$-\frac{1}{5}$
5	y_1	$\frac{9}{5}$	1	0	$\frac{7}{5}$	$\frac{1}{5}$	$\frac{2}{5}$
		$z_j - c_j$	0	0	$\frac{17}{5}$	$\frac{29}{5}$	$M - \frac{2}{5}$

(i) *Let a new variable $x_6 \geq 0$ be introduced in the problem with a cost coefficient 18 assigned to it in the objective function. The vector corresponding to x_6 be (3, 2). Find the effect of this addition of a variable on the optimality of the optimal solution of the original problem.*

(ii) *What will happens on the optimality and feasibility of the current solution, if the decision variable $x_3 \geq 0$ is deleted from the original problem?* [BESU(MSc) 2007]

Solution: (i) From optimal table it is obvious that x_4, $x_5 \geq 0$ are respectively the slack and the artificial variables. If B be the optimal basis, then

$$B^{-1} = \begin{pmatrix} \frac{2}{5} & -\frac{1}{5} \\ \frac{1}{5} & \frac{2}{5} \end{pmatrix}, \quad \boldsymbol{c_B} = (12 \quad 5).$$

After the addition of a new variable $x_6 \geq 0$, the corresponding $\boldsymbol{y_6}$ row is given by

$$\boldsymbol{y_6} = B^{-1}\boldsymbol{a_6} = \begin{pmatrix} \frac{2}{5} & -\frac{1}{5} \\ \frac{1}{5} & \frac{2}{5} \end{pmatrix}\begin{pmatrix}3\\2\end{pmatrix} = \begin{pmatrix}\frac{4}{5}\\ \frac{7}{5}\end{pmatrix}.$$

Now,

$$z_6 - c_6 = \mathbf{c_B y_6} - c_6 = (12 \quad 5)\begin{pmatrix} \frac{4}{5} \\ \frac{7}{5} \end{pmatrix} - 18 = -\frac{2}{5} < 0.$$

Thus, the post-optimal problem violates the condition of optimality, whereas condition of feasibility maintained. To find the revised optimal solution we proceed as follows.

		c_j	5	12	6	0	$-M$	18	
c_B	B	x_B	y_1	y_2	y_3	y_4	y_5	y_6	MR
12	y_2	$\frac{8}{5}$	0	1	$\frac{1}{5}$	$\frac{2}{5}$	$-\frac{1}{5}$	$\frac{4}{5}$	2
5	y_1	$\frac{9}{5}$	1	0	$\frac{7}{5}$	$\frac{1}{5}$	$\frac{2}{5}$	$\boxed{\frac{7}{5}}$	$\frac{9}{7}\rightarrow$
		$z_j - c_j$	0	0	$\frac{17}{5}$	$\frac{29}{5}$	$M-\frac{2}{5}$	$-\frac{7}{5}\uparrow$	

		c_j	5	12	6	0	$-M$	18
c_B	B	x_B	y_1	y_2	y_3	y_4	y_5	y_6
12	y_2	$\frac{4}{7}$	$-\frac{4}{7}$	1	$-\frac{3}{5}$	$\frac{2}{7}$	$-\frac{3}{7}$	0
18	y_6	$\frac{9}{7}$	$\frac{5}{7}$	0	1	$\frac{1}{7}$	$\frac{2}{7}$	1
		$z_j - c_j$	1	0	$\frac{24}{5}$	6	M	0

Since all $z_j - c_j \geq 0$, the optimum basic feasible solution is obtained. Hence, the new solution is $x_1^* = 0$, $x_2^* = \frac{4}{7}$, $x_3^* = 6$, $x_4^* = 0$, $x_5^* = 0$, $x_6^* = \frac{9}{7}$, $Z_{\max} = \frac{210}{7}$.

(ii) Since the decision variable $x_3 \geq 0$ is not in the current optimum basis

$$\mathbf{x_B} = \begin{pmatrix} x_2 \\ x_1 \end{pmatrix} = \begin{pmatrix} \frac{8}{5} \\ \frac{9}{5} \end{pmatrix},$$

therefore, the deletion of x_3 does not effect the current optimum basic feasible solution. So the previous solution remains for the new problem as well.

Example 4.4.3. *After obtaining the optimum basic feasible solution to the problem:*

Maximise $Z = 3x_1 + 2x_2$

subject to $x_1 + 2x_2 \leq 6$

$2x_1 + x_2 \leq 8$

$-x_1 + x_2 \leq 1$

$x_2 \leq 2$

$x_1, x_2 \geq 0.$

A new constraint of the form $x_1 \leq 4$ is added to the model. Check whether the new addition alters the optimum solution. If instead of $x_1 \leq 4$, the new constraint is $x_1 \leq 3$, then what will happen about the optimum solution?

[BESU(MSc) 2011; MBA(CU) 2004]

Solution: The optimum table is given below:

Optimum table:

		c_j	3	2	0	0	0	0
c_B	B	x_B	y_1	y_2	y_3	y_4	y_5	y_6
2	y_2	$\frac{4}{3}$	0	1	$\frac{2}{3}$	$-\frac{1}{3}$	0	0
3	y_1	$\frac{10}{3}$	1	0	$-\frac{1}{3}$	$\frac{2}{3}$	0	0
0	y_5	3	0	0	-1	1	1	0
0	y_6	$\frac{2}{3}$	0	0	$-\frac{2}{3}$	$\frac{1}{3}$	0	1
		$z_j - c_j$	0	0	$\frac{1}{3}$	$\frac{4}{3}$	0	0

The current optimum basic feasible solution of the problem is $x_1^* = \frac{10}{3}, x_2^* = \frac{4}{3}, Z_{\max} = \frac{38}{3}$.

Obviously, the additional constraint $x_1 \le 4$ satisfies the current solution so that the post-optimal addition of the constraint does not alter the solution.

But the constraint $x_1 \le 3$, which is not satisfied by the current solution. Here is what we do to recover feasibility. First put the constraint in the standard form by introducing slack variable

$$x_1 + \cdots + x_7 = 3, \quad x_7 \ge 0.$$

An alternative approach for determining the new optimal basic feasible solution is as follows (This is equivalent to the method applied in Ex. 4.4.1).

In the current optimum basic feasible solution x_1 is a basic variable and we must substitute it out in terms of non-basic variables. From the optimal table, we have $x_1 - \frac{1}{3}x_3 + \frac{2}{3}x_4 = \frac{10}{3}$.

Thus, the new constraint expressed in terms of the current non-basic variables becomes

$$\frac{10}{3} + \frac{1}{3}x_3 - \frac{2}{3}x_4 + x_7 = 3$$
$$\Rightarrow \frac{1}{3}x_3 - \frac{2}{3}x_4 + x_7 = -\frac{1}{3}.$$

Note that the negative right-hand side indicates infeasibility since given $x_3 = x_4 = 0, x_7 = -\frac{1}{3} < 0$, which violates the requirement $x_7 \ge 0$.

The modified constraints is now placed to the current optimal table and then use usual *dual-simplex* method.

		c_j	3	2	0	0	0	0	0	
c_B	B	x_B	y_1	y_2	y_3	y_4	y_5	y_6	y_7	
2	y_2	$\frac{4}{3}$	0	1	$\frac{2}{3}$	$-\frac{1}{3}$	0	0	0	
3	y_1	$\frac{10}{3}$	1	0	$-\frac{1}{3}$	$\frac{2}{3}$	0	0	0	
0	y_5	3	0	0	-1	1	1	0	0	
0	y_6	$\frac{2}{3}$	0	0	$-\frac{2}{3}$	$\frac{1}{3}$	0	1	0	
0	y_7	$-\frac{1}{3}$	0	0	$\frac{1}{3}$	$\left(-\frac{2}{3}\right)$	0	0	1	$\rightarrow$
		$z_j - c_j$	0	0	$\frac{1}{3}$	$\frac{4}{3}\uparrow$	0	0	0	

		c_j	3	2	0	0	0	0	0
c_B	B	x_B	y_1	y_2	y_3	y_4	y_5	y_6	y_7
2	y_2	$\frac{3}{2}$	0	1	$\frac{1}{2}$	0	0	0	$-\frac{1}{2}$
3	y_1	3	1	0	0	0	0	0	1
0	y_5	$\frac{5}{2}$	0	0	$-\frac{1}{2}$	0	1	0	$\frac{3}{2}$
0	y_6	$\frac{1}{2}$	0	0	$-\frac{1}{2}$	0	0	1	$\frac{1}{2}$
0	y_4	$\frac{1}{2}$	0	0	$-\frac{1}{2}$	1	0	0	$-\frac{3}{2}$
		$z_j - c_j$	0	0	1	0	0	0	2

Revised optimum solution is $x_1^* = 3$, $x_2^* = \frac{3}{2}$, $Z_{\max} = 12$. The new solution has worse optimum value of Z than before the constraint is added. This is always expected since the addition of a new binding constraint can never improve the value of Z.

4.5 EXERCISE 4

1. Solve the LPP.

   Maximise $Z = 5x_1 + 12x_2 + 4x_3$

   subject to $x_1 + 2x_2 + x_3 \leq 5$

   $2x_1 - x_2 + 3x_3 = 2$

   $x_1, x_2, x_3 \geq 0.$

   Find the effect of changing the requirement vector $(5,2)^T$ to $(7,2)^T$ on the optimum solution.

   [CU(MSc) 2002]

2. The optimal solution table of the following LPP is given below. Find the separate ranges of b_1, b_2 and b_3 consistent with the current optimal solution.

   Maximise $Z = -x_1 + 2x_2 - x_3$

   subject to $3x_1 + x_2 - x_3 \leq 10$

   $-x_1 + 4x_2 + x_3 \geq 6$

   $x_2 + x_3 \leq 4$

   $x_1, x_2, x_3 \geq 0.$

		c_j	−1	2	−1	0	0	0	$-M$
c_B	B	x_B	x_1	x_2	x_3	x_4	x_5	x_6	x_a
0	x_4	6	3	0	−2	1	0	−1	0
2	x_2	4	0	1	1	0	0	1	0
0	x_5	10	1	0	3	0	1	4	−1
		$z_j - c_j$	1	0	3	0	0	2	M

[Meerut(MSc) 1993]

3. Consider the LPP.

Maximise $Z = 3x_1 + 5x_2 + 4x_3$

subject to $2x_1 + 3x_2 \leq 8$

$2x_2 + 5x_3 \leq 10$

$3x_1 + 2x_2 + 4x_3 \leq 15$

$x_1, x_2, x_3 \geq 0.$

The optimum table is given below:

		c_j	3	5	4	0	0	0
c_B	B	x_B	y_1	y_2	y_3	y_4	y_5	y_6
5	y_2	$\frac{50}{41}$	0	1	0	$\frac{15}{41}$	$\frac{8}{41}$	$-\frac{10}{41}$
4	y_3	$\frac{62}{41}$	0	0	1	$-\frac{6}{41}$	$\frac{5}{41}$	$\frac{4}{41}$
3	y_1	$\frac{89}{41}$	1	0	0	$-\frac{2}{41}$	$-\frac{12}{41}$	$\frac{15}{41}$
		$z_j - c_j$	0	0	0	$\frac{45}{41}$	$\frac{24}{41}$	$\frac{11}{41}$

(i) How much c_3 and c_4 can be increased till the optimal solution given above ceases to be optimal?

(ii) Find the range over b_2 that can be changed for maintaining the feasibility of the solution.

[BESU(MSc) 2006, CU(MSc) 1998, JNU(Comp. Sc MTech) 1993]

4. Consider the problem: Maximise $Z = 45x_1 + 100x_2 + 30x_3 + 50x_4$

subject to $7x_1 + 10x_2 + 4x_3 + 9x_4 \leq 1200$

$3x_1 + 40x_2 + x_3 + x_4 \leq 800$

$x_1, x_2, x_3, x_4 \geq 0.$

The optimal table for this problem is given below:

		c_j	45	100	30	50	0	0
c_B	B	x_B	y_1	y_2	y_3	y_4	y_5	y_6
30	y_3	$\frac{800}{3}$	$\frac{5}{3}$	0	1	$\frac{7}{3}$	$\frac{4}{15}$	$-\frac{1}{15}$
100	y_2	$\frac{40}{3}$	$\frac{1}{30}$	1	0	$-\frac{1}{30}$	$-\frac{1}{150}$	$\frac{2}{75}$
		$z_j - c_j$	$\frac{25}{3}$	0	0	$\frac{50}{3}$	$\frac{22}{3}$	$\frac{2}{3}$

If a new variable x_7 is added to this problem with a column $\begin{pmatrix} 10 \\ 10 \end{pmatrix}$ and $c_7 = 120$, find the change in the optimal solution. [BESU(MSc) 2003; MBA(CU) 1996]

5. Solve the problem: Maximise $Z = x_1 + 5x_2 + 3x_3$

subject to $x_1 + 2x_2 + x_3 = 3$

$2x_1 - x_2 = 4$

$x_1, x_2, x_3 \geq 0.$

If the objective function is changed to maximise $Z^* = 2x_1 + 5x_2 + 2x_3$, will there be any change in the current optimal solution? If so, find the new optimal solution. [BU(MSc) 1996]

6. Solve the LPP: Maximise $Z = 45x_1 + 100x_2 + 30x_3 + 50x_4$

subject to $7x_1 + 10x_2 + 4x_3 + 9x_4 \leq 1200$

$3x_1 + 40x_2 + x_3 + x_4 \leq 800.$

(i) Find the effect of changing the cost coefficients c_1 and c_4 from 45 and 50 to 40 and 60 respectively.

(ii) What happens if changing c_1 to 40 and c_2 to 90?

(iii) Changing c_3 from 30 to 24? [BESU(MSc) 2009, CU(MSc Appl) 1997, VU(MSc) 1999]

7. Given the LPP: Minimise $Z = x_2 - 3x_3 + 2x_5$

subject to $3x_2 - x_3 + 2x_5 \leq 7$

$-2x_2 + 4x_3 \leq 12$

$-4x_2 + 3x_3 + 8x_5 \leq 10$

$x_2, x_3, x_5 \geq 0.$

The optimal table is:

		c_j	0	−1	+3	0	−2	0
c_B	B	x_B	y_1	y_2	y_3	y_4	y_5	y_6
1	y_2	4	$\frac{2}{5}$	1	0	$\frac{1}{10}$	$\frac{4}{5}$	0
−3	y_3	5	$\frac{1}{5}$	0	1	$\frac{3}{10}$	$\frac{2}{5}$	0
0	y_6	11	1	0	0	$-\frac{1}{2}$	10	1
		$z_j - c_j$	$\frac{1}{5}$	0	0	$\frac{4}{5}$	$\frac{12}{5}$	0

(a) Formulate *dual problem* for this primal problem.

(b) What are the optimal values of dual variables?

(c) How much c_5 can be decreased before x_5 goes into solution?

(d) How much can be 7 in first constraint be increased before the basis would change?

[IAS(Main) 2001, Roorke(MTech) 1977, ISI(OR) 1979]

8. Consider the following table which represents the optimal solution to some LPP.

		c_j	2	4	1	3	2	0	0	0
c_B	B	x_B	y_1	y_2	y_3	y_4	y_5	y_6	y_7	y_8
2	y_1	3	1	0	0	−1	0	$\frac{1}{2}$	$\frac{1}{5}$	−1
4	y_2	1	0	1	0	2	1	−1	0	$\frac{1}{2}$
1	y_3	7	0	0	1	−1	−2	5	$-\frac{3}{10}$	2
		$z_j - c_j$	0	0	0	2	0	2	$\frac{1}{10}$	2

(i) If the additional constraint $2x_1 + 3x_2 - x_3 + 2x_4 + 4x_5 \leq 5$ is annexed to the system, will there be any change in the optimal solution? Justify your answer. [BESU(MSc) 2004; MBA(CU) 1992]

(ii) If an additional constraint $2x_1 + 3x_2 - x_3 + 2x_4 + 4x_5 < 1$ is added to the system, then show that the current optimal solution is not optimal and the new optimal solution is $x_1^* = 3$, $x_2^* = 0$, $x_3^* = 9$, $x_4^* = 0$, $x_5^* = 1$, $Z_{max} = 17$.

9. The optimal solution of the LPP: Maximise $Z = 3x_1 + 4x_2 + x_3 + 7x_4$

$$\begin{aligned} \text{subject to } 8x_1 + 3x_2 + 4x_3 + x_4 &\le 7 \\ 2x_1 + 6x_2 + x_3 + 5x_4 &\le 3 \\ x_1 + 4x_2 + 5x_3 + 2x_4 &\le 8 \\ x_1,\ x_2,\ x_3,\ x_4 &\ge 0 \end{aligned}$$

is: $x_1^* = \frac{16}{19}$, $x_4^* = \frac{5}{19}$, $x_7^* = \frac{126}{19}$, $Z_{\max} = \frac{83}{19}$.

The variable x_4 is deleted from the above problem. Then show that this post-optimal deletion of the variable changes the above optimal solution. Find the new solution. [Roorkee(MSc Appl) 1996]

10. Consider the LPP: Minimise $Z = 8x_1 + 3x_2 + 6x_3 + 3x_4$

$$\begin{aligned} \text{subject to } \quad x_2 + 4x_3 + 5x_4 &\le 3 \\ 3x_1 \quad + 2x_3 \quad &\le 5 \\ x_1 + 2x_2 \quad + x_4 &\le 6 \\ x_1,\ x_2,\ x_3,\ x_4 &\ge 0. \end{aligned}$$

Will the optimal solution to the above problem remain optimal if the requirement vector $[3,5,6]^T$ changes to $[3,10,6]^T$? Justify in favour of your answer. [CU(MSc Appl) 1983]

11. Following is the optimal table for some LPP.

		c_j	2	1	1	2	0
c_B	B	x_B	y_1	y_2	y_3	y_4	y_5
2	y_1	3	1	0	−1	3	2
1	y_2	4	0	1	4	−3	−2
		$z_j - c_j$	0	0	1	3	2

(i) Find the limitations of the values of c_3, c_4, c_5 for which the current optimal solution will remain optimal.

(ii) Find the optimal solution to the problem, if c_3 increases to 3.

(iii) Find the limitations of the values of c_1 for which the current optimal solution remains optimal.

(iv) Find the optimal solution to the problem, if c_1 be increased to 5.

[CU(MSc Appl) 1981, 1992; BESU(MSc) 2004, 2008]

12. Consider the problem: Maximise $Z = 2x_2 - 5x_3$

$$\begin{aligned} \text{subject to } x_1 + \quad x_3 &\ge 2 \\ 2x_1 + x_2 + 6x_3 &\le 6 \\ x_1 - x_2 + 3x_3 &= 0 \\ x_1,\ x_2,\ x_3 &\ge 0. \end{aligned}$$

(a) Write the dual.

(b) Solve the primal; then find the solution to the dual.

(c) Suppose that the right-hand side of the primal is changed from $(2,6,0)^T$ to $(2,5,10)$. Find the new optimal solution.

(d) Suppose that the coefficients of x_2 and x_3 in the objective function are changed from $(2,-5)$ to $(1,1)$. Find the new solution.

13. Let x_B be the optimum solution to the LPP: Maximise $Z = cx$

subject to $Ax = b$

$x \geq 0.$

Is it possible to obtain an LPP, which has an unbounded solution by changing b alone?

14. The optimum simplex tableau for a maximisation problem with '$\leq$' constraints is

		c_j	*	*	0	0	0
c_B	B	x_B	y_1	y_2	y_3	y_4	y_5
0	y_2	2	0	1	$\frac{1}{2}$	$-\frac{1}{2}$	0
*	y_1	$\frac{3}{2}$	1	0	$-\frac{1}{8}$	$\frac{3}{8}$	0
0	y_3	4	0	0	1	-2	1
		$z_j - c_j$	0	0	$\frac{1}{4}$	$\frac{1}{4}$	0

where y_1, y_2 are the decision variables and y_3, y_4, y_5 are the slack variables.

(i) Complete the '*' positions.

(ii) Suppose that it is decided to increase the right-hand side of one of the constraints. Which one do you recommend for expansion and why? What is the maximum amount of increase in this case? Find the corresponding new value of the objective function.

15. Give an LPP: Maximise $Z = 5x_1 + 2x_2 + 3x_3$

subject to $x_1 + 5x_2 + 2x_3 \leq b_1$

$x_1 - 5x_2 - 6x_3 \leq b_2$

$x_1, x_2, x_3 \geq 0$

where b_1, b_2 are constants. For specific values of b_1 and b_2, the optimal solution is

		c_j	5	2	3	0	0
c_B	B	x_B	y_1	y_2	y_3	y_4	y_5
5	y_1	30	1	b	2	1	0
0	y_5	10	0	c	-8	-1	1
		$z_j - c_j$	0	a	7	d	e

where a, b, c, d, e are constants. Determine:

(i) The value of b_1 and b_2 that yield the given optimal solution.

(ii) The optimal dual solution.

(iii) The value of a, b, c in the optimal tableau. [IAS(Main) 2002]

16. Given the LPP: Maximise $Z = 6x_1 + 8x_2$

subject to $5x_1 + 10x_2 \leq 60$

$4x_1 + 4x_2 \leq 40$

$x_1, x_2 \geq 0.$

(i) Show that the post-optimal addition of a new constraint $7x_1 + 2x_2 \leq 65$ to be a redundant constraint and the current optimality will not be affected after the inclusion of new constraint into the existing LP model.

(ii) *The addition of* $6x_1 + 3x_2 \leq 48$ *affects the optimality.* — Justify this statement with arguments.

ANSWERS

1. Optimum solution: $x_1^* = \frac{9}{5}$, $x_2^* = \frac{8}{5}$, $x_3^* = 0$, $Z_{\max} = \frac{141}{5}$. (i) Optimum solution changed to: $x_1^* = \frac{11}{5}$, $x_2^* = \frac{12}{5}$, $x_3^* = 0$, $Z_{\max} = \frac{199}{5}$.

2. $4 \le b_1^* \le \infty$, $-\infty < b_2^* \le 16$, $\frac{3}{2} \le b^* \le 10$, whereas usual notation denoted in the chapter as $b_k^* = b_k + \delta b_k \ \forall\ k$.

3. (i) $\frac{5}{4} \le c_3^* \le \frac{23}{2}$, $-\infty < c_4^* < \frac{45}{41}$; (ii) $\frac{15}{4} \le b_2^* \le \frac{209}{12}$.

4. Post-optimal addition of new variable changes the optimal solution. The changed optimal solution is: $x_3^* = \frac{400}{3}$, $x_7^* = \frac{200}{3}$ (basic), $x_1^* = x_2^* = x_4^* = x_5^* = x_6^* = 0$ (non-basic), $Z_{\max} = 12{,}000$.

5. Current optimal solution: $x_1^* = 2$, $x_2^* = 0$, $x_3^* = 1$, $Z_{\max} = 5$. New objective function changes the current optimal solution. Changed optimal solution: $x_1^* = \frac{11}{5}$, $x_2^* = \frac{2}{5}$, $x_3^* = 0$, $Z_{\max} = \frac{32}{5}$.

6. Current optimal solution: $x_1^* = 0$, $x_2^* = \frac{40}{3}$, $x_3^* = \frac{800}{3}$, $x_4^* = 0$, $Z_{\max} = \frac{28{,}000}{3}$. (i) Current optimal solution remains optimal. (ii) Changed optimal solution: $x_1^* = 0$, $x_2^* = \frac{40}{3}$, $x_3^* = \frac{800}{3}$, $x_4^* = 0$, $Z_{\max} = 9200$. (iii) Changed optimal solution: $x_1^* = 160$, $x_2^* = 8$, $x_3^* = 0$, $x_4^* = 0$, $Z_{\max} = 8000$.

7. (a) Maximise $W = -7y_1 - 12y_2 - 10y_3$

$$\begin{aligned}\text{subject to } -3y_1 + 2y_2 + 4y_3 &\le 1\\ -y_1 + 4y_2 + 3y_3 &\ge 3\\ -2y_1 \qquad - 8y_3 &\le 2\\ y_1, y_2, y_3 &\ge 0.\end{aligned}$$

(b) $y_1^* = \frac{1}{5}$, $y_2^* = \frac{4}{5}$, $y_3^* = 0$.
(c) $\delta c_5 > \frac{12}{5}$.
(d) $\delta b_1 < -1$.

9. New solution: $x_1^* = \frac{11}{4}$, $x_2^* = \frac{5}{21}$, $x_7^* = \frac{5123}{58}$, $Z_{\max} = \frac{139}{42}$.

11. (i) $-\infty < c_3^* \le 2$, $-\infty < c_4^* \le 5$, $-\infty < c_5^* \le 2$, (ii) $x_1^* = 4$, $x_3^* = 1$, $x_2^* = x_4^* = 0$, (iii) $1 \le c_1 \le 3$, (iv) $x_1^* = \frac{13}{4}$, $x_3^* = 1$, $x_2^* = x_4^* = 0$.

12. (i) Minimise $W = 2v_1 + 6v_2$

$$\begin{aligned}\text{subject to } v_1 + 2v_2 + v_3 &\ge 0\\ v_2 - v_3 &\ge 2\\ v_1 + 6v_2 + 3v_3 &\ge -5\\ v_1, v_2 &\ge 0,\ v_3 \text{ unrestricted.}\end{aligned}$$

(ii) $v_1^* = 0$, $v_2^* = \frac{2}{3}$, $v_3^* - \frac{4}{3}$.
(iii) New solution: $x_1^* = 5$, $x_2^* = 3$, $x_3^* = 0$.
(iv) New solution is degenerate and remains the same as $x_1^* = 2, x_2^* = 2$, $x_3^* = 0$.

14. (ii) Either resource $1(b_1)$ or resource $2(b_2)$ can be considered for expansion. $\delta b_1 \le 12$ and $\delta b_2 \le 2$. New z for given δb_1 is 8 and new z for given $\delta b_2 = \frac{11}{2}$.

15. (i) $b_1 = 30$, $b_2 = 40$. (ii) $v_1^* = 5$, $v_2^* = 0$. (iii) $a = 23$, $b = 5$, $c = -10$.

Chapter 5

Integer Linear Programming

5.1 INTRODUCTION

All the problems in the prior chapters that we have treated wherein all basic variables including slack or surplus variables were permitted to take any non-negative real values (continuous or fractional). It was done since in many situations it was quite possible and made sense to have fractional solutions. For example, it is quite sensible to use 10.25 kg of raw material, 2.30 hours of man power, etc. But there are many problems, particularly in business and industry, where quite often the fractional solutions are unrealistic, because the units are not divisible. For example, it is meaningless to produce 5.67 tables or to open 4.25 shopping mall or to run 1.23 machines to produce a product, etc. In such cases, integer programming plays a key role where some or all the required variables are integer valued. Transportation problems, assignment problems, etc. are IPP, since the decision variables are either zero or one. Many other decision problems can necessitate integer programming models, one category of which problems deals with the sequencing, scheduling and routing decisions. This is the main reasons why integer programming is so important for marginal decisions.

5.2 DEFINITIONS

An LPP in which some or all of the variables are required to be an integer valued is called IPP. If all the variables are to be integer valued then the problem is called a *pure integer programme.* Otherwise, the problem is called *mixed integer programme.* Further, if all the variables in the optimum solution are allowed to take values either 0 or 1 in *do* or *not to do* type decisions, then the problem is called *zero-one integer programme.*

5.3 CUTTING PLANE CONSTRAINTS

Consider a pure integer programme.

Maximise $Z = \boldsymbol{cx}$ (5.3a)

subject to $A\boldsymbol{x} = \boldsymbol{b}$

$\boldsymbol{x} \geq \boldsymbol{0}$ and are integers,

where $A = (a_{ij})_{m \times n}$, $\boldsymbol{c} = (c_1, c_2, \ldots, c_n)$, $\boldsymbol{x} = (x_1, x_2, \ldots, x_n)^T$, $\boldsymbol{b} = (b_1, b_2, \ldots, b_m)^T$.

The problem (5.3a) with integer restriction deleted shall be called *related* LPP. The basic idea in cutting plane algorithm are as follows:

Given a pure IPP, solve the related LPP. If the optimum table contains only integer valued variables, then that must be the optimal solution of IPP. But if some variable in the optimum solution is not an integer, then a new constraint is added to the original problem and the new related LPP is solved. Again, we check whether the new optimum solution satisfies the integer requirement solution to the original IPP. If, on the other hand, some of the variables are still not an integer, then again a new constraint is added and the process is continued until one such related LPP is found to have an all integer optimum solution. As these are hyperplanes which cut off a portion of the feasible region of the related LPP, the constraints are called cutting planes.

We now derive the mathematical form of cutting planes.

Mathematical Formulation

Ignoring the integer restriction of the problem (5.3a) let us first solve the related LPP by usual simplex method and for simplicity we shall assume that the optimal solution contains first m columns of A in the basis B. Hence, A can be partitioned into two sub-matrices $A = [B, R]$, where B contains first m columns of A and R contains remaining $(n - m)$ columns of A. The corresponding optimal solution of the problem $\boldsymbol{x}^* = [\boldsymbol{x}^*_B, \boldsymbol{x}^*_R]^T$, where the non-basic variables $\boldsymbol{x}^*_R = \boldsymbol{0}$.

Now, the constraint equation $A\boldsymbol{x} = \boldsymbol{b}$ gives

$$[B, R]\begin{bmatrix} \boldsymbol{x}^*_B \\ \boldsymbol{x}^*_R \end{bmatrix} = \boldsymbol{b} \Rightarrow B\boldsymbol{x}^*_B + R\boldsymbol{x}^*_R = \boldsymbol{b} \Rightarrow (B^{-1}B)\,\boldsymbol{x}^*_B + (B^{-1}R)\,\boldsymbol{x}^*_R = B^{-1}\boldsymbol{b} \Rightarrow \boldsymbol{x}^*_B = B^{-1}\boldsymbol{b} - (B^1 R)\,\boldsymbol{x}^*_R. \tag{5.3b}$$

Since R consists of the columns of A we can express (5.3b) in terms of the columns of the simplex table namely

$$\boldsymbol{y}_0 = B^{-1}\boldsymbol{b} \text{ and } \boldsymbol{y}_j = B^{-1}\boldsymbol{a}_j. \tag{5.3c}$$

From (5.3b) using (5.3c),

$$\boldsymbol{x}^*_B = \boldsymbol{y}_0 - \sum_{j \in N} y_j x_j, \tag{5.3d}$$

where $N = \{j | x_j \text{ is a non-basic variable}\}$.

$\boldsymbol{x}^*_B$ represents the optimal basis of the related LPP of problem (5.3a). Suppose that the rth basic variable of $\boldsymbol{x}^*_B$ is not an integer but we want it to be an integer. To do so let us write (5.3d)

$$x_{Br} = y_{r0} - \sum_{j \in N} y_{rj} x_j. \tag{5.3e}$$

In the current optimal solution all x_j for $j \in N$ are zero so that y_{r0} is not an integer.

Let

$$y_{r0} = W_{r0} + f_{r0}, \quad y_{rj} = W_{rj} + f_{rj}, \tag{5.3f}$$

where W_{r0}, W_{rj} are integral parts and $0 < f_{r0}, f_{rj} < 1$ are fractional parts of y_{r0} and y_{rj} respectively. Then (5.3e) becomes

$$x_{Br} = \left(W_{r0} - \sum_{j\in N} W_{rj}x_j\right) + \left(f_{r0} - \sum_{j\in N} f_{rj}x_j\right) = [I] + \{f\}, \tag{5.3g}$$

where $[I]$ and $\{f\}$ are respectively integral part and fractional part of x_{Br}.

If we wish to modify the current solution so that the new solution is integer, then we make $\{f\}$ to be an integer.

Since each $f_{rj} > 0$ and $x_j \geq 0$ imply $\sum_{j\in N} f_{rj}x_j \geq 0$.

Hence, the quantity $\{f\} = f_{r0} - \sum_{j\in N} f_{rj}x_j$ consists of a positive quantity $\sum_{j\in N} f_{rj}x_j$ subtracted from another positive quantity f_{r0} which is less than unity. Therefore, the entire quantity cannot be a positive integer. If it is to be an integer, then it must be a negative integer or zero.

Therefore,

$$\boxed{\{f\} = \left(f_{r0} - \sum_{j\in N} f_{rj}x_j\right) \leq 0.} \tag{5.3h}$$

(5.3h) is the required cutting plane constraint derived by Gomory in the case of pure integer programme. This constraints is added to the optimal table of the related LPP and then solved by *dual-simplex* method.

Important Notes

1. Every integer feasible solution of original IPP will satisfy this constraint.
2. If some y_{ij} be negative, even then a non-negative fractional part of it as required may be obtained. For example, $\left(-2\frac{2}{3}\right)$ can be written as $\left(-3+\frac{1}{3}\right)$, whereby the non-negative fractional part $\frac{1}{3}$ has been separated.
3. In our above discussion, we have not considered how to determine the cutting plane constraint if more than one basic variable in the optimum table of the related LPP are not an integer. In most frequently employed technique, the x_{Br} whose fractional part f_{r0} is largest is used to find the cutting plane constraint (5.3h).

Example 5.3.1. *Use Gomory's cutting plane to solve the problem.*

Maximise $Z = x_1 - x_2$

subject to $x_1 + 2x_2 \leq 4$

$6x_1 + 2x_2 \leq 9$

$x_1, x_2 \geq 0$ *and are integers.*

Solution: We first find the optimal solution of the related LPP. The standard form of the related LPP is

Maximise $Z = x_1 - x_2 + 0x_3 + 0x_4$

subject to $x_1 + 2x_2 + x_3 = 4$

$6x_1 + 2x_2 + x_4 = 9$

$x_1, x_2 \geq 0$, decision variables

$x_3, x_4 \geq 0$, slack variables.

Now, solve the problem by simplex method as follows:

		c_j	1	−1	0	0	
c_B	B	x_B	y_1	y_2	y_3	y_4	MR
0	y_3	4	1	2	1	0	$\frac{4}{1}$
0	y_4	9	6	2	0	1	$\frac{9}{6}$ →
		$z_j - c_j$	−1↑	1	0	0	

		c_j	1	−1	0	0
c_B	B	x_B	y_1	y_2	y_3	y_4
0	y_3	$\frac{5}{2}$	0	$\frac{5}{3}$	1	$-\frac{1}{6}$
1	y_1	$\frac{3}{2}$	1	$\frac{1}{3}$	0	$\frac{1}{6}$
		$z_j - c_j$	0	$\frac{4}{3}$	0	$\frac{1}{6}$

All $z_j - c_j \geq 0$ and $x_B > 0$ so optimal basic feasible solution of the related LPP has been reached and is given by $x_1^* = \frac{3}{2}, x_2^* = 0, Z_{\max} = \frac{3}{2}$.

Observations. The decision variable $x_1^* = \frac{3}{2}$ is not an integer but we require it to be an integer. To obtain the integer solution we use Gomory's cutting plane constraint.

Here $y_{20} = \frac{3}{2} = 1 + \frac{1}{2}, \quad W_{20} = 1 \quad f_{20} = \frac{1}{2}$

$y_{22} = \frac{1}{3} = 0 + \frac{1}{3}, \quad W_{22} = 0 \quad f_{22} = \frac{1}{3}$

$y_{24} = \frac{1}{6} = 0 + \frac{1}{6}, \quad W_{24} = 0 \quad f_{24} = \frac{1}{6}$

$$\therefore f_{r0} - \sum_{j \in N} y_{rj} x_j \leq 0 \Rightarrow \frac{1}{2} - \left(\frac{1}{3}x_2 + \frac{1}{6}x_4\right) \leq 0 \Rightarrow -\frac{1}{3}x_2 - \frac{1}{6}x_4 \leq -\frac{1}{2} \Rightarrow -\frac{1}{3}x_2 - \frac{1}{6}x_4 + x_5 = -\frac{1}{2}.$$

We add a new slack variable $x_5 \geq 0$ in the new constraint and compute the following table with additional constraint.

		c_j	1	−1	0	0	0
c_B	B	x_B	y_1	y_2	y_3	y_4	y_5
0	y_3	$\frac{5}{2}$	0	$\frac{5}{3}$	1	$-\frac{1}{6}$	0
+1	y_1	$\frac{3}{2}$	1	$\frac{1}{3}$	0	$\frac{1}{6}$	0
0	y_5	$-\frac{1}{2}$	0	$-\frac{1}{3}$	0	$\left(-\frac{1}{6}\right)$	1 →
		$z_j - c_j$	0	$\frac{4}{3}$	0	$\frac{1}{6}$↑	0

We see that the solution is optimum as all $z_j - c_j \geq 0$ but it is not feasible, $\boldsymbol{y_5}$ being negative. Hence, we apply *dual-simplex* method. $\boldsymbol{y_5}$ leaves the basis and since

$$\max\left\{\frac{4/3}{-1/3}, \frac{1/6}{-1/6}\right\} = \max\{-4, -1\} = -1,$$

$\boldsymbol{y_4}$ enters the basis. The new table is thus

		c_j	1	−1	0	0	0
c_B	B	x_B	y_1	y_2	y_3	y_4	y_5
0	y_3	3	0	2	1	0	−1
1	y_1	1	1	0	0	0	1
0	y_4	3	0	2	0	1	−6
		$z_j - c_j$	0	1	0	0	1

This gives us an optimal solution which is integral.

Thus, the required integer solution is $\hat{x}=1$, $\hat{x}=0$, $Z_{\max}=1$.

Example 5.3.2. *Using Gomory's cutting plane method solve the following pure* IPP.

Maximum $Z=2x_1+2x_2$

subject to $5x_1+3x_2\leq 8$

$x_1+2x_2\leq 4$

$x_1,\ x_2\geq 0$ *and are integers.* [CU(MSc Appl) 1989, 1992; BESU(MSc) 2001, 2007]

Solution: We first find the optimal solution of the related LPP by introducing slack variables $x_3,\ x_4\geq 0$ to the two given constraints respectively. The following is the *optimal table* of the related LPP obtained by usual simplex method.

Optimum table:

		c_j	2	2	0	0
c_B	B	x_B	y_1	y_2	y_3	y_4
2	y_1	$\frac{4}{7}$	1	0	$\frac{2}{7}$	$-\frac{3}{7}$
2	y_2	$\frac{12}{7}$	0	1	$-\frac{1}{7}$	$\frac{5}{7}$
		z_j-c_j	0	0	$\frac{2}{7}$	$\frac{4}{7}$

Optimal basic feasible solution of the related LPP: $x_1^*=\frac{4}{7}$, $x_2^*=\frac{12}{7}$, $Z_{\max}=\frac{32}{7}$.

Observation. Neither of the decision variables are non-integer but we require both of them as integral solution.

Here $x_{B1}=x_1^*=\frac{4}{7}=0+\frac{4}{7}$, $W_{10}=0$, $f_{10}=\frac{4}{7}$

$x_{B2}=x_2^*=\frac{12}{7}=1+\frac{4}{7}$, $W_{20}=1$, $f_{20}=\frac{5}{7}$.

Since $f_{20}>f_{10}$ we take $x_{B2}=x_2^*$ to calculate cutting plane: $y_{23}=-\frac{1}{7}=-1+\frac{6}{7}$, $W_{23}=-1$, $f_{23}=\frac{6}{7}$

$y_{24}=\frac{5}{7}=0+\frac{5}{7}$, $W_{24}=0$, $f_{24}=\frac{5}{7}$.

$$\left(f_{r0}-\sum_{j\in N}f_{rj}x_j\right)\leq 0\Rightarrow\frac{5}{7}-\left(\frac{6}{7}x_3+\frac{5}{7}x_4\right)\leq 0\Rightarrow-\frac{6}{7}x_3+\frac{5}{7}x_4\leq-\frac{5}{7}\Rightarrow-\frac{6}{7}x_3-\frac{5}{7}x_4+x_5=-\frac{5}{7}.$$

This constraint is added to the previous optimum table and we apply dual-simplex method.

		c_j	2	2	0	0	0	
c_B	B	x_B	y_1	y_2	y_3	y_4	y_5	
2	y_1	$\frac{4}{7}$	1	0	$\frac{2}{7}$	$-\frac{3}{7}$	0	
2	y_2	$\frac{12}{7}$	0	1	$-\frac{1}{7}$	$\frac{5}{7}$	0	
0	y_5	$-\frac{5}{7}$	0	0	$\left(-\frac{6}{7}\right)$	$-\frac{5}{7}$	1	$\rightarrow$
		z_j-c_j	0	0	$\frac{2}{7}\uparrow$	$\frac{4}{7}$	0	

$$\max\left\{\frac{2/7}{-6/7},\frac{4/7}{-5/7}\right\}=\max\left\{-\frac{1}{3},-\frac{4}{5}\right\}=-\frac{1}{3}.$$

$\boldsymbol{y}_5$ leaves the basis and $\boldsymbol{y}_3$ enters the basis.

		c_j	2	2	0	0	0
c_B	B	x_B	y_1	y_2	y_3	y_4	y_5
2	y_1	$\frac{1}{3}$	1	0	0	$-\frac{2}{3}$	$\frac{1}{3}$
2	y_2	$\frac{11}{6}$	0	1	0	$\frac{5}{6}$	$-\frac{1}{6}$
0	y_3	$\frac{5}{6}$	0	0	1	$\frac{5}{6}$	$-\frac{7}{6}$
		$z_j - c_j$	0	0	0	$\frac{1}{3}$	$\frac{1}{3}$

From this table, we get a feasible and optimal solution but that too is non-integral. We again construct a new cutting plane following the same rule with $x_{B2} = x_2^*$ as the variable and the new constraint is

$$-\frac{5}{6}x_4 - \frac{5}{6}x_5 < -\frac{5}{6} \Rightarrow -\frac{5}{6}x_4 - \frac{5}{6}x_5 + x_6 = -\frac{5}{6}.$$

		c_j	2	2	0	0	0	0
c_B	B	x_B	y_1	y_2	y_3	y_4	y_5	y_6
2	y_1	$\frac{1}{3}$	1	0	0	$-\frac{2}{3}$	$\frac{1}{3}$	0
2	y_2	$\frac{11}{6}$	0	1	0	$\frac{5}{6}$	$-\frac{1}{6}$	0
0	y_3	$\frac{5}{6}$	0	0	1	$\frac{5}{6}$	$-\frac{7}{6}$	0
0	y_6	$-\frac{5}{6}$	0	0	0	$-\frac{5}{6}$	$-\frac{5}{6}$	1 $\rightarrow$
		$z_j - c_j$	0	0	0	$\frac{1}{3}\uparrow$	$\frac{1}{3}$	0

$\boldsymbol{y}_6$ leaves and $\boldsymbol{y}_4$ enters the basis.

		c_j	2	2	0	0	0	0
c_B	B	x_B	y_1	y_2	y_3	y_4	y_5	y_6
2	y_1	1	1	0	0	0	1	$-\frac{4}{5}$
2	y_2	1	0	1	0	0	-1	1
0	y_3	0	0	0	1	0	-2	1
0	y_4	1	0	0	0	1	1	$-\frac{6}{5}$
		$z_j - c_j$	0	0	0	0	0	$\frac{2}{5}$

Finally, we arrive at feasible and optimal integral solution as $\hat{x}_1 = 1, \hat{x}_2 = 1, Z_{\max} = 4$.

5.4 MIXED IPP

Consider a mixed IPP.

Maximise $Z = \boldsymbol{cx}$

subject to $A\boldsymbol{x} = \boldsymbol{b}$ (5.4a)

$\boldsymbol{x} \geq \boldsymbol{0}$

x_j for $j \in I$ is an integer. The set I consists of the subscripts corresponding to those decision variables which are required to be an integral value and

$$A = \left(a_{ij}\right)_{m \times n}, \quad \boldsymbol{x} = (x_1, x_2, \ldots, x_n)^T, \quad \boldsymbol{c} = (c_1, c_2, \ldots, c_n), \quad \boldsymbol{b} = (b_1, b_2, \ldots, b_m)^T.$$

In this section let us now derive the *cutting plane* constraint of mixed integer program (5.4a).

First we solve the related LPP of (5.4a) and suppose in the optimum table the rth basic variable is not an integer but we require it to be an integer. Then as before from (5.3e),

$$x_{Br} = y_{r0} - \sum_{j \in N} y_{rj} x_j, \tag{5.4b}$$

where $N = \{j | x_j$ is a non-basic variable$\}$.

Put $y_{r0} = W_{r0} + f_{r0}$, where $0 < f_{r0} < 1$ is the fraction part of y_{r0} in (5.4b)

$$x_{Br} = W_{r0} + f_{r0} - \sum_{j \in N} y_{rj} x_j$$

x_{Br} is to be an integer provided

$$\left(f_{r0} - \sum_{j \in N} y_{rj} x_j\right) = x_{Br} - W_{r0} = \text{an integer.} \tag{5.4c}$$

Let $N^+ = \left\{j \,|\, y_{rj} \geq 0,\ j \in N\right\}$

$N^- = \left\{j \,|\, y_{rj} < 0,\ j \in N\right\}$.

From (5.4c),

$$f_{r0} - \sum_{j \in N^+} y_{rj} x_j - \sum_{j \in N^-} y_{rj} x_j = \text{an integer.} \tag{5.4d}$$

Case 1. $\sum_{j \in N} y_{rj} x_j \geq 0$.

From (5.4c),

$$\sum_{j \in N} y_{rj} x_j = f_{r0} + P, \text{ where } P = \{0, 1, 2, \ldots\} \text{ is a set of non-negative integers}$$

$$\Rightarrow \sum_{j \in N} y_{rj} x_j \geq f_{r0} \Rightarrow \sum_{j \in N^+} y_{rj} x_j + \sum_{j \in N^-} y_{rj} x_j \geq f_{r0}.$$

Since $\sum_{j \in N^-} y_{rj} x_j < 0$ for any feasible solution to (5.4a) we must have

$$\sum_{j \in N^+} y_{rj} x_j \geq f_{r0}. \tag{5.4e}$$

Case 2. $\sum_{j \in N} y_{rj} x_j < 0$.

From (5.4c),

$$\sum_{j\in N} y_{rj}x_j = f_{r0} - P, \text{ where } P=\{1,2,3,\dots\} \text{ is a set of strictly positive integers}$$

$$\Rightarrow \sum_{j\in N^+} y_{rj}x_j + \sum_{j\in N^-} y_{rj}x_j \le f_{r0} - 1.$$

Again, since $\sum_{j\in N^+} y_{rj}x_j \ge 0$ for any feasible solution to (5.4a) we must have

$$\sum_{j\in N^-} y_{rj}x_j \le f_{r0} - 1. \tag{5.4f}$$

As $0 < f_{r0} < 1$ and $f_{r0} - 1 < 0$, $\frac{f_{r0}}{f_{r0}-1} < 0$.

$$\therefore \sum_{j\in N^-} \left(\frac{f_{r0}}{f_{r0}-1}\right) y_{rj}x_j \ge f_{r0}. \tag{5.4g}$$

Combining (5.4e) and (5.4g), we get

$$\boxed{\sum_{j\in N^+} y_{rj}x_j + \sum_{j\in N^-} \left(\frac{f_{r0}}{f_{r0}-1}\right) y_{rj}x_j \ge f_{r0}.} \tag{5.4h}$$

(5.4h) represents the cutting plane constraint for mixed integer program (5.4a).

Further Extension

In deriving (5.4h) we cannot consider the case when some of the non-basic variables may also require to be an integer valued. If we incorporate this additional requirement then a further development of cutting plane (5.4h) is necessary. For this further extension let us define two sets

$$N_I = \{j \mid x_j \text{ is non-basic and required to be an integer}\}$$
$$N_C = \{j \mid x_j \text{ is non-basic and not required to be an integer}\}$$
$$N_C^+ = \{j \mid y_{rj} \ge 0 \quad j \in N_c\} = N^+ \cap N_C$$
$$N_C^- = \{j \mid y_{rj} < 0 \quad j \in N_c\} = N^- \cap N_C.$$

From (5.4c),

$$f_{r0} - \sum_{j\in N_I} W_{rj}x_j - \sum_{j\in N_I} f_{rj}x_j - \sum_{j\in N_C} y_{rj}x_j = \text{integer}$$

$$\Rightarrow f_{r0} - \sum_{j\in N_I} f_{rj}x_j - \sum_{j\in N_C} y_{rj}x_j = \text{integer}. \tag{5.4i}$$

If we apply the same argument to (5.4i) which we apply to (5.4d) to obtain cutting plane (5.4h), then we will get the following modified cutting plane constraint of a mixed integer program as

$$\boxed{\sum_{j\in N_I} f_{rj}x_j + \sum_{j\in N_C} y_{rj}x_j + \sum_{j\in N_C} \left(\frac{f_{r0}}{f_{r0}-1}\right) y_{rj}x_j \ge f_{r0}.} \tag{5.4j}$$

Example 5.4.1. *Solve the following mixed* IPP.

Maximise $Z = 4x_1 + 6x_2 + 2x_3$

subject to

$$\begin{aligned} 4x_1 - x_2 &\le 5 \\ -x_1 + 6x_2 &\le 5 \\ -x_1 + x_2 + x_3 &\le 5 \\ x_1, x_2, x_3 &\ge 0. \end{aligned}$$

x_1, x_3 *are integers but* x_2 *not necessarily to be an integer.*

Solution: By introducing slack variables $x_4, x_5, x_6 \ge 0$ to the constraints respectively and using simplex algorithm, we get the following optimum basic feasible solution of the related LPP.

		c_j	4	6	2	0	0	0
C_B	B	x_B	y_1	y_2	y_3	y_4	y_5	y_6
4	y_1	$\frac{5}{2}$	1	0	0	$\frac{3}{10}$	$\frac{1}{5}$	0
6	y_2	$\frac{5}{4}$	0	1	0	$\frac{1}{20}$	$\frac{1}{5}$	0
2	y_3	$\frac{25}{4}$	0	0	1	$\frac{1}{4}$	0	1
		$z_j - c_j$	0	0	0	2	2	2

Optimum solution of related LPP is $x_1^* = \frac{5}{2}$, $x_2^* = \frac{5}{4}$, $x_3^* = \frac{25}{4}$, $Z_{\max} = 30$.

Neither x_1^* nor x_3^* is an integer. To find the integer optimal solution we construct the cutting plane constraint.

$$\sum_{j \in N^+} y_{rj} x_j + \sum_{j \in N^-} \left(\frac{f_{r0}}{f_{r0} - 1} \right) y_{rj} x_j \ge f_{r0} \Rightarrow \frac{3}{10} x_4 + \frac{1}{5} x_5 \ge \frac{1}{2} \quad \left[\because \max\{f_{10}, f_{30}\} = \frac{1}{2} \right]$$

$$\Rightarrow -\frac{3}{10} x_4 - \frac{1}{5} \le -\frac{1}{2}.$$

Adding slack variable $x_7 \ge 0$ to this new constraint and using dual-simplex method, we have the following table.

		c_j	4	6	2	0	0	0	0
C_B	B	x_B	y_1	y_2	y_3	y_4	y_5	y_6	y_7
4	y_1	$\frac{5}{2}$	1	0	0	$\frac{3}{10}$	$\frac{1}{5}$	0	0
6	y_2	$\frac{5}{4}$	0	1	0	$\frac{1}{20}$	$\frac{1}{5}$	0	0
2	y_2	$\frac{25}{4}$	0	0	1	$\frac{1}{6}$	0	1	0
0	y_7	$-\frac{1}{2}$	0	0	0	$\left(-\frac{3}{10}\right)$	$-\frac{1}{5}$	0	1 →
		$z_j - c_j$	0	0	0	2↑	2	2	0

The above table shows that the solution is optimum but not feasible. By dual-simplex method y_7 leaves the basis.

Since $\max\left\{ \frac{2}{-3/10}, \frac{2}{-1/5} \right\} = -\frac{20}{3}$, y_4 enters the basis.

		c_j	4	6	2	0	0	0	0
c_B	B	x_B	y_1	y_2	y_3	y_4	y_5	y_6	y_7
4	y_1	2	1	0	0	0	0	0	1
6	y_2	$\frac{7}{6}$	0	1	0	0	$\frac{1}{6}$	0	$\frac{1}{6}$
2	y_3	$\frac{35}{3}$	0	0	1	0	$-\frac{1}{6}$	1	$\frac{5}{6}$
0	y_4	$\frac{5}{3}$	0	0	0	1	$\frac{2}{3}$	0	$-\frac{10}{3}$
		z_j-c_j	0	0	0	0	$\frac{2}{3}$	0	$\frac{20}{3}$

The table indicates the optimum basic feasible solution as $x_1^* = 2$, $x_2^* = \frac{7}{6}$ and $x_3^* = \frac{35}{6}$. Still x_3^* is not an integer, so further another cutting plane constraint is required.

$$\sum_{j\in N^+} y_{rj}x_j + \sum_{j\in N^-}\left(\frac{f_{r0}}{f_{r0}-1}\right) y_{rj}x_j \geq f_{r0} \Rightarrow \frac{5}{6}x_7 + \frac{5/6}{\frac{5}{6}-1}\left(-\frac{1}{6}\right)x_5 \geq \frac{5}{6} \quad \left[\because f_{30} = \frac{5}{6}\right]$$

$$\Rightarrow -\frac{5}{6}x_5 - \frac{5}{6}x_7 \leq -\frac{5}{6}.$$

Again, adding slack variable $x_8 \geq 0$ and solving the problem with the new constraint:

		c_j	4	6	2	0	0	0	0	0
c_B	B	x_B	y_1	y_2	y_3	y_4	y_5	y_6	y_7	y_8
4	y_1	2	1	0	0	0	0	0	1	0
6	y_2	$\frac{7}{6}$	0	1	0	0	$\frac{1}{6}$	0	$\frac{1}{6}$	0
2	y_3	$\frac{35}{6}$	0	0	1	0	$-\frac{1}{6}$	1	$\frac{5}{6}$	0
0	y_4	$\frac{5}{3}$	0	0	0	1	$\frac{2}{3}$	0	$-\frac{10}{3}$	0
0	y_8	$-\frac{5}{6}$	0	0	0	0	$-\frac{5}{6}$	$-\frac{5}{6}$	0	1 →
		z_j-c_j	0	0	0	0	$\frac{2}{3}$	2	$\frac{20}{3}$	0

y_8 leaves the basis and since $\max\left\{\frac{2/3}{-5/6}, \frac{2}{-5/6}\right\} = -\frac{4}{5}$, y_5 enters the basis.

		c_j	4	6	2	0	0	0	0	0
c_B	B	x_B	y_1	y_2	y_3	y_4	y_5	y_6	y_7	y_8
6	y_1	2	1	0	0	0	0	0	1	0
6	y_2	1	0	1	0	0	0	0	$\frac{1}{6}$	$\frac{1}{5}$
2	y_3	6	0	0	1	0	0	1	$\frac{5}{6}$	$-\frac{1}{5}$
0	y_4	1	0	0	0	1	0	0	$-\frac{10}{3}$	$\frac{4}{5}$
0	y_5	1	0	0	0	0	1	0	0	$\frac{6}{5}$
		z_j-c_j	0	0	0	0	0	2	$\frac{20}{3}$	$\frac{4}{5}$

All $x_B > 0$ and $z_j - c_j \geq 0$ and x_1 and x_3 are integers. Hence, the optimal solution of the mixed IPP is $x_1^* = 2$, $x_2^* = 1$, $x_3^* = 6$, $Z_{\max} = 26$.

5.5 BRANCH AND BOUNDS TECHNIQUE

This technique has the potential to become one of the most powerful procedures for solving a pure IPP. Consider a pure integer program defined in (5.3a). The followings are the computational steps to be followed in branch and bounds technique.

Step 1. By ignoring the integer restriction first solve the related LPP. If all x_j are integers, then we obtain the desired optimal solution, but if at least one x_j is not an integer, then go to next step.

Step 2. Select one of the non-integers x_j. Suppose, for some $j = k$, x_k is not an integer. Write $x_k = \omega_k + f_k$, where ω_k is an integral part and $0 < f_k < 1$ is the fractional part of x_k. According to this technique we add each of the constraints $x_k \leq \omega_k$ and $x_k \geq \omega_k + 1$ individually to the constraint set of the original problem and then solve the resulting two related sub-LPPs.

Step 3. For each of the two solutions thus obtained in *Step* 2 we face the following situations:

(i) If the solutions obtained in *Step* 2 for both the cases are feasible integer solutions, compare its objective functional value with the best feasible solution thus found. Save the better of the two. Select another non-integer x_j, if any, and return to *Step* 2.

(ii) If the resulting related sub-LPP has no feasible solution, then select another non-integer x_j, if any, and return to *Step* 2.

(iii) If the solution is not a feasible integer solution, then repeat the process of *Step* 2 on the constraint set of the related LPP.

Step 4. The process terminates when all possibilities in *Step* 2 have been exhausted.

Example 5.5.1. *Use branch and bounds technique to solve the following* IPP.

$$\text{Maximise } Z = x_1 + x_2$$

$$\begin{aligned} \text{subject to } 8x_1 + 63x_2 &\leq 273 \\ 4x_1 - 3x_2 &\leq 10 \\ x_1, x_2 &\geq 0 \text{ and are integers.} \end{aligned}$$

Solution: We begin by solving the related LPP, which will give (Fig. 1) $x_1 = 5\frac{1}{4}$, $x_2 = 3\frac{2}{3}$, $Z_{\max} = 8\frac{11}{12}$.

Since neither x_1 nor x_2 is an integer we choose either variable to begin the next step. We arbitrarily select x_1 to form two branches $x_1 \leq 5$ or $x_1 \geq 6$. These will create two nodes (2A) and (2B) corresponding to two new related sub LPP. The node (2B) has no feasible solution. Hence, no further branches coming out from this node. At node (2A), we have the following optimal feasible solution (Fig. 2): $x_1 = 5$, $x_2 = 3\frac{44}{63}$, $Z_{\max} = 8\frac{44}{63}$.

As x_2 is the only non-integral value, as before we form two branches $x_2 \leq 3$ and $x_2 \geq 4$ coming out from the node (2A) to form two new nodes (3A) and (3B) respectively. Solving the related sub-LPP corresponding to (3A) (Fig. 3) and (3B) (Fig. 4), we get the following optimal basic feasible solutions:

$$x_1 = 4\tfrac{3}{4}, \quad x_2 = 3, \quad Z_{\max} = 7\tfrac{3}{4} \quad \text{[from (3A)]}$$
$$x_1 = 2\tfrac{5}{8}, \quad x_2 = 4, \quad Z_{\max} = 6\tfrac{5}{8} \quad \text{[from (3B)].}$$

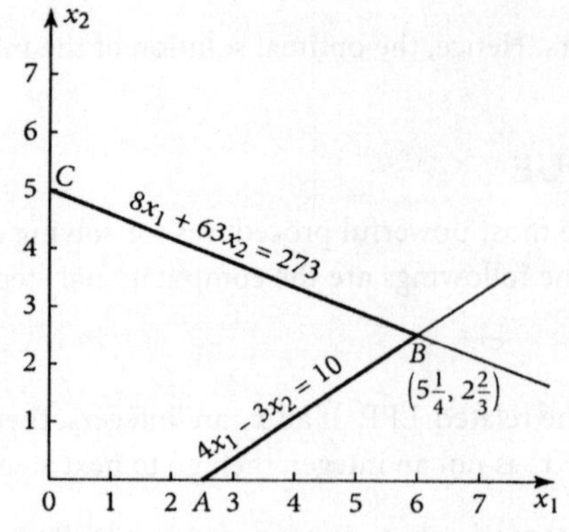

Fig. 1

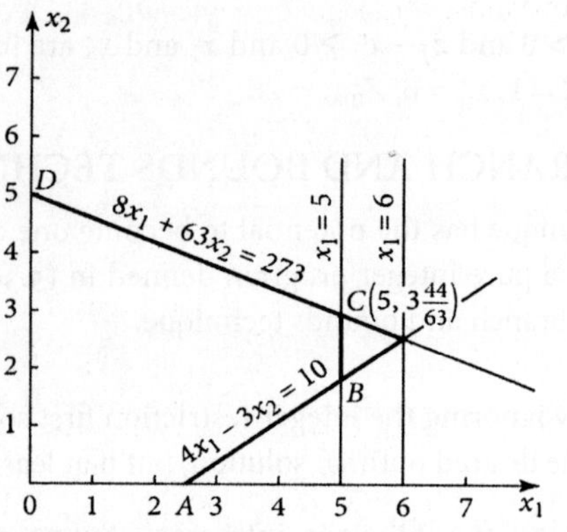

Fig. 2

Observe that node (3A) yields a larger value of Z than node (3B). Therefore, by this technique we use node (3A) since it has a better potential for approaching the ultimate optimal integral solution. At (3A) the only non-integer variable is x_1 so that again another two branches $x_1 \leq 4$ and $x_1 \geq 5$ are coming out from this node to form two new nodes (4A) and (4B) respectively. Upon solving the related sub-LPP, node (4B) indicates no feasible solution and node (4A) gives the ultimate all integral solutions (Fig. 5): $\hat{x}_1 = 4$, $\hat{x}_2 = 3$, $Z_{\max} = 7$.

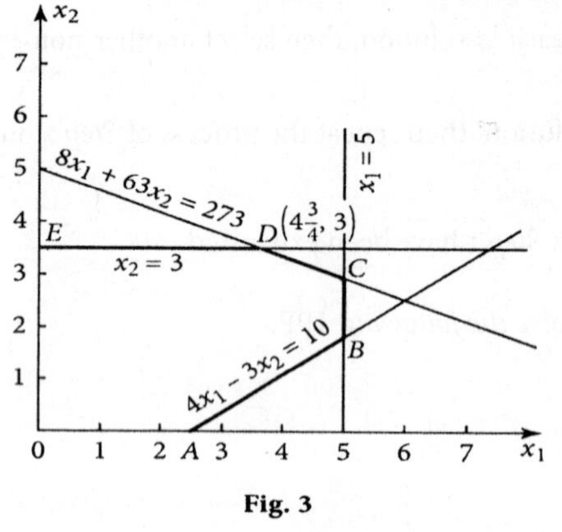

Fig. 3

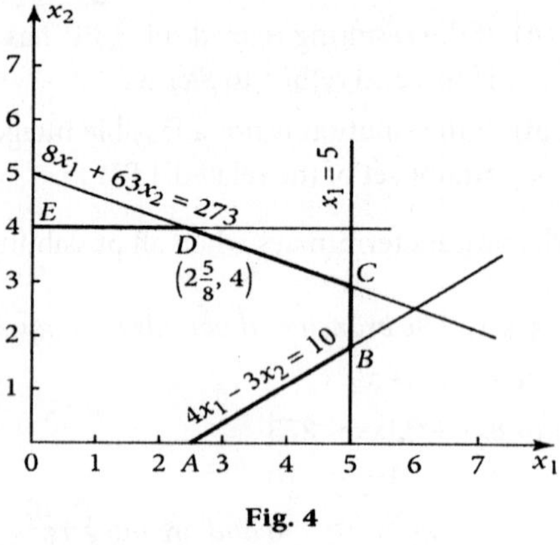

Fig. 4

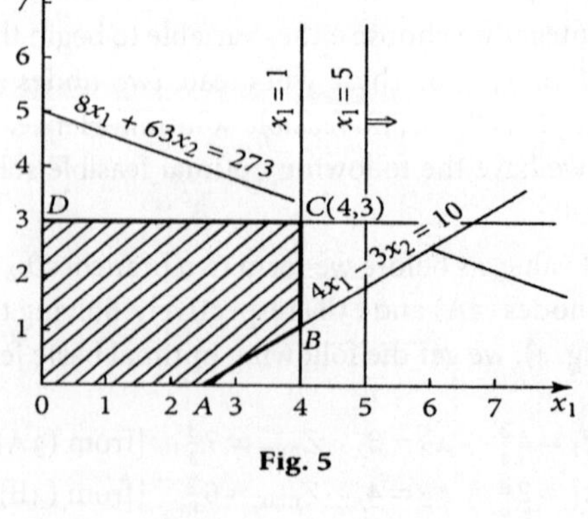

Fig. 5

The above illustration can be represented in a diagram known as *tree solution.*

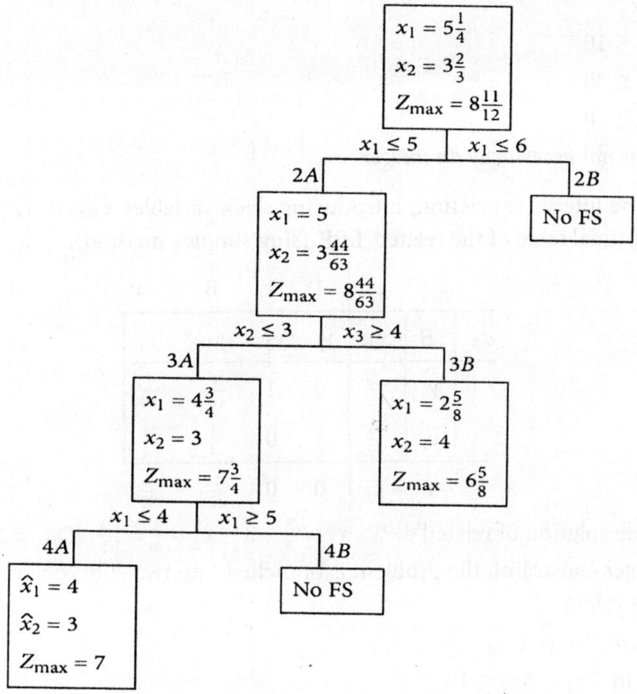

Important Note

In the second step of the above example we arbitrarily select x_1 to form two branches $x_1 \leq 5$ and $x_2 \geq 6$. Instead of x_1 if one can take x_2 to form the branches, $x_2 \leq 3$ and $x_2 \geq 4$, then the corresponding *tree solution* is given below (In this technique there exists no particular rule to the above choice).

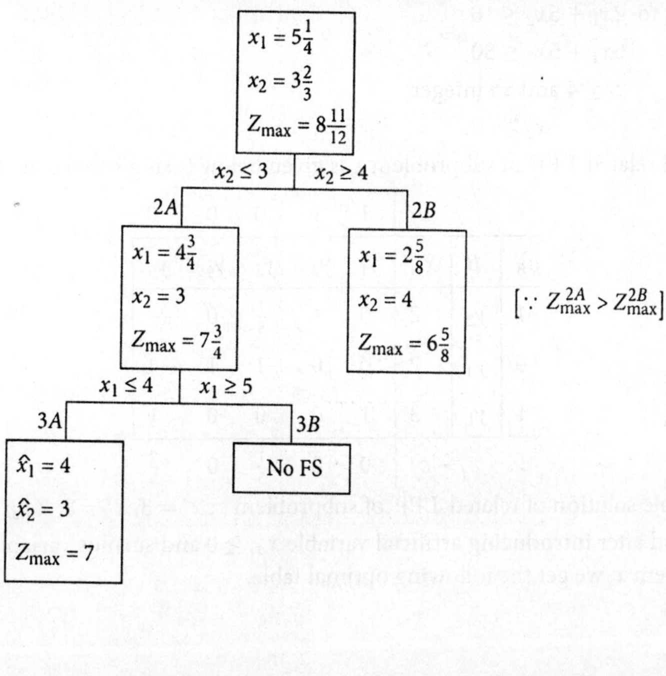

Example 5.5.2. *Solve the following mixed IPP by branch and bounds technique.*

Maximise $Z = x_1 + x_2$

subject to $2x_1 + 5x_2 \leq 16$

$6x_1 + 5x_2 \leq 30$

$x_1, x_2 \geq 0.$

x_1 *is an integer but* x_2 *is not necessarily an integer.*

Solution: Neglecting the integer restriction, introducing slack variables $x_3 \geq 0$, $x_4 \geq 0$ to the constraints, we get the following optimal table of the related LPP (sing simplex method).

		c_j	1	1	0	0
c_B	B	x_B	y_1	y_2	y_3	y_4
1	y_2	$\frac{9}{5}$	0	1	$\frac{3}{10}$	$-\frac{1}{10}$
1	y_1	$\frac{7}{2}$	1	0	$-\frac{1}{4}$	$\frac{1}{4}$
		$z_j - c_j$	0	0	$\frac{1}{20}$	$\frac{3}{20}$

Optimal basic feasible solution of related LPP: $x_1^* = \frac{7}{2} = 3\frac{1}{2}$, $x_2^* = \frac{9}{5} = 1\frac{4}{5}$, $Z_{\max} = 5\frac{3}{10}$.

Since only x_1 is integer constraint, the problem is branched into two subproblems using one of the following additional constraints.

Subproblem 1. Maximise $Z = x_1 + x_2$

subject to $2x_1 + 5x_2 \leq 16$

$6x_1 + 5x_2 \leq 30$

$0 \leq x_1 \leq 3$ and an integer

$x_2 \geq 0.$

Subproblem 2. Maximise $Z = x_1 + x_2$

subject to $2x_1 + 5x_2 \leq 16$

$6x_1 + 5x_2 \leq 30$

$x_1 \leq 4$ and an integer

$x_2 \geq 0.$

The optimal table of related LPP of subproblem 1 is given below (using simplex method).

		c_j	1	1	0	0	0
c_B	B	x_B	y_1	y_2	y_3	y_4	y_5
1	y_2	2	0	1	$\frac{1}{5}$	0	$-\frac{2}{5}$
0	y_4	2	0	0	-1	1	-4
1	y_1	3	1	0	0	0	1
		$z_j - c_j$	0	0	$\frac{1}{5}$	0	$\frac{3}{5}$

Optimal basic feasible solution of related LPP of subproblem 1: $x_1^* = 3$, $x_2^* = 2$, $Z_{\max} = 5$.

Using Big-M method after introducing artificial variable $x_{a_1} \geq 0$ and surplus variable $x_5 \geq 0$ to the new constraint of subproblem 2, we get the following optimal table.

	c_j		1	1	0	0	0	$-M$
c_B	B	x_B	y_1	y_2	y_3	y_4	y_5	y_{a_1}
0	y_3	2	1	0	1	1	-4	⋮
1	y_2	$\frac{6}{5}$	0	1	0	$\frac{1}{5}$	$\frac{6}{5}$	⋮
1	y_1	4	0	0	0	0	-1	⋮
		$z_j - c_j$	0	0	0	$\frac{1}{5}$	$\frac{1}{5}$	

Optimal solution of the related LPP of subproblem 2: $x_1^* = 4$, $x_2^* = \frac{6}{5} = 1\frac{1}{5}$, $Z_{\max} = 5\frac{1}{5}$.

Since $Z_{\max}$ (subproblem 2) > $Z_{\max}$ (subproblem 1), we accept the following integral optimal solution according to branch and bounds technique: $\hat{x}_1 = 4$, $\hat{x}_2 = \frac{6}{5} = 1\frac{1}{5}$, $Z_{\max} = 5\frac{1}{5}$.

5.6 EXERCISE 5

1. (a) Explain the basic difference between a pure and mixed IPP.

   (b) Given an IPP: Maximise $Z = \boldsymbol{cx}$

   subject to $A\boldsymbol{x} = \boldsymbol{b}$

   $\boldsymbol{x} \geq \boldsymbol{0}$ and are integers.

   Under certain conditions to be stated by you show that the cutting plane constraint for solving the above IP can be put in the form:

   $$f_{r0} - \sum_{j \in N} f_{rj} x_j \leq 0,$$

   where the symbols have their usual meaning (as stated in the Ch. 5). Hence, obtain the cutting plane constraint of a certain IP whose related LPP gives a non-integer solution with the following optimal table.

	c_j		2	2	0	0
c_B	B	x_B	y_1	y_2	y_3	y_4
2	y_1	$\frac{4}{7}$	1	0	$\frac{2}{7}$	$-\frac{3}{7}$
2	y_2	$\frac{12}{7}$	0	1	$-\frac{1}{7}$	$\frac{5}{7}$
		$z_j - c_j$	0	0	$\frac{2}{7}$	$\frac{4}{7}$

[BESU(Eng) 2005, BESU(MSc) 2007]

2. Consider the IPP: Maximise $f(x) = 15x_1 + 32x_2$

   subject to $7x_1 + 16x_2 \leq 52$

   $3x_1 - 2x_2 \leq 9$

   $x_1, x_2 \geq 0$ and are integers.

   (a) Ignoring the integer restrictions, show that the optimal solution to the related LPP is $(x_1^*, x_2^*) = (4, \frac{3}{2})$.

   (b) Show that the integer points (4, 1) and (4, 2), obtained by rounding the optimal solution $(4, \frac{3}{2})$ of the related LPP are infeasible solutions to the given IPP.

   (c) Find an optimal solution to the IPP by using *Gomory's cutting plane* method.

[BESU(MSc) 2004, JNU(Comp.Sc) 2009]

3. Solve the following all integer programming problem by *Gomory's cutting plane algorithm*:

(a) Maximise $Z = x_1 - x_2$

subject to $x_1 + 2x_2 \leq 4$

$6x_1 + 2x_2 \leq 9$

$x_1, x_2 \geq 0$ and are integers.

[Roorke(MTech) 1979]

(b) Maximise $Z = 7x_1 + 9x_2$

subject to $-x_1 + 3x_2 \leq 6$

$7x_1 + x_2 \leq 35$

$x_i \geq 0$ (x_i is an integer, $i = 1,2$).

[MBA(CU) 2001, ISI(OR) 1975]

(c) Maximise $Z = 4x_1 + 5x_2 + x_3$

subject to $3x_1 + 2x_2 \leq 10$

$x_1 + 4x_2 \leq 11$

$3x_1 + 3x_2 + x_3 \leq 13$

$x_i \geq 0$ (x_i is an integer, $i = 1,2,3$).

[CU(MSc APPl) 1987, BESU(MSc) 2003]

(d) Minimise $Z = -3x_1 - 4x_2$

subject to $3x_1 + 2x_2 \leq 8$

$x_1 + 4x_2 \leq 10$

$x_i \geq 0$ (x_i is an integer, $i = 1,2$).

[VU(MSc) 1998]

(e) Maximise $Z = 4x_1 + 3x_2$

subject to $3x_1 + 4x_2 \leq 12$

$4x_1 + 2x_2 \leq 9$

$x_1, x_2 \geq 0$ and are integers.

[BESU(MSc) 2001, 2004; JNU(Com Sc.) 2007]

(f) Maximise $Z = 3x_1 + x_2 + 3x_3$

subject to $-x_1 + 2x_2 + x_3 \leq 4$

$4x_2 - 3x_3 \leq 2$

$x_1 - 3x_2 + 2x_3 \leq 3$

$x_1, x_2, x_3 \geq 0$ and are integers.

[CU(MSc Appl) 1986]

(g) Maximise $Z = 3x_1 + 4x_2$

subject to $3x_1 + 2x_2 \leq 8$

$x_1 + 4x_2 \leq 10$

$x_1, x_2 \geq 0$ and are integers.

[CU(MSc Appl) 1993, Madras U 1978]

(h) Maximise $Z = 2x_1 + x_2$

subject to $2x_1 + 5x_2 \leq 17$

$3x_1 + 2x_2 \leq 10$

$x_1, x_2 \geq 0$ and are integers.

4. Show that under certain assumption to be stated by you, the cutting plane constraints for solving a mixed integer LP defined by:

Maximise $Z = \boldsymbol{cx}$

subject to $A\boldsymbol{x} = \boldsymbol{b}$

$\boldsymbol{x} \geq \boldsymbol{0}$

and x_j is an integer for $j \in I$, the set I consists of subscripts corresponding to those variables which are required to be an integer, can be expressed in the form:

$$\sum_{j \in N^+} y_{rj} x_j + \sum_{j \in N^-} \left(\frac{f_{r0}}{f_{r0} - 1} \right) y_{rj} x_j \geq f_{r0}$$

the symbols having their usual meaning (as mentioned in the Ch. 5). [IAS(Main) 2003]

5. Solve the following *mixed integer problem* by *cutting planes method*:

(a) Maximise $Z = x_1 + x_2$

subject to $2x_1 + 4x_2 \leq 16$

$6x_1 + 5x_2 \leq 30$

$x_1 \geq 0$ and is an integer.

$x_2 \geq 0$

(b) Maximise $Z = -3x_1 + x_2 + 3x_3$

subject to $-x_1 + 2x_2 + x_3 \leq 4$

$2x_2 - \frac{3}{2}x_3 \leq 1$

$x_1 - 3x_2 + 2x_3 \leq 3$

$x_1, x_2 \geq 0$, $x_3 \geq 0$ and is an integer.

(c) Maximise $Z = x_1 + x_2$
subject to $3x_1 + 2x_2 \leq 5$
$x_2 \leq 2$
$x_1 \geq 0$ and is an integer.
$x_2 \geq 0$

(d) Minimise $Z = x_1 - 3x_2$
subject to $x_1 + x_2 \leq 5$
$-2x_1 + 4x_2 \leq 11$
$x_1 \geq 0$
$x_2 \geq 0$ and is an integer.

6. (a) Explain the computational procedure to be followed in *branch and bounds* technique for the solution of a pure integer linear programs.

(b) Suppose that the basic variable associated with current node of a maximisation branch and bounds algorithm is defined by

$$x_\mu = \beta_\mu - \sum_{j=1}^{n} \alpha_\mu^j \sigma_j.$$

Branching is effected by the two constraints $x_\mu - [\beta_\mu] \leq 0$ and $x_\mu - [\beta_\mu] - 1 \geq 0$. Let P_d and P_u be the lower bounds on the true degradation in the optimum objective value as a result of activating the first and second constraints. Show by using the *dual-simplex* algorithm, that under the assumption of no change in basis.

$$P_d = \min_{j \in J^+} \left\{ \frac{(z_j - c_j) f_\mu}{\alpha_\mu^j} \right\}, \quad P_u = \min_{j \in J^-} \left\{ \frac{(z_j - c_j)(f_\mu - 1)}{\alpha_\mu^j} \right\},$$

where $(z_j - c_j)$ is the objective coefficients of the jth non-basic variable at the current node, $f_\mu = \beta_\mu - [\beta_\mu]$ and $J^+(J^-)$ is the set of non-basic subscripts for which $\alpha_\mu^j > 0 \left(\alpha_\mu^j < 0\right)$.

7. Use the *branch and bounds* algorithm to solve the following IPP:

(a) Maximise $Z = 9x_1 + 10x_2$
subject to $2x_1 + 5x_2 \leq 15$
$x_1 \leq 3$
$x_1, x_2 \geq 0$ and are integers.
[BESU(MSc) 2005]

(b) Minimise $Z = x_1 - 3x_2$
subject to $x_1 + x_2 \leq 5$
$-x_1 + 2x_2 \leq \frac{11}{2}$
$x_1 \geq 0,\ x_2 \geq 0$ and are integer.
[CU(MSc Appl) 1997]

(c) Minimise $Z = 9x_1 + 10x_2$
subject to $x_1 \leq 9$
$x_2 \leq 8$
$4x_1 + 3x_2 \geq 40$
$x_1 \geq 0,\ x_2 \geq 0$ and is an integer.

(d) Minimise $Z = 9x_1 + 10x_2$
subject to $x_1 \leq 9$
$x_2 \leq 8$
$4x_1 + 3x_2 \geq 40$
$x_1, x_2 \geq 0$ and are integers.

(e) Maximise $Z = x_1 + x_2$
subject to $4x_1 - x_2 \leq 10$
$2x_1 + 5x_2 \leq 10$
$4x_1 - 3x_2 \leq 6$
$x_1, x_2 \geq 0$ and are integers.
[IISc(Dip Man) 1997]

(f) Maximise $Z = 7x_1 + 9x_2$
subject to $-x_1 + 3x_2 \leq 6$
$7x_1 + x_2 \leq 35$
$0 < x_1, x_2 \leq 7$, x_1, x_2 are integers.
[IISc(Dip Man) 2006]

8. The owner of a readymade garment store makes two types of shirts S_1 and S_2. He makes a profit of ₹ 1 and ₹ 4 per shirt on S_1 and S_2 respectively. He has two tailors A and B at his disposal to stitch the shirts. Tailors A and B can devote at most 7 hours and 15 hours per day respectively. Both these shirts are to be stitched by both the tailors. Tailor A and Tailor B spend 2 hours and 5 hours respectively in stitching a shirt S_1 and 4 hours and 3 hours respectively in stitching a shirt S_2. How many shirts of both the types should be stitched in order to maximise the daily profit?
   (a) Set up and solve the LPP.
   (b) If the optimal solution be not integer valued, then use Gomory's cutting plane techniques to find the integer valued optimal solution. [BESU(MSc) 2010]

ANSWERS

1. (b) Cutting plane: $6x_3 + 5x_4 \geq 5$ or, $5x_1 + 4x_2 \leq 9$.
2. (c) Integer optimal solution: $\hat{x}_1 = 0$, $\hat{x} = 3$.
3. (a) $\hat{x}_1 = 1, \hat{x}_2 = 0, Z_{\max} = 1$ (b) $\hat{x}_1 = 0, \hat{x}_2 = 2, Z_{\max} = 18$
   (c) $\hat{x}_1 = 2, \hat{x}_2 = 2, \hat{x}_3 = 1, Z_{\max} = 19$ (d) $\hat{x}_1 = 1, \hat{x}_2 = 2, Z_{\min} = -11$
   (e) $\hat{x}_1 = 1, \hat{x}_2 = 2, Z_{\max} = 10$ (f) $\hat{x}_1 = 5, \hat{x}_2 = 2, \hat{x}_3 = 2, Z_{\max} = 23$
   (g) $\hat{x}_1 = 1, \hat{x}_2 = 2, Z_{\max} = 11$ (h) $\hat{x}_1 = 3, \hat{x}_2 = 0, Z_{\max} = 6$
5. (a) $x_1^* = 4, x_2^* = \frac{6}{5}, Z_{\max} = \frac{26}{5}$ (b) $x_1^* = 0, x_2^* = \frac{8}{7}, x_3^* = 1, Z_{\max} = \frac{29}{7}$
   (c) $x_1^* = 0, x_2^* = 2, Z_{\max} = 2$ (d) $x_1^* = \frac{17}{2}, x_2^* = 2, Z_{\min} = \frac{5}{2}$
7. (a) $x_1^* = 2, x_2^* = 2, Z_{\max} = 38$ (b) $x_1^* = \frac{1}{2}, x_2^* = 3, Z_{\min} = -\frac{10}{11}$
   (c) $x_1^* = \frac{17}{2}, x_2^* = 2, Z_{\min} = \frac{193}{2}$ (d) $x_1^* = 9, x_2^* = 2, Z_{\min} = 101$
   (e) $x_1^* = 2, x_2^* = 1, Z_{\max} = 3$ (f) $x_1^* = 4, x_2^* = 3, Z_{\max} = 55$
8. (a) Formulation: Maximise $x_{S_1} + 4x_{S_2}$

$$\begin{aligned} \text{subject to } 2x_{S_1} + 4x_{S_2} &\leq 7 \\ 5x_{S_1} + 4x_{S_2} &\leq 15 \\ x_{S_1}, x_{S_2} &\leq 0 \end{aligned}$$

   Optimal solution: $x_{S_1}^* = 0, x_{S_2}^* = \frac{7}{4}, Z_{\max} = 7$.
   (b) Integer valued optimal solution: $\hat{x}_{S_1} = 1, \hat{x}_{S_2} = 1, Z_{\max} = 5$.

Chapter 6

Linear Programming: Advanced Topics

OVERVIEW

This chapter presents the *advanced topics* of linear programming. Our primary objective is to utilise the theory to present new solution algorithms that are computationally more efficient than the method already discussed in earlier chapter. These algorithms include composite simplex, bounded variables technique, parametric linear programming and lastly revised simplex method. We wish to emphasise that all these algorithms utilise the exact steps of simplex method as presented earlier. The only difference occurs in the details of the computations for identifying the entering and leaving variables.

Since matrix algebra is used throughout this chapter, you are expected to review the chapter on *relevant mathematical background* of this book, if you have not already studied matrices. However, the only elementary concept of matrices is needed for understanding the presentation.

6.1 COMPOSITE SIMPLEX METHOD FOR SOLUTION OF LP MODEL

The process of obtaining an initial basic feasible solution of an LPP requires the addition of a number of artificial variables whose number will be very large for a large scale LP model. Many algorithms have been developed to reduce such number of artificial variables, even allowing some of the basic variables to be negative. Then, by different computational procedures these artificial variables in the initial basis are driven to zero while the negative artificial variable are forced to be non-negative (e.g., two-phase simplex method). The *composite simplex method* becomes computationally superior method for such an initial basic feasible solution to the problem. It is, therefore, the modification of phase I of regular two-phase method for the solution of LP model.

In composite simplex method, we first convert all inequality constraints of the LP model into the form

$$\sum_{j=1}^{n} a_{ij}x_j \le b_i : b_i > \text{ or } < 0 \text{ for } i = 1,2,\ldots,m. \tag{6.1a}$$

Then introduce slack variables to make them equations. Further, if there are any equality constraints, then in order to find the initial basis (if needed) add artificial variables. Thus, in composite simplex method initial basis composed of decision, slack (i.e., legitimate) variables and artificial variables.

Suppose, the.initial basis is not a feasible solution. Obviously, there are two possible sources of infeasibility:

1. Artificial variables appear in the basis at positive level.
2. Negative variables which are artificial or legitimate (slack or decision variables).

Let $P = \{i \mid x_{B_i} \ge 0 \text{ and } x_{B_i} \text{ artificial}\}$
$N = \{i \mid x_{B_i} < 0\}.$ (6.1b)

Note that we shall also include artificial variable in the basis at a zero level in P since it is required to derive such variables out of the basis. Now, if we take b_i to be the current value of the ith basic variable, then the ith row of the simplex iteration can be expressed as the equation of the form:

$$x_{B_i} + \sum_{j=1}^{n} y_{ij}x_j = b_i \text{ or, } x_{B_i} = b_i - \sum_{j=1}^{n} y_{ij}x_j. \tag{6.1c}$$

Next we define a total infeasibility ω of the solution by

$$\omega = \sum_{i \in P \cup N} |x_{B_i}| = \sum_{i \in P} x_{B_i} - \sum_{i \in N} x_{B_i}. \tag{6.1d}$$

Clearly, ω is always non-negative and the solution is a feasible solution, if and only if $\omega = 0$. In the composite simplex method, selection of vectors to enter and leave the basis are made in such a way so as to ω decreases at each iterations until an initial basic feasible solution is found.

Using (6.1c) and (6.1d)

$$\omega = \sum_{i \in P}\left[b_i - \sum_{j=1}^{n} y_{ij}x_j\right] - \sum_{i \in N}\left[b_i - \sum_{j=1}^{n} y_{ij}x_j\right] = \left(\sum_{i \in P} b_i - \sum_{i \in N} b_i\right) + \sum_{j=1}^{n}\left[\sum_{i \in N} y_{ij} - \sum_{i \in P} y_{ij}\right] x_j. \tag{6.1e}$$

The only variables x_j appearing in (6.1e) are currently non-basic variables.

Let $d_j = \sum_{i \in N} y_{ij} - \sum_{i \in P} y_{ij}.$ (6.1f)

Then $\omega = \text{constant} + \sum_{j=1}^{n} d_j x_j.$ (6.1g)

Hence, ω will decrease if we choose a vector x_j to enter the basis such that $d_j < 0$. The quantity d_j are analogous to $(z_j - c_j)$ of usual simplex method. Therefore, we shall choose the entering vector y_k, where

$$d_k = \min_j \{d_j \mid d_j < 0\}. \tag{6.1h}$$

In fact, the rule (6.1h) produces the greatest rate of decrease in the total infeasibility ω just as taking most negative $\left(z_j - c_j\right)$ in the simplex method which yields the greatest rate of increase in the objective function.

But if $d_j \geq 0$ for all j and the constant term in (6.1g) is non-negative, then the problem has no feasible solution, since in this case $\omega > 0$ and it cannot be decreased further. Now having determined the entering vector we must decide which will be the departing vector. To do this task consider the following simplex transformation rule and three possible cases separately:

$$\hat{x}_{B_i} = x_{B_i} - \theta y_{ik} : i \neq r$$
$$\hat{x}_{Br} = \frac{x_{Br}}{y_{rk}} = \theta \quad : i = r. \tag{6.1i}$$

Case 1. $x_{B_r} \geq 0$. This corresponds to the situation in the regular simplex method in which no non-negative variable will become negative so long as r is chosen in such a way that

$$\frac{x_{B_r}}{y_{rk}} = \min_i \left\{ \frac{x_{B_i}}{y_{ik}} \middle| y_{ik} > 0 \right\}.$$

But since all x_{B_i} may not be non-negative in composite simplex method we modify the above rule slightly and let

$$\theta_1 = \frac{x_{Br_1}}{y_{r_1 k}} = \min_i \left\{ \frac{x_{B_i}}{y_{ik}} \middle| \begin{matrix} y_{ik} > 0 \text{ and} \\ x_{B_i} \geq 0 \end{matrix} \right\}. \tag{6.1j}$$

If there is a tie for the above minimum we choose r_1 corresponding to an artifrcial variable, if possible. If we were to use decision (6.1j) exclusively to select the vector to leaves the basis we would ensure that no currently non-negative variable becomes negative. However, this decision does nothing to improve the status of the variable which are currently negative. So we investigate the next cases.

Case 2. $x_{B_i} \leq 0$ and artificial variables. By (6.1i) we can make a negative artificial variable $x_{B_{r_2}}$ to zero or out of the basis and replace it with the legitimate variable at a positive level, if $y_{r_2 k} < 0$. However, to ensure that no other negative artificial variables x_{B_i} becomes positive we must have to select r_2 such that

$$\theta_2 = \frac{x_{B_{r_2}}}{y_{r_2 k}} = \min_i \left\{ \frac{x_{B_i}}{y_{ik}} \middle| \begin{matrix} x_{B_i} \leq 0 \text{ and artificial} \\ y_{ik} < 0 \end{matrix} \right\}. \tag{6.1k}$$

It should be careful about that if $\theta_2 \leq \theta_1$, then we can remove the r_2th basic variable but, if $\theta_2 > \theta_1$, we cannot remove r_2th basic variable without introducing new infeasibilities.

Case 3. $x_{B_i} < 0$ and legitimate (slack and decision variables in composite simplex). In this case we now consider the effect of removing a negative legitimate from the basis. Since it is always desirable to increase these variables as much as possible, let

$$\theta_3 = \frac{x_{B_{r_3}}}{y_{r_3 k}} = \max_i \left\{ \frac{x_{B_i}}{y_{ik}} \middle| \begin{matrix} y_{B_i} < 0 \text{ and legitimate} \\ x_{ik} < 0 \end{matrix} \right\}. \tag{6.1l}$$

Once again, if $\theta_3 \leq \theta_1$, we can remove the r_3th basic variable without introducing any new infeasibility, whereas, if $\theta_3 > \theta_1$, we cannot do so.

Now combining the three possible cases a logical criterion for selecting the departing vector from the basis is:

Select r_2th basic variable, if $\theta_2 \le \theta_1 < \infty$, otherwise, r_1th basic variable, if $\theta_1 < \theta_3$, or r_3th basic variable, if $\theta_1 \ge \theta_3$. (6.1m)

To summarise, the method for the solution of a large scale LP model: We use the usual simplex table and regular simplex transformation formula (6.1i) and choose the entering vector according to (6.1h) and departing vector by computing $\theta_1, \theta_2, \theta_3$ using expression (6.1j), (6.1k) and (6.1l) respectively and finally employing the rule given in (6.1m). The method terminates when $\omega = 0$ and gives us the required optimal solution of the problem.

Example 6.1.1. *Solve the following* LPP *by composite simplex method.*

Maximise $Z = x_1 + 3x_2$

subject to
$$\begin{aligned} 2x_1 + x_2 + x_3 &\le 10 \\ 2x_1 + x_2 - 2x_3 &\ge 2 \\ x_1 + 2x_2 \quad &= 4 \\ x_1 \quad - 2x_3 &= -2 \\ x_1, x_2, x_3 &\ge 0. \end{aligned}$$

[BESU(MSc) 2005]

Solution: We add a slack variable $x_4 \ge 0$ to the first constraint. Multiply the second constraint by (-1) and then add a slack variable $x_5 \ge 0$ to it. Add artificial variables $x_{a_1} \ge 0$, $x_{a_2} \ge 0$ to the third and fourth constraints respectively. Thus, the set of constraints are

$$\begin{aligned} x_1 + x_2 + x_3 + x_4 \quad &= 10 \\ -2x_1 - x_2 + 2x_3 \quad + x_5 \quad &= -2 \\ x_1 + 2x_2 \quad + x_{a_1} &= 4 \\ x_1 \quad - 2x_3 \quad + x_{a_2} &= -2 \\ x_1, x_2, x_3, x_4, x_5, x_{a_1}, x_{a_2} &\ge 0. \end{aligned}$$

The initial basic solution is $x_4 = 10$, $x_5 = -2$, $x_{a_1} = 4$, $x_{a_2} = -2$.

The composite simplex iterations are as follows

(T 1)

y_B	x_B	y_1	y_2	y_3	y_4	y_5	y_{a_1}	y_{a_2}
y_4	10	1	1	1	1	0	0	0
y_5	−2	−2	(−1)	2	0	1	0	0 →
y_{a_1}	4	1	2	0	0	0	1	0
y_{a_2}	−2	1	0↑	−2	0	0	0	1

The current level of infeasibility: $P = \{i \mid x_{B_i} \ge 0 \text{ and artificial}\} = \{3\}$

$$N = \{i \mid x_{B_i} < 0\} = \{2, 4\}.$$

$\omega = x_{B_3} - x_{B_2} - x_{B_4} = 4 + 2 + 2 = 8.$

Now calculate d_1, d_2, d_3 for non-basic variables: $d_1 = y_{21} + y_{41} - y_{31} = -2 + 1 - 1 = -2$

$$d_2 = y_{22} + y_{42} - y_{32} = -1 + 0 - 2 = 3$$
$$d_3 = y_{23} + y_{43} - y_{33} = 2 - 2 - 0 = 0$$

$d_k = \min_j \{d_j \mid d_j < 0\} = d_2$. Therefore, d_2 is minimum and hence $\mathbf{y_2}$ enters the basis.

$$\theta_1 = \min_i \left\{ \frac{x_{B_i}}{y_{i2}} \middle| \begin{array}{l} x_{B_i} \geq 0 \\ y_{i2} > 0 \end{array} \right\} = \min\left\{ \frac{x_{B_1}}{y_{12}}, \frac{x_{B_3}}{y_{32}} \right\} = \min\left\{ \frac{10}{1}, \frac{4}{2} \right\} = 2$$

$$\theta_2 = \min_i \left\{ \frac{x_{B_i}}{y_{i2}} \middle| \begin{array}{l} x_{B_i} < 0 \text{ and artificial} \\ y_{i2} < 0 \end{array} \right\} = \frac{x_{B_4}}{y_{42}} = +\infty$$

$$\theta_3 = \max_i \left\{ \frac{x_{B_i}}{y_{i2}} \middle| \begin{array}{l} x_{B_i} < 0 \text{ and legitimate} \\ y_{i2} > 0 \end{array} \right\} = \frac{x_{B_{12}}}{y_{22}} = \frac{-2}{-1}.$$

We have $\theta_1 = \theta_3$, $x_{B_2} = \mathbf{y_5}$ leaves the basis.

(T 2)

y_B	x_B	y_1	y_2	y_3	y_4	y_5	y_{a_1}	y_{a_2}	
y_4	8	−1	0	3	1	1	0	0	
y_2	2	2	1	−2	0	−1	0	0	
y_{a_1}	0	−3	0	(4)	0	2	1	0	→
y_{a_2}	−2	1	0	−2	0	0	0	1	

$P = \{3\}$, $N = \{4\}$, $\omega = 0 - (-2) = 2$.

$d_1 = y_{41} - y_{31} = 1 + 3 = 4$

$d_3 = y_{43} - y_{33} = -2 - 4 = -6$

$d_5 = y_{45} - y_{35} = 0 - 2 = -2$

$\mathbf{y_3}$ enters the basis.

$$\theta_1 = \min\left\{ \frac{x_{B_1}}{y_{13}}, \frac{x_{B_3}}{y_{33}} \right\} = \min\left\{ \frac{8}{3}, \frac{0}{4} \right\} = 0$$

$$\theta_2 = \frac{x_{B_4}}{y_{34}} = \frac{-2}{-2} = 1$$

$$\theta_3 = \infty.$$

$\therefore$ $\theta_1 < \theta_3$, $x_{B_3} = \mathbf{y_{a_1}}$ leaves the basis.

(T 3)

y_B	x_B	y_1	y_2	y_3	y_4	y_5	y_{a_2}	
y_4	8	$\frac{5}{4}$	0	0	1	$-\frac{1}{2}$	0	
y_2	2	$\frac{1}{2}$	1	0	0	0	0	
y_3	0	$-\frac{3}{4}$	0	1	0	$\frac{1}{2}$	0	
y_{a_2}	−2	$(-\frac{1}{2})$↑	0	0	0	1	1	→

$P = \phi, N = \{4\}, \omega = 0 - (-2) = 2$.

$d_1 = y_{41} = -\frac{1}{2}$

$d_5 = y_{45} = 1$

y_1 enters the basis.

$$\theta_1 = \min\left\{\frac{x_{B_1}}{y_{11}}, \frac{x_{B_2}}{y_{12}}\right\} = \min\left\{\frac{8}{5/4}, \frac{2}{1/2}\right\} = 4$$
$$\theta_2 = \frac{x_{B4}}{y_{41}} = 4$$
$$\theta_3 = \infty.$$

$\therefore\ \theta_2 = \theta_1 < \theta_3,\ x_{B_4} = y_{a_2}$ leaves the basis.

(T 4)

y_B	x_B	y_1	y_2	y_3	y_4	y_5
y_4	3	0	0	0	1	2
y_2	0	0	0	0	0	1
y_3	3	0	0	1	0	−1
y_1	4	1	0	0	0	−2

(T 4) clearly indicates that an optimum basic feasible solution has been reached since $\omega = 0$ as $P = \phi$ and $N = \phi$. The required optimum solution is $\langle x_1^* = 4,\ x_2^* = 0,\ x_3^* = 3,\ Z_{\max} = 4\rangle$.

Example 6.1.2. *Use composite simplex method to solve the following* LPP.

Maximise $Z = 2x_1 + 8x_2 + 5x_3 + 6x_4$

subject to
$$\begin{aligned} 3x_1 - 4x_2 &\le -12 \\ x_3 &\le 3 \\ x_4 &\le 4 \\ 5x_1 + x_2 &\le 6 \\ x_1 + 4x_2 + 5x_3 + 2x_4 &\le 8 \\ x_1, x_2, x_3, x_4 &\ge 0. \end{aligned}$$

[BESU(MSc) 2007]

Solution: To start composite simplex iteration first write the constraints by introducing slack variables x_5, x_6, x_7, x_8, $x_9 \ge 0$ respectively.

$$\begin{aligned} 3x_1 - 4x_2 + x_5 &= -12 \\ x_3 + x_6 &= 3 \\ x_4 + x_7 &= 4 \\ 5x_1 + x_2 + x_8 &= 6 \\ x_1 + 4x_2 + 5x_3 + 2x_4 + x_9 &= 8 \\ x_j \ge 0,\ j = 1 - 9. \end{aligned}$$

(T 1)

y_B	x_B	y_1	y_2	y_3	y_4	y_5	y_6	y_7	y_8	y_9	
y_5	−12	0	0	3	(−4)	1	0	0	0	0	→
y_6	3	0	0	1	0	0	1	0	0	0	
y_7	4	0	0	0	1	0	0	1	0	0	
y_8	6	5	1	0	0	0	0	0	1	0	
y_9	8	1	4	5	2↑	0	0	0	0	1	

$P=\phi, N=\{1\}, \omega=-x_{B_1}=12.$

$d_1=y_{11}=1$

$d_2=y_{12}=0$

$d_3=y_{13}=3$

$d_4=y_{14}=-4 \rightarrow \boldsymbol{y_4}$ enters the basis.

$$\theta_1=\min\left\{\frac{x_{B_3}}{y_{34}},\frac{x_{B_5}}{y_{54}}\right\}=\min\left\{\frac{4}{1},\frac{8}{2}\right\}=4$$

$$\theta_2=\infty$$

$$\theta_3=\frac{x_{B_1}}{y_{14}}=\frac{12}{4}=3.$$

$\therefore\ \theta_3<\theta_1,\ x_{B_1}=\boldsymbol{y_5}$ leaves the basis.

(T 2)

y_B	x_B	y_1	y_2	y_3	y_4	y_5	y_6	y_7	y_8	y_9
y_4	3	0	0	$-\frac{3}{4}$	1	$-\frac{1}{4}$	0	0	0	0
y_6	3	0	0	1	0	0	1	0	0	0
y_7	1	$\frac{1}{4}$	0	$\frac{3}{4}$	0	$\frac{1}{4}$	0	1	0	0
y_8	6	5	1	0	0	0	0	0	1	0
y_9	2	$\frac{3}{2}$	4	$\frac{13}{2}$	0	$\frac{1}{2}$	0	0	0	1

$P=\phi$ and also $N=\phi$ so that $\omega=0$ and hence optimal basic feasible solution has been reached and is given by $\left\langle x_1^*=0,\ x_2^*=0,\ x_3^*=0,\ x_4^*=3,\ Z_{\max}=18\right\rangle$.

6.2 BOUNDED VARIABLES TECHNIQUE FOR SOLUTION OF LP MODEL

Applications of LP exist, wherein addition to the usual constraints, some or all variables are bounded from above and below. Let us define the problem.

Maximise $Z=\boldsymbol{cx}$

subject to $A\boldsymbol{x}=\boldsymbol{b}$

$$\boldsymbol{L}\leq\boldsymbol{x}\leq\boldsymbol{U} \tag{6.2a}$$

where $\boldsymbol{x}=\begin{pmatrix}x_1\\x_2\\\vdots\\x_n\end{pmatrix}$, $C=(c_1,c_2,\ldots,c_n)$, $A=\left(a_{ij}\right)_{m\times n}$, $\boldsymbol{b}=\begin{pmatrix}b_1\\b_2\\\vdots\\b_m\end{pmatrix}$, $U\geq L\geq 0$.

The elements of L and U for an unbounded variable are 0 and ∞. The problem can be solved by the regular simplex method.

The constraints of (6.2a) are written in the form

$$\left.\begin{aligned}A\boldsymbol{x}&=\boldsymbol{b}\\ \boldsymbol{x}+\boldsymbol{x_s}&=\boldsymbol{U}\\ \boldsymbol{x}-\boldsymbol{x}_s'&=L\\ \boldsymbol{x},\boldsymbol{x_s},\boldsymbol{x}_s'&\geq 0\end{aligned}\right\}. \tag{6.2b}$$

$\boldsymbol{x_s}, \boldsymbol{x}_s'$ are slack and surplus variables respectively.

The problem includes $3(m+n)$ variables and $3m+2n$ constraints. However, the size can be reduced considerably through the use of special techniques.

Consider first the lower bound constraints

$$\boldsymbol{x} = \boldsymbol{L} + \boldsymbol{x}'_s. \tag{6.2c}$$

Using (6.2c) eliminate $\boldsymbol{x}$ from all the remaining constraints. The new variables of the problem becomes $\boldsymbol{L}$ and $\boldsymbol{x}'_s$. Obviously, there is no chance; in this case $\boldsymbol{x}$ may violate the non-negativity restriction; as both $\boldsymbol{L}$ and $\boldsymbol{x}'_s$ are non-negative.

In fact, the main problem arises with upper bound variables, since there is no guarantee that $\boldsymbol{x} = \boldsymbol{U} - \boldsymbol{x}_s$ will remain non-negative. To get rid of this difficulty we use the following procedure.

The upper bound problem may be written as

Minimise $Z = \boldsymbol{cx}$

$$\left.\begin{aligned} \text{subject to } A\boldsymbol{x} &= \boldsymbol{b} \\ \boldsymbol{x} + \boldsymbol{x}_s &= \boldsymbol{U} \\ \boldsymbol{x},\ \boldsymbol{x}_s &\geq 0 \end{aligned}\right\}. \tag{6.2d}$$

It is assumed that $\boldsymbol{b}$ is a non-negative vector so that the problem (6.2d) is initially feasible. Now, the inclusion of the constraints $\boldsymbol{x} + \boldsymbol{x}_s = \boldsymbol{U}$ in the simplex tableau, one can account for their effect by modifying the feasibility condition. The optimality conditions remains the same as in the regular simplex method.

Thus, in developing the new feasibility condition two major points be considered.

(i) The non-negativity and upper bound constraints for the entering vector.

(ii) The non-negativity and upper bound constraints for those variables (basic) that may be affected by introducing the entering vector.

Mathematical Illustration

First consider the LPP without the upper bounds. Let x_j be a non-basic variable, which is selected to enter the solution. Let $x_{Bi} = x^*_{B_i}$ be the ith variable of the current basic solution $\boldsymbol{x_B}$. Then introduction of x_j into the solution gives

$$x_{B_i} = x^*_{B_i} - \alpha^j_i x_j, \tag{6.2e}$$

where α^j_i is the ith element of $\boldsymbol{\alpha}^j = \boldsymbol{B}^{-1}\boldsymbol{P_j}$, where $\boldsymbol{P_j}$ is the vector of A corresponding to x_j.

According to the guidelines above, x_j remains feasible if

$$0 \leq x_j \leq u_j. \tag{6.2f}$$

Again, x_{B_i} remains feasible if

$$0 \leq x^*_{B_i} - \alpha^j_i x_j \leq u_i,\ i = 1,2,\ldots,m. \tag{6.2g}$$

Since the introduction of x_j into the solution requires that it must be non-negative introduce, condition (6.2f), so it is taken care of by observing the upper bound on x_j. For non-negativity condition from (6.2g), $x_{B_i} = x^*_{B_i} - \alpha^j_i x_j \geq 0$, which implies that only $\alpha^j_i > 0$ may cause $x_{B_i} < 0$. Let η_1 represent the maximum value of x_j. Then

$$\eta_1 = \min_i \left\{ \frac{x^*_{B_i}}{\alpha^j_i} \,\middle|\, \alpha^j_i > 0 \right\}, \tag{6.2h}$$

which is analogous to the feasible condition of the regular simplex method.

Now to guarantee that x_{B_i} will not exceed its upper bound, it is necessary that $x_{B_i} = x^*_{B_i} + \left(-\alpha^j_i\right) x_j \le u_i$, eventually the condition violated if $\alpha^j_i < 0$. Therefore, by letting η_2 represent the maximum value of x_j

$$\eta_2 = \min_i \left\{ \frac{u_i - x^*_{B_i}}{-\alpha^j_i} \,\middle|\, \alpha^j_i < 0 \right\}. \tag{6.2i}$$

Finally, let η denote the maximum value of x_j that does not violate any of the conditions above. Then

$$\eta = \min\{\eta_1, \eta_2, u_j\}. \tag{6.2j}$$

If $\eta = u_j = \eta_1 = \eta_2$, the tie may be broken arbitrarily.

In the above derivation, the entering vector x_j is assumed to be at zero level before it is introduced into the solution. To maintain the validity of the results, every non-basic variable x_k at upper bound can be put at zero level by the substitution $x_k = u_k - x'_k : 0 \le x'_k \le u_k$.

Hence, selection of entering and departing (leaving) vectors of the procedure are as follows. Let x_{B_r} be the variable corresponding to $\eta = \min\{\eta_1, \eta_2, u_j\}$. Then

(i) If $\eta = \eta_1$, x_{B_r} leaves the solution and x_j enters by using the regular simplex method.

(ii) If $\eta = \eta_2$, x_{B_r} leaves and x_j enters. Here, x_{B_r} being non-basic at its upper bound must be substituted out by using $x_{B_r} = u_r - x'_{B_r}$.

(iii) If $\eta = u_j$, x_j is substituted at its upper bound $u_j - x'_j$ but remains non-basic.

Example 6.2.1. *Using the bounded variable technique, solve the following* LPP.

Maximise $Z = 3x_1 + 5x_2 + 2x_3$

subject to $x_1 + x_2 + 2x_3 \le 14$

$2x_1 + 4x_2 + 3x_3 \le 43$

$0 \le x_1 \le 4,\ 7 \le x_2 \le 10,\ 0 \le x_3 \le 3.$

[CU(MSc Appl) 2001]

Solution: Since x_2 has a positive lower bound, substitute $x_2 = x'_2 + 7$, then $0 \le x'_2 \le 3$ and modified LPP is:

Maximise $Z = 3x_1 + 5x'_2 + 2x_3 + 35$

subject to $x_1 + x'_2 + 2x_3 \le 7$ (P)

$2x_1 + 4x'_2 + 3x_3 \le 15$

$0 \le x_1 \le 4,\ 0 \le x'_2 \le 3,\ 0 \le x_3 \le 3.$

By introducing slack variables $x_4, x_5 \ge 0$, the starting tableau becomes:

(T 1)

		c_j	3	5	2	0	0
c_B	y_B	x_B	y_1	y'_2	y_3	y_4	y_5
0	y_4	7	1	1	2	1	0
0	y_5	15	2	4	3	0	1
		$z_j - c_j$	−3	−5↑	−2	0	0

y'_2 entering vector $(z_2 - c_2 = -5)$

$$\alpha^2 = \begin{pmatrix} 1 \\ 4 \end{pmatrix} > 0, \qquad \eta_1 = \min\left\{\frac{7}{1}, \frac{15}{4}\right\} = 3.75.$$

Since all $\alpha_i^2 > 0$, it follows that $\eta_2 = \infty$.

$\therefore\ \eta = \min\{3.75, \infty, 3\}$ because $\eta = u_2$, x_2' is substituted at its upper limit but it remains non-basic. Putting $x_2' = u_2 - x_2'' = 3 - x_2''$, the new tableau becomes:

(T 2)

		c_j	3	−5	2	0	0	
c_B	y_B	x_B	y_1	y_2''	y_3	y_4	y_5	
0	y_4	4	1	−1	2	1	0	
0	y_5	3	(2)	−4	3	0	1	→
		$z_j - c_j$	−3↑	5	−2	0	0	

Note. After substituting $x_2' = 3 - x_2''$ in previous problem (P) the modified LPP

Maximise $Z = 3x_1 - 5x_2'' + 2x_3 + 50$

subject to $x_1 - x_2'' + 2x_3 + x_4 = 4$

$2x_1 - 4x_2'' + 3x_3 + x_5 = 3$

which gives (T 2) above.

Select y_1 as the entering vector $(z_1 - c_1 = -3)$

$$\alpha^1 = \begin{pmatrix}1\\2\end{pmatrix} > 0, \qquad \eta_1 = \min\left\{\frac{4}{1}, \frac{3}{2}\right\} = \frac{3}{2} \text{ (corresponding to } y_5).$$

$$\eta_2 = \infty$$

$$\eta = \min\left\{\frac{3}{2}, \infty, 4\right\} = \frac{3}{2} = \eta_1.$$

Introduce y_1, drop y_5.

(T 3)

		c_j	3	−5	2	0	0	
c_B	y_B	x_B	y_1	y_2''	y_3	y_4	y_5	
0	y_4	$\frac{5}{2}$	0	+1	$\frac{1}{2}$	1	$-\frac{1}{2}$	
3	y_1	$\frac{3}{2}$	1	(−2)	$\frac{3}{2}$	0	$\frac{1}{2}$	→
		$z_j - c_j$	0	−1↑	$\frac{5}{2}$	0	$\frac{3}{2}$	

Select y_2'' as the entering vector

$$\alpha^2 = \begin{pmatrix}1\\-2\end{pmatrix} < 0, \qquad \eta_1 = \frac{5}{2}$$

$$\eta_2 = \frac{4 - \frac{3}{2}}{-(-2)} = \frac{5}{4} \text{ (corresponding to } y_1)$$

$$\eta = \min\left\{\frac{5}{2}, \frac{5}{4}, 3\right\} = \frac{5}{4}.$$

Since $\eta = \eta_2$ introduce y_2'' into the basis and drop y_1, then substitute x_1 out of its upper bound $4 - x_1'$ thus by removing y_1 and introducing y_2'', the tableau becomes:

(T 4)

		c_j	3	−5	2	0	0
c_B	y_B	x_B	y_1	y_2''	y_3	y_4	y_5
0	y_4	$\frac{13}{4}$	$\frac{1}{2}$	0	$\frac{5}{4}$	1	$-\frac{1}{4}$
−5	y_2''	$-\frac{3}{2}$	$-\frac{1}{2}$	1	$-\frac{3}{4}$	0	$-\frac{1}{4}$
		$z_j - c_j$	$\frac{1}{2}$	0	$\frac{7}{4}$	0	$\frac{5}{4}$

Now by substituting $x_1 = 4 - x_1'$, the final tableau becomes

(T 5)

		c_j	−3	−5	2	0	0
c_B	y_B	x_B	y_1'	y_2''	y_3	y_4	y_5
0	y_4	$\frac{5}{4}$	$-\frac{1}{2}$	0	$\frac{5}{4}$	1	$-\frac{1}{4}$
−5	y_2''	$\frac{5}{4}$	$\frac{1}{2}$	1	$-\frac{3}{4}$	0	$-\frac{1}{4}$
		$z_j - c_j$	$\frac{1}{2}$	0	$\frac{7}{4}$	0	$\frac{5}{4}$

(T 5) is now optimal and feasible. The optimal solution in terms of original variables x_1, x_2, x_3 is found as follows:

$x_1' = 0$ gives $x_1 = 4$.

$x_2'' = \frac{5}{4}$ gives $x_2' = 3 - \frac{5}{4} = \frac{7}{4}$ imply $x_2 = x_2' + 7 = \frac{7}{4} + 7 = \frac{35}{4}$ and $x_3 = 0$.

$\therefore$ required optimal solution: $\left\langle x_1^* = 4,\ x_2^* = \frac{35}{4},\ x_3^* = 0,\ Z_{\max} = \frac{223}{4}\right\rangle$.

Remark. It is noticed that on old basic variable x_{B_i} can become non-basic only if the introduction of the entering variable x_j at level η causes x_{B_i} to be at zero level or at its upper bound. This means that if $\eta = u_j$, x_j cannot be made basic, since no x_{B_i} can be dropped from the solution, and thus, x_j should remain non-basic but at its upper bound.

6.3 PARAMETRIC LINEAR PROGRAMMING MODEL

We know from *sensitivity analysis* that how sensitive is the optimum solution to perturbation in the parameters? A natural extension of this question is also of interest. One is interested in determining not only the critical amount of perturbation at which optimum basic feasible solution $\boldsymbol{x_B}$ just stops being optimum but also various basic solutions that become optimum, one after the other, as the perturbation is extended further and further beyond the initial point. This information is achieved by means of an iterative computational procedure called *parametric linear programming.* It investigates the behaviour of an optimum solution as a result of predetermined linear variations in the parameters of the problem.

The purpose of parametric LP is to minimise the additional computational effort required to obtain the indicated results. In the most general form the parameters vary as some implicit function of several independent parameters of arbitrary degree. The problem of parametric programming has not yet been solved for higher degree. The only case in which considerable work has been done is the parametric programming problem in which the parameters occur in first degree, particularly when a single parameter occurs linearly in the availability or requirement vector and the cost vector.

6.3.1 Parametric Changes in Cost Vector ($\boldsymbol{c}$)

We assume the existence of an optimum basic feasible solution with $\boldsymbol{B}$ as optimum basis has already been obtained for the LPP given by

Maximise $Z = \boldsymbol{cx}$

subject to $A\boldsymbol{x} = \boldsymbol{b}$ (6.3a)

$\boldsymbol{x} \geq \boldsymbol{0}$

where $\boldsymbol{c} = (c_1, c_2, \ldots, c_n)$, $\boldsymbol{x} = (x_1, x_2, \ldots, x_n)^T$, $A = \left(a_{ij}\right)_{m\times n}$, $b = (b_1, b_2, \ldots, b_m)^T$.

Let the cost vector $\boldsymbol{c}$ of problem (6.3a) be replaced by

$$\boldsymbol{c}^* = \boldsymbol{c} + \theta\,\hat{\boldsymbol{c}}, \tag{6.3b}$$

where $\hat{\boldsymbol{c}}$ is a predetermined specified n-component vector and θ is a scalar parameter. We are confined only to the cases in which $\underline{\boldsymbol{c}^*}$ defined in (6.3b) is a linear function of single parameter θ and lies on a straight line in the Euclidian space. Also we note that for the original LP model (6.3a), the cost vector is $\boldsymbol{c}$ when $\theta = 0$. As θ varies the feasible region as well as $\boldsymbol{x_B}$ remains unaltered but net evaluation $\left(z_j - c_j\right)$ changes. For any value of θ, the net evaluation $\left(z_j^n - c_j^n\right)$ for new problem is given by (n stands for new):

$$\begin{aligned} z_j^n - c_j^n &= \boldsymbol{c}_B^n \boldsymbol{y}_j - \boldsymbol{c}_j^n = (\boldsymbol{c}_B + \theta\,\hat{\boldsymbol{c}}_B)\,\boldsymbol{y}_j - \left(c_j + \theta\,\hat{c}_j\right) = \left(\boldsymbol{c}_B\boldsymbol{y}_j - c_j\right) + \theta\left(\hat{\boldsymbol{c}}_B\boldsymbol{y}_j - \hat{c}_j\right) \\ &= \left(z_j - c_j\right) + \theta\left(\hat{\boldsymbol{c}}_B\boldsymbol{y}_j - \hat{c}_j\right), \end{aligned} \tag{6.3c}$$

where $\hat{\boldsymbol{c}}_B$ contains those component of $\hat{c}$ which corresponds to the component of $\boldsymbol{c}$ in c_B.

The current basic feasible solution $\boldsymbol{x_B}$ will remain optimum as long as $z_j^n - c_j^n \geq 0$

$$\begin{aligned} \text{or, } \theta &\geq -\frac{z_j - c_j}{\beta_j}\,\bigg|\, \beta_j = \hat{c}_B y_j - \hat{c}_j > 0 \\ &\leq -\frac{z_j - c_j}{\beta_j}\,\bigg|\, \beta_j - \hat{c}_B y_j - \hat{c}_j < 0, \end{aligned} \tag{6.3d}$$

$$\text{i.e., } \max_j \left\{ -\frac{\alpha_j}{\beta_j} \,\bigg|\, \beta_j > 0 \right\} \leq \theta \leq \min_j \left\{ -\frac{\alpha_j}{\beta_j} \,\bigg|\, \beta_j < 0 \right\} \tag{6.3e}$$

where $\alpha_j = z_j - c_j$.

Again, $z_j^n - c_j^n = \left(z_j - c_j\right) + \theta\left(\hat{c}_B y_j - \hat{c}_j\right)$ indicates that if $\hat{c}_B y_j - \hat{c}_j \geq 0$, then automatically $z_j^n - c_j^n \geq 0$, since $z_j - c_j \geq 0$.

Hence, the *upper* and *lower* bounds of θ, so as the maintain the optimality of $\boldsymbol{x_B}$ are given by

$$\bar{\theta} \leq \theta \leq \underline{\theta} \tag{6.3f}$$

$$\text{where } \bar{\theta} = \max_j \begin{cases} -\dfrac{\alpha_j}{\beta_j} \,\bigg|\, \beta_j > 0 \\ -\infty \,|\, \beta_j \leq 0 \end{cases}, \qquad \underline{\theta} = \min_j \begin{cases} -\dfrac{\alpha_j}{\beta_j} \,\bigg|\, \beta_j < 0 \\ +\infty \,|\, \beta_j \geq 0 \end{cases} \tag{6.3g}$$

Obviously, $\boldsymbol{x_B}$ ceases to be optimum as soon as θ exceeds the value

$$\theta^* = \min_j \left\{ \frac{\alpha_j}{\beta_j} \,\bigg|\, \beta_j < 0 \right\}. \tag{6.3h}$$

Suppose, $\boldsymbol{x_B}$ be the non-basic variable for which (6.3h) occurs. Then for $j = k$,

$$\theta^* = -\frac{\alpha_k}{\beta_k} = -\frac{z_k - c_k}{\hat{c}_B y_k - \hat{c}_k}.$$

When $\theta=\theta^*$, the net evaluation $z_k^n - c_k^n = 0$ and the resulting LP model becomes

$$\begin{aligned} &\text{Maximise } Z^n = \boldsymbol{c}^*\boldsymbol{x} = (\boldsymbol{c}+\boldsymbol{\theta}^*\hat{\boldsymbol{c}})\,\boldsymbol{x} \\ &\text{subject to } \ A\boldsymbol{x}=\boldsymbol{b} \\ &\qquad\qquad \boldsymbol{x}\geq \boldsymbol{0}. \end{aligned} \tag{6.3i}$$

(6.3i) have at least two optimum solutions:

(i) The current optimum solution.

(ii) The new optimum solution (alternative optima) that results when x_k enters the basis.

Let us denote the two solutions under (i) and (ii) are $\boldsymbol{x}^{(1)}$ and $\boldsymbol{x}^{(2)}$ respectively. When θ increases beyond θ^*, the net evaluation $z_k^n - c_k^n$ becomes negative so that $\boldsymbol{x}^{(2)}$ replaces $\boldsymbol{x}^{(1)}$ as a unique optimum solution.

Even after having obtained $\boldsymbol{x}^{(2)}$ one may still wish to continue the investigation by considering larger value of θ. The question which now arises is — How much further can θ be increased beyond the value θ^* called *initial critical value* before the new solution $\boldsymbol{x}^{(2)}$ ceases to be optimum?

The answer can be obtained by performing a second analysis which will give *second critical value* and a new alternative optimum solution $\boldsymbol{x}^{(3)}$. If it is repeated a number of times, a basic feasible solution will be found which remains optimum.

Thus, the *parametric programming,* if performed will conclude that it will generate a sequence of *critical values* $\theta^{(1)},\theta^{(2)},\ldots,\theta^{(p)}$ and a sequence of solutions $\boldsymbol{x}^{(1)},\boldsymbol{x}^{(2)},\ldots,\boldsymbol{x}^{(p)},\boldsymbol{x}^{(p+1)}$ such that

$$\begin{aligned} \boldsymbol{x} &= \boldsymbol{x}^{(1)} && \text{is optimum if } \theta\in[0,\theta^{(1)}] \\ &= \boldsymbol{x}^{(2)} && \text{is optimum if } \theta\in[\theta^{(1)},\theta^{(2)}] \\ &= \ldots \\ \boldsymbol{x} &= \boldsymbol{x}^{(p+1)} && \text{is optimum if } \theta^{(p)}\leq\theta. \end{aligned}$$

Example 6.3.1. *Consider the following parametric* LP *model:*

$$\begin{aligned} &\textit{Maximise } Z=(\theta-1)x_1+x_2 \\ &\textit{subject to } \ x_1+2x_2\leq 10 \\ &\qquad 2x_1+\ x_2\leq 11 \\ &\qquad x_1-2x_2\leq \ 3 \\ &\qquad\quad x_1,\,x_2\geq \ 3. \end{aligned}$$

Perform a complete parametric programming analysis. Identify all critical values of parameter θ and all optimum basic feasible solution. [ISI(SQC/OR) 2002, BESU(MSc) 2000, 2004]

Solution:

Step 1. Put $\theta=0$ and introduce slack variables $x_3,\,x_4,\,x_5\geq 0$ in the constraints, using regular simplex method, we get the following optimum table (The intermediate steps are left for the reader).

Optimum table (for $\theta=0$):

		c_j	-1	1	0	0	0	
c_B	y_B	x_B	y_1	y_2	y_3	y_4	y_5	MR
1	y_2	5	$\frac{1}{2}$	1	$\frac{1}{2}$	0	0	10
0	y_4	6	$\boxed{\frac{3}{2}}$	0	$-\frac{1}{2}$	1	0	4 →
0	y_5	13	2	0	1	0	1	$\frac{13}{2}$
		z_j-c_j	$\frac{3}{2}$ ↑	0	$\frac{1}{2}$	0	0	

An optimum basic feasible solution $x_B = \begin{pmatrix} 0 \\ 5 \end{pmatrix}$.

Step 2. When $\theta \neq 0$, c_1 is changed from -1 to $(\theta - 1)$, where θ is an unknown parameter.

Here, $c^* = c + \theta \hat{c} = (-1 \quad 1 \quad 0 \quad 0 \quad 0) + \theta(1 \quad 0 \quad 0 \quad 0 \quad 0)$.

$$\hat{c}_B = (0,0,0) \qquad \hat{c}_B y_1 - \hat{c}_1 = (0,0,0)\begin{pmatrix} \frac{1}{2} \\ \frac{3}{2} \\ 2 \end{pmatrix} - 1 = -1$$

(For non-basic)

$$\hat{c}_B y_3 - \hat{c}_3 = (0,0,0)\begin{pmatrix} \frac{1}{2} \\ \frac{1}{2} \\ 0 \end{pmatrix} - 0 = 0$$

$$\hat{c}_B y_j - \hat{c}_j = 0 \text{ for all basic variable}$$

$$\theta^{(1)} = \min_j \left\{ -\frac{z_j - c_j}{\hat{c}_B y_j - \hat{c}_j} \,\middle|\, \hat{c}_B y_j - \hat{c}_j < 0 \right\} = \left\{ \frac{-3/2}{-1} \right\} = \frac{3}{2}.$$

The current optimum solution $x_B = \begin{pmatrix} 0 \\ 5 \end{pmatrix}$ will remain optimum as long as θ does not exceed $\theta^{(1)} = \frac{3}{2}$.

However, when $\theta = \theta^{(1)} = \frac{3}{2}$ an alternative optima is introduce. The adjusted net evaluations are:

$$z_1^n - c_1^n = (z_1 - c_1) + \theta\left(\hat{c}_B y_1 - \hat{c}_1\right) = \frac{3}{2} + \frac{3}{2}(-1) = 0$$

$$z_3^n - c_3^n = (z_3 - c_3) + \theta\left(\hat{c}_B y_3 - \hat{c}_3\right) = \frac{1}{2} + \frac{3}{2}(0) = \frac{1}{2}.$$

As the non-basic variable x_1 has a net evaluation 0 it can be introduced into the basic by removing x_4 by regular simplex method to produce an alternative optimum solution as follows.

Alternative optima: $\theta = \frac{3}{2}$ objective function: $\max Z = \left(\frac{3}{2} - 1\right) x_1 + x_2$.

		c_j	$\frac{1}{2}$	1	0	0	0	
c_B	y_B	x_B	y_1	y_2	y_3	y_4	y_5	MR
1	y_2	3	0	1	$\frac{2}{3}$	$-\frac{1}{3}$	0	$\frac{9}{2}$
$\frac{1}{2}$	y_1	4	1	0	$-\frac{1}{3}$	$\frac{2}{3}$	0	×
0	y_5	5	0	0	$\boxed{\frac{5}{3}}$	$-\frac{4}{3}$	1	3 →
		$z_j - c_j$	0	0	$\frac{1}{2}$↑	0	0	

When θ is increased above $\theta^{(1)} = \frac{3}{2}$, the new solution $x_B = \begin{pmatrix} 4 \\ 3 \end{pmatrix}$ becomes the unique optimum.

Step 3. In order to determine the value at which $\boldsymbol{x_B} = \begin{pmatrix} 4 \\ 3 \end{pmatrix}$ ceases to be optimum we proceed similarly, as follows.

Here, $\hat{c}_B = (0, 1, 0)$.

$$\hat{c}_B y_3 - \hat{c}_3 = (0 \quad 1 \quad 0) \begin{pmatrix} \frac{2}{3} \\ -\frac{1}{3} \\ \frac{5}{3} \end{pmatrix} - 0 = -\frac{1}{3}, \qquad \hat{c}_B y_4 - \hat{c}_4 = (0 \quad 1 \quad 0) \begin{pmatrix} -\frac{1}{2} \\ \frac{2}{3} \\ -\frac{4}{3} \end{pmatrix} - 0 = \frac{2}{3}.$$

$$\theta_2 = \frac{-1/2}{-1/3} = \frac{3}{2}.$$

To find new alternative optima when θ reaches the relative value of $\frac{3}{2}$ w.r.t. adjusted post-optimal problem

$$z_3^n - c_3^n = \frac{1}{2} + \frac{3}{2}\left(-\frac{1}{3}\right) = 0, \qquad z_4^n - c_4^n = 0 + \frac{3}{2}\left(\frac{2}{3}\right) = 1.$$

New cost vector

$$\hat{c}^* = \boldsymbol{c}_{\text{current}} + \theta_2 \hat{c} = \left[\boldsymbol{c}_{\text{original}} + \theta^{(1)}\hat{c}\right] + \theta\hat{c} = \boldsymbol{c}_{\text{original}} + \left(\theta^{(1)}\hat{c}\right)\hat{c}$$

$$= \boldsymbol{c}_{\text{original}} + \theta^{(2)}\hat{c} : \theta^{(2)} = \theta^{(1)} + \theta_2 = \tfrac{3}{2} + \tfrac{3}{2} = \tfrac{6}{2} = 3.$$

New objective function: $\max Z = (3-1)x_1 + x_2 = 2x_1 + x_2$.
Introduce x_3 (as net evaluation is zero) and drop x_5 to produce new alternative optima.

		c_j	2	1	0	0	0
c_B	y_B	x_B	y_1	y_2	y_3	y_4	y_5
1	y_2	1	0	1	0	$\frac{1}{5}$	$-\frac{2}{5}$
2	y_1	5	1	0	0	$\frac{2}{5}$	$\frac{1}{5}$
0	y_3	3	0	0	1	$-\frac{4}{5}$	$\frac{3}{5}$
		$z_j - c_j$	0	0	0	1	0

When θ is increased beyond $\theta^{(2)}$, the solution $x_B = \begin{pmatrix} 5 \\ 1 \end{pmatrix}$ becomes the unique optimum. For next we see that

$$\hat{c}_B = (0 \quad 1 \quad 0), \quad \hat{c}_B y_4 - \hat{c}_4 = (0 \quad 1 \quad 0) \begin{pmatrix} \frac{1}{5} \\ \frac{2}{5} \\ \frac{4}{5} \end{pmatrix} - 0 = \frac{2}{5}, \quad \hat{c}_B y_5 - \hat{c}_5 = (0 \quad 1 \quad 0) \begin{pmatrix} -\frac{2}{5} \\ \frac{1}{5} \\ \frac{3}{5} \end{pmatrix} - 0 = \frac{1}{5}.$$

Conclusion. All $\hat{c}_B y_j - \hat{c}_j \geq 0$ and hence all the adjusted net evaluation remains non-negative whatever θ may be.

Therefore, the sequence of optimum solutions and corresponding critical values of the problem by parametric programming analysis for unknown parameter θ are given by:

$$\boldsymbol{x}^{(1)} = \begin{pmatrix} 0 \\ 5 \end{pmatrix} \text{ in } 0 < \theta \leq \frac{3}{2}, \quad \boldsymbol{x}^{(2)} = \begin{pmatrix} 4 \\ 3 \end{pmatrix} \text{ in } \frac{3}{2} < \theta \leq 3, \quad \boldsymbol{x}^{(3)} = \begin{pmatrix} 5 \\ 1 \end{pmatrix} \text{ in } 3 \leq \theta.$$

6.3.2 Parametric Changes in Availability Vector ($\boldsymbol{b}$)

Let the LP model before parameterisation is defined as

Maximise $Z = \boldsymbol{cx}$

subject to $A\boldsymbol{x} = \boldsymbol{b}$

$\boldsymbol{x} \geq \boldsymbol{0}$

where $\boldsymbol{b}$ is the known availability (or requirement) vector. Let $\boldsymbol{b}$ changes to $\boldsymbol{b}^* = \boldsymbol{b} + \theta \hat{\boldsymbol{b}}$.

Then the LP model after parametrisation is reduced to

Maximise $Z = \boldsymbol{cx}$

subject to $A\boldsymbol{x} = \boldsymbol{b} + \theta \hat{\boldsymbol{b}}$

$\boldsymbol{x} \geq \boldsymbol{0}$

where $\hat{\boldsymbol{b}}$ is the given and predetermined variation vector and θ is an unknown parameter. Now our aim is to determine the family of basic feasible optimal solutions for variable θ.

Here, $\theta = 0$, the parametric LP model is converted to original LP model. By regular simplex method first we solve to find the optimal basic feasible solution of the original LP model neglecting the parametric restriction.

Let $\boldsymbol{x}_B$ be the optimum basic feasible solution with $\boldsymbol{B}$ as optimum basis. Then $\boldsymbol{x}_B = \boldsymbol{B}^{-1}\boldsymbol{b}$.

As θ changes from zero to a positive or negative value the basic feasible solution changes and the new values are given by

$$\boldsymbol{x}_B^* = \boldsymbol{B}^{-1}\left(\boldsymbol{b} + \theta \hat{\boldsymbol{b}}\right) = \boldsymbol{B}^{-1}\boldsymbol{b} + \theta \boldsymbol{B}^{-1}\hat{\boldsymbol{b}} = \boldsymbol{x}_B + \theta \boldsymbol{B}^{-1}\boldsymbol{b}.$$

Obviously, a change in θ has no effect on the values of c_j and hence on values of $\left(z_j - c_j\right)$.

The new solution remains feasible if $x_B^* \geq 0$ or, $\boldsymbol{x}_B + \theta \boldsymbol{B}^{-1}\hat{\boldsymbol{b}} \geq 0$

$$\Rightarrow \theta \geq \frac{-\boldsymbol{x}_B}{\boldsymbol{B}^{-1}\hat{\boldsymbol{b}}} \bigg| \boldsymbol{B}^{-1}\hat{\boldsymbol{b}} > 0$$

$$\leq \frac{-\boldsymbol{x}_B}{\boldsymbol{B}^{-1}\hat{\boldsymbol{b}}} \bigg| \boldsymbol{B}^{-1}\hat{\boldsymbol{b}} < 0.$$

If $\theta_1 = \max\left\{ \dfrac{-\boldsymbol{x}_B}{\boldsymbol{B}^{-1}\hat{\boldsymbol{b}}} \bigg| \boldsymbol{B}^{-1}\hat{\boldsymbol{b}} > 0 \right\}$, $\theta_2 = \min\left\{ \dfrac{-\boldsymbol{x}_B}{\boldsymbol{B}^{-1}\hat{\boldsymbol{b}}} \bigg| \boldsymbol{B}^{-1}\hat{\boldsymbol{b}} < 0 \right\}$.

Then the possible range of θ so that new solution remains feasible is

$$\theta_1 \leq \theta \leq \theta_2. \tag{6.3j}$$

If at least one $\boldsymbol{B}^{-1}\hat{\boldsymbol{b}}$ is negative, then there exists a *critical value* θ^* given by

$$\theta^* = \min\left\{ \frac{-\boldsymbol{x}_B}{\boldsymbol{B}^{-1}\hat{\boldsymbol{b}}} \bigg| \boldsymbol{B}^{-1}\hat{\boldsymbol{b}} < 0 \right\}.$$

In fact, when $\theta = \theta^*$, an alternative solution is obtained and when $\theta > \theta^*$, an improved solution of the problem is obtained.

Example 6.3.2. *Consider the parametric* LP *model.*

$$\begin{aligned} &\textit{Maximise } Z = 3x_1 + 2x_2 + 5x_3 \\ &\textit{subject to } x_1 + 2x_2 + x_3 \le 430 + \theta \\ &\qquad 3x_1 \qquad + 2x_3 \le 460 - 4\theta \\ &\qquad x_1 + 4x_2 \qquad \le 420 - 4\theta \\ &\qquad x_1,\ x_2,\ x_3 \ge 0 \end{aligned}$$

Determine the range of the unknown parameter θ for which the solution remains optimum basic feasible.

[BESU(MSc) 2005]

Solution:

Step 1. For $\theta = 0$, the non-parametric LP model is solved by simplex method by introducing slack variable $x_4 \ge 0$, $x_5 \ge 0$ and $x_6 \ge 0$. The following table represents the optimal solution of the problem without parametric restriction (The intermediate tables are left for readers).

Optimum table:

		c_j	3	2	5	0	0	0
c_B	y_B	x_B	y_1	y_2	y_3	y_4	y_5	y_6
2	y_2	100	$-\frac{1}{4}$	1	0	$\frac{1}{2}$	$-\frac{1}{4}$	0
5	y_3	230	$\frac{3}{2}$	0	1	0	$\frac{1}{2}$	0
0	y_6	20	2	0	0	-2	1	1
		$z_j - c_j$	4	0	0	1	2	0

The optimal table gives

$$B^{-1} = \begin{pmatrix} \frac{1}{2} & -\frac{1}{4} & 0 \\ 0 & \frac{1}{2} & 0 \\ -2 & 1 & 1 \end{pmatrix}, \quad x_B = \begin{pmatrix} 100 \\ 230 \\ 20 \end{pmatrix}, \quad B^{-1}\hat{b}_1 = \begin{pmatrix} \frac{1}{2} & -\frac{1}{4} & 0 \\ 0 & \frac{1}{2} & 0 \\ -2 & 1 & 1 \end{pmatrix} \begin{pmatrix} 1 \\ -4 \\ 4 \end{pmatrix} = \begin{pmatrix} \frac{3}{2} \\ -2 \\ -10 \end{pmatrix}.$$

First critical value $= \theta^*_{\text{first}} = \min\left\{\dfrac{-x_B}{B^{-1}\hat{b}_1} \,\middle|\, B^{-1}\hat{b}_1 < 0\right\} = \min\left\{-\dfrac{230}{-2}, \dfrac{20}{-10}\right\} = 2$, which corresponds to $x_{B_3} \equiv y_6$.

Then the solution will remain an optimal basic feasible over the interval $[0, 2]$.

Step 2. (i) At $\theta = 2$, the optimum simplex table will be:

		c_j	3	2	5	0	0	0
c_B	y_B	x_B	y_1	y_2	y_3	y_4	y_5	y_6
2	y_2	103	$-\frac{1}{4}$	1	0	$\frac{1}{2}$	$-\frac{1}{4}$	0
5	y_3	226	$\frac{3}{2}$	0	1	0	$\frac{1}{2}$	0
0	y_6	0	0	0	0	$\boxed{-2}$	1	1 →
		$z_j - c_j$	4	0	0	1↑	2	0

(ii) At $\theta > 2$, the basic y_6 becomes negative, the solution becomes infeasible but optimal. To find optimal basic feasible solution we employ *dual-simplex* method, where y_6 leaves and y_4 enters the basis. The improved optimum table becomes:

		c_j	3	2	5	0	0	0
c_B	y_B	x_B	y_1	y_2	y_3	y_4	y_5	y_6
2	y_2	103	$\frac{1}{4}$	1	0	0	0	$\frac{1}{4}$
5	y_3	226	$\frac{3}{2}$	0	1	0	$\frac{1}{2}$	0
0	y_4	0	0	0	0	1	$-\frac{1}{2}$	$-\frac{1}{2}$
		$z_j - c_j$	5	0	0	0	$\frac{5}{2}$	$\frac{1}{2}$

Step 3. To search for second critical value of parameter θ

$$B^{-1} = \begin{pmatrix} 0 & 0 & \frac{1}{4} \\ 0 & \frac{1}{2} & 0 \\ 1 & -\frac{1}{2} & -\frac{1}{2} \end{pmatrix}, \quad B^{-1}\hat{b}_1 = \begin{pmatrix} 0 & 0 & \frac{1}{4} \\ 0 & \frac{1}{2} & 0 \\ 1 & -\frac{1}{2} & -\frac{1}{2} \end{pmatrix} \begin{pmatrix} 1 \\ -4 \\ -4 \end{pmatrix} = \begin{pmatrix} -1 \\ -2 \\ 5 \end{pmatrix}.$$

$$\theta^*_{\text{second}} = \min\left\{-\frac{103}{-1}, -\frac{226}{-2}\right\} = 103$$

corresponds to $x_{B_1} \equiv y_2$ and the solution becomes optimum basic feasible solution over the interval [2, 103].

Observe that for $\theta > 103$, the basic variable y_2 becomes negative but all the entries in that row are positive so that no replacement ratio is found in *dual-simplex* method, which indicates that for $\theta > 103$ there exists no feasible solution.

Conclusion. The parametric programming analysis of the model gives the following solutions:

$$x_1^* = [0, 100, 230]^T \qquad \text{if } \theta \in [0, 2]$$

$$x_2^* = [0, 103, 226]^T \qquad \text{if } \theta \in [2, 103]$$

$$x_3^* = \text{no feasible solution if } \theta > 103.$$

6.4 REVISED SIMPLEX METHOD

The simplex method discussed earlier in Ch. 2, performs calculations on the entire table during each iteration. If an LP model involves a large number of variables, it will require a large storage space and consume much time on a computer. Some computational techniques have been developed which require much less computer storage and time. Two such important and efficient computational techniques are: *Revised simplex* method and *Bounded variable* method. The second one has already been illustrated in details in Sec. 6.2 of this chapter. Let us now explain the revised simplex method and its computational details as follows.

6.4.1 Product-Form of Inverse

We first show how the inverse $\boldsymbol{B}^{-1}$ can be computed for the successive iterations in a manner that is particularly suited for the simplex computations. This information is then used to develop the computational details of the revised simplex method.

Given the current basis $\boldsymbol{B}$, the next basis $\boldsymbol{B}_{\text{next}}$ in the immediately succeeding iteration will differ from $\boldsymbol{B}$ in one column only. The product-form procedure then computes the next inverse $\boldsymbol{B}_{\text{next}}^{-1}$ by premultiplying the current inverse $\boldsymbol{B}^{-1}$ by a newly constructed matrix $\boldsymbol{P}$.

$\boldsymbol{I}_m = (\boldsymbol{e}_1, \boldsymbol{e}_2, \dots, \boldsymbol{e}_i, \dots, \boldsymbol{e}_m)$, the identity matrix, where $\boldsymbol{e}_i$ is the unit column vector with a 1-element in the ith place and zero otherwise.

Suppose, we are given $\boldsymbol{B}$ and $\boldsymbol{B}^{-1}$ and assume that the vector $\boldsymbol{V}_r$ in $\boldsymbol{B}$ is replaced by a new vector $\boldsymbol{V}_j$.

Define $\boldsymbol{\sigma}^j = \boldsymbol{B}^{-1}\boldsymbol{V}_j$ so that σ_k^j is the kth column of $\boldsymbol{\sigma}^j$. Then the new inverse $\boldsymbol{B}_{\text{next}}^{-1}$ can be computed as follows: $\boldsymbol{B}_{\text{next}}^{-1} = \boldsymbol{P}\boldsymbol{B}^{-1}$, where $\boldsymbol{P} = (\boldsymbol{e}_1, \boldsymbol{e}_2, \dots, \boldsymbol{e}_{r-1}, \boldsymbol{\eta}, \boldsymbol{e}_{r+1}, \dots, \boldsymbol{e}_m)$ and

$$\eta = \begin{pmatrix} -\sigma_1^j/\sigma_r^j \\ -\sigma_2^j/\sigma_r^j \\ \vdots \\ +1/\sigma_r^j \\ \vdots \\ -\sigma_m^j/\sigma_r^j \end{pmatrix} \begin{matrix} \\ \\ \\ \longrightarrow r\text{th position} \\ \\ \\ \end{matrix}$$

provided $\sigma_r^j \neq 0$. If $\sigma_r^j = 0$, B_{next}^{-1} does not exist.

In fact, $\boldsymbol{P}$ is obtained from $\boldsymbol{I}_m$ by replacing the rth column $\boldsymbol{e}_r$ by $\boldsymbol{\eta}$.

Example 6.4.1. *Suppose,* $\boldsymbol{B} = \begin{pmatrix} 2 & 1 & 0 \\ 0 & 2 & 0 \\ 4 & 0 & 1 \end{pmatrix}$. *Then* $B^{-1} = \begin{pmatrix} \frac{1}{2} & -\frac{1}{4} & 0 \\ 0 & \frac{1}{2} & 0 \\ -2 & 1 & 1 \end{pmatrix}$.

If, for example, the third column vector $V_3 = \begin{pmatrix} 0 \\ 0 \\ 1 \end{pmatrix}$ of $\boldsymbol{B}$ changed to $V_3^* = \begin{pmatrix} 2 \\ 1 \\ 5 \end{pmatrix}$, we can find the new inverse as follows:

$$\boldsymbol{\sigma}^3 = \boldsymbol{B}^{-1}\boldsymbol{V}_3^* = \begin{pmatrix} \frac{1}{2} & -\frac{1}{4} & 0 \\ 0 & \frac{1}{2} & 0 \\ -2 & 1 & 1 \end{pmatrix} \begin{pmatrix} 2 \\ 1 \\ 5 \end{pmatrix} = \begin{pmatrix} \frac{3}{4} = \sigma_1^3 \\ \frac{1}{2} = \sigma_2^3 \\ 2 = \sigma_3^3 \end{pmatrix}$$

$$\boldsymbol{\eta} = \begin{pmatrix} -\frac{3/3}{2} \\ -\frac{1/2}{2} \\ +\frac{1}{2} \end{pmatrix} = \begin{pmatrix} -\frac{3}{8} \\ -\frac{1}{4} \\ \frac{1}{2} \end{pmatrix} \longrightarrow r = 3 \text{ position}$$

$$\boldsymbol{B}_{\text{next}}^{-1} = \boldsymbol{P}\boldsymbol{B}^{-1} = \begin{pmatrix} 1 & 0 & -\frac{3}{8} \\ 0 & 1 & -\frac{1}{4} \\ 0 & 0 & \frac{1}{2} \end{pmatrix} \begin{pmatrix} \frac{1}{2} & -\frac{1}{4} & 0 \\ 0 & \frac{1}{2} & 0 \\ -2 & 1 & 1 \end{pmatrix} = \begin{pmatrix} \frac{5}{4} & -\frac{5}{8} & -\frac{3}{8} \\ \frac{1}{2} & \frac{1}{4} & -\frac{1}{4} \\ -1 & \frac{1}{2} & \frac{1}{2} \end{pmatrix}.$$

6.4.2 Computational Procedure of the Revised Simplex Method

The steps of revised simplex method are essentially those of regular simplex method. Given the starting basis **I**, we determine its associated objective coefficients vector $\boldsymbol{c_B}$ depending on whether the starting basic variables are slack and/or artificial.

Step 1. Determination of entering vector $\boldsymbol{V_j}$: Compute $\boldsymbol{Y} = \boldsymbol{c_B}\boldsymbol{B}^{-1}$ for every non-basic vector $\boldsymbol{V_j}$ and $z_j - c_j = \boldsymbol{Y}\boldsymbol{V_j} - c_j$.

For maximisation/minimisation LP model, the entering vector $\boldsymbol{V_j}$ is selected to have the most negative/positive. If there is a tie-break, tie arbitrarily. If all $z_j - c_j \geq 0/\leq 0$, the optimum solution is reached and is given by $\boldsymbol{x_B} = \boldsymbol{B}^{-1}\boldsymbol{b}$ and $Z = \boldsymbol{c_B}\boldsymbol{x_B}$.

Otherwise, GO TO next step.

Step 2. Determination of departing vector $\boldsymbol{V_r}$: With respect to entering vector $\boldsymbol{V_j}$ compute (i) values of current basic variables: $\boldsymbol{x_B} = \boldsymbol{B}^{-1}\boldsymbol{b}$ (ii) Coefficients of the entering variables: $\boldsymbol{\sigma}^j = \boldsymbol{B}^{-1}\boldsymbol{V_j}$.

The departing vector $\boldsymbol{V_r}$ for both maximisation and minimisation must be associated with

$$\mu = \min_k \left\{ \frac{(\boldsymbol{B}^{-1}\boldsymbol{b})_k}{\sigma_k^j} \,\middle|\, \sigma_k^j > 0 \right\},$$

where $(\boldsymbol{B}^{-1}\boldsymbol{b})_k$ and σ_k^j are the kth elements of $\boldsymbol{B}^{-1}\boldsymbol{b}$ and $\boldsymbol{\sigma}^j$. If all $\sigma_k^j \leq 0$, the problem has no bounded solution.

Step 3. Determination of the next basis: We have $\boldsymbol{B}_{\text{next}}^{-1} = \boldsymbol{P}\boldsymbol{B}^{-1}$.

Now, set $\boldsymbol{B}^{-1} = \boldsymbol{B}_{\text{next}}^{-1}$ and GO TO *Step* 1.

The process terminates if all $z_j - c_j \geq 0/\leq 0$ for maximisation/minimisation LP model and gives us the required optimal solution.

Example 6.4.2. *Maximise* $Z = 3x_1 + 2x_2$

$$\begin{aligned} \textit{subject to}\quad x_1 + 2x_2 + x_3 \quad\quad\quad &= 6 \\ 2x_1 + x_2 \quad + x_4 \quad\quad &= 8 \\ -x_1 + x_2 \quad\quad + x_5 \quad &= 1 \\ x_2 \quad\quad\quad + x_6 &= 2 \\ x_1, x_2, \ldots, x_6 &\geq 0. \end{aligned}$$

[CU(MSc) 1989, JU(MSc) 1992]

Solution: *First iteration:* $\boldsymbol{x_B} = (x_3, x_4, x_5, x_6)^T$

$$\boldsymbol{c_B} = (0, 0, 0, 0)$$

$$\boldsymbol{B} = (V_3, V_4, V_5, V_6) = I_4$$

$$\boldsymbol{B^{-1}} = I_4.$$

(i) Computation of $z_j - c_j$ for non-basic V_1 and V_2

$$\boldsymbol{Y} = \boldsymbol{c_B} B^{-1} = (0,0,0,0),\ z_1 - c_1 = (0,0,0,0)\begin{pmatrix}1\\2\\-1\\0\end{pmatrix} - 3 = -3,\ z_2 - c_2 = (0,0,0,0)\begin{pmatrix}2\\1\\1\\1\end{pmatrix} - 2 = -2.$$

V_1 is the entering vector.

(ii) Computation of leaving vector given V_1 enters the basis

$$\boldsymbol{x_B} = \boldsymbol{B^{-1}b} = \boldsymbol{I_4 b} = \boldsymbol{b} = \begin{pmatrix}6\\8\\1\\2\end{pmatrix},\ \sigma^1 = \boldsymbol{B^{-1}} V_1 = \boldsymbol{I_4} V_1 = V_1 = \begin{pmatrix}1\\2\\-1\\0\end{pmatrix},\ \mu = \min\left\{\frac{6}{1}, \frac{8}{2}\right\} = 4$$

corresponding to x_4 so that V_4 is the leaving vector.

(iii) Computation of next basis inverse, where V_1 replaces V_4 and $\boldsymbol{\sigma}^1 = \begin{pmatrix}1\\2\\-1\\0\end{pmatrix}$.

Now

$$\eta = \begin{pmatrix} -\frac{1}{2} \\ +\frac{1}{2} \\ -\left(\frac{-1}{2}\right) \\ \frac{0}{2} \end{pmatrix} = \begin{pmatrix} -\frac{1}{2} \\ \frac{1}{2} \\ \frac{1}{2} \\ 0 \end{pmatrix},\quad \boldsymbol{B}_{\text{next}}^{-1} = \boldsymbol{P}\boldsymbol{B}^{-1} = \boldsymbol{P} I_4 = P = \begin{pmatrix} 1 & -\frac{1}{2} & 0 & 0 \\ 0 & \frac{1}{2} & 0 & 0 \\ 0 & \frac{1}{2} & 1 & 0 \\ 0 & 0 & 0 & 1 \end{pmatrix}$$

The new basis vector $\boldsymbol{x_B} = (x_3,\ x_1,\ x_5,\ x_6)^T$

$$\boldsymbol{c_B} = (0,\ 3,\ 0,\ 0).$$

Second iteration:

(i) Computation of $\left(z_j - c_j\right)$ for non-basic V_2 and V_4

$$c_B B^{-1} = (0, 3, 0, 0)\begin{pmatrix} 1 & -\frac{1}{2} & 0 & 0 \\ 0 & \frac{1}{2} & 0 & 0 \\ 0 & \frac{1}{2} & 1 & 0 \\ 0 & 0 & 0 & 1 \end{pmatrix} = \left(0, \frac{3}{2}, 0, 0\right)$$

$$z_2 - c_2 = \left(0, \frac{3}{2}, 0, 0\right)\begin{pmatrix} 2 \\ 1 \\ 1 \\ 1 \end{pmatrix} - 2 = -\frac{1}{2}, \quad z_4 - c_4 = \left(0, \frac{3}{2}, 0, 0\right)\begin{pmatrix} 0 \\ 1 \\ 0 \\ 0 \end{pmatrix} - 0 = \frac{3}{2}.$$

V_2 is the entering vector.

(ii) Computation of leaving vector w.r.t. to entering vector V_2

$$x_B = B^1 b = \begin{pmatrix} 1 & -\frac{1}{2} & 0 & 0 \\ 0 & \frac{1}{2} & 0 & 0 \\ 0 & \frac{1}{2} & 1 & 0 \\ 0 & 0 & 0 & 1 \end{pmatrix}\begin{pmatrix} 6 \\ 8 \\ 1 \\ 2 \end{pmatrix} = \begin{pmatrix} 2 \\ 4 \\ 5 \\ 2 \end{pmatrix}, \quad \sigma^2 = B^1 V_2 = \begin{pmatrix} 1 & -\frac{1}{2} & 0 & 0 \\ 0 & \frac{1}{2} & 0 & 0 \\ 0 & \frac{1}{2} & 1 & 0 \\ 0 & 0 & 0 & 1 \end{pmatrix}\begin{pmatrix} 2 \\ 1 \\ 1 \\ 1 \end{pmatrix} = \begin{pmatrix} \frac{3}{2} \\ \frac{1}{2} \\ \frac{3}{2} \\ 1 \end{pmatrix}.$$

$$\mu = \min\left\{\frac{2}{3/2}, \frac{4}{1/2}, \frac{5}{3/2}, \frac{2}{1}\right\} = \frac{4}{3}$$

corresponds to x_3 as a result, V_3 is the leaving vector.

(iii) Computation of next basic inverse, where V_2 replaces V_3 and

$$\sigma^2 = \begin{pmatrix} \frac{3}{2} \\ \frac{1}{2} \\ \frac{3}{2} \\ 1 \end{pmatrix}, \quad \eta = \begin{pmatrix} +\frac{1}{3/2} \\ -\frac{1/2}{3/2} \\ -\frac{3/2}{3/2} \\ -\frac{1}{3/2} \end{pmatrix} = \begin{pmatrix} \frac{2}{3} \\ -\frac{1}{3} \\ -1 \\ -\frac{2}{3} \end{pmatrix}.$$

$$B_{\text{next}}^{-1} = \begin{pmatrix} \frac{2}{3} & 0 & 0 & 0 \\ -\frac{1}{3} & 1 & 0 & 0 \\ -1 & 0 & 1 & 0 \\ -\frac{2}{3} & 0 & 0 & 1 \end{pmatrix} \begin{pmatrix} 1 & -\frac{1}{2} & 0 & 0 \\ 0 & \frac{1}{2} & 0 & 0 \\ 0 & \frac{1}{2} & 1 & 0 \\ 0 & 0 & 0 & 1 \end{pmatrix} = \begin{pmatrix} \frac{2}{3} & -\frac{1}{3} & 0 & 0 \\ -\frac{1}{3} & \frac{2}{3} & 0 & 0 \\ -1 & 1 & 1 & 0 \\ -\frac{2}{3} & \frac{1}{3} & 0 & 1 \end{pmatrix}.$$

The new basic vector $\boldsymbol{x_B} = (x_2, x_1, x_5, x_6)^T$

$\boldsymbol{C_B} = (2, 3, 0, 0)$

Third iteration: (i) Computation of $z_j - c_j$ for non-basic $\boldsymbol{V_3}, \boldsymbol{V_4}$

$$\boldsymbol{c_B B^{-1}} = (2, 3, 0, 0) \begin{pmatrix} \frac{2}{3} & -\frac{1}{3} & 0 & 0 \\ -\frac{1}{3} & \frac{2}{3} & 0 & 0 \\ -1 & 1 & 1 & 0 \\ -\frac{2}{3} & \frac{1}{3} & 0 & 1 \end{pmatrix} = \left(\frac{1}{3}, \frac{4}{3}, 0, 0\right)$$

$$z_3 - c_3 = \left(\frac{1}{3}, \frac{4}{3}, 0, 0\right) \begin{pmatrix} 1 \\ 0 \\ 0 \\ 0 \end{pmatrix} - 0 = \frac{1}{3}, \quad z_4 - c_4 = \left(\frac{1}{3}, \frac{4}{3}, 0, 0\right) \begin{pmatrix} 0 \\ 1 \\ 0 \\ 0 \end{pmatrix} - 0 = \frac{4}{3}.$$

Since all $z_j - c_j \geq 0$, the last basis gives the optimal basic feasible solution as under:

Optimal solution:

$$\begin{pmatrix} x_2^* \\ x_1^* \\ x_5^* \\ x_6^* \end{pmatrix} = \boldsymbol{B^{-1}b} = \begin{pmatrix} \frac{2}{3} & -\frac{1}{3} & 0 & \\ -\frac{1}{3} & \frac{2}{3} & 0 & 0 \\ -1 & 1 & 1 & 0 \\ -\frac{2}{3} & \frac{1}{3} & 0 & 1 \end{pmatrix} \begin{pmatrix} 6 \\ 8 \\ 1 \\ 2 \end{pmatrix} = \begin{pmatrix} \frac{4}{3} \\ \frac{10}{3} \\ 3 \\ \frac{2}{3} \end{pmatrix}$$

$$Z_{\max} = \boldsymbol{c_B x_B} = (2,\ 3,\ 0,\ 0)\begin{pmatrix} \frac{4}{3} \\ \frac{10}{3} \\ 3 \\ \frac{2}{3} \end{pmatrix} = \frac{38}{3}.$$

6.4.3 Computational Advantages of Revised Simplex Method

The *revised simplex* method offers two added advantages from the stand point of the use of the digital computer for solving large scale LP model.

1. It can reduce the volume of computations.
2. It uses the computer memory efficiently.

The revised method can involve less computations than regular simplex method. Savings in the use of computer memory can result because the revised method deals primarily with the basis $\boldsymbol{B}$. In the regular method on the other hand, the entire tableau must be stored in the computer memory.

The revised method unlike regular method, has the potential to alleviate the problem of machine round-off error. Specifically, methods can be used to minimise the effect of round-off error on the accuracy of $\boldsymbol{B}^{-1}$ and hence all the revised iteration computations.

6.5 EXERCISE 6

1. Discuss the method of finding the entering and leaving vectors in *composite simplex* method for obtaining the optimal solution of a large scale LPP. What is the basic difference of this method from usual simplex method? **[CU(MSc Appl) 1984]**

2. Solve the following LPP by *composite simplex* method:

(a) Maximise $Z = x_1 + 4x_2$

subject to
$$\begin{aligned} x_1 + x_2 + x_3 &\le 15 \\ 2x_1 + x_2 - 2x_3 &\ge 3 \\ x_1 + 2x_2 &= 6 \\ x_1 - 2x_3 &= -3 \end{aligned}$$
$x_1,\ x_2,\ x_3 \ge 0.$

(b) Minimise $Z = 5x_1 + 3x_2 + 4x_3 + 2x_4$

subject to
$$\begin{aligned} 3x_1 + 2x_2 + x_3 + x_4 &= 10 \\ x_1 + x_2 + 3x_3 + 4x_4 &= 18 \\ 2x_1 + 3x_2 + 2x_3 + 3x_4 &= 16 \end{aligned}$$
$x_j \ge 0,\ j = 1,2,3,4.$

(c) Minimise $Z = 3x_1 + x_2 + 4x_3 + 7x_4$

subject to
$$\begin{aligned} 3x_1 - x_2 + 2x_3 - 3x_4 &\ge 3 \\ 4x_1 + 2x_2 - 4x_3 - x_4 &\ge 6 \\ -2x_1 + 5x_2 + 4x_3 + 6x_4 &\ge 7 \end{aligned}$$
$x_k \ge 0,\ k = 1,2,3,4.$

3. State the computational procedure for solving an LPP with upper bound conditions.

4. Solve the following LPP by using *bounded variable* technique:

(a) Maximise $Z = 3x_1 + 2x_2$

subject to $x_1 - 3x_2 \leq 3$

$x_1 - 2x_2 \leq 4$

$2x_1 + x_2 \leq 20$

$-x_1 + x_2 \leq 6$

$x_1 + 3x_2 \leq 30$

$0 \leq x_1 \leq 8$

$0 \leq x_2 \leq 6.$

(b) Maximise $Z = 2x_1 + x_2$

subject to $x_1 + 2x_2 \leq 10$

$x_1 + x_2 \leq 6$

$x_1 - x_2 \leq 2$

$x_1 - 2x_2 \leq 1$

$0 \leq x_1 \leq 3$

$0 \leq x_2 \leq 2.$

[CU(MSc Appl) 1996]

(c) Maximise $Z = 4y_1 + 2y_2 + 6y_3$

subject to $4y_1 - y_2 \leq 9$

$-y_1 + y_2 + 2y_3 \leq 8$

$-3y_1 + y_2 + 4y_3 \leq 12$

$1 \leq y_1 \leq 3$

$0 < y_2 \leq 5$

$0 \leq y_3 \leq 2.$

(d) Minimise $Z = 3x_1 + 5x_2 + 2x_3$

subject to $x_1 + 2x_2 + 2x_3 \leq 10$

$2x_1 + 4x_2 + 3x_3 \leq 15$

$0 \leq x_1 \leq 4$

$0 \leq x_2 \leq 3$

$0 \leq x_3 \leq 3.$

5. Consider the LPP

Minimise $W = \sum_{j=1}^{n} c_j^0 v_j$

subject to $\sum_{j=1}^{n} a_{ij} v_j = u_i,\ j = 1,2,\ldots,m$

$v_j \geq 0,\ j = 1,2,\ldots,n.$

Let $(v_1^0, v_2^0, \ldots, v_n^0)$ be the optimal solution to the problem and $(v_1', v_2', \ldots, v_n')$ be its optimal solution, if c_j^0 is replaced by c_j', for all j. Prove that

$$\sum_{j=1}^{n}\left(c_j' - c_j^0\right)\left(v_j' - v_j^0\right) \leq 0.$$

What can you say about x_k' as compared with x_k^0 if

$$c_j' < c_j^0 \text{ for } j = k$$
$$= c_j^0 \text{ for } j \neq k?$$

[IAS(Main) 2002]

6. Explain the basic idea involved in parametric LP. How does it differ from post-optimal analysis?

7. Perform a complete parametric programming analysis. Identify all *critical values* of the parameter and the optimal solutions of the following problems:

(a) Maximise $Z = 3(1+\theta)x_1 + 2x_2 + (5-6\theta)x_3$

subject to $x_1 + 2x_2 + x_3 \leq 430$

$3x_1 + 2x_3 \leq 460$

$x_1 + 4x_2 \leq 420$

$x_1,\ x_2,\ x_3 \geq 0,$

where θ is a non-negative parameter.

[BESU(MSc) 2004, MBA(CU) 1998]

(b) Maximise $Z = (3-6\lambda)x_1 + (2-2\lambda)x_2 + (5+5\lambda)x_3$

subject to $x_1 + 2x_2 + x_3 \leq 430$

$3x_1 + 2x_3 \leq 460$

$x_1 + 4x_2 \leq 420$

$x_1,\ x_2,\ x_3 \geq 0.$

where λ is a parameter.

[IIT(MSc Maths) 1990, Meerut(MSc) 1998]

(c) Minimise $Z=\lambda(x_1-x_2)-x_3+x_4$

subject to $3x_1-3x_2-x_3+x_4\geq 5$

$2x_1-2x_2+x_3-x_4\leq 3$

$x_1,\ x_2,\ x_3,\ x_4\geq 0,$

where λ is a parameter.

(d) Maximise $Z=(6-\lambda)x_1+(12-\lambda)x_2+(4-\lambda)x_3$

subject to $3x_1+4x_2+x_3\leq 2$

$x_1+3x_2+2x_3\leq 1$

$x_1,\ x_2,\ x_3>0,$

where λ is a parameter.

(e) Maximise $Z=3x_1+2x_2+5x_3$

subject to $x_1+2x_2+x_3\leq 430+500\theta$

$3x_1+2x_3\leq 460+100\theta$

$x_1+4x_2\leq 420-200\theta$

$x_1,\ x_2,\ x_3\geq 0,$

where θ is the non-negative parameter.

(f) Maximise $Z=3x_1+4x_2+x_3+7x_4$

subject to $8x_1+3x_2+4x_3+x_4\leq 7-\theta$

$2x_1+6x_2+x_3+5x_4\leq 3+3\theta$

$x_1+4x_2+5x_3+2x_4\leq 8+\theta$

$x_1,\ x_2,\ x_3,\ x_4\geq 0,$

where θ is a parameter.

[BESU(MSc) 2009, ISI(OR) 1998]

(g) Maximise $Z=7x_1+4x_2+6x_3+5x_4$

subject to $2x_1+x_2+2x_3+x_4\leq 10+\theta$

$2x_1-x_2+4x_3+4x_4\leq 26-\theta$

$3x_1+x_2-2x_3+3x_4\leq 45-\theta$

$x_1,\ x_2,\ x_3,\ x_4\geq 0,$

where θ is a parameter.

8. (a) Compare regular simplex method with revised simplex method. Is there any advantages of the revised simplex method over the standard simplex method?

(b) Use *revised simplex* method to solve the following LPP.

(i) Maximise $Z=6x_1-2x_2+3x_3$

subject to $2x_1-x_2+2x_3\leq 2$

$x_1+4x_3\leq 4$

$x_1,\ x_2,\ x_3\geq 0.$

[BESU(MSc) 2003, Roorkee(MTech) 1984]

(ii) Maximise $Z=30x_1+23x_2+29x_3$

subject to $6x_1+5x_2+3x_3\leq 26$

$4x_1+2x_2+5x_3\leq 7$

$x_1,\ x_2,\ x_3\geq 0.$

[CU(MSc Stat) 1997, CU(MSc Appl) 1999]

(iii) Maximise $Z=-2x_1-x_2$

subject to $x_1+x_2\geq 2$

$x_1+x_2\leq 4$

$x_1,\ x_2\geq 0.$

(iv) Minimise $W=2x_3-2x_4-x_5$

subject to $x_1-2x_3+x_4+x_5=4$

$x_2+3x_3-x_4+2x_5=2$

$x_i\geq 0,\ (i=1,\ 2,\ 3,\ 4,\ 5).$

(v) Maximise $V=78x_2+212x_3-124x_5+6x_7+17x_8+10x_9$

subject to $x_3+x_4-8x_5+2x_7-x_8-3x_9=33$

$6x_2-x_3+x_5+x_6-2x_7+4x_8=27$

$x_1+4x_2+x_3-5x_5+x_8+x_9=86$

$x_i\geq 0$ for all i.

(vi) Maximise $Z=x_2$

subject to $x_1-x_2\geq 0$

$2x_1+3x_2\geq -6$

$x_1,\ x_2\geq 0.$

(vii) Maximise $Z=2x_1+x_2+2x_3$

subject to $4x_1+3x_2+8x_3\leq 12$

$4x_1+x_2+12x_3\leq 8$

$4x_1-x_2+3x_3\leq 8$

$x_1,\ x_2,\ x_3\geq 0.$

(viii) Minimise $Z=2x_1+x_2$

subject to $3x_1+x_2=3$

$4x_1+3x_2\geq 6$

$x_1+2x_2\leq 3$

$x_1,\ x_2\geq 0.$

ANSWERS

2. (a) $x_1^* = 6,\ x_2^* = 0,\ x_3^* = \frac{9}{2},\ x_4^* = \frac{9}{2},\ Z_{\max} = 6.$ (b) $x_1^* = 2,\ x_2^* = 0,\ x_3^* = 0,\ x_4^* = 4,\ Z_{\min} = 18.$
(c) $x_1^* = \frac{6}{5},\ x_2^* = \frac{53}{25},\ x_3^* = \frac{16}{35},\ x_4^* = 0,\ Z_{\min} = \frac{1321}{245}.$

4. (a) $x_1^* = 7,\ x_2^* = 6,\ Z_{\max} = 33.$ (b) Do yourself.
(c) $y_1^* = 3,\ y_2^* = 5,\ y_3^* = 2,\ Z_{\max} = 34.$ (d) $x_1^* = 4,\ x_2^* = \frac{7}{4},\ x_3^* = 0,\ Z_{\min} = \frac{83}{4}.$

7. (a)
$$\begin{aligned}(x_1^*, x_2^*, x_3^*) &= (0, 100, 230) &&: 0 \le \theta \le \tfrac{1}{3}\\ &= \left(10, 102\tfrac{1}{2}, 215\right) &&: \tfrac{1}{3} \le \theta \le \tfrac{5}{12}\\ &= \left(\tfrac{460}{3}, \tfrac{200}{3}, 0\right) &&: \theta \ge \tfrac{5}{12}.\end{aligned}$$

(b)
$$\begin{aligned}(x_1^*, x_2^*, x_3^*) &= (0, 100, 230): && -\tfrac{2}{3} \le \lambda \le 1\\ &= (0, 0, 230) &&: \lambda \ge 1\\ &= (0, 105, 200): && -1 \le \lambda \le -\tfrac{2}{3}.\end{aligned}$$

(c)
$$\begin{aligned}(x_1^*, x_2^*, x_3^*, x_4^*) &= \left(\tfrac{8}{5}, 0, 0, \tfrac{1}{5}\right): -2 \le \lambda \le 3\\ &= \text{no solution exists for } \lambda > 3.\end{aligned}$$

(d)
$$\begin{aligned}(x_1^*, x_2^*, x_3^*) &= \left(\tfrac{2}{5}, \tfrac{1}{5}, 0\right) &&: 0 \le \lambda \le 3\\ &= \left(0, \tfrac{1}{3}, 0\right) &&: 3 \le \lambda \le 9\\ &= (0, 0, 0) &&: 9 \le \lambda.\end{aligned}$$

(e)
$$\begin{aligned}(x_1^*, x_2^*, x_3^*) &= (0, 100 + 225\theta, 230 + 50\theta): 0 \le \theta \le \tfrac{1}{55}\\ &= (0, 150 - 50\theta, 230 + 50\theta): \tfrac{1}{55} \le \theta \le 2.1\\ &= \text{no feasible solution exists for } \theta > 2.1.\end{aligned}$$

(f)
$$\begin{aligned}(x_1^*, x_2^*, x_3^*, x_4^*) &= \left(\tfrac{16}{19}, 0, 0, \tfrac{5}{19}\right) &&: 0 \le \theta \le 4\\ &= (0, 0, 0, 3) &&: 4 \le \theta \le 7\\ &= \text{no feasible solution for } \theta \ge 7.\end{aligned}$$

(g)
$$\begin{aligned}(x_1^*, x_2^*, x_3^*, x_4^*) &= (0, 0, 0, 10) &&: 0 \le \theta \le 2\\ &= (0, 0, 0, 12) &&: 2 \le \theta \le \tfrac{11}{2}\\ &= \left(0, \tfrac{7}{2}, 0, 12\right) &&: \tfrac{11}{2} \le \theta \le \tfrac{35}{2}\\ &= \left(0, \tfrac{55}{2}, 0, 0\right) &&: \tfrac{35}{2} \le \theta \le \tfrac{59}{2}\\ &= \text{no feasible solution, if } \theta \ge \tfrac{52}{2}.\end{aligned}$$

8. (b) (i) $x_1^* = 4,\ x_2^* = 6,\ x_3^* = 0,\ Z_{\max} = 12.$ (ii) $x_1^* = 0,\ x_2^* = \frac{7}{2},\ x_3^* = 0,\ Z_{\max} = \frac{161}{2}.$
(iii) $x_1^* = 4,\ x_2^* = 0,\ Z_{\max} = -8.$ (iv) $x_1^* = 0,\ x_2^* = 0,\ x_3^* = 6,\ x_4^* = 16,\ x_5^* = 0,\ W_{\min} = -20.$
(v) $x_7^* = 92\frac{1}{2},\ x_8^* = 53,\ x_9^* = 33$ and remaining $x_i = 0.$ (vi) Unbounded solution.
(vii) $x_1^* = \frac{3}{2},\ x_2^* = 2,\ x_3^* = 0,\ Z_{\max} = 5.$ (viii) $x_1^* = \frac{3}{5},\ x_2^* = \frac{6}{5},\ Z_{\max} = \frac{12}{5}.$

Chapter 7

Transportation Model and Sequencing Problem

7.1 TRANSPORTATION MODEL

This section of this chapter presents the transportation model. In the obvious sense, the model deals with the determination of a minimum cost plan for transporting a single commodity from a number of sources to a number of destinations. The model can be extended in a direct manner to cover practical situations in the areas of inventory control, employment scheduling, personnel assignment, cash flow and many others. The model also can be modified to account for multiple commodities. The transportation model is basically an LP. However, its special structure allows development of a solution procedure, called the *transportation technique,* that is computationally more efficient.

7.1.1 Formulation of Transportation Problem

Let m be the number of origins and n be the number of destinations. The cost of transporting one unit of the commodity from origin i to destination j is c_{ij}. Let $a_i \geq 0$ for all $i = 1,2,\ldots,m$ be the quantity of the commodity available at origin i and $b_j \geq 0$ for all $j = 1,2,\ldots,n$ be the quantity required at destination j. If $x_{ij} \geq 0$ is the quantity transported from origin i to destination j, then the general formulation of the transportation problem is:

$$\text{Minimise } Z = \sum_{i=1}^{m}\sum_{j=1}^{n} c_{ij}x_{ij} \tag{7.1a}$$

$$\text{subject to } \sum_{j=1}^{n} x_{ij} = a_i,\ i = 1,2,\ldots,m \tag{7.1b}$$

$$\sum_{i=1}^{m} x_{ij} = b_j,\ j = 1,2,\ldots,n \tag{7.1c}$$

$$x_{ij} \geq 0. \tag{7.1d}$$

The above represents an LP with (mn) variables and $(m+n)$ constraints.

A transportation problem is said to be *balanced,* if

$$\sum_{i=1}^{m} a_i = \sum_{j=1}^{n} b_j.$$

Otherwise, it is said to be *unbalanced.*

Suppose,
$$\sum_{i=1}^{m} a_i > \text{or} < \sum_{j=1}^{n} b_j,$$

then a fictitious destination or fictitious origin with requirement

$$\sum_{i=1}^{m} a_i - \sum_{j=1}^{n} b_j$$

or with available quantity

$$\sum_{j=1}^{n} b_j - \sum_{i=1}^{m} a_i$$

can be taken so that unit cost of transportation to this destination from all the m origins or unit cost of transportation from origin to all n-destinations will be taken as zero. This way an unbalanced problem can be converted into balanced problem.

7.1.2 Some Important Results

Result 1. A necessary and sufficient condition for the existence of a feasible solution to the transportation problem is that

$$\sum_{i=1}^{m} a_i = \sum_{j=1}^{n} b_j.$$

Proof. (Necessity). Given a feasible solution (x_{ij}), $i = 1,2,\ldots,m$, $j = 1,2,\ldots,n$ exists. From (7.1b) and (7.1c), we get

$$\sum_{i=1}^{m}\sum_{j=1}^{n} x_{ij} = \sum_{i=1}^{m} a_i \text{ and } \sum_{j=1}^{n}\sum_{i=1}^{m} x_{ij} = \sum_{j=1}^{n} b_j.$$

Since the left sides are equal, the right sides must be equal. Thus,

$$\sum_{i=1}^{m} a_i = \sum_{j=1}^{n} b_j.$$

(Sufficiency). Given

$$\sum_{i=1}^{m} a_i = \sum_{j=1}^{n} b_j = T \neq 0 \text{ (say)}$$

define $x_{ij} = \dfrac{a_i b_j}{T}$, $i = 1,2,\ldots,m$, $j = 1,2,\ldots,n.$ (7.1e)

As $a_i \geq 0$, $b_j \geq 0\ \forall\ i$ and j $\displaystyle\sum_{j=1}^{n} x_{ij} = \frac{a_i}{T}\sum_{j=1}^{n} b_j = a_i$ for $i = 1,2,\ldots,m$

$$\sum_{i=1}^{m} x_{ij} = \frac{b_j}{T}\sum_{i=1}^{m} a_i = b_i \text{ for } j = 1,2,\ldots,n.$$

Hence, constraints (7.1b), (7.1c) and (7.1d) of the transportation problem are satisfied. Thus, x_{ij} defined by (7.1e) gives us a feasible solution.

Result 2. The number of basic variables in a transportation problem is at most $(m+n-1)$.

Proof. The $(m+n)$ constraints of a transportation problem are

$$\sum_{j=1}^{n} x_{ij} = a_i, \ i = 1,2,\ldots,m \tag{7.1f}$$

$$\sum_{i=1}^{m} x_{ij} = b_j, \ j = 1,2,\ldots,n \tag{7.1g}$$

Now $\sum_{i=1}^{m}\sum_{j=1}^{n} x_{ij} = \sum_{i=1}^{m} a_i = \sum_{j=1}^{n} b_j.$

Again, $\sum_{j=1}^{n-1}\sum_{i=1}^{m} x_{ij} = \sum_{j=1}^{n-1} b_j.$

$$\therefore \sum_{i=1}^{m}\sum_{j=1}^{n} x_{ij} - \sum_{j=1}^{n-1}\sum_{i=1}^{m} x_{ij} = \sum_{j=1}^{n} b_j - \sum_{j=1}^{n-1} b_j \text{ or, } \sum_{i=1}^{m}\left(\sum_{j=1}^{n} x_{ij} - \sum_{j=1}^{n-1} x_{ij}\right) = b_n \text{ or, } \sum_{i=1}^{m} x_{in} = b_n$$

which is the nth constraint of (7.1g). Therefore, one of the $(m+n)$ constraints is redundant and may be removed from the set of constraints. This will indicate that a basis consists of at most $(m+n-1)$ variables. In fact, a non-degenerate basic feasible solution to a transportation problem will consist of at most $(m+n-1)$ positive variable, the other being zero. By fundamental theorem of LP we conclude that one of these basic feasible solutions will be optimal.

7.1.3 Determination of Initial Basic Feasible Solution

A transportation problem can be represented by a tableau of the following type:

Destinations

		D_1	D_2		D_j		D_{n-1}	D_n	
	O_1	c_{11}	c_{12}	…	c_{1j}	…	…	c_{1n}	a_1
	O_2	c_{21}	c_{22}	…	c_{2j}	…	…	c_{2n}	a_2
		⋮	⋮		⋮			⋮	
Origins	O_i	c_{i1}	c_{i2}	…	c_{ij}	…	…	c_{in}	a_i
		⋮	⋮		⋮			⋮	
	O_m	c_{m1}	c_{m2}	…	c_{mj}	…	…	c_{mn}	a_m
		b_1	b_2		b_j			b_n	

The above table has (mn) cells arranged in m rows and n columns. The cell in the ith row and jth column of the table is called (i,j) cell. In the transportation table a sequence of cells is said to form a *loop,* if

(i) each adjacent pair of cells either lies in the same column or in the same row;
(ii) not more than two consecutive cells in the sequence lie in the same row or in the same column;
(iii) the first and the last cells in the sequence lie either in the same row or in the same column;
(iv) the sequence must involve at least two rows or two columns of the table.

Illustration of Loops

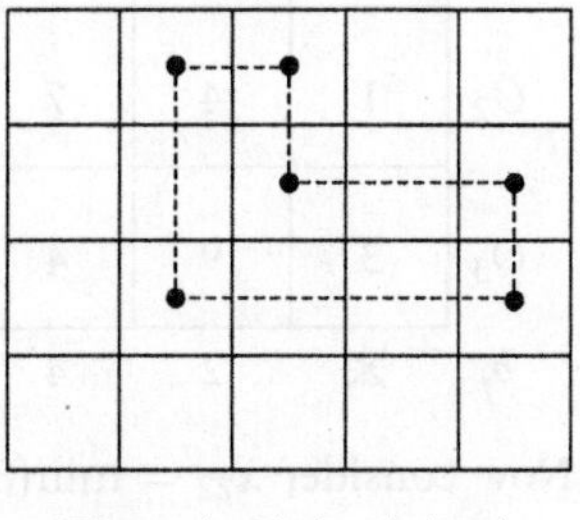

Fig. 1 (1,2) (1,3) (2,3) (2,5) (3,5) (3,2)

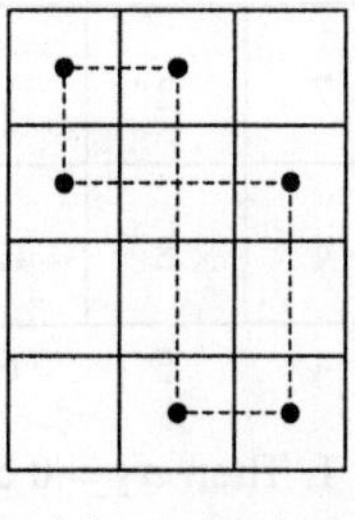

Fig. 2 (1,1) (1,2) (4,2) (4,3) (2,3) (2,1)

Note that every loop contains an *even* number of cells; every row or column either contains no cells or an even number of cells in the loop. Therefore, a set of cells S_c of a transportation table is said to contain a loop if the set S_c or a subset of S_c can be sequenced to form a loop.

(A) North-West Corner Rule (NWCR)

The procedures involved in this method — Make the first assignment to the upper left-hand cell which is called *North-West corner.* Take $x_{11} = \min(a_1, b_1)$ if $x_{11} = a_1$, then row 1 can be deleted. If $x_{11} = b_1$, then column 1 can be deleted. In the first case, replace b_1 by $(b_1 - a_1)$ and in the second case, replace a_1 by $(a_1 - b_1)$. If $a_1 = b_1$, then $x_{11} = a_1 = b_1$ so that row 1 as well as column 1 can be deleted. This gives an indication that a degenerate basic feasible solution will be obtained, that is less than $(m + n - 1)$ positive basic variables will be obtained. After first assignment a new matrix will appear which are called reduced matrix. Repeat the process until all quantities are exhausted. This is possible when the problem is balanced.

Example 7.1.1. *By North-West corner rule find the basic feasible solution of the transportation problem.*

	D_1	D_2	D_3	D_4	D_5	a_i
O_1	2	11	10	3	7	4
O_2	1	4	7	2	1	8
O_3	3	9	4	8	12	9
b_j	3	3	4	5	6	

Solution: $\sum_{i=1}^{3} a_i = \sum_{j=1}^{5} b_j = 21$. So it is a balanced problem.

First take $x_{11} = \min(4,3) = 3$. Now, $b_1 = 3-3 = 0$ and replace $a_1 = 4-3 = 1$. This gives

Table 1

	D_1	D_2	D_3	D_4	D_5	a_i
O_1	$x_{11}=3$ 2	11	10	3	7	1
O_2	1	4	7	2	1	8
O_3	3	9	4	8	12	9
b_j	✗	3	4	5	6	

Now, $x_{12} = \min(1,3) = 1$. Then $a_1 = 0$ and $b_2 = -3-1 = 2$.

Table 2

	D_1	D_2	D_3	D_4	D_5	a_i
O_1	$x_{11}=3$ 2	$x_{12}=1$ 11	10	3	7	✗
O_2	1	4	7	2	1	8
O_3	3	9	4	8	12	9
b_j	✗	2	4	5	6	

Now consider $x_{22} = \min(8,2) = 2$, $b_2 = 0$ and $a_2 = 8-2 = 6$.

Table 3

	D_1	D_2	D_3	D_4	D_5	a_i
O_1	$x_{11}=3$ 2	$x_{12}=1$ 11	10	3	7	✗
O_2	1	4	7	2	1	6
O_3	3	9	4	8	12	9
b_j	✗	✗	4	5	6	

$x_{23} = \min\{6,4\} = 4$, $b_3 = 0$, $a_2 = 6-4 = 2$.

Table 4

	D_1	D_2	D_3	D_4	D_5	a_i
O_1	$x_{11}=3$ 2	$x_{12}=1$ 11	10	3	7	✗
O_2	1	$x_{22}=2$ 4	$x_{23}=4$ 7	2	1	2
O_3	3	9	4	8	12	9
b_j	✗	✗	✗	5	6	

$x_{24} = \min\{2,5\} = 2$, $a_2 = 0$, $b_4 = 5-2 = 3$.

Table 5

	D_1	D_2	D_3	D_4	D_5	a_i
O_1	$x_{11}=3$ 2	$x_{12}=1$ 11	10	3	7	✗
O_2	1	$x_{22}=2$ 4	$x_{23}=4$ 7	$x_{24}=2$ 2	1	✗
O_3	3	9	4	8	12	9
b_j	✗	✗	✗	3	6	

$x_{34} = \min\{9,3\} = 3$, $b_4 = 0$, $a_4 = 9-3 = 6$.

Table 6

	D_1	D_2	D_3	D_4	D_5	a_i
O_1	$x_{11}=3$	$x_{12}=1$				✗
O_2		$x_{22}=2$	$x_{23}=4$	$x_{24}=2$		✗
O_3				$x_{34}=3$	$x_{35}=6$	6
b_j	✗	✗	✗	✗	6	

Therefore, the basic feasible solution of the problem by NWCR:

$$\langle x_{11}=3,\ x_{12}=1,\ x_{22}=2,\ x_{23}=4,\ x_{24}=2,\ x_{34}=3,\ x_{35}=6\rangle .$$

Here, $m+n-1 = 3+5-1 = 7$ and we have obtained seven positive x_{ij}'s. This gives us a non-degenerate basic feasible solution.

(B) The Vogel Approximation Method (VAM)

The following rules are followed in VAM.

Rule 1. For each row of matrix (c_{ij}) first select the lowest cost c_{ik} and then next lowest cost c_{ir}. Take the difference $(c_{ik} - c_{ir})$ and display them alongside the table by enclosing (•). Similarly, compute the differences for each column.

Rule 2. Identify the largest difference under (•) among all the rows and columns. If a tie occurs, select any one arbitrarily. Let the largest difference corresponds to 1st row and let c_{12} be the smallest cost in the 1st row, then allocate $x_{12} = \min(a_1, b_2)$ and delete the 1st row or the 2nd column in the usual manner.

Rule 3. Recompute the row and column differences for the reduced matrix and go to *Rule* 2. Repeat the process till all the availabilities and requirements are satisfied.

Remember that VAM determines an initial basic feasible solution which is very close to the optimum solution and consequently the number of iterations required to attain the optimal is less in this method.

Example 7.1.2. *Apply* VAM *to find initial basic feasible solution.*

	D_1	D_2	D_3	D_4	a_i
O_1	21	16	25	13	11
O_2	17	18	14	23	13
O_3	32	27	18	41	19
b_j	6	10	12	15	

[KU 1995]

Solution:

Table 1

	D_1	D_2	D_3	D_4	a_i
O_1	21	16	25	$x_{14} = 11$ 13	11(3)
O_2	17	18	14	23	13(3)
O_3	32	27	18	41	19(9)
b_j	6 (4)	10 (2)	12 (4)	15 (10)	

$$\sum_{i=1}^{3} a_i = \sum_{j=1}^{4} b_j = 43.$$

So it is a balanced problem. Use *Rule* 1 given above. The largest difference is (10) and is obtained in 4th column. The minimum cost in the 4th column is $c_{14} = 13$. Allocate $x_{14} = \min(11, 15) = 11$ and delete the 1st row. The reduced matrix is:

Table 2

	D_1	D_2	D_3	D_4	a_i
O_2	17	18	14	$x_{24} = 4$ 23	13(3)
O_3	32	27	18	41	19(9)
b_j	6 (15)	10 (9)	12 (4)	4 (18)	

The maximum difference is (18) it is in the 4th column. The minimum cost in 4th column $c_{24} = 23$. Allocate $x_{24} = \min(13, 4) = 4$ and delete 4th column.

Table 3

	D_1	D_2	D_3	a_i
O_2	$x_{21}=6$ 17	18	14	9(4)
O_3	32	27	18	19(9)
b_j	6 (15)	10 (9)	4 (4)	

1st column corresponds to maximum difference (15) and $c_{21} = 17$ is the minimum cost in 1st column. $x_{21} = \min(9,6) = 6$. Delete 1st column.

Table 4

	D_2	D_3	a_i
O_2	18	14	3(4)
O_3	27	$x_{33}=12$ 18	19(9)
b_j	10 (9)	4 (4)	

There is a tie, select 3rd row and allocate $x_{33} = \min(19,12) = 12$ and delete 3rd column.

Table 5

	D_2	a_i
O_2	$x_{22}=3$ 18	3(18)
O_3	$x_{32}=7$ 27	7(27)
	10 (9)	

The largest difference (27) and it is in 3rd row. Allocate $x_{32} = \min(7,10) = 7$ delete 3rd row and finally allocate $x_{22} = \min(3,3) = 3$.

Therefore, the initial basic feasible solution of the problem by VAM is $x_{14} = 11$, $x_{24} = 4$, $x_{21} = 6$, $x_{33} = 12$, $x_{22} = 3$, $x_{32} = 7$.

This gives us a non-degenerate basic feasible solution. The value of the objective function is: $13\times 11 + 23\times 4 + 17\times 6 + 18\times 12 + 18\times 3 + 27\times 7 = 796$.

(C) The Matrix Minima Method

In this method, the cell with the minimum cost c_{ij} is chosen and allocate by taking $x_{ij} = \min(a_i, b_j)$. If $x_{ij} = a_i$ delete ith row and go for reduced matrix but if $x_{ij} = b_j$, delete jth column and proceed with reduced matrix. The process continues till all quantities are allocated. If the cell with the minimum be not unique then any one is selected arbitrarily.

Example 7.1.3. *Find the initial basic feasible solution by matrix minima method.*

	D_1	D_2	D_3	D_4	a_i
O_1	5	8	3	6	30
O_2	4	5	7	4	50
O_3	6	2	4	6	20
b_j	30	40	20	10	

Solution: It is balanced transportation problem as $\sum_{i=1}^{3} a_i = \sum_{j=1}^{4} b_j = 100$.

The lowest cost in cost matrix (c_{ij}) is $c_{32} = 2$. Hence, allocate $x_{32} = \min(20,40) = 20$, delete 3rd row and replace $b_2 = 40 - 20 = 20$.

Table 1

	D_1	D_2	D_3	D_4	a_i
O_1	5	8	$x_{13}=20$ 3	6	30
O_2	4	5	7	4	50
O_3	6	$x_{32}=20$ 2	4	6	20✕
b_j	30	~~40~~ 20	20	10	

Next minimum cost in reduced matrix of *Table 1* $c_{13}=3$. Allocate $x_{13}=\min(30,20)=20$, delete 3rd column and replace $a_1=30-20=10$.

Table 2

	D_1	D_2	D_4	a_i
O_1	5	8	6	10
O_2	$x_{21}=30$ 4	5	$x_{24}=10$ 4	~~50~~ 40
b_j	30	20	10✕	

The minimum cost $c_{21}=c_{24}=4$, choose arbitrarily $c_{24}=4$ and allocate $x_{24}=\min\{50,10\}=10$, delete 4th column. Next minimum cell $c_{21}=4$ and allocate $x_{21}=\min(40,30)=30$, delete 1st column and go to next reduced table.

Table 3

	D_2	a_i
O_1	$x_{12}=10$ 8	10
O_2	$x_{22}=10$ 5	~~10~~
b_j	~~20~~ 10	

Minimum cell $c_{22}=5$, allocate $x_{22}=\min\{10,20\}=10$, delete 2nd row and finally allocate $x_{12}=10$.

Therefore, the required initial basic feasible solution by matrix minima method is: $x_{13}=20$, $x_{32}=20$, $x_{21}=30$, $x_{24}=10$, $x_{12}=10$, $x_{22}=10$.

This also gives a non-degenerate basic feasible solution. The cost corresponding to this solution is $20\times3+20\times2+30\times4+10\times4+10\times8+10\times5=390$.

7.1.4 Optimality Test of the Basic Feasible Solution

Consider a balanced transportation problem with the origin capacities a_i and the destination requirements b_j with costs c_{ij} in the (i,j) cell. First find an initial basic feasible solution by using any one method discussed in Sec. 7.1.3 and then test the optimality of the basic feasible solution by performing the following steps.

Step 1. Enter the initial basic feasible solution in the upper left corner of the basic cells.

Step 2. For all occupied cells, determine a set of $(m+n)$ numbers u_i and $v_j, i=1,2,\dots,m, j=1,2,\dots,n$ such that $c_{ij}=u_i+v_j$.

Take one u_i or v_j arbitrarily and equate it to zero. This choice is also made for that u_i or v_j for which the corresponding row or column contains maximum number of occupied cells. Then solve for the remaining u_i's and v_j's. Enter them in circles in the upper right corners of the corresponding unoccupied cells.

Step 3. For unoccupied or non-basic cells evaluate $D_{ij}=c_{ij}-\bar{c}_{ij}$, where $\bar{c}_{ij}=u_i+v_j$ and test the following

(i) if all $D_{ij}>0$, then the solution is optimal and unique,

(ii) if all $D_{ij}>0$, and at least one $D_{ij}=0$, then the solution is optimal but not unique,

(iii) if at least one $D_{ij} < 0$, then the solution is not optimal and we search a new basic feasible solution and go on to the next step.

Step 4. To find a new basic feasible solution, we include in it that cell for which D_{ij} is minimum negative. We allocate maximum amount possible in this cell. Take for example, $x_{pq} = \theta$, a non-negative real number and try to balance the rows and columns of the problem. This can be done by subtracting and adding θ alternatively to the *basic cells*, which will make a *loop*. The maximum value of θ, which makes these cells non-negative is taken as the true value of θ and for this true value, the cell which equals zero is taken as non-basic. If more than one cells equals zero, then any cell can be taken as non-basic. After that, *Steps* 2 and 3 are repeated until an optimal basic feasible solution is obtained.

Example 7.1.4. *Solve the adjoining transportation problem.*

	D_1	D_2	D_3	D_4	a_i
O_1	2	3	11	7	6
O_2	1	0	6	1	1
O_3	5	8	15	9	10
b_j	7	5	3	2	

[IAS 1996]

Solution: $\sum_{i=1}^{3} a_i = \sum_{j=1}^{4} b_j = 17$; it is a balanced transportation problem.

Step 1. Let us find the initial basic feasible solution by using VAM (following the procedure explained in details in Ex. 7.1.2).

Table 1

	D_1	D_2	D_3	D_4	a_i
O_1	2	3	11	7	6 (1)
O_2	1	0	6	[1] 1	1 (1)
O_3	5	8	15	9	10 (3)
b_j	7 (1)	5 (3)	3 (5)	2 (6) ↑	

Table 2

	D_1	D_2	D_3	D_4	a_i
O_1	2	[5] 3	11	7	6 (1)
O_3	5	8	15	9	10 (3)
b_j	7 (3)	5 (5) ↑	3 (4)	1 (2)	

Table 3

	D_1	D_3	D_4	a_i
O_1	[1] 2	11	7	1 (5) ←
O_3	5	15	9	10 (4)
b_j	7 (3)	3 (4)	1 (2)	

Table 4

	D_1	D_3	D_4	a_i
O_3	5	[3] 15	9	10 (4)
b_j	6 (5)	3 (15)↑	1 (9)	

Table 5

	D_1	D_4	a_i
O_3	[6] 5	[1] 9	7 (4)
b_j	6 (5)	1 (9) ↑	

The initial basic feasible solution: $x_{24} = 1$, $x_{12} = 5$, $x_{11} = 1$, $x_{33} = 3$, $x_{31} = 6$, $x_{34} = 1$, which gives a non-degenerate basic feasible solution.

Step 2. Perform optimality test using $(u - v)$ method discussed in Sec. 7.1.4.

Table 6

	D_1	D_2	D_3	D_4	u_i
O_1	[1] 2	[5] 3	(−1) 11	(1) 7	−3
O_2	(4) 1	(2) 0	(−1) 6	[1] 1	−8
O_3	[6] 5	(2) 8	[3] 15	[1] 9	0
v_j	5	6	15	9	

Enter the initial basic feasible solution in the upper left corner of the basic cells. To test the optimality, we construct u_i and v_j and to find the cell evaluation for the unoccupied (non-basic) cells $\left(D_{ij} = c_{ij} - \left(u_i - v_j\right)\right)$ shown in circles.

Now, we have the following conclusions and further investigations.

(i) A negative value in a non-basic cell indicates that a better solution can be obtained by allocating units to this cell so that current basic feasible solution is not optimum.

(ii) A zero value in a non-basic cell indicates that the solution is optimum but still an improved alternative optima can be found.

Table 7. Cell evaluation matrix

	D_1	D_2	D_3	D_4
O_1			−1	1
O_2	4	2	−1	
O_3		2		

Important remark. From the cell evaluation matrix, identify the cell with the most negative cell evaluation. This is the rate by which total transportation cost can be reduced if one unit is allocated to this cell. In case more units are allocated, the cost will come down proportionately. Therefore, as many units as possible will be allocated to this cell to bring down the cost by maximum amount. In case of tie in cell evaluation, the cell, wherein maximum allocation can be made is selected. This cell is now called the *identified cell.* With respect to *simplex method,* this identified cell is currently the non-basic cell that has been decided to make basic by making allocation in it.

In the present problem both the tied cells will have the same maximum allocation of unit. Select cell (1, 3) arbitrarily. Write down again the table of initial basic feasible solution that is to be improved.

Table 8

	D_1	D_2	D_3	D_4	a_i
O_1	1 (−)	5	✓ (+)		6
O_2				1	1
O_3	6 (+)		3 (−)	1	10
b_j	7	5	3	2	

Check mark (✓) indicates the identified cell. Having decided the vacant cell that is to be made basic, the next thing is to decide which basic cell should be made non-basic by changing its present allocation to zero. Trace a closed path in the matrix which has the following characteristics.

(a) it begins and terminates in the identified cell;

(b) it can be traced clockwise or anticlockwise;

(c) it consists of a series of alternate horizontal and vertical lines only.

Make a new allocation in the identified cell by entering the smallest allocation on the path that has assigned a negative sign. Add and subtract this new allocation from the cells. This causes one basic cell to became zero and other cell remain non-negative. The basic cell whose allocation has been made zero, leaves the solution.

Table 9

	D_1	D_2	D_3	D_4	a_i
O_1	1−1		−1+1		6
O_2				1	1
O_3	6+1		3−1	1	10
b_j	7	5	3	2	

Table 10

	D_1	D_2	D_3	D_4
O_1	2	[5] 3	[1] 11	7
O_2	1	0	6	[1] 1
O_3	[7] 5	8	[2] 15	[1] 9

The improved basic feasible solution: $x_{12} = 5$, $x_{13} = 1$, $x_{24} = 1$, $x_{31} = 7$, $x_{33} = 2$, $x_{34} = 1$ (from *Table* 10). This is also a non-degenerate basic feasible solution.

Step 3. Optimality test for improved basic feasible solution.

Table 11

	D_1	D_2	D_3	D_4	u_i
O_1	(1) 2	[5] 3	[1] 11	(2) 7	1
O_2	(4) 1	(1) 0	(−1) 6	[1] 1	−3
O_3	[7] 5	(1) 8	[2] 15	[1] 9	5
v_j	0	2	10	4	

Table 12. Cell evaluation matrix

	D_1	D_2	D_3	D_4
O_1	1			2
O_2	4	1	−1	
O_3		1		

Since one cell evaluation (shown in circle) is negative the 2nd feasible solution is not optimal.

Table 13

	D_1	D_2	D_3	D_4
O_1		5	1	
O_2			(+) +1	(−) 1−1
O_3	7		(−) 2−1	(+) 1+1

$\longrightarrow$

	D_1	D_2	D_3	D_4
O_1		5	1	
O_2			1	
O_3	7		1	2

The third basic feasible solution: $x_{12}=5$, $x_{13}=1$, $x_{23}=1$, $x_{31}=7$, $x_{33}=1$, $x_{34}=2$.

Step 4. Optimality test for third basic feasible (non-degenerate) solution.

Table 14

	D_1	D_2	D_3	D_4	u_i
O_1	(1) 2	[5] 3	[1] 11	(2) 7	1
O_2	(5) 1	(2) 0	[1] 6	(1) 1	−4
O_3	[7] 5	(2) 8	[1] 15	[2] 9	5
v_j	0	2	10	4	

Since all the cell values are positive, the third non-degenerate basic feasible solution gives the unique optimal solution and is given by $\langle x_{12}^*=5,\ x_{13}^*=1,\ x_{23}^*=1,\ x_{31}^*=7,\ x_{33}^*=1,\ x_{34}^*=2\rangle$.

Example 7.1.5. *Obtain an optimal basic feasible solution to the following transportation problem.*

	D_1	D_2	D_3	D_4	a_i
O_1	19	30	50	10	7
O_2	70	30	40	60	9
O_3	40	8	70	20	18
b_j	5	8	7	14	

[VU(H) 2002, KU(MSc) 1982]

Solution:

Step 1. It is a balanced transportation problem. Using VAM as done in Ex. 7.1.4, we get the following non-degenerate initial basic feasible solution: $x_{11}=5$, $x_{14}=2$, $x_{23}=7$, $x_{24}=2$, $x_{32}=8$, $x_{34}=10$.

Step 2. Test of optimality.

Table 1

	D_1	D_2	D_3	D_4	u_i
O_1	[5] 19	(32) 30	(60) 50	[2] 10	0
O_2	(1) 70	(−18) 30	[7] 40	[2] 60	50
O_3	(11) 40	[8] 8	(70) 70	[10] 20	10
v_j	19	−2	−10	10	

Enter the initial basic feasible solution in the upper left corner of the basic cell. Now, construct u_i and v_j and then find the cell evaluation for unoccupied cell using $D_{ij} = c_{ij} - \bar{c}_{ij} : \bar{c}_{ij} = u_i + v_j$, which are shown in circles.

Table 1 shows that $D_{22} = -18 < 0$. Hence, the basic feasible solution is not optimal. To find second set of basic feasible solution we follow the same rule discussed in details in Ex. 7.1.4.

Table 2. Cell evaluation.

	D_1	D_2	D_3	D_4
O_1				
O_2			2 (+)	2−2 (−)
O_3			(−) 8−2	(+) 10+2

→

	D_1	D_2	D_3	D_4	a_i
O_1	[5] 19	30	50	[2] 10	7
O_2	70	[2] 30	[7] 40	60	9
O_3	40	[6] 8	70	[18] 20	18
b_j	5	8	7	14	

The second basic feasible solution: $x_{11} = 5$, $x_{14} = 2$, $x_{22} = 2$, $x_{23} = 7$, $x_{32} = 6$, $x_{34} = 12$, which is also a non-degenerate solution.

Step 3. Test of optimality of second basic feasible solution.

Table 3

	D_1	D_2	D_3	D_4	u_i
O_1	[5] 19	(32) 30	(42) 50	[2] 10	0
O_2	(19) 70	[2] 30	[7] 40	(18) 60	32
O_3	(11) 40	[6] 8	(52) 70	[12] 20	10
v_j	19	−2	8	10	

Table 3 indicates all $D_{ij} > 0$ (number under circle in unoccupied cells). Therefore, the second non-degenerate basic feasible solution is the unique optimal solution and is given by

$$\langle x_{11}^* = 5,\ x_{14}^* = 2,\ x_{22}^* = 2,\ x_{23}^* = 7,\ x_{32}^* = 6,\ x_{34}^* = 12 \rangle$$

and the optimal cost $= 5 \times 19 + 2 \times 10 + 2 \times 30 + 7 \times 40 + 6 \times 8 + 12 \times 20 = 743$.

Example 7.1.6. *A product is produced by four factories F_1, F_2, F_3, F_4. The unit production costs in them are ₹2, ₹3, ₹1 and ₹5 respectively. Their production capacities are: F_1 — 50 units, F_2 — 70 units, F_3 — 30 units, F_4 — 50 units. These factories supply the product to four stores S_1, S_2, S_3 and S_4, demands of which are 25, 35, 105 and 20 units respectively. Unit transport cost in rupees from each factory to each store is given in the* *table below. Determine the extent of deliveries from each of the factories to each of the stores so that the total production and transportation cost is minimum.*

	S_1	S_2	S_3	S_4
F_1	2	4	6	11
F_2	10	8	7	5
F_3	13	3	9	12
F_4	4	6	8	3

[PTU(MBA) 2002, ISI(SQCOR) 1995]

Solution: First of all we shall form a new table of unit costs which consists of both production and transportation costs. The new cost matrix is given below.

	S_1	S_2	S_3	S_4	Production Capacity a_i
F_1	2+2	4+2	6+2	11+2	50
F_2	10+3	8+3	7+3	5+3	70
F_3	13+1	3+1	9+1	12+1	30
F_4	4+5	6+5	8+5	3+5	50
Demand b_j	25	35	105	20	

Since

$$\sum_{i=1}^{4} a_i \neq \sum_{j=1}^{4} b_j$$

it is an unbalanced transportation problem with surplus capacity = 15 units. Therefore, we create a dummy store S_5 with associated cost coefficients which are taken as zero. Therefore, the starting cost matrix becomes:

	S_1	S_2	S_3	S_4	S_5	a_i
F_1	4	6	8	13	0	50
F_2	13	11	10	8	0	70
F_3	14	4	10	13	0	30
F_4	9	11	13	8	0	50
b_j	25	35	105	20	15	

Now using VAM, we get the following initial non-degenerate basic feasible solution: $x_{11} = 25$, $x_{12} = 5$, $x_{13} = 20$, $x_{23} = 70$, $x_{32} = 30$, $x_{43} = 15$, $x_{44} = 20$, $x_{45} = 15$.

Test of optimality:

	S_1	S_2	S_3	S_4	S_5	u_i
F_1	[25] 4	[5] 6	[20] 8	(10) 13	(5) 0	4
F_2	(7) 13	(3) 11	[70] 10	(3) 8	(3) 0	6
F_3	(12) 14	[30] 4	(4) 10	(12) 13	(7) 0	2
F_4	(0) 9	(0) 11	[15] 13	[20] 8	[15] 0	9
v_j	0	2	4	–1	–9	

Enter the basic feasible solution in the upper left corner of the basic cell. Now construct u_i and v_j by usual procedure and finally find the cell evaluation D_{ij} of unoccupied cells which are displayed under circles. Since all D_{ij} are non-negative and at least one $D_{ij} = 0$, the current initial basic feasible solution is optimal but not unique. There exists alternate optimal solution. Therefore, one of the optimal solutions becomes $\langle x_{11}^* = 25,\ x_{12}^* = 5,\ x_{13}^* = 20,\ x_{23}^* = 70,\ x_{32}^* = 30,\ x_{43}^* = 15,\ x_{44}^* = 20,\ x_{45}^* = 15 \rangle$.

With optimum transportation plus product cost = ₹1465.

Remark. In connection with this particular problem, the practical significance of demand being 15 units less than production capacity is that the company may cut down the production of 15 units at the factory, where it is uneconomical, i.e., at factory F_4.

Example 7.1.7. *So far, we have considered minimisation transportation problem by using cost matrix. Let us now consider the following profit matrix which is a maximisation problem.*

	Sale Agencies					*Capacity*
	S_1	S_2	S_3	S_4	S_5	a_i
F_1	15	17	12	11	11	140
F_2	5	9	7	15	7	190
F_3	14	15	16	20	10	115
Demand b_j	74	94	69	39	119	

Solution:

$$\sum_{i=1}^{3} a_i \neq \sum_{j=1}^{5} b_j$$

it is an unbalanced problem.

We first make it a balanced problem by creating a dummy sale agency S_6 to take up the excess capacity of 50 units. The associated unit profit is zero in each cell. Next the profit matrix so obtained by introducing dummy column converted into loss matrix by changing the signs of all the cell values as given in the following table.

Table 1

	S_1	S_2	S_3	S_4	S_5	S_6	a_i
F_1	−15	−17	−12	−11	−11	0	140
F_2	−5	−9	−7	−15	−7	0	190
F_3	−14	−15	−16	−20	−10	0	115
b_j	74	94	69	39	119	50	

Using VAM find the initial basic feasible solution. Then test the optimality by (u-v) method exactly in a similar manner as done in Exs 7.1.4 and 7.1.5. The second basic feasible solution give the unique optimal solution and is given (intermediate part of the solution are left for my readers)

$\langle x_{11}^* = 46,\ x_{12}^* = 94,\ x_{24}^* = 21,\ x_{25}^* = 119,\ x_{26}^* = 50,\ x_{31}^* = 28,\ x_{33}^* = 69,\ x_{34}^* = 18\rangle$

and optimum profit (use original profit max) is ₹5292. Note that the production capacity of F_2 remains unused by 50 units and yields no profit.

7.1.5 Degeneracy in Transportation Problem

The degeneracy in transportation problem may occur at the very initial stage or any subsequent stage when the number of individual independent allocations be less than $(m+n-1)$. To resolve this degeneracy, we allocate a very small positive quantity ϵ to one or more of empty cells, generally to the lowest cost cells and consider these cells to be the occupied cells. In fact, with this choice of ϵ, the original problem is not changed. Since it does not violate the row and column restrictions, ultimately it is to be omitted in the optimal solution.

Example 7.1.8. *Solve the adjoining balanced transportation problem.*

	D_1	D_2	D_3	a_i
O_1	8	7	3	60
O_2	3	8	9	70
O_3	11	3	5	80
b_j	50	80	80	

[CU(H) 1989, KU(H) 1987]

Solution: To find initial basic feasible solution, we use VAM and get the following degenerate solution: $x_{13} = 60,\ x_{21} = 50,\ x_{23} = 20,\ x_{32} = 80$ [since $m+n-1 = 4 < 5$].

Table 1

	D_1	D_2	D_3
O_1	8	7	[60] 3
O_2	[50] 3	8	[20] 3
O_3	11	[80] 3	5

Table 2

	D_1	D_2	D_3	u_i
O_1	(11) 8	ε 7	[60] 3	0
O_2	[50] 3	(−5) 8	[20] 3	6
O_3	(18) 11	[80] 3	(6) 5	−4
v_j	−3	7	3	

Now we add a small positive quantity ϵ to a cell such that this does not result in forming a loop among the occupied cells. If it is so, then unique determination of u_i and v_j will not be possible. Keeping it in mind, allocate ϵ to the cell (1,2) and then compute u_i, v_j.

Enter the basic feasible solution to the upper left corner of the basic cell $D_{ij} = c_{ij} - \left(u_i + v_j\right)$ for unoccupied cell are displayed under circles which shows that $D_{22} = -5 < 0$. We allocate maximum possible unit to (2,2) cells and adjust this additional allotment such that the cell (1,2) becomes empty.

Table 3

	D_1	D_2	D_3
O_1		ε−ε	60+ε
O_2		+ε	20−ε
O_3			

	D_1	D_2	D_3	u_i
O_1	(11) 8	(5) 7	60 3	−6
O_2	50 3	(ε) 8	20 9	0
O_3	(13) 11	80 3	(1) 5	−5
v_j	3	8	9	

All D_{ij} (as shown under circles) are non-negative. An optimality has been reached. Occupied cells are basic cells. Hence, approaching $\epsilon \to 0$, we get the following optimal solution $\left\langle x_{13}^* = 60,\ x_{21}^* = 50,\ x_{23}^* = 20,\ x_{32}^* = 80 \right\rangle$ and minimum cost = 750.

7.2 ASSIGNMENT PROBLEMS

Suppose, the manager of a firm may be interested in finding the best *assignment* of m jobs to his m employees. Let c_{ij} be the cost of ith job to the jth employee. We can represent the cost or effectiveness matrix in the form as shown in the adjoining figure.

JOBS \ EMPLOYEE	E_1	E_2	...	E_m
J_1	c_{11}	c_{12}	...	c_{1m}
J_2	c_{21}	c_{22}	...	c_{2m}
⋮	⋮	⋮	...	⋮
J_m	c_{m1}	c_{m2}	...	c_{mm}

In an assignment problem as only one job is assigned to one employee, the above cost matrix in general is a square matrix of order $m \times m$. The main objective in this problem is that the assignment is to be made in such a way that each job can be associated with one and only one employee so that the overall cost is *minimum*.

7.2.1 Mathematical Formulation

Let c_{ij} is the cost of assigning the ith job to the jth facility. Then mathematically an assignment problem is to determine variables $x_{ij}, i, j = 1, 2, \ldots, m$ which will

$$\text{Minimise } Z = \sum_{i=1}^{m} \sum_{j=1}^{m} c_{ij} x_{ij} \text{ (Total cost)}$$

$$\text{subject to } \sum_{j=1}^{m} x_{ij} = 1 \ \forall\ i = 1, 2, \ldots, m \tag{7.2a}$$

$$\sum_{i=1}^{m} x_{ij} = 1 \ \forall\ j = 1, 2, \ldots, m \tag{7.2b}$$

$$\text{where } x_{ij} = \begin{cases} 1, & \text{if } i\text{th job is assigned to } j\text{th facility} \\ 0, & \text{if } i\text{th job is not assigned to } j\text{th facility.} \end{cases}$$

The constraints (7.2a) insure that only one job is assigned to one facility and (7.2b) insures that only one facility should be assigned to one job, so that an assignment is a *one to one* mapping. This can be viewed as LPP which is, in fact, a (0–1) LP model.

7.2.2 Some Useful Results

Result 1. If in an assignment problem we add or subtract some constants to/from row or column, then the new problem and original problem have the same optimal solution.

Proof. Let x_{ij} solves the problem stated in (7.2.1).

We define the new problem as

$$\text{Minimise } Z^* = \sum_{i=1}^{m}\sum_{j=1}^{m} c^*_{ij} x_{ij}, \text{ where } c^*_{ij} = c_{ij} \pm \alpha_j \pm \beta_j$$

$$\text{subject to } \sum_{j=1}^{m} x_{ij} = 1,\ i = 1,2,\ldots,m \tag{7.2c}$$

$$\sum_{i=1}^{m} x_{ij} = 1,\ j = 1,2,\ldots,m \tag{7.2d}$$

and $x_{ij} = 1$ or 0 for $i, j = 1,2,\ldots,m$.

Now

$$\text{minimise } Z^* = \sum_{i=1}^{m}\sum_{j=1}^{m} c^*_{ij} x_{ij} = \sum_{i=1}^{m}\sum_{j=1}^{m}\left(c_{ij} \pm \alpha_i \pm \beta_j\right) x_{ij}$$

$$= \sum_{i=1}^{m}\sum_{j=1}^{m} c_{ij} x_{ij} \pm \sum_{i=1}^{m} \alpha_i \sum_{j=1}^{m} x_{ij} \pm \sum_{j=1}^{m} \beta_j \sum_{i=1}^{m} x_{ij}$$

$$= Z \pm \sum_{i=1}^{m} \alpha_i \pm \sum_{j=1}^{m} \beta_j \text{ [by (7.2c) and (7.2d)].}$$

As $\sum_{i=1}^{m} \alpha_i$ and $\sum_{j=1}^{m} \beta_j$ are constant quantities, Z^* is minimum when Z is minimum. Hence, follow the required result.

Result 2. If all $c_{ij} \geq 0$ and a solution with $x_{ij} = x^*_{ij}$ is obtained to the assignment problem such that

$$\sum_{i=1}^{m}\sum_{j=1}^{m} c_{ij} x^*_{ij} = 0,$$

then the present solution is an optimal solution.

Proof. As $c_{ij} \geq 0$, then value of

$$Z = \sum_{i=1}^{m}\sum_{j=1}^{m} c_{ij} x_{ij} \geq 0.$$

Hence, its minimum value is zero which is attained when $x_{ij} = x^*_{ij}$ and the result follows accordingly.

7.2.3 Computational Procedure of an Assignment Problem

Considering the *cost matrix* and assuming all entries in the matrix are *positive*, we describe below the computational procedure to be followed for finding the optimum assignment of an assignment problem.

Step 1. Subtract the minimum element of each row in the cost matrix from all elements of respective rows (row reduction). The matrix has now at least one zero in every row. Then subtract the minimum element of each column from all the elements of the respective column (column reduction). This will provide us the *starting cost matrix*.

Step 2. Draw the *minimum* possible number of horizontal and vertical lines to cover all the zeros of the starting cost matrix. With this operation we may face the following two situations:

(i) The number of lines (N) so drawn may be equal to the order (m) of the cost matrix. In this situation an *optimum assignment* has been reached.

(ii) The number of lines so drawn is less than the order of the cost matrix ($N < m$).

When situation (i) occurs to find the optimum assignment we follow the next step.

Step 3. Write the matrix consisting of only zero elements by performing operations in *Step* 1 and *Step* 2. Then starting with the first row, examine all the rows which contain *only one zero* (row operation). Mark this zero under rectangle ▭, where an assignment will be made.

Apply similar procedure to the column (column operation) only after all the rows have been completely examined. As there is no *unmarked zero* is left we immediately have an optimum solution.

But whenever the situation (ii) occurs, follow the following step.

Step 3A. Search the *smallest element* after performing *Step* 1 and *Step* 2 among the *uncovered* element left after drawing the lines. Subtract this smallest element from all uncovered elements and at the same time add this smallest element to the elements lying at the point of intersection of horizontal and vertical lines. *Do not touch* the elements through which only one line passes. This operation will create a new MODIFIED MATRIX with more zeros.

Go to *Step* 2 with this modified matrix. If a complete assignment be not still available then repeat *Step* 3A and *Step* 2 successively and finally apply *Step* 3.

Step 4. Repeat *row and column* operations of *Step* 3 until one of the following two cases arise.

Case 1. There will be no unmarked zero left.

Case 2. There lie more than one unmarked zero in one row or column.

For **Case 1** process stops and we have exactly one *marked* zero in each row and each column.

For **Case 2** mark under ▭ one of the unmarked zeros arbitrarily and ignore the remaining zeros in that row or column. Repeat the process until no unmarked zero is left.

The procedure described above is called *Hungarian method* as it is based on the works of two famous Hungarian mathematicians König and Egerváry.

Example 7.2.1. *Find the optimal assignment and minimum cost for the following assignment problem.*

	1	2	3	4
A	10	12	19	11
B	5	10	7	8
C	12	14	13	11
D	8	15	11	9

[KU(H) 1994, BESU(ME) 2005]

Solution: The minimum elements of the rows A, B, C, D are respectively (10,5,11,8). We subtract these elements from all the elements of the respective rows yielding *Table* 1.

Table 1

	1	2	3	4
A	0	2	9	1
B	0	5	2	3
C	1	3	2	0
D	0	7	3	1

Table 1 shows the matrix has at least one zero in every row. Now the minimum elements of the columns 1, 2, 3, 4 respectively (0,2,2,0). We subtract these elements from all the elements of the respective columns giving the *starting cost matrix* in *Table* 2.

Table 2

	1	2	3	4
A	0	0	7	1
B	0	3	0	3
C	1	1	0	0
D	0	5	1	1

Now we draw the minimum number of horizontal and vertical lines to cover all the zeros of the starting matrix. The number of lines $N = 4 =$ order of the cost matrix so that a complete assignment will be possible from this matrix. Now follow *Step* 3 of Hungarian method.

Example 7.2.2. *Solve the following assignment problem whose cost matrix is given below.*

	a	b	c	d
1	18	26	17	11
2	13	28	14	26
3	38	19	18	15
4	19	26	24	10

[CU(H) 1987, 2002]

Solution: Using the same procedure as described in details in Ex. 7.2.1 the starting cost matrix of the problem is given by:

Table 1

	a	*b*	*c*	*d*
1	7	11	5	0
2	0	11	0	13
3	23	0	2	0
4	9	12	12	10

Draw minimum number of horizontal and vertical lines to cover all zeros of *Table* 1, which shows that number of lines $N = 3 < 4 = m$, order of matrix. So we follow *Step* 3A of the method. The smallest element among the uncovered elements by the lines is 2. We subtract 2 from each uncovered element and add 2 to the element at the point of intersection of horizontal and vertical lines but untouch those elements through which the lines pass. This will create a modified cost matrix given in *Table* 2.

Table 2

a	*b*	*c*	*d*
5	11	3	0
0	13	0	15
21	0	0	0
7	12	10	0

Again, $N = 3 < 4 = m$, order of matrix. Now smallest element among uncovered elements = 3. Perform the same operation which will give a second modified cost matrix given in *Table* 3.

Table 3

	1	2	3	4
A	~~0~~	[0]		
B	~~0~~		[0]	
C			~~0~~	[0]
D	[0]			

Assignments are made in the cell (4, 1), (1, 2), (3, 4) and (2, 3) for the fourth, first, third and second rows respectively, which contains only one zero in each. Cross of zeros lying on the corresponding columns marked zeros. Hence, the optimal assignment schedule will be A ⟶ 2, B ⟶ 3, C ⟶ 4, D ⟶ 1 (represents a one-one mapping) and minimum cost = 12 + 7 + 11 + 8 = 38.

Table 3

	a	*b*	*c*	*d*
1	2	8	0	0
2	0	13	0	18
3	22	0	0	3
4	4	9	7	0

Table 4

	a	*b*	*c*	*d*
1			[0]	~~0~~
2	[0]		~~0~~	
3		[0]	~~0~~	
4				[0]

Now $N = 4 \doteq$ order of matrix, an optimum assignment has been reached. To find the assignment follow the following.

Single zero row in cell (4, 4) assigns first zero in that row under ▭ and cross of all zero in the corresponding column. Next single zero in cell (2, 1) assigns second assignment thereunder ▭ and cross of zero in the corresponding row. Proceeding in this manner, we get the following optimal assignment schedule:

$$\langle 1 \longrightarrow c,\ 2 \longrightarrow a,\ 3 \longrightarrow b,\ 4 \longrightarrow d \rangle ..$$

Minimum cost = 17 + 13 + 19 + 10 = 59.

Example 7.2.3. *Solve the following assignment problem whose cost matrix is given below.*

	I	II	III	IV	V
A	6	5	8	11	16
B	1	13	16	1	13
C	16	11	8	8	8
D	9	14	12	10	16
E	10	13	11	8	16

[BU(H) 1996]

Solution: Using the same procedure, we get the following starting cost matrix.

The minimum lines to cover all zeros of starting matrix are 4, which is less than the order 5 of the matrix. So we search for the smallest element among the uncovered element, which is 3 and perform *Step* 3A to get *Table* 2.

Table 1

	I	II	III	IV	V
A	1	0	3	6	11
B	0	12	15	0	9
C	8	3	0	0	0
D	0	5	3	1	7
E	2	5	3	0	8

Table 2

	I	II	III	IV	V
A	4	0	3	0	11
B	0	9	12	0	6
C	11	3	0	3	0
D	0	2	0	1	4
E	2	2	0	0	5

Now the minimum number of lines is equal to the order of the matrix so that an optimum solution has been reached. To find the optimum assignment consider *Table* 3 and *Table* 4.

Table 3

	I	II	III	IV	V
A		[0]			
B	[0]			~~0~~	
C			~~0~~		[0]
D	~~0~~		[0]		
E			~~0~~	[0]	

Table 4

	I	II	III	IV	V
A		[0]			
B	~~0~~			[0]	
C			~~0~~		[0]
D	[0]		~~0~~		
E			[0]	~~0~~	

Single zero row in cell (1,2) in both tables assigns first in that cell under ▭. Then there is no other single zero in the row of both tables. Now examine single column which is the fifth column and assigns there. Cross off all zeros in that column and row.

Next we observe that there lie more than one unmarked zero in row as well as column. In *Table* 3 mark zero in (2, 1) cell and cross off zero in that particular row and column but in *Table* 4 mark zero in (2, 4) cell and similarly cross off all other zeros in that row and column. This will be done arbitrarily as mentioned in *Step* 4 and we get the following two alternate optimal assignments.

(i) A ⟶ II, B ⟶ I, C ⟶ V, D ⟶ III, E ⟶ IV

or, (ii) A ⟶ II, B ⟶ IV, C ⟶ V, D ⟶ I, E ⟶ III

and Minimum cost = 34.

7.2.4 Different Forms of An Assignment Problem

(A) Unbalanced Assignment Problem

When the number of facilities is not equal to the number of jobs (i.e., when the matrix is rectangular) such a problem is called an *unbalanced assignment problem.* Since the Hungarian method requires a square matrix, fictitious facilities or jobs may be added and zero costs be assigned to the corresponding cells of the matrix. These cells are then treated with the same way as the real cost cells during the solution procedure.

Example 7.2.4. *A manufacturer of electronic equipment has just received a sizeable contract and plans to subcontract a part of the job. He has solicited bids for 6 subcontracts from 3 firms. Each job is sufficiently large and any firm can take only one job. The table below shows the bids as well as the cost estimates (in lakh of rupees) for doing the job internally. Not more than three jobs can be performed internally.*

Find the optimal assignment that will result in minimum total cost. [IAS(Main) 2002]

Job / Firm	J_1	J_2	J_3	J_4	J_5	J_6
F_1	44	67	41	53	48	64
F_2	46	69	40	45	45	68
F_3	43	73	37	51	44	62
Internal	50	65	35	50	46	63

Solution: The problem involves a rectangular cost matrix of order 4×6. As three jobs can be performed internally we convert it into a square matrix of order 6×6 as follows.

Now using row and then column reduction, we get *Table* 2.

Table 1

	J_1	J_2	J_3	J_4	J_5	J_6
F_1	44	67	41	53	48	64
F_2	46	69	40	45	45	68
F_3	43	73	37	51	44	62
I_1	50	65	35	50	46	63
I_2	50	65	35	50	46	63
I_3	50	65	35	50	46	63

Table 2

	J_1	J_2	J_3	J_4	J_5	J_6
F_1	0	0	0	7	2	0
F_2	3	3	0	0	0	5
F_3	3	10	0	9	2	2
I_1	12	4	0	10	6	5
I_2	12	4	0	10	6	5
I_3	12	4	0	10	6	5

The minimum number of lines covering all zeros is only 3(< 6). Hence, optimal assignment cannot be made in the current feasible solution. Proceeding similarly as in previous examples, we get the following.

Table 3

	J_1	J_2	J_3	J_4	J_5	J_6
F_1	0	0	2	7	2	0
F_2	3	3	2	0	0	5
F_3	1	8	0	7	0	0
I_1	10	2	0	8	4	3
I_2	10	2	0	8	4	3
I_3	10	2	0	8	4	3

min line $N = 4 < 6$

Table 4

	J_1	J_2	J_3	J_4	J_5	J_6
F_1	0	0	4	7	2	0
F_2	3	3	4	0	0	5
F_3	1	8	2	7	0	0
I_1	8	0	0	6	2	1
I_2	8	0	0	6	2	1
I_3	8	0	0	6	2	1

min line $N = 5 < 6$

Table 5

	J_1	J_2	J_3	J_4	J_5	J_6
F_1	0	1	5	7	2	0
F_2	3	4	5	0	0	5
F_3	1	9	3	7	0	0
I_1	7	2	0	5	1	0
I_2	7	2	0	5	1	0
I_3	7	2	0	5	1	0

Number of lines = $N = 6$, current feasible solution becomes optimum. To find optimal assignment we construct as shown in the adjoining *Table* 6.

Table 6

	J_1	J_2	J_3	J_4	J_5	J_6
F_1	[0]					✗
F_2				[0]	✗	
F_3					[0]	
I_1		[0]	✗			✗
I_2		✗	[0]			✗
I_3		✗	✗			[0]

Optimal assignment schedule: $F_1 \longrightarrow J_1$, $F_2 \longrightarrow J_4$, $F_3 \longrightarrow J_5$, $I_1 \longrightarrow J_2$, $I_2 \longrightarrow J_3$, $I_3 \longrightarrow J_6$.

Associated minimum cost = ₹296 lac.

(B) Maximisation Problem

Sometimes the assignment problem may be a maximisation problem (with a profit matrix). Before the Hungarian method be applied the problem has to be changed to minimisation. This conversion may be done in either of the following two ways:

(i) The largest element of the profit matrix is selected and then a new *cost matrix* is formed whose elements are obtained by subtracting all the elements from the largest element.

(ii) By multiplying the matrix elements by (-1).

The Hungarian method can then be applied to this equivalent minimisation problem to obtain the optimal assignment.

Example 7.2.5. *The captain of Indian cricket team has to allot five middle order batsmen. The average runs scored by each batsman at these positions are as follows.*

(i) *Find the assignment of batsmen to position, which will give maximum number of runs.*

(ii) *If another batsman B_6 with the following average runs in batting position as given below joins the team, should he be included in the team? If so, who will be replaced by him?*

Batsman	*Batting position*				
	P_1	P_2	P_3	P_4	P_5
B_1	40	40	35	25	50
B_2	42	30	16	25	27
B_3	50	48	40	60	50
B_4	20	19	20	18	25
B_5	58	60	59	55	53

Batsman	*Batting position*				
	P_1	P_2	P_3	P_4	P_5
B_6	54	52	38	50	49

[JNU(Comp) 1999]

Solution: (i) The largest element is 60, the equivalent minimisation problem is:

Performing the row and the column reduction, we get *Table* 2.

Table 1

	P_1	P_2	P_3	P_4	P_5
B_1	20	20	25	35	10
B_2	18	30	44	35	33
B_3	10	12	20	0	10
B_4	40	41	40	42	35
B_5	2	0	1	5	7

Table 2

	P_1	P_2	P_3	P_4	P_5
B_1	10	10	14	25	0
B_2	0	12	25	17	15
B_3	10	12	19	0	10
B_4	5	6	4	7	0
B_5	2	0	0	5	7

Table 3

	P_1	P_2	P_3	P_4	P_5
B_1	6	6	10	21	0
B_2	0	12	25	17	19
B_3	10	12	19	0	14
B_4	1	2	0	3	0
B_5	2	0	0	5	11

Number of lines $N = 4 < 5$, current feasible solution is not optimum.

Minimum number of lines $N = 5$. Therefore, optimum solution has been reached and we get *Table* 4 for optimum assignment.

Table 4

	P_1	P_2	P_3	P_4	P_5
B_1					[0]
B_2	[0]				
B_3				[0]	
B_4			[0]		✗
B_5		[0]	✗		

Optimum assignment policy: Batsman⟶Position⟶No. of runs

B_1	P_5	50
B_2	P_1	42
B_3	P_4	60
B_4	P_3	20
B_5	P_2	60
		232

(ii) Assignment matrix if batsman B_6 joins the team is:

	P_1	P_2	P_3	P_4	P_5
B_1	40	40	35	25	50
B_2	42	30	16	25	27
B_3	50	48	40	60	50
B_4	20	19	20	18	25
B_5	58	60	59	55	53
B_6	45	52	38	50	49

This is an unbalanced assignment problem. First making it balanced by adding a dummy column P_D and then transforming it into a minimisation problem by usual method, we get *Table* 5.

Row reduction and then column reduction will give *Table* 6.

Table 5

	P_1	P_2	P_3	P_4	P_5	P_D
B_1	20	20	25	35	10	60
B_2	18	30	44	35	33	60
B_3	10	12	20	0	10	60
B_4	40	41	40	42	35	60
B_5	2	0	1	5	7	60
B_6	15	8	22	10	11	60

Table 6

	P_1	P_2	P_3	P_4	P_5	P_D
B_1	10	10	14	25	0	25
B_2	0	12	25	17	15	17
B_3	10	12	19	0	10	35
B_4	5	6	4	7	0	0
B_5	2	0	0	5	7	35
B_6	7	0	13	2	3	7

Minimum number of lines $N = 6$, current solution becomes optimal and is given in *Table* 7.

Table 7

	P_1	P_2	P_3	P_4	P_5	P_D
B_1					[0]	
B_2	[0]					
B_3				[0]		
B_4					⊠	[0]
B_5		⊠	[0]			
B_6		[0]				

Optimal assignment policy after the inclusion of batsman B_6 in Indian team:

Batsman⟶	Batting position⟶	No. of runs
B_1	P_5	50
B_2	P_1	42
B_3	P_4	60
B_4	P_D	0
B_5	P_3	59
B_6	P_2	52
		263

Conclusion. Since the number of runs increases, batsman B_6 should be included in the team. Obviously, in place of B_4 batsman B_6 enters into the Indian team.

(C) Impossible Assignment

Sometime due to certain restrictions we do not permit the assignment of a particular facility to a particular job. To tackle such problems we assign a very large cost to the corresponding cell. Such job will then be automatically excluded from further consideration.

Example 7.2.6. *Consider the problem of assigning the operators to the machines. The assignment cost in rupees are given in the table. Operator O_2 cannot be assigned to machine M_2 and operator O_5 cannot be assigned to machine M_4. Find the optimal cost of assignment.* [BESU(BE) 2010]

	M_1	M_2	M_3	M_4	M_5
O_1	8	4	2	6	1
O_2	0	–	5	5	4
O_3	3	8	9	2	6
O_4	4	3	1	0	3
O_5	9	5	8	–	5

Solution: The problem indicates that two assignments are impossible. Therefore, we put a very large cost 10 in the cells (2, 2) and (5, 4), then proceed as usual. Performing first row reduction and then column reduction, we get *Table 1*.

Minimum number of lines $N = 5$, which is equal to order of the matrix. Current basic solution is therefore optimal and is given in *Table 2*.

Table 1

	M_1	M_2	M_3	M_4	M_5
O_1	7	3	0	5	0
O_2	0	10	4	5	4
O_3	1	6	6	0	4
O_4	4	3	0	0	3
O_5	4	0	2	5	0

Table 2

	M_1	M_2	M_3	M_4	M_5
O_1			✗		[0]
O_2	[0]				
O_3				[0]	
O_4			[0]	✗	
O_5		[0]			✗

Optimal assignment: $O_1 \longrightarrow M_5, O_2 \longrightarrow M_1, O_3 \longrightarrow M_4, O_4 \longrightarrow M_3, O_5 \longrightarrow M_2$.

Minimum cost = 1 + 0 + 2 + 1 + 5 = ₹9.

(D) Negative Cost

If the cost matrix contains some negative cost, then we add to each element of the rows and columns a quantity, sufficient to make all the cell elements of the cost matrix non-negative. Then we apply the usual assignment procedure.

Example 7.2.7. *Solve the following assignment problem whose cost matrix is given.*

[JNU(Comp) 1992, IAS 1990]

	J_1	J_2	J_3	J_4
M_1	2	−1	−1	−2
M_2	1	0	−2	−1
M_3	1	−1	−2	0
M_4	2	2	1	1

Solution: First of all we make all the cell elements non-negative by adding 3 to each element of the matrix and get *Table* 1.

Table 1

	J_1	J_2	J_3	J_4
M_1	5	2	2	1
M_1	4	3	1	2
M_1	4	2	1	3
M_1	5	5	4	4

Table 2

	J_1	J_2	J_3	J_4
M_1	3	0	1	0
M_2	2	1	0	1
M_3	2	0	0	2
M_4	0	0	0	0

Now row reduction and column reduction will give *Table* 2.

Minimum number of lines $N = 4$, which is equal to the order of the cost matrix. Hence, an optimal solution has been reached and is given by *Table* 3.

Table 3

	J_1	J_2	J_3	J_4
M_1		~~0~~		[0]
M_2			[0]	
M_3		[0]	~~0~~	
M_4	[0]	~~0~~	~~0~~	~~0~~

Optimal assignment: $M_1 \longrightarrow J_4$, $M_2 \longrightarrow J_3$, $M_3 \longrightarrow J_2$, $M_4 \longrightarrow J_1$.

Minimum cost $= (-2)+(-2)+(-1)+2 = -3$.

(E) Alternate Optimal Solution

Sometimes, it is possible to have two or more ways to strike off all zero elements in the reduced matrix for a given problem. In such cases, there will be alternate optimal solutions. How to find alternate solution that is already mentioned in computational procedures. In fact, an alternate optimal solutions offer a great flexibility to the management since it can select the one which is most suitable to its requirement.

Ex. 7.2.3 illustrate an alternate optimal solution of a given problem.

7.3 TRAVELLING SALESMAN PROBLEM

Suppose, a salesman wants to visit a certain number of cities from his headquarters. The distances (or cost or time) of journey between every pair of cities be denoted by c_{ij}, distance from city i to city j is assumed to be known. The problem is: Salesman starting from its home city visiting each city only once and return to his home city in the shortest possible distance (or at the least cost or in the least time).

Given n cities and distance c_{ij}, the salesman starts from city 1, then any permutation of $2, 3, \ldots, n$ represents the number of possible ways for his tour. So, there are $(n-1)!$ possible ways for his tour. The problem is to select the optimal route that could achieve the salesman's objective.

$$\text{Let } x_{ij} = \begin{cases} 1, & \text{if the salesman goes directly from city } i \text{ to city } j \\ 0, & \text{otherwise.} \end{cases}$$

Then the problem: Minimise $Z = \sum_{i=1}^{n}\sum_{j=1}^{n} c_{ij}x_{ij}$ (Total distance)

$$\text{subject to } \sum_{j=1}^{n} x_{ij} = 1, \quad i = 1,2,\ldots,n$$

$$\sum_{i=1}^{n} x_{ij} = 1, \quad i = 1,2,\ldots,n.$$

Furthermore, $c_{ii} = \infty$ by convention as x_{ij} can never be unity for $i = j$ as a city cannot follow the same city.

We express below the matrix form of the problem.

From \ To	A_1	A_2	...	A_n
A_1	∞	c_{12}	...	c_{1n}
A_2	c_{21}	∞	...	c_{2n}
⋮	⋮	⋮		⋮
A_n	c_{n1}	c_{n2}	...	∞

Travelling salesman problem is therefore very similar to *assignment problem.* The only difference being that the former has an additional restrictions, which will ensure that the round trip will consist of a connected sequence ending in the starting point. Such a connected sequence without any sub-loop is called a *tour.*

If the tour restriction is relaxed, then the problem can be solved by the *Hungarian method* and the minimum objective value for this assignment problem is the lower bound of the cost of the tour.

But there may be cases, where the solution will not satisfy this additional restrictions. In such a case, the *enumerative method* is applied after the problem is solved by the *assignment technique.*

Example 7.3.1. *Solve the travelling salesman problem with the following cost matrix $\left[c_{ij}\right]_{5\times5}$, where c_{ij} is the cost of travelling from city i to city j.*

[KU(MSc) 1995, BESU(BE) 2009]

	1	2	3	4	5
1	∞	4	7	3	4
2	4	∞	6	3	4
3	7	6	∞	7	5
4	3	3	7	∞	7
5	4	4	5	7	∞

Solution: Using Hungarian method, performing first row reduction and then column reduction, we form the following starting matrix in *Table* 1.

Table 1

	1	2	3	4	5
1	∞	1	3	0	1
2	1	∞	2	0	1
3	2	1	∞	2	0
4	0	0	3	∞	4
5	0	0	0	3	∞

Number of lines $N = 4 <$ order of the matrix. So, go to next step.

Table 2

	1	2	3	4	5
1	∞	0	2	0	0
2	0	∞	1	0	0
3	2	1	∞	3	0
4	0	0	3	∞	4
5	0	0	0	3	∞

Number of lines $N = 5$, which is equal to the order of the matrix.

Table 3

	1	2	3	4	5
1	∞	×0	2	[0]	×0
2	[0]	∞	(1)	×0	×0
3	2	1	∞	3	[0]
4	×0	[0]	3	∞	4
5	×0	×0	[0]	3	∞

The optimum assignment is $1 \longrightarrow 4$, $2 \longrightarrow 1$, $3 \longrightarrow 5$, $4 \longrightarrow 2$, $5 \rightarrow 3$ with minimum cost ₹20.

This assignment schedule does not provide us the solution of travelling salesman problem as it gives $1 \longrightarrow 4 \longrightarrow 2 \longrightarrow 1$ without passing through 3 and 5.

Now we try to find the next best solution which satisfies this restriction. The next non-zero minimum element in the cost matrix is 1. So, we bring 1 into the solution but the element 1 occurs at two places. We consider all cases separately until, we get an optimal solution.

We start with making an assignment at (2, 3) cell under circle ◯ instead of zero assignment at (2, 1). This will give the assignment schedule $1 \longrightarrow 4$, $4 \longrightarrow 2$, $2 \longrightarrow 3$, $3 \longrightarrow 5$, $5 \longrightarrow 1$.

Again, when an assignment is made at (3, 2) cell instead of zero assignment at (3, 5), the schedule is $1 \longrightarrow 5$, $5 \longrightarrow 3$, $3 \longrightarrow 2$, $2 \longrightarrow 4$, $4 \longrightarrow 1$.

In both cases the minimum cost is 21.

Example 7.3.2. *Solve the travelling salesman problem, given the following* (5×5) *matrix.* [VU(H) 1998]

	1	2	3	4	5
1	∞	14	10	24	41
2	6	∞	10	12	10
3	7	13	∞	8	15
4	11	14	30	∞	17
5	6	8	12	16	∞

Solution: Row reduction and column reduction will produce *Table* 1.

Minimum number of lines to cover all zeros is equal to the order of the matrix. So we go to next *Table* 2.

Table 1

	1	2	3	4	5
1	∞	2	0	13	27
2	0	∞	4	5	0
3	0	4	∞	0	4
4	0	1	19	∞	2
5	0	0	6	9	∞

Table 2

	1	2	3	4	5
1	∞	2	[0]	13	27
2	×0	∞	4	5	[0]
3	×0	4	∞	[0]	4
4	[0]	1	19	∞	2
5	×0	[0]	6	9	∞

The optimum assignment is: $1 \longrightarrow 3$, $2 \longrightarrow 5$, $3 \longrightarrow 4$, $4 \longrightarrow 1$, $5 \longrightarrow 2$ with minimum cost $= 10 + 10 + 8 + 11 + 8 = 47$.

This assignment does not provide us the solution of travelling salesman problem. It gives $1 \longrightarrow 3 \longrightarrow 4 \longrightarrow 1$ without passing through 2 and 5.

Following the same procedure as done in Ex. 7.3.1, we get *Table* 3.

Table 3

	1	2	3	4	5
1	∞	2	$\boxed{0}$	13	27
2	$\not{0}$	∞	4	5	$\boxed{0}$
3	$\not{0}$	4	∞	$\boxed{0}$	4
4	$\not{0}$	(1)	19	∞	2
5	$\boxed{0}$	$\not{0}$	6	9	∞

The optimal assignment schedule: $1 \longrightarrow 3 \longrightarrow 4 \longrightarrow 2 \longrightarrow 5 \longrightarrow 1$.

Minimum cost = 10 + 8 + 14 + 10 + 6 = 48.

Remark. A similar type of problem is encountered when n items. I_i, $i = 1,2,\ldots,n$ are to be processed in a machine within a scheduled time. The set-up cost of the processing machine when the item I_i is followed by I_j is given to be c_{ij}.

$$\text{Also } x_{ij} = \begin{cases} i, & \text{if } I_i \text{ be followed by } I_j \text{ directly} \\ 0, & \text{otherwise.} \end{cases}$$

For obvious reason $c_{ii} = \infty$ as one item cannot follow the same item.

Such type of problem is known as *production scheduling* problem, which is, therefore, required to find a sequence of these n items for processing such that the total set-up cost is minimum.

7·4 SEQUENCING PROBLEM

The sequencing problem involves the determination of an optimal order or optimal sequence of performing a series of jobs by a number of facilities that are arranged in a specific order so as to optimise the total involved time. The general sequencing problem may be defined as follows:

Let there be n jobs $\langle J_1, J_2, \ldots, J_n \rangle$ to be performed one at a time on each of m machine $\langle M_1, M_2, \ldots, M_m \rangle$. The sequence of the machines in which each job should be performed is given in advance. The actual or expected time required by the jobs on each of the machines is also given. Therefore, the general sequencing is to find the sequence out of $(n!)^m$ possible sequences which minimise the total elapsed time, that is the time between the start of the job in the first machine till the completion of last job on the last machine.

The following basic assumptions are usually made while dealing with sequencing problems:

(i) Each job once started on a machine is to be performed till the completion on that particular machine.
(ii) The processing time on each machine is known in advance. It should be remembered that such a time is independent of the order of the jobs in which they are to be processed.
(iii) The time taken by each job in changing over from one machine to another is negligible.
(iv) No machine can process more than one job at a time.
(v) No job is to be given priority. The order of completion of jobs is independent of sequence of jobs.
(vi) Only one machine of each type is available.
(vii) The cost of in-process inventory for each job is same and negligibly small.

7.4.1 Basic Terms

Some of the basic terms used in sequencing problem are:

(i) *Number of machines.* It refers to the number of service facilities through which a job must pass before it is assumed to be completed.
(ii) *Process order.* It refers to the order or sequence in which given machines are required for completing the job.
(iii) *Process time.* It indicates the time required by a job on each machine.
(iv) *Total elapsed time.* It is time interval between starting the first job and completing the last job including the *idle time,* if any, in a particular order by the given set of machines.
(v) *Idle time.* It is the time for which a machine does not have a job to process.

(vi) *No passing rule.* This rule maintains the order in which jobs are to be processed on a given machine. For example, if n jobs $\langle J_1, J_2, \ldots, J_n \rangle$ are to be processed through three machines $\langle M_1, M_2, M_3 \rangle$ in the order M_1, M_2, M_3, then this rule will mean that each job $J_i (i = 1,2,\ldots,n)$ will go through machine M_1 first, then to M_2 and finally to M_3.

7.4.2 Different Sequencing Problems

(A) *n*-Jobs, 1-Machine Problem

That a number of jobs are to be processed on a single facility is quite common in actual practice. For example,

(i) a number of patients waiting for a doctor,
(ii) a number of cars served from a single service station,
(iii) a number of programmes waiting for a computer, etc.

Consider a static job shop, where n different jobs with known processing times are processed on a single machine. The shop is static in the sense that any new job that arrives there does not disturb the processing of n jobs. So it is assumed that on arrival of a new job it waits for consideration in the next batch.

Let n = Number of different jobs $\langle J_1, J_2, \ldots, J_n \rangle$; t_i = Processing time of job $J_i (i = 1,2,\ldots,n)$
W_i = Waiting time for job i; F_i = Flow time for job $i = W_i + t_i$
c_i = Completion time for job i; d_i = Due time (date) for job i
L_i = Lateness of job $i = c_i - d_i$; E_i = Earliness of job $i = d_i - c_i$.

(a) Shortest Processing Time Rule (SPTR)

Sequencing of jobs in a way that the job with *least* processing time is picked up first, followed by next *smallest* processing time and so on. This is known as SPTR and achieves the following objectives:

(i) Minimising mean waiting time (W_i)
(ii) Minimising mean flow time (F_i)
(iii) Minimising mean lateness
(iv) Minimising mean number of jobs waiting as in process inventory.

In case importance of jobs varies, a weight w_i is assigned to each job. On the basis of larger value indicating greater importance, processing times divided by weights and jobs are sequenced in order of increasing (t_i/w_i)

$$\text{Weight mean flow time (WMFT)} = \left(\frac{\Sigma_i w_i F_i}{\Sigma_i w_i} \right).$$

This particular rule is called *weighted shortest processing time rule* (WSPTR).

Example 7.4.1. *Eight jobs $\langle J_1, J_2, \ldots, J_8 \rangle$ are to be processed on a single machine. The processing times, due dates, and importance weights of the jobs are represented below.*

Job	*Processing time* t_i(min)	*Due date* d_i(min)	*Importance weight* w_i	t_i/w_i
J_1	5	15	1	5.0
J_2	8	10	2	4.0
J_3	6	15	3	2.0
J_4	3	25	1	3.0
J_5	10	20	2	5.0
J_6	14	40	3	4.7
J_7	7	45	2	3.5
J_8	3	50	1	3.0

Assume that no new jobs arrive thereafter, determine using SPTR and WSPTR:

(i) Optimal sequence (ii) Completion time of the jobs
(iii) Mean flow and weighted mean flow times (iv) Average in process inventory
(v) Lateness, mean lateness and maximum lateness (vi) Number of jobs actually late.

Solution: Using SPTR.

(i) Optimal sequence: $J_4 \longrightarrow J_8 \longrightarrow J_1 \longrightarrow J_3 \longrightarrow J_7 \longrightarrow J_2 \longrightarrow J_5 \longrightarrow J_6$.

(ii) Completion time (min): $3 \longrightarrow 6 \longrightarrow 11 \longrightarrow 17 \longrightarrow 24 \longrightarrow 32 \longrightarrow 42 \longrightarrow 56$.

(iii) Mean flow time $= \dfrac{3+6+11+17+24+32+42+56}{8} = 2.3875$ min.

(iv) Number of jobs waiting: J_8 during 0–3, J_7 during 3–6, J_6 during 6–11, J_5 during 11–17, J_4 during 17–24, J_3 during 24–32, J_2 during 32–42, J_1 during 42–56.

$$\text{Average} = \frac{8\times3+7\times3+6\times5+5\times6+\times4\times7+3\times8+2\times10+1\times14}{3+3+5+6+7+8+10+14} = 3.41 \simeq 3 \text{ jobs.}$$

(v) Lateness of various jobs:

Jobs →	J_4 —	J_8 —	J_1 —	J_3 —	J_7 —	J_2 —	J_5 —	J_6
Lateness → (min)	−22	−44	−4	2	−21	22	22	16

$$\text{Mean lateness} = \frac{-22-44-4+2-21+22+22+16}{8} = -3.625 \text{ min.}$$

Maximum late = 22 min.

(vi) Number of jobs actually late = 4.

Using WSPTR.

(i) In table (t_i/w_i) values are shown. Therefore, as per non-decreasing (t_i/w_i), the optimal sequence is: $J_3 \longrightarrow J_4 \longrightarrow J_8 \longrightarrow J_7 \longrightarrow J_2 \longrightarrow J_6 \longrightarrow J_1 \longrightarrow J_5$.

(ii) Completion time (min): 6—9—12—19—27—41—46—56.

(iii) Mean flow time $= \dfrac{6+9+12+19+27+41+46+56}{8} = 27$ min.

$$\text{Weighted mean flow time} = \frac{3\times6+1\times9+1\times12+2\times19+2\times27+3\times41+1\times46+2\times56}{3+1+1+2+2+3+1+2}$$

$= 27.47$ min.

(iv) Number of jobs waiting in process: J_8 during 0–6, J_7 during 6–9, J_6 during 9–12, J_5 during 12–19, J_4 during 19–27, J_3 during 27–41, J_2 during 41–46, J_1 during 46–56.

$$\text{Average} = \frac{8\times6+7\times3+6\times3+5\times7+4\times8+3\times14+2\times5+1\times10}{6+3+3+7+8+14+5+10} \Rightarrow 3.86 \text{ job} \simeq 4 \text{ jobs.}$$

(v) Lateness of various jobs:

Jobs →	J_3 —	J_4 —	J_8 —	J_7 —	J_2 —	J_6 —	J_1 —	J_5
Lateness → (min)	−9	−16	−38	−26	17	1	31	36

$$\text{Mean lateness} = \frac{-9-16-38-26+17+1+31+36}{8} = -0.5 \text{ min.}$$

Maximum late = 36 min.

(vi) Number of jobs actually late = 4.

(B) *n*-Job, 2-Machine Problem

The iterative procedure for determining the optimal sequence for n-jobs $\langle J_1, J_2, \ldots, J_n \rangle$ on 2 machines $\langle M_1, M_2 \rangle$ can be summarised as following (Given processing order M_1, M_2).

Step 1. Represent the jobs along with their processing times in a table as shown below, where M_{ij} is the processing time of ith machine on jth job for $i = 1,2$ and $j = 1,2,\ldots,n$.

Jobs / Machines	J_1	J_2	J_3	...	J_n
M_1	M_{11}	M_{12}	M_{13}	...	M_{1n}
M_2	M_{21}	M_{22}	M_{23}	...	M_{2n}

Step 2. Examine the columns for processing times on machines M_1 and M_2 and find $\min_j \{M_{1j}, M_{2j}\}$. If the minimum time occurs for the first machine M_1, then do the corresponding job in the first available position in the sequence. But if the minimum time occurs for the second machine M_2, do the corresponding job in the last available position in the sequence.

Step 3. If there is a tie in the minimum, then we face the following obvious situations

(i) $\min_j \{M_{1j}, M_{2j}\} = M_{1k} = M_{2r}$. Then do the kth job first and rth job last.

(ii) Tie for minimum occurs from same machine M_1, then select arbitrarily the job to process first (Generally, the corresponding time of machine M_2 is considered and which one is minimum that is taken first and then the other).

(iii) Similarly, follow if tie for minimum occurs from same machine M_2.

Step 4. Cross off the jobs already assigned and repeat *Step* 1 and *Step* 3 placing the jobs next to first or next to last until all jobs have been assigned. This will give a sequence of jobs, which is the *optimal sequence*, where the total involved or elapsed time is minimum.

Step 5. Calculation of times:

(i) T = total elapsed time $= \sum_{j=1}^{n} M_{2j} + \sum_{j=1}^{n} I_{2j}$, where M_{2j} = time required for processing of jth job on M_2; I_{2j} = time for which M_2 remains idle after processing $(j-1)$th job and before starting work on jth job.

(ii) I_{M_1} = idle time for $M_1 = T-$ (time when the last job in an optimal sequence finishes on M_1).

(iii) I_{M_2} = idle time for M_2 = time at which the first job in an optimal sequence finishes on $M_1 + \sum_{j=2}^{n}$ [(time when the jth job in an optimum sequence starts on M_1) – (time when $\overline{j-1}$th job in an optimum sequence finishes on M_2)].

Example 7.4.2. *There are seven jobs each of which has to go through machines M_1 and M_2 in the order M_1, M_2. Processing times in hours are given as:*

Job :	J_1	J_2	J_3	J_4	J_5	J_6	J_7
M_1	3	12	15	6	10	11	9
M_2	8	10	10	6	12	1	3

Determine a sequence of these jobs that will minimise the total elapsed time T. Also find T and idle time for machines M_1 and M_2.

[IAS 1988, BESU(MSc) 2010]

Solution: Using the procedure given above: $\min\{M_{1j}, M_{2j}\} = 1$ corresponds to M_{26} (Machine 2 Job J_6). Do J_6 last

						J_6.

The reduced set of processing times becomes:

Job :	J_1	J_2	J_3	J_4	J_5	J_7
M_1	3	12	15	6	10	9
M_2	8	10	10	6	12	3

$\min\{M_{1j}, M_{2j}\} = 3$ corresponds to M_{11} and M_{27}. According to rules, J_1 is scheduled first and J_7 next to J_6 as shown below

J_1					J_7	J_6

Next reduced set of processing times becomes:

Job:	J_2	J_3	J_4	J_5
M_1	12	15	6	10
M_2	10	10	6	12

$\min\{M_{1j}, M_{2j}\} = 6$ for both M_{14} and M_{24}. We may choose arbitrarily as follows:

J_1	J_4				J_7	J_6

J_1				J_4	J_7	J_6

Further, reduced set of processing times:

Job:	J_2	J_3	J_5
M_1	12	15	10
M_2	10	10	12

$\min\{M_{1j}, M_{2j}\} = 10$ for M_{15}, M_{22} and M_{23}. According to rule stated earlier the *optimal sequences* are shown below.

J_1	J_4	J_5	J_3	J_2	J_7	J_6

J_1	J_5	J_2	J_3	J_4	J_7	J_6

Now, we can calculate the different times corresponding to either of the optimal sequences. The elapsed time and idle times for machines M_1 and M_2 will be same for either sequence. Let us calculate by taking first optimal sequence schedule (Reader may check by considering second optimal sequence schedule).

	M_1		M_2		
Job	Time-in	Time-out	Time-in	Time-out	I_{M_2}
J_1	0	3	3	11	3
J_4	3	9	11	17	0
J_5	9	19	19	31	2
J_3	19	34	34	44	3
J_2	34	46	46	56	2
J_7	46	55	56	59	0
J_6	55	66	66	67	7

T = Minimum elapsed time = 67 hours.

I_{M_1} = Idle time for machine $M_1 = 67 - 66 = 1$ hour.

I_{M_2} = Idle time for machine $M_2 = 17$ hours.

Mathematical Illustration

Let there be n jobs $\langle J_1, J_2, \ldots, J_n \rangle$ processed through two machines $\langle M_1, M_2 \rangle$ in the order M_1, M_2. A job is assigned to machine M_1 first and after it has been completely processed on M_1, then it is assigned to M_2. If the machine M_2 is not free at that moment for processing the same job, then the job has to wait in a waiting line for its turn on machine M_2 so that passing is not allowed. As before, M_{ij} be the time required for processing ith job on the jth machine ($i = 1, 2$ and $j = 1, 2, \ldots, n$). Since passing is not allowed, machine M_1 will be busy in processing all the n jobs one by one while machine M_2 may remain *idle* after completion of one job and before starting of another job. Therefore, our obvious objective is to minimise the idle time of M_2. Let I_{2j} ($j = 1, 2, \ldots, n$) be the time for which machine M_2 remains idle after finishing $(j-1)$th job and before starting ith job. Hence, the total elapsed time T is given by $T = \sum_{j=1}^{n} M_{2j} + \sum_{j=1}^{n} I_{2j}$, where some of I_{2j} ($j = 1, 2, \ldots, n$) may be zero (as shown in Ex. 7.4.2).

The problem now is to minimise T but as $\sum_{j=1}^{n} M_{2j}$ represent the total time for which M_2 has to work and hence it is fixed, so we have to minimise $\sum_{j=1}^{n} I_{2j}$.

A very convenient method for a sequence of jobs to minimise $\sum_{j=1}^{n} I_{2j}$ is well explained by GNATT CHART described below.

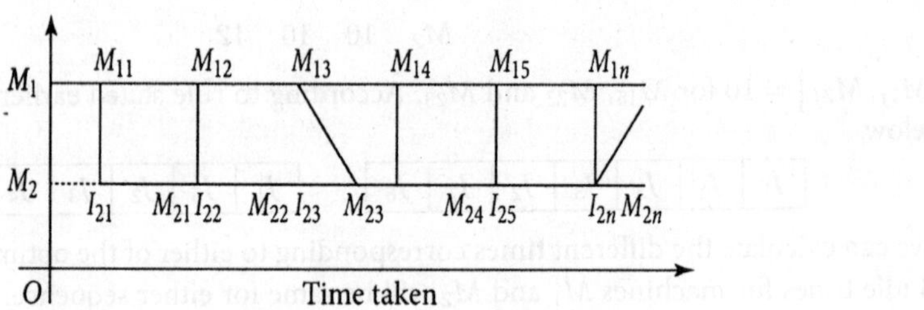

From chart: $I_{21} = M_{11}$.

$I_{22} = M_{11} + M_{12} - I_{21} - M_{21} : M_{11} + M_{12} > I_{21} + M_{21}$

$= 0$ otherwise.

$\therefore\ I_{22} = \max\{M_{11} + M_{12} - I_{21} - M_{21}, 0\}$.

$I_{21} + I_{22} = \max\{M_{11} + M_{12} - M_{21}, M_{11}\}$ since $I_{21} = M_{11}$.

In general, $$D_n(S) = \sum_{j=1}^{n} I_{2j} = \max\left\{\left(\sum_{j=1}^{n-1} M_{1j} - \sum_{j=1}^{n-1} M_{2j}\right), \left(\sum_{j=1}^{n-1} M_{1j} - \sum_{j=1}^{n-2} M_{2j}\right), \ldots M_{11}\right\}.$$

Our actual problem is to find a sequence $\langle S^* \rangle$ for processing jobs $\langle j_1, j_2, \ldots, j_n \rangle$ so that $D_n(S^*) \le D_n(S)$ for all $\langle S \rangle$ other than $\langle S^* \rangle$ or in other words, we have to determine an *optimal sequence* so as to minimise $D_n(S)$. This can be achieved iteratively by a stepwise procedure mentioned earlier.

Example 7.4.3. *A book-binder has one printing machine M_1 and one binding machine M_2 and manuscripts of six different books $\langle B_1, B_2, B_3, B_4, B_5, B_6 \rangle$. The time required to perform the printing and binding operations for each book is shown below.*

Machines \ Books	B_1	B_2	B_3	B_4	B_5	B_6
M_1	30	120	50	20	90	110
M_2	80	100	90	60	30	10

Determine the optimal sequence and corresponding different optimal times (in hours).

[CU(MCA) 2005, BESU(MSc) 2006]

Solution: First find $\min\{M_{1j}, M_{2j}\} = M_{26} = 10$. Do B_6 last (Notre that order of work is M_1, M_2 as obviously manuscripts are subject to printing first and then binding)

					B_6

First reduced processing times:

Books:	B_1	B_2	B_3	B_4	B_5
M_1	30	120	50	20	90
M_2	80	100	90	60	30

$\min\{M_{1j}, M_{2j}\} = 20 = M_{14}$. Do B_4 first.

B_4					B_6

Second reduced processing times:

Books:	B_1	B_2	B_3	B_5
M_1	30	120	50	90
M_2	80	100	90	30

$\min\{M_{1j}, M_{2j}\} = 30$ corresponding to M_{11} as well as M_{25}. According to rule B_1 next to the first and B_5 next to the last:

B_4	B_1			B_5	B_6

Third reduced processing times:

Books	B_2	B_3
M_1	120	50
M_2	100	90

$\min\{M_{1j}, M_{2j}\} = 50$ corresponding to M_{13}. Therefore, the optimal sequence is

B_4	B_1	B_3	B_2	B_5	B_6

Calculation of times:

	M_1		M_2		
Books	Time-in	Time-out	Time-in	Time-out	I_{M_2}
B_4	0	20	20	80	20
B_1	20	50	80	160	0
B_3	50	100	160	250	0
B_2	100	220	250	350	0
B_5	220	310	350	380	0
B_6	310	420	420	430	40

T = Optimal involved time = 430 hours.

I_{M_1} = Idle time for machine $M_1 = 430 - 420 = 10$ hours.

I_{M_2} = Idle time for machine $M_2 = 60$ hours.

(C) *n*-Job 3-Machine Problem

Let there be n jobs $\langle J_1, J_2, \ldots, J_n \rangle$ each of which is to be processed through 3 machines $\langle M_1, M_2, M_3 \rangle$ in the order M_1, M_2; M_3. The iterative scheme for determining an *optimal sequence* of jobs are as follows:

Step 1. Find $\{\min M_{1j}, \max M_{2j}, \min M_{3j}\}$ for $j = 1, 2, \ldots, n$ and check whether $\min M_{1j} \geq \max M_{2j}$ or, $\min M_{3j} \geq \max M_{2j}$.

If no inequality is satisfied, the method fails. Otherwise, go to next step.

Step 2. Convert the 3-machine problem to 2-machine problem by introducing two arbitrary machines G and H such that

$$\left.\begin{array}{l} M_{Gj} = M_{1j} + M_{2j} \\ M_{Hj} = M_{2j} + M_{3j} \end{array}\right\} \forall\, j = 1, 2, \ldots, n.$$

Step 3. Determine the optimal sequence of n jobs on 2 machines G and H in the order G, H by the process described in (B) of this Sec. 7.4. Calculation of times are based on the original machines $\langle M_1, M_2, M_3 \rangle$ by considering the optimal sequence. Accordingly the idle times are calculated.

Example 7.4.4. *Solve the following sequencing problem (Given order M_1, M_2, M_3).*

Machines \ Jobs	A	B	C	D	E	F	G
M_1	3	8	7	4	9	8	7
M_2	4	3	2	5	1	4	3
M_3	6	7	5	11	5	6	12

Solution: The problem becomes a 7-job and 3-machine problem.

$\min M_{1j} = 3$, $\max M_{2j} = 5$ and $\min M_{3j} = 5$.

The condition $\min M_{3j} = \max M_{2j}$ is satisfied. So we consider two machines P and Q such that

$$\left.\begin{array}{l} M_{Pj} = M_{1j} + M_{2j} \\ M_{Qj} = M_{2j} + M_{3j} \end{array}\right\} \forall\, j = 1, 2, \ldots, 7.$$

The modified problem becomes:

Jobs	A	B	C	D	E	F	G
P	7	11	9	9	10	12	10
Q	10	10	7	16	6	10	15

$\min\{M_{Pj}, M_{Qj}\} = 5 \langle$corresponds to $M_{QE}\rangle$; do job E last.

						E

First reduced processing times:

Jobs	A	B	C	D	E	F	G
P	7	11	9	9	10	12	10
Q	10	10	7	16	6	10	15

$\min\{M_{Pj}, M_{Qj}\} = 7$ for M_{PA} and M_{QC} so that job A is done first and job C next to last.

A				C	E

Second reduced processing times:

Jobs	B	D	F	G
P	11	9	12	10
Q	10	16	10	15

$\min\{M_{Pj}, M_{Qj}\} = 9$ for M_{PD}. Do job D next to the first.

A	D			C	E

Third reduced processing times:

Jobs	B	F	G
P	11	12	10
Q	10	10	15

$\min\{M_{Pj}, M_{Qj}\} = 10$ for M_{PG}, M_{QB} and M_{QF}.
→ from same ←
machine Q

According to rules, we have the following optimal sequence of jobs.

A	D	G	F	B	C	E

Calculation of times:

	M_1		M_2			M_3		
Jobs	Time-in	Time-out	Time-in	Time-out	I_{M_2}	Time-in	Time-out	I_{M_3}
A	0	3	3	7	3	7	13	7
D	3	7	7	12	0	13	24	0
G	7	14	14	17	2	24	36	0
F	14	22	22	26	5	36	42	0
B	22	30	30	33	4	42	49	0
C	30	37	37	39	4	49	54	0
E	37	46	46	47	7	54	59	0

T = Minimum elapsed time = 59 hours.

I_{M_1} = Idle time for machine $M_1 = 59 - 46 = 13$ hours.

I_{M_2} = Idle time for machine $M_2 = 25 + (59 - 47) = 37$ hours.

I_{M_3} = Idle time for machine $M_3 = 7$ hours.

Example 7.4.5. *There are five jobs each of which is to be processed through three machines A, B, C in the order A, B, C. Processing times in hours are:*

Jobs	A	B	C
1	3	4	7
2	8	5	9
3	7	1	5
4	5	2	6
5	4	3	10

Determine all possible optimum sequences and minimum elapsed time. Also find the idle time for the three machines and waiting time for the jobs. [JNU(Comp) 2008, BESU(MSc) 1999]

Solution: Here, $\min M_{Aj} = 3$, $\max M_{Bj} = 5$ and $\min M_{Cj} = 5$. The condition is satisfied and the equivalent problem involving 5 jobs and two fictitious machines G and H.

Jobs	G	H
1	7	11
2	13	14
3	8	6
4	7	8
5	7	13

Examining columns G and H, we find that the smallest value is 6 hours under column H for job 3. Thus, we schedule job 3 last. Further, examining the columns G and H we find the next minimum is 7 hours under column G for jobs 1, 4 and 5. Since all the values are in the same column G we schedule job 4 first since it has lowest entry 8 in column H, job 1 next as it has next entry 11 in column H and job 5 next to job 1 since it has higher entry 13 in column H (We can also select arbitrarily as mentioned in the discussion); job 2 is now scheduled next to job 3 and the optimal sequence becomes

4	1	5	2	3

Obviously, the other optimal sequences, because of ties will be:

4	1	5	2	3

1	4	5	2	3

1	5	4	2	3

5	1	4	2	3

5	4	1	2	3

The minimum elapsed time can be calculated corresponding to any optimal sequence. Consider the first optimal sequence and calculate times as follows:

	A		B		C	
Jobs	Time-in	Time-out	Time-in	Time-out	Time-in	Time-out
4	0	5	5	7	7	13
1	5	8	8	12	13	20
5	8	12	12	15	20	30
2	12	20	20	25	30	39
3	20	27	27	28	39	44

T = Minimum elapsed time = 44 hours.

I_A = Idle time for $A = 44-27 = 17$ hours.

I_B = Idle time for $B = 5 + 1 + 5 + 2 + (44-28) = 29$ hours.

I_C = Idle time for $C = 7$ hours.

Minimum elapsed time and idle times for machine *A, B* and *C* will be same for other optimal sequences.

There is no waiting of jobs between machines *A* and *B*, the jobs have to wait for loading on machine *C* for $(1 + 5 + 5 + 11) = 22$ hours resulting in some extra in-process inventory cost.

(D) *n* Jobs *m* Machines Problem

This is a general sequencing problem, when there are *n* jobs $\langle J_1, J_2, \ldots, J_n \rangle$ each of which is to be processed through *m* machines $\langle M_1, M_2, \ldots, M_m \rangle$. The iterative procedure for obtaining the optimal sequence is as follows.

Step 1. Find $\min M_{1j}, \min M_{mj}$ for $j = 1,2,\ldots,n$ and max of each $M_{2j}, M_{3j}, \ldots, M_{m-1j}$.

Check whethermin $M_{1j} \geq \max M_{ij}$ for $i = 2,3,\ldots,m-1$

or, $\min M_{mj} \geq \max M_{ij}$ for $i = 2,3,\ldots,m-1$

If the inequalities are not satisfied, then the method fails, otherwise go to next step.

Step 2. Convert *m* machines problem into 2 machines problem by introducing two fictitious machines *G* and *H* such that

$$M_{Gi} = \sum_{\mu=1}^{m-1} M_{\mu i} \text{ and } M_{Hi} = \sum_{\nu=1}^{m-1} M_{\nu i}.$$

Step 3. Determine the optimal sequence of *n* jobs through 2 machines *G* and *H* and calculate the times similarly as before.

Remark. In *Step* 2, if it happens that $M_{2j} + M_{3j} + \cdots + M_{n-1j}$ is a fixed constant, then determine the optimal sequence for *n* jobs through 2 machines by using M_1 and M_m and taking order as M_1, M_m provided *Step* 1 is strictly followed by original problem.

Example 7.4.6. *Solve the following 4 jobs 6 machines sequencing problem.*

Jobs	M_1	M_2	M_3	M_4	M_5	M_6
A	18	8	7	2	10	25
B	17	6	9	6	8	19
C	11	5	8	5	7	15
D	20	5	3	4	8	12

Solution: $\min M_{1j} = 11$, $\min M_{6j} = 12$, $\max\left(M_{2j}, M_{3j}, M_{4j}, M_{5j}\right) = (8,9,6,10)$.

$\min M_{1j} > \max M_{1j},\ i = 2,3,4,5$

also $\min M_{6j} > \max M_{1j},\ i = 2,3,4,6$.

The condition is satisfied and the equivalent problem involving 6 jobs and 2 machines *G* and *H*, where

$$M_{Gj} = \sum_{\mu=1}^{5} M_{G\mu} \text{ and } M_{Hj} = \sum_{\nu=1}^{6} M_{A\mu},$$

is given by

	Machines	
Jobs	G	H
A	45	52
B	46	48
C	36	40
D	39	31

$\min\{M_{Gj}, M_{Hj}\} = 31$ for job *D* under machine *H*, we schedule job *D* last. Next $\min\{M_{Gj}, M_{Hj}\} = 36$ for job *C* under machine *G*; so do job *C* first. Again, $\min\{M_{Gj}, M_{Hj}\} = 45$, which is under machine *G*, job *A*. We schedule job *A* next to first and finally job *B* next to job *A*. Thus, we get the following optimal sequence.

C	A	B	D

Calculation of times: (T_i = time-in and T_o = time-out).

	M_1		M_2		M_3		M_4		M_5		M_6	
Jobs	T_i	T_O	T_i	T_O	T_i	T_O	T_i	T_O	T_i	T_O	T_i	T_O
C	0	11	11	16	16	24	24	29	29	26	36	51
A	11	29	29	37	27	44	44	46	46	56	56	81
B	29	46	46	52	52	61	61	67	67	75	81	100
D	46	66	66	70	70	73	73	77	77	85	100	112

T = Total elapsed time = 112 hours.

I_{M_1} = Idle time for $M_1 = 112-66 = 46$ hours.

I_{M_2} = Idle time for $M_2 = (11+13+9+14)+(112-70) = 89$ hours.

I_{M_3} = Idle time for $M_3 = (16+13+8+9)+(112-73) = 85$ hours.

I_{M_4} = Idle time for $M_4 = (24+15+15+6)+(112-77) = 95$ hours.

I_{M_5} = Idle time for $M_5 = (29+10+11+2)+(112-85) = 79$ hours.

I_{M_6} = Idle time for $M_6 = (36+5+0+0) = 41$ hours.

Example 7.4.7. *This is an example of a 5 jobs $\langle J_1, J_2, J_3, J_4, J_5\rangle$ and 4 machines $\langle M_1, M_2, M_3, M_4\rangle$ sequencing problem.*

	J_1	J_2	J_3	J_4	J_5
M_1	10	12	8	15	16
M_2	3	2	4	1	5
M_3	5	6	4	7	3
M_4	14	7	12	8	10

This particular problem shows that: $\min M_{1j} \geq \max M_{ij},\ i = 2,3$

$\min M_{4j} \geq \max M_{ij},\ i = 2,3$

and at the same time $M_{2j} + M_{3j} = 8$ (a constant quantity). This type of sequencing problem will be solved by considering M_1 and M_4 as two machines.

Here $\min\{M_{1j}, M_{4j}\} = 7$ for M_{42}, do J_2 last

$= 8$ for M_{13} and M_{44}, schedule J_3 first and J_4 next to the last

$= 10$ for M_{11} and M_{45}.

The optimum sequence becomes: | J_3 | J_1 | J_5 | J_4 | J_2 |.

7.5 EXERCISE 7

1. In a (3×3) transportation problem let x_{ij} be the amount shipped from source i to destination j and c_{ij}, the corresponding per unit transportation cost. The supplies at sources 1, 2 and 3 are 15, 30 and 85 units and the demands at destinations 1, 2 and 3 are 20, 30 and 80 units. Assuming that the starting solution obtained by the north-west corner method gives the optimal basic solution to the problem, let the associated values of the multipliers for sources 1, 2 and 3 be 2, 3 and 5 and those of destinations 1, 2 and 3 be 2, 5 and 10.
   (a) Find the total optimal transportation cost.
   (b) What are the smallest values of c_{ij} for the non-basic variables that will keep the solution optimal?

2. Solve the adjoining transportation model by using north-west corner method and Volgel's approximation method (VAM) to obtain the starting solution. Compare the computations:

1	2	6	7
0	4	2	12
3	1	5	11
10	10	10	

3. Find the starting solution in the adjoining transportation problem by the (a) North-west corner method (b) Matrix-minima method (c) VAM method. Obtain the optimal solution by using the best starting solution.

10	20	5	7	10
13	9	12	8	20
4	15	7	19	30
14	7	1	0	40
3	12	5	19	50
60	60	20	10	

4. For the balanced transportation problem, prove that set of optimal solutions is unaffected if the cost matrix (c_{ij}) is replaced by the cost matrix (b_{ij}), where $b_{ij} = c_{ij} + p_i + q_j$ and p_i, q_j are real numbers. What would happen to the set of optimum solutions if the matrix (c_{ij}) is replaced by the cost matrix (αc_{ij}), where α is a given positive number?

5. In the balanced transportation problem, if all a_i, b_j are integers and if b_j is replaced by $b_j + \frac{1}{n}$ for all $j = 1, 2, \ldots, n$ and a_m by $a_m + 1$, then prove that the new balanced transportation problem is never degenerate for a basic feasible solution.

6. Find the optimal (minimum) solution of the following transportation problem:

(a)

	D_1	D_2	D_3	D_4	D_5	a_i
O_1	3	4	6	8	8	20
O_2	2	10	0	5	8	30
O_3	7	11	20	40	3	15
O_4	1	0	9	14	16	13
b_j	40	6	8	18	6	

[KU(MSc) 1991, BESU(BE) 2000]

(b)

	D_1	D_2	D_3	D_4	a_i
O_1	5	3	6	4	30
O_2	3	4	7	8	15
O_3	9	6	5	8	15
b_j	10	25	18	7	

[JU(MSc) 1983, CU(H) 1992]

(c)

	a	b	c	d	e	f	a_i
A	5	3	7	3	8	5	3
B	5	6	12	5	7	11	4
C	2	1	3	4	8	2	2
D	9	6	10	5	10	9	8
b_j	3	3	6	2	1	2	

[CU(H) 2001, MCA(WBUT) 2005]

(d)

	D_1	D_2	D_3	a_i
O_1	0	2	1	5
O_2	2	1	5	10
O_3	2	4	3	5
b_j	5	5	10	

[CU(H) 1993]

(e)

	D_1	D_2	D_3	D_4	D_5	D_6	a_i
O_1	1	2	1	4	5	2	30
O_2	3	3	2	1	4	3	50
O_3	4	2	5	9	6	2	75
O_4	3	1	7	3	4	6	20
b_j	20	40	30	10	50	25	

[Delhi(MSc) 1968, JNU(Comp Sc) 2001]

(f)

	D_1	D_2	D_3	D_4	a_i
O_1	8	10	7	6	50
O_2	12	9	4	7	40
O_3	9	11	10	8	30
b_j	25	32	40	33	

[IGNOU(MBA) Dec 2006, Delhi(MSc) 1975]

(g)

	D_1	D_2	D_3	D_4	D_5	D_6	a_i
O_1	9	12	9	6	9	10	5
O_2	7	3	7	7	5	5	6
O_3	6	5	9	11	3	11	2
O_4	6	8	11	2	2	10	9
b_j	4	4	6	2	4	2	

[IAS(Main) 1995, Meerut(MSc) 2000, 1995]

(h)

	D_1	D_2	D_3	D_4	D_5	a_i
S_1	4	7	3	8	2	4
S_2	1	4	7	3	8	7
S_3	7	2	4	7	7	9
S_4	4	7	2	4	7	2
b_j	8	3	7	2	2	

(i)

	D_1	D_2	D_3	D_4	D_5	a_i
S_1	2	11	10	3	7	4
S_2	1	4	7	2	1	8
S_3	3	9	4	8	12	9
b_j	3	3	4	5	6	

7. Is $x_{13} = 50, x_{14} = 20, x_{21} = 55, x_{31} = 30, x_{32} = 35, x_{34} = 25$ an optimal solution of the adjoining transportation problem?
If not, modify it to obtain a better solution.

[IISc (1991)]

	D_1	D_2	D_3	D_4	a_i
S_1	6	1	9	3	70
S_2	11	5	2	8	55
S_3	10	12	4	7	90
b_j	85	35	50	45	

8. Find the minimum cost of the adjoining unbalanced transportation problem.

	D_1	D_2	D_3	a_i
O_1	4	3	2	10
O_2	1	5	0	13
O_3	3	8	6	12
b_j	8	5	4	

[CU(H) 1982]

9. Solve the adjoining unbalanced transportation problem.

	D_1	D_2	D_3	D_4	D_5	a_i
O_1	1	3	0	5	1	20
O_2	−6	5	10	3	−5	34
O_3	2	−4	3	2	0	11
b_j	10	8	15	12	8	

10. Define an assignment problem. Let $C = (c_{ij})$ and $B = (b_{ij})$ be two $n \times n$ matrices, where $b_{ij} = c_{ij} - d_i - e_j$, d_i, e_j are arbitrary constants. Then show that an optimal solution to the assignment problem with the cost matrix B is also an optimal solution to the assignment problem with the cost matrix C, and vice versa.

11. *If P is a non-empty subset of the points of matrix* $C = (c_{ij})$, *then the maximum number of independent points that can be selected in P is equal to the minimum number of lines covering all the elements of P.* — Prove it.

12. There are four men and each of them has to perform one of the four tasks. The men differ in their efficiency and ability to complete the tasks. The estimate of the time required by each person to complete each task as shown in the adjoining. Assign a task to each man so as to *minimise the total time* spent on the four assignments.

		Man			
		A	B	C	D
Task	a	18	26	17	11
	b	14	28	14	26
	c	38	19	18	15
	d	19	26	24	10

13. A machine shop purchased a drilling machine and two lathes of different capacities. The positioning of the machines among four possible locations on the shop-floor is important from the standpoint of materials handling. Given the *cost estimate per unit of time* of materials handling as shown in the adjoining table. Determine the optimal location of the three machines.

[CU(H) 2005, MCA(WBUT) 2009]

		Location			
		1	2	3	4
Machine	L_1	12	9	12	9
	D	15	unsuitable	13	20
	L_2	4	8	10	6

14. There are five pumps available for developing five wells. The efficiency of each pump in producing the maximum yield in each well is shown in the adjoining table. In what way should the pumps be assigned so as to *maximise* the overall efficiency? [IAS(Main) 1993]

		Efficiency well				
		W_1	W_2	W_3	W_4	W_5
Pump	P_1	45	40	65	30	55
	P_2	50	30	25	60	30
	P_3	25	20	15	20	40
	P_4	35	25	30	25	20
	P_5	80	60	60	70	50

15. There are four engineers available for designing four projects. Engineer E_1 is not competent to design project P_3. Given the time estimate required by each engineer to design a given project in the adjoining table. Find an assignment which *minimise the total time.*

		Project			
		P_1	P_2	P_3	P_4
Engineer	E_1	10	3	unsuitable	8
	E_2	4	13	1	5
	E_3	3	7	2	10
	E_4	8	6	1	9

16. A construction company has to move four large cranes from old construction site to new construction site. The distance in kilometres between the old and new locations are as given in the adjoining table. The crane at O_3 cannot be used at N_2 but all the cranes can work equally well at any of the other new sites. Determine a plan for moving the cranes that will *minimise* the total distance involved in the move.

		New cons. sites			
		N_1	N_2	N_3	N_4
Old cons. sites	O_1	15	20	13	40
	O_2	38	42	15	20
	O_3	25	17	30	18
	O_4	18	30	40	35

17. (a) Consider the problem of assigning four operations to four machines. The assignment costs in rupees are given below. Operator O_1 cannot be assigned to machine M_3. Also O_3 cannot be assigned to M_4. Find the optimal assignment.

		Machine			
		M_1	M_2	M_3	M_4
Operator	O_1	5	5	–	2
	O_2	7	4	2	3
	O_3	9	3	5	–
	O_4	7	2	6	7

(b) Suppose that in problem (a) a fifth machine M_5 is made available, its respective assignment costs to the four operators are 2, 1, 2 and 8. The new machine M_5 replaces an existing one if the replacement can be justified economically. Reformulate the problem as an assignment model and find the optimal solution.

18. Solve the following assignment models

(a)

	A	B	C	D	E
a	3	8	2	10	3
b	8	7	2	9	7
c	6	4	2	7	5
d	8	4	2	3	5
e	9	10	6	9	10

(b)

	I	II	III	IV	V
1	3	9	2	3	7
2	6	1	5	6	6
3	9	1	7	10	3
4	2	5	4	2	1
5	9	6	2	4	6

[CU(H) 1987, CU(P) 2000]

(c)

	a	b	c	d
1	18	26	17	11
2	13	28	14	26
3	38	19	18	15
4	19	26	24	10

[CU(H) 1987, 2002]

(d)

	I	II	III	IV	V
A	1	3	2	3	6
B	2	4	3	1	5
C	5	6	3	4	6
D	3	1	4	2	2
E	1	5	6	5	4

19. Find the minimum cost for the 5×5 assign- ment problem whose cost coefficients are as given in adjoining table.

[Roorkee(ME) 1977, BESU(BE) 2004, 2006]

	a	b	c	d	e
1	−2	−4	−8	−6	−1
2	0	−9	−5	−5	−4
3	−3	−8	−9	−2	−6
4	−4	−3	−1	0	−3
5	−9	−5	−8	−9	−5

20. Assign four trucks 1, 2, 3, 4 to vacant spaces 7, 8, 9, 10, 11 and 12 so that the distance travelled is minimised. The matrix adjoining shows the distance. [ISI(OR) 1992, KU(MSc) 2001]

	1	2	3	4
7	4	7	3	7
8	8	2	5	5
9	4	9	6	9
10	7	5	4	8
11	6	3	5	4
12	6	8	7	3

21. What is the travelling salesman problem? Which situations can be treated as the travelling salesman problem? How does its solution differ from the solution of the assignment problem?

22. A machine operator processes five types of items on his machine each week and must choose a sequence for them. The set-up cost per change depends on the items at present on the machine and the set-up to be made, according to adjoining table.

If he processes each type of item once and only once each week, how should he sequence the items on this machine?

[IAS(Main) 1991, CU(MSc Appl) 1988]

From item \ To item	A	B	C	D
A	∞	4	7	3
B	4	∞	6	3
C	7	6	∞	7
D	3	3	7	∞

23. Solve the adjoining travelling salesman problem so as to minimise the cost per cycle.

[IIT(MTech) 1980, MCA(WBUT) 2004]

From city \ To city	C_1	C_2	C_3	C_4	C_5
C_1	∞	10	25	25	10
C_2	1	∞	10	15	2
C_3	8	9	∞	20	10
C_4	14	10	24	∞	15
C_5	10	8	25	27	∞

24. A travelling salesman has planned to visit five cities. He would like to start from a particular city, visit each city only once and return to starting city. The travelling cost in rupees is given in the table adjoining. Find the least cost route.

[MCA(IGNOU) 2001, CU(MSc Appl) 1986]

From \ To	A	B	C	D	E
A	∞	7	5	3	5
B	7	∞	8	4	3
C	3	8	∞	6	2
D	3	4	6	∞	2
E	5	3	2	2	∞

25. Find the least cost route for the following travelling salesman problem.

		To city						
		C_1	C_2	C_3	C_4	C_5	C_6	C_7
From city	C_1	∞	8	14	8	6	10	3
	C_2	8	∞	12	7	6	5	5
	C_3	10	9	∞	13	5	13	10
	C_4	7	6	13	∞	7	10	8
	C_5	7	4	9	10	∞	6	9
	C_6	8	5	13	7	6	∞	4
	C_7	4	5	11	9	6	5	∞

26. Solve the travelling salesman problem given by the following data: $c_{12}=20$, $c_{13}=4$, $c_{14}=10$, $c_{23}=6$, $c_{34}=6$, $c_{25}=10$, $c_{35}=6$ and $c_{45}=20$, where $c_{ij}=c_{ji}$ and there is no route between cities i and j if a value of c_{ij} be not shown above.

27. (a) Explain the following terms in the context of sequencing problems: (i) Total elapsed time and idle time, (ii) Process order and (iii) No passing rule.
(b) Write down the computational procedure to be followed for obtaining the optimal sequence in n jobs through m machines sequencing problem, state the assumptions made in sequencing.

28. A company has six jobs on hand. All the jobs have to go through 2 machines M_1 and M_2. The time required for the jobs on each machines, in hours, is given adjoining. Find the optimal sequence and the minimum elapsed time.

[CU(MSc Appl.) 1985]

		Job					
		A	B	C	D	E	F
Macine	M_1	1	4	6	3	5	2
	M_2	3	6	8	8	1	5

29. Five jobs are performed, first on machine X and then on machine Y. The time taken in hours by each job on each machine is given adjoining. Determine the optimum sequence of jobs that minimises the total elapsed time to complete the jobs. Also compute the minimum time.

[JNU(Comp Sc) 1982, BESU(MSc) 2002]

		Job				
		A	B	C	D	E
Macine	X	12	4	20	14	22
	Y	6	14	16	18	10

30. Given the adjoining data:
Order of processing job ACB and sequence suggested jobs $J_5 \longrightarrow J_3 \longrightarrow J_6 \longrightarrow J_2 \longrightarrow J_1 \longrightarrow J_4$.
(a) Determine the total elapsed time for the sequence suggested.
(b) Is the given sequence optimal?
(c) If your answer to (b) is negative, determine optimal sequence and total elapsed time associated with it.

[BESU(MSc) 2007, MCA(IGNOU) 2005]

		Job					
		J_1	J_2	J_3	J_4	J_5	J_6
Machine	A	12	10	9	14	7	9
	B	7	6	6	5	4	4
	C	6	5	6	4	2	4

31. We have five jobs, each of which must go through A, B and C in the order A, B, C. Processing times in hours are given in the adjoining table. Obtain the optimal sequence.

Machine \ Job	1	2	3	4	5
A	8	10	6	7	11
B	5	6	2	3	4
C	4	9	8	6	5

32. Find the sequence for the following 8 jobs that will minimise the total elapsed time for the completion of all jobs. Each job is processed in the order C, A, B. The entries give the time in hours on the machines.

Machine \ Job	J_1	J_2	J_3	J_4	J_5	J_6	J_7	J_8
A	4	6	7	4	5	3	6	2
B	8	10	7	8	11	8	9	13
C	5	6	2	3	4	9	15	11

33. Four jobs 1, 2, 3, 4 are to be processed on each of the five machines A, B, C, D and E in the order ABCDE. Find the total minimum elapsed time if no passing of jobs is permitted.

[BESU(MSc) 2008, CU(MSc Appl) 1995]

Job \ Machine	A	B	C	D	E
1	7	5	2	3	9
2	6	6	4	5	10
3	5	4	5	6	8
4	8	3	3	2	6

34. Solve the adjoining sequencing problem giving an optimal solution when no passing is allowed.

Machine \ Job	J_1	J_2	J_3	J_4	J_5
M_1	14	7	12	8	10
M_2	5	6	4	7	3
M_3	3	2	4	1	5
M_4	10	12	8	15	16

35. Six jobs $\langle J_1, J_2, \ldots, J_6\rangle$ are required to be processed on four machines $\langle M_1, M_2, M_3, M_4\rangle$ in that order. Using the processing time given in adjoining table, determine the optimal sequence of the job performance. [BESU(MSc) 2009, Roorke(ME) 1997]

Job \ Machine	M_1	M_2	M_3	M_4
J_1	12	6	6	8
J_2	8	3	6	12
J_3	13	4	6	9
J_4	9	2	4	14
J_5	10	6	7	12
J_6	12	7	2	10

36. Solve the adjoining sequencing problem giving an optimal solution, if passing is not allowed.

Jobs \ Machines	M_1	M_2	M_3	M_4
A	13	8	7	14
B	12	6	8	19
C	9	7	8	15
D	8	5	6	15

37. Processing times and due dates for six jobs waiting to be processed at a work station are given in the adjoining table. Determine the sequence of jobs, average flow time, average days late and average number of jobs at the work station by using SPTR method.

Job	Processing time (days)	Due date (days)
A	4	14
B	16	32
C	8	8
D	20	34
E	10	30
F	18	30

ANSWERS

1. (a) $c_{11}=0, c_{21}=5, c_{22}=8, c_{32}=10, c_{33}=15$; (b) $c_{12}\geq 3, c_{13}\geq 8, c_{23}\geq 13, c_{31}\geq 7$.

2. North-west corner: $x_{11}=7, x_{21}=3, x_{22}=9, x_{32}=1, x_{33}=10, Z=94$

   VAM: $x_{11}=7, x_{21}=2, x_{23}=10, x_{31}=1, x_{32}=10, Z=40$

3. VAM has the best starting solution and yields the optimum in three iterations: $x_{13}=10$, $x_{22}=20$, $x_{31}=30$, $x_{42}=30$, $x_{44}=10$, $x_{51}=30$, $x_{52}=10$, $x_{53}=10$, $z=820$.

6. (a) $x_{11}=20$, $x_{21}=4$, $x_{23}=8$, $x_{24}=18$, $x_{31}=9$, $x_{35}=6$, $x_{41}=7$, $x_{42}=6$, $Z_{\min}=246$.

   (b) $x_{12}=23$, $x_{14}=7$, $x_{21}=10$, $x_{22}=2$, $x_{23}=3$, $x_{33}=15$, $Z_{\min}=231$.

   (c) $x_{12}=1$, $x_{16}=2$, $x_{21}=3$, $x_{25}=1$, $x_{33}=2$, $x_{42}=2$, $x_{43}=4$, $x_{44}=2$, $Z_{\min}=103$.

   (d) $x_{13}=x_{21}=x_{22}=x_{33}=5, Z_{\min}=35$.

   (e) $x_{11}=20$, $x_{13}=10$, $x_{23}=20$, $x_{24}=10$, $x_{25}=20$, $x_{32}=40$, $x_{35}=10$, $x_{36}=25$, $x_{45}=20$, $Z_{\min}=440$.

   (f) $x_{11}=25$, $x_{12}=2$, $x_{14}=23$, $x_{23}=40$, $x_{32}=30$, $Z_{\min}=848$.

   (g) $x_{13}=5$, $x_{22}=4$, $x_{26}=2$, $x_{31}=1$, $x_{33}=1$, $x_{41}=3$, $x_{44}=2$, $x_{45}=4$, $Z_{\min}=112$.

   (h) $x_{11}=1$, $x_{13}=1$, $x_{15}=2$, $x_{21}=7$, $x_{32}=3$, $x_{33}=6$, $x_{44}=2$, $Z_{\min}=56$.

   (i) $x_{11}=3$, $x_{12}=1$, $x_{22}=2$, $x_{23}=4$, $x_{24}=2$, $x_{34}=3$, $x_{35}=6$, $Z_{\min}=153$.

7. $x_{12}=30$, $x_{14}=40$, $x_{22}=5$, $x_{23}=50$, $x_{31}=85$, $x_{34}=5$, $Z_{\min}=1160$.

8. Minimum cost = 23.

9. $x_{13}=5$, $x_{14}=15$, $x_{21}=22$, $x_{24}=4$, $x_{25}=8$, $x_{32}=8$, $x_{34}=3$.

12. $A\longrightarrow b$, $B\longrightarrow c$, $C\longrightarrow a$, $D\longrightarrow d$, Minimum time =59.

13. $L_1\longrightarrow 2$, $D\longrightarrow 3$, $L_2\longrightarrow 1$ or, $L_1\longrightarrow 4$, $D\longrightarrow 3$, $L_2\longrightarrow 1$.

14. $P_1\longrightarrow W_3$, $P_2\longrightarrow W_4$, $P_3\longrightarrow W_5$, $P_4\longrightarrow W_2$, $P_5\longrightarrow W_1$.

15. $E_1\longrightarrow P_2$, $E_2\longrightarrow P_4$, $E_3\longrightarrow P_1$, $E_4\longrightarrow P_3$.

16. Move cranes from old sites O_1, O_2, O_3 and O_4 to new sites N_2, N_3, N_4 and N_1 respectively.

17. (a) $O_1\longrightarrow M_4$, $O_2\longrightarrow M_3$, $O_3\longrightarrow M_2$, $O_4\longrightarrow M_1$; (b) M_5 replaces M_1.

18. (a) $a\longrightarrow E$, $b\longrightarrow C$, $c\longrightarrow B$, $d\longrightarrow D$, $c\longrightarrow A$.

    (b) $1\longrightarrow$ I, $2\longrightarrow$ II, $3\longrightarrow$ V, $4\longrightarrow$ IV, $5\longrightarrow$ III.

(c) $1 \longrightarrow c, 2 \longrightarrow a, 3 \longrightarrow b, 4 \longrightarrow d$.

(d) $A \longrightarrow$ I, $B \longrightarrow$ IV, $c \longrightarrow$ III, $D \longrightarrow$ II, $E \longrightarrow$ V or, $A \longrightarrow$ II, $B \longrightarrow$ IV, $c \longrightarrow$ III, $D \longrightarrow$ V, $E \longrightarrow$ I.

19. $1 \longrightarrow c, 2 \longrightarrow b, 3 \longrightarrow e, 4 \longrightarrow a, 5 \longrightarrow d$.

20. $7 \longrightarrow 3, 8 \longrightarrow 2, 9 \longrightarrow 1, 12 \longrightarrow 4$.

22. $A \longrightarrow D \longrightarrow B \longrightarrow C \longrightarrow A$

and Minimum cost =19

$A \longrightarrow C \longrightarrow B \longrightarrow D \longrightarrow A$.

23. $C_1 \longrightarrow C_5 \longrightarrow C_2 \longrightarrow C_3 \longrightarrow C_4 \longrightarrow C_1$ Minimum cost = 62.

24. $A \longrightarrow D \longrightarrow B \longrightarrow E \longrightarrow C \longrightarrow A$

or Least cost = ₹17

$A \longrightarrow C \longrightarrow E \longrightarrow B \longrightarrow D \longrightarrow A$.

25. $C_1 \longrightarrow C_7 \longrightarrow C_2 \longrightarrow C_6 \longrightarrow C_4 \longrightarrow C_3 \longrightarrow C_5 \longrightarrow C_1$, Least cost = 45.

26. $1 \longrightarrow 3 \longrightarrow 2 \longrightarrow 5 \longrightarrow 4 \longrightarrow 1$, Minimum cost = 49.

28. | A | F | D | B | C | E | Minimum time = 32 hours.

29. | B | D | C | E | A | Minimum time = 48 hours.

30. (a) 73 hours, (b) No, (c) Optimal sequence $J_1 \longrightarrow J_3 \longrightarrow J_2 \longrightarrow J_4 \longrightarrow J_6 \longrightarrow J_5$ and elapsed time = 67 hours.

31. | 3 | 2 | 4 | 1 | 5 | Minimum time = 51 hours.

32. | J_4 | J_5 | J_3 | J_1 | J_2 | J_8 | J_7 | J_6 | Minimum time = 61 hours.

33. | 1 | 3 | 2 | 4 | Minimum time = 51 units. Machines A, B, C, D and E remain idle for 25, 33, 37, 35 and 18 respectively in units of time.

34. | J_2 | J_4 | J_5 | J_1 | J_3 | Minimum elapsed time = 76 units. Idle time 25, 51, 61, 15 units respectively.

35. | J_4 | J_2 | J_5 | J_1 | J_3 | J_6 | or | J_4 | J_2 | J_5 | J_1 | J_6 | J_3 |

36. | D | C | B | A |. Minimum total elapsed time = 82 units. Idle time for M_1 = 40 units. Idle time for M_2 = 56 units. Idle time for M_3 = 53 units. Idle time for M_4 = 19 units.

37. | A | C | E | B | F | D |. Average flow time = 34.67 days. Average days late = 13 days. Average number of jobs at the work station = 2.74.

Chapter 8

Decision Theory and Games

8.1 INTRODUCTION

Everyday we make many decisions and occasionally we make an important decision that can have immediate or long term effects on our real life. A decision, in general, may be defined as the selection by the decision-maker of an act, considered to be best according to some predesigned standard from among the several options. The decision-making process is of significant importance in different branches of science and technology. In economics it is important to ensure optimal functioning of industrial organisation. In social science it is used to organise the function and development of social processes. In management it is necessary to determine the course of action for an organisation over a short or long period. In technology it is important in design and production of machine tools, equipment, etc. In all the cases, the main objective is to made rational decision. The rational decision is to be taken on the basis of some optimal principles.

The availability of partial or imperfect information about a problem leads to two types of decision-making situations: (i) *Decision under uncertainty* and (ii) *Decision under risk.*

8.2 STEPS IN DECISION THEORY APPROACH

Step 1. Determine the various alternative courses of action for choices from which the final decision is to be made.

Step 2. Identify the possible outcomes, called *states* of nature or *events* for the decision problem. Note that, events are beyond the control of decision-maker.

Step 3. Construct a *payoff matrix.* If there are m alternative courses of actions $A_1, A_2, \ldots, A_m$ and n states of nature $S_1, S_2, \ldots, S_n$, then payoff matrix will be represented as

States \ Action	A_1	A_2	...	A_m
S_1	a_{11}	a_{12}	...	a_{1m}
S_2	a_{21}	a_{22}	...	a_{2m}
⋮	⋮	⋮		⋮
S_n	a_{n1}	a_{n2}	...	a_{nm}

where a_{ij}, the payoff resulting from combination of ith state and jth action.

Step 4. The decision-maker will decide the criterion, which results in largest payoff. The criterion may be economic, quantitative or qualitative (for examples, profit, market share, etc.).

Example 8.2.1. *A firm manufactures three types of electric bulbs. The fixed and variable costs per bulb are given below.*

Bulbs	*Fixed cost (₹)*	*Variable cost (₹)*
B_1	25	10
B_2	35	8
B_3	55	5

The likely demand per day of the products is: *Poor demand* (D_p) 300
Moderate demand (D_M) 700
High demand (D_H) 1100.

Solution: Payoff = Sales revenue−Cost (Fixed + Variable).

$D_P B_1 = 300 \times 60 - 25 - 300 \times 10 = 14975$
$D_P B_2 = 300 \times 60 - 35 - 300 \times 8 = 15565$
$D_P B_2 = 300 \times 60 - 55 - 300 \times 5 = 16445$
$D_M B_1 = 700 \times 60 - 25 - 700 \times 10 = 34975$
$D_M B_2 = 700 \times 60 - 35 - 700 \times 8 = 36365$
$D_M B_2 = 700 \times 60 - 55 - 700 \times 5 = 38445$
$D_P B_1 = 1100 \times 60 - 25 - 1100 \times 10 = 54975$
$D_P B_2 = 1100 \times 60 - 35 - 1100 \times 8 = 57165$
$D_H B_2 = 1100 \times 60 - 55 - 1100 \times 5 = 60445$

Payoff Matrix

		Demand		
		D_P	D_M	D_H
Events	B_1	14975	34975	54975
	B_2	15565	35365	57165
	B_3	16445	38445	60445

8.3 DECISION UNDER UNCERTAINTY

This section introduce a number of criteria for making decision under uncertainty on the basis of the assumption that no probability distribution are available. The methods to be presented here includes.

(A) The Laplace Criterion, (B) The Minimax (Maximin) Criterion,
(C) The Savage Criterion, (D) The Hurwicz Criterion.

The informations utilised in making decision under uncertainty usually summarised in the form of a matrix with its row representing possible *actions* and columns representing possible future *states* of the system.

Associated with each action and each states there exists an outcome that evaluates the gain or loss resulting from taking such action when a given state occurs. Therefore, if a_i represent the ith action

$(i = 1,2,\dots,m)$ and θ_j represents the jth state $(j = 1,2,\dots,n)$, then $v\left(a_i,\theta_j\right)$ will represent the associated outcome. In general, $v\left(a_i,\theta_j\right)$ may be a continuous function of a_i and θ_j. Under discrete conditions, this information is arranged in a matrix as shown below.

$$\begin{array}{c|cccc|} & \theta_1 & \theta_2 & \dots & \theta_n \\ \hline a_1 & v(a_1,\theta_1) & v(a_1,\theta_2) & \dots & v(a_1,\theta_n) \\ a_2 & v(a_2,\theta_1) & v(a_2,\theta_2) & \dots & v(a_2,\theta_n) \\ \vdots & \vdots & \vdots & & \\ a_m & v(a_m,\theta_1) & v(a_m,\theta_2) & \dots & v(a_m,\theta_n) \\ \hline \end{array}$$

(A) Laplace Criterion

This is based on what is known as *Laplace principle of insufficient reason* in information system. Since the probability associated with the occurrence of $\theta_1,\theta_2,\dots,\theta_n$ are unknown, we do not have enough information to conclude that these probabilities will be different. For, if this is not so, we should be able to determine these probabilities, and the situation will no longer be a decision under uncertainty. Thus, because of insufficient reason to believe otherwise the states $\theta_1,\theta_2,\dots,\theta_n$ are equally likely to occur. When this conclusion is established, the problem is converted to a *decision under risk*, where one selects the action a_i, yielding the largest expected gain, that is one selects the action a_i^* corresponding to

$$\max_{\substack{a_i \\ i=1,2,\dots,n}} \left\{ \frac{1}{n}\sum_{j=1}^{n} v\left(a_i,\theta_j\right) \right\},$$

where $\frac{1}{n}$ is the probability that $\theta_j (j = 1,2,\dots,n)$ occurs.

Example 8.3.1. *A recreational facility must be decided on the level of supplies it must stock to meet the needs of its customers during one of the holidays. The exact number of customers are not known, but it is expected to be in one of four categories 200, 250, 300 or 350 customers. Four level of supplies are suggested with level i ideal if the number of customers falls in category i. Deviation from the ideal levels results in additional costs either because of stocking extra supplies needlessly or because of failing to supply as per demand. The table below provides these costs in thousand of dollars.*

		Customer category			
		θ_1	θ_2	θ_3	θ_4
	a_1	5	10	18	25
Supplies level	a_2	8	7	8	23
	a_3	21	18	12	21
	a_4	30	22	19	15

Obtain the solution by Laplace criteria.

Solution: The Laplace criteria assumes that θ_j $(j = 1,2,3,4)$ are equally likely to occur so that $P\left(\theta = \theta_j\right) = \frac{1}{4}\ \forall\, j = 1,2,3,4$ and the expected costs for the different actions:

$$E(a_1) = \tfrac{1}{4}(5+10+18+25) = 14.5$$

$$\boxed{E(a_2) = \tfrac{1}{4}(8+7+8+23) = 11.5} \leftarrow \text{Minimum}$$

$$E(a_3) = \tfrac{1}{4}(21+18+12+21) = 18.0$$

$$E(a_4) = \tfrac{1}{4}(30+22+19+15) = 21.5$$

Since the matrix is a cost payoff, by taking minimum the best level of inventory according to *Laplace criterion* is a_2^*.

(B) The Minimax (Maximin) Criterion

This is the most conservative criterion since it is based on making the best out of the worst possible conditions. If the outcome $v\left(a_i,\theta_j\right)$ represents loss, the decision-maker then for action $a_i (i=1,2,\ldots,m)$, the worst loss regardless of what θ_j $(j=1,2,\ldots,n)$ may be is $\max\limits_{\theta_j}\left\{v\left(a_i,\theta_j\right)\right\}$.

The *minimax* criterion then selects the action a_i associated with

$$\min_{a_i}\max_{\theta_j}\left\{v\left(a_i,\theta_j\right)\middle|\begin{array}{l}i=1,2,\ldots,m\\ j=1,2,\ldots,n\end{array}\right\}.$$

In a similar manner, if $v\left(a_i,\theta_j\right)$ represents gain, then *maximum* criterion select the action a_i for which

$$\max_{a_i}\min_{\theta_j}\left\{v\left(a_i,\theta_j\right)\middle|\begin{array}{l}i=1,2,\ldots,m\\ j=1,2,\ldots,n\end{array}\right\}.$$

Example 8.3.2. *Consider the same payoff of Ex. 8.3.1 and obtain the solution by minimax criterion.*

		Customer category			
		θ_1	θ_2	θ_3	θ_4
	a_1	5	10	18	25
Supplies	a_2	8	7	8	23
level	a_3	21	18	12	21
	a_4	30	22	19	15

Solution: Since $v\left(a_i,\theta_j\right)$ represents cost, we find solution by minimax criterion.

	θ_1	θ_2	θ_3	θ_4	$\max\limits_{\theta_j} v\left(a_i,\theta_j\right)$
a_1	5	10	18	25	25
a_2	8	7	8	23	23
a_3	21	18	12	21	21 $\leftarrow \min\limits_{a_i}\max\limits_{\theta_j} v\left(a_i,\theta_j\right)$
a_4	30	22	19	15	30

Therefore, the minimax strategy is action a_3^*.

(C) The Savage Criterion

The minimax criterion is extremely conservative to the extent that it may sometime lead to illogical conclusions. Consider the following loss payoff matrix.

	θ_1	θ_2	$\max\limits_{\theta_j} v\left(a_i,\theta_j\right)$
a_1	1100	90	1100
a_2	1000	1000	1000 $\leftarrow \min\limits_{a_i}\max\limits_{\theta_j} v\left(a_i,\theta_j\right)$

A minimax criterion applied to the above payoff cost matrix yields optimal action a_2^*. But intuitively we are tempted to choose the action a_1^* since there is a chance that if $\theta=\theta_2$, only 90 units will be lost, whereas it is certain that a_2^* will yield a loss of 1000 whether $\theta=\theta_1$ or, $\theta=\theta_2$.

The *savage criterion* rectifies this point by constructing a new loss matrix in which $v(a_i, \theta_j)$ is replaced by $L(a_i, \theta_j)$ and is defined by

$$L(a_i,\theta_j)=\begin{cases}\max\limits_{a_k} v(a_k,\theta_j)-v(a_i,\theta_j), & \text{if } v \text{ is a profit}\\ v(a_i,\theta_j)-\min\limits_{a_k} v(a_k,\theta_j), & \text{if } v \text{ is a loss.}\end{cases}$$

This means that $L(a_i, \theta_j)$ is the difference between the best choice in the column of θ_j and the values of $v(a_i, \theta_j)$ in the same column. In essence $L(a_i, \theta_j)$ is the representation of the *regret* of the decision-maker as a result of missing the best choice corresponding to a given future state θ_j. The function $L(a_i, \theta_j)$ is referred to as the *regret matrix.*

For above example $L(a_i, \theta_j)$ is:

	θ_1	θ_2	$\max\limits_{\theta_j} L(a_i,\theta_j)$
a_1	100	0	100 ← $\min\limits_{a_i}\max\limits_{\theta_j} L(a_i,\theta_j)$
a_2	0	910	910

The minimax criterion yields action a_1^*, which is expected for logical conclusion.

Hence, whether $v(a_1, \theta_j)$ is a profit or a loss function, $L(a_i, \theta_j)$ is a regret function which in both cases represents a loss function and consequently only *minimax* criterion can be applied to $L(a_i, \theta_j)$ (never applied maximin criteria).

Example 8.3.3. *Consider the same* Ex. 8.3.1 *as taken earlier and apply savage criterion to find its solution.*

Customer category

		θ_1	θ_2	θ_3	θ_4
Supplies level	a_1	5	10	18	25
	a_2	8	7	8	23
	a_3	21	18	12	21
	a_4	30	22	19	15

Solution: *Regret matrix* $L(a_i, \theta_j)$ is given by

	θ_1	θ_2	θ_3	θ_4	$\max\limits_{\theta_j} L(a_i,\theta_j)$
a_1	0	3	10	10	10
a_2	3	0	0	8	8 ← $\min\limits_{a_i}\max\limits_{\theta_j} L(a_i,\theta_j)$
a_3	16	11	4	6	16
a_4	25	15	11	0	25

Therefore, savage criterion suggests that the best course of action is a_2^*.

(D) The Hurwicz Criterion

This criterion represents the range of attitude from the most optimistic to the most pessimistic. Under the most optimistic conditions one would select the action yielding $\max\limits_{a_i} \max\limits_{\theta_j}$, where it is assumed that $v(a_i, \theta_j)$ represents *gain* or *profit.*

Similarly, under the most pessimistic conditions the choice of action corresponds to $\max\limits_{a_i} \min\limits_{\theta_j} v(a_i, \theta_j)$.

The *Hurwicz criterion* strikes a balance between extreme pessimism and extreme optimism by weighing the above two conditions by the respective weight λ and $(1-\lambda)$ such that $\lambda \in [0,1]$.

If $v\left(a_i, \theta_j\right)$ presents profit, select the action that yields

$$\max_{a_i}\left[\lambda \max_{\theta_j} v\left(a_i, \theta_j\right)+(1-\lambda)\min_{\theta_j} v\left(a_i, \theta_j\right)\right].$$

In case, where $v\left(a_i, \theta_j\right)$ presents loss, the choice will be corresponding to

$$\min_{a_i}\left[\lambda \min_{\theta_j} v\left(a_i, \theta_j\right)+(1-\lambda)\max_{\theta_j} v\left(a_i, \theta_j\right)\right].$$

The parameter $\lambda \in [0,1]$ is known as *index of optimism.*

Remarks

1. When $\lambda = \begin{cases} 1, & \text{Hurwicz criterion is } \textit{too optimistic} \\ 0, & \text{Hurwicz criterion is } \textit{too pessimistic.} \end{cases}$
2. Generally, value of $\lambda \in [0,1]$ can be taken depending on whether the decision-maker leans towards pessimism or optimism. However, $\lambda = \frac{1}{2}$ seems to be a reasonable choice.

Example 8.3.4. *Referred to the same* Ex. 8.3.1.

	θ_1	θ_2	θ_3	θ_4
a_1	5	10	18	25
a_2	8	7	8	23
a_3	21	18	12	21
a_4	30	22	19	15

Solution: Apply Hurwicz criterion to the above cost payoff matrix:

	$\min_{\theta_j} v\left(a_i, \theta_j\right)$	$\max_{\theta_j} v\left(a_i, \theta_j\right)$	$P=\lambda \min_{\theta_j} v\left(a_i, \theta_j\right)+(1-\lambda)\max_{\theta_j} v\left(a_i, \theta_j\right)$ (Here taking $\lambda = 1/2$)
a_1	5	25	15 } $\min_{a_i} P$.
a_2	7	23	15 }
a_3	12	21	16.5
a_4	15	30	22.5

Therefore, the best choice of action is either a_1^* or a_2^*.

Example 8.3.5. *A farmer wants to decide which of the three crops he should plant on his 10 acres farm. The profit from each depends on the rainfall during growing season. The farmer has categorised the amount of rainfall as high, medium and low. His estimated profit for each is given below.*

	Estimated conditional profit (₹)		
Rainfall	*Crop* A	*Crop* B	*Crop* C
High	8000	3500	5000
Medium	4500	4500	5000
Low	2000	5000	4000

If the farmer wishes to plant only one crop, decide which should be his best crop using (i) *The Laplace criterion and* (ii) *Hurwicz criterion (Given index of optimism* $\lambda = 0.6$). [ISI(Dip) 1992, BESU(MSc) 2011]

Solution: (i) The Laplace criterion

	Crop A	Crop B	Crop C
High	8000	3500	5000
Medium	4500	4500	5000
Low	2000	5000	4000

$$E(\text{Crop A}) = \tfrac{1}{3}(8000+4500+2000) = 4833.33 \longleftarrow \text{Maximum}$$

$$\boxed{E(\text{Crop B}) = \tfrac{1}{3}(3500+4500+5000) = 4333.33}$$

$$E(\text{Crop C}) = \tfrac{1}{3}(5000+5000+4000) = 4666.66$$

Since the matrix is a profit payoff, by taking maximum the best crop according to Laplace criterion is: Crop A.

(ii) Hurwicz criterion

$v(a_i,\theta_j)$	High	Medium	Low
Crop A	8000	4500	2000
Crop B	3500	4500	5000
Crop C	2000	5000	4000

	$\min\limits_{\theta_j} v(a_i,\theta_j)$	$\max\limits_{\theta_j} v(a_i,\theta_j)$	$P=(0.6)\max\limits_{\theta_j} v(a_i,\theta_j)+(0.4)\min\limits_{\theta_j} v(a_i,\theta_j)$
Crop A	8000	2000	5600⟶ max P
Crop B	5000	3500	4400 (as it is a profit)
Crop C	5000	2000	3800

The best crop according to Hurwicz criterion is also: Crop A.

8.4 DECISIONS UNDER RISK

Under this environment, most decisions may have to be made under conditions of risk. Here more than one state of nature exist and the decision-maker has sufficient information to assignment probabilities to each of the states. Decisions under risk are usually based on one of the following criteria.

(A) Expected value criterion, (B) Expected opportunity loss criterion,

(C) Expected value of perfect information.

Each of these criteria will now be explained with examples.

(A) Expected Value Criterion (EVC)

The expected value criterion for a given course of action is the weighted average payoff, which is the sum of the payoff for each state of nature. Let n be the number of states of nature, p_i is the probability of occurrence of state of nature i, σ_{ij} is the payoff for the ith state of nature and jth course of action, then mathematically EVC is given by

$$\text{EVC}\left(A_j\right) = \sum_{i=1}^{n} \sigma_{ij} p_i.$$

To find EVC $\left(A_j\right)$ we first list conditional profit of each act-event combination along with corresponding event probabilities. For each act determine the expected conditional profits. Then determine EVC of each act and finally select the act, which gives the optimal EVC. That is the course of action, a_k is optimal (maximum payoff) if and only if EVC $(A_k) = \max\limits_j \text{EVC}\left(A_j\right)$.

Example 8.4.1. *A newspaper boy has the following probabilities of selling a popular magazine. Cost of each magazine is 30 paise and sale price of each is 50 paise. He cannot return unsold magazines. How many copies should he order?*

[CU(MBA) 2001, JNU(Com Sc) 1989]

No. of copies sold	*Probability*
10	0.10
11	0.15
12	0.20
13	0.25
14	0.30

Solution: Here there is no reason for newspaper boy to buy less than 10 and more than 14 magazines.

Now payoff = 20 × copies sold − 30 × copies unsold and construct the following table of conditional profit (in paise).

		Possible stock of magazine				
Demand	Probability	10	11	12	13	14
10	0.10	200	170	140	110	80
11	0.15	200	220	190	160	130
12	0.20	200	220	240	210	180
13	0.25	200	220	240	260	230
14	0.30	200	220	240	260	280

In the next step, we have to find the expected value of each decision alternative by multiplying its conditional profit and associated probability and adding the resulting values as shown in the following table.

		Expected profit				
Demand	Probability	10	11	12	13	14
10	0.10	20	17	14	11	8
11	0.15	30	33	28.5	24	19.5
12	0.20	40	44	48	42	36.5
13	0.25	50	55	60	65	57.5
14	0.30	60	66	72	78	84
Total expected profit		200	215	222.5	220	205
				↑Optimum		

The newspaper boy must, therefore, order 12 copies of magazine to earn highest possible average profit of 222.5.

Remark. Of course, there is no guarantee that he will make a profit of 222.5 p the next day. However, if he stocks 12 copies each day under conditions given, then he will have average profit 222.5 p per day. Because the choice of any one of other four possible stock of actions will result in a lower daily profit (as shown in the table).

(B) Expected Opportunity Loss Criterion (EOL)

An alternative way of maximising expected payoff considering *regret* or *opportunity loss* is choosing a course of A_j for each state of nature S_i. This is defined as the difference between the payoff value of the most favourable course of action having highest payoff with zero regret and the payoff for the course of action A_j in the event of outcome S_i. If r_{ij} represents such quantity, then

$$r_{ij} = \max_{i \le j \le m} \sigma_{ij} - \sigma_{ij} : 1 \le i \le n, \tag{8.4a}$$

where σ_{ij} payoff of ith state of nature S_i and jth course of action A_j.

The expected regret for adapting the courses of action A_j is

$$\text{ER}\left(A_j\right) = \sum_{i=1}^{n} r_{ij} p_i.$$

Now we show that among all course of actions the expected regret is minimum when the expected value of the payoff is maximum.

$$\text{ER}\left(A_j\right) = \sum_{i=1}^{n} r_{ij} p_i = \sum_{i=1}^{n} p_i \left[\max_{i \le j \le m} \sigma_{ij} - \sigma_{ij}\right] = \sum_{i=1}^{n} p_i \max_{1 \le j \le m} \sigma_{ij} - \sum_{i=1}^{n} p_i \sigma_{ij} = K - \text{EVC}\left(A_j\right), \tag{8.4b}$$

where $K = \sum_{i=1}^{n} p_i \max_{1 \le j \le m} \sigma_{ij}$ is constant for entire payoff matrix. The right-hand side of (8.4b) is minimum when $\text{EVC}\left(A_j\right)$ is maximum (that is, expected value of the payoff is maximum).

Therefore, for calculating EOL, first construct the conditional profit table for each act-event combination along the corresponding probabilities. Then for each state of nature calculate the opportunity loss by using (8.4a). After that determine the expected regret and finally choose that action, which corresponds to minimum.

(C) Expected Value of Perfect Information (EVPI)

$K = \sum_{i=1}^{n} \max_{1 \le j \le m} \sigma_{ij}$ is called *expected profit* with perfect information (EPPI). It represents maximum attainable profit in the given state of nature. The term *perfect information* is used here in the sense that the decision-maker is in position to choose maximum profit among all courses of action in every state of nature of his decision problem.

The minimum expected regret $\min_{1 \le j \le m} \text{ER}\left(A_j\right) = K - \text{EVC}^*\left(A_j\right)$ is called the *expected value* of perfect information (EVPI). It represents the maximum expected cost, which the decision-maker should be prepared in order to obtain perfect information.

Example 8.4.2. *Consider the same* Ex. 8.4.1.

Solution: As obtained in Ex. 8.4.1 the payoff matrix is given by

Demand	Probability	Possible stock of magazine				
		10	11	12	13	14
10	0.10	200	170	140	110	80
11	0.15	200	200	190	160	130
12	0.20	200	200	240	210	180
13	0.25	200	220	240	260	230
14	0.30	200	220	240	260	280

Now regret or opportunity loss using (8.4a) and corresponding $\text{ER}\left(A_j\right)$ is given in the following table.

Demand (No. of copies)	Probability (p_i)	Possible stock (r_{ij}) 10	11	12	13	14	Possible action ($r_{ij}p_i$) 10	11	12	13	14
10	0.10	0	30	60	90	120	0	3	6	9	12
11	0.15	20	0	30	60	90	3	0	4.5	9	13.5
12	0.20	40	20	0	30	60	8	4	0	6	12
13	0.25	60	40	20	0	30	15	10	5	0	7.5
14	0.30	80	60	40	20	0	24	18	12	6	0
						$\text{ER}(A_j) = \Sigma r_{ij}p_i \longrightarrow$	50	35	27.5	30	45
									↑Optimal (minimum)		

The best choice is to have a stock of 12 copies of magazine.

Since EOL is an alternative decision for decision-making under risk, the results will always be the same as those obtained by EVC. Thus, only one of two methods should be applied to reach a decision.

Example 8.4.3. *An electrical equipment manufacturing company wants to increase its existing capacity. It has narrowed down the alternatives to two approaches* (a) *expansion at a cost of ₹80 lakh or* (b) *modernisation at a cost of ₹50 lakh. Both approaches would require the same time for implementation. The management believes that over the required payback period, the demand will be either high or moderate. Since high demand is considered less likely, the probability is set at 0.35. If the demand is high, expansion would gross an estimated additional cost of ₹120 lakh, but for modernisation only ₹60 lakh. On the other hand, if the demand is moderate, the corresponding figures would be ₹70 lakh for expansion and ₹50 lakh for modernisation. Calculate* EVC's ERs *for the courses of action and determine the optimal with* EVPI. [MBA(CU) 2002, IAS(Main) 1997]

Solution: Based on the information given in the problem we obtain the following conditional payoff matrix.

States of nature and probabilities		Courses of action A_1 (Expand)	A_2 (Modernise)
S_1 (High demand)	0.35	120−80 = 40	60−50 = 10
S_2 (Moderate demand)	0.65	70−80=−10	50−50 = 0

$\text{EVC}(A_1) = 0.35 \times 40 + 0.65 \times (-10) = ₹7.5$ lakh

$\text{EVC}(A_2) = 0.35 \times 10 + 0.65 \times (0) \quad = ₹3.5$ lakh

For *maximum* EVC the company should adopt expansion with expected profit of ₹7.5 lakh.

The regret table is obtained from the payoff table as

States	Probabilities	Actions A_1	A_2
S_1	0.35	40−40 = 0	40−10 = 30
S_2	0.65	0 (−10) = 10	0−0

$\text{ER}(A_1) = 0.35 \times 0 + 0.65 \times 10 = ₹6.5$ lakh

$\text{ER}(A_2) = 0.35 \times 30 + 0.65 \times 0 = ₹10.5$ lakh

For *minimum* ER the company should expand as was concluded before with the minimum regret EVPI of ₹6.5 lakh.

8.5 DECISION-TREE ANALYSIS

A *decision-tree* is a graphic display of various decision alternatives and the sequence of events. In constructing a tree diagram, it is the convention to use the symbol ▭ to indicate the decision point and ○ to denote the situation of uncertainty or event. Branches coming out of decision point are nothing but representation of immediate mutually exclusive alternatives open to the decision-maker. Branches emerging from event point ○ represents all possible situations.

The basic advantage of tree diagram is that another act subsequent to the happening of each event may also be represented. The resulting outcomes or payoff for each act-event combination may be indicated in the tree diagram at the outer end of each branch.

Tree Diagram

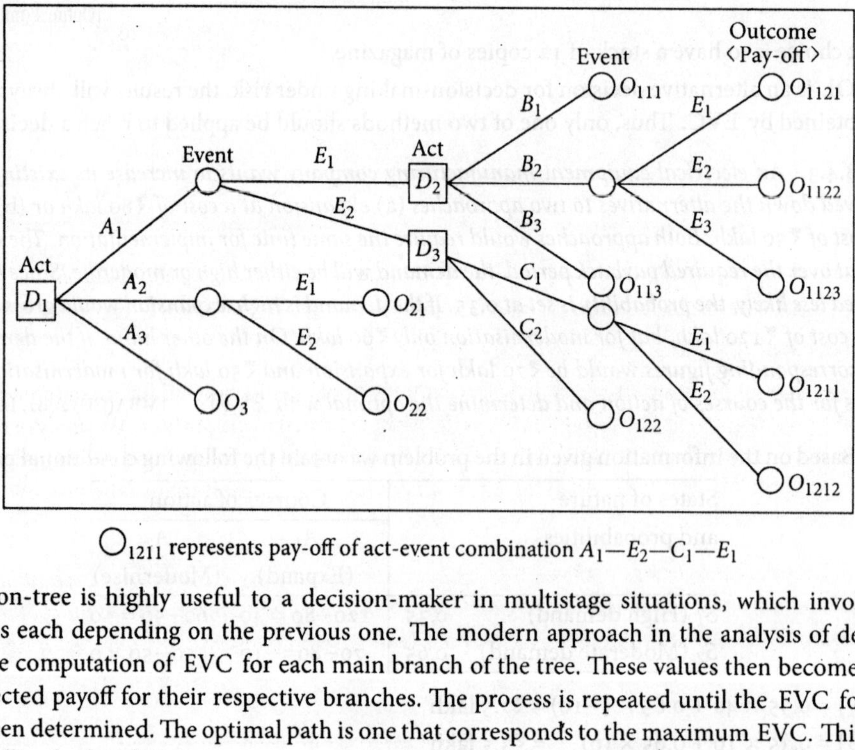

○$_{1211}$ represents pay-off of act-event combination A_1—E_2—C_1—E_1

A decision-tree is highly useful to a decision-maker in multistage situations, which involve a series of decisions each depending on the previous one. The modern approach in the analysis of decision-tree involves the computation of EVC for each main branch of the tree. These values then become the conditional expected payoff for their respective branches. The process is repeated until the EVC for the given path has been determined. The optimal path is one that corresponds to the maximum EVC. This technique is called *Rolling back technique.*

Example 8.5.1. *A businessman has two independent investments* A *and* B *available to him, but he lacks the capital to undertake both of them simultaneously. He can choose to take* A *first and then to stop or if* A *is successful, then to take* B *or vice versa. The probability of success on* A *is* 0.7 *while on* B *it is* 0.4. *Both investments require an initial capital of* ₹2000 *and both return nothing if the venture is unsuccessful. Successful completion of* A *will return* ₹3000 *(over cost) and that of* B *will return* ₹5000 *(over cost).*

Draw the decision-tree and determine the best strategy.

Solution: By rolling back technique the *tree-diagram* is as shown below:

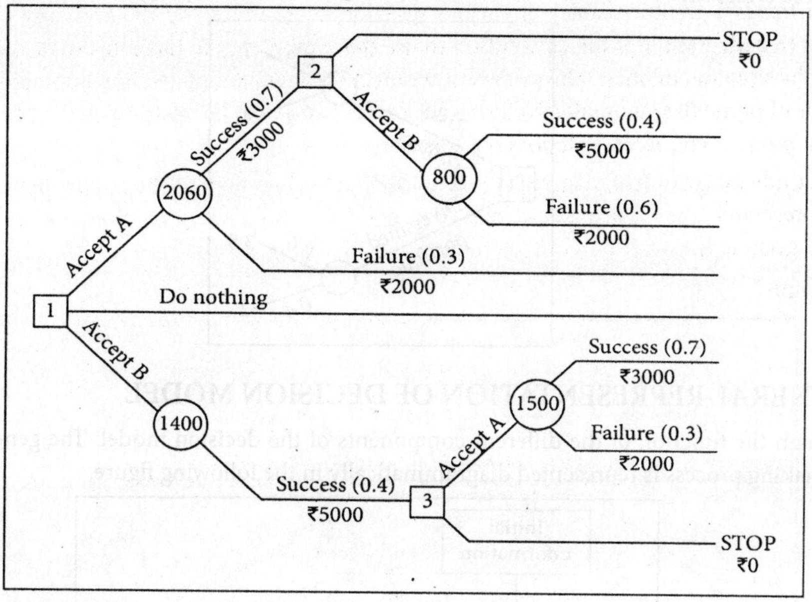

Conclusion. Optimal decision is to accept investment A and if successful the investment B.

Brief Explanation of Rolling Back Technique

Since it is possible to evaluate an immediate decision without considering all future outcomes, one begins the analysis at the end of the tree. The last decision point is primarily important. We analyse this point and take the decision which yields optimal EVC and then roll back to the last but one decision point, make the same EVC analysis for decision and roll back to the preceding decision point. The process continues till the initial point is reached.

Example 8.5.2. *A manager has a choice* (i) *a risky contact promising ₹7 lakh with probability 0.6 and ₹4 lakh with probability 0.4,* (ii) *A diversified portfolio consisting of two contracts with independent outcomes each promising ₹3.5 lakh with probability 0.6 and 2 lakh with probability 0.4. Construct a decision-tree for using* EVC.

Solution:

Events	Probability	Conditional Payoff		Expected Payoff	
		Contract	Portfolio	Contract	Portfolio
E_1	0.6	7	3.5	4.2	2.1
E_2	0.4	4	2	1.6	0.8
			EVC⟶	5.8	2.9
				↑Optimal	

The manager must go in for risky contract, which will give him a higher EVC of ₹5.8 lakh.

Decision-tree Diagram

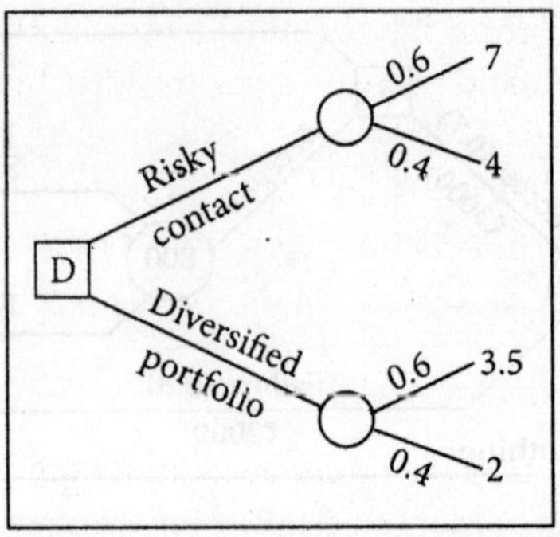

8.6 GENERAL REPRESENTATION OF DECISION MODEL

Let us explain the function of the different components of the decision model. The general structure of decision-making process is represented diagrammatically in the following figure.

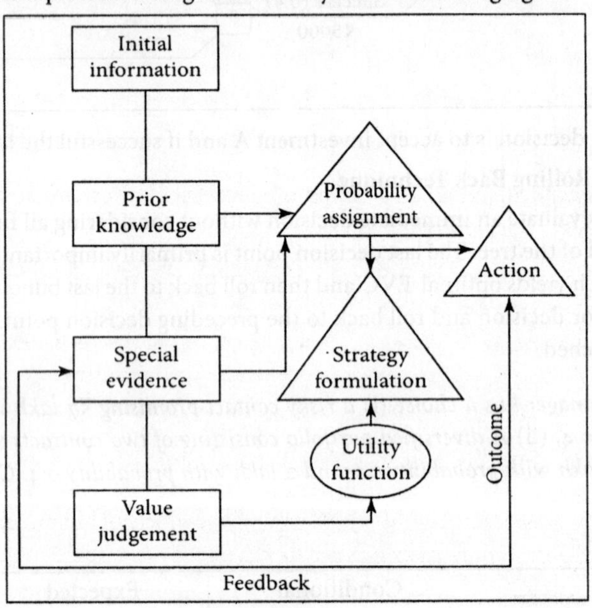

Discussion

The box labelled prior knowledge and that labelled special evidence combine to give triangular box labelled probability assignment. This part operates on Baye's equation to produce posterior probability. Mathematically, let us consider the set $\Lambda = \{E_1, E_2, \ldots, E_n\}$ of mutually exclusive and exhaustive elementary events, which may represent different states of a system of a decision problem. Let Ω denote the data or prior knowledge about the system and $\sigma_i^\circ = P(E_i/\Omega)$ represent the prior probability of states $E_i (i = 1, 2, \ldots, n)$. If some additional new data, say special evidence S, are available, the posterior probability is given by

$$\sigma_i = P(E_i/S\Omega) = \frac{P(E_i/\Omega)P(S/E_i\Omega)}{\sum_{i=1}^{n} P(E_i/\Omega)P(S/E_i\Omega)}.$$

The posterior probability, we shall call it simply probability distribution, constitutes the content elements of triangular box labelled probability assignment. Again, the different alternatives of the decision problem may be of different utilities and they form the constituents of elliptic box labelled utility function. The triangular box labelled strategy formulation serves to put together the probability and utility to obtain a strategy objective function on the basis of which one can formulate the *decision rule*. The output of the strategy formulation is the action, which in fact the basis of the *rational decision*. The action may serve as a feedback to provide more data, which may be used by the decision-maker later on provided the decision-maker gets a second chance.

8.7 GAME THEORY

The criteria for decisions under uncertainty are developed under the assumption that *nature* is the opponent. This section deals with decisions under uncertainty involving two or more intelligent opponents in which each opponent aspires to optimise his own decision at the expense of the other opponents.

In *game theory*, an opponent is referred to as a *player*. Each player has a number of choices, finite or infinite, called *strategies*. The *outcomes* or *payoffs* of a game are summarised as functions of the different strategies for each player. A game with two players, where a gain of one player equals a loss to the other, is known as *two-person zero-sum game*. In such a game, it suffices to express the outcomes in terms of the payoff to one player. A matrix similar to the one used in decision under uncertainty is usually used here to summarise the payoffs to the players whose strategies are given by the rows of the matrix.

8.7.1 Some Definitions

1. *Strategy*. It is the predetermined rule by which a player decides his course of action from his list of courses of actions during the game.
2. *Pure strategy*. It is the decision rule to always select a particular course of action. It is usually represented by a number with which the course of action is associated.
3. *Mixed strategy*. Mathematically, a mixed strategy of a player with m possible courses of action is a set S of m non-negative numbers, whose sum is unity, where each number represents the probability with which each course of action is chosen. Hence, if p_i is the probability of choosing course i, then $S = \{p_1, p_2, \ldots, p_m\}$, where $\sum_{i=1}^{m} p_i = 1$ and $p_i \geq 0 \; \forall \; i = 1, 2, \ldots, m$.

   In fact, a pure strategy is a special case of mixed strategy in which all but one p_i are zero so that a player may be able to choose only m pure strategies but he has an infinite number of mixed strategies to choose from.
4. *Payoff*. It is the outcome of the game. Let player P_1 have m courses of action and player P_2 have n courses of action. Then the game can be described by a pair of matrices, which can be constructed by the following rules:
   (a) Row designations for each matrix are the courses of action available to player P_1.
   (b) Column designations for each matrix are the courses of action available to player P_2.
   (c) The cell entry a_{ij} is the payment to P_1 in P_1's payoff matrix, when P_1 chooses the course of action i and P_2 chooses the course of action j.
   (d) In a two-person zero-sum game, the cell entries in P_2's payoff will be the negative of the corresponding cell entries in P_1's payoff matrix. P_1 is called *maximising player* as he would try to maximise the gains, while P_2 is called *minimising player* as he always would try to minimise his losses.

$$\text{Player } P_1 \quad \overset{\text{Player } P_2}{\begin{array}{c|ccccccc|} & 1 & 2 & \cdots & j & \cdots & n \\ \hline 1 & a_{11} & a_{12} & \cdots & a_{1j} & \cdots & a_{1n} \\ 2 & a_{21} & a_{22} & \cdots & a_{2j} & \cdots & a_{2n} \\ \vdots & \vdots & & & & & \\ i & a_{i1} & a_{i2} & \cdots & a_{ij} & \cdots & a_{in} \\ \vdots & \vdots & & & & & \\ m & a_{m1} & a_{m2} & \cdots & a_{mj} & \cdots & a_{mn} \\ \hline \end{array}}$$

P_1's payoff matrix

$$\text{Player } P_1 \quad \overset{\text{Player } P_2}{\begin{array}{c|ccccccc|} & 1 & 2 & \cdots & j & \cdots & n \\ \hline 1 & -a_{11} & -a_{12} & \cdots & -a_{1j} & \cdots & -a_{1n} \\ 2 & -a_{21} & -a_{22} & \cdots & -a_{2j} & \cdots & -a_{2n} \\ \vdots & \vdots & & & & & \\ i & -a_{i1} & -a_{i2} & \cdots & -a_{ij} & \cdots & -a_{in} \\ \vdots & \vdots & & & & & \\ m & -a_{m1} & -a_{m2} & \cdots & -a_{mj} & \cdots & -a_{mn} \\ \hline \end{array}}$$

P_2's payoff matrix

Note that the sum of payoff matrices of P_1 and P_2 is a null matrix. Here the objective is to determine the optimal strategies of both the players that result in optimum payoff to each irrespective of strategy used by other.

(e) *Optimal strategy.* The strategy that puts the player in the most preferred position irrespective of the strategy of his opponent is called an *optimal strategy.*

8.7.2 Rules for Game Theory

The basic rules employed in solving games are described below:

Rule 1. Look for a pure strategy (Saddle point)

The steps required to detect a saddle point are:

(i) At the right of each row, write the row minimum and put the largest of them within ( ).

(ii) At the bottom of each column, write column maximum and right the smallest of them within ( ).

(iii) If these two elements are same, the cell, where the corresponding row and column meet is a saddle point and the element in that cell is the value of the game. Therefore, saddle point is the number, which is lowest in its row and highest in its column.

(iv) If the two elements within ( ) are unequal, there is no saddle point and value of game lies between these two values.

(v) If there are more than one saddle point, then there will be more than one solution, each solution corresponding to each saddle point.

For examples:

$$P_1 \overset{P_2}{\begin{bmatrix} 3 & 2 \\ -2 & -3 \\ -4 & -5 \end{bmatrix}} \begin{array}{c} (2) \\ -3 \\ -5 \end{array} \qquad \begin{array}{l} \text{Stategies: } P_1 \text{ row 1, } P_2 \text{ column 2} \\ \text{Saddle point: (1, 2)} \\ \text{Game value} = +2 \end{array}$$
$$\quad 3 \quad (2)$$

$$P_1 \overset{P_2}{\begin{bmatrix} 16 & 4 & 0 & 14 & -2 \\ 10 & 8 & 6 & 10 & 12 \\ 2 & 6 & 4 & 8 & 14 \\ 8 & 10 & 2 & 2 & 0 \end{bmatrix}} \begin{array}{c} -2 \\ (6) \\ 2 \\ 0 \end{array} \qquad \begin{array}{l} \text{Strategies: } P_1 \text{ row 2, } P_2 \text{ column 3} \\ \text{Saddle point: (2, 3)} \\ \text{Game value} = +6 \end{array}$$
$$\quad 16 \quad 10 \quad (6) \quad 14 \quad 14$$

Remarks

1. The game is said to be *fair* if maximin value = minimax value = 0 and is said to *strictly determinable* if maximin value = minimax value $\neq 0$.
2. Always look for a saddle point while attempting to solve a game. If the given problem has a saddle point but is solved by other methods, the resulting solution will be incorrect.

Example 8.7.1. *For what value of a, the game with adjoining payoff matrix is strictly determinable?* [Roorke(MTech) 1985]

Player

		Q_1	Q_2	Q_3
	P_1	a	6	−2
Player	P_2	−1	a	−7
	P_3	−2	4	a

Solution: Ignoring whatever the value of a may be, the given payoff matrix represents:

Player

	Q_1	Q_2	Q_3	Row minima
P_1	a	6	−2	2
P_2	−1	a	−7	−7
P_3	−2	4	a	−2
Column maxima	−1	6	2	

Maximin value = 2, Minimax value = −1.

$\therefore$ value of the game $V(G)$ lies between −1 and 2; $-1 \leq V(G) \leq 2$.

For strictly determinable game since maximin value = minimax value, we must have $-1 \leq a \leq 2$.

Example 8.7.2. *Find the ranges of values of p, q which will render the entry (2, 2), a saddle point, for the adjoining game.* [NET Ent 1996, CU(H) 1987]

Player B

		B_1	B_2	B_3
	A_1	2	4	5
Player A	A_2	10	7	q
	A_3	4	p	6

Solution: First ignoring the values of p and q we determine the maximin and minimax values of payoff matrix which are given by Maximin value = 7

Minimax value = 7

Since the entry (2, 2) is the saddle point for the game, this imposes the condition on p as $p \leq 7$ and on q as $q \geq 7$, which are therefore the required ranges for p and q.

Rule 2. Reduce game by dominance. If no pure strategies exist, the next step is to eliminate certain strategies (rows and/or columns) by *dominance.* Rows and/or columns of the payoff matrix that are inferior to at least one of the remaining rows and/or columns are deleted from further consideration. The resulting game can be solved for some mixed strategy as discussed in next rule.

For example, let us take the adjoining 3 × 3 game, matrix reduction by dominance.

Player Q

		Q_1	Q_2	Q_3
	P_1	0	−2	7
Player P	P_2	2	5	6
	P_3	3	−3	8

This matrix has no saddle point. Obviously player Q will not play strategy Q_3 since this will result in heaviest losses to him and highest gain to player P. He can do better by playing column Q_1 or Q_2. Thus, column Q_3 is to be deleted and strategy Q_3 is called *dominated strategy*.

Dominance rule for columns is: Every value in the dominating column(s) must be less than or equal to the corresponding value of the dominated column. The resulting matrix is

Player P \ Player Q	Q_1	Q_2
P_1	0	−7
P_2	2	5
P_3	3	−3

It is clear from above matrix that player P will not play row P_1 since it will give him return lower than given by row P_2. Hence, row P_1 is dominated by row P_2 and can be deleted.

Dominance rule for rows is: Every value in the dominating row(s) must be greater than or equal to the corresponding value of the dominated row. The resulting matrix is:

Player P \ Player Q	Q_1	Q_2
P_2	2	5
P_3	3	−3

This is a 2 × 2 matrix, which can be easily solved after next rule discussed.

Again, *a given strategy* is also said to be *dominated* if it is inferior to some average of the two or more *pure strategies*. To illustrate this let us consider the adjoining game.

Player A \ Player B	B_1	B_2	B_3
A_1	6	1	3
A_2	0	9	7
A_3	2	3	4

This game has no saddle point. Further, none of the pure strategies of player A is inferior to any of the other pure strategies. However, the average of A's first and second pure strategies given as $\left(\frac{6+0}{2}, \frac{1+9}{2}, \frac{3+7}{2}\right) = (3, 5, 5)$, which is obviously superior to A's third pure strategy. Therefore, third strategy may be deleted from the matrix. The resulting matrix becomes:

	B_1	B_2	B_3
A_1	6	1	3
A_2	0	9	7

Remarks

1. The rules for dominance discussed above are used when the payoff matrix is a profit matrix for player A and a loss matrix for player B. If otherwise, the rules get reversed.
2. Always look for dominance when solving a game.

Rule 3. Solve a mixed strategy. In case, where there is no saddle point and dominance has been used to reduce the game matrix, player will resort to mixed strategies. A few different methods will exist to optimise the winning of each payer and to solve the game.

Method 1. Shortcut method for finding optimum strategies and game value.

It consists of the following steps:

(i) Subtract the two digits in column 1 and write the difference under column 2.

(ii) Subtract the two digits in column 2 and write the difference under column 1.

(iii) Similarly, proceed for the two rows.

These values are called *oddments*. They are the frequencies with which the players must use their course of action in their optimum strategies.

Example 8.7.3. *In a game of matching coins, player A wins ₹2 if there are two heads, wins nothing if there are two tails and loses ₹1 when there are one head and one tail. Determine the payoff matrix, best strategies for each player and value of the game to player A (This is a two-person zero-sum game without saddle point.)*

[MBA(CU) 1998, Delhi(MTech) 1978]

Solution: The payoff matrix for *A*:

		Player B	
		H	*T*
Player A	*H*	2	−1
	T	−1	0

Since there is no saddle point, the optimal strategies will be mixed strategies. Using the steps of *Method* 1, we get in the adjoining table.

		Player B			
		H	*T*		
Player A	*H*	2	−1	1	$\frac{1}{4}=0.25$
	T	−1	0	3	$\frac{3}{4}=0.75$
		1	3		
		$\frac{1}{4}=0.25$,	$\frac{3}{4}=0.75$		

For optimum game or gains, player A should use strategy H for 25% of the time and strategy T for 75% of the time while player B should use strategy H 25% of the time and strategy T 75% of the time.

Value of game to A = ₹$\frac{1\times2-1\times3}{1+3}=-\frac{1}{4}$.

Example 8.7.4. *Solve the game by using the principle of dominance.* [JNU(Com Sc) 1988, CU(Stat) 2002]

		Player B					
		I	II	III	IV	V	VI
	1	4	2	0	2	1	1
	2	4	3	1	3	2	2
Player B	3	4	3	7	−5	1	2
	4	4	3	4	−1	2	2
	5	4	3	3	−2	2	2

Solution: The payoff matrix has no saddle point. From player A's point of view row 1 is dominated by row 2 and row 5 is dominated by row 4. Accordingly, row 1 and row 5 are deleted and we get the reduced matrix as

		Player B					
		I	II	III	IV	V	VI
	2	4	3	1	3	2	2
Player B	3	4	3	7	−5	1	2
	4	4	3	4	−1	2	2

Now from player B's point of view, columns I and II are dominated by columns IV, V and VI, also column VI is dominated by column V. Therefore, columns I, II and VI are deleted.

		Player B		
		III	IV	V
	2	1	3	2
Player A	3	7	−5	1
	4	4	−1	2

None of the single rows or columns dominates another row or column. However, column V is dominated by the average of columns III and IV.

$$\begin{pmatrix}(1+3)/2\\(7-5)/2\\(4-1)/2\end{pmatrix}=\begin{pmatrix}2\\1\\3/2\end{pmatrix}$$

So column V is deleted and we obtain the matrix:

		Player B	
		III	IV
	2	1	3
Player A	3	7	−5
	4	4	−1

Further, row 4 is dominated by average of row 2 and 3. Hence, row 4 is deleted. The resulting 2 × 2 game is shown in the right side:

		Player B			
		III	IV		
Player A	2	1	3	12	$\frac{6}{7}$
	3	7	−5	2	$\frac{1}{7}$
		8	6		
		$\frac{4}{7}$	$\frac{3}{7}$		

Solving this game by shortcut method, we have

Optimal strategy for Player A $\left(0,\frac{6}{7},\frac{1}{7},0,0\right)$.

Optimal strategy for Player B $\left(0,0,\frac{4}{7},\frac{3}{7},0,0\right)$.

Value of game $G=\frac{1\times8+3\times6}{8+6}=\frac{26}{14}=\frac{13}{7}$.

Method 2. *Algebraic method for finding optimum strategies and game value.* While applying this method it is assumed that x and $(1-x)$ be the probabilities of selecting strategies by Player A, and y and $(1-y)$ be the probabilities of selecting strategies by Player B. To illustrate this method let us consider the following (2×2) two-person zero-sum game without any saddle point, having payoff matrix is as shown in the right side:

		Player B	
		B_1	B_2
Player A	A_1	a_{11}	a_{12}
	A_2	a_{21}	a_{22}

[IAS 1987]

We want to find optimal mixed strategies, and value of the game.

Here, the expected value of the game to Player A is

$$E(x,y)=xya_{11}+(1-x)ya_{21}+x(1-y)a_{12}+(1-x)(1-y)a_{22}.$$

In order to determine the optimum values of x and y, we use

$$\frac{\partial}{\partial x}E(x,y)=0\Rightarrow ya_{11}-ya_{21}+(1-y)a_{12}-(1-y)a_{22}=0 \tag{1}$$

$$\frac{\partial}{\partial y}E(x,y)=0\Rightarrow xa_{11}+(1-x)a_{21}-xa_{12}-(1-x)a_{22}=0. \tag{2}$$

From (1),

$$y^*=\frac{a_{22}-a_{12}}{(a_{11}+a_{22})-(a_{12}+a_{21})}$$

and from (2),

$$x^*=\frac{a_{22}-a_{21}}{(a_{11}+a_{22})-(a_{12}+a_{21})}$$

gives the optimal mixed strategies, and the value of the game is

$$G=E(x^*y^*)=\frac{a_{11}a_{22}-a_{12}a_{21}}{(a_{11}+a_{22})-(a_{12}+a_{21})} \text{ (by substituting } x^* \text{ and } y^*)$$

Example 8.7.5. *A game has the payoff* $A=\begin{bmatrix}0 & 1\\ 2 & 1\end{bmatrix}$. *Show that* (i) $E(x,y)=1-2y\left(x-\frac{1}{2}\right)$, (ii) *In the solution of the game the second player follows a pure strategy while the first player has infinite number of mixed strategies.*

[CU(H) 2008]

Solution: Suppose, A uses first and second pure strategies with probabilities x and $(1-x)$ and B first and second pure strategies with probabilities y and $(1-y)$

$$\begin{aligned}E(x,y) &= 0\cdot x\cdot y+1\cdot x(1-y)+2(1-x)y+(1-x)(1-y)\cdot 1 = x(1-y)+2(1-x)y+(1-x)(1-y)\\ &= x(1-y)+(1-x)(2y+1-y)=x(1-y)+(1-x)(1+y)=x-xy+1-x+y-xy\\ &= 1-2xy+y=1-2y\left(x-\tfrac{1}{2}\right).\end{aligned}$$

For optimality: $\frac{\partial}{\partial x}E(x,y)=0 \Rightarrow y=y_1=0$ and $y_2=1-y_1=1$

$\frac{\partial}{\partial y}E(x,y)=0 \Rightarrow 1-2x=0 \Rightarrow x=x_1=\frac{1}{2}$ and $x_2=1-x_1=\frac{1}{2}$.

B's optimum strategy is (0,1) indicating B should always use his second pure strategy, whereas A's optimum mixed strategy is $\left(\frac{1}{2},\frac{1}{2}\right)$ indicating A can use his supporting strategies, either singly or in any proportion. Hence, B has one optimum pure strategy, while A has infinite number of optimum mixed strategies.

Value of the game $= 1-2.0\left(0-\frac{1}{2}\right)=1$.

8.7.3 Rectangular Game

The payoff for a rectangular game can be given by $m\times n$, where Player A has m possible courses of action and Player B has n possible courses of action and the payoff matrix is $(a_{ij})_{m\times n}$.

It can be shown mathematically that:

(i) Each rectangular game has a unique specific value $V(G)$.

(ii) There exists for Player A a best strategy $X=\left\{x_1,x_2,\ldots,x_m \,\middle|\, \sum_{i=1}^{m} x_i=1\right\}$ with at least an expected gain, which is equal to value of the game $V(G)$.

(iii) Similarly, for Player B there exists a best strategy $Y=\left\{y_1,y_2,\ldots,y_n \,\middle|\, \sum_{j=1}^{n} y_j=1\right\}$ and at least a loss of $V(G)$.

Without going into details it should be noted that the unknowns $x_1,x_2,\ldots,x_m,y_1,y_2,\ldots,y_n$ and $V(G)$ can be found from the relations:

$$\left.\begin{aligned}&x_1+x_2+\cdots+x_m=1\\ &y_1+y_2+\cdots+y_n=1\\ &x_1a_{1j}+x_2a_{2j}+\cdots+x_ma_{mj}\geq V(G),\ j=1,2,\ldots,n\\ &y_1a_{i1}+y_2a_{i2}+\cdots+y_na_{in}\geq V(G),\quad i=1,2,\ldots,m\\ &x_i\geq 0,\ y_j\geq 0\end{aligned}\right\} \tag{8.7a}$$

Example 8.7.6. *Consider the following rectangular game and solve it.*

Player B

		B_1	B_2	B_3
	A_1	−1	2	1
Player A	A_2	1	−2	2
	A_3	3	4	−3

Solution: (x_1, x_2, x_3) and (y_1, y_2, y_3) be the probabilities of the optimal strategies of Player A and Player B respectively and V is the value of the game.

Then from (8.7a),

$$\begin{aligned}
x_1 + x_2 + x_3 &= 1 \\
y_1 + y_2 + y_3 &= 1 \\
-x_1 + x_2 + 3x_3 &\geq V \\
2x_1 - 2x_2 + 4x_3 &\geq V \\
x_1 + 2x_2 - 3x_3 &\geq V \\
-y_1 - 2y_2 + 2y_3 &\leq V \\
y_1 - 2y_2 + 2y_3 &\leq V \\
3y_1 + 4y_2 - 3y_3 &\leq V \\
x_1, x_2, x_3, y_1, y_2, y_3 &\geq 0
\end{aligned}$$

We have eight equations in seven unknowns. Taking all inequalities as equalities these linear equations can be solved to find the values of the unknowns. If these solutions satisfy the non-negativity restrictions as well as all the inequalities then these solutions will give the optimal strategies and the value of the game.

For this particular problem we easily solve these equations, and the optimal strategies for Player A and Player B are found to be $\left(\frac{17}{46}, \frac{10}{23}, \frac{9}{46}\right)$ and $\left(\frac{7}{23}, \frac{6}{23}, \frac{10}{23}\right)$ respectively with the value of the game, $V = \frac{15}{23}$.

Example 8.7.7. *Solve the following rectangular game.*

		Player B	
		B_1	B_2
	A_1	−2	−4
Player A	A_2	−1	3
	A_3	1	2

Solution: (x_1, x_2, x_3) and (y_1, y_2) be the probabilities of the optimal strategies of Player A and Player B respectively and V is the value of the game.

Then from (8.7a),

$$\begin{aligned}
x_1 + x_2 + x_3 &= 1 && \dots (1) \\
y_1 + y_2 &= 1 && \dots (2) \\
-2x_1 - x_2 + x_3 &\geq V && \dots (3) \\
-4x_1 + 3x_2 + 2x_3 &\geq V && \dots (4) \\
-2y_1 - 4y_2 &\leq V && \dots (5) \\
-y_1 + 3y_2 &\leq V && \dots (6) \\
y_1 + 2y_2 &\leq V && \dots (7) \\
x_1, x_2, x_3, y_1, y_2 &\geq 0 && \dots (8)
\end{aligned}$$

We have six unknowns. The first step towards solution is to assume all the inequalities as equalities and we get

$$\begin{aligned}
x_1 + x_2 + x_3 &= 1 && \dots (1.1) \\
y_1 + y_2 &= 1 && \dots (2.1) \\
-2x_1 - x_2 - x_3 &= V && \dots (3.1) \\
-4x_1 + 3x_2 + 2x_3 &= V && \dots (4.1) \\
-2y_1 - 4y_2 &= V && \dots (5.1) \\
-y_1 + 3y_2 &= V && \dots (6.1) \\
y_1 + 2y_2 &= V && \dots (7.1)
\end{aligned}$$

Now, $y_2 = 1 - y_1$ and $-2y_1 - 4(1 - y_1) = V \Rightarrow 2y_1 - 4 = V$.
Again, $-y_1 + 3(1 - y_1) = V \Rightarrow -4y_1 + 3 = V$.
$\therefore 6y_1 = 7 \Rightarrow y_1 = \frac{7}{6}$, which is unacceptable, as $0 \le y_1 \le 1$.
Therefore, if we assume (5) and (6) as equalities, we do not get a solution.

A general procedure is, then, to assume one inequality and other relations as equalities. If we again meet with a contradiction, we assume other inequalities until a solution is finally reached. However, these computations can be made simpler with the help of the following results.

Results. (i) if $x_1 a_{1j} + x_2 a_{2j} + \cdots + x_m a_{mj} > V$, then $y_j = 0$, (ii) if $y_1 a_{i1} + y_2 a_{i2} + \cdots + x_n a_{in} > V$, then $x_i = 0$.

Let us apply these results.

If $-2x_1 - x_2 + x_3 > V$, then $y_1 = 0$ and eqs (1.1), (3.1) and (7.1) can be true, only if $y_2 = 0$. Therefore, $y_1 + y_2 = 0$, which is contradicted by eq. (2.1).

Similarly, a contradiction is obtained if $-4x_1 + 3x_2 + 2x_3 > V$.

Now, if $-2y_1 - 4y_2 < V$, then $x_1 = 0$ and eqs (1.1), (3.1) and (4.1) will lead to the contradiction. Proceeding in this manner, we finally find that only the following relations lead to a solution.

$$x_1 + x_2 + x_3 = 1 \quad \ldots \quad (1.2)$$
$$y_1 + y_2 = 1 \quad \ldots \quad (2.2)$$
$$-2x_1 - x_2 + x_3 = V \quad \ldots \quad (3.2)$$
$$-4x_1 + 3x_2 + 2x_3 > V \quad \ldots \quad (4.2)$$
$$-2y_1 - 4y_2 < V \quad \ldots \quad (5.2)$$
$$-y_1 + 3y_2 < V \quad \ldots \quad (6.2)$$
$$y_1 + 2y_2 = V \quad \ldots \quad (7.2)$$

From relation (4.2), $y_2 = 0$ so that $y_1 = 1$. From (5.2), $x_1 = 0$ and (6.2), $x_2 = 0$ so that $x_3 = 1$. Substituting the values of y_1 and y_2 in (7.2), $V = 1$.

$\therefore$ optimum strategy for Player A (0,0,1). Optimum strategy for Player B (1,0). Value of the game $V = 1$.

8.7.4 Method of Sub-games for $2 \times n$ or $m \times 2$ Games

This method subdivides the given $2 \times n$ or $m \times 2$ game into a number of 2×2 sub-games, each of which is then solved and optimal strategies are determined. While trying to solve, first find out for each sub-game if a saddle point exists and the sub-game has a pure strategy. In case there is no saddle point, then solve the sub-game by shortcut or algebraic method.

Example 8.7.8. *Solve the following* 2×3 *games by the method of sub-games.*

[Roorker(MSc) 1979, CU(H) 1989, 2007]

		Player B		
		B_1	B_2	B_3
Player A	A_1	1	3	11
	A_2	8	5	2

Solution: The game has no saddle point and also it cannot be reduced by the property of dominance. The given 2×3 matrix can be split up into three 2×2 sub-games.

Sub-game I:

	B_1	B_2	Row minimum
A_1	1	3	1
A_2	8	5	(5)
Column maximum	8	(5)	

Sub-game I has a saddle point (A_2, B_2) and solution is:
Player A: Strategy A_2
Player B: Strategy B_2.
Game value = 5.

Sub-game II:

	B_2	B_3		
A_1	3	11	3	$\frac{3}{11}$
A_2	5	2	8	$\frac{8}{11}$
	9	2		
	$\frac{9}{11}$	$\frac{2}{11}$		

It has no saddle point.
The solution is:
Player A's strategy: $\left(\frac{3}{11}, \frac{8}{11}\right)$
Player B's strategy: $\left(\frac{9}{11}, \frac{2}{11}\right)$.
Value of game $= \frac{3\times3+5\times8}{3+8} = 4.46.$

Sub-game III:

	B_1	B_3		
A_1	1	11	6	$\frac{3}{8}$
A_2	8	2	10	$\frac{5}{8}$
	9	7		
	$\frac{9}{16}$	$\frac{7}{16}$		

It has no saddle point. The complete solution is:
Player A's strategy: $\left(\frac{3}{8}, \frac{5}{8}\right)$.
Player B' strategy: $\left(\frac{9}{16}, \frac{7}{16}\right)$.
Game value $= \frac{1\times6+10\times8}{6\times10} = 5.37.$

Conclusion. Player B has the flexibility to play any two out of the courses of action available to him. However, he will follow those strategies for which the loss occurring to him is the minimum. *Since the value for all sub-games are positive,* Player A *is the winner.* Therefore, Player B will play sub-game for which his loss is minimum. Hence, the required solution to the problem is $A\left(\frac{3}{11}, \frac{8}{11}\right)$, $B\left(0, \frac{9}{11}, \frac{2}{11}\right)$, $V = 4.46$.

8.7.5 Graphical Method for $2 \times n$ or $m \times 2$ Games

Graphical method is only applicable to those games in which one of the players has two strategies only. The advantage of this method is that it is relatively first. It reduces the $2 \times n$ or $m \times 2$ into 2×2 size by identifying and eliminating the dominating strategies.

It is assumed that the game has no saddle point. Player A has two strategies A_1 and A_2 with probabilities x_1 and $x_2 = 1 - x_1$, where $0 \le x_1 \le 1$, Player B has n strategies $B_1, B_2, \ldots, B_n$ with probabilities $y_1, y_2, \ldots, y_n$, where $\sum_{j=1}^{n} y_i = 1$ and $y_j \ge 0$, $j = 1, 2, \ldots, n$. The objective is to determine the optimal values of x_1 and x_2.

Expected payoff for Player A corresponding to strategies of B:

B's strategies	A's expected payoff
1	$a_{11}x_1 + a_{21}(1-x_1) = (a_{11} - a_{21})x_1 + a_{21}$
2	$a_{12}x_1 + a_{22}(1-x_1) = (a_{12} - a_{22})x_1 + a_{22}$
⋮	
n	$a_{1n}x_1 + a_{2n}(1-x_1) = (a_{1n} - a_{2n})x_1 + a_{2n}$

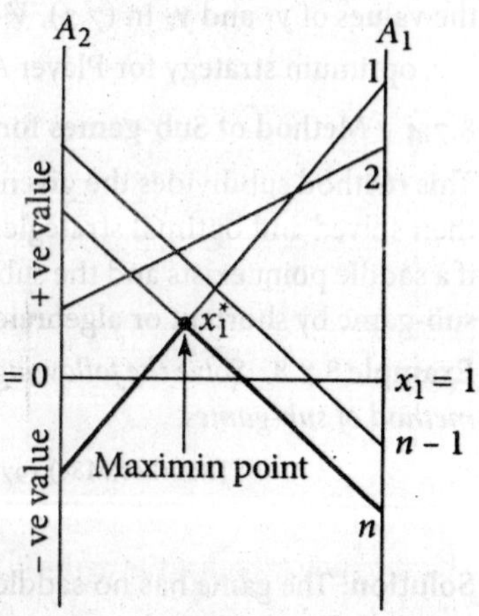

Fig. 1

A's expected payoff varies linearly with x_1. According to maximin for mixed strategies, A should select that value of x_1, which maximises his minimum expected payoff. This can be done by plotting the above lines as a function of x_1 (Fig. 1). When A chooses strategy A_1, $x_1 = 1$ and probability of taking strategy A_2, $x_2 = 0$. Probability x_1 is represented by horizontal line and A_1 and A_2 by two vertical lines unit distance apart. A's expected payoffs are represented by the sloping lines. A number is allotted to each line corresponding to B's pure strategy. The *lower boundary* gives the minimum expected payoff to A. Since A is maximising player, the highest point on this lower boundary gives the *maximum* expected payoff to A and hence, the optimum value x_1^* (in Fig. 1). The two *optimum strategies* for Player B are given by the two lines which passes through maximin point x_1^* so that $2 \times n$ game is reduced to 2×2 game and can be solved by the methods already discussed.

Exactly in the similar way for $m \times 2$ games we can get minimax point, which will be the *lowest point* on the *upper boundary*. Thus, we conclude that any $(2 \times n)$ or $(m \times 2)$ game can be reduced to (2×2) game by graphical method.

Example 8.7.9. *Solve* (2×4) *game by graphical method.* [MBA(CU) 2005, CU(H) 2008]

		Player B			
		1	2	3	4
Player A	1	3	3	4	0
	2	5	4	3	7

Solution: The game has no saddle point. But by dominance rule column 2 dominates column 1 and gives us the reduced matrix

		Player B		
		2	3	4
Player A	1	3	4	0
	2	4	3	7

Expected payoffs of A:

$$3x_1 + 4(1 - x_1) = 4 - x_1$$
$$4x_1 + 3(1 - x_1) = 3 + x_1$$
$$0x_1 + 7(1 - x_1) = 7 - 7x_1$$

Graphical Representation

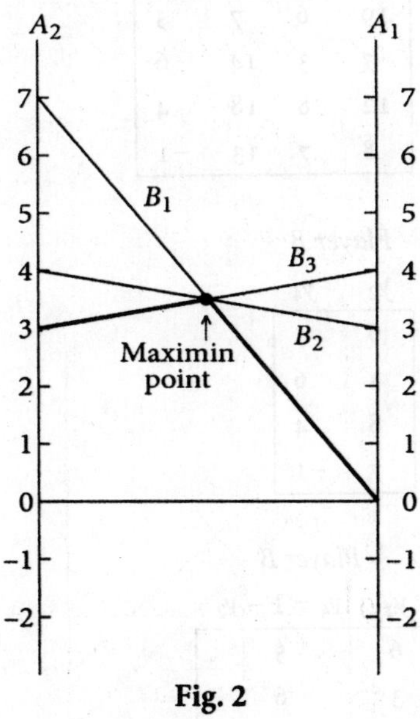

Fig. 2

Graph indicates that the game is reduced to two 2×2 games, which can be solved by shortcut method.

Game 1.

		Player B			
		2	3		
Player A	1	3	4	1	$\frac{1}{2}$
	2	4	3	1	$\frac{1}{2}$
		1	1		
		$\frac{1}{2}$	$\frac{1}{2}$		

Player A: Optimum strategy $\left(\frac{1}{2}, \frac{1}{2}\right)$.

Player B: Optimum strategy $\left(0, \frac{1}{2}, \frac{1}{2}, 0\right)$.

Value of game $v = \frac{3\times1+4\times1}{1+1} = \frac{7}{2}$.

Game 2.

		Player B			
		3	4		
Player A	1	4	3	4	$\frac{1}{2}$
	2	0	7	4	$\frac{1}{2}$
		7	1		
		$\frac{7}{8}$	$\frac{1}{8}$		

Player A: Optimum strategy $\left(\frac{1}{2}, \frac{1}{2}\right)$.

Player B: Optimum strategy $\left(0, 0, \frac{7}{8}, \frac{1}{8}\right)$.

Value of game $v = \frac{7\times4+1\times0}{7+1} = \frac{7}{2}$.

Example 8.7.10. *Solve graphically the following* (2×4) *rectangular game.*

		Player B			
		B_1	B_2	B_3	B_4
Player A	A_1	1.	3	0	2
	A_2	3	0	1	−1

Solution: Graphical representation.

Graph clearly indicates the 2 × 2 sub-matrix, which provides the optimal solution of the game.

	B_3	B_4		
A_I	0	2	2	$\frac{1}{2}$
A_{II}	1	−1	2	$\frac{1}{2}$
	3	1		
	$\frac{3}{4}$	$\frac{1}{4}$		

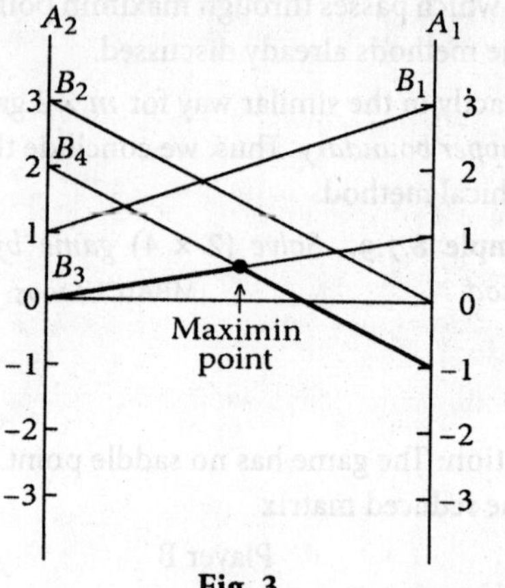

Fig. 3

The optimum strategy for Player A is $\left(\frac{1}{2}, \frac{1}{2}\right)$ and that for Player B is $\left(0, 0, \frac{3}{4}, \frac{1}{4}\right)$, and value of game $v = \frac{3\times0+1\times1}{3+1} = \frac{1}{4}$.

Remark. B_1 and B_2 are dominated strategies as is obvious from the graph as well as from the payoff matrix.

Example 8.7.11. *Using graphical method solve the game.* [JNU(Comp Sc) 2007, IAS 1998]

Player B

		y_1	y_2	y_3	y_4
Player A	x_1	19	6	7	5
	x_2	7	3	14	6
	x_3	12	8	18	4
	x_4	8	7	13	−1

Solution: The game has no saddle point. Column 1 and Column 3 are dominated by Columns 2 and 4 and the reduced matrix becomes:

Player B

		y_2	y_4
Player A	x_1	6	5
	x_2	3	6
	x_3	8	4
	x_4	7	−1

Again, Row 3 dominates Row 4 and the matrix is reduced to:

Player B

		y_2	$y_4 = 1 - y_2$
Player A	x_1	6	5
	x_2	3	6
	x_3	8	4

This matrix can be solved by graphical method. B's expected payoff corresponding to A's pure strategies are given by

A's pure strategies	B's expected payoff
x_1	$6y_2 + 5(1 - y_2) = y_2 + 5$
x_2	$3y_2 + 6(1 - y_2) = -3y_2 + 6$
x_3	$8y_2 + 4(1 - y_2) = 4y_2 + 4$

Graphical Representation

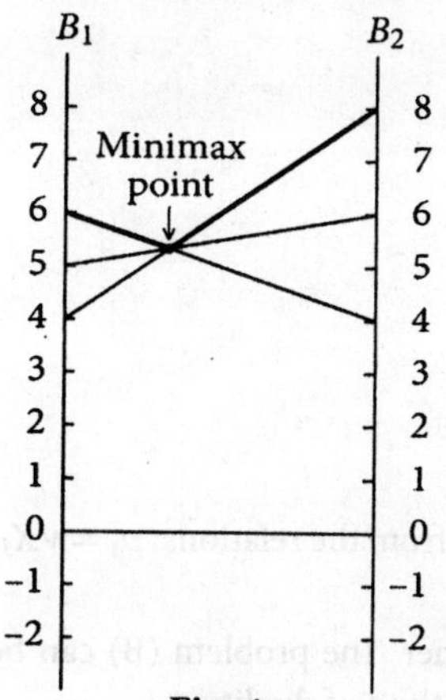

Fig. 4

Since Player B wishes to minimise his maximum expected losses, the two lines, which intersect at lower point of the upper bound show the two courses of action. A should choose his best strategy x_1 and x_2 and we have the following resulting 2×2 game.

		Player B			
		y_2	y_4		
Player A	x_1	6	5	3	$\frac{3}{4}$
	x_2	3	6	1	$\frac{1}{4}$
		1	3		
		$\frac{1}{4}$	$\frac{3}{4}$		

Optimum strategies are:

Player A $\left(\frac{3}{4}, \frac{1}{4}, 0, 0\right)$

Player B $\left(0, \frac{1}{4}, 0, \frac{3}{4}\right)$

Value of game $v = \frac{6\times1+3\times5}{1+3} = \frac{21}{4}$.

8.7.6 Relation between Game and LPP

Game theory bears a strong relationship to LP, since every finite two-person zero-sum game can be expressed as an LP model and conversely. If there is no saddle point, dominance is unsuccessful in reducing the game and the method of matrices also fails, the LP offers the best method of solution.

Consider a game with payoff $\left(a_{ij}\right)_{m\times n}$. The maximising Player A has m mixed strategies with probabilities $\{p_1, p_2, \ldots, p_m\}$ such that

$$\sum_{i=1}^{m} p_i = 1 \text{ and } p_i \geq 0 \;\forall\; i = 1, 2, \ldots, m. \tag{8.7b}$$

Now, our first objective is to show that this problem can be transformed to an LPP before it is solved.

The expected gain to A when the minimising Player B chooses his jth course of action is $\sum_{i=1}^{m} a_{ij}x_j$. Let

$$\min_j \left\{\sum_{i=1}^{m} a_{ij}x_j\right\} = v,$$

then A expects to get at least v. Therefore, we must have

$$\sum_{i=1}^{m} a_{ij}x_j \geq v \;\forall j. \tag{8.7c}$$

Hence, $p_1, p_2, \ldots, p_m$ are to be so determined as to satisfy (8.7b) and maximises v.

(A) To put the above problem in standard LPP divide (8.7b) and (8.7c) by v, which is positive. If v is not positive (as indicated by the presence of some negative element in the payoff matrix, make it positive by adding sufficient large positive quantity so that v becomes positive). Taking $\frac{p_i}{v} = X_i$, $i = 1, 2, \ldots, m$ we can write the problem for Player A as

Maximise V = Minimise $V^{-1} = X_1 + X_2 + \cdots + X_m$

subject to $a_{1j}X_1 + a_{2j}X_2 + \cdots + a_{mj}X_m \geq 1, j = 1,\ldots,n$

$x_i \geq 0, \quad i = 1,\ldots,m.$

(B) Similarly, the problem for Player B

Maximise $\frac{1}{V}$ = Minimise $V^{-1} = Y_1 + Y_2 + \cdots + Y_n$

subject to $a_{i1}Y_1 + a_{i2}Y_2 + \cdots + a_{in}Y_n \leq 1, i = 1,2,\ldots,m$

$$Y_j = \frac{q_j}{v}, \; j = 1,2,\ldots,n,$$

where $\{q_1, q_2, \ldots, q_n\}$ probabilities of B's n mixed strategies.

After obtaining X_i, Y_j by solving problems (A) and (B) we can find p_i and q_j from the relations: $p_i = vX_i$, $q_j = vY_j$.

Remark. The problems (A) and (B) as mentioned above are *dual* to each other. The problem (B) can be solved by regular simplex method while problem (A) can be solved by the method of duality.

Example 8.7.12. *Solve the game by the* LP *method.*

[CU(H) 2005, VU(H) 2008]

		Player B		
		1	2	3
Player A	1	3	−4	2
	2	1	−3	−7
	3	−2	4	7

Solution: (x_1, x_2, x_3) and (y_1, y_2, y_3) be the probabilities with which A and B select their pure strategies. It is clear that the game has no saddle point and the matrix cannot be reduced by dominance rule so that it cannot be solved by earlier methods. Further, the game value lies between −2 and +3. Therefore, it is possible that the value of the game (v) may be negative or zero. Therefore, a positive constant λ is added to all the elements of the matrix, which is more than the maximin value, i.e., $\lambda > 2$. Take $\lambda = 3$, the matrix is modified to:

		Player B		
		1	2	3
Player A	1	6	−1	5
	2	4	0	−4
	3	1	7	10

LP problem from Player B's point of view.

Minimise V

$$\left.\begin{aligned} \text{subject to } 6y_1 - y_2 + 5y_3 &\leq V \\ 4y_1 \qquad - 4y_3 &\leq V \\ y_1 + 7y_2 + 10y_3 &\leq V \\ y_1 + y_2 + y_3 &= 1 \\ y_1, y_2, y_3 &\geq 0 \end{aligned}\right\} \quad (P1)$$

where $Y_j = \frac{y_j}{V}$, $j = 1,2,3$.

An equivalent form of (P1)

$$\left.\begin{aligned} 6Y_1 - Y_2 + 5Y_3 &\leq 1 \\ 4Y_1 \qquad - 4Y_3 &\leq 1 \\ Y_1 + 7Y_2 + 10Y_3 &\leq 1 \\ Y_1 + Y_2 + Y_3 &= \tfrac{1}{V} \\ Y_1, Y_2, Y_3 &\geq 0 \end{aligned}\right\} \quad (P2)$$

Solve (P2) by simplex method:

Standard form of (P2)

Maximize $\frac{1}{V} = Y_1 + Y_2 + Y_3 + 0Y_4 + 0Y_5 + 0Y_6$

subject to
$$4Y_1 - Y_2 + 5Y_3 + Y_4 = 1$$
$$4Y_1 - 4Y_3 + Y_5 = 1$$
$$Y_1 + 7Y_2 + 10Y_3 + Y_6 = 1$$
$$Y_1, Y_2, Y_3 \geq 0$$
$Y_4, Y_5, Y_6 \geq 0$, slack variables.

The optimum table of the above problem by usual simplex iterations is given below (Initial and one intermediate iteration are left for the reader).

		c_j	1	1	1	0	0	0
C_B	Y_B	B	Y_1	Y_2	Y_3	Y_4	Y_5	Y_6
1	Y_1	8/43	1	0	45/43	7/43	0	1/43
0	Y_5	11/43	0	0	−352/43	−28/43	1	−4/43
1	Y_2	5/43	0	1	55/43	−1/43	0	6/43
		$z_j - c_j$	0	0	57/48	16/43	0	7/43

Optimal solution: $Y_1 = \frac{8}{43}$, $Y_2 = \frac{5}{43}$, $Y_3 = 0$, $\frac{1}{V} = \frac{13}{43}$.

Value of the game for the modified matrix $V = \frac{43}{13}$.

Now $y_1 = VY_1 = \frac{43}{13} \cdot \frac{8}{43} = \frac{8}{13}$, $y_2 = \frac{5}{13}$, $y_3 = 0$.

Again, for duality concept discussed in earlier chapter Player A's best strategies from optimum table is given by $X_1 = \frac{16}{43}$, $X_2 = 0$, $X_3 = \frac{7}{43}$.

$x_1 = X_1 \times V = \frac{6}{43} \times \frac{43}{13} = \frac{6}{13}$. $\quad x_2 = X_2 \times V = 0$. $\quad x_3 = X_3 \times V = \frac{7}{43} \times \frac{43}{13} = \frac{7}{13}$.

Conclusion. Optimal strategies of Player A: $\left(\frac{6}{13}, 0, \frac{7}{13}\right)$. Optimal strategies of Player B: $\left(\frac{7}{13}, \frac{5}{13}, 0\right)$. Value of the game of original problem $v^* = V - 3 = \frac{4}{13}$.

Example 8.7.13. *For the adjoining rectangular game write down both primal and dual* LP *problems.*

[ISI(Dip) 1981, IISc(Dip) 1977]

Player Y

		y_1	y_2	y_3	y_4
Player X	x_1	5	7	4	10
	x_2	4	3	7	9
	x_3	1	2	5	6

Solution: (x_1, x_2, x_3) and (y_1, y_2, y_3, y_4) be the probabilities with which X and Y select their pure strategies. Let the value of the game is V.

LPP from Y's point of view.

Maximise $\frac{1}{V}$

subject to
$$5y_1 + 7y_2 + 4y_3 + 10y_4 \leq V$$
$$4y_1 + 3y_2 + 7y_3 + 9y_4 \leq V$$
$$y_1 + 2y_2 + 5y_3 + 6y_4 \leq V \qquad \text{(P1)}$$
$$y_1 + y_2 + y_3 + y_4 \leq 1$$
$$y_j \geq 0,\ j = 1, 2, 3, 4.$$

(P1) has equivalent form as

Maximise $\frac{1}{V} = Y_1 + Y_2 + Y_3 + Y_4$

subject to
$$5Y_1 + 7Y_2 + 4Y_3 + 10Y_4 \leq 1$$
$$4Y_1 + 3Y_2 + 7Y_3 + 9Y_4 \leq 1 \qquad \text{(P2)}$$
$$Y_1 + 2Y_2 + 5Y_3 + 6Y_4 \leq 1$$
$$Y_1, Y_2, Y_3, Y_4 \geq 0 \text{ and } Y_j = \frac{y_j}{V} \Big| j = 1, 2, 3, 4.$$

Similarly, LPP from X's point of view.

Minimise $\frac{1}{V}$

$$\text{subject to } 5x_1+4x_2+x_3 \geq V$$
$$7x_1+3x_2+2x_3 \geq V$$
$$4x_1+7x_2+5x_3 \geq V \qquad \text{(P3)}$$
$$10x_1+9x_2+6x_3 \geq V$$
$$x_1+x_2+x_3=1$$
$$x_1, x_2, x_3 \geq 0$$

(P3) has equivalent form as

Minimise $\frac{1}{V}=X_1+X_2+X_3$

$$\text{subject to } 5X_1+4X_2+X_3 \geq 1$$
$$7X_1+3X_2+2X_3 \geq 1$$
$$4X_1+7X_2+5X_3 \geq 1 \qquad \text{(P4)}$$
$$10X_1+9X_2+6X_3 \geq 1$$
$$X_1, X_2, X_3 \geq 0 \text{ and } X_i=\frac{x_i}{V} \,\Big|\, i=1, 2, 3$$

If (P2) is regarded as a primal, then (P4) is its associated dual and vice versa. Solution of (P4) can be obtained from the solution (Optimal table) of P2 by usual simplex method.

8.8 EXERCISE 8

1. (a) Indicate the difference between decision-making under risk and uncertainty in statistical decision theory.
   (b) Explain with suitable examples: (i) Laplace criterion (ii) Regret criterion (iii) Savage criterion and (iv) Hurwicz criterion in the decision-making problems.

2. The research department of M/s. Hindustan Lever has recommended to the marketing department to launch a shampoo of three different types. The marketing manager has to decide one of the types of shampoo to be launched under the following estimated payoffs for various levels of sales.

	Estimated levels of sales		
Types of shampoo	15,000	10,000	5,000
S1 Egg shampoo	30	10	10
S2 Clinic shampoo	40	15	5
S3 Deluxe shampoo	55	20	3

   What will be the marketing manager's decision if (a) Maximin (b) Laplace (c) Regret criterion is applied?

3. Consider the following payoff (profit) matrix: No probabilities are known for the occurrence of nature states. Compare the solutions obtained by each of the following criteria: (a) Laplace (b) Maximin (c) Savage (d) Hurwicz (Assume that $\lambda=1/2$). [MCA(BESU) 1991, MBA(CU) 2003]

	θ_1	θ_2	θ_3	θ_4	θ_5
a_1	15	10	0	−6	17
a_2	3	14	8	9	2
a_3	1	5	14	20	−3
a_4	7	19	10	2	0

4. A gamble at a horse race is considering placing a bet on a specific horse. There are four possible alternatives and four states of nature with the following payoff.
   (a) What is the maximin strategy?
   (b) What strategy should be selected as per Hurwicz criterion? ($\lambda=1/2$)
   (c) What is the best strategy by savage criterion?
   (d) What is the best strategy by Laplace criterion?

	States of nature			
Strategies	A wins	B wins	C wins	All lose
Bet A	7	−2	−2	−2
Bet B	3	3	−2	−2
Bet C	2	2	2	−2
Do not Bet	0	0	0	0

5. One of N machines is to be selected for producing a lot whose size Q could assume any value between Q_1 and $Q_2 (Q_1 \le Q_2)$. The production cost for machine i is $c_i = k_i + \alpha_i Q$.
Given: $Q_1 = 1000$ and $Q_2 = 4000$ and the right-side table:

Machine (i)	k_i	α_i
1	100	5
2	40	12
3	150	3
4	90	8

Solve the problem by each of the following criteria: (a) Laplace (b) Minimax (c) Savage (d) Hurwicz (Assume that $\lambda = 0.5$). [Roorkee 2001]

6. An investor was considering stock purchases in two companies. He determined the following payoff table contingent upon whether company A or B wins a competition for share of the market.

State	Strategies a_1 (invest in A)	a_2 (invest in B)
Q_1 : Win A	30	0
Q_2 : Win B	40	80

(a) What is the maximin strategy? The minimax strategy?
(b) At what probability of A's winning in the expected value of the two strategies the same?
[*Hints.* $30p + 40(1-p) = 0 \cdot p + 80 \cdot (1-p)$.] [MBA(CU) 1986]

7. Let x be an r.v. representing cost and $f(x)$ be its probability mass function. Suppose that $u(x)$ is the utility function of x. Show that the expected value of $u(x)$, $E(u(x))$ can be expanded as a series around the point $E(x)$ and that the resulting expansion can be approximated by

$$E(u(x)) \cong U(E(x)) + K \text{ Var}(x).$$

Determine the expression for K and show that K >or< 0 according as x represents loss and profit. [ISI(SQC OR) 1993]

8. A newspaper boy buys his newspaper for ₹0.20 each and sells it for ₹0.40 each. Any paper not sold by the end of the day becomes useless for him. His problem is to determine the optimum number of papers that he should buy. If he stocks more, his profit is reduced to the extent of cost of unsold newspapers, and if he stocks less, he loses the opportunity to earn more profits. An analysis of past records shows the probability distribution of demand of newspapers as given in the adjoining table.

Demand	Probability
0	0.20
10	0.25
20	0.40
30	0.10
40	0.05

Find the optimum number of newspapers he should stock? [BESU(MSc) 2008, JNU(Com Sc) 1997]

9. A well-known department store advertises female fashion garments from time to time in the Sunday press. Only one garment is advertised on each occasion. The statistical probability of demand at various levels after each advertisement is as follows:

Demand (No. of garments)	After advertising in one newspaper	After advertising in two newspapers
30	0.10	0
40	0.25	0.15
50	0.40	0.35
60	0.25	0.40
70	0	0.10

The garment advertised to sell at ₹35 costs ₹15 to make and can be disposed of, if unsold, for ₹10.

(a) Calculate how many garments should be purchased by the stores in order to maximise expected gross profit after advertising in (i) one newspapers (ii) two newspapers.

(b) Calculate the amount, if any, of the expected net profit under conditions (i) and (ii) of (a).

[BESU(MSc) 2011]

[*Hints*. Prepare the payoff as usual. Then calculate EMV for probabilities of demand on advertising in one newspaper and two newspapers independently.]

10. A wholesaler of sports goods has an opportunity to buy 5000 pairs of skis that have been declared surplus by the government. The wholesaler will pay ₹50 per pair and can obtain ₹100 a pair by selling skis to retailers. The wholesalers is in doubt as to how many pairs he will be able to sell. Any skis left over can be sold to discount outlets at ₹20 a pair. The wholesaler assigns probabilities to demand as follows.

(a) Compute the conditional monetary and expected monetary values.

(b) Compute the expected profit with a perfect predicting device.

(c) Compute the EVPI.

Retailer's demand (Pairs)	Probability
1000	0.6
3000	0.3
5000	0.1

11. Mr Amit has ₹10,000 to invest in one of the three products A, B, C. The return on his investment depends on whether the economy experiences inflation recession, or no change at all. His possible returns under each economic condition are given in the adjoining table.

	States of nature		
Strategy	Inflation	Recession	No change
A	2000	1200	1500
B	3000	800	1000
C	2500	1000	1800

What should he decide using the pessimistic, optimistic and regret criteria?

12. A company buys certain items, which is sold for ₹16 and costs ₹12. A tabulation of recent demand for the product appears as follows.

Quantity sold	80	81	82	83	84	85
No. of days	14	36	70	30	20	10

Further, demand for this product during next 30 days should be comparable to past demand.

(a) What is the expected profit and loss from stocking 83 units?

(b) What is the expected profit under uncertainty?

(c) What would be the maximum expected profit certainty if this were possible?

13. The probability distribution of monthly sales of an item is as follows.

The cost of carrying inventory (unsold during the month) is ₹30 per unit per month and cost of unit shortage is ₹70. Determine optimum stock to minimise expected cost.

Monthly sales (*units*)	0	1	2	3	4	5	6
Probabilities	0.01	0.06	0.25	0.30	0.22	0.10	0.06

14. A small industry finds from past data and the cost of making an item is ₹25, the selling price of the item is ₹30, if it is sold within a week and it could be disposed of at ₹20 per item at the end of the week.

Weekly sales	<3	4	5	6	7	<8
No. of sales	0	10	20	40	30	0

[*Hints.* Conditional profit = $\begin{cases} 5D & : D \geq S \quad D \to \text{Demand} \\ 10D - 5D : D < S & S \to \text{Stock.}] \end{cases}$

Find the optimum number of items per week the industry should produce.

15. What do you understand by decision-tree analysis? What is node in a decision-tree? What is rolling back technique in decision-tree analysis?

16. LIC company is evaluating four alternative single period investment opportunities whose return are based on the state of the economy. The possible states of the economy and the associated probability distribution is as follows.

State	Fair	Good	Great
Probability	0.2	0.5	0.3

	State of economy		
Alternative	Fair (in ₹)	Good (in ₹)	Great (in ₹)
W	1000	3000	6000
X	500	4500	6800
Y	0	5000	8000
Z	4000	6000	8500

Using *decision-tree* approach, determine the expected return for each alternative. Which alternative investment proposal would you recommend if the expected monetary value criterion is to be employed?

17. The IOC is considering whether to go for an offshore oil drilling contract to be awarded in Mumbai high. If they bid, value would be ₹600 million with a 65% chance of gaining the contract. They may set-up a new drilling operation or move already existing operation, which has proved successful, to new site. The probability of success and expected returns are as follows.

	New drilling operations		Existing operations	
Outcome	Probability	Expected revenue (₹ million)	Outcome	Expected revenue (₹ million)
Success	0.75	800	0.85	700
Failure	0.25	200	0.15	350

If the corporation do not bid or lose the contact, they can use the ₹600 million to modernise their operation. This would result in a return of either 5% or 8% on the sum invested with probabilities 0.45 and 0.55 (Assume that all costs and revenues have been discounted to present value).

(a) Construct a decision-tree for the problem showing clearly the course of action.

(b) By applying an appropriate decision criterion, recommended whether or not the IOC should bit the contract.

18. Mr Ram is interested in developing and marketing a new drug. The cost of extensive research to develop the drug would be ₹10,000. The manager of the research programme said that there was 60% chance that the drug would be developed successfully. The market potential is assessed as follows with the present value of profits.

Market conditions	Probability	Present value of profit (in ₹)
Large market potential	0.1	550,000
Moderate market potential	0.5	240,000
Low market potential	0.4	80,000

The present value figures do not include the cost of research. While Ram was considering this proposal, another similar proposal came up which also required the investment of ₹100,000. The present value of profit for the second proposal is ₹120,000. The return on the investment in the second proposal is almost certain.
Draw a decision-tree for Mr Ram indicating all choices and events. What decision Mr Ram should take regarding the investment of ₹100,000?

19. Consider the following data on daily net profit.

		Demand (D_j)				
		50	100	150	200	250
Order size (Q_i)	75	950	1200	575	−675	−1425
	150	50	1700	2000	2250	1600
	225	−850	850	2550	3550	4525
	300	−1800	600	1800	2000	5000

(a) Find the best order size based on.the savage minimax regret criterion.

(b) Also obtain the best order size based on Hurwicz criterion.

20. Consider the two matrix game with payoff matrices $A=(a_{ij})$ and $B=(b_{ij})$, where $b_{ij}=a_{ij}+\omega$. Show that an optimal strategy for one game is also an optimal strategy for the other game.

21. The following matrix represents the return (in ₹) on fixed investments relative to inflation, stability and recession.

$$\begin{array}{l} \\ \text{Bank interest} \\ \text{Bonds} \\ \text{Stocks} \end{array} \begin{array}{c} \begin{array}{ccc} \text{Recession} & \text{Stability} & \text{Inflation} \end{array} \\ \begin{pmatrix} 40 & 50 & 30 \\ 25 & 55 & 75 \\ -60 & 45 & 100 \end{pmatrix} \end{array}$$

What percentage should be invested in each category?

22. Solve the games with the following payoff matrices (a) by the graphical method (b) by linear programming.

(a) $\overset{A}{B\begin{pmatrix} 2 & -3 & -1 & 1 \\ 0 & 2 & 1 & 2 \end{pmatrix}}$ (b) $\overset{A}{B\begin{pmatrix} 1 & 0 & 4 & 1 \\ 0 & -4 & -3 & 1 \end{pmatrix}}$ (c) $\overset{A}{B\begin{pmatrix} -1 & 0 \\ 0 & 4 \\ -4 & 3 \\ 2 & -4 \end{pmatrix}}$

23. Solve the following matrix game:

(a) $B\overset{A}{\begin{pmatrix} 4 & 3 & 1 & 4 \\ 2 & 5 & 6 & 3 \\ 1 & 0 & 7 & 0 \end{pmatrix}}$ [CU(H) 1984] (b) $B\overset{A}{\begin{pmatrix} 0 & -2 & 1 \\ 2 & 0 & -2 \\ -1 & 2 & 0 \end{pmatrix}}$ [KU 1985]

24. Consider the two-person zero-sum game with the payoff

$$k(x,y)=\sum_{i=1}^{n} p_i x_i \exp(-k_i y_i/x_i),\ k_i>0.$$

Show that the optimal strategy y^* is given by

$$y_i^*=\begin{cases}\dfrac{1}{k_i}\log(p_i/\lambda), & \text{if } p_i>\lambda\\ 0, & \text{if } p_i\le\lambda\end{cases}$$

where λ is determined from the condition $\sum_{i=1}^{n} y_i^*=1$. [CSIR(JRF) 1992, IAS(Main) 1996]

25. Use the dominance relations to solve the following matrix games:

(a) $B\overset{A}{\begin{pmatrix} 2 & 0 & 3 \\ 3 & -1 & 1 \\ 5 & 2 & -1 \end{pmatrix}}$ [JU 1997] (b) $B\overset{A}{\begin{pmatrix} 4 & 2 & 2 & 1 \\ 2 & 3 & 5 & 4 \\ 3 & 2 & 1 & 1 \\ 2 & 1 & 2 & 1 \end{pmatrix}}$ [VU 2002]

26. Two firms A and B are determining their sales strategies for a competitive product. Each firm has three alternatives. The payoff (in thousand of ₹) to firm A for three alternatives is

$$\text{Firm A}\overset{\text{Firm B}}{\begin{pmatrix} 1 & 2 & 3 \\ 3 & 2 & 1 \\ 4 & 2 & 0 \end{pmatrix}}.$$

What should be firm A's strategy to maximise its profit?

27. Find the range of values for p and q that will render the entry (2, 2), a saddle point, in the following games.

(a) $A\overset{B}{\begin{pmatrix} 1 & q & 6 \\ p & 5 & 10 \\ 6 & 2 & 3 \end{pmatrix}}$ (b) $A\overset{B}{\begin{pmatrix} 2 & 4 & 5 \\ 10 & 7 & q \\ 4 & p & 6 \end{pmatrix}}$ [CU(H) 1986]

28. Indicate whether the values of the following games are greater than, less than, or equal to zero.

(a) $A\overset{B}{\begin{pmatrix} 1 & 9 & 6 & 0 \\ 2 & 3 & 8 & 4 \\ -5 & -2 & 10 & -3 \\ 7 & 4 & -2 & -5 \end{pmatrix}}$ [ISI(Dip) 1994] (b) $A\overset{B}{\begin{pmatrix} 3 & 7 & -1 & 3 \\ 4 & 8 & 0 & -6 \\ 6 & -9 & -2 & 4 \end{pmatrix}}$ [CU(H) 1997]

29. Let σ_{ij} be the (i,j)th element of the payoff matrix with m and n strategies respectively. Prove that

$$\max_i \min_j \sigma_{ij} \leq \min_j \max_i \sigma_{ij}.$$

30. Formulate the following game as an LP model and obtain its solution:

$$\begin{array}{cc} & B \\ A & \begin{pmatrix} 8 & 9 & 3 \\ 2 & 5 & 6 \\ 4 & 1 & 7 \end{pmatrix}. \end{array}$$

31. Solve the following games by reducing them to 2×2 games by graphical method.

(a) $\begin{array}{cc} & B \\ A & \begin{pmatrix} 3 & 0 & 6 & -1 & 7 \\ -1 & 5 & -2 & 2 & 1 \end{pmatrix}. \end{array}$ (b) $\begin{array}{cc} & B \\ A & \begin{pmatrix} 0 & 4 & -8 & -5 & 1 \\ 1 & 5 & 8 & -4 & 0 \end{pmatrix} \end{array}$ (c) $\begin{array}{cc} & B \\ A & \begin{pmatrix} 1 & 3 & 11 \\ 8 & 5 & 2 \end{pmatrix}. \end{array}$

[MBA(DU) 1996] [DU 1991, '84]

32. Show that for the game $\begin{array}{cc} & B \\ A & \begin{pmatrix} 5 & 50 & 50 \\ 1 & 1 & 1/10 \\ 10 & 1 & 10 \end{pmatrix} \end{array}$, the strategies $\left(\frac{1}{6}, 0, \frac{5}{6}\right)$ for player A and $\left(\frac{49}{54}, \frac{5}{54}, 0\right)$ for player B are optimal.

33. Write both primal and dual LPP corresponding to the following rectangular game:

$$\begin{array}{cc} & Y \\ X & \begin{pmatrix} 5 & 7 & 4 & 10 \\ 4 & 3 & 7 & 9 \\ 1 & 2 & 5 & 6 \end{pmatrix}. \end{array}$$

34. Solve the following game by the *method of sub-games:*

$$\begin{array}{ccc} & & \text{Player B} \\ & & \begin{array}{ccc} B_1 & B_2 & B_3 \end{array} \\ \text{Player A} & \begin{array}{c} A_1 \\ A_2 \end{array} & \begin{pmatrix} 1 & 3 & 11 \\ 8 & 5 & 2 \end{pmatrix}. \end{array}$$

[Roorkee(MSc) 1974, DU(MSc) 1972]

35. Show that for the game $\begin{pmatrix} a & -b \\ -c & d \end{pmatrix}$, where $a,b,c,d \geq 0$, the optimal strategies are $A\left(\frac{c+d}{E}, \frac{a+b}{E}\right)$, $B\left(\frac{b+d}{E}, \frac{a+c}{E}\right)$, where $E = a+b+c+d$. Find the value of the game and state the condition for which the game is fair.

[CU(H) 1984, KU 1985]

36. In a two-person game, each player simultaneously shows either one or two fingers. If the number of the fingers matches, then the player wins a rupee from player B, otherwise A pays B a rupee. Show that the payoff matrix for this game is:

$$\begin{array}{ccc} & & B \\ & & \begin{array}{cc} 1 & 2 \end{array} \\ A & \begin{array}{c} 1 \\ 2 \end{array} & \begin{pmatrix} 1 & -1 \\ -1 & 1 \end{pmatrix}. \end{array}$$

Solve this game by reducing it to LPP.

[CU(H) 1982, VU 1997]

37. Show that if the dominance occurs in the payoff matrix of a 2×2 game, then there is a saddle point. Is the converse true?

38. Use dominance to reduce the payoff matrices and solve the games with the following payoff matrices:

(a) $A \overset{B}{\begin{pmatrix} -5 & 3 & 1 & 20 \\ 5 & 5 & 4 & 6 \\ -4 & -2 & 0 & -5 \end{pmatrix}}$ [CU(H) 1985]

(b) $A \overset{B}{\begin{pmatrix} 1 & 7 & 2 \\ 0 & 2 & 7 \\ 5 & 1 & 6 \end{pmatrix}}$ [CU(MSc) 1975]

(c) $A \overset{B}{\begin{pmatrix} 3 & 2 & 4 & 0 \\ 2 & 4 & 2 & 4 \\ 4 & 2 & 4 & 0 \\ 0 & 4 & 0 & 8 \end{pmatrix}}$. [CU(MSCc) 1976, JU 1993]

39. Use *algebraic method* to solve the game given by the following matrices:

(a) $A \overset{B}{\begin{pmatrix} -5 & -1 & -1 \\ 4 & 0 & 2 \\ -5 & 2 & 0 \end{pmatrix}}$ [Roorke(MTech) 1992]

(b) $A \overset{B}{\begin{pmatrix} -1 & 2 & 1 \\ 1 & -2 & 2 \\ 3 & 4 & -3 \end{pmatrix}}$. [IIT(MTech) 1973]

40. Two players independently select one of stone, paper and scissor and simultaneously disclose their choices. The rules of the game are that the stone beats the scissor, the scissor beats the paper and the paper beats the stone. Suppose that there is a scope of one point for winning, (−1) point for losing and 0 if both the players select the same object. Find the payoff matrix, and show that the game is symmetric. Find also the optimal strategies for each payer by reducing it to an LP model.

[CU(H) 1991, CSII(JRF) 1989]

ANSWERS

2. (a) Maximin: S1, (b) Laplace: S3, (c) Regret: S3.
3. (a) Laplace: a_4, (b) Maximin: a_2, (c) Savage: a_2, (d) Hurwicz: a_4.
4. (a) Do not bet, (b) Bet A, (c) Bet B, (d) Bed C.
5. All criteria select machine 3.
6. (a) a_1, a_2; (b) $\frac{4}{7}$.
8. Optimum number of newspaper = 20.
9. (a) (i) 60, (ii) 60; (b) (i) ₹900, (ii) ₹1037.50.
10. (a)EVM: ₹50 thousand, ₹54 thousand, ₹10 thousand, (b) ₹100,000. (c) ₹46000.
11. Pessimistic: A ₹120, Optimistic: B ₹300, Regret: C ₹50.
12. (a) Profit: ₹338.72, Loss: ₹11.28; (b) EMV: ₹328.72; EVPI: ₹32.72.
13. Cost function = $\begin{cases} 70(D-S) & : D \geq S \\ 200(S-D) & : D < S \end{cases}$

    where D is demand, S is stock.

    Optimum stock to minimise cost = 4 units/month.
14. Maximum EMV= ₹48.60, produce 6 items.

16.

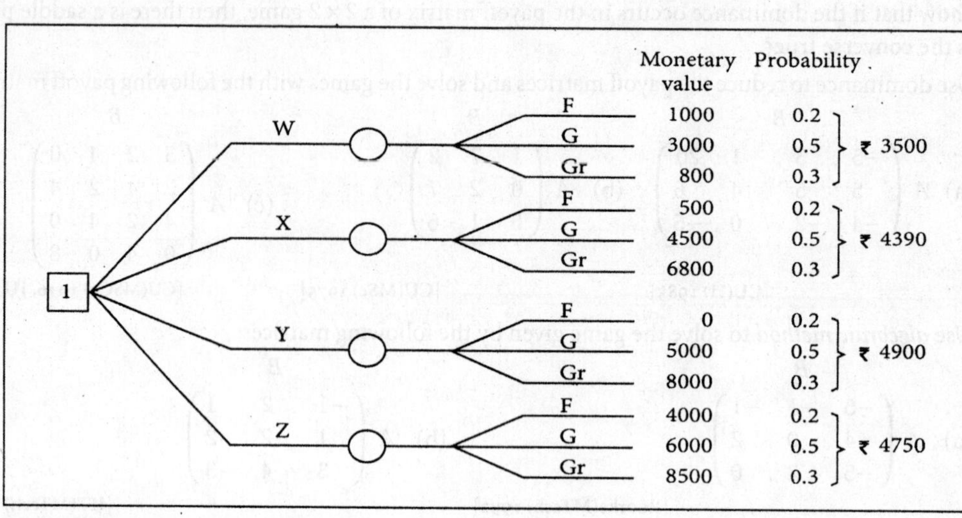

EMV(W) = 1000 × 0.2 + 3000 × 0.5 + 6000 × 0.3 = ₹3500

EMV(X) = ₹4390

EMV(Y) = ₹4900

EMV(Z) = ₹4750.

Alternative Y is the best with maximum return of ₹4900.

17. (a) *Decision-tree:*

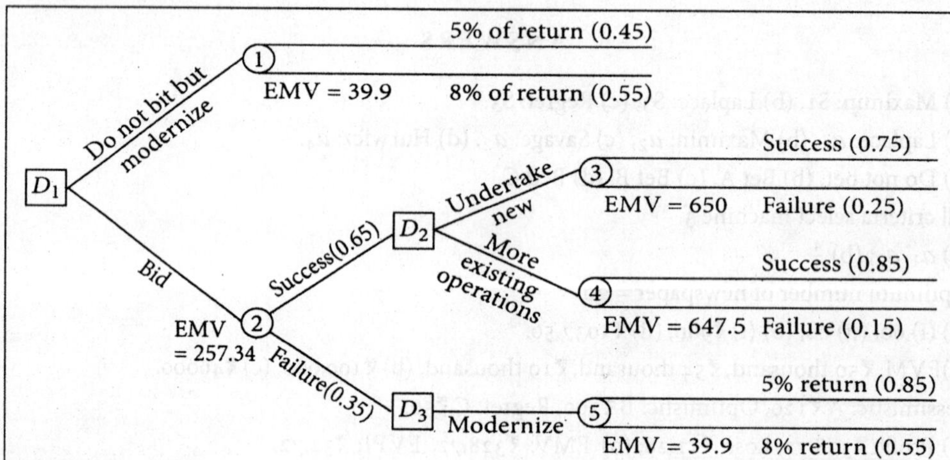

(b) Since the EMV at nod 2 is largest, made decision to launch the product in whole country.

18. Mr Ram should develop the new drug (expected present value of the net profit = ₹124,200.)

19. Savage minimax regret criterion = 225 units. Hurwicz criterion = 225 units.

21. Invest $\frac{250}{3}$ per cent in bank and $\frac{50}{3}$ per cent in bonds. Return = $v = \frac{75}{2}$.

22. (a) $A\left(\frac{1}{2},0,\frac{1}{2},0\right)$, $B\left(\frac{1}{4},\frac{3}{4}\right)$, $V=\frac{1}{2}$. (b) $B(1,0)$, $A(0,1,0,0)$, $V=0$. (c) $A\left(\frac{4}{5},\frac{1}{5}\right)$, $B\left(0,\frac{3}{5},0,\frac{2}{5}\right)$, $V=\frac{4}{5}$.

23. (a) Fair game. Optimal strategies for players A and B are respectively $A(0,1,0,0)$, $B(0,1,0)$.

25. (a) $A\left(0,\frac{2}{3},\frac{1}{3}\right)$, $B\left(\frac{1}{2},0,\frac{1}{2}\right)$, $V=1$. (b) Optimal strategy for both players $\left(\frac{1}{3},\frac{2}{3},0,0\right)$ with $V=\frac{8}{3}$.

26. For firm A $\left(\frac{2}{3},0,\frac{1}{3}\right)$. For firm B $\left(\frac{1}{2},0,\frac{1}{2}\right)$. $V=2$.

27. (a) $p \geq 5$ and $q \leq 5$, (b) $p \leq 7$ and $q \geq 7$.

28. (a) $2 < V < 4$, (b) $-1 < V < 0$.

30. Optimal solution: $A\left(\frac{21}{52},\frac{12}{52},\frac{19}{52}\right)$, $B\left(\frac{2}{13},\frac{3}{13},\frac{8}{13}\right)$, $V=\frac{67}{13}$.

31. (a) $A\left(\frac{3}{7},\frac{4}{7}\right), B\left(\frac{3}{7},0,0,\frac{4}{7},0\right), v=\frac{5}{7}$; (b) $A_2, B_4, v=-4$; (c) $A\left(\frac{3}{11},\frac{8}{11}\right), B\left(0,\frac{2}{11},\frac{9}{11}\right), v=\frac{49}{11}$.

33. (a)
$$\begin{aligned} 5Y_1+7Y_2+4Y_3+10Y_4 &\leq 1 \\ 4Y_1+3Y_2+7Y_3+9Y_4 &\leq 1 \\ Y_1+2Y_2+5Y_3+6Y_4 &\leq 1 \\ Y_1+Y_2+Y_3+Y_4 &\leq \tfrac{1}{V} \\ Y_i \geq 0,\ i=1,2,3,4 & \end{aligned}$$

(b)
$$\begin{aligned} 5X_1+4X_2+3X_3 &\geq 1 \\ 7X_1+3X_2+2X_3 &\geq 1 \\ 4X_1+7X_2+5X_3 &\geq 1 \\ 10X_1+9X_2+6X_3 &\geq 1 \\ X_1+X_2+X_3 &\leq \tfrac{1}{V} \\ X_j \geq 0,\ j=1,2,3,4 & \end{aligned}$$

(a) is the dual of (b) and vice versa.

34. $A\left(\frac{3}{11},\frac{8}{11}\right), B\left(0,\frac{9}{11},\frac{2}{11}\right), V=\frac{49}{11}$.

35. $V=\frac{ad-bc}{E}$, game is fair if $ad-bc=0$.

36. $A\left(\frac{1}{2},\frac{1}{2}\right), B\left(\frac{1}{2},\frac{1}{2}\right), V=0$.

38. (a) $A\left(0,\frac{15}{16},\frac{1}{16}\right)$, $B\left(0,0,\frac{3}{16},\frac{13}{16}\right)$, $V=4$; (b) $A\left(\frac{2}{5},0,\frac{3}{5}\right)$, $B\left(\frac{3}{5},\frac{2}{5},0\right)$, $V=\frac{17}{5}$; (c) $A\left(0,0,\frac{2}{3},\frac{1}{3}\right)$, $B\left(0,0,\frac{2}{3},\frac{1}{3}\right), V=\frac{8}{3}$.

39. (a) $A\left(0,\frac{7}{11},\frac{4}{11}\right), B\left(\frac{2}{11},\frac{9}{11},0\right), V=\frac{8}{11}$; (b) $A\left(\frac{17}{46},\frac{10}{23},\frac{9}{46}\right), B\left(\frac{7}{23},\frac{6}{23},\frac{10}{23}\right), V=\frac{15}{23}$.

40.
$$\begin{array}{c} \quad B \\ A\begin{pmatrix} 0 & 1 & -1 \\ -1 & 0 & 1 \\ 1 & -1 & 0 \end{pmatrix} \end{array}, A\left(\tfrac{1}{3},\tfrac{1}{3},\tfrac{1}{3}\right),\ B\left(\tfrac{1}{3},\tfrac{1}{3},\tfrac{1}{3}\right),\ V=0.$$

Chapter 9

Network Techniques

9.1 PROJECT MANAGEMENT BY CPM-PERT

A project is defined as a combination of interrelated activities all of which must be executed in a certain order to achieve a goal. In a large or complex project involving a number of interrelated activities requiring men, machines, materials, it is possible for the management to make and execute an optimum schedule just by intuition, based on organisational capacities and work experience. A systematic logical approach has becme a necessity. A number of methods applying network scheduling techniques have been developed. CPM and PERT are two of the many network techniques, which are widely used for planning, scheduling and controlling large scale as well as complex projects. CPM and PERT are basically time oriented methods in the sense that they both lead to the determination of a time schedule of a project. The significance difference between two approaches are given below.

CPM

1. Since CPM was developed in connection with a construction of a project which consisted of routine tasks whose resource requirements and duration were known with certainty, it is basically deterministic.
2. CPM is suitable for establishing a trade off optimum balancing between schedule time and cost of the project.
3. CPM is used for projects involving activities of a repetitive nature.

PERT

1. Since PERT was developed in connection with an R & D work, it had to cope with the uncertainties which are associated with such activities. In PERT the total project is regarded as a random variable, and, therefore, associated probabilities are calculated so as to characterise it.
2. It is an event-oriented network, because in the analysis of network, emphasis is given to important stages of completion of task rather than to the activities required to be performed to reach a particular task.

3. PERT is normally used for projects involving activities of non-repetitive nature in which time estimates are uncertain.
4. It helps in pinpointing critical areas in a project so that necessary adjustments can be made to meet the scheduled completion date of the projects.

9.1.1 Network Diagram Representations

The network diagram represents the interdependencies and precedence relationship among the activities of the project. An *arrow* is commonly used to represent an activity, with its head indicating the direction of the progress in the project. The precedence relationship between the activities is specified by using events. An *event* represents a point in time that signifies the completion of some activities and the beginning of new ones. The beginning and end points of an activity are thus described by two events known as the *tail* and *head* events. Each activity is represented by a directed arc and each event is represented by a node.

The figure $(i) \longrightarrow (j)$ shows an example of a typical representation of an activity (i, j) with its tail event i and head event j.

Again, the figure:

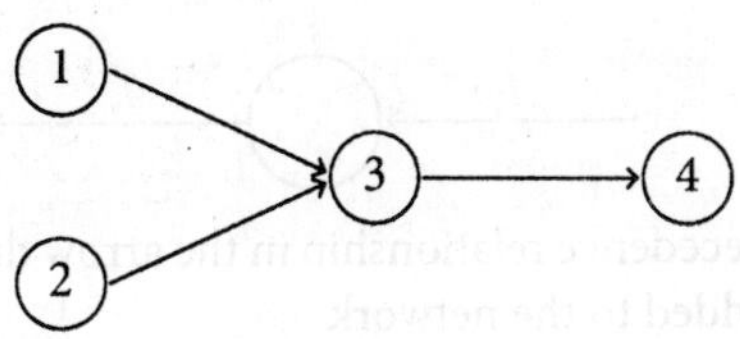

shows another example, where activities (1, 3) and (2, 3) must be completed before activity (3, 4) can start. In general, the direction of progress in each activity is specified by assigning a smaller number to the tail event compared with the number of its head event.

The rules for constructing the arrow diagram will be summarised as follows.

Rule 1. Each activity is represented by one and only one arrow in the network. No single activity can be represented twice in the network. For example, laying down a pipe may be done in sections rather than as one job.

Rule 2. No two activities can be identified by the same head and tail events. This situation arise when two or more activities can be performed concurrently.

An example is shown in figure, where activities a and b have the same end events. The procedure is to introduce a *dummy* activity either between a and one of the end events or between b and one of the end events. The modified representations after introducing the dummy D_m are shown below.

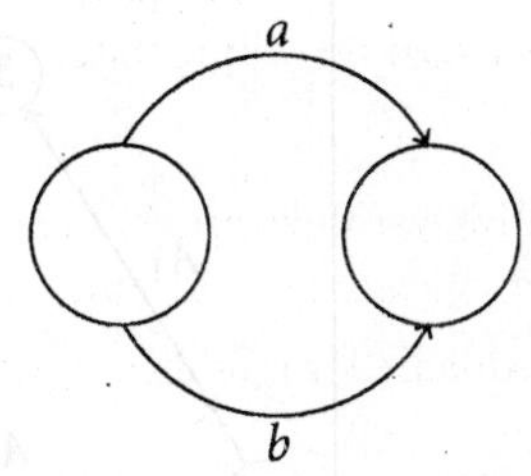

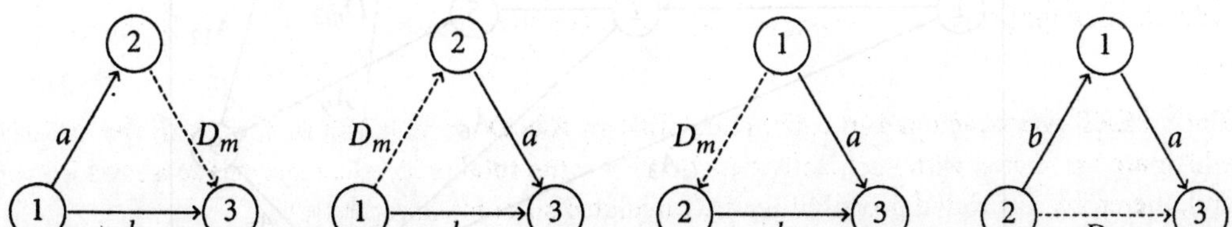

Dummy activities are also useful in establishing logical relationships in the arrow diagram that cannot otherwise be represented correctly. Suppose that in a certain project jobs J_1 and J_2 must precede J_3 while job J_4 is preceded by job J_2 only.

The figure:

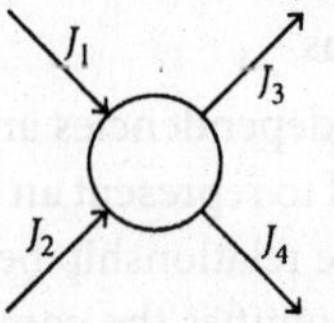

shows the incorrect way, since although the relationship among J_1, J_2 and J_3 is correct, the diagram implies that J_4 must be preceded by both J_1 and J_2. The correct representation using dummy D_m is shown below.

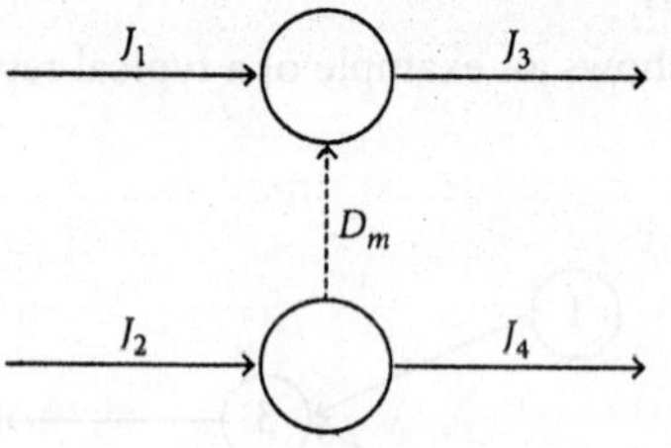

Rule 3. To ensure the correct precedence relationship in the arrow diagram, the following questions must be answered as every activity is added to the network.

(i) What activities must be completed immediately before this activity can start?

(ii) What activities must follow this activity?

(iii) What activities must occur concurrently with this activity?

Example 9.1.1. *Construct the arrow diagram comprising activities $A_1, A_2, \ldots, A_{12}$ such that the following relationships are satisfied. (a) A_1, A_2, A_3, the first activities of the project, can start simultaneously; (b) A_1 and A_2 precede A_4; (c) A_2 precedes A_5, A_6, A_8; (d) A_6 and A_3 precede A_7; (e) A_5 and A_8 precede A_9, A_{10}; (f) A_3, A_4, A_6, A_{10} precede A_{11}; (g) A_{11} precede A_{12}; (h) A_9, A_7 and A_{12} are the terminal activities of the project.*

Solution:

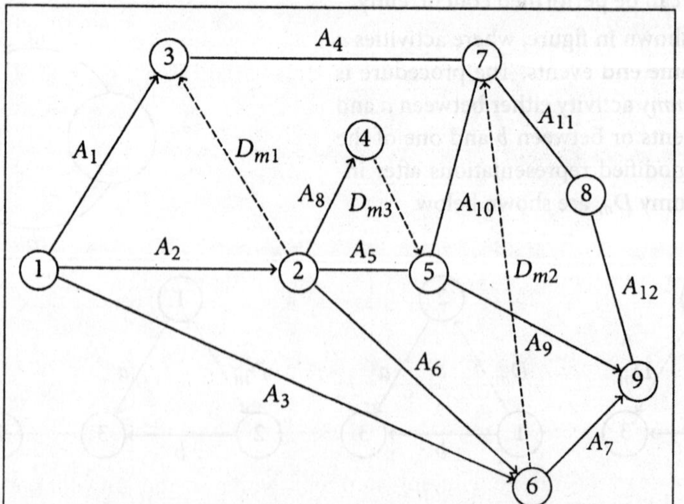

Remark. The dummy activities D_{m_1} and D_{m_2} are used to establish correct precedence relationship. D_{m_3} is used to identify activities A_5 and A_8 with unique end events. The events of the project are numbered such that their ascending order indicates the direction of progress in the project.

9.1.2 Fulkerson's Law for Numbering an Event

A standard procedure developed by Fulkerson, is most commonly used for numbering an event in a network diagram. Main steps of this law are:

(i) A start event is the one, which has arrows emerging from it but none entering it. This is the start event and number it as unity (1).

(ii) Delete all arrows emerging from numbered event (1). This will create one or more new start events. Number them as (2), (3), etc.

(iii) Go on repeating this process until the end event is reached.

Example 9.1.2. *Draw a network for the following project and number the events according to Fulkerson's law.* (a) *A is the start event and K is the end event,* (b) *A precedes B,* (c) *J is the successor event to F,* (d) *C and D are successor events to B,* (e) *D is the preceding event to G,* (f) *E and F occur after event C,* (g) *E precedes F,* (h) *C restrains the occurrence of G, and G precedes H,* (i) *H precedes J, and K succeeds J,* (j) *F restrains the occurrence of H.*

[CU(H) Stat 1994]

Solution:

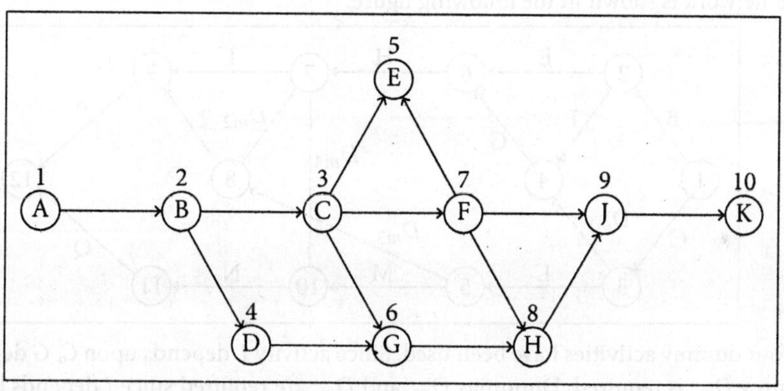

In this problem the events *A, B, C, D, E, F, G, H, J* and *K* constitute the network. The diagram is shown in the above figure. Along the nodes are given their numbers as obtained by *Fulkerson's law.*

Example 9.1.3. *Number the events according to Fulkerson's law of the following network.*

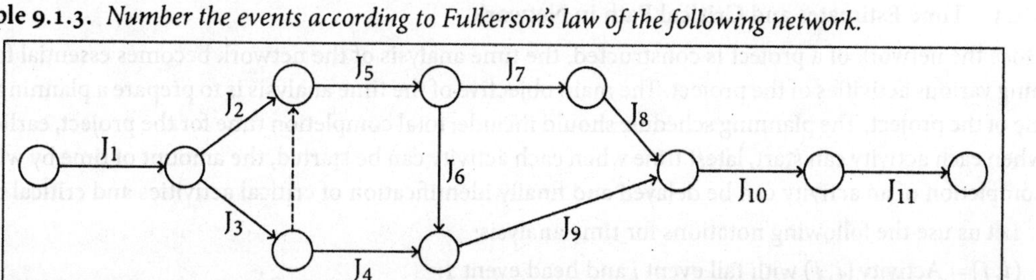

Solution: The bottom event is the only event from jobs, which is emerging out but none entering it. This is number 1. Delete arrow emerging from 1, which will create one new starting event from which jobs are emerging out but none entering. This is number 2. Continuing in this way we reach at the end event. The corresponding numbered network is shown below.

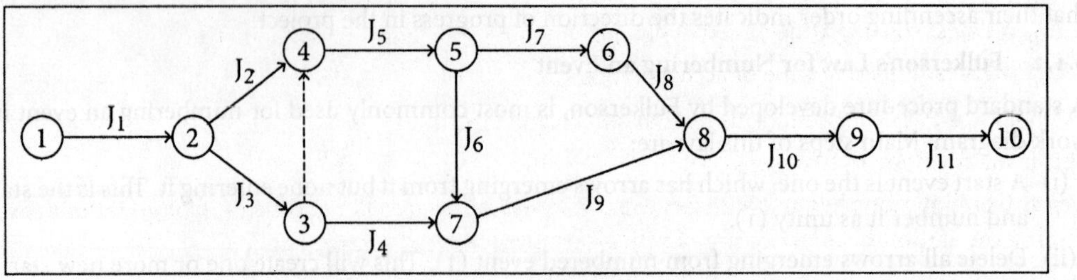

Remark. Fulkerson's procedure has certain distinct advantages when the network is large. First this procedure always detects a *close loop* in the network if there is any. In the network a close loop represents an *impossible events.* Secondly, the numbers are smaller towards the start and become larger in the end.

Example 9.1.4. *Construct a network diagram for a project comprising of activities B, C, E, F, G, H, I, J, L, M, N, P and Q such that the following precedence relationships are satisfied.*

$B < E, F;\ C, F < G;\ C < L;\ E, G < H;\ H, L < I;\ H < J;\ L < M;\ L < M;\ H, M < N;\ I, J < P, N < Q.$

[JNU(ME) 2004, KU(MSc) 2008]

Solution: The network is shown in the following figure:

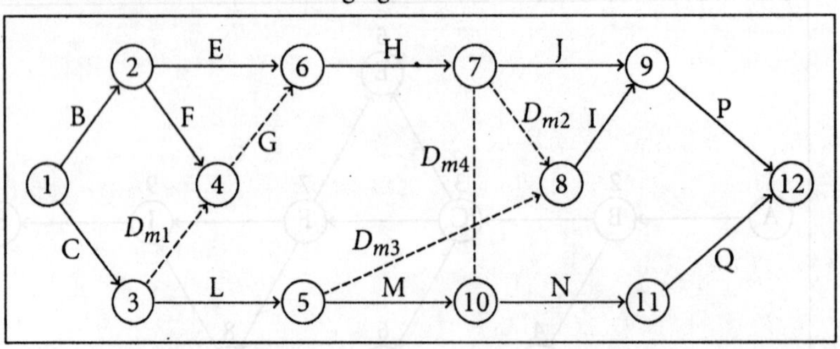

Note that four dummy activities have been used. Since activity L depends upon C, G depends upon both F and C, dummy D_{m_1} is required. Dummies D_{m_2} and D_{m_3} are required since I depends both on H and L, while J depends only on H. Activity N depends both on H and M, while J depends on H. These precedence orders are established by employing D_{m_4}. The events of the network are numbered using Fulkerson's law.

9.1.3 Time Estimates and Critical Path in Network

Once the network of a project is constructed, the time analysis of the network becomes essential for planning various activities of the project. The main objective of the time analysis is to prepare a planning schedule of the project. The planning schedule should include: total completion time for the project, earliest time when each activity can start, latest time when each activity can be started, the amount of time by which the completion of an activity can be delayed and finally identification of critical activities and critical path.

Let us use the following notations for time analysis:

(i, j) = Activity (i, j) with tail event i and head event j;

E_i = Earliest occurrence time of event i;

L_j = Latest allowable occurrence time of event j;

D_{ij} = Estimated completion time of activity (i, j);

$E_{s_{ij}}$ = Earliest starting time of activity (i, j);
$E_{f_{ij}}$ = Earliest finish time of activity (i, j);
$L_{s_{ij}}$ = Latest starting time of activity (i, j);
$L_{f_{ij}}$ = Latest finishing time of activity (i, j).

(A) Forward Pass Computations for Earliest Event Time

This is mainly done in two steps:

Step 1. Computations begin from start event and move towards the end event. Computations start by assuming the earliest occurrence time for the start project event is zero.

Step 2.

(i) Earliest starting time of activity (i, j) is the earliest event time of the tail and event, $E_{s_{ij}} = E_i$.

(ii) Earliest finish time of activity (i, j) is the earliest starting time + the activity time, $E_{f_{ij}} = E_{s_{ij}} + D_{ij} = E_i + D_{ij}$.

(iii) Earliest event time for event j is the maximum of the earliest finish times of all activities ending into the event, $E_j = \max_i \left(E_{f_{ij}}\right)$ for all immediate predecessor of (i, j)

$$= \max_i \left\{E_i + D_{ij}\right\}.$$

(B) Backward Pass Computations for Latest Allowable Event Time

This is done in the following steps:

Step 1. For ending event assume $E = L$, where all E's have been computed by *forward pass computations*.

Step 2.

(i) Following the similar argument for activity (i, j): $L_{f_{ij}} = L_j$.

(ii) Latest starting time of activity (i, j) = latest completion of (i, j)– activity time: $L_{s_{ij}} = L_{f_{ij}} - D_{ij} = L_j - D_{ij}$.

(iii) $L_i = \min_j \left(L_{s_{ij}}\right)$ for all immediate successors of (i, j)

$$= \min_j \left\{L_{f_{ij}} - D_{ij}\right\} = \min_j \left\{L_j - D_{ij}\right\}.$$

(C) Computations of Floats and Slack Times

(i) The amount of time by which the completion of an activity could be delayed beyond the earliest expected completion time without effecting the overall project duration time is known as *total float*.

Mathematically, total float $\left(T_{f_{ij}}\right)$ can be calculated by the formula:

$$T_{f_{ij}} = \text{(Latest start} - \text{Earliest start) for activity } (i, j)$$
$$= L_{s_{ij}} - E_{s_{ij}} = L_j - D_{ij} - E_i = \left(L_j - E_i\right) - D_{ij}.$$

The concept of floats is useful for the management in representing under utilised resources and flexibility of the schedule and the extent to which the resources will be utilised on different activities.

(ii) Event slack for a given event is defined as the difference between the latest event and the earliest event times.

Mathematically, for a given activity (i, j): Head event slack = $L_j - E_j$, Tail event slack = $L_i - E_i$.

(D) Location of Critical Path

Since the slack of an event is the difference between the latest and the earliest event times, the event with zero slack times are called *critical events*.

Therefore, an event i is said to be *critical*, if $E_i = L_i$.

Again, since the difference between the latest start time and earliest start time of an activity is called as *total float* the activities with zero total float are known as *critical activities*.

The sequence of critical activities in a network is called the *critical path*. This path is the longest path from the starting event to ending event and taken the minimum time to complete the project. The critical path identifies all critical activities of the project. The method of determining such a path is best explained by the following numerical examples.

Example 9.1.5. *Identify the critical path in respect to following network (Activity times in number of days are indicated on the network).*

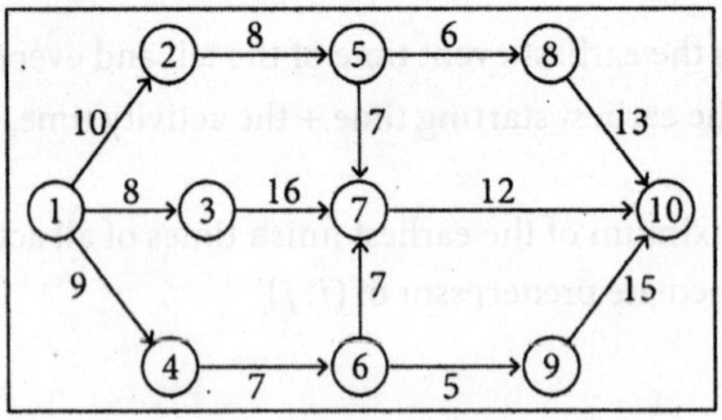

[CU(MSc) 2006, BESU(MSc) 2010]

Solution: To determine the critical path compute the earliest start E_i and latest finish L_j for each task (i, j). The calculations are done as follows: $E_1 = 0$

$$E_2 = E_1 + D_{12} = 0 + 10 = 10$$
$$E_3 = E_1 + D_{13} = 0 + 8 = 8$$
$$E_4 = E_1 + D_{14} = 0 + 9 = 9$$
$$E_5 = E_2 + D_{25} = 10 + 8 = 18$$
$$E_6 = E_4 + D_{46} = 9 + 7 = 16.$$

To determine the value of E_7 since there are three incoming tasks (3, 7), (5, 7), (6, 7):

$$E_7 = \max_i \{E_i + D_{i7}\},\ i = 3, 5, 6 = \max\{24, 25, 23\} = 25.$$

Similarly, $E_8 = 24$, $E_9 = 21$, $E_{10} = 37$.

The value of L_i are calculated backwards as follows: $L_{10} = E_{10} = 37$

$$L_9 = L_{10} - D_{9,10} = 37 - 15 = 22$$
$$L_8 = L_{10} - D_{8,10} = 37 - 13 = 24$$
$$L_7 = 37 - 12 = 25$$
$$L_6 = 7,\ L_5 = 18,\ L_4 = 17,\ L_3 = 9,\ L_2 = 10,\ L_1 = 0.$$

Network analysis table

Activity		Earliest time		Latest time		Total float
(i, j)	D_{ij}	Start	Finish	Start	Finish	$L_j - E_i - D_{ij}$
		E_i	$E_i + D_{ij}$	$L_j - D_{ij}$	L_j	
(1, 2)	10	0	10	0	10	0
(1, 3)	8	0	8	1	9	1
(1, 4)	9	0	9	8	17	8
(2, 5)	8	10	18	10	18	0
(4, 6)	7	9	16	10	17	1
(3, 7)	16	8	24	9	25	1
(5, 7)	7	18	25	18	25	0
(6, 7)	7	16	23	18	25	2
(5, 8)	6	18	24	18	24	0
(6, 9)	5	16	21	17	22	1
(7, 10)	12	25	37	25	37	0
(8, 10)	13	24	37	24	37	0
(9, 10)	15	21	36	22	37	1

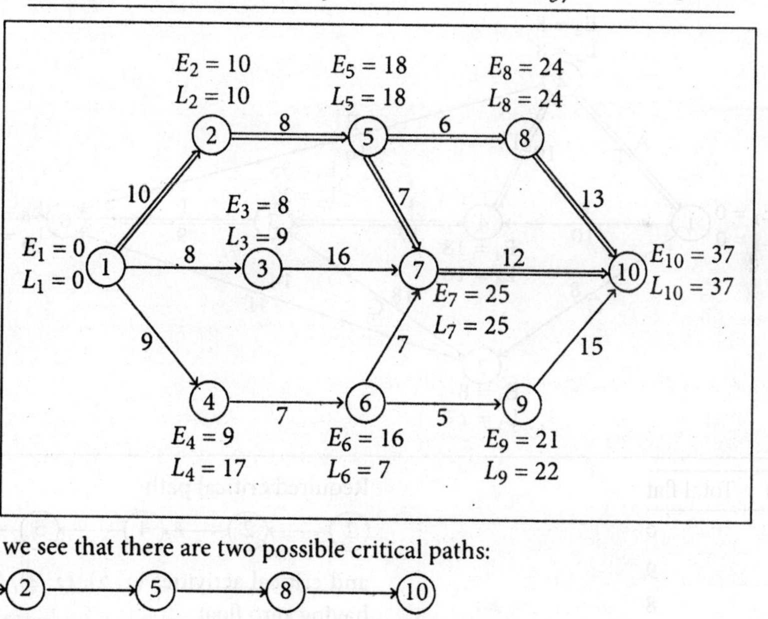

From the table we see that there are two possible critical paths:

(i) 1 → 2 → 5 → 8 → 10

(ii) 1 → 2 → 5 → 7 → 10

Example 9.1.6. *Tasks A, B, C, D, E, F, G, H, I constitute a project. The precedence relationships are: A < D, A < E, B < F, D < F, C < G, C < H, F < I, G < I. Draw a network. Identify the critical path. The time, in days, of each task is as follows:*

Task	A	B	C	D	E	F	G	H	I
Time	8	10	8	10	16	17	18	14	9

[IIT(Roorkee MSc) 1976, JNU(Comp.Sc) 1989]

Solution:

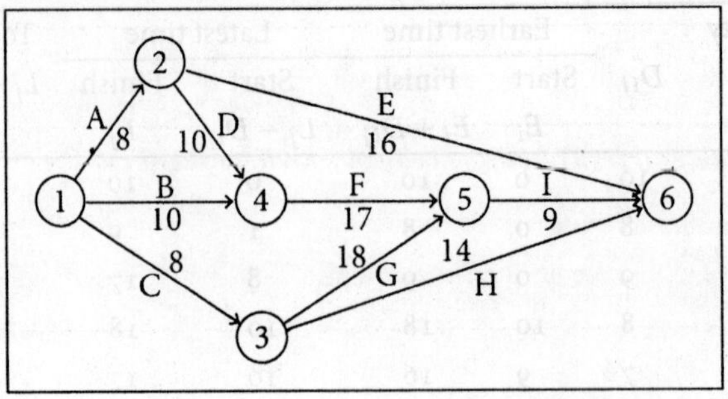

$E_1 = 0$
$E_2 = E_1 + D_{12} = 8$
$E_3 = E_1 + D_{13} = 8$
$E_4 = \max\{0+10, 8+10\} = 18$
$E_5 = \max\{18+17, 8+18\} = 35$
$E_6 = \max\{8+16, 35+9, 8+14\}$

$L_6 = E_6 = 0$
$L_5 = L_6 - D_{56} = 35$
$L_4 = L_5 - D_{45} = 18$
$L_3 = \min\{44-14, 35-18\} = 17$
$L_2 = \min\{44-16, 18-10\} = 8$
$L_1 = \min\{8-8, 17-8, 18-10\} = 0$

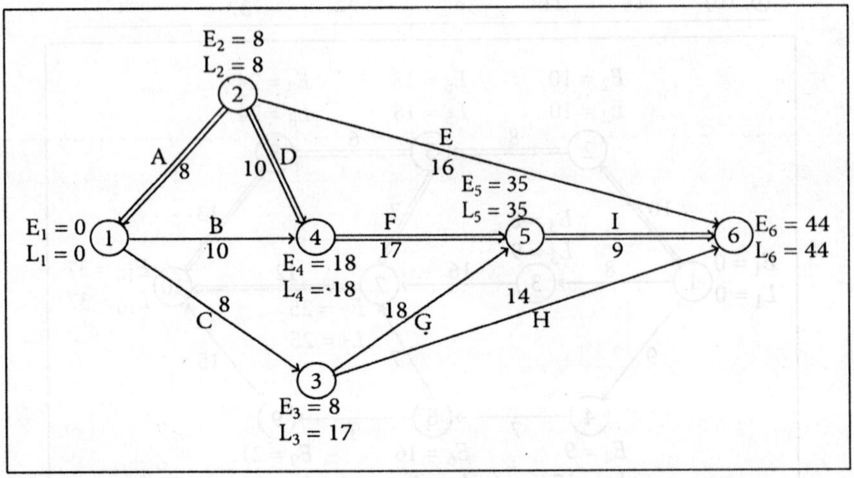

Activity (i, j)	Total flat
(1, 2)	0
(1, 3)	9
(1, 4)	8
(2, 4)	0
(2, 6)	20
(3, 5)	9
(3, 6)	22
(4, 5)	0
(5, 6)	0

Required critical path:

(1) → (2) → (4) → (5) → (6)

and critical activities (1, 2), (2, 4), (4, 5) and (5, 6) having zero float.

Example 9.1.7. *A project schedule has the following characteristics.*

Activity	1–2	1–3	2–4	3–4	3–5	4–9	5–6	5–7	6–8	7–8	8–10	9–10
Time (Days)	4	1	1	1	6	5	4	8	1	2	5	7

(i) *Construct a network diagram;* (ii) *Indicate critical activities;* (iii) *Find the critical path and duration of the project.*

[IAS 2001, CU(MSc) 2005]

Solution:

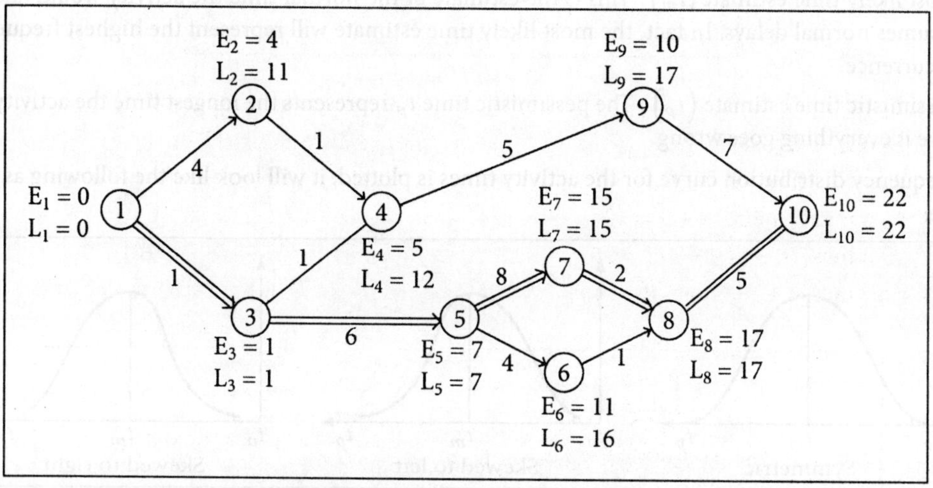

Calculation of E and L are exactly similar as detailed shown in Ex. 9.3.2. We represent the calculation in the tabular form.

Activity	Duration	Earliest Start	Earliest Finish	Latest Start	Latest Finish	Total float
1–2	4	0	4	7	11	7
1–3	1	0	1	0	1	0
2–4	1	4	5	11	12	7
3–4	1	1	2	11	12	10
3–5	6	1	7	1	7	0
5–7	8	7	15	7	15	0
5–6	4	7	11	12	16	5
7–8	2	15	17	15	17	0
6–8	1	11	12	16	17	5
4–9	5	5	10	12	17	7
9–10	7	10	17	15	22	5
8–10	5	17	22	17	22	0

Critical path is: (1) → (3) → (5) → (7) → (8) → (10)

Critical activities: (1, 3), (3, 5), (5, 7), (7, 8), (8, 10).

Duration of the project = 1 + 6 + 8 + 2 + 5 = 22 days.

9.1.4 Programme Evaluation and Review Technique (PERT)

In the network analysis discussed so far, it is assumed that the time values are deterministic. In PERT analysis, time duration of each activity is no longer a single time estimate, but is an r.v. characterised by some probability distribution—usually a β-distribution. To estimate the parameters of the β-distribution (the mean and variance) the PERT system is based on *three time estimates*. They are:

(i) Optimistic time estimate (t_o): This is the shortest possible time in which the activity can be finished. Obviously, it assumes that everything goes very well.

(ii) Most likely time estimate (t_m): This is the estimate of the normal time the activity would take. This assumes normal delays. In fact, the most likely time estimate will represent the highest frequency of occurrence.

(iii) Pessimistic time estimate (t_p): The pessimistic time t_p represents the longest time the activity could take if everything goes wrong.

If a frequency distribution curve for the activity times is plotted, it will look like the following as shown in figure:

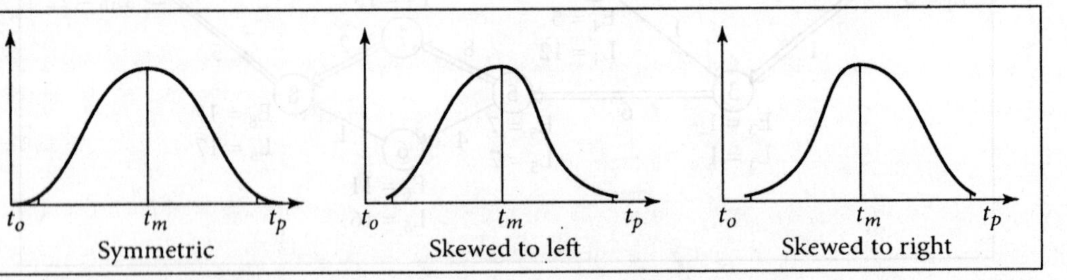

Though the curve is not fully described by the mean (μ) and the standard deviation (σ), yet in PERT analysis the following relations are approximated for μ and σ.

$$t_e = \mu = \text{expected time of an activity is taken equal to mean} = \frac{t_o + 4t_m + t_p}{6}$$

$$\sigma = \frac{t_p - t_o}{6} = \text{standard deviation.}$$

The expected time is used as the activity duration and standard deviation is used to find the probability of completing the whole project by a given data with the following procedure.

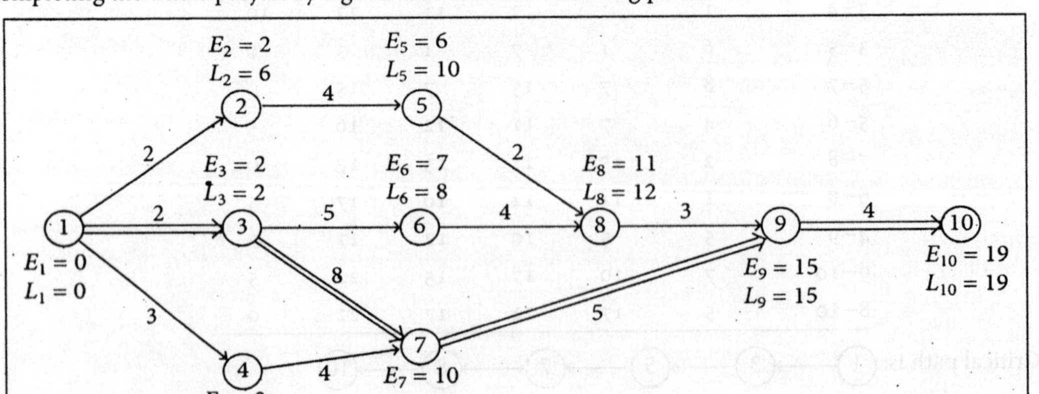

Consider the above network. Table 1 gives three time estimates for each activity, the expected value and the variance.

Table 1.

Activity	Time estimate			Expected time	Variance
	t_o	t_m	t_p	$t_o = \frac{1}{6}\left(t_o + 4t_m + t_p\right)$	$\sigma^2 = \left(\frac{t_p - t_o}{6}\right)^2$
1–2	1.0	2.0	3.0	2	4/36
1–3	1.5	2.0	2.5	2	1/36
1–4	1.5	1.75	3.5	2	4/36
2–5	3.0	3.5	7.0	4	16/36
3–6	4.0	4.5	8.0	5	16/36
3–7	6.0	8.25	9.0	8	9/36
4–7	3.0	3.50	7.0	4	16/36
5–8	2.0	2.0	2.0	2	0
6–8	2.0	4.0	6.0	4	16/36
7–9	2.0	5.0	8.0	5	36/36
8–9	2.0	3.0	4.0	3	4/36
9–10	2.5	4.25	4.5	4	4/36

Expected values are calculated, these are used in finding the critical path. The critical path calculations are same as before. Find *E*'s, *L*'s and total floats as usual taking t_e's. The above example indicates the critical path is (1) ⟶ (3) ⟶ (7) ⟶ (9) ⟶ (10). However, the interpretations of critical path is now different. In this case the expected duration of the job is 19 days, which implies that there are times when this would have taken time less than or more than 19 days. Therefore, the meaning of the expected duration is that–if the same job is performed again under similar conditions, the average duration is 19 days. If the job takes 19 days, then there is probability value associated with it which can be calculated under some assumptions. Since duration of each activity is an r.v., the duration of a path, which consists of a set of activities will also an r.v. To calculate the exact distribution of duration of a path will be difficult and for overall decisions it is enough to know the mean and the variance.

In the above example, the expected duration of the project is 19 days and the variance of this path is 50/36. If the exact probability distribution of the path is known, it would have been easy to find out the probability of completing the project in a given time.

Since the variance of the path is known, the *Chebyshev inequality* $P(|x - \mu| > \tau\sigma) \leq \frac{1}{\tau^2}$ could be used to get an estimate of probability for a given duration but PERT users, however, have used *central limit theorem* to claim that probability distribution of time for each event could be considered as *normal.* This in fact, a *strong assumption,* which greatly simplifies calculations.

Therefore, assuming the normality, the probability of project being completed by a certain date can be evaluated easily.

For this particular example let us find probability of project duration (*D*) 20 days, then

$$P[D \leq 20] = P\left[\frac{D-\mu}{\sigma} \leq \frac{20-\mu}{\sigma}\right],$$

where μ is the mean of the distribution and σ is standard deviation. Now $\frac{D-\mu}{\sigma}$ is a normalised value usually written as *z*.

$$P(D \le 20) = P\left(z \le \frac{20-19}{\sqrt{50/36}}\right) = P(z \le 0.85) = 0.80 \text{ (from standard normal table).}$$

The physical meaning of this is: If the job is done 100 times under almost identical conditions, then there will be 80 occasions when it will take 20 days or less to complete the job.

Advantages

1. One of the main advantages of PERT approach to the management of a large scale project is in binding for contractual dates to finish the project.
2. The manager would like to know the duration of the project that will have 95% chance of being completed by the following way.

Let t_s be the scheduled duration such that

$$P(t \le t_s) = 0.95 \text{ or, } P\left(\frac{t-\mu}{\sigma} \le \frac{t_s-\mu}{\sigma}\right) = 0.95 \text{ or, } P\left(z \le \frac{t_s-\mu}{\sigma}\right) = 0.95$$

$$\text{or, } \frac{t_s-\mu}{\sigma} = 1.64 \ [\because z_{0.95} = 1.64 \text{ from table}]$$

$$\text{or, } t_s = \mu + 1.64\sigma = 19 + \sqrt{\frac{50}{36}} \times 1.64 = 20.90 \simeq 21 \text{ days.}$$

Remark. The β-distribution was chosen possibly because (i) it is a *unimodal* distribution, (ii) finite non-negative end points, (iii) symmetric β-density is

$$f(x, \alpha, \beta) = \frac{1}{B(\alpha+1, \beta+1)} x^{\alpha}(1-x)^{\beta}, \ 0 < x < 1, \alpha+1, \beta+1 > 0$$

where $B(\alpha, \beta) = \dfrac{\Gamma(\alpha)\Gamma(\beta)}{\Gamma(\alpha+\beta)}$, $\Gamma(\alpha)$ is a gamma function.

Example 9.1.8. *In the network shown below the three time estimates for the activities are indicated. Number the events according to Fulkerson's law and calculate the variance and expected time for each activity.*

[CU(H) Stat 1995]

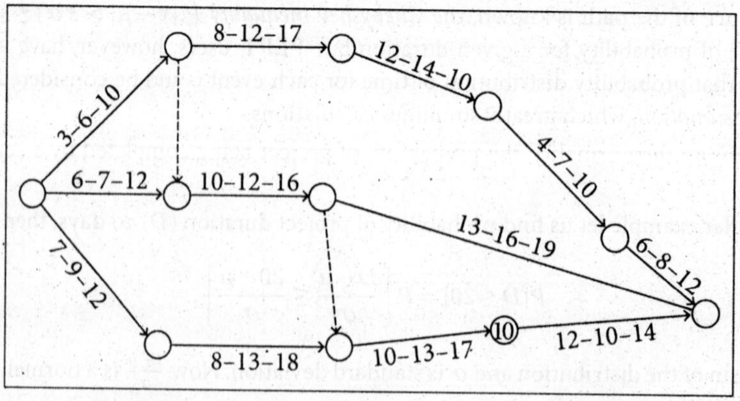

Solution: Number the events according to Fulkerson's law.

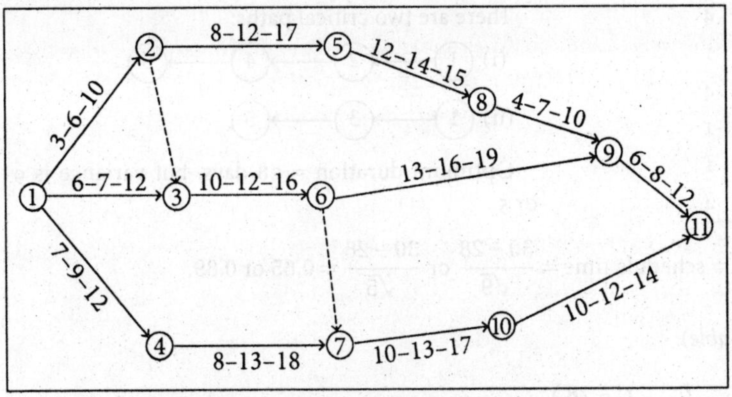

Activity	t_o	t_m	t_p	t_e	σ^2
1–2	3	6	10	6.2	1.36
1–3	6	7	12	7.7	1.00
1–4	7	9	12	9.2	0.69
2–3	0	0	0	0	0
2–5	8	12	17	12.2	2.25
3–6	10	12	15	12.2	0.69
4–7	8	13	19	13.2	3.36
5–8	12	14	15	13.9	0.25
6–5	8	9	10	9.0	0.11
6–9	13	16	19	16.0	1.00
8–9	4	7	10	7.0	1.00
7–10	10	13	17	13.2	1.36
9–11	6	8	12	8.4	1.00
10–11	10	12	14	12.0	0.66

Using the formula $t_e = \frac{1}{6}\left(t_o + 4t_m + t_p\right)$ and $\sigma^2 = \frac{1}{36}\left(t_p - t_o\right)^2$ compute the adjoining table.

Example 9.1.9. *Assuming that the expected times are normally distributed, find the probability of meeting the scheduled date as given for the network. Scheduled project completion time is 30 days. Also find the date on which the project manager can complete the project with a probability of* 0.95.

	Days		
Activity $\langle i-j \rangle$	*Optimistic* (t_o)	*Most likely* (t_m)	*Pessimistic* (t_p)
1-2	2	5	14
1-3	9	12	15
2-4	5	14	17
3-4	2	5	8
4-5	6	6	12
3-5	8	17	20

[ISI(Dip) 1996]

Solution:

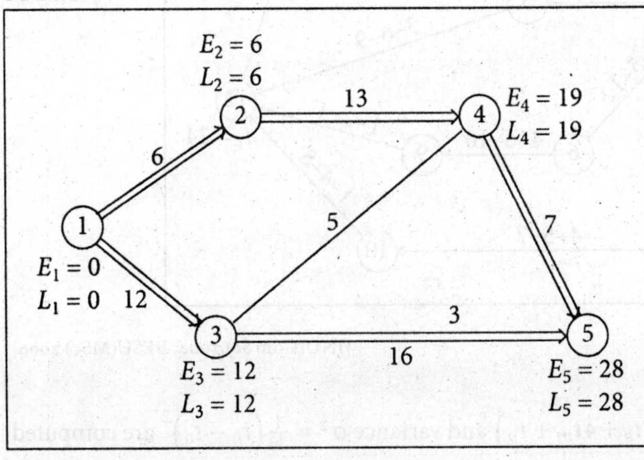

The expected activity time

$$t_e = \tfrac{1}{6}\left(t_o + 4t_m + t_p\right)$$

and the activity variance

$$\sigma^2 = \tfrac{1}{36}\left(t_p - t_o\right)^2$$

are calculated in the following table.

Activity $\langle i-j \rangle$	t_o	t_m	t_p	t_e	σ^2
1–2	2	5	14	6	4
1–3	9	12	15	12	1
2–4	5	14	17	13	4
3–4	2	5	8	5	1
4–5	6	6	12	7	1
3–5	8	17	20	16	4

For the *critical path* determine E and L and corresponding floats.

There are two critical paths:

(i) (1) ⟶ (2) ⟶ (4) ⟶ (5)

(ii) (1) ⟶ (3) ⟶ (5)

Optimum duration = 28 days, but variance is 9 or 5.

Now, $D_i = \dfrac{t_s - 28}{\sqrt{9}}$ or $\dfrac{t_s - 28}{\sqrt{5}}$: t_s = schedule time $= \dfrac{30-28}{\sqrt{9}}$ or $\dfrac{30-28}{\sqrt{5}} = 0.65$ or 0.89.

$P(z \le D_i) = 0.71$ or 0.81 (from *Table*).

Again, $P\left(z \le \dfrac{t_s - 28}{3}\right) = 0.95$ or, $P\left(z \le \dfrac{t_s - 28}{\sqrt{5}}\right) = 0.95$.

$$\therefore\ t_s = 28 + 3 \times 1.64 \text{ or, } 28 + \sqrt{5} \times 1.64 \quad [\because z_{0.95} = 1.64]$$
$$= 32.92 \text{ or } 31.60 \simeq 33 \text{ or } 32 \text{ days.}$$

Example 9.1.10. *A PERT network is shown below. The activity times in days are given along the arrows. The scheduled times for some important events are given along the nodes. Determine the critical path and probabilities of meeting the scheduled dates for the specified events. Tabulate the results and determine slack for each event.*

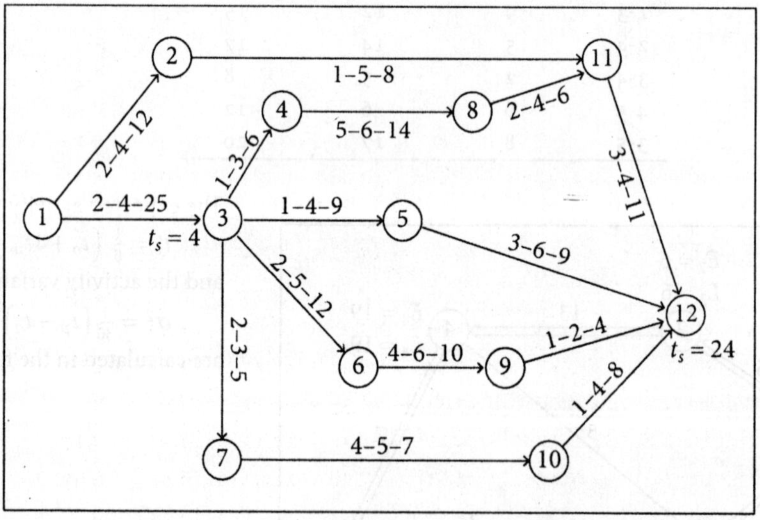

[JNU(Com Sc) 2004, BESU(MSc) 2006]

Solution: The expected activity times $t_e = \frac{1}{6}\left(t_o + 4t_m + t_p\right)$ and variance $\sigma^2 = \frac{1}{36}\left(t_p - t_o\right)^2$ are computed below.

Activity	t_o	t_m	t_p	t_e	σ^2
1−2	2	4	12	5	2.78
1−3	2	4	25	7.17	14.69
2−11	1	5	8	4.83	1.36
3−4	1	3	6	3.17	0.69
3−5	1	4	9	4.33	1.78
3−6	2	5	12	5.67	2.78
3−7	2	3	5	3.17	0.25
4−8	5	6	14	7.17	2.25
5−2	3	6	9	6.00	1.00
6−9	4	6	10	6.33	1.00
7−10	4	5	7	5.17	0.25
8−11	2	4	6	4.00	0.44
9−12	1	2	4	2.17	0.25
10−12	1	4	8	4.17	1.36
11−12	3	4	11	5.00	1.78

The earliest, latest and total floats are calculated in the following table.

Activity	Expected duration (t_e)	Earliest Start	Earliest Finish	Latest Start	Latest Finish	Total float
1−2	5.00	0	5.00	11.68	16.68	11.68
1−3	7.17	0	7.17	0	7.17	0
2−11	4.83	5.00	9.83	16.68	21.51	11.68
3−4	3.17	7.17	10.34	7.17	10.34	0
3−5	4.33	7.17	11.50	16.18	20.51	9.01
3−6	5.67	7.17	12.84	12.33	18.00	5.16
3−7	3.17	7.17	10.34	14.00	17.17	6.83
4−8	7.17	10.34	17.51	10.34	17.51	0
5−12	6.00	11.50	17.50	20.51	26.51	9.01
6−9	6.33	12.84	19.17	18.01	24.34	5.17
7−10	5.17	10.34	15.51	17.17	22.34	6.83
8−11	4.00	17.51	21.51	17.51	21.51	0
9−12	2.17	19.17	21.34	24.34	26.51	5.17
10−12	4.17	15.51	19.68	22.34	26.51	6.83
11−12	5.00	21.51	26.51	21.51	26.51	0

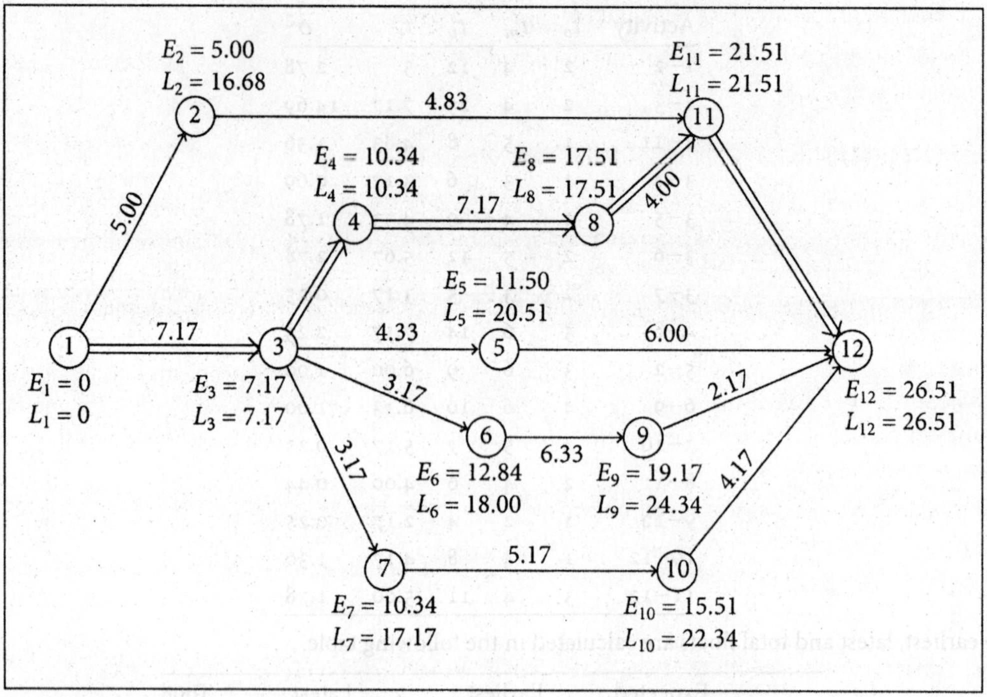

(i) Critical path is (1) → (3) → (4) → (8) → (11) → (12).

Optimum duration along critical path: $7.17+3.17+7.17+4.00+5.00=26.51$.

(ii) Probability of completing the project in the scheduled completion time as given by t_s = 24 days at node (12)

$$z=\frac{24-26.51}{\sqrt{14.69+0.69+2.25+0.44+1.78}}=\frac{-2.51}{\sqrt{19.85}}=-0.5634.$$

$$\therefore\ P(t_s \le 24)=1-\text{value of probability for } z=0.5634$$
$$=1-0.7146 \text{ [from table]}$$
$$=29.54\%.$$

(iii) Probability that event (3) will occur on scheduled date t_s at (3) = 4 (given).

$$E=L=7.17; \quad z=\frac{4-7.17}{\sqrt{14.69}}=-0.8271.$$

$P(t_s(3)\le 4)=1-0.7956=20.44\%$.

(iv) Probability that event (5) meeting the scheduled date t_5 at (5) = 12 (given).

Variance of path = 14.69 + 1.78 = 16.47.

$t_s = 12$
$E = 11.50$

$$z=\frac{12-11.50}{\sqrt{16.47}}=0.123.$$

$t_s = 12$
$L = 20.51$

$$z=\frac{12-20.51}{\sqrt{16.47}}=-2.1.$$

∴ required probability = 50.89% and (1−0.982) = 0.018.

Therefore, the probability of meeting the scheduled date in case of event (5) is less than 54.89 with minimum of 0.018.

9.2 MINIMUM SPANNING TREE PROBLEM

We know a network (undirected) not containing any loop is called a *tree graph.* Given an undirected network of nodes connected by arcs of given length. Now our main objective is which tree graph connecting all the nodes of the network, possesses minimum total length. The connection between any two nodes may be direct or indirect, passing through other nodes. For examples, connecting a group of villages in a district by paved roads, providing telecom cable connection to householders living in a specified area or connecting a set of cities by high power transmission and gas pipe lines, are problems of the same nature. A simple method of finding the *minimal spanning tree* was given by J W Kruskal (1956). The method essentially consists of adding a *safe arc* (which does not result in a loop) of smallest length to the growing minimum spanning tree.

We now state *Kruskal's algorithm* as follows:

Let the nodes be $1, 2, \ldots, n$, then the method consists of:

Rule 1. Sort the arc lengths in increasing order of magnitude. Set S, the set of nodes of minimum spanning tree = ϕ.

Rule 2. Select shortest length (ties may be broken arbitrarily) arc $(i, j): i \neq j$ and $i, j \notin S$.

Rule 3. Set $S = S \cup \{i, j\}$ if $S = \{1, 2, \ldots, n\}$ connecting all nodes stop. Else if S consists of unconnected branches go to *Rule* 4, otherwise go to *Rule* 2.

Rule 4. Connect the unconnected branches by *shortest arcs*. Then stop.

Illustration. Consider the network.

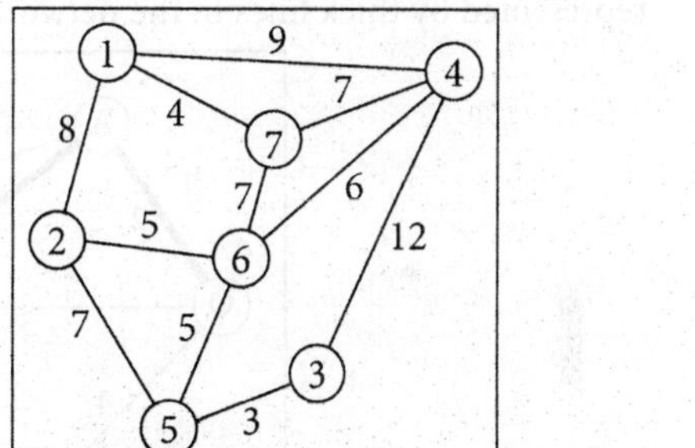

The arcs in increasing order of magnitude of length are: (3, 5), (1, 7), (2, 6), (5, 6), (4, 6), (2, 5), (6, 7), (4, 7), (1, 2), (1, 4) and (3, 4).

Rule 2 and *Rule* 3 of Kruskal's algorithm yields:

Iteration 1. Shortest arc (3, 5), $S = \{3, 5\}$.

Iteration 2. Shortest arc (1, 7), $S = \{3, 5, 1, 7\}$.

Iteration 3. Shortest arc (2, 6) [arc (5, 6) could also be chosen], $S = \{3, 5, 1, 7, 2, 6\}$.

Iteration 4. Shortest arc (5, 6), $S = \{3, 5, 1, 7, 2, 6\}$.

Iteration 5. Shortest arc (4, 6), $S = \{3, 5, 1, 7, 2, 6, 4\}$.

Iteration 6. Shortest arc (6, 7) [arc (4, 7) could have been alternatively chosen]. All nodes are now connected.

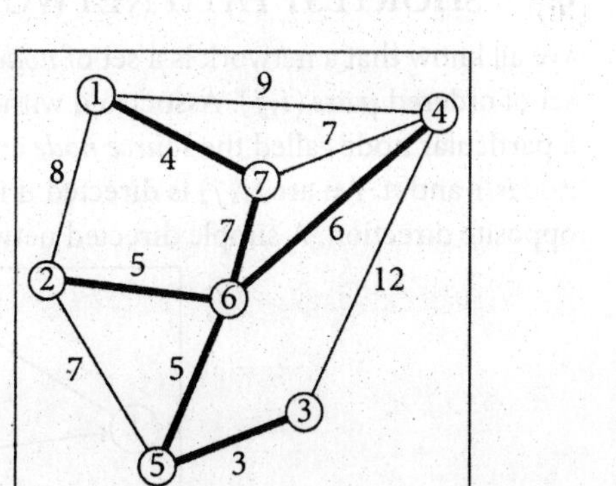

The minimal spanning tree is shown by the thick lines in the adjoining diagram.

Example 9.2.1. *The Millennium Park management needs to determine under which roads telephone lines should be installed to connect all stations with a minimum total length of lime (in miles) using the data given in the following network.*

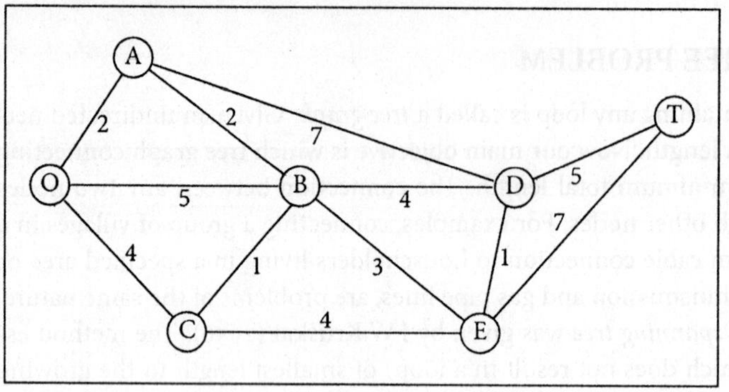

[JU(Comp.Sc) 2002, BESU(MCA) 1992]

Solution: Select node O to start. The unconnected node closest to node O is A; connect A to nod O. The unconnected node closest to node O or A is node B (closest to A); connect node B to node A. The unconnected node closest to node O, A or B is node C (closest to B); connect node C to node B. The unconnected node closest to O, A, B or C is E (closest to B); connect node E to B. The unconnected node closest to node O, A, B, C or E is node D closest to E. Connect node D to node E. Finally, the only connected node is T, which is closest to node D. Connect node T to node D. We get the following minimum spanning tree represented by thick lines in the network (The total length of the branches is 14 miles).

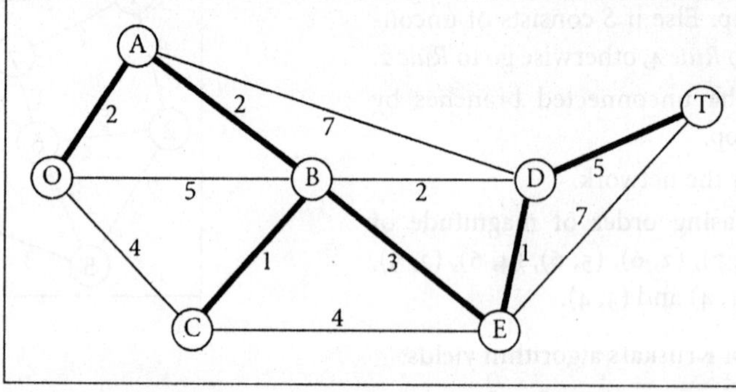

9.3 SHORTEST PATH NETWORK PROBLEM

We all know that a network is a set of *nodes* consisting of elements 1, 2, ..., n linked by *arcs* defined by the set of ordered pairs (i, j). Associated with each arc generally speaking, is some kind of flow, starting from a particular node called the *source node* and ending at another called *sink node.* These are usually taken as nodes 1 and n. An arc (i, j) is directed if it allows positive flow in the direction i to j and zero flow in the opposite direction. A simple directed network is shown below:

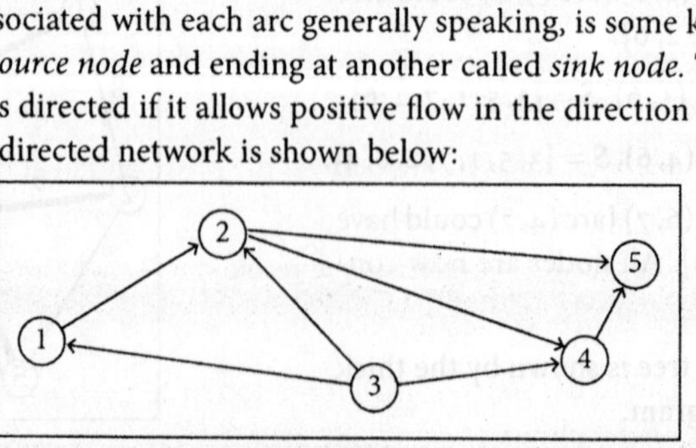

A path is a sequence of distinct arc s, joining a set of nodes regardless of the direction of flow in each arc. For example, in the above figure two paths 1 and 5 are (1) → (2) → (5) and (1) → (3) → (4) → (5). A path forms a *loop* or *cycle* if it connects a node to itself. For example, (1) → (2) → (3) → (1) is a loop.

In transport organisations, one of the objectives is to find the shortest path to a particular node to any of the other nodes in a network. Determination of the shortest path using the following two well-known methods (A) Dijkstra's algorithm (B) Floyd's algorithm are discussed in this section.

(A) Dijkstra's Algorithm

The steps of the algorithm are summarised below.

Step 1. Form a *distance matrix* from start node to all other nodes. If there is no direct arc from the start node to another node, the corresponding distance is assumed as ∞. Let the currently selected node (start node) be S.

Step 2. Find the smallest of the distances from the node S to all other unselected nodes in the distance matrix. Let it be D and corresponding node is N. Check whether N is a neighbour of the start node. If yes, do (a), otherwise do (b).

(a) Select the arc connecting the start node and N and then go to *Step* 3.

(b) Find the iteration among the preceding iterations in which the distance to N from the start node is different from D. Select the arc connecting the selected node of that iteration and the selected node N of the present iteration. Then go to *Step* 3.

Step 3. Check whether N is the required destination. If no, go to *Step* 4, otherwise go to *Step* 6.

Step 4. From the *distance matrix* according to following guidelines: For each of the unselected neighbour of N, find its new distance by adding D to its distance from N, and *update* its old distance from the start node in the distance matrix if the new distance is smaller than its old distance. Transfer the data of the last node of the distance matrix to the column corresponding to the recently selected node N. This reduces the matrix column size by 1 in every iteration.

Step 5. Set S = N and go to *Step* 2.

Step 6. Locate the shortest path in the following ways:

(a) Fix the selected node of last iteration as the last node of the shortest path.

(b) Traverse back through iterations and identify the iteration (say, *j*th iteration) at which the distance of the recently selected node is different.

(c) Prefix the selected node of *j*th iteration in the partially formed shortest path.

(d) Check whether the node selected at *j*th iteration is the source node. If not, go to next point (e), otherwise go to point (f).

(e) Treat the selected node in the *j*th iteration as the recently selected node and go to (b) of *Step* 6.

(f) Construction of *shortest path* is complete.

Illustrative example. Let us find the shortest path from node 1 to node 9 of the following *distance network* using Dijkstra's algorithm in details.

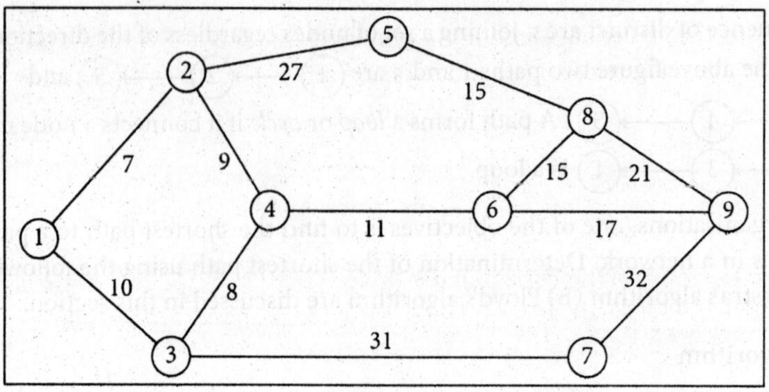

[JNU(Comp.Sc) 2010, NIMS(MCA) 1989]

Iteration 1. Distance matrix from the start node 1 to all other nodes.

$$\begin{pmatrix} 2 & 3 & 4 & 5 & 6 & 7 & 8 & 9 \\ \hline \underset{\uparrow}{7} & 10 & \infty & \infty & \infty & \infty & \infty & \infty \end{pmatrix}$$

(The distance for all other nodes from node 1 is assumed as ∞).

The smallest distance D = 7 and the corresponding node N is 2. Since the node 2 is a neighbour of the start node, select the arc 1−2. Again, as node 2 is not the required destination, go to next iteration.

Iteration 2. For node 2(N) nodes 4 and 5 are the unselected neighbours. Then $D+d_{24}=7+9=16$, where d_{24} is the actual distance from node 2 to node 4. Since this distance $<\infty$ update the distance to node 4 as 16. Similarly, $D+d_{25}=34<\infty$, update the distance to node 5 as 34. Transfer the data of node 9 to the position of node 2. This will form new distance matrix.

$$\begin{pmatrix} 9 & 3 & 4 & 5 & 6 & 7 & 8 \\ \hline \infty & \underset{\uparrow}{10} & 16 & 34 & \infty & \infty & \infty \end{pmatrix}$$

Smallest distance D = 10 and corresponding node N is 3. Since node 3 is neighbour of the start node, select the arc 1−3. Node 3 is not the required destination.

Iteration 3. Following similarly as *Iteration* 2, we get the following new distance matrix.

$$\begin{pmatrix} 9 & 8 & 4 & 5 & 6 & 7 \\ \hline \infty & \infty & \underset{\uparrow}{16} & 34 & \infty & 41 \end{pmatrix}$$

Smallest is 16 and corresponding node 4. Since N is not a neighbour of the start node *Step* 2(b) of the given algorithm: The iteration among the preceding iterations in which the distance to N from the starting node is different from D is the *Iteration* 1. The node selected in that iteration is 2, so select the arc 2−4. Further, node 4 is not the required destination.

Iteration 4. Distance matrix

$$\begin{pmatrix} 9 & 8 & 7 & 5 & 6 \\ \hline \infty & \infty & 41 & 34 & \underset{\uparrow}{27} \end{pmatrix}$$

Smallest distance 27 and corresponding node 6. Since N is not a neighbour of the start node, again perform *Step* 2(b).

The iteration among the preceding iterations in which the distance to N from the starting node is different from D in *Iteration* 3, the node selected is 4 and select the arc 4–6. Further, 6 is not the required destination.

Iteration 5.

$$\left(\frac{9 \quad 8 \quad 7 \quad 5}{44 \quad 42 \quad 41 \quad 34_{\uparrow}}\right)$$

Smallest distance D = 34 and the corresponding node (N) is 5. Since N is not a neighbour of the start node, follow *Step* 2(b) and select arc 2–5. Again, 5 is not the required destination.

Iteration 6.

$$\left(\frac{9 \quad 8 \quad 7}{44 \quad 42 \quad 41_{\uparrow}}\right)$$

Smallest distance D = 41 and the corresponding node (N) is 7. Since it is not the neighbour of start node, use *Step* 2(b) similarly; and select arc 3–7. Further, 7 is not the required destination.

Iteration 7.

$$\left(\frac{9 \quad 8}{44 \quad 42_{\uparrow}}\right)$$

Smallest distance D = 42 and the corresponding node (N) is 8. Since it is not the neighbour of start node, use *Step* 2(b) and select arc 6–8, but 8 is not the required destination.

Iteration 8.

$$\left(\frac{9}{44_{\uparrow}}\right)$$

Distance D = 44 and corresponding node (N) is 9. Since 9 is not a neighbour of start node, the iteration among the preceding iterations in which the distance to N from the starting node is different from D is *Iteration* 4. The node selected in that iteration is 6, so select the arc 6–9. Since 9 is the required destination we locate the shortest path based on the guidelines given in *Step* 6. The following figure shows the network of final solution.

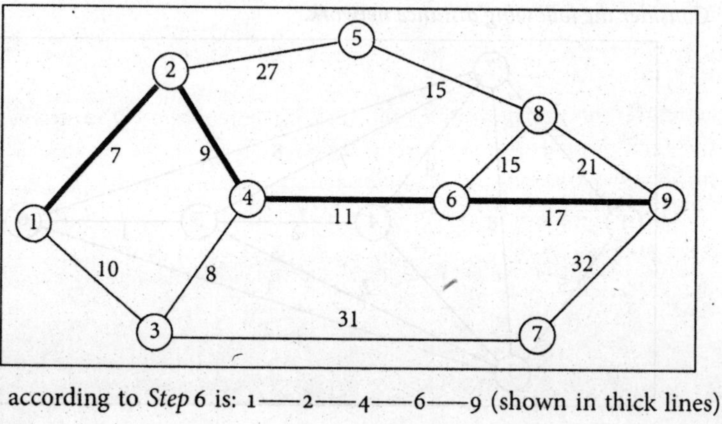

The shortest path according to *Step* 6 is: 1——2——4——6——9 (shown in thick lines) and the corresponding distance is 44.

(B) Floyd's Algorithm

Floyd's algorithm is used to find the shortest path and the corresponding distance from any source node to any destination node in a given distance network. This algorithm is based on the following steps.

Step 1. Set $k = 0$.

Step 2. From the initial distance matrix $\left(I_D^0\right)$ and the initial precedence matrix $\left(I_P^0\right)$ from the distance network. The distance as well as precedence matrices are of order $n \times n$. In the distance matrix, between any two nodes, if there is no direct arc, then the corresponding distance is assumed as ∞. The diagonal elements of the initial distance matrix are assumed as 0. In the initial precedence matrix the diagonal elements are assumed as '–' and the other entries in the ith row are assumed as i for $i = 1, 2, \ldots, n$.

Step 3. Set $k = k + 1$.

Step 4. Find the distance matrix $\left(I_D^k\right)$ for all the cell, where $i \neq j$ using the formula

$$I_{D_{ij}}^k = \min\left[I_{D_{ij}}^{k-1}, \left(I_{D_{ik}}^{k-1} + I_{D_{kj}}^{k-1}\right)\right].$$

Step 5. Find the precedence matrix $\left(I_P^k\right)$ for all the cell, where $i \neq j$ using the formula

$$\begin{aligned} I_{P_{ij}}^k &= I_{P_{kj}}^{k-1} \; : \; I_{D_{ij}}^k \neq I_{D_{ij}}^{k-1} \\ &= I_{P_{ij}}^{k-1} \text{ otherwise.} \end{aligned}$$

Step 6. If $k = n$ is the order of the matrix, then go to *Step* 7, otherwise repeat *Step* 4.

Step 7. Find the shortest distance from the final distance matrix $\left(I_D^n\right)$ and trace the corresponding shortest path from the final precedence matrix $\left(I_P^n\right)$ by using the following guidelines.

(a) Let the source node be S and destination node D.

(b) Fix node D as the last node.

(c) Find the value from the final precedence matrix $\left(I_P^n\right)$ for the row corresponding to node S and the column corresponding to D. Let it be N*. Prefix N* in the partially formed shortest path.

(d) Check whether N* is equal to S if not set D = N* and go to *Step* 7(c), otherwise go to *Step* 7(e).

(e) The path constructed is the required *shortest path* from the source node S to the distance node D.

Example 9.3.1. *Consider the following distance network.*

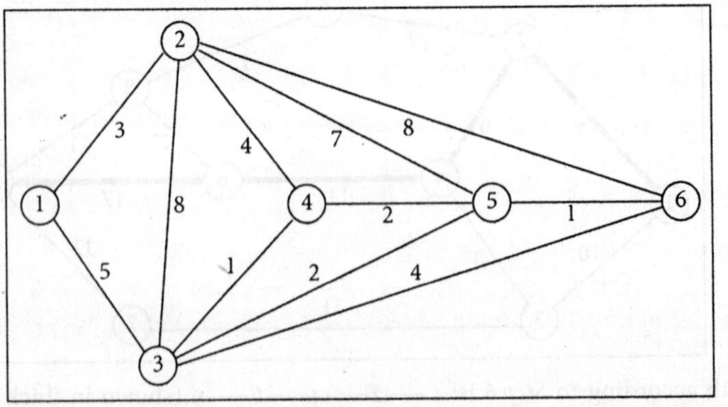

(i) *Applying Floyd's algorithm generate the final distance matrix and precedence matrix.*

(ii) *Locate the shortest path and the corresponding distance from the source node to the destination node* 1——6.

Solution: (i) Applying the steps as indicated in Floyd's algorithm we reach the final distance matrix $\left(I_D^6\right)$ and final precedence matrix $\left(I_P^6\right)$ through *Iteration* 0 to *Iteration* 6 as follows.

Iteration 0

$$I_D^{(o)} = \begin{array}{c} \\ 1 \\ 2 \\ 3 \\ 4 \\ 5 \\ 6 \end{array} \begin{array}{c} \begin{matrix} 1 & 2 & 3 & 4 & 5 & 6 \end{matrix} \\ \begin{pmatrix} 0 & 3 & 5 & \infty & \infty & \infty \\ 3 & 0 & 8 & 4 & 7 & 8 \\ 5 & 8 & 0 & 1 & 2 & 4 \\ \infty & 4 & 1 & 0 & 2 & \infty \\ \infty & \infty & 2 & \infty & 0 & 1 \\ \infty & 8 & 4 & \infty & 1 & 0 \end{pmatrix} \end{array} \qquad I_P^{(o)} = \begin{array}{c} \\ 1 \\ 2 \\ 3 \\ 4 \\ 5 \\ 6 \end{array} \begin{array}{c} \begin{matrix} 1 & 2 & 3 & 4 & 5 & 6 \end{matrix} \\ \begin{pmatrix} - & 1 & 1 & 1 & 1 & 1 \\ 2 & - & 2 & 2 & 2 & 2 \\ 3 & 3 & - & 3 & 3 & 3 \\ 4 & 4 & 4 & - & 4 & 4 \\ 5 & 5 & 5 & 5 & - & 5 \\ 6 & 6 & 6 & 6 & 6 & - \end{pmatrix} \end{array}$$

Iteration 1

$$I_D^{(1)} = \begin{pmatrix} 0 & 3 & 5 & \infty & \infty & \infty \\ 3 & 0 & 8 & 4 & 7 & 8 \\ 5 & 8 & 0 & 1 & 2 & 4 \\ \infty & 4 & 1 & 0 & 2 & \infty \\ \infty & \infty & 2 & \infty & 0 & 1 \\ \infty & 8 & 4 & \infty & 1 & 0 \end{pmatrix} \qquad I_P^{(1)} = \begin{pmatrix} - & 1 & 1 & 1 & 1 & 1 \\ 2 & - & 2 & 2 & 2 & 2 \\ 3 & 3 & - & 3 & 3 & 3 \\ 4 & 4 & 4 & - & 4 & 4 \\ 5 & 5 & 5 & 5 & - & 5 \\ 6 & 6 & 6 & 6 & 6 & - \end{pmatrix}$$

Iteration 2

$$I_D^{(2)} = \begin{pmatrix} 0 & 3 & 5 & 7 & 10 & 11 \\ 3 & 0 & 8 & 4 & 7 & 8 \\ 5 & 8 & 0 & 1 & 2 & 4 \\ 7 & 4 & 1 & 0 & 2 & 12 \\ \infty & \infty & 2 & \infty & 0 & 1 \\ 11 & 8 & 4 & 12 & 1 & 0 \end{pmatrix} \qquad I_P^{(2)} = \begin{pmatrix} -1 & 1 & 1 & 2 & 2 & 2 \\ 2 & - & 2 & 2 & 2 & 2 \\ 3 & 3 & - & 3 & 3 & 3 \\ 2 & 4 & 4 & - & 4 & 2 \\ 5 & 5 & 5 & 5 & - & 5 \\ 2 & 6 & 6 & 2 & 6 & - \end{pmatrix}$$

Iteration 3

$$I_D^{(3)} = \begin{pmatrix} 0 & 3 & 5 & 6 & 7 & 9 \\ 3 & 0 & 8 & 4 & 7 & 8 \\ 5 & 8 & 0 & 1 & 2 & 4 \\ 6 & 4 & 1 & 0 & 2 & 5 \\ 7 & 10 & 2 & 3 & 0 & 1 \\ 9 & 8 & 4 & 5 & 1 & 0 \end{pmatrix} \qquad I_P^{(3)} = \begin{pmatrix} - & 1 & 1 & 3 & 3 & 3 \\ 2 & - & 2 & 2 & 2 & 2 \\ 3 & 3 & - & 3 & 3 & 3 \\ 3 & 4 & 4 & - & 4 & 3 \\ 3 & 3 & 5 & 3 & - & 5 \\ 3 & 6 & 6 & 3 & 6 & - \end{pmatrix}$$

Iteration 4

$$I_D^{(4)} = \begin{pmatrix} 0 & 3 & 5 & 6 & 7 & 9 \\ 3 & 0 & 5 & 4 & 6 & 8 \\ 5 & 5 & 0 & 1 & 2 & 4 \\ 6 & 4 & 1 & 0 & 2 & 5 \\ 7 & 7 & 2 & 3 & 0 & 1 \\ 9 & 8 & 4 & 5 & 1 & 0 \end{pmatrix} \qquad I_P^{(4)} = \begin{pmatrix} - & 1 & 1 & 3 & 3 & 3 \\ 2 & - & 4 & 2 & 4 & 2 \\ 3 & 4 & - & 3 & 3 & 3 \\ 3 & 4 & 4 & - & 4 & 3 \\ 3 & 4 & 5 & 3 & - & 5 \\ 3 & 6 & 6 & 3 & 6 & - \end{pmatrix}$$

Iteration 5

$$I_D^{(5)} = \begin{pmatrix} 0 & 3 & 5 & 6 & 7 & 8 \\ 3 & 0 & 5 & 4 & 6 & 7 \\ 5 & 5 & 0 & 1 & 2 & 3 \\ 6 & 4 & 1 & 0 & 2 & 3 \\ 7 & 7 & 2 & 3 & 0 & 1 \\ 8 & 8 & 3 & 4 & 1 & 0 \end{pmatrix} \qquad I_P^{(5)} = \begin{pmatrix} - & 1 & 1 & 3 & 3 & 5 \\ 2 & - & 4 & 2 & 4 & 5 \\ 3 & 4 & - & 3 & 3 & 5 \\ 3 & 4 & 4 & - & 4 & 5 \\ 3 & 4 & 5 & 3 & - & 5 \\ 3 & 6 & 5 & 3 & 6 & - \end{pmatrix}$$

Iteration 6

$$I_D^{(6)} = \begin{array}{c} \\ 1 \\ 2 \\ 3 \\ 4 \\ 5 \\ 6 \end{array}\!\!\begin{array}{c} \begin{array}{cccccc} 1 & 2 & 3 & 4 & 5 & 6 \end{array} \\ \begin{pmatrix} 0 & 3 & 5 & 6 & 7 & 8 \\ 3 & 0 & 5 & 4 & 6 & 7 \\ 5 & 5 & 0 & 1 & 2 & 3 \\ 6 & 4 & 1 & 0 & 2 & 3 \\ 7 & 7 & 2 & 3 & 0 & 1 \\ 8 & 8 & 3 & 4 & 1 & 0 \end{pmatrix} \end{array} \qquad I_P^{(6)} = \begin{array}{c} \\ 1 \\ 2 \\ 3 \\ 4 \\ 5 \\ 6 \end{array}\!\!\begin{array}{c} \begin{array}{cccccc} 1 & 2 & 3 & 4 & 5 & 6 \end{array} \\ \begin{pmatrix} - & 1 & 1 & 3 & 3 & 5 \\ 2 & - & 4 & 2 & 4 & 5 \\ 3 & 4 & - & 3 & 3 & 5 \\ 3 & 4 & 4 & - & 4 & 5 \\ 3 & 4 & 5 & 3 & - & 5 \\ 3 & 6 & 5 & 3 & 6 & - \end{pmatrix} \end{array}$$

(ii) Here the source node (S) is 1 and destination node (D) is 6. According to *Step 7* of Floyd's algorithm the shortest path from node 1 to note 6 is: 1——3——5——6 and corresponding distance = 8 (as shown in the figure below by thick lines).

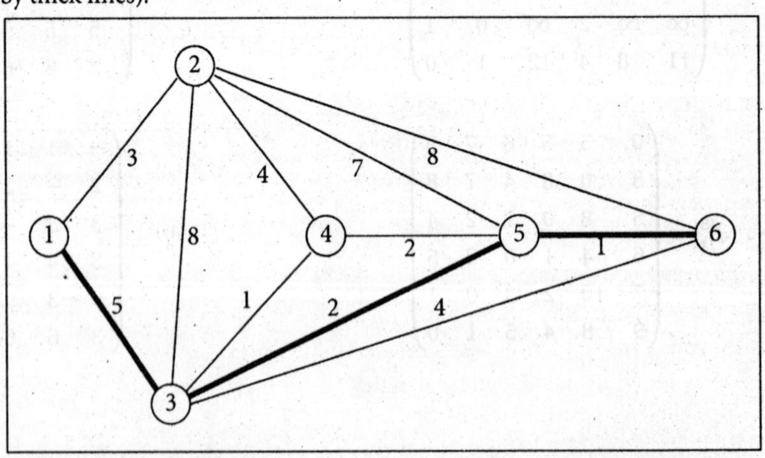

Remark

1. The shortest path from node 5 to node 1 is: 5——3——1 and corresponding distance = 7.
2. Shortest path from node 5 to node 2 is: 5——3——4——2 and corresponding distance = 7.

9.4 EXERCISE 9

1. (a) Define *critical path, slack time* and *dummy activity* with reference to PERT and CPM.
   (b) In PERT, the approach is probabilistic.—Explain.
   (c) What is the type of theoretical distribution used in the determination of expected time in PERT? Give the equations for the expected time and variance.
   (d) How does PERT technique help a project manager in decision-making.
2. Construct the arrow diagram comprising activities, A, B, C, ..., P that satisfies the following precedence relationships.
   (a) A, B and C, the first activities of the project, can start simultaneously.
   (b) Activities D, E and F start immediately after A is completed.
   (c) Activities I and G start after both B and D are completed.
   (d) Activity H starts after both C and G are completed.
   (e) Activities K and L succeed activity I.
   (f) Activity J succeeds both E and H.
   (g) Activities M and N succeed F but cannot start until E and H are completed.
   (h) Activity O succeeds M and L.
   (i) Activity P succeeds J, L and O.
   (j) Activities K, N and P are the terminal jobs of the project.
3. An architect has been awarded a contract to prepare a plan for an urban renewal project. The job consists of the following activities and their estimated times.

Activity	A	B	C	D	E	F	G	H	I	J	K	L
Preceding activity	–	–	–	A, B	B	B	F, C	B	E, H	E, H	C, D, F, J	K
Duration (*days*)	3	4	2	5	1	3	6	4	4	2	1	5

Draw the network and find the project critical path. [CU(MCom) 2004, DU(MBA) 2007]

4. The R and D department is planning to bid on a project for the development of a new communication system for commercial planes. The accompanying table shows the activities, times and sequence required.
   (a) Draw the network diagram.
   (b) What is the critical path?
   (c) Suppose, you want to shorten the completion time as much as possible and have the option of shortening any or all of B, C, D and G each by two weeks. Which would you shorten?
   (d) What is the new critical path and earliest completion time?

Activity	Immediate predecessor	Time (Weeks)
A	–	3
B	A	2
C	A	4
D	A	4
E	B	6
F	C, D	6
G	D, F	2
H	D	3
I	E, G, H	3

5. For the following network the time estimates $\left(t_o - t_m - t_p\right)$ are given. Find the probabilities that the different events will occur without delay.

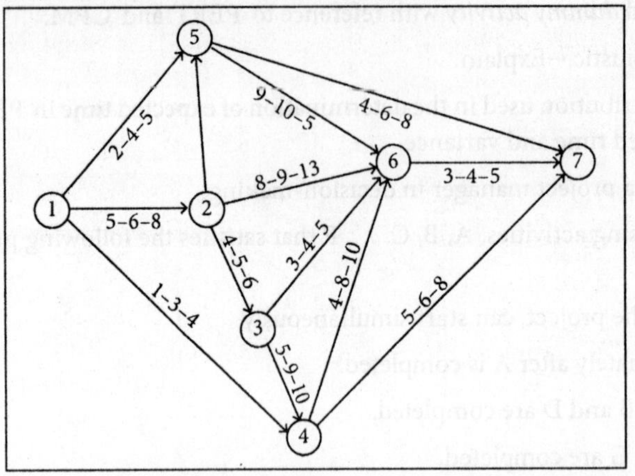

[BESU(BE) 2012, MBA(CU) 1998]

6. The following table summarises the activities for relocating 1700 feet of 13.8 kilovolt overhead primary line due to the widening of the road section in which the line is presently installed. Draw the network model and carry out the critical path computations.

Activity	Description	Immediate predecessor(s)	Duration (day)
A	Job review	—	1
B	Advice customers of temporary outage	A	5
C	Requisition	A	1
D	Scout job	A	5
E	Secure poles and materials	C, D	3
F	Distribute poles	E	3.5
G	Pole location coordination	D	5
H	Retake	G	5
I	Dig holes	H	3
J	Frame and set poles	F, I	4
K	Cover old conductor	F, I	1
L	Pull new conductor	J, K	2
M	Install remaining material	L	2
N	Sag conductor	L	2
O	Trim trees	D	2
P	De-energise and switch lines	B, M, N, O	1
Q	Energise and phase new line	P	5
R	Clean up	Q	1
S	Remove old conductor	Q	1
T	Remove old poles	S	2
U	Return material to stores	I	2

7. Consider the network consisting of the adjoining activities.
Find the probability of completing the project in 25 days. [BESU(MSc) 2009]

Activity	t_o	t_m	t_p
1–2	1	2	9
2–3	1	4	7
2–4	2	4	12
3–4	0	0	0
3–5	2	3	4
3–7	6	8	16
4–5	4	6	8
4–6	3	5	7
5–6	1/2	1	3/2
5–7	5	7	15
6–7	3	5	13

8. The following table gives the data for the activities of a small project.

Job $(i \to j)$	1–2	1–3	2–4	2–6	3–4	3–5	4–5	5–6
t_o (days)	1	5	3	1	8	2	5	2
t_m (days)	4	10	3	4	15	4	5	5
t_p (days)	7	17	3	7	26	8	5	8

(a) Draw the network and find the expected project completion time.

(b) What is the probability that it would takę five days more than the expected duration?

(c) Find the project completion time which will have 95% confidence.

[BESU(MSc) 2009, ICWA(Final, June) 1989]

9. For the data given find the following.

(a) The expected task times and their variances.

(b) The earliest expected and latest allowable occurrence time of each event.

(c) The critical path.

(d) The probability that task will be completed on schedule.

Task	A	B	C	D	E	F	G	H	I	J	K	L
t_o (days)	3	1	2	6	8	0	5	6	1	3	8	2
t_m (days)	5	2	4	8	12	0	7	9	2	6	15	4
t_p (days)	6	3	6	12	17	0	9	12	3	8	20	6

Precedence relationship: A and B can start immediately; C, D > A; E > B, C; F, H > E; G > D, F; J > G; I, K > H and L > J, I.

[JNU(Comp.Sc) 1982, MCA(WBUT) 1993]

10. Consider a task of obtaining ISO 9000, quality system certification of an organisation. The activities involved, dependence and estimated duration are given.

(a) Draw the network and find the expected duration of the task, which will have 95% confidence of completion [*Given*: $P(z < 1.645) = 0.95$].

(b) What is the minimum duration of completing the task? Compute its probability [*Given*: $P(z > 3) = 0$].

[IIT(MTech) 1994, BESU(MSc) 1998]

Activity	Dependence	t_p (weeks)	t_m (weeks)	t_o (weeks)
A	–	7	4	1
B	–	9	6	3
C	A	14	5	2
D	C	3	2	1
E	A, B	18	9	6
F	D	27	18	9
G	D, E	40	20	10
H	F, G	18	9	6
I	D, E	28	10	4
J	A, B	5	5	5

11. (a) What is the minimum spanning problem? Explain the steps of the following algorithms: (i) Dijkstra's algorithm (ii) Flyod's algorithm (iii) Kruskal's algorithm.

    (b) What is the shortest path problem? Give some practical applications of the shortest path problem.

12. Consider the distance network as shown.

    (a) Construct the distance network.

    (b) Find the shortest path from node 1 to node 9 by Dijkstra's algorithm.

Arc	Distance	Arc	Distance
1–2	8	3–6	6
1–3	5	4–5	8
1–4	7	4–6	12
1–4	16	5–8	7
2–3	15	6–8	9
2–6	3	6–9	15
2–7	4	7–9	12
3–4	5	8–9	6

13. Consider the details of a distance network as shown in adjoining table:

    (a) Construct the distance network.

    (b) Apply Floyd's algorithm and obtain the final matrices I_D^5 and I_p^5.

    (c) Find the shortest path and corresponding distance from node 1 to node 5.

Arc	Distance	Arc	Distance
1–2	3	2–4	7
1–3	8	3–4	2
1–4	10	3–5	8
2–3	4	4–5	6

14. Consider the details of a distance network as shown in the adjacent table.
   (a) Construct the distance network.
   (b) Find the minimum spanning tree using Kruskal's algorithm.
   [JNU(Comp.Sc) 1993, MCA(WBUT) 2007]

Arc	Distance	Arc	Distance
1–2	6	5–6	13
1–3	7	5–8	9
1–4	10	6–7	5
2–3	8	6–8	4
2–5	4	6–9	8
3–4	6	6–10	3
3–5	11	7–9	10
3–6	3	8–10	10
3–7	5	9–10	9
4–7	7		

15. Suppose that it is desired to establish a cable communication network that links the major cities shown in figure below. Determine how the cities are connected such that the total used cable mileage is minimised.

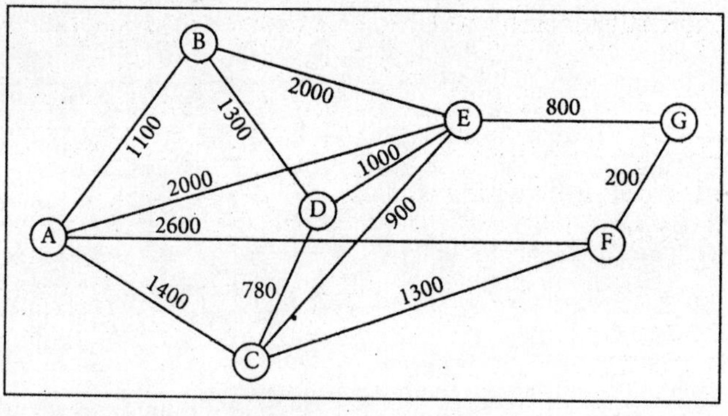

ANSWERS

3. Critical path: B ⟶ H ⟶ J ⟶ K ⟶ L, 16 days.
4. (b) A ⟶ C ⟶ F — G — I and A ⟶ D — F — G — I.
   (c) C, D, G each by 2 weeks.
   (d) A ⟶ B ⟶ E ⟶ I, A ⟶ C ⟶ F ⟶ G ⟶ I, A ⟶ D ⟶ F ⟶ G ⟶ I, 14 weeks.
5. Respective probabilities for events 2, 3, 4, 5, 6 and 7 are $\frac{1}{2}, \frac{1}{2}, \frac{1}{2}, \frac{1}{2}, 1, \frac{1}{2}$ and $\frac{1}{2}$.
6. Critical paths: (A, C, E, F, J, L, M, P, Q, S, T, U)
   (A, C, E, F, J, L, N, P, Q, S, Y, U)

   Duration = 22.1.
7. 86%.
8. (a) 36 days, (b) 90.9%, (c) 42.16 days.
9. Critical path A ⟶ C ⟶ E ⟶ H ⟶ K.
10. (a) 47.7 weeks, 57.2 weeks, (b) 25 weeks, Probability = 0.
12. (b) Shortest path 1—2—7—9 and corresponding total distance is 24.

13. (b)

$$I_D^5: \begin{array}{c} \\ 1 \\ 2 \\ 3 \\ 4 \\ 5 \end{array} \begin{array}{c} \begin{array}{ccccc} 1 & 2 & 3 & 4 & 5 \end{array} \\ \begin{pmatrix} 0 & 3 & 7 & 9 & 15 \\ 3 & 0 & 4 & 6 & 12 \\ 7 & 4 & 0 & 2 & 8 \\ 9 & 6 & 2 & 0 & 6 \\ 15 & 12 & 8 & 6 & 0 \end{pmatrix} \end{array} \qquad I_P^5: \begin{array}{c} \\ 1 \\ 2 \\ 3 \\ 4 \\ 5 \end{array} \begin{array}{c} \begin{array}{ccccc} 1 & 2 & 3 & 4 & 5 \end{array} \\ \begin{pmatrix} 0 & 1 & 2 & 3 & 3 \\ 2 & 0 & 2 & 3 & 3 \\ 2 & 3 & 0 & 3 & 3 \\ 2 & 3 & 4 & 0 & 4 \\ 2 & 3 & 5 & 5 & 0 \end{pmatrix} \end{array}$$

(c) 1—2—3—5, distance = 15.

14. Minimum spanning tree: 1–2, 1–3, 2–5, 3–4, 3–6, 3–7, 6–8, 6–9, 6–10, Distance = 46.

15. A⟶B⟶D⟶C⟶E⟶G⟶F. Length = 5080 miles.

Chapter 10

Queueing Models

10.1 INTRODUCTION

Queue is a common word that means a waiting line or sequence of customers or vehicles awaiting their turns to be attended to. It is formed when the number of customers arriving is grater than the number of customers being served during a period of time. Various queueing situations are:

Example	*Members of queue*	*Server(s)*
Bank counter	Accounts holders	Counter clerk
Library	Students	Counter clerk
Traffic signal	Vehicles	Signal point
Airport runways	Planes	Runways
Hospital	Patient	Doctor
Telephone booth	Customers	Telephones
Maintenance	Breakdown machines	Machines

Depending on the server status, the incoming customers either waits at the queue or gets served. In any service system involving queuing situations, the objective is to design the system in such a way that the average waiting time of the customers is minimised and the percentage utilisation of the server is maintained above a desired level.

A schematic representation of a simple queueing system that consists of a queue and a service station is shown in Fig. 1a.

This chapter discussed a number of queueing models that account for a variety of service operations. The models developed are basically applications of probability theory and stochastic process. The ultimate goal of solving these models is to determine the characteristics that measure the performance of the system.

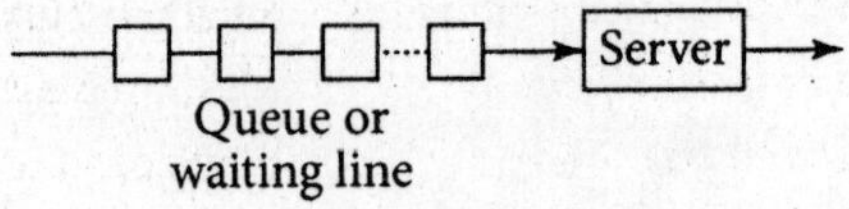

Fig. 1a Queueing system

10.2 BASIC ELEMENTS OF QUEUEING MODEL

The principal actors in a queueing situation are the *customer* and the *server.* Customer arrivals and service times are summarised in terms of probability distributions known as *arrivals* and *service* time distributions.

1. *Arrival* (*Input*): It represents the pattern in which customers arrive at the system. It is also represented by *inter-arrival time,* which is the time period between successive arrivals. The number of customers arriving per unit of time is called *arrival rate.*
2. *Service* (*Pattern*): The service pattern is similar to arrival pattern. The service system in which the customers may be served in batches in a fixed or variable size is known as *bulk service* system.

Although the pattern of arrivals and departures are the main factors in the analysis of queues, other factors also important in the development of the models which are discussed below.

3. *Service discipline*: The manner of choosing customers from the waiting lines to start service is referred as *service discipline.* The most common discipline is the FCFS (*first come, first served*), LCFS (last come, first served), SIRO (service in random order), etc.
4. Another factor deals with the design of the facility and the execution of service. When all servers offer the same service, the facility is said to have *parallel server.* When the facility may comprise a number of series stations through which the customers may pass before service is completed. In this case, waiting line may or may not be allowed between the stations. This situations are normally known as *queues in series.*
5. In certain situations, only a limited number of customers may be allowed (for example, for space limitation). Once the queue fills to capacity newly arriving customers are denied service and may not join the queue. This factor is called *queue size.*
6. *Customer behaviour*: Customers generally behave in three ways:
   (a) *Balking*: A customer may leave the queue because it is long and he has no time to wait or there is no sufficient waiting space.
   (b) *Reneging*: Some customers wait for some time in the queue but leave due to impatience without getting the service.
   (c) *Jockeying*: A server may speed up the rate of service when the waiting line builds up in size. A customer may *Jockey* from one line to another in hopes of reducing his/her waiting line.

We now see that the basic elements of queueing model depend on the following major factors:

1. *Arrival distribution* : Single or bulk arrivals
2. *Service time distributions* : Single or bulk service
3. *Service discipline* : Series, parallel or network stations
4. *Queue size* : Finite or infinite
6. *Customer behaviour* : Balking, reneging, jockeying.

10.3 POISSON AND EXPONENTIAL DISTRIBUTIONS IN QUEUEING MODEL

Consider queueing situation in which the number of arrivals and departures during an interval of time is controlled by the following conditions.

(i) The probability of an event (arrival or departure) occurring between times t and $t+\Delta t$ depends only on Δt, that is, the probability function has *stationary independent* increment.

(ii) During small time interval Δt, the probability of an event is positive and less than 1.

(iii) At most one event can occur during small time interval $\Delta t \ll$.

Let $p_n(t)=$ probability of n events occurring during time t.

Condition (i) implies that for $n=0$, $p_0(t+\Delta t)=p_0(t)\,p_0(\Delta t)$ (10.3a)

Condition (ii) implies that $0<p_0(\Delta t)<1$.

It can be shown that the solution of (10.3a) is $p_0(t)=e^{-kt}$: $t\geq 0$ and $k>0$ is a constant.

Our main aim is to show that k represents the *rate of arrival* (departures) per unit time when the event represents arrivals (departures).

For $\Delta t>0$ and $\Delta t \ll$, we have

$$p_0(\Delta t)=e^{-k\Delta t}=1-k\Delta t+\frac{(k\Delta t)^2}{2!}-\frac{(k\Delta t)^3}{3!}+\cdots\simeq 1-k\Delta t.$$

Again, from condition (iii), $p_1(\Delta t)=1-p_0(\Delta t)\simeq k\Delta t$ (for occurrence of at most one event).

Now, let $f(t)=$ pdf of the time interval t between the occurrence of successive events, $t\geq 0$.

$F(t)=$ cumulative density function (cdf) of t.

If T is the time interval since the occurrence of last event, then

$$P(t\geq T)=p_0(T)=e^{-kT}\Rightarrow\int_T^{\infty}f(t)\,dt=e^{-kT}\text{ and }1-F(T)=e^{-kT},\ T>0. \tag{10.3b}$$

Differentiating both sides of (10.3b) w.r.t. T, we get

$$f(T)=ke^{-kT}:\ T>0, \tag{10.3c}$$

which is an *exponential distribution*. Therefore, the time between the occurrence of successive event *follow an exponential distribution.*

$$E(T)=\frac{1}{k}\text{ or, }k=\frac{1}{E(T)}\text{ (events/unit time)} \tag{10.3d}$$

represents rate at which events are generated. Hence, k represents arrivals (departures) rate when the generated events represent arrivals (departures).

10.4 ARRIVAL PROCESS

According to the discussion above, events in this situation represent *pure arrival,* which means that customers once join the system, never leave. This process is also named as *pure birth.*

We want to derive an expression for the probability $p_n(t)$ of n arrivals during time interval t.

For $\Delta t > 0$ and very small, we have for $n > 0$

$$\begin{aligned} p_n(t+\Delta t) &= P\{n \text{ arrivals during } t \text{ and none during } \Delta t \text{ OR } (n-1) \text{ arrivals during } t \text{ and one during } \Delta t\} \\ &= p_n(t)\,p_0(\Delta t) + p_{n-1}(t)\,p_1(\Delta t)\ \forall\ n = 1, 2, \ldots \end{aligned}$$

and $p_0(t+\Delta t) = p_0(t)\,p_0(\Delta t)$, $n = 0$. (10.4a)

We replace k, the rate of event generation by standard notation λ representing the arrival rate.

Therefore, $p_0(\Delta t) = e^{-\lambda\Delta t} \simeq 1 - \lambda\Delta t$

$p_1(\Delta t) = 1 - p_0(\Delta t)\lambda\Delta t.$

From (10.4a), $p_n(t+\Delta t) \simeq p_n(t)(1-\lambda\Delta t) + p_{n-1}(t)\lambda\Delta t : n > 0$

$p_0(t+\Delta t) \simeq p_0(t)(1-\lambda\Delta t) \quad : n > 0$

$$\therefore \quad \frac{p_n(t+\Delta t) - p_n(t)}{\Delta t} \simeq -\lambda p_n(t) + \lambda p_{n-1}(t)$$

$$\frac{p_0(t+\Delta t) - p_0(t)}{\Delta t} \simeq -\lambda p_0(t).$$

As $\Delta t \to 0$, the equations reduce to $\left.\begin{aligned} p_n'(t) &= -\lambda p_n(t) + \lambda p_{n-1}(t) \\ p_0'(t) &= -\lambda p_0(t). \end{aligned}\right\}$ (10.4b)

(10.4b) are the differential difference equations.

From (10.4b), $\displaystyle\int \frac{dp_0(t)}{p_0(t)} = -\int \lambda\, dt \Rightarrow \log|p_0(t)| = -\lambda t + A.$

Using boundary conditions: $p_n(0) = \begin{cases} 1 : n = 0 \\ 0 : n > 0, \end{cases}$ we get $A = 0$.

Therefore, $p_0(t) = e^{-\lambda t}$. (10.4c)

Now from $n = 1$ from (10.4b)

$$\frac{dp_1(t)}{dt} + \lambda p_1(t) = \lambda p_0(t) = \lambda e^{-\lambda t}.$$

Integrating factor (IF) = $e^{\lambda \int dt} = e^{\lambda t}$.

$$e^{\lambda t}\frac{dp_1(t)}{dt} + \lambda e^{\lambda t} p_1(t) = \lambda p_0(t) e^{\lambda t} = \lambda\, dt \Rightarrow e^{\lambda t} p_1(t) = \lambda t + B.$$

At $t = 0$, $p_1(0) = B \Rightarrow B = 0$.

Therefore, $p_1(t) = \dfrac{(\lambda t)e^{-\lambda t}}{1!}$. (10.4d)

Let for particular $n = m$, the result is $p_m(t) = \dfrac{(\lambda t)^m e^{-\lambda t}}{m!}$. This is actually true and can be shown by mathematical induction as follows:

$$p'_{m+1}(t) + \lambda p_{m+1}(t) = \lambda p_m(t) = \lambda \cdot \frac{(\lambda t)^m e^{-\lambda t}}{m!} \Rightarrow \frac{d}{dt}\left[e^{\lambda t} p_{m+1}(t)\right] = \frac{\lambda(\lambda t)^m}{m!}$$

$$\Rightarrow p_{m+1}(t) e^{\lambda t} = \frac{(\lambda t)^{m+1}}{(m+1)!} \Rightarrow p_{m+1}(t) = \frac{(\lambda t)^{m+1} e^{-\lambda t}}{(m+1)!}.$$

Hence, for any $n = 0, 1, 2, \ldots$

$$p_n(t) = \frac{(\lambda t)^n e^{-\lambda t}}{n!}.$$

The distribution of $p_n(t)$ is thus *Poisson* with mean and variance (λt). Hence, an important conclusion is: *whereas the inter-arrival time is exponential with mean $1/\lambda$, the number of arrivals during time interval t is Poisson with mean λt.*

10.5 DEPARTURE PROCESS

The departure process assumes that the system starts with a given number of customers N who leave the facility at the rate of μ after being serviced. No new customers are allowed to join the system. The process is given the suggestive name *pure death.*

Using the results developed earlier, and taking $k = \mu$ represents departure rate, let $q_n(t) =$ probability of n departure during t.

As in the case, of *pure birth* for every small $\Delta t > 0$, we have $q_0(\Delta t) = e^{-\mu \Delta t} \simeq 1 - \mu \Delta t$

$$q_1(\Delta t) = 1 - q_0(\Delta t) \simeq \mu \Delta t.$$

Now for $n = N$, $\quad q_N(t + \Delta t) \simeq q_N(t) \cdot 1 + q_{N-1}(t)\mu \Delta t$ (10.5a)

for $1 \le n \le N$, $q_n(t + \Delta t) \simeq q_n(t)(1 - \mu \Delta t) + q_{n-1}(t)\mu \Delta t$

for $n = 0$, $\quad q_0(t + \Delta t) \simeq q_0(t)(1 - \mu \Delta t)$.

As before after simplification and taking limit as $\Delta t \to 0$, we get from (10.5a)

$$\left.\begin{aligned} q'_N(t) &= \mu q_{N-1}(t) && : n = N \\ q'_n(t) &= -\mu q_n(t) + \mu q_{n-1}(t) && : 1 \le n \le N \\ q'_0(t) &= -\mu q_0(t) && : n = 0 \end{aligned}\right\}. \tag{10.5b}$$

From (10.5b), $q_0(t) = A = e^{-\mu t}$.

For initial condition $q_0(0) = 1$, we get $A = 1$.

$$q_0(t) = e^{-\mu t}.$$

Now for $n = 1$,

$$q'_1(t) = -\mu q_1(t) + \mu e^{-\mu t} \Rightarrow q_1(t) = e^{-\mu t}\left(\int \mu e^{-\mu t} \cdot e^{\mu t}\, dt + B\right) = (\mu t + B) e^{-\mu t}.$$

Since $q_1(0) = 0$, $B = 0$,

$$q_1(t) = (\mu t) e^{-\mu t}.$$

It can be proved generally by induction (as we have proved in Sec. 10.4)

$$q_n(t) = \frac{e^{-\mu t}(\mu t)^n}{n!}, \quad n = 0, 1, \ldots, N-1. \tag{10.5c}$$

For $n = N$,

$$q'_N(t) = \mu q_{N-1}(t) = \mu \frac{(\mu t)^{N-1} e^{-\mu t}}{(N-1)}.$$

Using integration by parts, we get

$$q_N(t) = 1 - \sum_{n=0}^{N-1} \frac{(\mu t)^n e^{-\mu t}}{n!} = 1 - \sum_{n=0}^{N-1} q_n(t). \qquad (10.5d)$$

Let $p_n(t)$ = probability of n-customers remaining after t. Since the system starts initially with N customers, having n remained after t, it is equivalent to $(N-n)$ customers departing during t.

$$\therefore p_n(t) = q_{N-n}(t) = \frac{(\mu t)^{N-n} e^{-\mu t}}{(N-n)!} \quad : n = 1, 2, \ldots, N$$

$$= 1 - \sum_{n-1}^{n} \frac{(\mu t)^{N-n} e^{-\mu t}}{(N-n)!} \quad : n = 0. \qquad (10.5e)$$

This distribution of departure in time t follows *truncated Poisson distribution.*

10.6 CLASSIFICATIONS OF QUEUES

In this chapter we study queueing models in which both arrivals and departures take place simultaneously. Fig. 10.6a represents the parallel queueing system. It should be note that the number of customers in the system at any point in time is defined to include those in queue and in service.

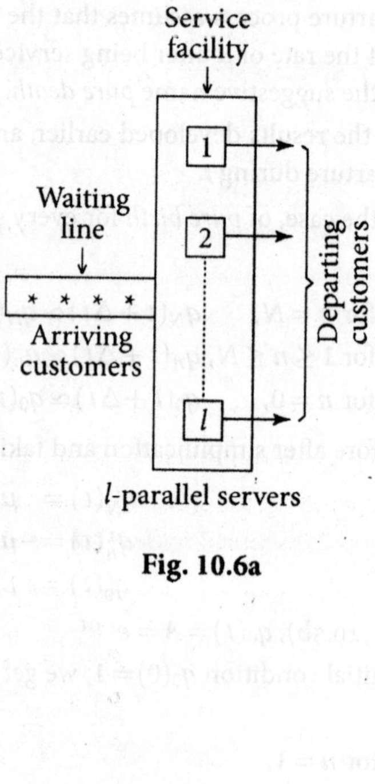

Fig. 10.6a

Generally, a queueing model has been universally standardised in the following format:

$$(a/b/c):(d/e/f)$$

where $a \equiv$ arrivals distribution,

$b \equiv$ service time (or departure) distribution,

$c \equiv$ number of parallel servers ($l = 1, 2, 3, \ldots, \infty$),

$d \equiv$ service discipline (e.g., FCFS, LCFS, SIRO),

$e \equiv$ maximum number allowed in the system (both in queue and in service)

$f \equiv$ size of calling source.

The standard notations replaces the symbols a and b for arrivals and departures by the following codes.

$M \equiv$ Poisson or Markovian arrival or departure distributions or equivalently exponential inter-arrival or service time distribution.

$E_k \equiv$ Erlangian or Gamma distribution of inter-arrival or service time distribution having parameter k.

$GI \equiv$ General independent distribution of arrivals and inter-arrival time.

$G \equiv$ General distribution of departures or service time.

For example, the notation (M/M/c) : (FCFS/∞/∞) means Poisson arrivals, Poisson service time, c-parallel servers. The service discipline is *first come first serve basis,* the system (queue + service) can hold a maximum of infinite customers and finally the source generating the arriving customers has an infinite capacity.

The above standard notation is known as *Kendall notations* as it was initially devised by D G Kendall.

As any queueing system operates as a function of time, we must decide whether we are interested in analysing the system under *transient* or *steady-state* conditions.

Transient state: A queueing system is said to be in transient state when its operating characteristics depend upon time.

Steady state: If the characteristics of the queueing system are independent of time, then a steady $p_n(t)$ state is said to prevail. If $p_n(t)$ be the probability that there are n situation, we have $\lim_{t\to\infty} p_n(t) = p_n$ (independent of t).

$\therefore\ p'_n(t) = 0.$

Although the basic equations of the various models that we develop here can be used to study the transient behaviour, our main analysis will concentrate on the steady state results.

10.7 DIFFERENT QUEUEING MODELS

Model 1: (M/M/1) : (FCFS/∞/∞)

The parameters of this model are:

1. Arrival rate follows Poisson distribution.
2. Service rate follows Poisson distribution.
3. Number of server is one.
4. First come first serve is the service discipline.
5. Maximum number of customers permitted in the system is infinite.
6. Size of the calling source is infinite.

The differential difference equations for $p_n(t)$ are derived using the same ideas with pure birth and pure death model discussed in Secs 10.4 and 10.5 respectively.

As before, for $\Delta t > 0$ and very small,

$$\begin{aligned} P\,(\text{zero arrival in } \Delta t) &= e^{-\lambda\Delta t} \simeq 1 - \lambda\Delta t \\ P\,(\text{one arrival in } \Delta t) &= 1 - e^{-\lambda\Delta t} \simeq \lambda\Delta t \\ P\,(\text{zero departure in } \Delta t) &= e^{-\mu\Delta t} \simeq 1 - \mu\Delta t \\ P\,(\text{one departure in } \Delta t) &= 1 - e^{-\mu\Delta t} \simeq \mu\Delta t \end{aligned} \tag{10.7a}$$

Now $p_n(t+\Delta t) = P\,(n$ is the system at t and no arrivals and no departures during $\Delta t)$
$+P\,(n-1$ in the system t, one arrival and no departure during $\Delta t)$
$+P\,(n+1$ in the system at t, no arrivals and one departure during $\Delta t) + \bigcirc(\Delta t)$

$$\therefore\ p_n(t+\Delta t) \simeq p_n(t)(1-\lambda\Delta t)(1-\mu\lambda t) + p_{n-1}(t)(\lambda\Delta t)(1-\mu\Delta t) + p_{n+1}(t)(1-\lambda\Delta t)(\mu\Delta t) : n > 0$$
$$p_0(t+\Delta t) \simeq p_0(t)(1-\lambda\Delta t)\cdot 1 + p_1(t)(\mu\Delta t)\cdot 1 \qquad : n = 0.$$

On minor simplification and taking $\Delta t \to 0$, we get

$$\begin{aligned} p_n'(t) &= \lambda p_{n-1}(t) + \mu p_{n+1}(t) - (\lambda+\mu)p_n(t) : n > 0 \\ p_0'(t) &= -\lambda p_0(t) + \mu p_1(t) \qquad : n = 0. \end{aligned} \tag{10.7b}$$

Steady-state Solution

As $t \to \infty$, $p_n'(t) \to 0$ and $p_n(t) \to p_n$ (independent of t) for $n = 0, 1, 2, \ldots$ in steady-state situation. Using this, we have from (10.7b)

$$\begin{aligned} -\lambda p_0 + \mu p_1 &= 0 \\ \lambda p_{n-1} + \mu p_{n+1} - (\lambda+\mu)p_n &= 0. \end{aligned} \tag{10.7c}$$

Let us solve the difference eq. (10.7c) as follows:

$$p_1 = \frac{\lambda}{\mu}p_0; \quad p_2 = \frac{\lambda+\mu}{\mu}p_1 - \frac{\lambda}{\mu}p_0 = \left(\frac{\lambda}{\mu}\right)^2 p_0; \quad p_3 = \frac{\lambda+\mu}{\mu}p_2 - \frac{\lambda}{\mu}p_1 = \left(\frac{\lambda}{\mu}\right)^3 p_0.$$

Therefore, for particular n : $p_n = \left(\frac{\lambda}{\mu}\right)^n p_0$. This is actually true and can be shown by mathematical induction.

From (10.7c),

$$\begin{aligned} p_{n+1} &= \frac{\lambda+\mu}{\mu}p_n - \frac{\lambda}{\mu}p_{n-1} = \frac{\lambda+\mu}{\mu}\left(\frac{\lambda}{\mu}\right)^n p_0 - \frac{\lambda}{\mu}\left(\frac{\lambda}{\mu}\right)^{n-1} p_0 \\ &= \left(\frac{\lambda}{\mu}\right)^{n+1} p_0 + \left(\frac{\lambda}{\mu}\right)^n p_0 - \left(\frac{\lambda}{\mu}\right)^n p_0 = \left(\frac{\lambda}{\mu}\right)^{n+1} p_0. \end{aligned}$$

Hence,

$$\boxed{p_n = \left(\frac{\lambda}{\mu}\right)^n p_0 \ \forall\ n \geq 0} \tag{10.7d}$$

To find p_0 we make use of

$$\sum_{n=0}^{\infty} p_n = 1 \Rightarrow \sum_{n=0}^{\infty}\left(\frac{\lambda}{\mu}\right)^n p_0 = 1 \Rightarrow p_0\left(1 - \frac{\lambda}{\mu}\right)^{-1} = 1 : \frac{\lambda}{\mu} < 1 \Rightarrow p_0 = \left(1 - \frac{\lambda}{\mu}\right).$$

Remark. *Steady-state solution exists* if $\lambda < \mu$ corresponding to $t \to \infty$. If $\lambda = \mu$, then there is *no queue.* Again, if $\lambda > \mu$, then the state is an *explosive state.*

$$\boxed{p_n = \left(\frac{\lambda}{\mu}\right)^n \left(1 - \frac{\lambda}{\mu}\right) = (1-\rho)\rho^n, \text{ where } \rho = \frac{\lambda}{\mu} < 1,\ n = 0, 1, 2, \ldots} \tag{10.7e}$$

(a) L_s = expected number of customers in the system

$$\begin{aligned} &= E(n) = \sum_{n=0}^{\infty} n p_n = \sum_{n=0}^{\infty} n(1-\rho)\rho^n = \rho(1-\rho)\sum_{n=0}^{\infty}\frac{d}{d\rho}(\rho^n) = \rho(1-\rho)\frac{d}{d\rho}\sum_{n=0}^{\infty}\rho^n \\ &= \rho(1-\rho)\frac{d}{d\rho}\left(\frac{1}{1-\rho}\right) = \frac{\rho}{1-\rho} = \frac{\lambda/\mu}{1-\frac{\lambda}{\mu}} = \frac{\lambda}{\mu-\lambda}. \end{aligned}$$

(b) L_q = expected number of customers in queue

$$= \sum_{n=1}^{\infty}(n-1)p_n = \sum_{n=1}^{\infty} np_n - \sum_{n=1}^{\infty} p_n = \sum_{n=0}^{\infty} np_n - \left[\sum_{n=0}^{\infty} p_n - p_0\right] = L_s - [1-(1-\rho)]$$

$$= \frac{\rho}{1-\rho} - 1 + (1-\rho) = \frac{\rho^2}{1-\rho} = \frac{\lambda^2}{\mu(\mu-\lambda)}.$$

(c) W_s = expected waiting time in (queue + service) system

$$= \frac{Ls}{\lambda} = \frac{\rho}{\lambda(1-\rho)} = \frac{1}{\mu(1-\rho)} = \frac{1}{\mu\left(1-\frac{\lambda}{\mu}\right)} = \frac{1}{\mu-\lambda}.$$

(d) W_q = expected waiting time in queue

$$= \frac{Lq}{\lambda} = \frac{\rho^2}{\lambda(1-\rho)} = \frac{\rho}{\mu(1-\rho)} = \frac{\lambda}{\mu^2\left(1-\frac{\lambda}{\mu}\right)} = \frac{\lambda}{\mu(\mu-\lambda)}.$$

(e) $V(n)$ = Fluctuation (variance) of queue

$$= E\left(n^2\right) - [E(n)]^2 = \sum_{n=0}^{\infty} n^2 p_n - L_S^2 = \sum_{n=0}^{\infty} n(n-1)p_n + L_S - L_S^2 = \frac{\rho}{(1-\rho)^2} = \frac{\lambda\mu}{(\mu-\lambda)^2}.$$

(f) *Waiting time distribution*: From (10.7e), p_n is shown to be independent of service discipline. Now we want to show how the pdf of the *waiting time* depends on the FCFS discipline of (M/M/1) : (FCFS/∞/∞) queueing model.

Let t^* be the amount of time a person just after arrival waits in the system, until his service is completed. On the basis of FCFS, if an arriving customer finds n_1 persons ahead of him in the system, then

$$t^* = \hat{t}_1 + t_2 + \cdots + t_{n_1+1},$$

where $\hat{t}_1$ is the time taken for the customer actually in service and $t_2, t_3, \ldots, t_{n_1+1}$ are service times for (n_1-1) customers in queue, so that t_{n_1+1} is the service time for the arriving customer.

Suppose, $\psi\left(t^*/n_1+1\right)$ be the *conditional pdf* of t^* given n_1 customers in the system ahead of the arriving customer. Since $\hat{t}_1, t_2, \ldots, t_{n_1+1}$ have the same *exponential distribution*, t^* is the sum of identically independent exponential distributions. This means that $\psi\left(t^*/n_1+1\right)$ is *gamma-distributed* with parameters (μ, n_1+1).

$$\therefore \psi\left(t^*\right) = \sum_{n_1=0}^{\infty} \psi\left(t^*/n_1+1\right) p_{n_1} = \sum_{n_1=0}^{\infty} \frac{\mu(\mu t^*)^{n_1} e^{-\mu t^*}}{n_1!}(1-\rho)\rho^{n_1} = (1-\rho)\mu e^{-\mu t^*} \sum_{n_1=0}^{\infty} \frac{(\lambda t^*)^{n_1}}{n_1!}$$

$$= (1-\rho)\mu e^{-\mu t^*} \cdot e^{\lambda t^*} = \mu(1-\rho)e^{-\mu(1-\rho)t^*} \; ; \; t^* > 0$$

which is also an exponential distribution with Mean $= E\left(t^*\right) = \dfrac{1}{\mu(1-\rho)} = W_s$ [from (c)]

= expected waiting time in the system.

Again, $E(n/n>0) = \dfrac{E(n)}{P(n>0)} = \dfrac{Ls}{1-p_0} = \dfrac{\rho}{(1-\rho)\rho} = \dfrac{1}{1-\rho}$

= expected length of non-empty queue.

Example 10.7.1. *Cars arriving at a petrol pump, having one petrol unit in Poisson fashion with an average of 10 cars per hour. The service time is distributed exponentially with mean of 3 minutes. Find* (i) *average number of cars in the system* (ii) *average waiting time in the queue* (iii) *average queue length* (iv) *probability that the number of cars in the systems is 10.*

Solution: Here, $\lambda = 10$/hour, $\mu = \frac{1}{3} \times 60 = 20$/hour, $\rho = \frac{\lambda}{\mu} = \frac{10}{20} = \frac{1}{2} < 1$.

(i) $L_s = \dfrac{\rho}{1-\rho} = \dfrac{1/2}{1/2} = 1$ car.

(ii) $W_q = \dfrac{L_q}{\lambda} = \dfrac{\rho}{\mu(1-\rho)} = \dfrac{1/2}{20 \times \frac{1}{2}} = \dfrac{1}{20} = 0.05 = 3$ min.

(iii) $L_q = \dfrac{\rho^2}{1-\rho} = \dfrac{1/4}{1/2} = \dfrac{1}{2} = 0.5$ car.

(iv) $p_{10} = \rho^{10}(1-\rho) = \left(1-\dfrac{1}{2}\right)\left(\dfrac{1}{2}\right)^{10} = \left(\dfrac{1}{2}\right)^{11} = \dfrac{1}{2^{11}}$.

Example 10.7.2. *Show that in* (M/M/1) : (FCFS/∞/∞) *queueing system* 36.8% *of the customers will wait more than average waiting time* W_s.

Solution: We know, $W_s = \dfrac{1}{\mu(1-\rho)}$, where $\rho = \dfrac{\lambda}{\mu} < 1$.

$$P(t^* > W_s) = 1 - \int_0^{W_s} \psi(t^*)\, dt = e^{-\mu(1-\rho)W_s} \text{ [after integration]}$$
$$= e^{-1} \simeq 0.368.$$

Hence, the result follows.

Remark. Obviously, probability will change with the change of service discipline and normally should be higher for the LCFS and SIRO disciplines.

Example 10.7.3. *Customers arrive at one counter of* UBI *according to Poisson pattern with mean* 10 *per hour. Service time per customer is exponential with mean* 5 *minutes. The space in front of the counter can accommodate a maximum of* 3 *cars including the customer in service. Others can wait outside this space.* (i) *What is the probability that an arriving customer can drive directly to the space in front of the counter?* (ii) *What is the probability that an arriving customer will have to wait outside the indicated space?* (iii) *How long is the arriving customer expected to wait before starting service?*

Solution: Here, $\lambda = 10$/hour, $\mu = \frac{1}{5} \times 60 = 12$ hour, $p_n = \rho^n(1-\rho)$, where $= \frac{\lambda}{\mu} = \frac{10}{12} < 1$.

(i) Arriving customer can drive directly to the space $= P(\text{i}) = p_0 + p_1 + p_2 = (1-\rho)(1+\rho+\rho^2)$

$$= \left(1 - \frac{10}{12}\right)\left[1 + \frac{10}{12} = \left(\frac{10}{12}\right)^2\right] = 0.42.$$

(ii) $P(\text{ii}) = 1 - P(\text{i}) = 1 - 0.42 = 0.58$.

(iii) $W_q = \dfrac{\rho}{\mu(1-\rho)} = \dfrac{10/12}{12\left(1-\frac{10}{12}\right)} = \dfrac{10/12}{2} = \dfrac{5}{12} = 0.417$ hours.

Model 2: (M/M/1) : (FCFS/N/∞)

The parameters of this model are:

1. Arrival rate follows Poisson distribution.
2. Service rate follows Poisson distribution.
3. Number of servers is one.

4. Service discipline is on *first come first serve* basis.
5. Maximum number of customers permitted in the system is N.
6. Size of the calling source is infinite.

The only difference in Model 2 from Model 1 is maximum number of customers allowed in the system is N instead of infinite so that in Model 2 maximum queue length is $(N-1)$.

For $0<n<N$, $p_n(t+\Delta t)\simeq p_n(t)(1-\lambda\Delta t)(1-\mu\Delta t)+p_{n-1}(t)\lambda\Delta t(1-\mu\Delta t)+p_{n+1}(t)(1-\lambda\Delta t)(\mu\Delta t)$

For $n=0$, $p_0(t+\Delta t)\simeq p_0(t)(1-\lambda\Delta t)\cdot 1+p_1(t)(\mu\Delta t)\cdot 1$

For $n=N$, $p_N(t+\Delta t)\simeq p_N(t)\cdot 1(1-\mu\Delta t)+p_{N-1}(\lambda\Delta t)(1-\mu\Delta t)$

For $n>N$, $p_n(t)=0$.

Now taking limit as $\Delta t\to 0$, we have
$$p'_n(t)=\lambda p_{n-1}(t)+\mu p_{n+1}(t)-(\lambda+\mu)p_n(t):0<n<N$$
$$p'_0(t)=-\lambda p_0(t)+\mu p_1(t) \qquad :n=0$$
$$p'_N(t)=-\mu p_N(t)+\lambda p_{N-1}(t) \qquad :n=N.$$

Steady-state solution $\mu p_{n+1}=(\lambda+\mu)p_n-\lambda p_{n-1}:0<n<N$
$$\mu p_1=\lambda p_0 \qquad :n=0$$
$$\mu p_N=\lambda p_{N-1} \qquad :n=N.$$

Adapting the same procedure as was done in Model 1, we have
$$p_n=\left(\frac{\lambda}{\mu}\right)^n p_0=\rho^n p_0:n\le N-1.$$

Also we see that for this value of p_n, the third difference equation holds for $n=N$.
$$\boxed{p_n=\rho^n p_0:\ \forall\, n\le N} \tag{10.7f}$$

To find p_0: $\displaystyle\sum_{n=0}^{N}p_n=1\Rightarrow 1=\sum_{n=0}^{N}p_0\rho^n=\begin{cases}p_0\dfrac{1-\rho^{N+1}}{1-\rho} & :\rho=\dfrac{\lambda}{\mu}\neq 1\\ p_0(N+1) & :\rho=\dfrac{\lambda}{\mu}=1.\end{cases}$

$$\therefore\ p_n=\begin{cases}\dfrac{(1-\rho)\rho^n}{1-\rho^{N+1}} & :\rho\neq 1\\ \dfrac{1}{N+1} & :\rho=1\end{cases}\qquad n=0,1,2,\dots,N. \tag{10.7g}$$

Remark. If $N\to\infty$, then $p_n=(1-\rho)\rho^n$, which is in agreement with the steady-state solution of *Model* 1, where the maximum number of customers allowed in the system is infinite.

(a) $\displaystyle L_s=\sum_{n=0}^{N}np_n=p_0\rho\sum_{n=0}^{N}n\rho^{n-1}=p_0\rho\frac{d}{d\rho}\sum_{n=0}^{N}\rho^n=p_0\rho\frac{d}{d\rho}\left[\frac{1-\rho^{N+1}}{1-\rho}\right]:\rho\neq 1$

$$=p_0\rho\frac{-(N+1)\rho^N(1-\rho)-(1-\rho^{N+1})(-1)}{(1-\rho)^2}=p_0\rho\frac{-(N+1)\rho^N+(N+1)\rho^{N+1}+1-\rho^{N+1}}{(1-\rho)^2}$$

$$=\begin{cases}\dfrac{\rho\left[1-(N+1)\rho^N+N\rho^{N+1}\right]}{(1-\rho)(1-\rho^{N+1})} & :\rho\neq 1\\ \dfrac{N}{2} & :\rho=1.\end{cases}$$

(b) $L_q = L_s - \sum_{n=1}^{N} p_n = \dfrac{\rho\left[1-(N+1)\rho^N + N\rho^{N+1}\right]}{(1-\rho)(1-\rho^{N+1})} - \dfrac{\rho(1-\rho^N)}{1-\rho^{N+1}}$

$= \dfrac{\rho^2\left[1+(N-1)\rho^N - N\rho^{N-1}\right]}{(1-\rho)(1-\rho^{N+1})} : \rho \neq 1.$

(c) Since the probability that a customer does not join the system is equal to p_N, the ratio of customers joining the system must be equal to $P(n > N) = 1 - p_N$.
It then follows that the *effective arrival rate* is given by $\lambda_{\text{effective}} = \lambda(1-p_N)$.

(d) $W_q = \dfrac{L_q}{\lambda_{\text{effective}}} = \dfrac{L_q}{\lambda(1-p_N)}$.

(e) $W_s = W_q + \dfrac{1}{\mu} = \dfrac{L_q}{\lambda(1-p_N)} + \dfrac{1}{\mu}$.

(f) $L_s = L_q + \dfrac{\lambda_{\text{effective}}}{\mu} = L_q + \dfrac{\lambda(1-p_N)}{\mu} \Rightarrow L_s - L_q = \dfrac{\lambda(1-p_N)}{\mu} \Rightarrow \lambda_{\text{effective}} = \mu\left(L_s - L_q\right)$.

Example 10.7.4. *Trains arrived at the yard every 15 minutes and the service time is 33 minutes. If the line capacity of the yard is limited to 4 trains, find (i) the probability that the yard is empty (ii) the average number of trains in the system.* [MBA(CU) 1989, PUBE 1996]

Solution: Here, $\lambda = \frac{1}{15}$/min, $\mu = \frac{1}{33}$/min, $\rho = \frac{\lambda}{\mu} = 2.2$, $N = 4$.

(i) $p_0 = \dfrac{-(1-\rho)}{\rho^{N+1}-1} = \dfrac{\rho-1}{\rho^{N+1}-1} = \dfrac{1.2}{(2.2)^5-1} = 0.0237.$

(ii) $L_s = \sum_{n=0}^{N} np_n = 0 + p_1 + 2p_2 + 3p_3 + 4p_4 = p_0\left(\rho + 2\rho^2 + 3\rho^3 + 4\rho^4\right)$

$= 0.0237\left[2.2 + 2(2.2)^2 + 3(2.2)^3 + 4(2.2)^4\right] = 0.0237[2.2 + 9.68 + 31.94 + 93.70] = 3.26.$

Example 10.7.5. *At a railway station only one train is handled at a time. The railway yard is sufficient only for two trains to wait while the other is given signal to leave the station. Trains arrive at the station at an average rate of 6 per hour and the railway station can handle them on an average of 12 per hour. Assuming Poisson arrival and exponential service distribution find the steady state for various number of trains in the system. Also find average waiting time of a new train coming into the yard.* [IAS(Main) 2002]

Solution: Given: $\lambda = 6$/hour, $\mu = 12$/hour, $\rho = \frac{\lambda}{\mu} = 0.5$.

Maximum queue length = 2, maximum trains in the system = $N = 3$.

$$p_0 = \frac{1-\rho}{1-\rho^{N+1}} = \frac{1-0.5}{1-(0.5)^4} = 0.53$$

$$p_1 = p_0\rho = 0.53 \times (0.5) = 0.265$$

$$p_2 = p_0\rho^2 = 0.53 \times (0.5)^2 = 0.13$$

$$p_3 = p_0\rho^3 = 0.53 \times (0.5)^3 = 0.066.$$

$$L_s = 1 \cdot p_1 + 2 \cdot p_2 + 3 \cdot p_3 = 1 \times 0.265 + 2 \times 0.13 + 3 \times 0.066 = 0.723.$$

$$L_q = \frac{1 - N\rho^{N-1} + (N-1)\rho^N}{(1-\rho)(1-\rho^{N+1})} \times \rho^2 = 0.267.$$

$$\lambda_{\text{effective}} = \lambda(1-p_N) = 6(1-p_3) = 6(1-0.066) = 5.604.$$

$\therefore\ W_q$ = average waiting time of a new train coming into the yard

$$= \frac{L_q}{\lambda_{\text{effective}}} = \frac{0.267}{5.604} = 0.0476 \text{ hours.}$$

Model 3: (M/M/c) : (FCFS/∞/∞)

The parameters of this model are defined as follows:

1. Arrival rate follows Poisson distribution.
2. Service time follows Poisson distribution.
3. Number of server is *c*.
4. Service discipline is *first come first serve.*
5. The maximum number of customers permitted in the system is infinite.
6. Size of the calling source is infinite.

To analyse Model 3 we shall develop a generalised single server model in which both the arrival and service rates depend on n, that is λ_n and μ_n. The objective would be to derive a general expression for steady-state probabilities p_n. By putting $\lambda_n = \lambda$ and $\mu_n = \mu n$ for $n < c$ and $\mu_n = c\mu$ for $n \geq c$ we can obtain all the measures for (M/M/c) model.

Let us use the notation $(M_n/M_n/1)$:(FCFS/∞/∞) to indicate the arrival and service rates λ_n, μ_n, which depend on n so that

P (zero arrival during Δt given n in the system) $\cong 1 - \lambda_n \Delta t$.

P (zero departure during Δt given n in the system) $\simeq 1 - \mu_n \Delta t$.

Then $p_{n(t+\Delta t)} \simeq p_n(t)(1-\lambda_n\Delta t)(1-\mu_n\Delta t) + p_{n-1}(t)(\lambda_n\Delta t)(1-\mu_n\Delta t) + p_{n+1}(t)(1-\lambda_n\Delta t)(\mu_{n+1}\Delta t) : n > 0$

$p_0(t+\Delta t) \simeq p_0(t)(1-\lambda_0\Delta t)\cdot 1 + p_1(t)(1-\lambda_1\Delta t)\mu_1\Delta t \quad : n > 0$

Under the basic assumption that at most one (arrival or departure) can occur during small time $\Delta t > 0$.

Now as before taking limit as $\Delta t \to 0$, the differential difference equations become:

$$p_n'(t) = -(\lambda_n + \mu_n)\, p_n(t) + \lambda_{n-1} p_{n-1}(t) + \mu_{n+1} p_{n+1}(t) : n > 0$$

$$p_0'(t) = -\lambda_0 p_0(t) + \mu_1 p_1(t) \quad : n = 0.$$

Steady-state equations: $-(\lambda_n + \mu_n)\, p_n + \lambda_{n-1} p_{n-1} + \mu_{n+1} p_{n+1} = 0 : n > 0$

$$-\lambda_0 p_0 + \mu_1 p_1 = 0 : n = 0.$$

$$\left.\begin{aligned} \text{or,}\quad p_1 &= \frac{\lambda_0}{\mu} p_0 \\ \text{and } p_{n+1} &= \frac{\lambda_n + \mu_n}{\mu_{n+1}} p_n - \frac{\lambda_{n-1}}{\mu_{n+1}} p_{n-1} : n > 0 \end{aligned}\right\} \tag{10.7h}$$

Starting from p_1 and successively computing $p_2, p_3, \ldots$ using (10.7h) we can show by mathematical induction:

$$p_n = \frac{\lambda_0 \lambda_1 \ldots \lambda_{n-1}}{\mu_1 \mu_2 \ldots \mu_n} p_0 : n \geq 1. \tag{10.7i}$$

Now

$$\sum_{n=0}^{\infty} p_n = 1 \Rightarrow p_0 + \sum_{n=1}^{\infty} p_n = 1 \Rightarrow p_0 = \frac{1}{1 + \sum_{n=0}^{\infty} \prod_{i=1}^{n} \frac{\lambda_{i-1}}{\mu_i}}.$$

$$\therefore\ p_n = \left(\frac{\lambda_0\lambda_1\ldots\lambda_{n-1}}{\mu_1\mu_2\ldots\mu_n}\right) \times \left(\frac{1}{1+\sum_{n=0}^{n}\prod_{i=1}^{n}\frac{\lambda_{i-1}}{\mu_i}}\right) \tag{10.7j}$$

Now we come to point, where we derive for the Model 3: (M/M/c) : (FCFS/∞/∞)

$$\lambda_n = \lambda \qquad \forall\ n \geq 0$$

$$\mu_n = \begin{cases} n\mu & \forall\ n \leq c \\ c\mu & \forall\ n \geq c. \end{cases}$$

For $n \leq c : p_n = \dfrac{\lambda^n}{\mu(2\mu)(3\mu)\ldots(n\mu)} p_0 = \dfrac{\lambda^n}{n!\mu^n} p_0$

$n \geq c : \quad = \dfrac{\lambda^n}{\mu(2\mu)\ldots(c-1)\mu c\mu(c\mu)(c\mu)\ldots(c\mu)} p_0 = \dfrac{\lambda^n}{c!\, c^{n-c}\mu^n} p_0$

$\leftarrow (n-c)$ times $\rightarrow$

taking $\rho = \lambda/\mu$.

$$p_n = \begin{cases} \left(\dfrac{\rho^n}{n!}\right) p_0 & : 0 \leq n \leq c \\ \left(\dfrac{\rho^n}{c^{n-c}c!}\right) p_0 & : n > c \end{cases} \tag{10.7k}$$

where $p_0 = \left\{\sum_{n=0}^{c-1}\dfrac{\rho^n}{n!} + \dfrac{\rho^c}{c!(1-\rho/c)}\right\}^{-1}$.

(a) $L_q = \sum_{n=c}^{\infty}(n-c)p_n = \sum_{v=0}^{\infty} v\, p_{v+c} = \sum_{v=0}^{\infty}\dfrac{v\rho^{v+c}}{c^v\, c!} p_0 = p_0\dfrac{\rho^c}{c!}\cdot\dfrac{\rho}{c}\sum_{v=0}^{\infty} v\left(\dfrac{\rho}{c}\right)^{v-1} \quad \left[\because \dfrac{\rho}{c} < 1\right]$

$= p_0 \dfrac{\rho^{c+1}}{c\, c!}\left[\dfrac{1}{\left(1-\frac{\rho}{c}\right)^2}\right] = \dfrac{\rho^{c+1}}{(c-1)!\,(c-\rho)^2} p_0 = \dfrac{c\rho\cdot\rho^c}{c!\,(c-\rho)^2} p_0$

$= \dfrac{c\rho}{(c-\rho)^2}\left(\dfrac{\rho^c}{c!}p_0\right) = \dfrac{c\rho}{(c-\rho)^2} p_c \quad \left[\because p_c = \dfrac{\rho^c}{c!} p_0 \text{ [from (10.7k)]}\right]$

(b) $L_s = L_q + \rho = \dfrac{c\rho}{(c-\rho)^2} p_c + \rho.$

(c) $W_q = \dfrac{L_q}{\lambda}.$

(d) $W_s = W_q + \dfrac{1}{\mu}.$

Remark. If $\lambda_n = \lambda\ \forall\ n \geq 0$ and $\mu_n = \mu\ \forall\ n > 1$, then

$$p_0 = \left[1 + \sum_{n=1}^{\infty}\left(\frac{\lambda}{\mu}\right)^n\right]^{-1} = \left[1 + \frac{\lambda/\mu}{\left(1-\frac{\lambda}{\mu}\right)}\right]^{-1} \quad : \frac{\lambda}{\mu} < 1$$

$$= \left[1 + \frac{\rho}{1-\rho}\right]^{-1} \quad : \rho < 1$$

$$= 1 - \rho.$$

$\therefore\ p_n = \rho^n(1-\rho)\ \forall\ n \geq 0$, which is the same as that of Model 1 (M/M/1) : (FCFS/∞/∞).

Example 10.7.6. *At a central warehouse, vehicles arrive at the rate of 18 per hour and the arrival rate follows Poisson distribution. The unloading time of the vehicles follows exponential distribution and the unloading rate is 6 vehicles per hour. There are 4 unloading crews. Find the following (i) p_0 and p_3 (ii) L_q, L_s, W_q and W_s.*

Solution: Given: $\lambda = 18$/hour, $\mu = 6$/hour, $c = 4$, $\rho = \frac{\lambda}{\mu} = \frac{18}{6} = 3$, $\frac{\rho}{c} = \frac{3}{4} < 1$.

(i) $$p_0 = \left\{\sum_{n=0}^{c-1}\frac{\rho^n}{n!} + \frac{\rho^c}{c!\,(1-\rho/c)}\right\}^{-1} = \left\{\sum_{n=0}^{3}\frac{3^n}{n!} + \frac{3^4}{4!\,(1-3/4)}\right\}^{-1} = 0.0377.$$

$$p_n = \frac{\rho^n}{n!}p_0,\ 0 \leq n \leq c.$$

$$p_3 = \frac{\rho^3}{3!}p_0 = \frac{3^3}{3!} \times 0.0377 = 0.1697.$$

(ii) $$L_q = \frac{\rho^{c+1}}{(c-1)!\,(c-\rho)^2}p_0 = \frac{3^5}{3! \times 1}0.0377 = 1.53 \simeq 2 \text{ vehicles}.$$

$$L_s = L_q + \rho = 1.53 + 3 = 4.53 \simeq 5 \text{ vehicles}.$$

$$W_q = \frac{L_q}{\lambda} = \frac{1.53}{18} = 0.085 \text{ hour}.$$

$$W_s = W_q + \frac{1}{\mu} = 0.085 + \frac{1}{6} = 0.252 \text{ hours}.$$

Model 4: (M/M/c) : (FCFS/N/∞), $c < N$

This model is defined by the following parameters.

1. Arrival rate follows Poisson distribution.
2. Service rate follows Poisson distribution.
3. Number of servers is c.
4. Service discipline is general (*first come first serve basis*).
5. Maximum number of customers allowed in the system is N.
6. Size of the calling source is infinite.

In this model the maximum queue length is $= N - c$. Therefore, λ_n and μ_n for the current model are given by

$$\lambda_n = \begin{cases}\lambda & : 0 \leq n < N \\ 0 & : n \geq N\end{cases} \qquad \mu_n = \begin{cases}n\mu & : 0 \leq n \leq c \\ c\mu & : c \leq n \leq N\end{cases}$$

Therefore, the expression for p_n of Model 4 is $p_n = \begin{cases}\dfrac{\rho^n}{n!}p_0 & : 0 \leq n \leq c \\ \dfrac{\rho^n p_0}{c!\,c^{n-c}} & : c \leq n \leq N\end{cases}$

where $$p_0 = \begin{cases}\left[\displaystyle\sum_{n=0}^{c-1}\frac{\rho^n}{n!} + \frac{\rho^c(1-\rho/c)^{N-c+1}}{c!\,(1-\rho/c)}\right]^{-1} & : \dfrac{\rho}{c} \neq 1 \\ \left[\displaystyle\sum_{n=0}^{c-1}\frac{\rho^n}{n!} + \frac{\rho^c}{c!}(N-c+1)\right]^{-1} & : \dfrac{\rho}{c} = 1.\end{cases}$$

Note that p_0 is different from the expression p_0 obtained in *Model* 3.

(a) $$L_q = \sum_{n=c+1}^{N}(n-c)p_n = \sum_{j=1}^{N-c} j\,p_{j+c} = p_0 \frac{\rho^{c+1}}{c!\cdot c}\sum_{j=1}^{N-c} j\left(\frac{\rho}{c}\right)^{j-1}$$
$$= p_0 \frac{\rho^{c+1}}{(c-1)!\,(c-\rho)^2}\left\{1-\left(\frac{\rho}{c}\right)^{N-c} - (N-c)\left(\frac{\rho}{c}\right)^{N-c}\left(1-\frac{\rho}{c}\right)\right\}$$

Again, $$L_q = \sum_{n=c+1}^{N}(n-c)\,p_n = \sum_{n=0}^{N} np_n - \sum_{n=0}^{c} np_n - c\left(1-\sum_{n=0}^{c}\right) = L_s - \left\{c - \sum_{n=0}^{c}(c-n)\,p_n\right\}$$
$$= L_s - (c - c^*),$$

where $c^* = \sum_{n=0}^{c}(c-n)\,p_n$ = expected number of idle servers.

(b) $\lambda_{\text{effective}} = \lambda(1-p_N)$.

As $L_q = L_s - (c-c^*) \Rightarrow L_s = L_q + (c-c^*) = L_q + \dfrac{\lambda_{\text{effective}}}{\mu}$.

$\therefore\ c - c^* = \dfrac{\lambda_{\text{effective}}}{\mu} \Rightarrow \lambda_{\text{effective}} = \lambda(1-p_N) = \mu(c-c^*)$ = effective arrival rate.

[Since $(c-c^*)$ = expected number of busy channels, $\mu(c-c^*)$ = actual number served per unit time = effective arrival rate.]

Example 10.7.7. *A telephone exchange has two long distance operators. The telephone company finds that during the peak load, long distance calls arrive in a Poisson fashion at an average rate of 15 per hour. The length of service on these calls is approximately exponentially distributed with mean length 5 minutes.*

(i) *What is the probability that a subscriber will have to wait for his long distance call during the peak hours of the day?*

(ii) *If the subscriber will wait and are serviced in turn, what is the expected waiting time?*

Solution: Given: $c = 2, \lambda = \frac{15}{60} = \frac{1}{4}, \mu = \frac{1}{5}, \rho = \frac{\lambda}{c\mu} = \frac{5}{8}$.

$$p_0 = \left[\sum_{n=0}^{c-1}\frac{(c\rho)^n}{n!} + \frac{(c\rho)^c}{c!\,(1-\rho)}\right]^{-1} = \left[\sum_{n=0}^{1}\frac{(5/4)^n}{n!} + \frac{(5/4)^2}{2!\,(1-5/8)}\right]^{-1} = \frac{3}{13}.$$

(i) $$P(W>0) = \frac{(\lambda/\mu)^c}{c!\,(1-\rho)}p_0 = \frac{\left(\frac{5}{4}\right)^2\left(\frac{3}{13}\right)}{2!\,(1-5/8)} = 0.48.$$

(ii) $$W_q = \frac{L_q}{\lambda} = \frac{1}{\lambda}\cdot\frac{\rho(c\rho)^2}{c!\,(1-\rho)^2}p_0 = \frac{4\times(5/8)(5/4)^2\times\frac{3}{13}}{2!\,(1-5/8)} = 3.2 \text{ minutes}.$$

Model 5: (M/M/c) : (FCFS/N/N) $c < N$

This model has the following parameters.

1. Arrival rate follows Poisson distribution.
2. Service rate follows Poisson distribution.
3. Number of servers is c.
4. Service discipline is general (FCFS).
5. Maximum number in the system is N.
6. Size of the calling source is also N.

This model satisfies the following assumptions:

$$\lambda_n = \begin{cases} (N-n)\lambda & : 0 \le n \le N \\ 0 & : n \ge N \end{cases} \qquad \mu_n = \begin{cases} n\mu & : 0 \le n \le c \\ c\mu & : c < n \le N \\ 0 & : n \ge N \end{cases}$$

The steady-state formulae are $p_n = \begin{cases} {}^N C_n \rho^n p_0 & : 0 \le n \le c \\ {}^N C_n \dfrac{n!\,\rho^n}{c!\,c^{n-c}} p_0 & : c \le n \le N \end{cases}$

where $p_0 = \left[\sum_{n=0}^{c} {}^N C_n \rho^n + \sum_{n=c+1}^{N} {}^N C_n \dfrac{n!\,\rho^n}{c!\,c^{n-c}} \right]^{-1}$.

Proceeding similarly as before, we get

(a) $L_q = \sum_{n=c+1}^{N} (n-c) p_n$.

(b) $L_s = L_q + (c - c^*) = L_q + \dfrac{\lambda_{\text{effective}}}{\mu}$, where $c^* = \sum_{n=0}^{c} (c-n) p_n$ and $\lambda_{\text{effective}} = \mu (c - c^*)$.

(c) $W_q = \dfrac{L_q}{\lambda_{\text{effective}}}$ and $W_s = \dfrac{L_s}{\lambda_{\text{effective}}}$.

Model 6: (M/M/∞) : (FCFS/∞/∞)

The parameters of the model are:

1. Arrival rate follows Poisson distribution.
2. Service rate follows Poisson distribution.
3. Number of servers is infinite.
4. Service discipline is general (FCFS).
5. Infinite numbers of customers in the system.
6. The size of the calling source is infinite.

Such a model is known as *self-service model* because the customer himself is also the server and the number of servers is unlimited.

We have in this model $\lambda_n = \lambda \ \forall\, n \ge 0$

$\mu_n = n\mu \ \forall\, n \ge 0$.

Hence

$$p_n = \frac{\lambda^n}{n!\,\mu^n} p_0 = \frac{\rho^n}{n!} p_0.$$

Since

$$\sum_{n=0}^{\infty} p_n = 1 \Rightarrow p_0 \sum_{n=0}^{\infty} \frac{\rho^n}{n!} = 1 \Rightarrow p_0 e^{\rho} = 1 \Rightarrow p_0 = e^{-\rho}.$$

$$\therefore\ p_n = \frac{\rho^n e^{-\rho}}{n!},\ n = 0, 1, 2, \ldots$$

which is Poisson with mean $= E(n) = \rho$ and $\text{var}(n) = \rho$.

(a) $L_s = E(n) = \rho$.

(b) $W_s = \frac{1}{\mu}$ = the mean service time as each customer services himself.

(c) $L_q = W_q = 0$ because each customer services himself.

Model 7 (M/M/1) : (FCFS/N/N) $N > 1$

The parameters of this model are:

1. Arrival rate follows Poisson distribution.
2. Service rate follows Poisson distribution.
3. Single number of server.
4. General service (FCFS) discipline.
5. Maximum number allowed in the system is N.
6. Size of the calling source is N.

For this model: $\lambda_n = \begin{cases} (N-n)\lambda, & 0 \le n \le N \\ 0, & \text{otherwise.} \end{cases}$

$$\mu_n = \begin{cases} n\mu, & 0 \le n \le 1 \\ \mu, & 1 \le n \le N \\ 0, & \text{otherwise.} \end{cases}$$

Steady-state probability is given by

$$p_n = \begin{cases} {}^N C_n \rho^n p_0 & : 0 \le n \le 1 \\ {}^N C_n \dfrac{n!\,\rho^n}{1!\,.\,1^{n-1}} p_0 & : 1 \le n \le N, \end{cases}$$

where $p_0 = \left[\sum_{n=0}^{1} {}^N C_n \rho^n + \sum_{n=2}^{N} {}^N C_n \; n!\,\rho^n \right]^{-1}$.

(a) $L_q = N - \left(1 + \dfrac{1}{\rho}\right)(1 - p_0)$. (b) $L_s = N - \dfrac{1 - p_0}{\rho}$.

(c) $W_q = \dfrac{L_q}{\lambda_{\text{effective}}}$, $W_s = \dfrac{L_s}{\lambda_{\text{effective}}}$, $\lambda_{\text{effective}} = \mu(1 - p_0)$.

Example 10.7.8. *A cafeteria with self-service has an arrival rate of 12/hour. The average time taken by a person to collect and eat his meal is 20 minutes. Assume that the inter-arrival time are exponentially distributed, how many seats must the cafeteria have to accommodate each customer with probability 95%.* **[UGC(NET) 1995]**

Solution: Given: $\lambda = 12$ customers/hour, $\mu = \frac{60}{20} = 3$ customers/hour.

We have to find n such that $p_n = 0.95$.

Using *Model* 6 (self-service model), $p_n = \dfrac{e^{-\rho}\rho^n}{n!}$, where $\rho = \dfrac{\lambda}{\mu} = 4$

$$\Rightarrow 0.95 = \frac{e^{-4}4^n}{n!} \Rightarrow \frac{4^n}{n!} = \frac{0.95}{0.183} = 51.9.$$

From the trial and error, $n = 7$. Therefore, seven seats must be provided.

Example 10.7.9. *Arrival rate of telephone calls at a telephone booth are according to Poisson fashion with an average of 9 minutes between two consecutive arrivals. The length of telephone call is assumed to be exponentially distributed with mean 3 minutes.* (i) *Determine the probability that a person arriving at the booth will have to wait.* (ii) *Find the average queue length that is formed from time to time.* (iii) *What is the probability that an arrival will have to wait for more than 10 minutes before the phone is free?* (iv) *What is the probability he will have to wait for more than 10 minutes before the phone is available and the call is also complete?*

[MCA(CU) 1998, MBA(CU) 2002]

Solution: Given: $\lambda = \frac{1}{9}$/min, $\mu = \frac{1}{2}$/min, $\frac{\lambda}{\mu} = \rho = \frac{1}{3} = 0.33$.

(i) P (that a person will have to wait) $= \frac{\lambda}{\mu} = 0.33$.

(ii) Average queue length that is formed from time to time

$$= \frac{\text{Average length of queue}}{\text{Average length of non-empty queue}} = \frac{\lambda/\mu \times \lambda/\mu - \lambda}{(\lambda/\mu)^2} = \frac{\mu}{\mu - \lambda} = \frac{1/3}{1/3 - 1/9} = \frac{3}{2} = 1.5.$$

(iii) Using *Model* 1: Probability density function of (waiting + service) time distribution

$$= \psi(t) = \mu(1-\rho)e^{-\mu(1-\rho)}t = (\mu - \lambda)e^{-(\mu-\lambda)t} : t > 0.$$

But probability density function of waiting time only (excluding service) distribution

$$= \phi(t) = \begin{cases} \rho\mu(1-\rho)e^{-\mu(1-\rho)t} = \dfrac{\lambda}{\mu}(\mu - \lambda)e^{-(\mu-\lambda)t} : t > 0 \\ \mu\rho(1-\rho) \qquad\qquad = \dfrac{\lambda}{\mu}(\mu - \lambda) \qquad\qquad : t = 0 \end{cases}$$

$$\therefore P\,(\text{waiting time} \geq 10) = \int_{10}^{\infty} \frac{\lambda}{\mu}(\mu - \lambda)e^{-(\mu-\lambda)t}\,dt = \lim_{p \to \infty} \int_{10}^{p} \frac{\lambda}{\mu}(\mu - \lambda)e^{-(\mu-\lambda)t}\,dt$$

$$= \frac{\lambda}{\mu}(\mu - \lambda) \lim_{p \to \infty} \left[\frac{e^{-(\mu-\lambda)t}}{-(\mu - \lambda)}\right]_{10}^{p} = \frac{\lambda}{\mu} e^{-10(\mu-\lambda)} = \frac{1}{3}e^{-20/9} = \frac{1}{30} = 0.033.$$

(iv) $P(\text{waiting time + service} \geq 10) = \displaystyle\int_{10}^{\infty} (\mu - \lambda)e^{-(\mu-\lambda)t}\,dt = \lim_{p \to \infty}(\mu - \lambda)\left[\frac{e^{-(\mu-\lambda)t}}{-(\mu - \lambda)}\right]_{10}^{p}$

$$= e^{(\mu-\lambda)10} = e^{-20/9} = 0.1.$$

Example 10.7.10. *Problems arrive at a computer centre in a Poisson fashion at an average rate of 5 per day. The rules of the computer centre are that any man waiting to get his problem solved must aid the man whose problem is currently being solved. If the time to solve mean time of $\frac{1}{3}$ day and if the average solving time is inversely proportional to the number of people working on the problem, find the expected system time for a person entering the line.*

[MSc(DU) 1976, JNU(Comp) 1997, IAS(Main) 2004]

Solution: Given: $\lambda = 5$ problem per day, $\mu = 3$ problem per day.

The problem is based on the self-service model, where p_n is given by

$$p_n = \frac{e^{-\rho}\rho^n}{n!} : \rho = \frac{\lambda}{\mu} \text{ and } n = 0, 1, 2, \ldots, \infty.$$

Expected number of persons working at any instant

$$L_s = \sum_{n=0}^{\infty} np_n = \sum_{n=0}^{\infty} \frac{n \cdot e^{-\rho} \cdot \rho^n}{n!} = e^{-\rho} \cdot \rho \sum_{n=1}^{\infty} \frac{\rho^{n-1}}{(n-1)!} = \rho = \frac{\lambda}{\mu} = \frac{5}{3}.$$

$$W_s = \frac{L_s}{\lambda} = \frac{5/3}{5} = \frac{1}{3}\,\text{day} = \frac{24}{3} = 8 \text{ hours}.$$

10.8 INTRODUCTION TO NON-POISSON QUEUES

Queues in which arrivals and/or departures may not follow Poisson axioms are called non-Poisson queues. In this section we employed imbedded Markov chain techniques for studying two non-Poisson models (i) (M/G/1) : (GD/∞/∞) (ii) (GI/M/1) : (GD/∞/∞).

The technique by which non-Markovian queues are reduced to Markovian is called *imbedded Markov chain technique.* When one or more r.v.'s are added to convert a non-Markovian process into a Markovian, the technique involved in this conversion is called the *supplementary variable technique.* In fact, this technique is applied to (i) and (ii) mentioned earlier.

The concept of imbedded Markov chains was introduced by D G Kendall. In (M/G/1) model the transition matrix is determined by the probabilities that certain numbers of arrivals will occur during a service time. Similarly, (GI/M/1) transition matrix defined by the probabilities of certain numbers of departures during an inter-arrival time.

Model 8 (M/G/1) : (FCFS/∞/∞)

Let $s(t)$ be the pdf of the service time. If i customers are in the system at observation time, at the next observation time the number in the system k is given by

$$k=\begin{cases} j, & \text{if } i=0\\ i-1+j, & \text{if } i>0,\end{cases}$$

where $j=0,1,2,\ldots$ is the number of arrivals during a service time.

$$r_j=\int_0^{\infty}\frac{e^{-\lambda t}(\lambda t)^j}{j!}s(t)\,dt, \tag{10.8a}$$

where r_j be the probability that j-persons arrive during service time. Since arrivals occur according to Poisson with mean arrival rate λ, the expression of r_j is given in (10.8a).

Let p_n be the steady state probabilities that there are n customers in the system and the transition matrix between the beginning and the end of a service is given by

$$T=\begin{pmatrix} r_0 & r_1 & r_2 & r_3 & r_4 & \cdots\\ 0 & r_0 & r_1 & r_2 & r_3 & \cdots\\ 0 & 0 & r_0 & r_1 & r_2 & \cdots\\ 0 & 0 & 0 & r_0 & r_1 & \cdots\\ \cdots & \cdots & \cdots & \cdots & \cdots & \cdots\end{pmatrix} \tag{10.8b}$$

Now steady-state probabilities are given by

$$(p_0,p_1,p_2,\ldots)\,T=(p_0,p_1,p_2,\ldots)\ :\ n=0,1,2,\ldots$$

$$\Rightarrow p_0r_n+p_1r_n+p_2r_{n-1}+p_3r_{n-2}+\cdots+p_{n+1}r_0=p_n$$

$$\Rightarrow p_n=p_0r_n+\sum_{k=1}^{n+1}p_kr_{n+1-k}\ :\ n=0,1,2,\ldots \tag{10.8c}$$

$$\Rightarrow \sum_{n=0}^{\infty} z^n p_n = p_0 \sum_{n=0}^{\infty} z^n r_n + \sum_{n=0}^{\infty} z^n \left\{ \sum_{k=1}^{n+1} p_k r_{n+1-k} \right\} \text{ [using } z\text{-transform]}$$

$$= p_0 \sum_{n=0}^{\infty} z^n r_n + \frac{1}{z} \sum_{m=1}^{\infty} z^m \left\{ \sum_{k=0}^{m} p_k r_{m-k} - p_0 r_m \right\}. \tag{10.8d}$$

Suppose,

$$\sigma_m = \sum_{k=0}^{m} p_k r_{m-k},$$

which is the *convolution* of p_m and r_m. Since the z-transform of the convolution of two pdf's is the product of their z-transform, we have $\Omega(z) = P(z)R(z)$.

From (10.8d),

$$P(z) = p_0 R(z) + \frac{1}{z}\{\Omega(z) - \sigma_0\} - \frac{p_0}{z}\{R(z) - r_0\}.$$

Since $\sigma_0 = p_0 r_0$ and $\Omega(z) = P(z)R(z)$.

On some minor simplification, we get

$$P(z) = p_0 \left\{ \frac{R(z)(z-1)}{z - R(z)} \right\}. \tag{10.8e}$$

To find p_0 we use the condition,

$$P(1) = 1 = \lim_{z \to 1} p_0 \left\{ \frac{R(z)(z-1)}{z - R(z)} \right\} \left(\frac{0}{0} \text{ form} \right)$$

$$= p_0 \left\{ \frac{R(1)}{1 - R'(1)} \right\} \text{ (Applying L'Hôspital's rule)}$$

Since $R(1) = 1$, therefore, $p_0 = 1 - R'(1)$. (10.8f)

$$\text{Now } R(z) = \sum_{n=0}^{\infty} r_n z^n = \sum_{n=0}^{\infty} z^n \int_0^{\infty} \frac{e^{-\lambda t}(\lambda t)^n}{n!} s(t)\,dt = \int_0^{\infty} \left\{ \sum_{n=0}^{\infty} \frac{(z\lambda t)^n}{n!} \right\} e^{-\lambda t} s(t)\,dt$$

$$= \int_0^{\infty} e^{\lambda t z - \lambda t} s(t)\,dt = \int_0^{\infty} e^{\lambda t(z-1)} s(t)\,dt = E\left\{e^{\lambda t(z-1)}\right\}.$$

$$\therefore R'(1) = \left. \int_0^{\infty} (\lambda t) e^{\lambda t(z-1)} s(t)\,dt \right]_{z=1} = \lambda E(t).$$

From (10.8f), $p_0 = 1 - \lambda E(t)$.

(10.8e) gives

$$P(z) = \frac{(1 - \lambda E(t))(z-1)R(z)}{z - R(z)} \Big\}. \tag{10.8g}$$

Because of the complexity of $P(z)$ a general expression is not easily secured for $P(z)$. Any individual probability can be obtained by using the formula $P^{(n)}(0) = p_n n!$.

(a) $P^{(1)}(1) = E(n) = L_s =$ expected number in the system.

Now $L_s = P^{(1)}(1) = \lim_{z \to 1} P^{(1)}(z) = \lambda E(t) + \dfrac{R''(1)}{2[1 - \lambda E(t)]}$.

⟨Calculation is exactly similar as that of (10.8f)⟩

Where

$$R''(1) = \lambda^2 \left. \int_0^\infty t^2 e^{\lambda t(z-1)} s(t)\,dt \right]_{z=1} = \lambda^2 E\left(t^2\right) = \lambda^2\left[V(t) + \{E(t)\}^2\right].$$

$$V(t) = \text{Variance of } (t) = E\left(t^2\right) - \{E(t)\}^2.$$

$$\therefore\ L_s = \lambda E(t) + \frac{\lambda^2\left[V(t) + \{E(t)\}^2\right]}{2(1 - \lambda E(t))} : \lambda E(t) < 1.$$

Remark. From the property of *ergodicity of Markov chain* $\lambda E(t)$ must be less than one.

Model 9: (GI/M/1) : (FCFS/∞/∞)

Let $I(t)$ be the density function of inter-arrival time and μ be the service rate. If i customers are in the system at observation time then at the next observation time, the number k in the system is given by $k = i + 1 - j : 0 \le j \le i$, where j is the number of persons *serviced between two successive arrivals*.

Let V_j = Probability $\{j$ persons are serviced during time $t\}$.

As departures occur according to Poisson (M) with rate μ

$$V_j = \int_0^\infty \frac{(\mu t)^j e^{-\mu t}}{j!} I(t)\,dt. \tag{10.8h}$$

Transition matrix in this case is given by $T = (\tau_{ik}) = \begin{pmatrix} l_0 & V_0 & 0 & 0 & \cdots \\ l_1 & V_1 & V_0 & 0 & \cdots \\ l_2 & V_2 & V_1 & V_0 & \cdots \\ \vdots & \vdots & \vdots & \vdots & \cdots \end{pmatrix}$.

Note that $\tau_{ik} = V_{i+1-k} : 1 \le k \le i + 1$ and $i \ge 0$.

$$\tau_{i0} = 1 - \sum_{k=1}^{i+1} V_{i+1-k} = 1 - \sum_{k=0}^{i} V_{i-k} = 1 - \sum_{k=0}^{i} V_k = l_i.$$

The steady-state probabilities p_n are given by $(p_0, p_1, p_2, \ldots)\,T = (p_0, p_1, p_2, \ldots)$.

[Since T are *ergodic* for $\frac{1}{\mu E(t)} < 1$ and for all states, the corresponding *Markov chain* is ergodic subject to the same condition.]

$$p_k = \sum_{i=k-1}^{\infty} p_i \tau_{ik} = \sum_{j=0}^{\infty} p_{j+k-1} V_j : k \ge 1. \tag{10.8i}$$

To solve for p_n, consider the trial solution $p_n = As^n : A \neq 0$ is a constant and s is a parameter.

We observe that for $s = 0$, $p_n = 0$ and $s \ge 1$, the solution cannot define a probability distribution. Therefore, $0 < s < 1$.

From (10.8i),

$$As^n = \sum_{j=0}^{\infty} As^{j+n-1} V_j \Rightarrow s = \sum_{j=0}^{\infty} V_j s^j \equiv F(s).$$

To solve the equation $s = F(s)$, it is first noticed that $F(s)$ is a convex function in s. Also, $F(0) = V_0 > 0$, $F(1) = 1$.

From Fig. 10.8.2 it follows that $s = F(s)$ will have a solution in $0 < s < 1$, if at $s = 1$,

$$\frac{dF(s)}{ds} > 1 \Rightarrow F'(1) > 1.$$

Now $F(s) = \sum_{j=0}^{\infty} \int_0^{\infty} \frac{e^{-\mu t}(\mu t s)^j}{j!} I(t)\,dt$

$$= \int_0^{\infty} e^{-\mu t + \mu t s} I(t)\,dt = \int_0^{\infty} e^{-\mu t(1-s)} I(t)\,dt$$

$$F'(s) = \int_0^{\infty} e^{-\mu t(1-s)} \mu t\, I(t)\,dt, \quad F'(1) = \mu \int_0^{\infty} t\, I(t)\,dt = \mu E(t).$$

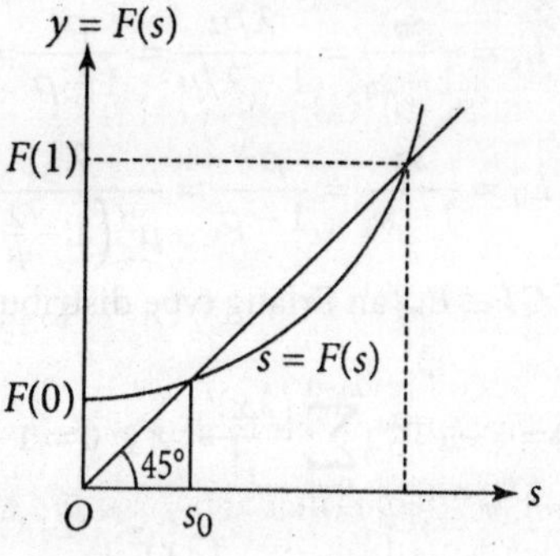

Fig. 10.8.2

$F'(1) > 1$ implies $\frac{1}{\mu E(t)} < 1$, which guarantees the *ergodicity* condition of the Markov chain mentioned earlier.

Let $s = s_0 : 0 < s_0 < 1$ be the solution of $s = F(s)$. It remains to find constant A.

$$\sum_{i=0}^{\infty} p_i = A \sum_{i=0}^{\infty} s_0^i = \frac{A}{1 - s_0} : 0 < s_0 < 1 \Rightarrow A = (1 - s_0).$$

Thus, $p_n = (1 - s_0)\, s_0^n : 0 < s_0 < 1$ and $n = 0, 1, 2, \ldots$ (10.8j)

p_n follows geometric distribution.

(a) $L_s = E(n) = \frac{s_0}{1 - s_0} : 0 < s_0 < 1,\ L_q = \frac{s_0^2}{1 - s_0}$.

(b) In particular, if $GI \equiv M$, then the model is reduced to (M/M/1) : (FCFS/∞/∞).

$$I(x) = \begin{cases} 1 - e^{-\lambda x} & : x \geq 0 \\ 0 & \text{otherwise} \end{cases} \quad \Bigg| \quad dI(x) = \lambda e^{-\lambda x} dx$$

$$F(s) = \int_0^{\infty} e^{-\mu x + \mu s x} dI(x) = \int_0^{\infty} \lambda e^{-\mu x + \mu s x - \lambda x} dx = \lambda \int_0^{\infty} e^{-\mu x\left[1 - \frac{\lambda}{\mu} - s\right]} dx = \frac{\lambda}{\mu\left[1 + \frac{\lambda}{\mu} - s\right]}.$$

$$F'(s) = \frac{\lambda}{\mu\left(1 + \frac{\lambda}{\mu} - s\right)^2}, \quad F'(1) = \frac{\lambda}{\mu \cdot \frac{\lambda^2}{\mu^2}} = \frac{\mu}{\lambda}.$$

$$F'(1) > 1 \Rightarrow \frac{\lambda}{\mu} = \rho < 1 \text{ (satisfied in M/M/1 queue).}$$

$$s = F(s) : 0 < s < 1 \Rightarrow s = \frac{\lambda}{\mu\left(1 + \frac{\lambda}{\mu} - s\right)} \Rightarrow s\mu\left(1 + \frac{\lambda}{\mu} - s\right) = \lambda \Rightarrow s\mu + s\lambda - s^2\mu = \lambda$$

$$\Rightarrow s\mu(1 - s) - \lambda(1 - s) = 0 \Rightarrow (1 - s)(s\mu - \lambda) = 0.$$

Since $s \neq 1,\ 0 < s_0 = \frac{\lambda}{\mu} < 1$.

$$\therefore\ p_n = (1 - s_0)\, s_0^n = \left(1 - \frac{\lambda}{\mu}\right)\left(\frac{\lambda}{\mu}\right)^n = (1 - \rho)\rho^n : \rho = \frac{\lambda}{\mu} < 1,$$

which is in agreement with (M/M/1) : (FCFS/∞/∞) queue of *Model* 1.

Also $L_s = \frac{s_0}{1-s_0} = \frac{\lambda/\mu}{1-\lambda/\mu} = \frac{\rho}{1-\rho} = \frac{\lambda}{\mu-\lambda}$

$$L_q = \frac{s_0^2}{1-s_0} = \frac{\rho^2}{1-\rho} = \frac{\lambda^2}{\mu^2\left(1-\frac{\lambda}{\mu}\right)} = \frac{\lambda^2}{\mu(\mu-\lambda)}.$$

(c) If $GI \equiv E_m$ an Erlang type distribution, then the model is $(E_m/\mathrm{M}/1):(\mathrm{FCFS}/\infty/\infty)$.

$$I(x) = 1 - e^{-\lambda x}\sum_{j=0}^{m-1}\frac{(\lambda x)^j}{j!} : x \geq 0 = 1 - e^{-\lambda x}\left[1 + \lambda x + \frac{(\lambda x)^2}{2!} + \cdots + \frac{(\lambda x)^{m_1}}{(m-1)!}\right]$$

$$\frac{dI(x)}{dx} = \lambda e^{-\lambda x}\left[1 + \lambda x + \frac{(\lambda x)^2}{2!} + \cdots + \frac{(\lambda x)^{m-1}}{(m-1)!}\right] - e^{-\lambda x}\left[1 + \lambda + \lambda^2 x + \cdots + \frac{(m-1)}{(m-1)!}(\lambda x)^{m-1}\right]$$

$$dI(x) = \frac{\lambda e^{-\lambda x}(\lambda x)^{m-1}}{(m-1)!}dx.$$

$$F(s) = \int_0^\infty e^{-\mu x(1-s)}\,dI(x) = \int_0^\infty e^{-\mu x(1-s)}\lambda e^{-\lambda x}\frac{(\lambda x)^{m-1}}{(m-1)!}dx = \frac{\lambda}{(m-1)!}\int_0^\infty (\lambda x)^{m-1}e^{-\lambda x\left[1-\frac{\mu}{\lambda}(1-s)\right]}dx$$

$$= \frac{\lambda}{(m-1)!}\int_0^\infty (\lambda x)^{m-1}e^{-\lambda x\eta}dx, \text{ where } \eta = 1 + \frac{\mu}{\lambda}(1-s)$$

$$= \frac{\lambda}{(m-1)!}\int_0^\infty \left(\frac{z}{\eta}\right)^{m-1} e^{-z}\cdot\frac{1}{\lambda\eta}dz \text{ [putting } z = \lambda x\eta]$$

$$= \frac{1}{(m-1)!\,\eta^m}\int_0^\infty e^{-z}z^{m-1}dz = \frac{1}{(m-1)!\,\eta^m}\Gamma(m) = \frac{(m-1)!}{(m-1)!\,\eta^m} = \frac{1}{\left[1-\frac{\mu}{\lambda}(1-s)\right]^m}.$$

Now

$$s = F(s) \Rightarrow s\left[1 - \frac{\mu}{\lambda}(1-s)\right]^m = 1 \Rightarrow sz^m = 1, \tag{10.8k}$$

where $z = 1 + \frac{\mu}{\lambda}(1-s) \Rightarrow \lambda z = \lambda + \mu(1-s) \Rightarrow s_0 = \frac{\lambda(1-z)+\mu}{\mu}$.

$$\therefore\ p_n = (1-s_0)\,s_0^n = \left[1 - \frac{\lambda(1-z)+\mu}{\mu}\right]\left[\frac{\lambda(1-z)+\mu}{\mu}\right]^n = \frac{\lambda}{\mu}(z-1)\left[\frac{\mu+\lambda(1-z)}{\mu}\right]^n. \tag{10.8l}$$

From (10.8k),

$$s_0 z^m = 1.$$

$$\frac{\lambda(1-z)+\mu}{\mu}z^m = 1 \Rightarrow \lambda(1-z)z^m + \mu z^m = \mu \Rightarrow \lambda z^m = \mu\left(\frac{z^{m-1}}{z-1}\right) = \mu\left[z^{m-1} + z^{m-2} + \cdots + 1\right]$$

$$\Rightarrow z^m - \frac{\lambda}{\mu}\left(z^{m-1} + z^{m-2} + \cdots + 1\right) = 0. \tag{10.8m}$$

(10.8m) gives possible values of z and (10.8l) gives the corresponding p_n of $(E_n/M/1):(\mathrm{FCFS}/\infty/\infty)$ model.

Throughout the chapter we noticed that the Poisson and exponential distributions play a key role in the queueing analysis. They characterise service facilities in which both arrivals and services are completely random. The important question regarding queueing theory is how good it is in practice. The limitations imposed by the mathematical analysis seems to make it difficult to find real applications that fit the model. However, the numerical examples introduced in this chapter show that queueing analysis yields results that may not be obvious intuitively.

10.9 EXERCISE 10

1. Consider the pure birth process, where the system starts with n_1 customers at $t = 0$. Derive the equations describing the system (with usual notation) and show that

$$p_n(t) = \frac{e^{-\lambda t}(\lambda t)^{n-n_1}}{(n-n_1)!} : n = n_1, n_1+, \ldots$$

2. A TV repairman finds that the time spent on his jobs has an exponential distribution with mean 30 minutes. If he repairs sets in the order in which they come in, and if the arrival of sets is approximately Poisson with an average rate of 10 per 8-hour day, what is the repairman's expected idle time each day? How many jobs are ahead of the average set just brought in?
3. Consider a simplified single-queue model in which the service mechanism allows for only one customer in the system. Customers that arrive while the facility is busy leave and never return. Suppose that, customers arrive completely randomly Poisson with rate λ per unit time and that the service time is exponential with mean value equal to $1/\mu$. Develop the difference equations representing the probabilities of the system and solve the associated steady-state model. Is the condition $\lambda < \mu$ essential for reaching steady state?
4. Customers arrive at a restaurant according to Poisson distribution at a rate of 20 per hour. The restaurant opens for business at 11:00 AM. Find the following:
   (a) The probability of having 20 customers in the restaurant at 11:12 AM given that there were 18 at 11:07 AM.
   (b) The probability that a new customer will arrive between 11:28 AM and 11:30 AM given that the last customer arrived at 11:25 AM.
5. A supermarket has two girls ringing up sales at the counters. If the service time for each customer is exponential with mean 4 minutes, and if people arrive in a Poisson fashion at the customer at the rate of 10 an hour.
   (a) What is the probability of having to wait for service?
   (b) What is the expected percentage of idle time for each girl?
6. In a bank, customers arrive in a Poisson stream with mean 36 per hour. The service time per customer is exponential with mean 0.035 hour. Assuming that the system can accommodate at most 30 customers at a time, how many tellers should be provided under each of the following conditions?
   (a) The probability of having more than 3 customers waiting is less than 0.20.
   (b) The expected number in the system does not exceed 3.
7. For (M/M/1) : (FCFS/N/∞), show that the two expressions for λ_{eff} are equivalent, namely $\lambda_{\text{eff}} = \lambda(1 - p_N) = \mu(L_s - L_q)$.
8. For the (M/M/1) : (FCFS/N/∞), find the formula for p_n and L_s, when $\rho = 1$.
9. A telephone exchange has two long distance operators. The telephone company finds that, during the peak load, long distance calls arrive in a Poisson manner at an average rate of 15 per hour. The length of service on this calls is approximately exponentially distributed with mean length 5 minutes.

What is the probability that a subscriber will have to wait for his long distance call during the peak hours of the day? If the subscribers wait and are serviced in turn, what is the expected waiting time?

10. In a self-service facility arrivals occur according to Poisson distribution with mean 50 per hour. Service time per customer is exponentially distributed with mean 5 minutes.
    (a) Find the expected number of customers in service.
    (b) What is the percentage of time the facility is idle?
11. For (M/M/c) : (FCFS/∞/∞) show that
    (a) The probability of someone is waiting $= \frac{\rho}{c-\rho} p_c$.
    (b) The expected number in the queue if it is given that it is not empty $= \frac{c}{c-\rho}$.
    (c) The expected waiting time in queue for customers who have.to wait $= \frac{1}{\mu(c-\rho)}$.
12. For (M/M/c) : (FCFS/N/∞) derive the steady state equations describing the situation for $N = c$, then show that

$$p_n = \begin{cases} \frac{\rho^n}{n!} p_0, & n = 0, 1, 2, \ldots, c \\ 0, & \text{otherwise,} \end{cases}$$

where $p_0 = \left\{ \sum_{n=0}^{c} \frac{\rho^n}{n!} \right\}^{-1}$.

13. At what average rate must a clerk at a supermarket work in order to insure a probability of 0.90 that the customer will not have to wait longer than 12 minutes? It is assumed that there is only one counter, to which customers arrive in a Poisson pattern at an average rate of 15 per hour. The length of service by the clerk has an exponential distribution.
14. A fast-food restaurant has one drive-in-window. It is estimated that cars arrive according to a Poisson distribution at the rate of 2 in every 5 minutes and that there is enough space to accommodate a line of 10 cars. Other arriving cars can wait outside this space, if necessary. It takes 1.5 minutes on the average to fill an order, but the service time actually varies according to an exponential distribution. Determine the following:
    (a) The probability that the facility is idle.
    (b) The expected number of customers waiting but currently not being served.
    (c) The probability that the waiting line will exceed the capacity of the space leading to the derive-in-window.
15. Show that for the special case of exponential service time with mean $1/\mu$, the results of (M/G/1): (FCFS/∞/∞) (*Model* 8) reduce to those of the (M/M/1):(FCFS/∞/∞).
16. (a) Show that for exponential inter-arrival time with mean $1/\lambda$, the results of (GI/M/1):(FCFS/∞/∞) reduce to those of the (M/M/1):(FCFS/∞/∞) model.
    (b) If GI $\equiv E_m$, an Erlang type distribution, then show that

$$p_n = \frac{\lambda}{\mu}(z-1)\left[\frac{\mu + \lambda(1-z)}{\mu}\right]^n,$$

where z is determined by the equation $z^m - \frac{\lambda}{\mu}(z^{m-1} + z^{m-2} + \cdots + 1) = 0$. **[IAS(Main) 2007]**

17. A branch of PNB has only one typist. Since the typing work varies in length (number of pages to be type), the typing rate is randomly distributed approximating a Poisson distribution with mean

service rate of 8 letters per hour. The letters arrive at a rate of 5 per hour during the entire 8-hour working day. If the typewriter is valued at ₹1.50 per hour, determine: (a) Equipment utilisation, (b) Average system time, (c) Average cost due to waiting on the part of typewriter.

18. If for a period of 2 hours in a day 8:00 AM to 10:00 AM trains arrive at the yard in every 20 minutes but the service time is 36 minutes, calculate for this period: (a) the probability that the yard is empty (b) the average number of trains at the yard. Capacity of the yard is limited to 4 trains only.

[CU(MSc) 2001, MBA(CU) 1997]

19. At present a servicing department provides answers through one channel, which on average can deal with 24 enquiries/hour at a cost of ₹3 per enquiry. Increasingly the customers are complaining that they have to wait for a long time and the department is considering alternative arrangements. There is either a two-channel system costing ₹100/hour and service rate of 15/hour in each, or a three-channel system costing ₹125/hour and service rate of 10/hour in each. Customers arrive at the rate of 20 hours. Average time a customer is in the system

$$= \frac{(\rho k)^k}{k!\,(1-\rho)^2 \cdot k\mu} p_0 + \frac{1}{\mu},$$

where $p_0 = \dfrac{k!\,(1-\rho)}{(\rho k)^k + k!\,(1-\rho)\left\{\sum_{n=0}^{k-1}\left(\dfrac{(\rho k)^n}{n!}\right)\right\}}$.

You are required to calculate:

(a) the average time a customer is in the system under the present arrangement,

(b) the extra charges per enquiry that would need to be made to recover the extra cost of each of the two arrangements proposed. [CSIR(JRF) 1989, JNU(MBA) 2000]

20. In the machine shop of a small scale industry, machines breakdown with a mean rate of 2 per hour. The maintenance shop of the industry has 2 machines who can attend the breakdown machines individually. The service rate of each of the mechanics is 1.5 machines per hour. Initially there are 5 working machines in the machine shop. Find (with usual notations mentioned in the chapter) p_0, L_q, L_s, W_q and W_s.

ANSWERS

2. Expected idle time = 3 hours, No. of jobs = $1\frac{2}{3}$ jobs.
3. $p_0'(t) = -\lambda p_0(t) + \mu p_1(t)$, $p_1'(t) = \lambda p_0(t) - \mu p_1(t)$. $\lambda < \mu$ is not essential for reaching steady state.
4. (a) $P(n=2/t=5 \text{ minutes}) = 0.262$; (b) $P(t \le 2 \text{ minutes}) = 0.486$.
5. (a) Probability = 0.167; (b) Idle time = 67%.
6. (a) Two tellers; (b) Two tellers.
9. Probability to wait = 0.48; Expected waiting time = 3.2 minutes.
10. (a) $L_s = 4.17$; (b) $p_0 = 0.015$.
13. 2.48 minutes per service.
14. (a) $p_0 = 0.4$; (b) $L_q = 0.9$ customer; (c) $P(\ge 1) = 0.00363$.
17. (a) Equipment utilisation $= \rho = \frac{\lambda}{\mu} = 0.625$; (b) Average system time $= \frac{1}{\mu-\lambda}$ = 20 minutes; (c) Idle cost = ₹4.50.

18. (a) $p_0 = \frac{\rho - 1}{\rho^{N+1} - 1} = 0.045$; (b) $L_s = 3.05$ trains.

19. (a) Average time a customer spends in the system $= \frac{1}{\mu - \lambda} = 15$ minutes; (b) For 2-service channel extra charges/enquiry = ₹1.40, For 3 service channel extra charges/enquiry = ₹2.65.

20. $\rho = \frac{\lambda}{\mu} = 1.33$, $p_0 = \left(\sum_{n=0}^{2} {}^5C_n (1.33)^n + \sum_{n=2+1}^{2} {}^5C_n \frac{n!(1.33)^n}{2^{n-1}\, 2!} \right)^{-1} = 0.0072$,

$$L_q = \sum_{n=2+1}^{5} (n-2)\, {}^5C_n \frac{n!(1.33)^n}{2!\, 2^{n-2}} p_0 = 1.604 \text{ machines},$$

$$\bar{c} = \sum_{n=0}^{c} (c-n) p_n = \sum_{n=0}^{2} (2-n) p_n = 2p_0 + p_1 = 0.06228,$$

$\lambda_{\text{eff}} = \mu(c - \bar{c}) = 1.5(2 - 0.06228) = 2.907$ per hour, $L_s = L_q + (c - \bar{c}) = 3.54172$ machines,

$$W_q = \frac{L_q}{\lambda_{\text{eff}}} = 0.552 \text{ hours}, \quad W_s = \frac{L_s}{\lambda_{\text{eff}}} = 1.2183 \text{ hours}.$$

Chapter 11

Replacement Analysis

11.1 INTRODUCTION

The study of replacement is concerned with situations that arise when some items such as a machine, men, electric bulbs, etc. need replacement due to their deteriorating efficiency, failure or breakdown. The efficiency or breakdown may be either gradual or all of a sudden. For examples, a machine becomes more and more expensive to maintain after a number of years, an electric bulb fails all of a sudden, pipelines is blocked after some years, an employee retired from his job, etc. In all such situations there is a need to formulate a most economic replacement policy for replacing faulty units or to take some remedial action to restore the efficiency of units.

Followings are the situations when the replacement of certain items is to be done:

1. Old item has failed and does not work at all or old item is expected to fail shortly.
2. The old item has deteriorated and works badly or requires expensive maintenance charges.
3. A better design of equipment has been developed.

The main objective of the problem is to decide the *best policy* to adapt with regard to replacement. The needs for replacement arise in different situation so that different types of decisions may have to be taken. For examples:

(a) It may be necessary to decide whether to wait for certain item to fail, which might cause some loss or to replace earlier at the expense of higher cost of the item.

(b) The expensive item can be considered individually to decide whether to replace now or, if not, when to reconsider the item to replace.

(c) It is necessary to decide whether to replace by the same item or by a different type of item.

In all such cases the ultimate aim is usually to enable the organisation concerned to *maximise profit*, or *minimise cost*.

11.2 VARIOUS REPLACEMENT MODELS

Generally, the maintenance cost of certain items always increases with time, and a stage comes when the maintenance cost becomes so high that it is better and more economical to replace the item with a new one. There may be a number of alternative choices and in each choice, we make a comparison between various alternatives by considering the cost due to waste, scarp, loss of output, damage of equipment, safcty risk, etc. In this section we shall deal with models for making such comparisons under different conditions by assuming that the suitable expressions for maintenance cost are readily available.

Model 1: Replacement of items whose maintenance cost increases with time and the value of money remains same during the period

Let C = capital cost of a certain item (say, machine).

$S(t)$ = the selling or scrap value of the item after t-years hence.

$f(t)$ = maintenance cost function of an item at time t.

n = optimal replacement period of the item.

Case 1. When t is a continuous variable.

$$T_m = \text{total maintenance cost incurred during } n \text{ years} = \int_0^n f(t)\,dt.$$

$$\begin{aligned} T &= \text{total cost incurred on the machine during } n \text{ years} \\ &= \text{capital cost} - \text{scrap value} + T_m \\ &= C - S(t) + \int_0^n f(t)\,dt. \end{aligned}$$

$$\begin{aligned} T_A &= \text{average annual total cost incurred on the machine} \\ &= \frac{1}{n}T = \frac{1}{n}\left[C - S(t) + \int_0^n f(t)\,dt\right]. \end{aligned}$$

Now, we have to determine that value of n, the optimal period for replacing the machine with a new machine so that the average annual total cost T_A is *minimum*.

$$\frac{dT_A}{dn} = -\frac{1}{n^2}\left[C - S(t) + \int_0^n f(t)\,dt\right] + \frac{1}{n}f(n)$$

$$\begin{aligned} \frac{dT_A}{dn} = 0 \Rightarrow f(n) &= \frac{C - S(t)}{n} + \frac{1}{n}\int_0^n f(t)\,dt : n \neq 0 \\ &= T_A \end{aligned}$$

$$\left.\frac{d^2 T_A}{dn^2}\right|_{T_A = f(n)} \geq 0.$$

Hence, *item should be replaced when the average cost becomes equal to current maintenance cost.* Using this result we can decide when to replace the machine, provided we have an explicit expression for the maintenance cost.

Case 2. When t is a discrete variable $T_A(n) = \dfrac{C - S(t)}{n} + \dfrac{1}{n}\sum_{t=1}^{n} f(t)$.

Using *finite difference* method, $T_A(n)$ will be minimum if $T_A(n+1) - T_A(n) \geq 0$ and $T_A(n) - T_A(n-1) \leq 0$.

Now

$$T_A(n+1)-T_A(n)=\left[\frac{C-S(t)}{n+1}+\frac{1}{n+1}\sum_{t=1}^{n+1}f(t)\right]-\left[\frac{C-S(t)}{n}+\frac{1}{n}\sum_{t=1}^{n}f(t)\right]$$

$$=\frac{1}{n+1}\left[C-S(t)+\sum_{t=1}^{n}f(t)+f(n+1)\right]-\frac{1}{n}\left[C-S(t)+\sum_{t=1}^{n}f(t)\right]$$

$$=\frac{f(n+1)}{n+1}+\sum_{t=1}^{n}f(t)\left[\frac{1}{n+1}-\frac{1}{n}\right]+[C-S(t)]\left(\frac{1}{n+1}-\frac{1}{n}\right)$$

$$=\frac{f(n+1)}{n+1}-\frac{1}{n(n+1)}\left[\sum_{t=1}^{n}f(t)+\{C-S(t)\}\right].$$

$$T_A(n+1)-T_A(n)\geq 0\Rightarrow\frac{f(n+1)}{n+1}\geq\frac{1}{n(n+1)}\left[\sum_{t=1}^{n}f(t)+\{C-S(t)\}\right]$$

$$\Rightarrow f(n+1)\geq T_A(n). \tag{11.2a}$$

Similarly, $$T_A(n)-T_A(n-1)\leq 0\Rightarrow f(n)\leq T_A(n-1). \tag{11.2b}$$

(11.2a) and (11.2b) suggest the optimal replacement policy as: *Replacement of the machine at the end of n years when the maintenance cost in the $(n+1)$th year is more than the average total cost in the nth year and the maintenance cost of the nth year is less than the previous year's average total cost.*

Example 11.2.1. *A truck-owner finds from his past records that the maintenance cost per year of a truck whose purchase price is ₹8000 is as below:*

Year	1	2	3	4	5	6	7	8
Maintenance cost	1000	1300	1700	2200	2900	3800	4800	6000
Resale price	4000	2000	1200	600	500	400	400	400

Determine at which time it is profitable to replace the truck? [MBA(CU) 2003, BESU(MSc) 2012]

Solution: Given the maintenance costs $f(t)$, which is discrete in the problem. Selling $S(t)$ and capital cost $C=$ ₹8000.

Let it be profitable to replace the truck after n years. Then n is determined by the minimum value of T_A. The value of T_A for each year are computed as follows.

Year (t)	$f(t)$	$\Sigma f(t)$	$S(t)$	$C-S(t)$	$T=C-S(t)+\Sigma f(t)$	$T_A=\frac{1}{n}T$
1	1000	1000	4000	4000	5000	5000
2	1300	2300	2000	6000	8300	4150
3	1700	4000	1200	6800	10800	3600
4	2200	6200	600	7400	13600	3400
5	2900	9100	500	7500	16600	3320
6	3800	12900	400	7600	20500	3417
7	4800	1770	400	7600	25300	3614
8	6000	23700	400	7600	31300	3913

Table 11.2.1a

From Table 11.2.1a, we see that during 5th year, T_A is minimum. Hence, the truck should be replaced after 5 years.

Example 11.2.2. (i) *An autorickshaw driver finds from his previous records that the cost per year of running an autorickshaw whose purchase price is ₹7000 is as given below.*

Year	1	2	3	4	5	6	7	8
Running cost (₹)	1100	1300	1500	1900	2400	2900	3500	4100
Resale price (₹)	3100	1600	850	475	300	300	300	300

At what age is the replacement due? [JNU(Comp) 2007]

(ii) *Another person has three autorickshaws of the same purchase price and cost of running each as in part* (i). *Two of these autorickshaws are* 2 *years old and the third one is* 1 *year old. He is considering a new type of autorickshaw with* 50% *more capacity than one of the old one at a unit price of* ₹9000. *He estimates that the running cost and resale price for the new auto will be as follows.*

Year	1	2	3	4	5	6	7	8
Running cost (₹)	1300	1600	1900	2500	3200	4100	5100	6200
Resale price (₹)	4100	2100	1100	600	400	400	400	400

Assuming that the loss of flexibility due to fewer vehicles is of no importance and that he will continue to have sufficient work for three of the old vehicles, what should be his policy? [BESU(MSc) 2012]

Solution: (i) The average annual cost for old autorickshaw is computed in **Table 11.2.2a.**

Year (n)	Resale value $S(t)$	Purchase price-resale $C-S(t)$	Maintenance cost $f(t)$	$\Sigma f(t)$	$T=C-S(t)$ $+\Sigma f(t)$	$T_A=\frac{1}{n}T$
1	3100	3900	1100	1100	5000	5000
2	1600	5400	1300	2400	7800	3900
3	850	6150	1500	3900	10050	3350
4	475	6525	1900	5800	12325	3081
5	300	6700	2400	8200	14900	2980
6	300	6700	2900	11100	17800	2967
7	300	6700	3500	14600	21300	3043
8	300	6700	4100	18700	25400	3175

Table 11.2.2a

From table it is evident that the old autorickshaw should be replaced at the end of 6th year.

(ii) Now, let us compute the average cost (annual) of the new autorickshaw of larger capacity. This is done in **Table 11.2.2b.**

Year (n)	$S(t)$ (₹)	$C-S(t)$ (₹)	$f(t)$ (₹)	$\Sigma f(t)$ (₹)	$T=C-S+\Sigma f(t)$ (₹)	$T_A=\frac{1}{n}T$ (₹)
1	4100	4900	1300	1300	6200	6200
2	2100	6900	1600	2900	9800	4900
3	1100	7900	1900	4800	12700	4233
4	600	8400	2500	7300	15700	3925
5	400	8600	3200	10500	19100	3820
6	400	8600	4100	14600	23200	3867
7	400	8600	5100	19700	28300	4043
8	400	8600	6200	25900	34500	4312

Table 11.2.2b

Conclusion. As the new autorickshaw has 50% more capacity than the old one, the minimum average annual cost of ₹3820 for the former is equivalent to ₹3820 $\times\frac{2}{3}$ = ₹2547 for the latter. Since this amount is less than ₹2967, the latter will be replaced by the new autorickshaw.

Having decided to replace the old vehicle by the new one, we now will determine as to when this replacement should be made. For the uniformity we assume that all the three old autorickshaws will be replaced by two larger new autorickshaws since they have 50% more capacity.

Total annual cost of one smaller autorickshaw during first year = ₹5000.

Total annual cost of one smaller autorickshaw during second year = (₹7800–5000) = 2800.

Total annual cost of one smaller autorickshaw during third year = ₹2250.

Total annual cost of one smaller autorickshaw during fourth, fifth and sixth years are ₹2275, ₹2575, ₹2900 respectively.

Total cost one year hence for two smaller autorickshaws aged two years and one autorickshaw aged one year = $2\times 2250+2800=$ ₹7300.

Similarly, total cost 2 years hence = $2\times 2275+2250=$ ₹6800

total cost 3 years hence = $2\times 2575+2275=$ ₹7425

total cost 4 years hence = $2\times 2900+2575=$ ₹8375.

And minimum average annual cost for two new autorickshaws = $2\times 3820=$ ₹7640.

As the total cost of old autorickshaws is less than the minimum average cost of the new autorickshaws till 3 years hence and becomes more only 4 year hence, the old autorickshaws should be replaced by the new larger ones three years hence.

Example 11.2.3. (i) *Machine M_1 costs ₹9000. Annual maintenance cost is ₹200 for first year and then increases by ₹2000 every year. Determine the best age at which to replace the machine. If the optimal replacement is followed, what will be the average yearly costs of owning and maintaining the machine?*

(ii) *Machine M_2 costs ₹10000. Annual maintenance cost is ₹400 for the first year and then increases by ₹800 every year. You now have a machine of Type M_1 which is one year old.*

Should you replace it with machine M_2? If so, when?

Solution: (i) The average annual cost for machine M_1 is computed in **Table 11.2.3a.**

Year (n)	$f(t)$	$\Sigma f(t)$	$S(t)$	$C-S(t)$	$T=C-S(t)$ $+\Sigma f(t)$	$T_A=\frac{1}{n}T$
1	200	200	×	9000	9200	9200
2	2200	2400	×	9000	11400	5700
3	4200	6600	×	9000	15600	5200
4	6200	12800	×	9000	21800	5450
5	8200	21000	×	9000	30000	6000

Table 11.2.3a

(a) The table indicates that the best age for the replacement of machine M_1 is 3rd year. (b) The average yearly cost of owning and operating for this period is ₹5200.

(ii) For mac...ne M_2, the average cost per year can similarly computed in **Table 11.2.3b.**

Year (n)	$f(t)$	$\Sigma f(t)$	$S(t)$	$C-S(t)$	$T=C-S(t)$ $+\Sigma f(t)$	$T_A=\frac{1}{n}T$
1	400	400	×	10000	10400	10400
2	1200	1600	×	10000	11600	5800
3	2000	3600	×	10000	13600	4533
4	2800	6400	×	10000	16400	4100
5	3600	10000	×	10000	20000	4000
6	4400	14400	×	10000	24400	4066

Table 11.2.3b

From **Table 11.2.3b** we see that machine M_2 should be replaced after 5 years and the average yearly cost of owning and operating for this is ₹4000.

Now an important observation is that: *The average total cost of one year old machine M_1 is ₹5700 during first year, ₹5200 during second year and ₹5450 during third year (from* **Table 11.2.3a**) *but from* **Table 11.2.3b** *the average total cost for machine M_2 does not exceed that of one year old machine M_1 in third year. Hence, machine M_1 should be replaced with machine M_2 during third year.*

Model 2: Replacement of items whose maintenance costs increase with time and the value of money also changes with time

Definitions. As money value changes with time, we calculate the *present worth* of the money to be spent in a few years. One rupee a year from now is equivalent to $(1.1)^{-1}$ rupee at the interest rate of 10% per year. Similarly, one rupee spent two years from now is equivalent to $(1.1)^{-2}$ today at the interest rate of 10% per year. Hence, one rupee spent n years from now is equivalent to $(1.1)^{-n}$ today at 10% interest rate.

The quantity $(1.1)^{-n}$ is called *present worth factor* (pwf) of one rupee spent in n years from now at 10% interest rate.

Generally, if r is the rate of interest per year, then $(1+r)^{-n}$ is called pwf of one rupee spent in n years from now.

Similarly, the expression $(1+r)^n$ is known as *payment compound amount factor* of one rupee spent in n years time.

The pwf of unit amount to be spent after one year is given by $v=(1+r)^{-1}$, where r is rate of interest. v is called *discount rate* or *depreciation value*. Obviously, $v<1$.

Now, if the maintenance cost increases with time and money value decreases at a constant rate, that is depreciation value is given, then we have to establish the following replacement policy in *Model* 2.

Replace the equipment if the next period's operating cost is greater than the weighted average of previous cost and do not replace the equipment if the next period's operating cost is less than the weighted average of previous cost.

Assumptions

1. The equipment under consideration has no resale value at the time of replacement.
2. The maintenance costs are incurred in the beginning of different time periods.

Let $C=$ purchase price of new equipment.

$R_n=$ operating cost at the beginning of nth year such that $R_{n+1}>R_n$ for all n.

$r=$ annual rate of interest.

$v=(1+r)^{-1}<1$ is the depreciation value per unit of money during one year.

$V(n)=$ present worth of all future costs of purchasing and operating the item with the policy of replacing the equipment at the end of each n years.

$$\begin{aligned}
&=\left[(C+R_1)+vR_2+v^2R_3+\cdots+v^{n-1}R_n\right] \qquad \text{(for 1 to } n \text{ years)}\\
&+\left[(C+R_1)v^n+v^{n+1}R_2+\cdots+v^{2n-1}R_n\right] \qquad \text{(for } n+1 \text{ to } 2n \text{ years)}\\
&+\left[(C+R_1)v^{2n}+v^{2n+1}R_2+\cdots+v^{3n-1}R_n\right] \qquad \text{(for } 2n+1 \text{ to } 3n \text{ years)}\\
&+\ldots\\
&=(C+R_1)\left[1+v^n+v^{2n}+\ldots\right]+R_2v\left[1+v^n+v^{2n}+\ldots\right]+R_3v^2\left[1+v^n+v^{2n}+\ldots\right]+\ldots\\
&+R_nv^{n-1}\left[1+v^n+v^{2n}+\ldots\right]\\
&=\left(C+R_1+R_2v+R_3v^2+\cdots+R_nv^{n-1}\right)\left(1+v^n+v^{2n}+\ldots\right)\\
&=\frac{F(n)}{1-v^n}, \text{ where } F(n)=C+R_1+R_2v+\cdots+R_nv^{n-1}.
\end{aligned}$$

By finite difference method $V(n)$ will be a minimum for that value of n for which

$$V(n+1)-V(n)>0 \text{ and } V(n)-V(n-1)<0. \tag{11.2c}$$

Now

$$V(n+1)-V(n)=\frac{F(n+1)}{1-v^{n+1}}-V(n)=\frac{\left[C+\sum_{k=1}^{n+1}v^{k-1}R_k\right]}{1-v^{n+1}}-V(n)=\frac{v^n\left[R_{n+1}-(1-v)V(n)\right]}{1-v^{n+1}} \tag{11.2d}$$

Similarly,

$$V(n)-V(n-1)=\frac{v^{n-1}\left[R_n-(1-v)V(n)\right]}{1-v^{n-1}}. \tag{11.2e}$$

As $v<1 \Rightarrow \dfrac{v^n}{1-v^{n+1}}\geq 0$.

From (11.2d) and (11.2e) and using conditions (11.2c), we have

$$R_n < (1-v)V(n) < R_{n+1} \Rightarrow R_n < \frac{C+R_1+R_2v+\cdots+R_nv^{n-1}}{1-v^n}(1-v) < R_{n+1}$$

$$\Rightarrow R_n < \frac{C+R_1+R_2v+\cdots+R_nv^{n-1}}{(1-v^n)(1+v+v^2+\ldots)} < R_{n+1}$$

$$\Rightarrow R_n < \frac{C+R_1+R_2v+\cdots+R_nv^{n-1}}{1+v+v^2+\cdots+v^{n-1}} < R_{n+1}$$

$$\Rightarrow R_n < W(n) < R_{n+1}, \qquad (11.2f)$$

where $W(n) = \dfrac{C+R_1+R_2v+\cdots+R_nv^{n-1}}{1+v+v^2+\cdots+v^{n-1}}$ = weighted average cost.

The value of n satisfying (11.2f) will be the best replacement age of the equipment.

Important Discussions

1. When the time value of money is not taken into consideration, the rate of interest $r = 0$ and $v \to 1$, then (11.2f) becomes

$$R_n < \frac{C+R_1+R_2+\cdots+R_n}{n} < R_{n+1}.$$

2. Let two machines M_1 and M_2 with all corresponding data be given. We have to determine the best replacement by the following ways.

   Step 1: First find best replacement age for machines M_1 and M_2 by using: $R_n < (1-v)V(n) < R_{n+1}$ and let the optimum replacement age for $M_1 = n_1$, $M_2 = n_2$.

   Step 2: Compare the weighted average cost $W(n)$ for each equipment by using:

$$W(n) = \frac{C+R_1+R_2v+\cdots+R_nv^{n-1}}{1+v+\cdots+v^{n-1}}.$$

   Step 3: Find $W(n_1)$ for machine M_1; $W(n_2)$ for machine M_2.

   If $W(n_1) < W(n_2)$ choose machine M_1

   $> W(n_2)$ choose machine M_2

   $= W(n_2)$ both machines are equally good.

Example 11.2.4. *Let the value of money be assumed to be 10% and suppose that machine M_1 is replaced after every 3 years, whereas machine M_2 is replaced after every six years. The yearly costs of both the machines are given below.*

Year	1	2	3	4	5	6
Machine M_1	1000	200	400	1000	200	400
Machine M_2	1700	100	200	300	400	500

Determine which machine should be purchased?

Solution: Here pwf $= \frac{100}{100+100} = \frac{10}{11}$.

Total discount cost (present worth) of machine M_1 for 3 years $= 1000 + 200 \times \frac{10}{11} + 400 \times \left(\frac{10}{11}\right)^2 =$ ₹1512 (approx).

Total discount cost of machine M_2 for 6 years $= 1700 + 100 \times \frac{10}{11} + 200 \times \left(\frac{10}{11}\right)^2 + 400\left(\frac{10}{11}\right)^4 + 500\left(\frac{10}{11}\right)^5 =$ ₹2765.

Average yearly cost for machine $M_1 = \frac{1512}{3} = ₹504$.
Average yearly cost for machine $M_2 = \frac{2765}{6} = ₹461$.
This shows the apparent advantage with machine M_2 but the comparison is unfair because the period of consideration is different. So if we consider 6 years period for machine M_1, then total discount cost of machine $M_1 = 1000 + 200 \times \frac{10}{11} + 400\left(\frac{10}{11}\right)^2 + 1000\left(\frac{10}{11}\right)^3 + 200\left(\frac{10}{11}\right)^4 + 400\left(\frac{10}{11}\right)^5 = ₹2647$.
Average yearly cost of machine $M_1 = \frac{2647}{6} = ₹441 <$ average yearly cost of machine M_2.
Hence, machine M_1 should be purchased.

Example 11.2.5. *A pipeline is due for repairs. It will cost ₹10000 and last for three years. Alternatively, a new pipeline can be laid at a cost of ₹30000 and lasts for 10 years. Assuming cost of capitals to be 10%, which alternative should be chosen?* [MBA(CU) 2002]

Solution: Here two types of pipelines for replacement (i) 10 years for new pipelines (ii) 3 years for existing pipelines.

$$v = \frac{100}{100+10} = \frac{10}{11} = 0.9091.$$

K_n = discount value of all future costs associated with the policy of replacing the equipment of n years assuming initial outlay as $C = C + Cv^n + Cv^{2n} + \cdots + \text{ to } \infty = \frac{C}{1-v^n}$.

For existing pipeline: $K_3 = \frac{10000}{1-(0.9091)^3} = ₹40211$.

For new pipeline: $K_{10} = \frac{30000}{1-(0.9091)^{10}} = ₹48820$.

Since $K_3 < K_{10}$, the existing pipeline should be continued.

Example 11.2.6. *A manufacturer is offered two machines M_1 and M_2. M_1 is priced at ₹5000 and running cost are estimated at ₹800 for each of the 5 years, increasing ₹200 per year in the 6th and subsequent years. Machine M_2 which have the same capacity as M_1 costs ₹2500 increasing by 200 per year thereafter. If money is worth 10% per year, which machine should be purchased? (Assume machines have negligible resale value).*

Solution: Here, $v = \frac{100}{100+1} = \frac{10}{11} = 0.9091$. For machine M_1, we construct **Table 11.2.6a**.

Year (n)	Maintenance charge R_n	pwf v^{n-1}	$R_n v^{n-1}$	$\Sigma R_n v^{n-1}$	$C + \Sigma R_n v^{n-1}$	Σv^{n-1}	$W(n)$
1	800	1	800	800	5800	1	5800.00
2	800	0.9091	727	1527	6527	1.9091	3418.88
3	800	0.8264	661	2188	7188	2.7355	2627.67
4	800	0.7513	601	2789	7789	3.4868	2233.85
5	800	0.6830	546	3335	8335	4.1698	1998.89
6	1000	0.6209	621	3956	8956	4.7907	1869.45
7	1200	0.5645	677	4633	9633	5.3552	1798.81
8	1400	0.5132	718	5351	10351	5.8684	1763.85
9	1600	0.4665	746	6097	11097	6.3349	1751.72
10	1800	0.4241	763	6860	11860	6.7590	1754.70

Table 11.2.6a

For machine M_2 we construct **Table 11.2.6b**.

Year (n)	Maintenance charge R_n	pwf v^{n-1}	$R_n v^{n-1}$	$\Sigma R_n v^{n-1}$	$C+\Sigma R_n v^{n-1}$	Σv^{n-1}	$W(n)$
1	1200	1	1200	1200	3700	10000	3700.00
2	1200	0.9091	1090.91	2290.91	4790.91	1.9091	2509.51
3	1200	0.8264	991.98	3282.89	5782.59	2.7353	2113.91
4	1200	0.7531	901.56	4184.35	6684.15	3.4868	1916.99
5	1200	0.6830	819.60	5003.95	7503.75	4.1698	1799.75
6	1200	0.6209	745.08	5744.03	8248.83	4.7907	1721.84
7	1400	0.5645	790.30	6534.33	9039.13	5.3552	1687.92
8	1600	0.5132	821.12	7355.45	9860.25	5.8684	1680.23
9	1800	0.4665	839.70	8195.15	10699.95	6.3349	1689.05
10	2000	0.4241	848.20	9043.35	11548.15	6.7590	1708.56

Table 11.2.6b

For machine M_1 : $1400 < 1751.72 < 1800$

$$R_8 < W(9) \quad < R_{10}$$

Machine M_1 should be replaced after 9 years.

For machine M_2 : $1400 < 1680.23 < 1800$

$$R_7 < W(8) \quad < R_9$$

Machine M_2 should be replaced after 8 years.

Since $W_{M_1}(9) > W_{M_2}(8)$. It is advisable to purchase machine M_2 instead of machine M_1.

Example 11.2.7. *The cost of a new machine is ₹5000. The maintenance cost during nth year is given by $M_n =$ ₹$500(n-1)$, where $n = 1, 2, \ldots$ If the discount rate per year is 0.05, after how many years will it be economical to replace the machine by a new one?* [MBA(CU) 1992, ICWA(Final) 1981]

Solution: Here, $v = \frac{1}{1+0.05} = 0.9523$. Construct the following **Table 11.2.7a** based on the data of the problem.

Year (n)	Maintenance cost R_n	pwf v^{n-1}	$R_n v^{n-1}$	$C+\Sigma R_n v^{n-1}$	Σv^{n-1}	$W(n)$
1	0	1.0000	0	5000	1.0000	5000
2	500	0.9523	476	5476	1.9523	2805
3	100	0.9070	907	6383	2.8593	2232
4	1500	0.8638	1296	7679	3.7231	2063
5	2000	0.8227	1645	9324	4.5458	2051
6	2500	0.7835	1959	11283	5.3293	2117

Table 11.2.7a

From **Table 11.2.7a** it is clear that it will be economical to replace the machine at the end of 5th year.

Model 3: Replacement of items that fail completely and suddenly

It is not easy to predict when a particular equipment will fail and its time of failure. The difficulty can be overcome by determining the probability distribution of failures. Assume that failure occurs only at the end of the period t. The objective is to find the value of t for which the total cost after replacement of an equipment is minimum.

(A) Individual Replacement Policy

Under this policy, an item is replaced immediately on its failure. In fact, this policy is very similar to the results of the following theorem:

Mortality theorem. A large population is subject to a given mortality law for a very long period of time. All deaths are immediately replaced by birth and no other enters or exists. Then age distribution becomes stable and that the number of deaths becomes constant which is equal to size of total population divided by the mean age at death.

Proof. Assume that death or failure occurs before the age of $(k+1)$ years, where k is an integer, that is life span of any item is between $t=0$ to $t=k$.

Define $\phi(t)=$ number of birth or replacement at time t.

$p(x)=P$ (death) or P (failure) just before the age $(x+1)$, that is, failure at the age x

$$\sum_{x=0}^{k} p(x)=1.$$

If $\phi(t-x)=$ number of birth at $t-x: t=k, k+1,\ldots,$ then new born attains age x at time t.

$\therefore$ expected number of death of such new borns before reaching the time $(t+1)$ (that is at time t)

$$=\sum_{x=0}^{k} p(x)\phi(t-x),\ t=k, k+1,\ldots$$

Since all deaths or failures at time t are immediately replaced by births or replacements at time $t+1$, we have

$$\phi(t+1)=\sum_{x=0}^{k} p(x)\phi(t-x),\ t=k, k+1,\ldots \tag{11.2g}$$

(11.2g) is the difference equation in t and can be solved by substituting $\phi(t)=A\alpha^{t}$, where A is a constant.

From (11.2g),

$$A\alpha^{t+1}=A\sum_{x=0}^{k} p(x)\alpha^{t-x}. \tag{11.2h}$$

Divide both side of (11.2h) by $A\alpha^{t-k}$

$$\alpha^{k+1}=\sum_{x=0}^{k} p(x)\alpha^{k-x}=\alpha^{k}\sum_{x=0}^{k} p(x)\alpha^{-x}=\alpha^{k}\left[p(0)+p(1)\alpha^{-1}+\cdots+p(k)\alpha^{-k}\right]$$

$$\Rightarrow \alpha^{k+1}-\alpha^{k}p(0)-\alpha^{k-1}p(1)-\cdots-p(k)=0. \tag{11.2i}$$

(11.2i) is a linear homogeneous equation of degree $(k+1)$ in α and is therefore exactly $(k+1)$ roots, say, $\{\alpha_0, \alpha_1, \ldots, \alpha_k\}$.

Now for $\alpha=1$: from (11.2i), $1-\sum_{x=0}^{k} p(x)=0$.

Hence, $\alpha=1$ is a root of (11.2i). Let it be $\alpha_0=1$.

Therefore, the general solution of eq. (11.2i) will be of the form

$$\phi(t) = A\alpha_0^t + A_1\alpha_1^t + \cdots + A_k\alpha_k^t = A_0 + A_1\alpha_1^t + \cdots + A_k\alpha_k^t. \tag{11.2j}$$

Again, from (11.2i) sum of the roots $= \alpha_0 + \alpha_1 + \cdots + \alpha_k = \dfrac{p(0)}{1} = p(0)$

$$\Rightarrow |\alpha_1 + \alpha_2 + \cdots + \alpha_k| = |p(0) - 1| < 1 \; [\because 0 \le p(0) \le 1]$$
$$\Rightarrow |\alpha_1| + |\alpha_2| + \cdots + |\alpha_1| < 1$$
$$\Rightarrow |\alpha_i| < 1, \; i = 1, 2, \ldots, k.$$

Hence, $\alpha_1^t, \alpha_2^t, \ldots, \alpha_k^t \to 0$ as $t \to \infty$.

From (11.2j), $\phi(t) = A_0$, which shows that number of death per unit time as well as number of births becomes constant.

Next, we have to find out A_0 : Let $\sigma(x) =$ probability of survivor for more than x years

$$= 1 - \text{probability (survivor will die before attaining age } x)$$
$$= 1 - \{p(0) + p(1) + \cdots + p(x-1)\}.$$

It is obvious that $\sigma(0) = 1$ (basic assumption).

Since the number of births as well as deaths becomes constant and each is equal to A_0, the expected number of survivors of age x is given by $A_0\sigma(x)$.

As deaths immediately replaced by birth, the size N of population remains constant

$$N = A_0 \sum_{x=0}^{k} \sigma(x) \Rightarrow A_0 = \frac{N}{\sum_{x=0}^{k} \sigma(x)}. \tag{11.2k}$$

From finite difference method, we know $\Delta x = (x+1) - x$ by taking $h = 1$.

$$\Delta\sigma(x) = \sigma(x+1) - \sigma(x).$$

$$\sum_{x=0}^{k} \sigma(x) \cdot 1 = \sum_{x=0}^{k} \sigma(x)\Delta x = (k+1)\sigma(k+1) - 0 \cdot \sigma(0) + \sum_{x=0}^{k} (x+1)[\sigma(x+1) - \sigma(x)]$$

$$= (k+1)\sigma(k+1) - \sum_{x=0}^{k} (x+1)\Delta\sigma(x). \tag{11.2l}$$

But $\sigma(k+1) = 1 - \{p(0) + p(1) + \cdots + p(k)\} = 0.$

$$\Delta\sigma(x) = \sigma(x+1) - \sigma(x) = \{1 - p(0) - p(1) - \cdots - p(x)\} - \{1 - p(0) - p(1) - \cdots - p(x-1)\}$$
$$= -p(x).$$

From (11.2l),

$$\sum_{x=0}^{k} \sigma(x) = 0 + \sum_{x=0}^{k} (x+1)\, p(x) = \sum_{y=1}^{k+1} y\, p(y-1) = \sum_{y=1}^{k+1} y\, p(\text{age at death } y)$$

$$= E(\text{age at death}) = \text{Mean age at death}. \tag{11.2m}$$

From (11.2k), $A_0 = \dfrac{N}{\text{Mean age at death}}$.

Hence, we conclude that age distribution is stable and ultimate rate of death can be obtained by dividing the size of the population by mean age at death.

(B) Group Replacement Policy

It is concerned with those items that either work or fail completely. It happens that a system contains a large number of items that are increasingly liable to failure with age. In this case, it is reasonable to replace all items irrespective of the facts that the items have failed or not failed with a provision that if any item fails before optimal time it may be individually replaced. Such a policy is called *group replacement policy.*

Group replacement policy is based on the following theorem.

Theorem. Let all the items in a system be replaced after a time interval t with a provision that individual replacement can be made if and when any item fails during this time period, then

1. Group replacement should be made at the end of the period t if the cost of individual replacement for the same period t is greater than the average cost per period through the end of the period t.
2. Group replacement should not be made at the end of the period t if the cost of individual replacement at the end of period $(t-1)$ is less than the average cost per period through the end of the tth period.

Proof. Let N = total number of items in the system.

$f(t)$ = number of items failing during time t.

$C(t)$ = total cost of group replacement after time period t.

C_g = cost of replacing item in a group.

C_I = cost of replacing an individual item.

With the above notations we can write $C(t) = NC_g + C_I(f(0) + f(1) + \cdots + f(t-1))$.

$A(t)$ = average cost of group replacement per unit period of time during a period t

$$= \frac{C(t)}{t} = \frac{NC_g + C_I[f(0) + f(1) + \cdots + f(t-1)]}{t}.$$

In order to determine replacement age, the average cost $A(t)$ should be minimum. From finite difference method the condition of minimum of $A(t)$ are $\Delta A(t-1) < 0$ and $\Delta A(t) > 0$.

$$\text{Now } \Delta A(t) = A(t+1) - A(t) = \frac{C(t+1)}{t+1} - \frac{C(t)}{t}$$

$$= \frac{NC_g + C_I[f(0) + f(1) + \cdots + f(t-1) + f(t)]}{t+1} - \frac{C(t)}{t}$$

$$= \frac{C(t) + C_I f(t)}{t+1} - \frac{C(t)}{t} = \frac{C_I f(t) - \frac{C(t)}{t}}{t+1}.$$

$$\Delta A(t) > 0 \Rightarrow C_I f(t) > \frac{C(t)}{t}.$$

Similarly, $\Delta A(t-1) < 0 \Rightarrow C_I f(t-1) < \dfrac{C(t)}{t}$.

$$\therefore\ C_I f(t-1) < \frac{C(t)}{t} < C_I f(t). \qquad (11.2n)$$

Again, $C_I f(t) > \frac{C(t)}{t} \Rightarrow \frac{C_I f(t)}{t+1} > \frac{C(t)}{t(t+1)} \Rightarrow \frac{C_I f(t)}{t+1} + \frac{C(t)}{t+1} > \frac{C(t)}{t+1}\left(\frac{1}{t}+1\right)$

$$\Rightarrow \frac{C_I f(t) + C(t)}{t+1} > \frac{C(t)}{t} \Rightarrow \frac{C(t+1)}{t+1} > \frac{C(t)}{t}$$

$\Rightarrow$ average cost for $(t+1)$ period is greater than average cost for t period.

$[\because C(t+1) = NC_g + C_I[f(0) + f(1) + \cdots + f(t-1) + f(t)] = C(t) + C_I f(t)]$.

Hence, the theorem is proved.

Example 11.2.8. *The following failure rates have been observed for certain type of light bulbs.*

Week	1	2	3	4	5
Percentage failed by the end of the week	10	25	50	80	100

There are 1000 bulbs in use and it costs ₹2 to replace an individual bulb, which has burnt out. If all the bulbs were replaced simultaneously it would costs 50 paise per bulb. It is proposed to replace all bulbs at fixed interval of time, weather or not they have burnt out and to continue replacing burnt out bulbs as an when they fail.

(i) *At what interval should all the bulbs be replaced?*

(ii) *At what group replacement price per bulb would a policy of strictly individual replacement becomes preferable to the adapted policy.* [MBA(CU) 2009, BESU(MSc) 2011]

Solution: Given 1000 bulbs are in use: $p_1 =$ probability of failure in 1st week $= \frac{10}{100} = 0.10$.

$p_2 =$ probability of failure in 2nd week $= \frac{25-10}{100} = 0.15$.

$p_3 =$ probability of failure in 3rd week $= \frac{50-25}{100} = 0.25$.

$p_4 =$ probability of failure in 4th week $= \frac{80-50}{100} = 0.30$.

$p_5 =$ probability of failure in 5th week $= \frac{100-80}{100} = 0.20$.

$\sum_{i=1}^{5} p_i = 1$, so, $p_i = 0$ for $i = 6, 7, 8, \ldots$.

Important conclusion. A bulb that has already lasted four weeks is sure to fail during fifth week.

$N_0 =$ number of bulbs in the beginning $= 1000$

$N_1 = N_0 p_1 = 1000 \times 0.10 = 100$

$N_2 = N_0 p_2 + N_1 p_1 = 160$

$N_3 = N_0 p_3 + N_1 p_2 + N_2 p_1 = 281$

$N_4 = N_0 p_4 + N_1 p_3 + N_2 p_2 + N_3 p_1 = 377$

$N_5 = N_0 p_5 + N_1 p_4 + N_2 p_3 + N_3 p_2 + N_4 p_1 = 350$

$N_6 = 0 + N_1 p_5 + N_2 p_4 + N_3 p_3 + N_4 p_2 + N_5 p_1 = 230$

$N_7 = 0 + 0 + N_2 p_5 + N_3 p_4 + N_4 p_3 + N_5 p_2 + N_6 p_1 = 250$, etc.

We observe that the expected number of bulbs burnt out in each week increases until 4th week, then decreases until the 6th week and again starts increasing. This pattern suggests that ultimately the system settles down to a steady state.

Expected life of each bulb = mean life $= \sum_{i=1}^{5} i p_i = 3.35$ weeks.

Also by *mortality theorem*: Number of failure in each week in steady state $= \frac{1000}{3.35} = 299$.

$\therefore$ the cost of replacing bulbs only on failure $= 2 \times 299$ [$\because$ given ₹2 per bulb]
$= ₹598.$

Since replacement of all 1000 bulbs simultaneously costs 0.50 per bulb and replacement of individual bulb on failure costs ₹2 the *average costs* for different group replacement policies are given below.

End of week	Cost of individual replacement	Cost of group replacement	Average cost per week
1	100 × 2 = 200	1000 × 0.50 + 100 × 2 = 700	700
2	160 × 2 = 320	700 + 160 × 2 = 1020	510
3	281 × 2 = 562	1020 + 281 + 2 = 1582	527

General Conclusion

1. Cost of individual replacement in third week is greater than average costs of two weeks. Therefore, it is reasonable to replace all the bulbs after every two weeks. Otherwise, average cost will start increasing.
2. Group replacement after one week costs ₹700 and the individual after one week costs ₹598. So, individual replacement is preferable.

Example 11.2.9. *At time zero all items in a system are new. Each item has a probability p of failing immediately before the end of the first month of the life and probability $q = 1 - p$ of failing immediately before the end of the second month (that is, all items fails by the end of the second month.) If all items are replaced as they fail, show that the expected number of failures at the end of the month x is given by $f(x) = \frac{N}{1+q}\left[1-(-q)^{x+1}\right]$, where N is the number of items in the system.*

Solution: $N_0 =$ number of items in the system in the beginning $= N$ (given).
$N_i =$ number of items expected to fail at the end of the ith month ($i = 1, 2, \ldots$), then
$N_1 = N_0 p = N(1-q)$
$N_2 = N_0 q + N_1 p = Nq + N(1-q)^2 = N(1-q+q^2)$
$N_3 = N_1 q + N_2 p = Nq(1-q) + N(1-q+q^2)(1-q) = N(1-q+q^2-q^3)$.
Let for a particular $i = k$, $N_k = N\left[1-q+q^2-q^3+\cdots+(-q)^k\right]$.
Now for $i = k+1$: $N_{k+1} = N_{k-1}q + N_k p$

$$= N\left[1-q+q^2-\cdots+(-q)^{k+1}q\right] + N\left[1-q+q^2-\ldots(-q)^k\right](1-q)$$
$$= N\left[1-q+q^2-\cdots+(-q)^{k+1}\right].$$

Hence, by mathematical induction the expected number of failures at the end of month x is given by

$$f(x) = N\left[1-q+q^2-\cdots+(-q)^x\right] = N\frac{1-(-q)^{x+1}}{1+q} \quad \text{(Proved).}$$

Remarks.

1. Average life of an item $= 1\cdot p + 2\cdot q = 1\cdot(1-q) + 2q = 1+q$. Average number of failure $= \frac{N}{1+q}$.
2. $f(x)$ at the end of month x will vary for different values of $(-q)^{x+1}$ and it will reach the steady state if $x \to \infty$.

$\therefore$ in steady state the expected number of failures $= \lim\limits_{x\to\infty} \dfrac{N\left(1-(-q)^{x+1}\right)}{1+q} = \dfrac{N}{1+q}$ $[q<1]$

$$= \frac{\text{Total number}}{\text{Mean age}} \quad \text{(Mortality law).}$$

Example 11.2.10. *An electronic equipment contains 500 resistors. When any resistor fails, it is replaced. The cost of replacement of a resistor individually is ₹20. If all the resistors are replaced at the same time, the cost per resistor is ₹5. The percentage of resistors surviving, S(i), at the end of month i is given below.*

Month (i)	0	1	2	3	4	5
$S(i)$	100	90	75	55	30	0

What is the optimum replacement plan?

Solution: p_i = probability of failure during month i.

$$p_1 = \frac{100-90}{100} = 0.10 \quad p_2 = \frac{90-75}{100} = 0.15 \quad p_3 = \frac{75-55}{100} = 0.20$$

$$p_4 = \frac{55-30}{100} = 0.25 \quad p_5 = \frac{30-0}{100} = 0.30.$$

N_i = number of resistors replaced at the end of ith month.

$N_0 = 500$

$N_1 = N_0 p_1 = 50$

$N_2 = N_0 p_2 + N_1 p_1 = 80$

$N_3 = N_0 p_3 + N_1 p_2 + N_2 p_1 = 116$

$N_4 = N_0 p_4 + N_1 p_3 + N_2 p_2 + N_3 p_1 = 159$

$N_5 = N_0 p_5 + N_1 p_4 + N_2 p_3 + N_3 p_2 + N_4 p_1 = 212.$

Determination of Individual Replacement Cost

Expected life of each resistor $= \sum_{i=1}^{5} i p_i = 3.5$ months.

Average number of failure/month $= \frac{500}{3.5} = 143$ (approx).

∴ cost of individual replacement = 143 × ₹20 = ₹2860.

Determination of Group Replacement Cost

Cost/resistor when replaced altogether = ₹5.

Cost/resistor when replaced individually = ₹20.

End of month (n)	Cost of replacement of 500 resistors at a time (1)	Cost of replacement of resistors individually during given replacement period (2)	Total cost (3) = (1) + (2)	Average cost per month $E = \frac{(3)}{n}$
1	2500	50 × 20 = 1000	3500	3500
2	2500	(50 + 80) × 20 = 2600	5100	2550
3	2500	(50 + 80 + 116) × 20 = 4920	7420	2473*
4	2500	(50 + 80 + 116 + 159) × 20 = 8100	10600	2650
5	2500	(50 + 80 + 116 + 159 + 212) × 20 = 12340	14840	2968

From above table it is clear that the average cost/month is minimum for the third month. Hence, the group replacement period is 3 months.

Conclusion. Individual replacement cost/month = ₹2860 and minimum group replacement cost/month = ₹2473, which is lesser than the individual. The group replacement policy is the best and hence all the resistors are to be replaced once in three months and the resistors which fail during this three months period are to be replaced individually.

11.3 EXERCISE 11

1. The following normality rates have been observed for a certain type of light bulbs.

Week	1	2	3	4	5
Percentage of failure by the end of week	10	25	50	80	100

There are 1000 bulbs in use, and it costs ₹1.00 to replace an individual bulb which has burnt out. If all the bulbs are replaced simultaneously, it would cost 25 per cent per bulb. It is proposed to replace bulbs at a fixed interval, whether or not they have burnt out, and to continue replacing burnt out bulbs as they fail. At what intervals should all the bulbs be replaced?

2. A large population is subject to a given mortality curve for a very long period of time. All deaths are immediately replaced by births, and there no other enters or exists. Show that the age distribution ultimately becomes stable and that the number of deaths per unit time becomes constant.

3. A company manufactures automobile batteries at a factory cost of ₹10 each. Battery life is subject to mortality as given in table below. The company has a guarantee policy under which if a battery fails during the first month after purchase, a refund of the full price of a new battery is made; if it fails during second month, a refund of 29/30 of the full price is given; during the third month, 28/30, and so on until the 30th month after purchase, at which time a refund of 1/30 of the full price is made. At what unit price should batteries be sold so that on average the company will break even? (Assume battery age is zero at the time of purchase).

Age in months	Probability of failure in next month	Age in months	Probability of failure in next month	Age in months	Probability of failure in next month
0	0.05	11	0	21	0.01
1	0	12	0	22	0.01
2	0	13	0	23	0.015
3	0	14	0	24	0.015
4	0	15	0	25	0.020
5	0	16	0	26	0.025
6	0	17	0.01	27	0.030
7	0	18	0.01	28	0.035
8	0	19	0.01	29	0.040
9	0	20	0.01	30	0.71
10	0				

[MBA(DU) 2002, BESU(MSc) 2010]

4. A computing machine has a large number of electronic tubes, each of which has a life normally distributed about a mean of 1200 hours with a standard deviation of 150 hours. If all tubes were to be replaced at fixed intervals on the night shift (when the computer is not normally used), the only costs would be the costs of labour and parts, which average about ₹3 a tube. Replacement of

individual tubes, which fail in service, costs about ₹8 for labour and parts, plus the cost of computer down time, which runs about ₹80 for an average tube failure. How frequently should all tubes be replaced.

5. A piece of equipment either can fail completely, so that it has to be scrapped, or may suffer a minor defect which can be repaired. The probability that it will not have to be scrapped before age t is $f(t)$. The conditional probability that it will need a repair in the interval t to $t+dt$ given that it is in running order at age t is $r(t)\,dt$. The probability of a repair or complete failure is dependent only on the age of the equipment, and not on the previous repair history. Each repair costs C_R and complete replacement costs C_R^*. For some considerable time the policy is to replace only on failure.

   (a) Derive a formula for the expected cost per unit time of the present policy of replacing only on failure.

   (b) It has been suggested that it might be cheaper to scrap equipment at some fixed age t_f, thus avoiding the higher risk of repairs with advancing age. Show that then expected cost per unit time of such a policy is

$$\frac{C_R \int_0^{t_f} f(u)r(u)\,du + C_R^*}{\int_0^{t_f} f(u)\,du}.$$

Hence, by differentiating this expression, find a condition to be satisfied by t_f for *minimum cost.*

[IAS(Main) 2003]

6. A firm is thinking of replacing particular machine whose cost price is ₹12000. The scrap price of this machine is only ₹200. The maintenance costs are found to be as follows:

Year	1	2	3	4	5	6	7	8
Maintenance cost (₹)	220	500	800	1200	1800	2500	3200	4000

Determine when the firm should get the machine replaced. [IIMS(Kol) 1996, MCom(Delhi) 1984]

7. An equipment which costs ₹15000 has to be replaced by a new equipment. The following data have been estimated.

Year	1	2	3	4	5	6	7	8
Resale value (₹)	12000	9500	7500	5700	4200	3900	2900	2000
Annual maintenance cost (₹)	600	800	1050	1400	2100	3500	5000	6800

Ignoring the time value of money and inflation when should the equipment be replaced?

[CU(MCom) 1989]

8. A machine costs ₹500. Operation and maintenance costs are zero for first year and increase by ₹100 every year. If money worth 5% every year, determine the best age at which the machine should be replaced. The resale value of the machine is negligibly small. What is the weighted average cost of owning and operating the machine?

9. Find the optimum replacement policy when minimises the total of all future discounted costs for an equipment, which costs ₹R and which needs maintenance cost of ₹$R_1, R_2, \ldots, R_n$, etc. ($R_{n+1} > R_n$) during the first year, second year, etc., respectively and further d is the depreciation value for unit of money during a year.

10. The cost of a new machine is ₹4000. The maintenance cost of nth year is given by $R_n = 500(n-1)$, $n = 1, 2, \ldots$. Suppose that the discount rate per year is 0.05. After how many years will it be economical to replace the machine by a new one? [CU(MSc Stat) 1984]

11. The probability of failure just before age n is shown below. If individual replacement costs ₹1.25 and group replacement costs ₹0.50 per item, find the optimal group replacement policy.

n	1	2	3	4	5	6	7	8	9	10	11
p_n	0.01	0.03	0.05	0.07	0.10	0.15	0.20	0.15	0.11	0.08	0.05

[CU(MCom) 1975, ISI(OR) 1997]

12. A computer contains 10000 resistors. When any resistor fails it is replaced. The cost of replacement of a resistor individually is ₹1 only. If all the resistors are replaced at the same time, the cost per resistor would be reduced to 35 paise. The percentage of resistors surviving at the end of the month t is given below.

Month	0	1	2	3	4	5	6
Surviving at the end of month	100	97	90	70	30	15	0

What is the optimum replacement plan? [ISI(Dip) 1971]

ANSWERS

1. It would be cheapest to replace all the bulbs every two weeks.
3. The break-even price = ₹11.00 (which is the sum of the factory cost and the expected return).
4. *Hints.* The average working life of a tube is 1200/16 or 75 days. Consider the cost of policies involving group replacement at the end of 50 days, at the end of 55 days, at the end of 60 days, etc.
5. (a) Expected cost of repair $= C_R \int_0^{\infty} f(u)r(u)\,du.$

$$\text{Total expected cost} = \frac{C_R \int_0^{\infty} f(u)r(u)\,du + C_R^*}{\int_0^{\infty} f(u)\,du} = C_R \int_0^{\infty} f(u)r(u)\,du + C_R^*.$$

(b) At a fixed age t_f.

$$\text{Expected cost of repair} = C_R \int_0^{t_f} f(u)r(u)\,du.$$

$$\text{Expected total cost} = C_R \int_0^{t_f} f(u)r(u)\,du + C_R^*.$$

$$\text{Expected cost per unit time} = \frac{C_R \int_0^{t_f} f(u)r(u)\,du + C_R^*}{\int_0^{t_f} f(u)\,du}.$$

6. 6th year (machine replaced). 7. To be replaced after 4 years, ₹3287.50.
9. The machine should be replaced after third year. The weighted average cost is ₹217.61.
10. After 4 years. 11. After every six weeks. 12. To be replaced every three months.

Chapter 12

Inventory Models

12.1 INTRODUCTION

Keeping an inventory (stock of goods) for future sale or use is very common in business. Retail firms, wholesalers, manufacturing companies and even blood banks — generally have its *inventory policy*, i.e., when and how much does it replenish? In a small firm the manager may keep track of his inventory and make these decisions. However, many companies have saved large sums of money by using *scientific inventory management.* The ultimate objective of any inventory model is to answer two most basic questions: (1) *How much to order?* (2) *When to order?*

The answer to the first one is expressed in terms of, what we say, the *order quantity.* It is the optimum amount that should be ordered every time; an order is placed and may vary with time depending on the situation under consideration. The answer to the second question depends on the type of the inventory system. The system may require *periodic review* or the system is under the *continuous review,* a *reorder point* is usually specified by the *inventory level* at which a new order must be placed.

The order quantity and reorder point mentioned above are usually determined by minimising the total inventory cost, which is the sum of some principal components and defined in the following manner:

$$\text{Total inventory cost} = \begin{pmatrix}\text{Purchasing}\\ \text{cost}\end{pmatrix} + \begin{pmatrix}\text{Set-up}\\ \text{cost}\end{pmatrix} + \begin{pmatrix}\text{Holding}\\ \text{cost}\end{pmatrix} + \begin{pmatrix}\text{Shortage}\\ \text{cost}\end{pmatrix}.$$

1. *Set-up cost.* This is the cost associated with setting up equipments before starting production. Set-up cost is in general independent of the quantity ordered for.
2. *Purchasing cost.* The cost of purchasing (or producing) a unit of an item is known as *purchasing* or *sometimes production cost.* This becomes an important component when the commodity unit price becomes dependent on the size of the order. This situation is usually expressed in terms of *quantity discount* or a *price break.*

3. *Holding cost.* The holding cost, which represents the cost of carrying inventory in stock, normally increases with the level of inventory. For example, space used for storage, money locked-up, insurance of stored equipments, taxes, etc.
4. *Shortage cost.* When an item cannot be supplied on the customer's demand, the penalty incurred for running out of stock is known as *shortage* or *penalty cost.* Obviously, it includes costs of customer's goodwill as well as potential loss in income.

The following figure illustrates the variation of four cost components of general inventory model as a function of inventory level.

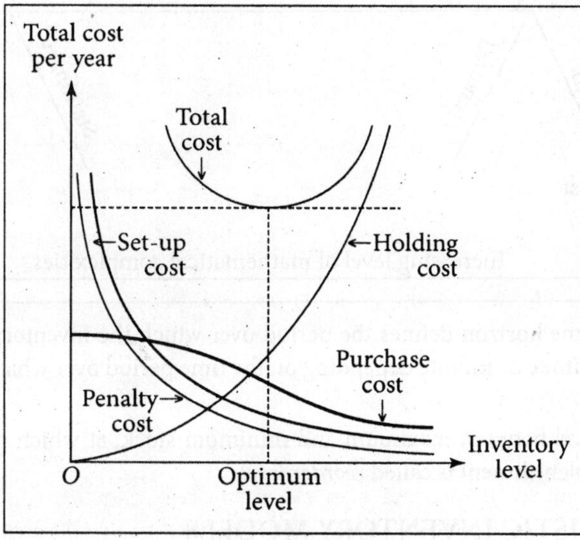

The *optimum inventory level* corresponds to the minimum total cost of all four components (see figure).

Remark. Note that an inventory model need not include all four types of costs. In practice, however, we can delete a cost component only if its effect on the total cost model is negligible. This point should be kept in mind, when we study the various *inventory models* in this particular chapter.

12.2 TYPES OF INVENTORY MODELS

The following figure illustrates the different classifications of demand, which is a key component in inventory models. A *deterministic demand* may be *static,* in the sense that the consumption rate remains constant w.r.t. time, or *dynamic,* where the demand is known with certainty but varies with time. The *probabilistic demand* has two similar classifications: *Stationary case* where probability density function of demand remains unchanged overtime, and in *non-stationary* case the probability density function varies with time.

Although the type of demand is a principal factor in the design of the inventory model, the following factors may also influence the way the model is formulated.

1. *Lead time.* The time gap between placing of an order and its actual arrival in the inventory is known as *lead time,* which may be deterministic or probabilistic.
2. *Order cycle.* The time period between placement of two successive orders is referred to as an order cycle. The order may be placed on the basis of either *continuous review* process or *periodic review* process. In continuous review the inventory level is checked continuously until a specified point is reached, where a new order is placed; while in periodic review the inventory level is reviewed at equal intervals of time and order is placed at such intervals.

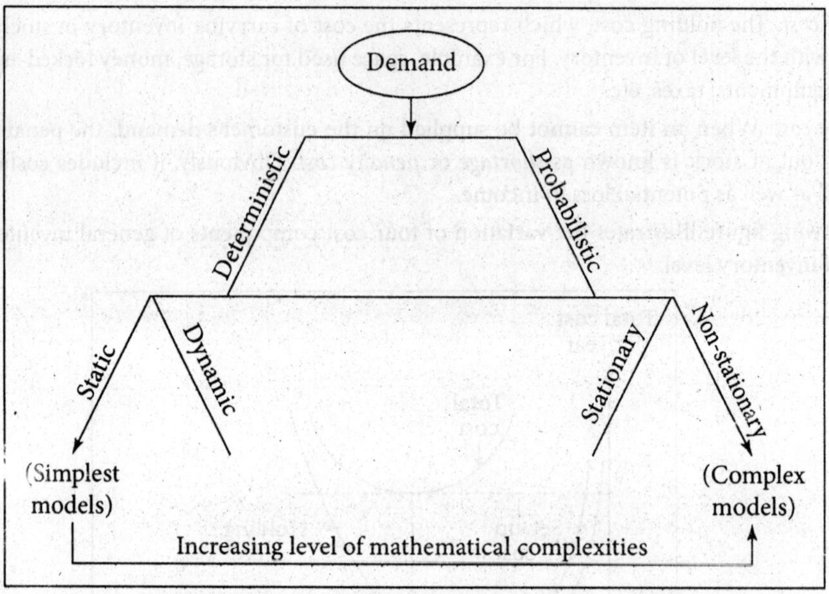

3. *Time horizon.* The time horizon defines the period over which the inventory level will be controlled. This horizon may be finite or infinite depending on the time period over which demand can be forecast reliably.
4. *Reorder level.* The level between maximum and minimum stock, at which purchasing or production activities start for replenishment is called *reorder level.*

12.3 DETERMINISTIC INVENTORY MODELS

The models presented in this section are meant to be illustrative of some inventory control systems. It is unlikely these models will fit a real situation exactly, but the objective of the presentation is to provide different ideas that can be adapted to specific inventory system.

Model 1: Single Item Static Model

In this model, demand is constant over time with instantaneous replenishment and no shortages. The following notations and assumptions are made in this model.

1. Demand occurs at a rate of β per unit time.
2. The highest level of inventory occurs when the order quantity x is delivered.
3. The inventory level reaches zero level x/β time units after the order quantity x is received.
4. K be the set-up cost incurred every time an order is placed.
5. H be the holding cost per unit inventory per unit time.

Total cost per unit time (TC) as a function of x may be written as

$$\text{TC}(x) = \text{Set-up cost per unit time + holding cost per unit time}$$

$$= \frac{K}{x/\beta} + H\left(\frac{x}{2}\right) = \frac{K\beta}{x} + \frac{Hx}{2} \qquad (12.3a)$$

Fig. 12.3.1a illustrates the variation of the inventory level.

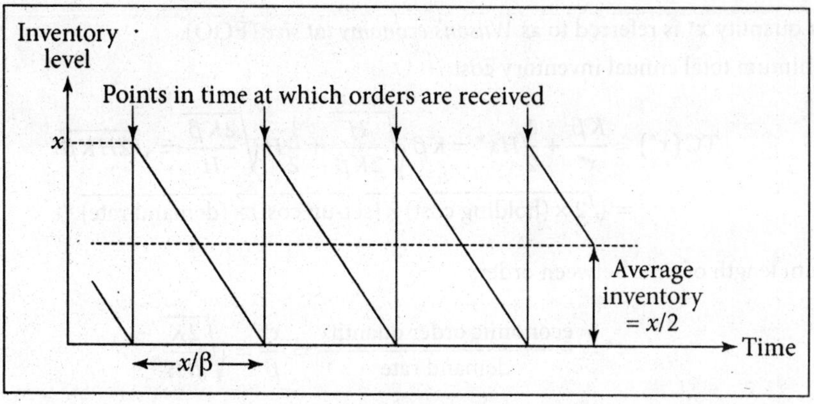

Fig. 12.3.1a

The smaller the order quantity x, the more frequent will be the placement of new orders. Again, larger order quantities indicate larger inventory level and consequently less frequent placement of orders. Because there are costs associated with placing orders and holding inventory in stock, the quantity x is selected to allow a compromise between two types of costs. This fact is represented in Fig. 12.3.1b below.

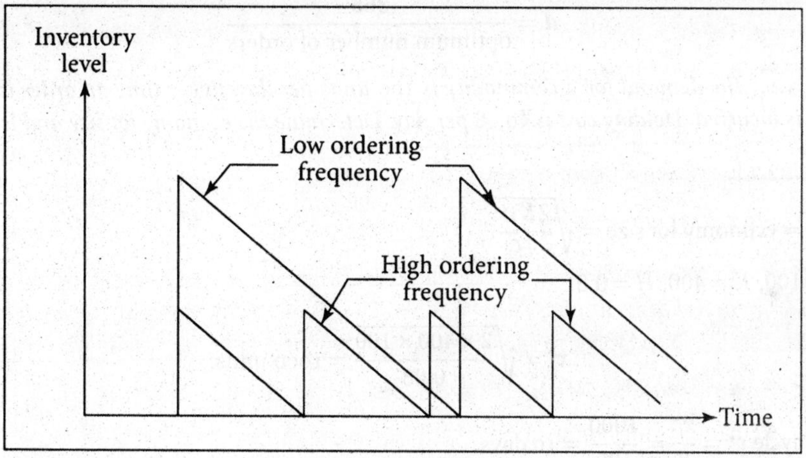

Fig. 12.3.1b

From Fig. 12.3.1a, length of each inventory cycle $= x/\beta$ and average inventory in stock $= x/2$.

Let us further assume that x is a continuous variable. Now our main objective is to minimise TC (x) w.r.t. x, which will give the optimum value x^* of x.

From (12.3a), $\dfrac{d\text{TC}(x)}{dx} = -\dfrac{K\beta}{x^2} + \dfrac{H}{2}$ $\qquad \dfrac{d^2\text{TC}(x)}{dx^2} = \dfrac{2K\beta}{x^3}$

$\dfrac{d\text{TC}(x)}{dx} = 0 \Rightarrow x = \sqrt{\dfrac{2K\beta}{H}}$ $\qquad \left.\dfrac{d^2\text{TC}(x)}{dx^2}\right|_{x=\sqrt{2K\beta/H}} > 0.$

1. Therefore, the optimum order quantity

$$x^* = \sqrt{\frac{2K\beta}{H}}. \tag{12.3b}$$

The order quantity x^* is referred to as *Wilson's economy lot size* (EOQ).

2. The minimum total annual inventory cost

$$\text{TC}(x^*) = \frac{K\beta}{x^*} + \frac{1}{2}Hx^* = K\beta\sqrt{\frac{H}{2K\beta}} + \frac{1}{2}H\sqrt{\frac{2K\beta}{H}} = \sqrt{2HK\beta}$$

$$= \sqrt{2 \times (\text{holding cost}) \times (\text{set-up cost}) \times (\text{demand rate})}. \tag{12.3c}$$

3. Optimum length of time between orders

$$t^* = \frac{\text{economic order quantity}}{\text{demand rate}} = \frac{x^*}{\beta} = \sqrt{\frac{2K}{\beta H}}. \tag{12.3d}$$

4. Optimum number of order placed

$$n^* = \frac{\beta}{x^*} = \sqrt{\frac{\beta H}{2K}}. \tag{12.3e}$$

5. Number of days of supply

$$d = \frac{365}{\text{optimum number of orders}}. \tag{12.3f}$$

Example 12.3.1. *The demand for a commodity is 100 units per day. Every time an order is placed, a fixed cost of ₹400 is incurred. Holding cost is ₹0.08 per day. Determine the economy lot size and length of cycle.*

[MSc(CU) 1987]

Solution: $x^* = \text{economy lot size} = \sqrt{\dfrac{2K\beta}{H}}.$

Here, $\beta = 100,\ K = 400,\ H = 0.8.$

$$x^* = \sqrt{\frac{2 \times 400 \times 100}{0.08}} = 1000 \text{ units.}$$

Length of cycle $t^* = \dfrac{x^*}{\beta} = \dfrac{1000}{100} = 10$ days.

Example 12.3.2. *A particular items has a demand of 9000 units/year. The cost of one procurement is ₹100 and the holding cost per unit is ₹2.40 per year. The replacement is instantaneous and no shortage are allowed. Determine* (i) *the economy lot size* (ii) *the number of orders per year* (iii) *the time between orders.*

[VU(MSc) 2000, NET(JRF) 1992]

Solution: Here, β = 9000 units/year, K = 100/procurement, H = 2.40 per year.

(i) Economy lot size $= x^* = \sqrt{\dfrac{2K\beta}{H}} = \sqrt{\dfrac{2 \times 100 \times 9000}{2.40}} = 866$ units/procurement.

(ii) Number of orders per year $= n^* = \dfrac{\beta}{x^*} = \dfrac{9000}{866} = 10.4.$

(iii) Time between orders $t^* = \dfrac{1}{n^*} = \dfrac{x^*}{\beta} = 1.15$ months between procurements.

Example 12.3.3. *Calculate* EOQ *in units and total variable cost for the following items assuming an ordering cost of ₹5 and a holding cost of 10%.*

Item	Annual demand (units)	Unit price (₹)
I_1	800	0.02
I_2	400	1.00
I_3	392	8.00
I_4	13800	0.20

[CU(MSc) 1999]

Solution:

Item I_1: $x^* = \sqrt{\dfrac{2K\beta}{H}} = \sqrt{\dfrac{2\times5\times800}{0.02\times\frac{10}{100}}} = 2000$ units.

$\text{TC}(x^*) = \sqrt{2KH\beta} = \sqrt{2\times5\times800\times0.02\times\frac{1}{2}} = ₹4.$

Item I_2: $x^* = \sqrt{\dfrac{2\times5\times400}{1.00\times\frac{1}{10}}} = 200$ units.

$\text{TC}(x^*) = \sqrt{2\times5\times400\times1.00\times\frac{1}{10}} = ₹20.$

Item I_3: $x^* = \sqrt{\dfrac{2\times5\times392}{8.00\times\frac{1}{10}}} = 70$ units.

$\text{TC}(x^*) = \sqrt{2\times5\times392\times8.00\times\frac{1}{10}} = ₹56.$

Item I_4: $x^* = \sqrt{\dfrac{2\times5\times13800}{0.20\times\frac{1}{10}}} = 2627$ units.

$\text{TC}(x^*) = \sqrt{2\times5\times13800\times0.20\times\frac{1}{10}} = ₹52.54.$

Model 2: Model with no Shortages and Several Production Runs of Unequal Lengths

Model 2 is based on all assumptions as in Model 1 except that the demand is uniform and the production runs differ in units. Let $t_1, t_2, \ldots, t_n$ denote the times of successive production runs such that

$$T = \sum_{i=1}^{n} t_i = \text{total time}.$$

The following Fig. 12.3.2 illustrates the behaviour of the model.

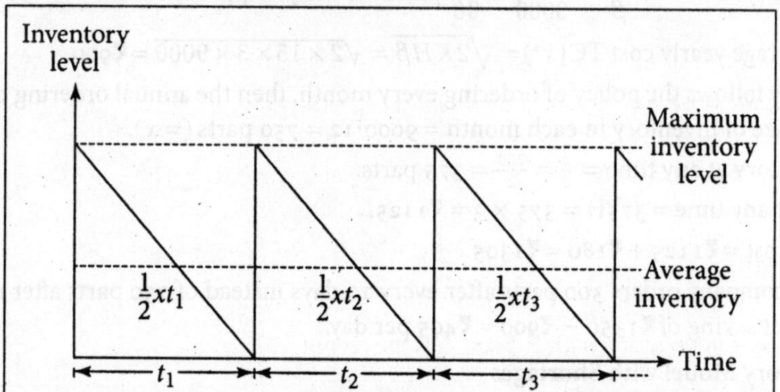

Fig. 12.3.2

Carrying cost for time period $T = \dfrac{1}{2}xH\sum_{i=1}^{n} t_i = \dfrac{1}{2}xHT.$

Set-up cost for the time period $T = \dfrac{\beta}{x}K$, since $nx = \beta$.

Total yearly variable inventory cost is given by $TC(x) = \frac{1}{2}xHT + \frac{K\beta}{x}$.

For optimum value of x, which minimises $TC(x)$,

$$\frac{dT(x)}{dx} = \frac{1}{2}HT - \frac{K\beta}{x^2} \qquad \frac{d^2TC(x)}{dx^2} = \frac{2K\beta}{x^3}$$

$$\frac{dT(x)}{dx} = 0 \Rightarrow x = \sqrt{\frac{2KB}{HT}} \qquad \left.\frac{d^2TC(x)}{dx^2}\right]_{x=\sqrt{2K\beta/HT}} > 0$$

Optimum value of x denoted by $x^* = \sqrt{\frac{2K\beta}{HT}}$ (12.3g)

and minimum value of $TC(x) = TC(x^*) = \sqrt{2HK \cdot \left(\frac{\beta}{T}\right)}$, (12.3h)

where β/T is the average rate of demand.

From eqs (12.3g) and (12.3h) we find that results for this model can be obtained if the demand rate β in Model 1 is replaced by average demand rate β/T.

Example 12.3.4. *A manufacturing company purchases 9000 parts of a machine for its annual requirements ordering one month requirement at a time. Each part costs ₹20. The ordering cost per order is ₹15 and the carrying charges are 15% of the average inventory per year. You have been assigned to suggest a more economical purchasing policy for the company. What advice would you offer and how much would it save for the company per year?*

Solution: Given: $\beta = 9000$ parts per year, $K = ₹15$ per order, $H = ₹20 \times 15/100 = ₹3$ each per year.

$\therefore$ optimal lot size $= x^* = \sqrt{\frac{2K\beta}{H}} = \sqrt{\frac{2 \times 9000 \times 15}{3}} = 300$ units.

Optimal order cycle $= t^* = \frac{x^*}{\beta} = \frac{300}{9000} = \frac{1}{30}$ years = 12 days (approx).

Minimum average yearly cost $TC(x^*) = \sqrt{2KH\beta} = \sqrt{2 \times 15 \times 3 \times 9000} = ₹900$.

If the company follows the policy of ordering every month, then the annual ordering cost is = ₹12 × ₹15 = ₹180 and lot size of inventory in each month = 9000/12 = 750 parts (= x).

Average inventory at any time $= \frac{x}{2} = \frac{750}{2} = 375$ parts.

Storage cost at any time = 375H = 375 × 3 = ₹1125.

Total annual cost = ₹1125 + ₹180 = ₹1305.

Hence, if the company orders 300 parts after every 12 days instead of 750 parts after every month, then there will be a net saving of ₹1350 − ₹900 = ₹405 per day.

Model 3: Inventory Model with Shortages

This model is an extension of the previous models by considering shortages. We discuss this model in three parts on the basis of some slightly different assumptions.

Part 1: Production is instantaneous.

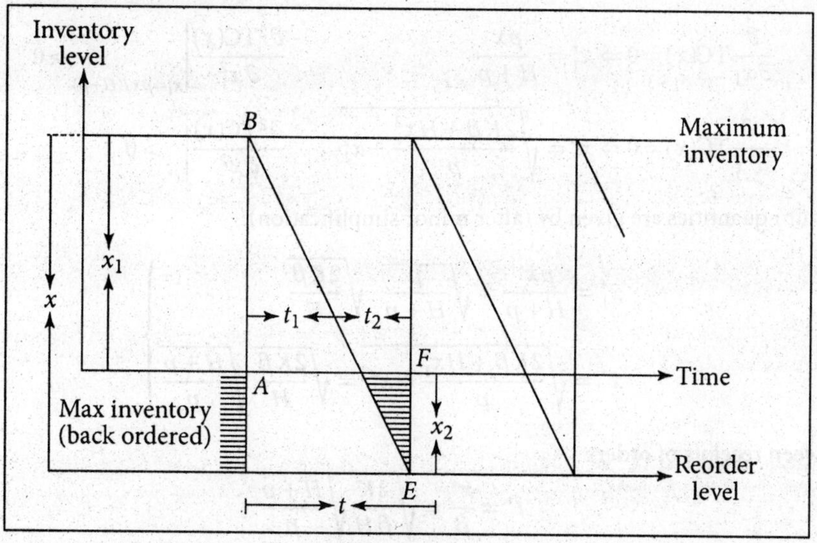

Fig. 12.3.3a

Here total inventory cost = ordering cost + carrying cost + shortage cost. Let p be the shortage cost per unit of time per unit quantity. We divide the total time period t into equal parts t_1 and t_2 such that $t = t_1 + t_2$.

In time t_1, the items are drawn from the inventory as needed and during t_2, orders for the item are being accumulated but not filled so that at the end of the interval t, an amount x is produced. The amount x has been divided into x_1 and x_2, where $x = x_1 + x_2$, x_1 denotes the amount, which goes into the inventory and x_2 is the amount which is immediately taken to satisfy unfilled demand.

$$\text{Now, } t_1 = \frac{x_1}{\beta},\ t_2 = \frac{x_2}{\beta} \text{ and } t = \frac{x}{\beta}. \tag{12.3i}$$

$$\text{Average inventory level} = \frac{(\text{average level over } t_1) + (\text{average level over } t_2)}{t_1 + t_2}$$

$$= \frac{\frac{x_1}{2} t_1 + 0 \cdot t_2}{t} = \frac{\frac{x_1}{2} \cdot \frac{x_1}{\beta}}{t} = \frac{x_1^2}{2\beta \cdot \frac{x}{\beta}} = \frac{x_1^2}{2x} \text{ [from (12.3i)]} \tag{12.3j}$$

$$\text{Carrying cost} = \frac{x_1^2}{2x} \times H = \frac{Hx_1^2}{2x}. \tag{12.3k}$$

$$\text{Average number of units on back order} = \frac{(\text{average level over } t_1) + (\text{average level over } t_2)}{t_1 + t_2}$$

$$= \frac{0 \cdot t_1 + \frac{x_2^2}{2} t_2}{t} = \frac{x_2^2}{2x}. \tag{12.3l}$$

$$\text{Shortage cost} = \frac{x_2^2}{2x} p = \frac{px_2^2}{2x}. \tag{12.3m}$$

$$\left.\begin{aligned} \therefore \text{TC}(x) &= \frac{\beta}{x} K + \frac{Hx_1^2}{2x} + \frac{px_2^2}{2x} \\ &= \frac{K\beta}{x} + \frac{Hx_1^2}{2x} + \frac{p(x - x_1)^2}{2x} \end{aligned}\right\} \tag{12.3n}$$

Our objective in this model is to calculate optimum values of x and x_1. We have from (12.3n)

$$\frac{\partial}{\partial x_1}\text{TC}(x)=0\Rightarrow x_1^*=\frac{px}{H+p} \qquad \left.\frac{\partial^2\text{TC}(x)}{\partial x_1^2}\right|_{x_1^*=px/(H+p)}>0$$

$$\frac{\partial}{\partial x}\text{TC}(x)=0\Rightarrow x^*=\sqrt{\frac{2K\beta+Hx_1^2}{p}+x_1^2} \qquad \left.\frac{\partial^2\text{TC}(x)}{\partial x^2}\right|_{x^*}>0$$

1. The optimum quantities are given by (after minor simplification)

$$\left.\begin{aligned}\hat{x}_1^*&=\frac{p\hat{x}^*}{H+p}=\sqrt{\frac{p}{H+p}}\cdot\sqrt{\frac{2K\beta}{H}}\\ \hat{x}^*&=\sqrt{\frac{2K\beta+Hx_1^*}{p}+x_1^{*2}}=\sqrt{\frac{2K\beta}{H}}\sqrt{\frac{H+p}{p}}\end{aligned}\right\} \qquad (12.3\text{o})$$

2. Time between receipts of orders

$$\hat{t}^*=\frac{\hat{x}^*}{\beta}=\sqrt{\frac{2K}{\beta H}}\sqrt{\frac{H+p}{p}}. \qquad (12.3\text{p})$$

3. Total optimum inventory cost

$$\text{TC}(\hat{x}^*)=\sqrt{2\beta KH}\sqrt{\frac{p}{H+p}}. \qquad (12.3\text{q})$$

4. Recorder level $=\hat{x}^*-\hat{x}_1^*=\hat{x}^*\left(1-\dfrac{p}{H+p}\right)$. (12.3r)

Remarks.

1. If $p\to\infty$, then $\text{TC}(\hat{x}^*)=\sqrt{2\beta KH}$, $\hat{x}^*\to\sqrt{\dfrac{2\beta K}{H}}$.
2. If $p\to 0$, $H>0$, then $\hat{x}_1^*\to 0$, $\hat{x}^*\to\infty$.
3. If $p=H$, then $\dfrac{p}{p+H}=\dfrac{1}{2}$ and $\hat{x}^*=\sqrt{\dfrac{4K\beta}{H}}$.

Part 2: Production is instantaneous and time is fixed.

In this part, time is fixed. Let $x=\beta t$, where as usual β is the demand rate per unit time, x is fixed economy lot size to meet the demand for the period t. From Fig. 12.3.3a, $x_1<x$. The amount x_1 is planned to meet demand during $t_1=\frac{x_1}{\beta}$. As set-up cost and time is constant,

$$\text{TC}(x)=\text{carrying cost + shortage cost}=\frac{x_1^2H}{2x}+\frac{(x-x_1)^2}{2x}p.$$

$$\frac{\partial}{\partial x_1}\text{TC}(x)=0\Rightarrow x_1=\frac{p}{p+H}x=\frac{p}{p+H}\beta t.$$

$$\left.\frac{\partial^2}{\partial x_1^2}\text{TC}(x)\right|_{x_1=p\beta t/(p+H)}>0 \text{ for all values of } x_1.$$

$\therefore\ \tilde{x}_1^*=\dfrac{p\beta t}{p+H}$ optimum value of x_1 when set-up cost is not under consideration due to fixed time.

(12.3s)

Part 3: Production is finite.

This part of inventory system is shown in the following Fig. 12.3.3b.

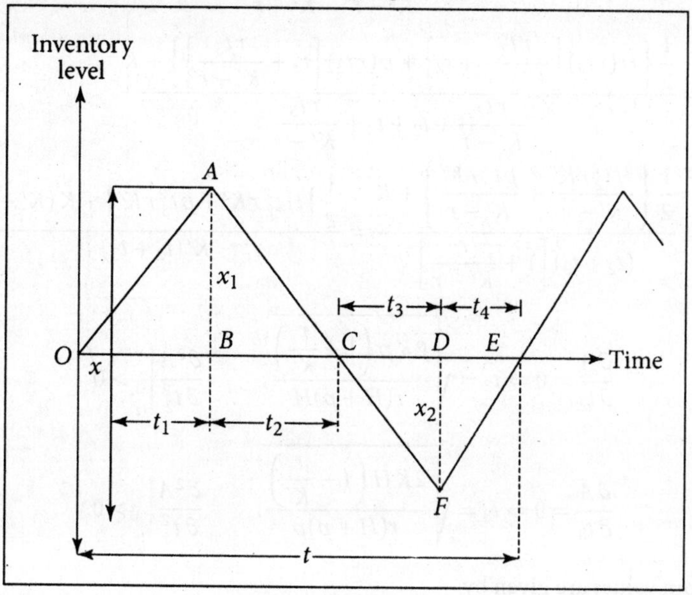

Fig. 12.3.3b

From figure: Holding cost $= H \times \Delta OAC = \frac{1}{2}Hx_1(t_1+t_2)$

Shortage cost $= p\Delta CEF = \frac{1}{2}px_2(t_3+t_4)$

$$A = \text{average cost/unit time} = \frac{\frac{1}{2}Hx_1(t_1+t_2)+\frac{1}{2}px_2(t_3+t_4)+K}{t_1+t_2+t_3+t_4}. \quad (12.3t)$$

The inventory is zero at O and during t_1, say, an amount $K't_1$ is produced and orders are filled at a rate r so that net increase x_1 in inventory during t_1 is

$$x_1 = K't_1 - rt_1 = (K'-r)\ t_1. \quad (12.3u)$$

After time t_1, the production is stopped and x_1 is used during t_2 and as the rate of use is r we must have

$$x_1 = rt_2. \quad (12.3v)$$

From (12.3u) and (12.3v),

$$t_1 = \frac{x_1}{K'-r} = \frac{rt_2}{K'-r}. \quad (12.3w)$$

As per the figure during t_3, shortages are accumulated at the rate r, so

$$x_2 = rt_3. \quad (12.3x)$$

Finally, during t_4, production rate is K and demand rate is r so that net rate of reduction of shortage is $(K'-r)$ and hence, we have

$$x_2 = (K'-r)\ t_4. \quad (12.3y)$$

From (12.3x) and (12.3y),

$$t_4 = \frac{x_2}{K'-r} = \frac{rt_3}{K'-r}. \tag{12.3z}$$

From (12.3t),
$$A = \frac{\frac{1}{2}\left\{H(rt_2)\left[\frac{rt_2}{K'-r}+t_2\right]+p(rt_3)\left[t_3+\frac{rt_3}{K'-r}\right]\right\}+K}{\frac{rt_2}{K'-r}+t_2+t_3+\frac{rt_3}{K'-r}}$$

$$= \frac{\frac{1}{2}\left\{\frac{Ht_2^2rK'}{K'-r}+\frac{pt_3^2rK'}{K'-r}\right\}+K}{(t_2+t_3)\left[1+\frac{r}{K'-r}\right]} = \frac{\frac{1}{2}\{Ht_2^2rK'+pt_3^2rK'\}+K(K'-r)}{K'(t_2+t_3)}. \tag{12.3A}$$

$$\frac{\partial A}{\partial t_2} = 0 \Rightarrow t_2 = \sqrt{\frac{2Kp\left(1-\frac{r}{K'}\right)}{r(H+p)H}}, \qquad \left.\frac{\partial^2 A}{\partial t_2^2}\right|_{t_2} > 0$$

$$\frac{\partial A}{\partial t_3} = 0 \Rightarrow t_3 = \sqrt{\frac{2KH\left(1-\frac{r}{K'}\right)}{r(H+p)p}}, \qquad \left.\frac{\partial^2 A}{\partial t_3^2}\right|_{t_3} > 0.$$

Therefore, optimum values are given by

$$t_2^* = \sqrt{\frac{2Kp\left(1-\frac{r}{K'}\right)}{r(H+p)H}}, \qquad t_3^* = \sqrt{\frac{2KH\left(1-\frac{r}{K'}\right)}{r(H+p)p}} \tag{12.3B}$$

$$A^* = \sqrt{\frac{2rHpK\left(1-\frac{r}{K'}\right)}{H+p}}, \qquad x^* = \sqrt{\frac{2rK(H+p)}{Hp\left(1-\frac{r}{K'}\right)}} \tag{12.3C}$$

$$x_1^* = \sqrt{\frac{2rp}{H}\left(1-\frac{r}{K'}\right)\left(\frac{p}{H+p}\right)}, \qquad x_2^* = \sqrt{\frac{2rHK\left(1-\frac{r}{K'}\right)}{(H+p)p}}. \tag{12.3D}$$

Example 12.3.5. *The demand for an item in a company is 18000 units per year and the company can produce the items at a rate of 3000 per month. The cost of one set-up is ₹500 and holding cost of 1 unit per month is 15 paise. The shortage cost of one unit is ₹20 per month. Determine:* (i) *Optimum production* (ii) *Optimum shortage* (iii) *Optimum production time and optimum cycle time* (iv) *Optimum inventory level.*

Solution: Here, $K = ₹500$, $H = ₹0.15$/month, $p = ₹20$, $K' = 3000$ units/month, $r = 18000$ units/year $=$ 1500 units/month.

(i) Optimum production
$$x^* = \sqrt{\frac{2rK(H+p)}{\left(1-\frac{r}{K'}\right)Hp}} = \sqrt{\frac{2K(H+p)}{Hp}\times\frac{K'r}{(K'-r)}}$$

$$= \sqrt{\frac{2\times 500(0.15+20)\times 1500\times 3000}{0.15\times 20(3000-1500)}}$$

$$= 4489 \text{ units (approx).}$$

(ii) Optimum shortages $x_2^* = \sqrt{\dfrac{2rHK(K'-r)}{K'p(H+p)}} = \sqrt{\dfrac{2\times 1500\times 500\times 0.15(3000-1500)}{3000\times 20\times(0.15+20)}}$

$= 18$ units (approx).

(iii) Optimum production time $= \dfrac{x^*}{K'} = \dfrac{4489}{3000} = 1.5$ months.

Optimum cycle time $= \dfrac{x^*}{r} = \dfrac{4489}{1500} = 3$ months.

(iv) Optimum inventory level $x_1^* = \sqrt{\dfrac{2rp}{H}\times\dfrac{K'-r}{K'}\times\dfrac{p}{H+p}}$

$= \sqrt{\dfrac{2\times 1500\times 200}{0.15}\times\dfrac{3000-1500}{3000}\times\dfrac{20}{0.15\times 20}}$

$= 2227$ units (approx).

Example 12.3.6. *A commodity is to be supplied at a constant rate of 200 units per day. Supplies of any amount can be had at any required time, but each order costs ₹50. Cost of holding the commodity in inventory is ₹2 per unit per day while delay in the supply of the items induces a penalty of ₹10 per unit per delay of 1 day. Find the optimal policy and the reorder cycle.*

Solution: Here, $\beta = 200$ units per day, $K = 50$ per order, $H = ₹2$ per unit per day, $p = ₹10$ per unit per day.

$$\hat{x}^* = \sqrt{\frac{2K\beta}{H}\left(\frac{H+p}{p}\right)} = \sqrt{\frac{2\times 50\times 200}{2}\left(\frac{2+10}{10}\right)} = 109.5 \text{ units.}$$

$$\hat{t}^* = \frac{\hat{x}^*}{\beta} = \frac{109.5}{200} = \frac{1}{2} \text{ day.}$$

Model 4: Inventory Model with Price Breaks

Consider the inventory model with instantaneous stock replenishment and no shortage. Assume the cost per unit is c_1 for $x < d$ and c_2 for $x \geq d$, where x is the quantity which is a price break or discount granted and $c_1 > c_2$.

TC = Total cost = purchasing cost + set-up cost + holding cost.

Now $TC_1(x) = \beta c_1 + \dfrac{k\beta}{x} + \dfrac{Hx}{2} : x < d$

$TC_2(x) = \beta c_2 + \dfrac{k\beta}{x} + \dfrac{Hx}{2} : x \geq d.$

Fig. 12.3.4a represents TC_1 and $TC_2(x)$.

Let x_m be the quantity at which the minimum values of $TC_1(x)$ and $TC_2(x)$ occur. Then as before (Model 1).

$$x_m = \sqrt{\frac{2K\beta}{H}}.$$

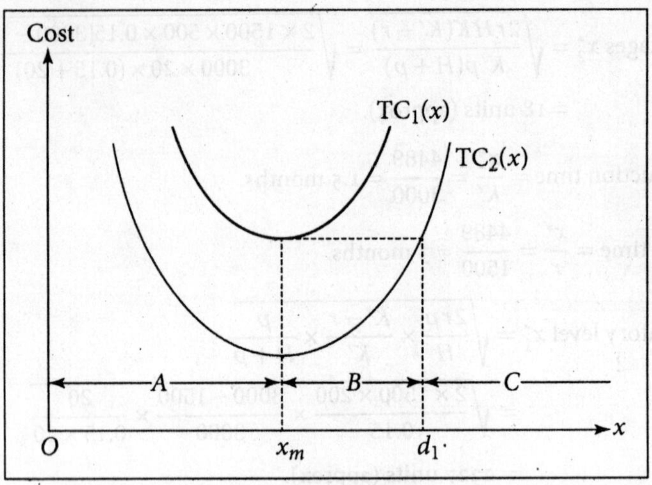

Fig. 12.3.4a

Fig. 12.3.4a indicates that optimum order quantity x^* depends on where the price break point d falls w.r.t. the zones A, B and C. Let these zones are defined by determining $d_1 > x_m$ from the equation

$$\mathrm{TC}_1(x_m) = \mathrm{TC}_2(d_1).$$

Now since $x_m = \sqrt{2K\beta/H}$, the solution of the equation will give the value of d_1. Zones are defined as follows: $0 \le d < x_m$: Zone A

$x_m \le d < d_1$: Zone B

$d \ge x_m$: Zone C.

Figs 12.3.4b, 12.3.4c and 12.3.4d illustrate clearly the situations.

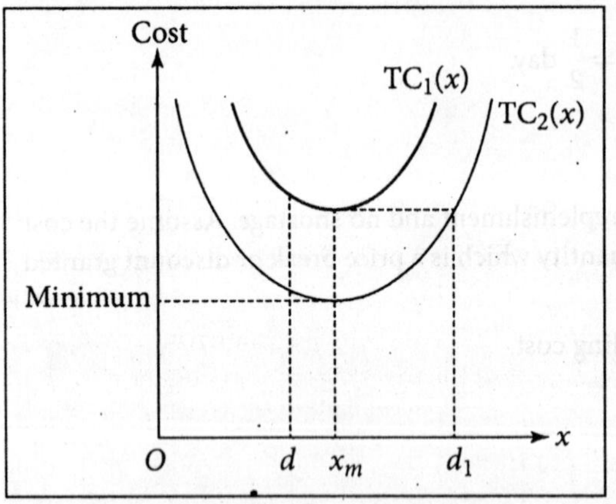

Fig. 12.3.4b Zone A

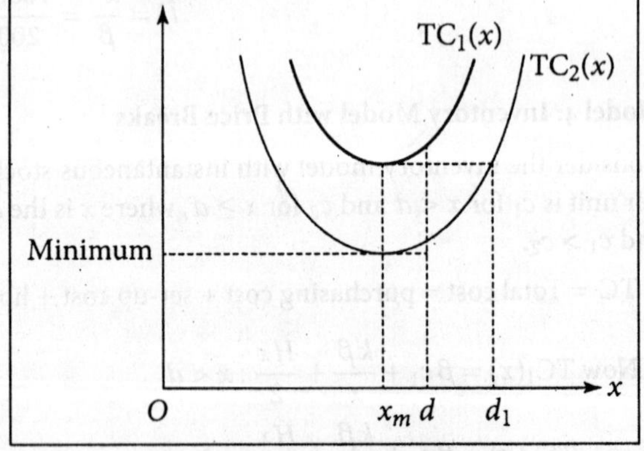

Fig. 12.3.4c Zone B

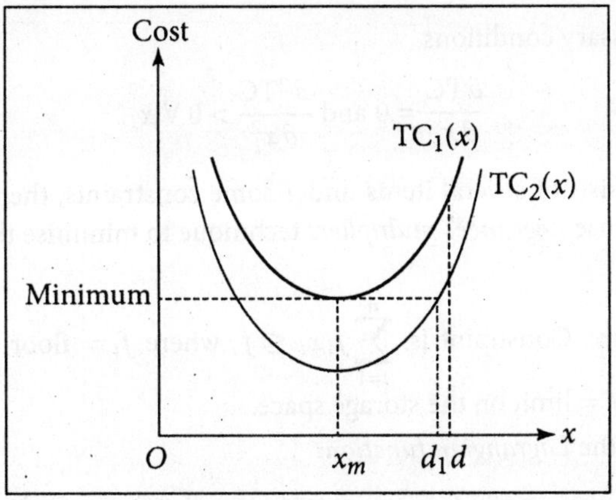

Fig. 12.3.4d Zone C

Therefore, the required optimum order quantity: $x^* = x_m : 0 \le d < x_m$, Zone A
$= d \;: x_m \le d < d_1$, Zone B
$= x_m : d \ge d_1$, Zone C,

where $x_m = \sqrt{2K\beta/H}$, and determine d_1 from equation $TC_1(x_m) = TC_2(d_1)$.

Example 12.3.7. *Consider $K = ₹10$, $H = ₹1$, $\beta = 5$ units, $d_1 = ₹2$, $d_2 = ₹1$ and $d = 15$ units.*

For solution first find $x_m = \sqrt{\dfrac{2K\beta}{H}} = \sqrt{\dfrac{2 \times 10 \times 5}{1}} = 10$ units.

Since $d > x_m$, it is necessary to check whether d is in Zone B or Zone C.

$$TC_1(x_m) = TC_2(d_1) \Rightarrow c_1\beta + \frac{K\beta}{x_m} + \frac{Hx_m}{2} = c_2\beta + \frac{K\beta}{d_1} + \frac{Hd_1}{2} \Rightarrow d_1^2 - 30d_1 + 100 = 0$$

$$\Rightarrow d_1 = 26.18 \text{ or, } d_1 = 3.82,$$

d_1 is selected as the maximum value. Since $x_m < d < d_1$, d is in Zone B so that $x^* = d = 15$ units.

$$TC_2(15) = c_2\beta + \frac{K\beta}{15} + \frac{H \times 15}{2} = 1 \times 5 + \frac{10 \times 5}{15} + \frac{1 \times 15}{2} = ₹15.38/\text{day}$$

is the associated total cost per unit time.

Model 5: Multi-item Inventory Model

Suppose, n = number of items, β_i = demand rate for ith item ($i = 1, 2, \ldots, n$), which is known and uniform, H_i = holding cost per unit of quantity of ith item, K_i = set-up cost for the ith item, x_i = quantity of ith item in inventory at the beginning.

As calculated in Model 1, the total cost per unit of time

$$TC = \sum_{i=1}^{n} \left\{ \frac{1}{2} x_i H_i + \frac{\beta_i K_i}{x_i} \right\}. \tag{12.3E}$$

As before, the optimum values of x_i for $i = 1, 2, \ldots, n$ is given by

$$x_i^* = \sqrt{\frac{2K_i\beta_i}{H_i}}$$

obtained by using the necessary conditions

$$\frac{\partial \text{TC}}{\partial x_i} = 0 \text{ and } \frac{\partial^2 \text{TC}}{\partial x_i^2} > 0 \;\forall\; x_i.$$

When the inventory consists of several items under some constraints, then after constructing the cost equation in such model we use *Lagrange's multipliers* technique to minimise the cost.

For examples:

1. *Limitation of storage space.* Constraint is: $\sum_{i=1}^{n} f_i x_i \le f$, where f_i = floor space requirement per unit square feet for ith item, f = limit on the storage space.
   To find x_i^* we formulate the *Lagrangian function*:

$$\mathcal{L} = \sum_{i=1}^{n} \left\{ \frac{1}{2} x_i H_i + \frac{\beta_i K_i}{H_i} \right\} + \lambda \left[\sum_{i=1}^{n} f_i x_i - f \right\},$$

where λ is a *Lagrange multiplier*. The necessary condition for $\mathcal{L}$ to be minimum is

$$\frac{\partial \mathcal{L}}{\partial x_i} = 0, \quad \frac{\partial \mathcal{L}}{\partial \lambda} = 0 \;\forall\; i = 1, 2, \ldots, n$$

$$\Rightarrow x_i^* = \sqrt{\frac{2K_i\beta_i}{H_i + 2\lambda f_i}} \text{ and } \sum_{i=1}^{n} f_i x_i^* = f.$$

2. *Limitation on capital investment.* The constraint is of the form: $\sum_{i=1}^{n} c_i x_i \le C$, where c_i = cost per unit of ith item, C = total capital.

Here, $\mathcal{L} = \sum_{i=1}^{n} \left\{ \frac{1}{2} x_i H_i + \frac{\beta_i K_i}{H_i} \right\} + \lambda \left\{ \sum_{i=1}^{n} c_i x_i - C \right\}.$

The optimum values of x_i is $x_i^* = \sqrt{\frac{2K_i\beta_i}{H_i + 2\lambda C_i}}$ and $\sum_{i=1}^{n} c_i x_i^* = C.$

12.4 PROBABILISTIC INVENTORY MODELS

This section presents different inventory models with probabilistic demand. The models discussed in earlier section seems to be unrealistic. In some reality the demand of an item is not known exactly, but it will follow some probability distribution. In probabilistic system the basic decision criterion used is the minimisation of expected cost or equivalently maximisation of expected profit.

12.4.1 Probabilistic Model 1: Single Period, Instantaneous Demand

Depending on the amount demanded r, the inventory position right after demand occurs may be either positive or negative (shortage). These two cases are shown in Figs 12.4.1a and 12.4.1b.

Given y, the amount in hand *after* an order is received:

$$\text{Holding inventory} = h(y) = \begin{cases} y - r & : r < y \\ 0 & : r \ge y \end{cases}$$

$$\text{Shortage inventory} = g(y) = \begin{cases} 0 & : r < y \\ r - y & : r \ge y \end{cases} \tag{12.4a}$$

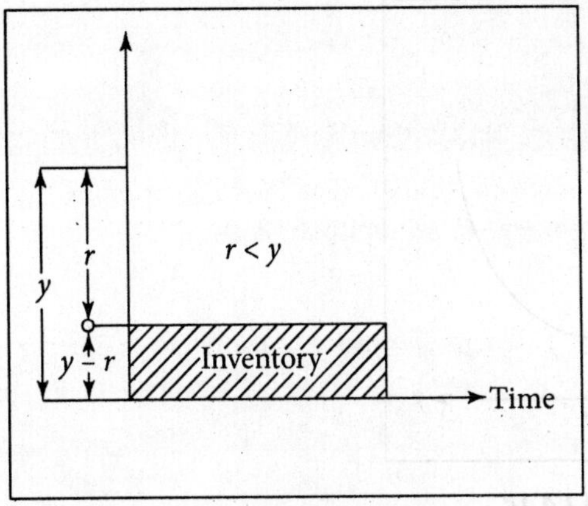

Fig. 12.4.1a

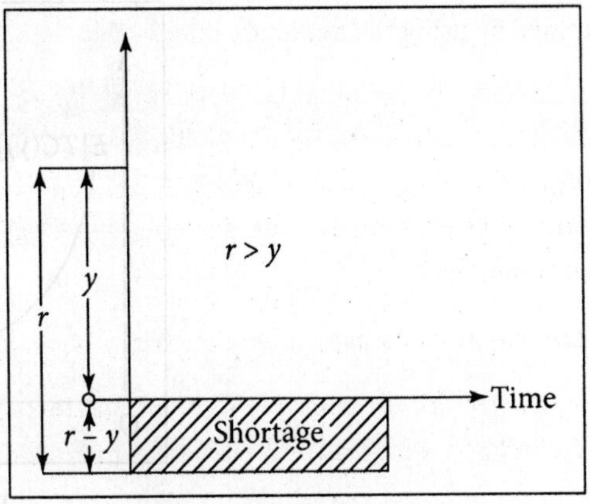

Fig. 12.4.1b

Let I be the amount in hand *before* an order is placed, and $f(r)$ be the probability density function (pdf) of demand. Let C_H and C_S be the holding and shortage costs per unit per period. Further, suppose C_P be the purchasing cost per unit. Assuming that no set-up cost is involved the expected cost for the period is then given by

$$E[\mathrm{TC}(y)] = C_P(y-I) + C_H\int_0^{\infty} h(y)f(r)\,dr + C_S\int_0^{\infty} g(y)f(r)\,dr$$

$$= C_P(y-I) + C_H\int_0^{y}(y-r)f(r)\,dr + C_S\int_y^{\infty}(r-y)f(r)\,dr \text{ [using (12.4a)].} \qquad (12.4b)$$

Now we know: Given $H(y) = \int_{\alpha(y)}^{\beta(y)} f(x,y)\,dx$, then

$$\frac{dH(y)}{dy} = \int_{\alpha(y)}^{\beta(y)} \frac{\partial f(x,y)}{\partial y}dx + f\{\beta(y),y\}\frac{\partial\beta(y)}{\partial y} - f\{\alpha(y),y\}\frac{\partial\alpha(y)}{\partial y}. \qquad (12.4c)$$

To obtain the optimal value of y, we have

$$\frac{\partial E\{\mathrm{TC}(y)\}}{\partial y} = C_P + C_H\int_0^{y} f(r)\,dr - C_S\int_y^{\infty} f(r)\,dr = 0 \Rightarrow C_P + C_H\int_0^{y} f(r)\,dr - C_S\left[1-\int_0^{y} f(r)\,dr\right] = 0$$

$$\Rightarrow (C_H + C_S)\int_0^{y} f(r)\,dr = C_S - C_P \Rightarrow \int_0^{y^*} f(r)\,dr = \frac{C_S - C_P}{C_H + C_S}. \qquad (12.4d)$$

Now, $\frac{\partial^2 E\{\mathrm{TC}(y)\}}{\partial y^2} = (C_H + C_S)\,f(y^*) > 0$, which shows that y^* corresponds to a minimum point. Also $E\{\mathrm{TC}(y)\}$ is a convex function. As y^* is unique the minimum is a global minimum. Graphically, the function $E\{\mathrm{TC}(y)\}$ is shown in Fig. 12.4.1c.

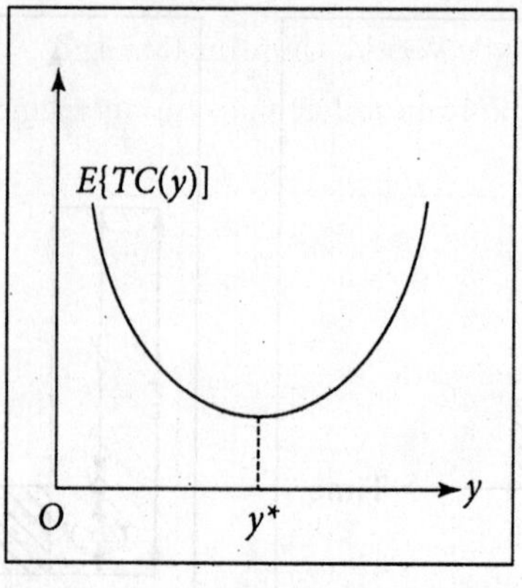

Fig. 12.4.1c

The value of y^* is selected such that $P\{r \le y^*\} = \dfrac{C_S - C_P}{C_H + C_S} : C_S > C_P$.

Therefore, optimum policy is that: Given I is in hand before an order is placed

$$\left.\begin{array}{l}\text{if } y^* > I, \text{ then order to be placed for } y^* - I, \text{ but} \\ \text{if } y^* \le I, \text{ obviously no order to be placed}\end{array}\right\}. \qquad (12.4e)$$

Discrete case. In place of continuous units suppose demand occurs in discrete manner. Then

$$\sigma(y) = E\{\text{TC}(y)\} = C_P(y - I) + C_H \sum_{r=0}^{y} (y - r)\, p(r) + C_S \sum_{r=y+1}^{\infty} (r - y)\, p(r),$$

where $p(r)$ is the probability mass function of demand.

Now the necessary conditions for a minimum are give by $\sigma(y-1) \ge \sigma(y)$ and $\sigma(y+1) \ge \sigma(y)$.

$$\begin{aligned}\text{Thus } \sigma(y-1) &= C_P(y - 1 - I) + C_H \sum_{r=0}^{y-1} (y - 1 - r)\, p(r) + C_S \sum_{r=y}^{\infty} (r - y + 1)\, p(r) \\ &= C_P(y - I) + C_H \sum_{r=0}^{y-1} (y - r)\, p(r) + C_S \sum_{r=y}^{\infty} (r - y)\, p(r) - C_H \sum_{r=0}^{y-1} p(r) + C_S \sum_{r=y}^{\infty} p(r) - C_P \\ &= \sigma(y) + (C_S - C_P) - (C_H + C_S) \sum_{r=0}^{y-1} p(r).\end{aligned}$$

$$\therefore\ \sigma(y-1) - \sigma(y) = (C_S - C_P) - (C_H + C_S)\, P\{r \le (y-1)\} \ge 0 \text{ or, } P\{r \le (y-1)\} \le \frac{C_S - C_P}{C_H + C_S}. \qquad (12.4f)$$

Similarly, $\sigma(y+1) \ge \sigma(y)$ gives

$$P\{r \le y\} \ge \frac{C_S - C_P}{C_H + C_S}. \qquad (12.4g)$$

Hence, the optimum value y^* satisfies the inequality

$$P\{r \le y^* - 1\} \le \frac{C_S - C_P}{C_H + C_S} \le P\{r \le y^*\}. \qquad (12.4h)$$

12.4.2 Probabilistic Model 2: Single Period, Uniform Demand

In this model demand occurs uniformly rather than instantaneously, during the period as shown in Figs 12.4.2a and 12.4.2b.

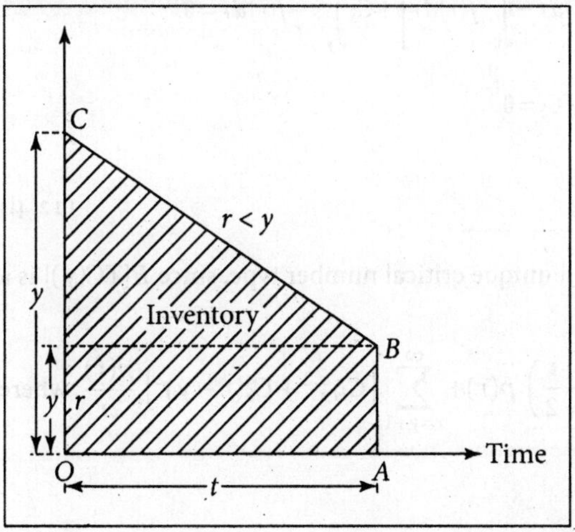

Fig. 12.4.2a

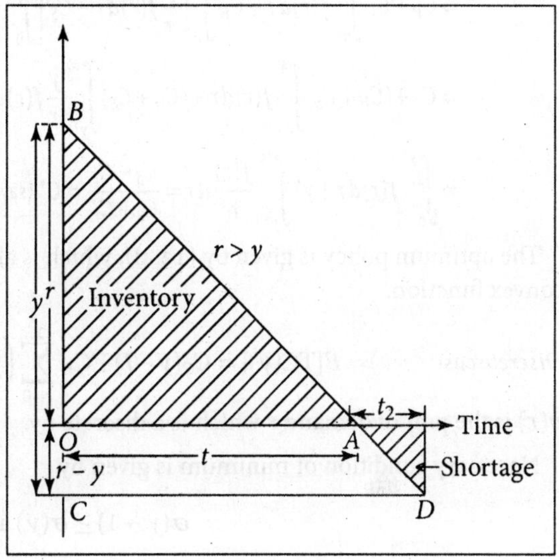

Fig. 12.4.2b

When $r < y$, no shortage occurs but when $r > y$, both the costs are involved. The units that build up an inventory may consist of either *continuous* or *discrete units.*

When $r \le y$, the total inventory is given by the area of the trapezium $OABC$

$$= \tfrac{1}{2}(AB + OC)OA = \tfrac{1}{2}(y - r + y)\,t.$$

Holding cost of carrying r units $= \tfrac{1}{2}C_H(y - r + y)\,t = \tfrac{1}{2}C_H(2y - r)\,t.$

When $r > y$ both costs are involved. Holding cost $= \tfrac{1}{2}C_H y\, t_1.$

$$\text{Shortage cost} = \tfrac{1}{2}C_S(r - y)\,t_2.$$

From similar triangle in Fig. 12.4.2b, $\dfrac{t_1}{t} = \dfrac{y}{r}$ and $\dfrac{t_2}{t} = \dfrac{r - y}{r}$.

$\therefore$ holding cost $= \dfrac{1}{2}C_H y \cdot \dfrac{y}{r}t = \dfrac{1}{2}C_H\dfrac{y^2}{r}t$. Shortage cost $= \dfrac{1}{2}C_S(r - y)\dfrac{(r-y)}{r}t = \dfrac{1}{2}C_S\dfrac{(r-y)^2}{r}t.$

As before let I be the amount in hand before an order is placed. C_P is the purchasing cost per unit.

Continuous case. Demand r is estimated as a continuous r.v. with pdf $f(r)$, where $0 \le r < \infty$,

$f(r) \ge 0 \ \forall\ r$ and $\displaystyle\int_0^\infty f(r)\,dr = 1.$

Assuming that no set-up cost is involved the expected cost per unit period ($t = 1$) is then given by

$$E[\mathrm{TC}(y)] = C_p(y - I) + C_H\left[\int_0^y \left(y - \frac{r}{2}\right) f(r)\,dr + \int_2^\infty \frac{y^2}{2r} f(r)\,dr\right] + C_S\int_0^\infty \frac{(r-y)^2}{2r} f(r)\,dr,$$

where C_H and C_S are defined in Model 1. Taking the first derivative and equating it to zero, we get

$$\frac{dE[\mathrm{TC}(y)]}{dy}=C_P+C_H\left[\int_0^y f(r)dr+\int_y^\infty \frac{y}{r}f(r)dr\right]-C_S\int_y^\infty \frac{r-y}{r}f(r)dr=0$$

$$\Rightarrow C_P+C_H\int_0^y f(r)dr+C_H\int_y^\infty \frac{y}{r}f(r)dr-C_S\left[\int_0^\infty f(r)dr-\int_0^y f(r)dr\right]+C_S\int_y^\infty \frac{y}{r}f(r)dr=0$$

$$\Rightarrow C_P+(C_H+C_S)\int_0^y f(r)dr+(C_H+C_S)\int_y^\infty \frac{y}{r}f(r)dr-C_S=0$$

$$\Rightarrow \int_0^{y^*} f(r)dr+y^*\int_{y^*}^\infty \frac{f(r)}{r}dr=\frac{C_S-C_P}{C_S+C_H}=C^*\text{ (say)}. \tag{12.4i}$$

The optimum policy is given by (12.4i), which is also a unique critical number type, since $E[\mathrm{TC}(y)]$ is a convex function.

Discrete case $\sigma(y)=E[\mathrm{TC}(y)]=C_P(y-I)+C_H\sum_{r=0}^{y}\left(y-\frac{r}{2}\right)p(r)+\sum_{r=y+1}^{\infty}\left[C_Hy^2+C_S(r-y)^2\right]\frac{p(r)}{2r}$, where $p(r)$ is the pmf of demand r which is a discrete r.v.

Necessary condition of minimum is given by

$$\sigma(y-1)\geq\sigma(y)\text{ and }\sigma(y+1)\geq\sigma(y).$$

$$\sigma(y+1)=C_P(y+1-I)+C_H\sum_{r=0}^{y+1}\left(y+1-\frac{r}{2}\right)p(r)+\sum_{r=y+2}^{\infty}\left[C_H(y+1)^2+C_S(r-y-1)^2\right]\frac{p(r)}{2r}$$

$$=C_P(y-I)+C_P+C_H\sum_{r=0}^{y}\left(y-\frac{r}{2}\right)p(r)+\sum_{r=y+1}^{\infty}\left[C_Hy^2+C_S(r-y)^2\right]\frac{p(r)}{2r}$$

$$+(C_H+C_S)\left[\sum_{r=0}^{y}p(r)+\left(y+\frac{1}{2}\right)\sum_{r=y+1}^{\infty}\frac{p(r)}{r}\right]$$

$$=\sigma(y)+(C_H+C_S)\sigma_1(y)-C_S+C_P$$

$$\Rightarrow\sigma(y+1)-\sigma(y)\geq 0\Rightarrow\sigma_1(y^*)\geq\frac{C_S-C_P}{C_S+C_H},$$

where $\sigma_1(y)=\sum_{r=0}^{y}p(r)+\left(y+\frac{1}{2}\right)\sum_{r=y+1}^{\infty}\frac{p(r)}{r}$.

Similarly, $\sigma(y-1)\geq\sigma(y)$ gives $\sigma_1(y^*-1)\leq\frac{C_S-C_P}{C_S+C_H}$.

Therefore, the optimum value y^* satisfies the inequality

$$\sigma_1(y^*-1)\leq\frac{C_S-C_P}{C_S+C_H}\leq\sigma_1(y^*)\text{ or, }\sigma_1(y^*-1)\leq C^*\leq\sigma_1(y^*), \tag{12.4j}$$

where $\sigma_1(y)=\sum_{r=0}^{y}p(r)+\left(y+\frac{1}{2}\right)\sum_{r=y+1}^{\infty}\frac{1}{r}p(r)$.

12.4.3 Probabilistic Model 3: Instantaneous Demand, Set-up Cost ($s-S$ Policy)

Consider the probabilistic Model 1 by taking into account of the set-up cost K. Then the total expected cost of the system inclusive of set-up cost is

$$E\{TC_1(y)\} = K + E\{TC(y)\},$$

where $E\{TC(y)\} = C_P(y-I)+C_H\int_0^y (y-r)f(r)\,dr + C_S\int_y^\infty (r-y)f(r)\,dr$, the minimum of which occurs at y^* satisfying

$$\int_0^{y^*} f(r)\,dr = \frac{C_S - C_P}{C_S - C_H}.$$

Since K is constant, the minimum value of $E\{TC_1(y)\}$ must also occur at y^*. The curves $E\{TC(y)\}$ and $E\{TC_1(y)\}$ are shown in Fig. 12.4.3a.

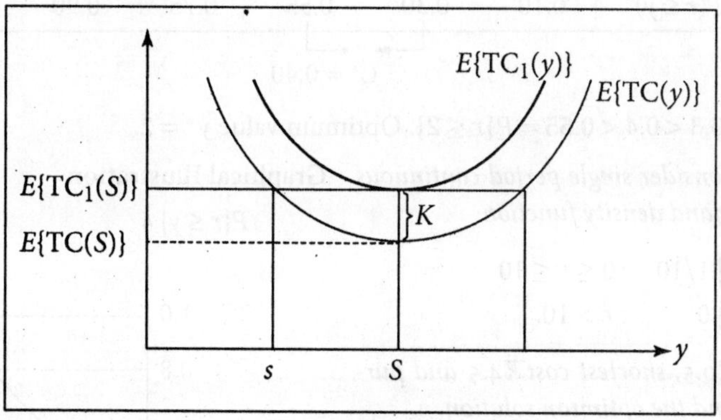

Fig. 12.4.3a

In the figure the value of S is equal to y^* and the value of s is determined from the equation

$$E\{TC(s)\} = E\{TC_1(s)\} \Rightarrow E\{TC(s)\} = K + E\{TC(S)\} : s < S.$$

Given I, the amount in hand before the order is placed, our main objective is how much should be ordered.

Now (i) if $I < s$, since I is already in hand, its cost is given by $E\{TC(y)\}$. If any additional amount $(y-I)$, is ordered $(y > I)$, the corresponding cost is $E\{TC_1(y)\}$, which includes set-up cost K. Therefore, from Fig. 12.4.3a,

$$\min_{y>I} E\{TC_1(y)\} = E\{TC_1(S)\} < E\{TC(I)\}.$$

That is, optimal inventory must reach $y^* = S$ and amount of order $S - I$.

(ii) If $s < I < S$, from Fig. 12.4.3a, $E\{TC(I)\} \le \min_{y>I} E\{TC_1(y)\} = E\{TC_1(S)\}$.

Hence, $y^* = I$ and obviously no order to be placed in this situation.

(iii) If $I > S$, again from Fig. 12.4.3a, $y > I$, $E\{TC(I)\} < E\{TC_1(y)\}$ and it clearly indicates that $y^* = s$ and less costly and no order to be placed.

Therefore, when the cost function is convex the optimality conditions of $(s-S)$ policy are given by:

$$\text{if } I < s : \text{order } S - I$$

$$\text{but if } I \ge s : \text{do not order at all.}$$

Remark. When convexity property is not satisfied, in general $(s-S)$ policy will cease to be optimal.

Example 12.4.1. *Consider the single period model with holding cost ₹1, shortage cost ₹4 and purchase cost ₹2. The demand density function is given by*

r	0	1	2	3	4	5
$f(r)$	0.10	0.20	0.25	0.20	0.15	0.10

Solution: $C^* = \dfrac{C_S - C_P}{C_S + C_H} = \dfrac{4-2}{4+1} = \dfrac{2}{5} = 0.4.$

The optimum solution is obtained by constructing the cumulative probability distribution, which is given below.

y	0	1	2	3	4	5
$P(r \le y)$	0.10	0.30	0.55	0.75	0.90	1.00

$C^* = 0.40$

Since $P\{r \le 1\} = 0.3 < 0.4 < 0.55 = P\{r \le 2\}$. Optimum value $y^* = 2$.

Example 12.4.2. *Consider single period continuous unit model with demand density function*

$$f(r) = \begin{cases} 1/10 & : 0 \le r \le 10 \\ 0 & : r > 10. \end{cases}$$

If the holding cost ₹0.5, shortest cost ₹4.5 and purchasing cost ₹0.5. Find the optimum solution.

Graphical Illustration

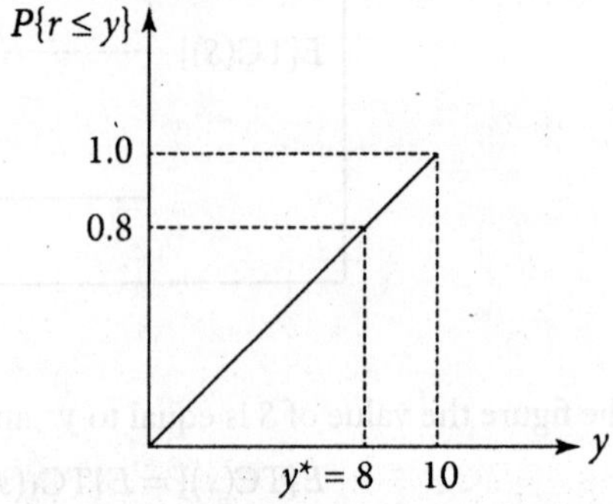

Solution: Optimum y^* satisfies

$$P\{r \le y^*\} = \int_0^{y^*} f(r)\,dr = \frac{C_S - C_P}{C_H + C_S}$$

$$\Rightarrow \int_0^{y^*} \frac{1}{10}\,dr = \frac{4.5-0.5}{4.5+0.5} = 0.8 \Rightarrow y^* = 0.8 \times 10 = 8.$$

Example 12.4.3. *If we use the data of Ex. 12.4.2 to probabilistic Model 2, then*

$$\int_0^{y^*} \frac{1}{10}\,dr + y^* \int_{y^*}^{10} \frac{1}{10r}\,dr = \frac{C_S - C_P}{C_H + C_S} = 0.8 \Rightarrow \frac{1}{10}(y^* - y^* \ln y^* + 2.3y^*) = 0.8 \Rightarrow 3.3y^* - y^* \ln y^* - 8 = 0.$$

The solution of this equation is obtained by numerical method. Solving numerically the solution is $y^* = 4.5$ (approx). Note the difference of results between Ex. 12.4.2 (instantaneous demand) and Ex. 12.4.3 (uniform demand).

Example 12.4.4. *Suppose, the demand of a bicycle has an exponential distribution given by*

$$f(r) = \begin{cases} \frac{1}{10^4} e^{-r/10^4}, & r \ge 0 \\ 0, & \text{otherwise.} \end{cases}$$

If the purchasing cost of a cycle is ₹20, shortage cost is ₹45 and holding cost ₹9, then find the optimum quantity to order by distributor of the bicycles company.

Solution: The optimum ordering quantity y^* satisfies

$$\int_0^{y^*} \frac{1}{10^4} e^{-r/10^4} dr = \frac{45-20}{45-9} = 0.6944 \Rightarrow 1 - e^{-y^*/10000} = 0.6944 \Rightarrow e^{-y^*/10000} = 1 - 0.6944 = 0.3056$$

$$\Rightarrow e^{-y^*/10000} = 0.3056 \Rightarrow -y^*/10000 = \ln(0.3056) \Rightarrow y^* = 11856.$$

Therefore, the distributor should stock 11856 bicycles.

Example 12.4.5. *Referring to the bicycles* Ex. 12.4.4, *we have* $y^* = S = 11856$.

If $K = 800, C_P = 20, C_S = 45, C_H = -9$, then from (s, S) policy model discussed in (12.4.3) s is obtained as follows.

$$E\{\text{TC}(s)\} = K + E\{\text{TC}(S)\} = 20s + 45\int_s^{\infty} (r-s)\frac{1}{10000}e^{-r/10000} dr - 9\int_0^s (s-r)\frac{1}{10000}e^{-r/10000} dr$$

$$= 800 + 45(11856) + 45\int_{11856}^{\infty} (r - 11856)\frac{1}{10000}e^{-r/10000} dr$$

$$-9\int_0^{11856} (11856 - r)\frac{1}{10000}e^{-r/10000} dr.$$

After simplification, we have $s = 10674$. Hence, the optimal policy calls for ordering up to $S = 11,856$ bicycles if the amount in hand is less than $s = 10674$, otherwise no order is placed.

12.4.4 Multi-period Inventory Models

In this section probabilistic models are considered for multi-period. Models with infinite period will be derived from the finite period by taking the limit as the period tends to infinity. All multi-period models are formulated by *dynamic programming* approach based on *Bellman's principle of optimality*.

Of all previous inventory models discussed so far the optimal policy is determined by minimising a cost function, solution in this section are based on the maximisation of profit function.

In multi-period model the discounted value of money should be taken into account unlike the single period models. If $\alpha < 1$ is the *discount factor* per period, an amount of money M after $n \geq 1$ periods is equivalent to $\alpha^n M$. Now, we shall develop some multi-period models under the following assumptions:

1. Demand distribution is stationary for all periods.
2. $f_i(r_i)$ is the demand density function for the period i.

Model A: Zero delivery lag and backlog

Let the finite planning horizon be up to N periods. Using the same notations as used in earlier sections and assuming that v is the revenue per unit, we can formulate the problem as a dynamic programming model as follows.

$$\phi_i(I_i) = \max_{y_i \geq I_i}\Big[-C_P(y_i - I_i) + \int_0^y [vr - C_H(y_i - r)\, f(r) dr]$$

$$+ \int_{y_i}^{\infty} [vy_i + \alpha v(r - y_i) - C_S(r - y_i)]\, f(r) dr + \alpha\int_0^{\infty} \phi_{i+1}(y_i - r)\, f(r) dr\Big], \quad (12.4k)$$

where (i) $\phi_i(I_i)$ = maximum total expected profit for periods $i, i+1, \ldots, N$, given that I_i amount is in hand before an order is placed in the ith period such that $\phi_{N+1}(y_N - r) = 0$; (ii) $\alpha v(r - y_i)$ in (12.4k) is included due to the reason that the amount $(r-y_i)$ is the unfilled demand in the ith period, which must be filled in the (i,j)th period so that the discounted return is $\alpha v\,(r-y_i)$.

(12.4k) represents the recursive equation and can be solved by dynamic programming approach, which is extremely difficult in this case. So we analyse this model by considering the eq. (12.4k) in the following form:

$$\phi(I)=\max_{y\geq I}\left[-C_P(y-I)+\int_0^y [vr-C_H(y-r)f(r)dr]+\int_0^\infty [vy+\alpha v(r-y)-C_S(r-y)]\,f(r)dr \right.$$
$$\left. +\alpha\int_0^\infty \phi(y-r)f(r)dr\right]. \quad (12.4l)$$

Let $[\bullet]=\psi(y)$.

Now $$\frac{\partial\psi(y)}{\partial y}=-C_P-C_H\int_0^y f(r)dr+\int_y^\infty [(1-\alpha)v+C_S]\,f(r)dr+\alpha\int_0^\infty \frac{\partial\phi(y-r)}{\sigma y}f(r)dr=0. \quad (12.4m)$$

The value of $\frac{\partial\phi(y-r)}{\partial y}$ is determined as follows: If there are $\delta>0$ units more in hand at the start of the next period, the profit for next period will increase by $C_P\delta$, for this much less has to be ordered. Therefore, $\frac{\partial\phi(y-r)}{\partial y}=C_P$.

From (12.4m), we get $$\int_0^{y^*} f(r)dr=\frac{C_S+(1-\alpha)(v-C_P)}{C_S+C_H+(1-\alpha)v}\left[\because \int_0^\infty f(r)dr=1\right].$$

The optimal policy for each period: Order y^*-I, if $I<y^*$

Otherwise, no order, if $I\geq y^*$

Following above if in the finite model y_i^* denotes the optimal inventory level for period i, we have then use the following relationship $y_N^*\leq y_{N-1}^*\leq\cdots\leq y_i^*\leq\ldots y_1^*\leq y^*$, (12.4n)

where y^* is the *single critical value* in the finite model.

Model B: Zero delivery lag and no backlog

This model is very similar to Model A with an exception that demand r exceeds the inventory level y_i in which case the next period start with $I_{i+1}=0$, that means unfilled demand is lost and hence does not result in any revenue.

Therefore, for no backlog case the N-period recursive equation becomes

$$\phi_i(I_i)=\max_{y_i\geq I_i}\left[-C_P(y_i-I_i)+\int_0^{y_i} [vr-C_H(y_i-r)]\,f(r)dr+\int_0^\infty [vy-C_S(r-y_i)]\,f(r)dr \right.$$
$$\left. +\alpha\left\{\int_0^{y_i}\phi_{i+1}(y_i-r)\,f(r)dr+\int_{y_i}^\infty \phi_{i+1}(0)f(r)dr\right\}\right]. \quad (12.4o)$$

The solution of (12.4o) by dynamic programming is also very much difficult. So we adapt the same procedure as in Model A and considering

$$\psi_1(y)=-C_P(y-I)+\int_0^y [vr-C_H(y-r)]\,f(r)dr+\int_y^\infty [vy-C_S(r-y)]\,f(r)dr$$
$$+\alpha\left\{\int_0^y \phi(y-r)f(r)dr+\int_0^\infty \phi(0)f(r)dr\right\}. \quad (12.4p)$$

$$\frac{\partial \psi_1(y)}{\partial y}=0 \Rightarrow -C_P - C_H\int_0^y f(r)dr+(v+C_S)\int_y^\infty f(r)dr+\alpha\int_0^y \frac{\partial \phi(y-r)}{\partial y}f(r)dr=0.$$

Using the result $\frac{\partial \phi(y-r)}{\partial y}=C_P$, we get $\int_0^{y^*} f(r)dr=\frac{v+C_S-C_P}{C_H+v+C_S-\alpha C_P}$.

As before the following relationship holds corresponding to optimal inventory level y_i^* of i

$$y_N^* \le y_{N-1}^* \le \cdots \le y_i^* \le \cdots < y_1^* \le y^*. \tag{12.4q}$$

12.5 EXERCISE 12

1. In the Model 1, suppose that stock is replenished uniformly (rather than instantaneously) at the rate of α. Consumption occurs at the uniform rate of β at every point in time. If x is the order size and no shortage is allowed, show that

   (a) Maximum inventory level at any point in time is $x\left(1-\frac{\beta}{\alpha}\right)$.

   (b) Total cost per unit time is $\text{TC}(x)=\frac{K\beta}{x}+\frac{H}{2}\left(1-\frac{\beta}{\alpha}\right)x$.

   (c) The economy lot size is $x^*=\sqrt{\frac{2K\beta}{H\left(1-\frac{\beta}{\alpha}\right)}}:\alpha>\beta$.

2. If stock is replenished instantaneously and no shortage is allowed, find the economy lot size, the associated total cost and length of time between two orders, when $K=$ ₹100, $H=$ ₹0.05 $\beta=30$ units/day [Notation is the same as stated in the chapter]. [MCA(WBUT) 2000]

3. A company currently replenishes its stock of a certain item by ordering supply to cover a one month demand. The annual demand of the item is 1500 units. It is estimated that it costs ₹20 every time an order is placed. The holding cost per unit inventory per month is ₹2 and no shortage is allowed. Determine the optimal order quantity and the time between orders.

4. A company stocks an item that is consumed at a rate of 50 units per day. It costs the company ₹25 each time an order is placed. A unit inventory held in stock for one week will cost ₹0.70. Determine the optimum number of orders rounded to an integer, that the company has to place each year. Assume that the company has a standing policy of not allowing shortage in demand. [MBA(DU) 1998]

5. A stockist has to supply 400 units of a product every Monday to his customers. He gets the product at ₹50 per unit from the manufacturer. The cost of ordering and transportation from the manufacturer is ₹75 per order. The cost of carrying inventory 7.5 per year of the cost of the product. Find (a) Economy lot size (b) The total optimal cost including the capital cost (c) The total weekly profit if the item is sold for ₹55 per unit.

6. A company uses ₹10000 worth of an item during the year. The ordering costs are ₹25 per order and carrying charges are 12.5% of the average inventory value. Find the economic order quantity, number of orders per year, time period per order and the total cost.

7. Determine EOQ for the following data: Annual demand : ₹100,000 worth of an item.

   Ordering cost : 1% of order value.

   Carrying cost : 20% of average inventory level.

   [CU(MCom) 2002]

8. A manufacturer uses ₹25000 worth of an item during the year. He has estimated the ordering cost as ₹50 per order and carrying cost as 12.5% of average inventory value. Find the optimal order size, number of order per year, time period per order and total cost. [MBA(IGNOU) 2002]

9. Given the following data for a particular inventory item: Usage : 500 units/week
Ordering cost : ₹40/order
Carrying cost : ₹1 per unit per week
Lead time : 3 weeks
Price : ₹50 per unit.
Determine the following: (a) EOQ (b) Cycle time (c) Reorder point (d) Average inventory level.

10. A purchase manager places order each time for a lot of 500 numbers of a particular item. From the available data the following results are obtained: Inventory carrying cost : 40%.
Ordering cost per order : ₹600.
Cost per unit : ₹50.
Annual demand : 1000 units.
Find out the loss to the organisation due to his ordering policy.

11. A company has a demand of 12000 units/year for an item and it can produce 2000 such items per month. The cost of one set-up is ₹400 and the holding cost per unit per month is ₹0.15. Find the optimum lot size and the total cost per year, assuming the cost of 1 unit as ₹4. Also find the maximum inventory, manufacturing time and total time. [MBA(CU) 1998, BESU(ME) 2001]

12. An item is produced at the rate of 50 items per day. The demand occurs at the rate of 25 items per day. If the set-up cost is ₹100 per set-up and holding cost is ₹0.01 per unit of item per day, find the economy lot size for one run, assuming that shortage are not permitted. Also find the time of cycle and minimum total cost for one run. [CU(MSc Appl) 1987, CU(MSc Stat) 2008]

13. A contractor supplies diesel engine to a truck manufacturer at the rate of 20 per day. He has to pay a penalty of ₹10 per engine per day for missing the scheduled delivery data. Holding cost of a complete engine is ₹12 per month. The manufacturing of engines starts with the beginning of the month and is completed at the end of the month. What should be the inventory level at the beginning of each month?

14. The product is sold at a rate of 50 pieces per day and is manufactured at the rate of 25 pieces per day. The set-up cost of the machines is ₹1000 and the shortage cost is found to be ₹0.0015 per piece per day. With labour charges of ₹3.20 per piece, material cost at ₹2.10 per piece and the overhead cost of ₹4.10 per piece, find the minimum cost batch size if the interest charges are 8 per cent (assume 300 working days in a year). Also compute the optimal number of orders in a year.

15. A trader stocks a particular seasonal product at the beginning of the season and cannot reorder. The item costs him ₹25 and he sells it at ₹50 each. For any item that cannot be met on demand, the trader has estimated a goodwill cost of ₹15. Any item unsold will have a salvage value of ₹10. Holding cost during the period is estimated to be 10% of the price. The probability of demand is as follows.

Units stocked	2	3	4	5	6
Probability of demand	0.35	0.25	0.20	0.15	0.05

Determine the optimal number of items to be stocked.

16. Some of the spare parts of a ship cost ₹50000 each. These spare parts can only be ordered together with the ship. If not ordered at the time the ship is constructed, these parts cannot be available in

need. Suppose that a loss of ₹4500,000 is suffered for each spare that is needed when none is available in the stock. Further, suppose that the probabilities that the spares will be needed as replacement during the life term of the class of ship discussed are

Spares required	Probability
0	0.900
1	0.40
2	0.25
3	0.20
4	0.10
5	0.05
7 or more	0

How many spare parts should be procured?

17. A baking company sells one of its types of cake by weight. It makes a profit of 95 paise a pound on every pound of cake sold on the day it is baked. It disposes of all cakes not sold on the day they are baked at a loss of 15 paise a pound. If demand is known to have probability density function $f(x)=0.03-0.0003x$, show that optimum amount I_m of cake the company should bake daily satisfies the equation $I_m^2-200I_m+5757=0$.

18. A fish-stall sells a variety of fish at the rate of ₹5 per kg on the day of the catch. If the stall fails to sell the catch on the same day, it pays for shortage at the rate of ₹0.30 per kg and the price fetched is ₹4.50 per kg on the next day. Past records show that there is an unlimited demand for fish one day old. The problem is to ascertain how much fish should be procured everyday so that the total expected cost is minimum. It has been found from past records that the daily demand follows an exponential distribution with pdf: $f(x)=0.02e^{-0.02x}$, $0\le x\le\infty$. [CU(MSc Stat) 1994]

19. The probability distribution of monthly sales of a certain item is as follows. The cost of holding inventory is ₹8 per unit per month. A stock of 5 items is maintained at the start of each month. If the shortage cost is proportional to both time and quantity short, find the imputed cost of shortage of unit item for unit time.

Monthly sales	0	1	2	3	4	5	6	7	8
Probability	0.01	0.04	0.25	0.30	0.23	0.08	0.05	0.03	0.01

20. Show that when considering the optimum level of inventory S_0, which minimises the total expected cost in case of continuous quantities, the condition to be satisfied is

$$\phi_0(S_0)=\frac{C_S}{C_H+C_S},\ \text{where } \phi(S_0)=\int_0^{S_0} f(r)\,dr.$$

Here, $f(r)$ = pdf of requirement of quantity r, C_S = shortage cost, C_H = the holding cost per unit of quantity per unit of time. [CU(MCom) 1976, ISI(OR) 1972]

21. The annual demand of a product is 10000 units. Each unit costs ₹100 if orders are placed in quantities below 200 units but for order of 200 or above the price is ₹95. The annual inventory holding cost is 10% of the value of the item and ordering cost is ₹5 per order. Find the economy lot size.

22. The purchasing cost per unit of a product is ₹10 and its holding cost per unit per period is ₹1. If the order quantity is 4 units, then show that the permissible range of shortage cost p under optimal conditions given the following demand pmf is $19\le p\le 35.7$.

r	0	1	2	3	4	5	6	7	8
$f(r)$	0.05	0.1	0.1	0.2	0.25	0.15	0.05	0.05	0.05

ANSWERS

2. $x^* = 346.6$, $t^* = 1155$, $TC(x) = 17.3$.
3. $x^* \simeq 50$ units, $t^* \simeq 12$ days.
4. Optimum number of order per year = 129.
5. (a) 912 units/order, (b) ₹20065.80 per week, (c) ₹1934.20 per week.
6. EOQ = ₹2000. Number of orders per year = 5. Time period per order = 73 days. Total cost = ₹10250.
7. EOQ = ₹10000.
8. Order size = ₹3,162. Number of order per year = 7.9. Time period = 1.52 months. Total cost = ₹559.
9. EOQ = 200 units. Cycle time = 0.4 days. Reorder point = 1500 units. Average inventory level = 100 units.
10. ₹1301.
11. (a) Optimum lot size = 3264 units. (b) Total cost per year = ₹50940. (c) Maximum inventory = 1632 units. (d) Manufacturing time = 0.136 years. (e) Total time = 0.272 years.
12. Economy lot size = 1000 items. Time cycle = 40 days. Minimum total cost = ₹200.
13. Inventory level = 577 engines/month.
14. Minimum cost batch size = 5586 pieces. Optimal number of orders in a year $\simeq$ 3 cycles/year.
15. Optimal number of items = 4 units.
16. Number of spare parts procured = 4.
18. Fish procured everyday so that the total expected cost is minimum = 100.
19. Range of values of imputed cost is (₹216, ₹570.25).

Chapter 13

Dynamic Programming

13.1 INTRODUCTION

Dynamic programming (DP) is a mathematical technique often useful for making a sequence of interrelated decisions. It provides a systematic procedure for determining the combination of decisions that maximises overall effectiveness. In contrast to LP, there does not exist a standard mathematical formulation of the DPP. Rather, DP is a general type of approach to problem solving, and the particular equations used must be developed to fit each individual situation. Therefore, a certain degree of ingenuity and insight into the general structure of DPP is required to recognise when a problem can be solved by DP procedures and how it would be done. These abilities can probably be best developed by an exposure to a wide variety of DP applications and a study of characteristics that are common to all these situations.

Mathematically, a DPP is a decision-making problem of n variables. The problem can be divided into subproblems each of which being a decision-making problem in one variable. The solution to a DPP is achieved sequentially starting from the initial to the next till the final situation is reached.

The main unifying idea in DPP is the *principle of optimality* due to *Bellman*, which states as follows:

An optimal policy has the property that whatever the initial state and initial decisions are, the remaining decisions must constitute an optimal policy with regard to the state resulting from the first decision.

The above principle basically tells us how a properly decomposed problem can be solved in stages through the use of recursive computations.

Before discussing the solutions, it will be worthwhile to know a little more about some fundamental concepts of DP. The first concept is *stage*. Already mentioned, the problem is broken down into subproblems and each subproblem is referred to as stage. A stage signifies a portion of decision problem for which a separate decision can be made. At each stage there are a number of alternatives and the decision-making process involves the sélection of one feasible alternative which may be called as *stage decision*.

The stage decision may not be optimal for the considered stage, but contributes to make an overall optimal decision for the entire problem.

The other important concept is *state*. The variable which specifies the condition of decision process and summarise the current status of the system is called *state variable*. The number of state variables should be as small as possible. With the increase in number of state variables, increases the difficulty of problem solving.

13.2 RECURSIVE EQUATION OF DP

Consider a situation wherein a certain quantity q of a resource is to be distributed among n number of different activities. The return F depends upon the activities and quantities of resource allotted to them and the objective is to maximise the total return.

If $f_i(q_i)$ denotes the return from the ith activity with the resource q_i, then the total return may be expressed as

$$F(q_1, q_2, \ldots, q_n) = f_1(q_1) + f_2(q_2) + \cdots + f_n(q_n) = \sum_{i=1}^{n} f_i(q_i). \tag{13.2a}$$

The quantity of resource q is limited, which gives rise to the constraint

$$q = \sum_{i=1}^{n} q_i, \; q_i \geq 0, \; i = 1, 2, \ldots, n. \tag{13.2b}$$

The problem is to maximise the total return given by eq. (13.2a) subject to the constraint (13.2b).

If $F_n(q) = \max\limits_{0 \leq q_i \leq q} \{F(q_1, q_2, \ldots, q_n) = \max\limits_{0 \leq q_i \leq q} \left\{ \sum\limits_{i=1}^{n} f_i(q_i) \right\}.$ (13.2c)

Then $F_n(q)$ is the maximum return from the distribution of resource q to the n activities. Let us now allocate the resource to the activities, one by one, starting from the last, i.e., the nth activity. An expression connecting $F_n(q)$ and $F_{n-1}(q)$ for arbitrary values of q and n may now be obtained with the help of *principle of optimality*. If q_n is the quantity of resource allocated to the nth activity such that $0 \leq q_n \leq q$, then regardless of the values of q_n, a quantity $(q - q_n)$ of the resource will be distributed among the remaining $(n-1)$ activities. Let $F_{n-1}(q - q_n)$ denote the return from the $(n-1)$ activity, then the total return from all the n activities will be $f_n(q_n) + F_{n-1}(q - q_n)$.

An optimal choice of q_n will maximise the above function and thus the fundamental DP model may be expressed as

$$F_n(q) = \underset{\substack{0 \leq q_n \leq q \\ n = 2, 3, \ldots}}{\text{maximise}} \left[f_n(q_n) + F_{n-1}(q - q_n) \right], \tag{13.2d}$$

where $F_1(q) = f_1(q)$ when $n = 1$ is obtained from (13.2c). (13.2e)

(13.2e) gives the return from the first activity when whole of the resource q is allotted to it. Once $F_1(q)$ is known, eq. (13.2d) provides a relation to evaluate $F_2(q), F_3(q), \ldots$ This recursive process ultimately leads to the value of $F_{n-1}(q)$ and finally $F_n(q)$ at which the process stops.

13.3 SUBDIVISION PROBLEM IN DYNAMIC PROGRAMMING

This type of problem deals with the division of a given quantity into a given number of parts. Let V be the quantity to be divided into n number of parts $(V_1, V_2, \ldots, V_n)$. Then the problem can be expressed as

$$\text{Maximise} \prod_{i=1}^{n} V_i$$

$$\text{subject to} \sum_{i=1}^{n} V_i = V \tag{13.3a}$$

$$V_i \geq 0,\ i = 1,2,\ldots,n. \tag{13.3b}$$

Such type of problem can be handled by DP, by considering each part as a stage. The alternatives at each stage are infinite, since V_i is continuous and may assume any non-negative value, satisfying the condition (13.3a).

The state of the system x_i at any stage i, represents the part of resource V, allocated to stage 1 through i inclusive. The recursion formula is then given as

$$F_1(x_1) = \max_{V_1 = x_1} \{V_1\} \tag{13.3c}$$

$$F_i(x_i) = \max_{0 \leq V_i \leq x_i} \{V_i F_{i-1}(x_i - V_i)\}. \tag{13.3d}$$

Example 13.3.1. *Let us consider the general case of dividing V into n parts $V_1, V_2, \ldots, V_n$ so as to maximise* $\prod_{i=1}^{n} V_i,\ V_i \geq 0$. [IAS 1993, BESU(MSc) 2007, MBA(CU) 2002]

Solution: Using the recursive eqs (13.3c) and (13.3d),

$$F_1(x_1) = \max_{V_1}\{V_1\}; \quad F_i(x_i) = \max_{0 \leq V_i \leq x_i} \{V_i F_{i-1}(x_i - V_i)\}.$$

For $i = 1$, $F_1(x_1) = x_1$, which means $V_1^* = x_1$.

For $i = 2$, $F_2(x_2) = \max\limits_{0 \leq V_2 < x_2} \{V_2 F_1(x_2 - x_1)\} = \max\limits_{V_2} V_2(x_2 - V_2)$, since $F_1(x_2 - V_2) = x_2 - V_2$

$= \max\limits_{V_2} \phi_1(V_2)$,

where $\phi_1(V_2) = V_2 x_2 - V_2^2$.

Differentiating w.r.t. V_2, $\dfrac{\partial \phi_1(V_2)}{\partial V_2} = 0 \Rightarrow V_2^* = \dfrac{x_2}{2}$.

$$\therefore\ F_2(x_2) = \frac{x_2}{2}\left(x_2 - \frac{x_2}{2}\right) = \left(\frac{x_2}{2}\right)^2.$$

It can be shown that the second derivative is negative, which is a sufficient condition for maxima.

Since $x_2 = V_1 + V_2$; $V_1 = x_2 - V_2 = x_2 - \dfrac{x_2}{2} = \dfrac{x_2}{2}$. Thus, for a two-stage problem, $V_1 = V_2 = \dfrac{x_2}{2}$.

For $i = 3$, $F_3(x_3) = \max\limits_{V_3}\{V_3 F_2(x_3 - V_3)\} = \max\limits_{V_3}\left\{V_3\left(\dfrac{x_3 - V_3}{2}\right)^2\right\} = \max\limits_{V_3} \phi_2(V_3)$,

where $\phi_2(V_3) = \dfrac{V_3(x_3 - V_3)^2}{4}$.

$$\frac{\partial \phi_2(V_3)}{\partial V_3} = 0 \Rightarrow V_3 = \frac{x_3}{3}.$$

Since only $V_3 = x_3/3$ satisfies the sufficiency condition for a maximum and also $V_3 \neq x_3$. Since $V_1 + V_2 + V_3 = x_3$,

$$F_3(x_3) = \frac{x_3}{3} \cdot \frac{\left(x_3 - \frac{x_3}{3}\right)^2}{4} = \left(\frac{x_3}{3}\right)^3.$$

$$V_3^* = \frac{x_3}{3}, \quad x_3 = V_1 + V_2 + V_3 = x_2 + V_3, \quad x_2 = x_3 - V_3 = x_3 - \frac{x_3}{3} = \frac{2}{3}x_3$$

but $V_1 = V_2 = \dfrac{x_2}{2} = \dfrac{x_3}{3}$.

$\therefore$ for three-stage problem, $V_1 = V_2 = V_3 = \dfrac{x_3}{3}$ with $F_3(x_3) = \left(\dfrac{x_3}{3}\right)^3$.

For n-stage problem, $V_1 = V_2 = V_3 = \cdots = V_n = \dfrac{x_n}{n}$ with $F_n(x_n) = \left(\dfrac{x_n}{n}\right)^n$.

But, $x_n = V$.

$$\therefore\ V_1 = V_2 = V_3 = \cdots = V_n = \frac{V}{n} \text{ with } F_n(V) = \left(\frac{V}{n}\right)^n.$$

Remark. Since $F_n(V) = \left(\dfrac{V}{n}\right)^n = \left(\dfrac{\sum_{i=1}^{n} V_i}{n}\right)^n$ and $F_n(V) = \max\limits_{V_i}\{V_1, V_2, \ldots, V_n\} = \max\limits_{V_i}\left[\prod_{i=1}^{n} V_i\right] \geq \prod_{i=1}^{n} V_i$.

$$\therefore\ \frac{\sum_{i=1}^{n} V_i}{n} \geq \left(\prod_{i=1}^{n} V_i\right)^{1/n}. \qquad \therefore \text{ AM} \geq \text{GM}.$$

Example 13.3.2. *Using* DP *solve the following non-linear programming problem* (NLPP).

Minimize $Z = y_1^2 + y_2^2 + y_3^2$

subject to $y_1 + y_2 + y_3 \geq 15$

$y_1,\ y_2,\ y_3 \geq 0.$ **[IAS 1995, CU(MSc Stat) 1984, MBA(WBUT) 2002]**

Solution: Let the state variables be x_1, x_2 and x_3 such that $x_3 = y_1 + y_2 + y_3$

$$x_2 = x_3 - y_3 = y_1 + y_2$$
$$x_1 = x_2 - y_2 = y_1.$$

The recursive equations are $F_3(x_3) = \min_{y_3}\left\{y_3^2 + F_2(x_2)\right\}$

$$F_2(x_2) = \min_{y_2}\left\{y_2^2 + F_1(x_1)\right\}$$
$$F_1(x_1) = \min_{y_1}\left\{y_1^2\right\} = y_1^2.$$

Since $x_1 = x_2 - y_2$ and $F_1(x_1) = y_1^2$, $F_2(x_2) = \min\limits_{y_2}\left\{y_2^2 + (x_2 - y_2)^2\right\} = \min\limits_{y_2} \phi_2(y_2)$,

where $\phi_2(y_2) = y_2^2 + (x_2 - y_2)^2$.

$$\phi_2'(y_2) = 0 \Rightarrow y_2 = \frac{x_2}{2} \text{ and } \phi''(y_2)\Big|_{y_2 = x_2/2} > 0.$$

$$\therefore\ F_2(x_2) = \left(\frac{x_2}{2}\right)^2 + \left(x_2 - \frac{x_2}{2}\right)^2 = \frac{x_2^2}{2}.$$

Now $F_3(x_3) = \min_{y_3} \{y_3^2 + F_2(x_2)\}$.

Since $x_2 = x_3 - y_3$, $F_2(x_2) = \frac{x_2^2}{2}$, $F_3(x_3) = \min_{y_3} \left\{ y_3^2 + \frac{(x_3 - y_3)^2}{2} \right\} = \min_{y_3} \phi_3(y_3)$,

where $\phi_3(y_3) = y_3^2 + \frac{(x_3 - y_3)^2}{2}$.

$$\phi_3'(y_3) = 0 \Rightarrow y_3 = \frac{x_3}{3} \text{ and } \phi_3''(y_3)\Big|_{y_3 = x_3/3} > 0.$$

$$\therefore F_3(x_3) = \left(\frac{x_3}{3}\right)^2 + \frac{\left(x_3 - \frac{x_3}{3}\right)^2}{2} = \frac{x_3^2}{3}.$$

Since $x_3 = y_1 + y_2 + y_3 \geq 15$ for minimum of $F_3(x_3)$, $y_1 + y_2 + y_3 = 15$ or, $x_3 = 15$.

$$F_3(x_3) = \frac{(15)^2}{3} = 75, \quad y_3 = \frac{x_3}{3} = 5, \quad y_2 = \frac{x_2}{2} = \frac{x_3 - y_3}{2} = \frac{15 - 5}{2} = 5.$$

$\therefore$ minimum value of $y_1^2 + y_2^2 + y_3^2 = 75$ with $y_1 = y_2 = y_3 = 5$.

Example 13.3.3. *Use DP to show that* $z = \sum_{i=1}^{z} p_i \ln p_i$ *subject to* $\sum_{i=1}^{n} p_i = 1$, $p_i \geq 0$, $i = 1, 2, \ldots, n$ *is minimum when* $p_1 = p_2 = \cdots = p_n = \frac{1}{n}$. **[IAS 1983, BESU(MSc) 2007, MSc(Delhi) 1993]**

Solution: The problem here is to subdivide unity into n parts so as to minimise the objective function $z = \sum_{i=1}^{n} p_i \ln p_i$.

Let $f_n(1) =$ minimum attainable sum of $p_i \ln p_i$.

For $n = 1$, $f_1(1) = \min_{0 < p_1 \leq 1} (p_1 \ln p_1) = 1 \ln 1$, which can be written as $f_1(t) = t \ln t$ as unity is divided only into $p_1 = 1$.

For $n = 2$, unity is divided into two parts p_1 and p_2 so that $p_1 + p_2 = 1$ or, $p_2 = 1 - p_1$, let $p_1 = x$, then $p_2 = 1 - x$.

$$f_2(1) = \min_{0 < x \leq 1} \{x \ln x + f_1(1 - x)\} = \min_{0 < x \leq 1} \{x \ln x + (1 - x) \ln(1 - x)\}.$$

In general, for n-stage: $f_n(1) = \min_{0 < x \leq 1} \{x \ln x + f_{n-1}(1 - x)\}$.

In stage 2, let $\phi_2(x) = x \ln x + (1 - x) \ln(1 - x)$.

$$\phi_2'(x) = 0 \Rightarrow x = \tfrac{1}{2} \in (0, 1] \text{ and } \phi_2''\left(\tfrac{1}{2}\right) > 0.$$

$$\therefore \phi_2(x) = \tfrac{1}{2} \ln \tfrac{1}{2} + \tfrac{1}{2} \ln \tfrac{1}{2} = 2\left(\tfrac{1}{2} \ln \tfrac{1}{2}\right),$$

which is of the form $\phi_2(t) = 2\left(\frac{t}{2} \ln \frac{t}{2}\right)$.

In stage 3, $f_3(1) = \min_{0 < x \leq 1} \{x \ln x + f_2(1 - x)\} = \min_{0 < x \leq 1} \left\{x \ln x + 2\left(\frac{1-x}{2} \ln \frac{1-x}{2}\right)\right\}$.

$$\phi_3(x) = x \ln x + 2\left(\tfrac{1-x}{2} \ln \tfrac{1-x}{2}\right) \quad \phi_3'(x) = 0 \Rightarrow x = \tfrac{1}{3} \in (0, 1]$$

$$\phi_3''\left(\tfrac{1}{3}\right) > 0 \qquad \phi_3(x) = 3\left(\tfrac{1}{3} \ln \tfrac{1}{3}\right).$$

In general, for n-stage: $\phi_n(x) = n\left(\frac{1}{n} \ln \frac{1}{n}\right)$.

$$f_n(1) = \min_{0<x\le 1} \{x \ln x + f_{n-1}(1-x)\} = n\left(\tfrac{1}{n}\ln\tfrac{1}{n}\right).$$

Optimal policy: $f_n(1) = \min \sum_{i=1}^{n} p_i \ln p_i = n\left(\tfrac{1}{n}\ln\tfrac{1}{n}\right)$, which gives $p_1 = p_2 = \cdots = p_n = \tfrac{1}{n}$.

Example 13.3.4. *Using Bellman's principle of optimality: minimise* $Z = y_1 + y_2 + \cdots + y_n$ *subject to* $y_1 y_2 \ldots y_n = b$, $y_i \ge 0$, $i = 1, 2, \ldots, n$. [IAS 1993, MSc(Delhi) 1976, BESU(MSc) 2001, MCA(WBUT) 2000]

Solution: The problem comprised of factorising a constant b into n factors such that the sum of the factors is minimum. It can be treated as an n-stage DPP.

Let $f_n(b) =$ minimum attainable value of $\sum_{i=1}^{n} y_i$, where $y_1, y_2, \ldots, y_n$ are factors of b.

Considering problem as single-stage: $n = 1$, $f_1(b) = b$

$$f_1(b) = \min_{y_1 = b} \{y_1\}.$$

Consider the problem as two-stage: $n = 2$ and factorising b into two factors y_1 and y_2, $y_1 \cdot y_2 = b$, let $y_2 = x$, $y_1 = b/x$, then

$$f_2(b) = \min\{y_1 + y_2\} = \min_{0\le x\le b}\left\{x + \frac{b}{x}\right\} \text{ or, } f_2(b) = \min_{0\le x\le b}\left\{x + f_1\left(\frac{b}{x}\right)\right\},$$

since $f_1\left(\frac{b}{x}\right) = \frac{b}{x}$.

Next consider three-stage: $n = 3$, $y_1 y_2 y_3 = b$, let $y_3 = x$, $y_1 y_2 = b/x$, then

$$f_3(b) = \min\{y_1 + y_2 + y_3\} = \min_{0\le x\le b}\left\{x + f_2\left(\frac{b}{x}\right)\right\}.$$

In the general form, for an i-stage: $f_i(b) = \min_{0\le x\le b}\left\{x + f_{i-1}\left(\frac{b}{x}\right)\right\}$, where $y_i = x$ and $y_1 y_2 \ldots y_{i-1} = b/x$.

Now, the optimum policy can be determined as follows:

$$f_1(b) = b,\ f_2(b) = \min_{0\le x\le b}\left\{x + f_1\left(\frac{b}{x}\right)\right\} = \min_{0\le x\le b}\left\{x + \frac{b}{x}\right\}$$

Let $\phi_2(x) = x + b/x$, $\phi_2'(x) = 0 \Rightarrow x = b^{1/2}$, $\phi_2''(b^{1/2}) > 0$.

$$f_2(b) = b^{1/2} + \frac{b}{b^{1/2}} = 2b^{1/2}.$$

Now $f_3(b) = \min_{0\le x\le b}\left\{x + f_2\left(\frac{b}{x}\right)\right\} = \min_{0\le x\le b}\left\{x + 2\left(\frac{b}{x}\right)^{1/2}\right\}.$

Let $\phi_3(x) = x + 2\left(\frac{b}{x}\right)^{1/2}$, $\phi_3'(x) = 0 \Rightarrow x = b^{1/3}$, $\phi_3''(b^{1/3}) > 0$.

$$f_3(b) = b^{1/3} + 2\left(\frac{b}{b^{1/3}}\right)^{1/2} = 3b^{1/3} \text{ and so on.}$$

For n-stage problem: $f_n(b) = nb^{1/n}$ and $x = b^{1/n}$.

The required optimal solution is: $y_1 = y_2 = \cdots = y_n = b^{1/n}$ and $f_n(b) =$ minimum attainable value of

$$\sum_{i=1}^{n} y_i = \sum_{i=1}^{n} b^{1/n} = nb^{1/n}.$$

Example 13.3.5. *Solve the following* NLPP *by* DP *technique. Minimise* $Z=\sum_{i=1}^{n} y_i^2$ *subject to* $\prod_{i=1}^{n} y_i = b$, $y_i \ge 0,\ i=1,2,\ldots,n.$ [MCA(JNU) 1997, CU(MSc Stat) 2006, MBA(CU) 1995]

Solution: The problem can be treated as n-stage DPP. Let $f_n(b)$ be the minimum attainable value of Z, when b is factorised into n parts.

For $n=1$, $y_1=b$ and $f_1(b)=\min_{y_1=b}\{y_1^2\}=b^2$.

For $n=2$, $y_1y_2=b$; if $y_2=x$, then $y_1=b/x$ and

$$f_2(b)=\min\{y_1^2+y_2^2\}=\min_{0\le x\le b}\left\{x^2+\left(\frac{b}{x}\right)^2\right\}=\min_{0\le x\le b}\left\{x^2+f_1\left(\frac{b}{x}\right)\right\}.$$

For $n=i$, $f_i(b)=\min_{0\le x\le b}\left\{x^2+f_{i-1}\left(\frac{b}{x}\right)\right\}$.

Now, $f_1(b)=b^2$, $f_2(b)=\min_{0\le x\le b}\left\{x^2+\frac{b^2}{x^2}\right\}$. If we take $\phi_2(x)=x^2+\frac{b^2}{x^2}$, then $\phi_2'(x)=0\Rightarrow x=b^{1/2}$, $\phi_2''(b^{1/2})>0$.

$\therefore f_2(b)=(b^{1/2})^2+\left(\frac{b}{b^{1/2}}\right)^2=2(b^{1/2})^2$.

Similarly, $f_3(b)=(b^{1/3})^2+2\frac{b}{b^{1/3}}=3(b^{1/3})^2$.

Continuing in the same way $f_n(b)=n(b^{1/n})^2$ and $y_1=y_2=\cdots=y_n=b^{1/n}$.

13.4 CHARACTERISTICS OF DP

The basic features which characterise DPP are presented below.

1. The problem can be divided into *stages*, with a policy decision required at each stage.
2. Each *stage* has a number of *states* associated with it. In general, the states are the various possible conditions in which the system might be at that stage of the problem. The number of states may be either finite or infinite.
3. The effect of the policy decision at each stage is to transform the current state into a state associated with next stage.
4. Given the current state, an optimal policy for the remaining stages is independent of the policy adopted in previous stages.
5. The solution procedure begins by finding the optimal policy for each state of the last stage. The solution of this one-stage problem is usually trivial.
6. A *recursive relationship* that identifies the optimal policy for each state at stage n, given the optimal policy for each state at stage $(n+1)$, is available.
7. Using this recursive relationship, the solution procedure moves forward/backward stage by stage — each time finding the optimal policy for each state of that stage — until it finds the optimal policy when starting at final/initial stage.

One way of categorising deterministic DPP is by the form of the objective function. Another categorisation is in terms of the nature of the set of states for the respective stages. In particular, the states might be represented by a *discrete* state variable or by a *continuous* state variable. In the continuous case the optimal decision at each stage are obtained by using the usual classical method of optimisation (Problems are already discussed). In the discrete case a tabular computational scheme is followed.

Example 13.4.1. *The World Health Council is devoted to improving health care in the underdeveloped countries of the world. It now has five medical teams available to allocate among three such countries to improve their medical care, health education, and training programme. Therefore, the council needs to determine how many teams (if any) to allocate to each of these countries to maximise the total effectiveness of the five teams. (For a particular country, this measure equals the countries increased life expectancy in years times its population). Table gives the estimated additional man-year of life (in multiple of 1000) for each country for each possible allocation of medical teams.*

No. of medical teams	*Thousands of additional man-years of life* Country 1	2	3
0	0	0	0
1	45	20	50
2	70	45	70
3	90	75	80
4	105	110	100
5	120	150	130

Table 1:
Data from World Health Council

Solution: This problem requires making three interrelated decisions, namely, how many medical teams to be allocated to each of the three countries. Therefore, even through there is no fixed sequence, these three countries can be considered as the three *stages* in a DP formulation. The decision variables $x_n (n = 1,2,3)$ would be the number of teams to be allocated to stage (country) n.

The identification of *stages* may not be readily apparent. To determine this, questions such as the following should be asked.

1. What is it that changes from one stage to the next?
2. Given that the decision have been made in the previous stages, how can the states of the situation at the current stage be described?
3. What information about the current state of affairs is necessary to determine the optimal policy hereafter?

On these bases, an appropriate choice for the *state of the system* is the number of medical teams still available for allocation.

Let $p_i(x_i)$ be the measure of effectiveness from allocating x_i medical teams to country i as given in Table 1. Thus, the objective is to choose x_1, x_2, x_3 so as to

$$\text{Maximise} \sum_{i=1}^{3} p_i(x_i)$$

$$\text{subject to} \sum_{i=1}^{3} x_i = 5.$$

x_i are non-negative integers.

Let $f_n(s, x_n)$ be the maximising value of the objective function, then

$$f_n(s,x_n) = p_n(x_n) + \max \sum_{i=n+1}^{3} p_i(x_i)$$

such that $\displaystyle\sum_{i=n}^{3} x_i = s$, x_i are non-negative integers,

for $n = 1,2,3$.

Now in addition $f_n^*(s) = \max\limits_{x_n=0,1,\ldots,s} f_{n(s,x_n)}$.

Therefore, $$f_n(s,x_n) = p_n(x_n) + f_{n+1}^*(s-x_n)$$

(with f_4^* defined to be zero). These basic relationships are summarised in the following figure.

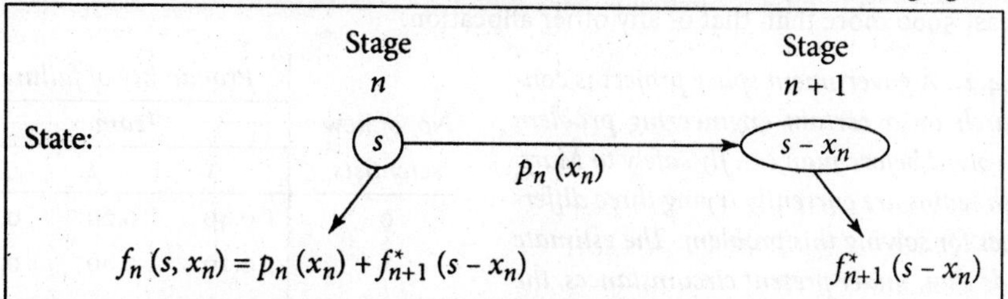

The recursive relationship relating the f_1^*, f_2^*, f_3^* functions for this problem is

$$f_n^*(s) = \max_{x_n=0,1,2,\ldots,s} \{p_n(x_n) + f_{n+1}^*(s-x_n)\},\ n = 1,2.$$

For the last stage $(n=3)$: $f_3^*(s) = \max\limits_{x_3=0,1,2,\ldots,s} p_3(x_3)$.

The resulting DP calculations are given below, beginning with the last stage ($n = 3$) and proceeding backward to the first stage ($n = 1$).

$n=3$:

s	$f_3^*(s)$	x_3^*
0	0	0
1	50	1
2	70	2
3	80	3
4	100	4
5	130	5

$n=2$: $$f_2(s,x_2) = p_2(x_2) + f_3^*(s-x_2)$$

S \ x_2	0	1	2	3	4	5	$f_2^*(S)$	x_2^*
0	0						0	0
1	50	20					50	0
2	70	70	45				70	0, 1
3	80	90	95	75			95	2
4	100	100	115	125	110		125	3
5	130	120	125	145	160	150	160	4

$n=1$: $$f_1(s,x_1) = p_1(x_1) + f_2^*(s-x_1)$$

S_1 \ x_1	0	1	2	3	4	5	$f_2^*(S)$	x_1^*
5	160	170	165	160	155	120	170	1

Thus, the optimal solution has $x_1^* = 1$, which makes $s = 5-1 = 4$ for $n = 2$; so $x_2^* = 3$, which makes $s = 4-3 = 1$ for $n = 3$, so $x_3^* = 1$. Since $f_1^*(5) = 170$, this $(x_1^*, x_2^*, x_3^*) = (1,3,1)$ allocation of medical teams to the three countries will yield an estimated total of 170 × 1000 = 170,000 additional man-years of life, which is at least 5000 more than that of any other allocation.

Example 13.4.2. *A government space project is conducting research on a certain engineering problem that must be solved before man can fly safely to Mars. Three research teams are currently trying three different approaches for solving this problem. The estimate has been made that, under present circumstances, the probability that the respective teams — call them 1, 2 and 3 — will not succeed is 0.40, 0.60 and 0.80 respectively. Thus, the current probability that all three teams will fail is (0.40) (0.60) (0.80) = 0.192. Since the objective is to minimise this probability, the decision has been made to assign two more top scientists among the three teams to lower it as much as possible.*

No. of new scientists	*Probability of failure* Team 1	Team 2	Team 3
0	0.40	0.60	0.80
1	0.20	0.40	0.50
2	0.15	0.20	0.30

Table 2: Data on the government space project problem

The adjoining table gives the estimated probability that the respective teams will fail when 0, 1 or 2 additional scientists are included with that team. The problem is to determine how to allocate the two additional scientists to minimise the probability that all three teams will fail. (Government space project problem). **[IAS (Main) 1998]**

Solution: The understanding structure of this problem is very similar to that of Ex. 13.4.1. In this case, scientists replace medical teams and research teams replace countries. Here *states* correspond to the research teams, and the *state* s is the number of new scientists still available for assignation at the stage. The decision variables $x_n (n = 1,2,3)$ are the number of additional scientists allocated to stage n.

Let $p_i(x_i)$ = probability of failure for team i if it is assigned x_i additional scientists, as given in **Table 2.** The government's objective is to choose x_1, x_2, x_3 so as to

$$\text{Minimise} \prod_{i=1}^{3} p_i(x_i)$$

$$\text{subject to} \sum_{i=1}^{3} x_i = 2$$

$x_i \geq 0$ and integers.

Consequently, $f_n(s, x_n) = p_n(x_n)$, minimum $\prod_{i=n+1}^{3} p_i(x_i)$ such that $\sum_{i=n}^{3} x_i = s$, $x_i \geq 0$ and integers

for $n = 1,2,3$. Thus, $f_n^*(s) = \min_{x_n \leq s} f_n(s, x_n)$

$$f_n(s, x_n) = p_n(x_n)\, f_{n+1}^*(s - x_n).$$

Therefore, the *recursive relationship* relating to f_1^*, f_2^* and f_3^* functions in this case is

$$f_n^*(s) = \min_{x_n \leq s} \left\{ p_n(x_n)\, f_{n+1}^*(s - x_n) \right\} \text{ for } n = 1,2$$

and when $n = 3$, $f_3^*(s) = \min_{x_3 \leq s} p_3(x_3)$.

The resulting DP calculations are given below in tabular form.

$n=3$

s	$f_3^*(s)$	s_3^*
0	0.80	0
1	0.50	1
2	0.30	2

$n=2$

x_2 \ s	$f_2(s,x_2)=p_2(x_2)\,f_3^*(s-x_2)$			$f_2^*(s)$	x_2^*
	0	1	2		
0	0.48			0.48	0
1	0.30	0.32		0.30	0
2	0.18	0.20	0.16	0.16	2

$n=1$

x_1 \ s	$f_1(s,x_1)=p_1(x_1)\,f_2^*(s-x_1)$			$f_2^*(s)$	x_1^*
	0	1	2		
2	0.064	0.060	0.072	0.060	1

Optimal solution. $x_1^*=1$, which makes $s=1$ at Stage 2, so that $x_2^*=0$, which makes $s=1$ at Stage 3, so that $x_3^*=1$.

Final conclusion. Teams 1 and 3 should each receive one additional scientist. The new probability that all three teams will fail would then be 0.060.

Example 13.4.3 (Cargo-loading problem). *Consider loading a vessel with stocks of n items. Each unit of item j has a weight σ_j and a value v_j ($j=1,2,\ldots,n$). The maximum cargo weight is Ω. It is required to determine the most valuable cargo load without exceeding the maximum weight of the vessel. Formulate this as a* DP *model and then solve by considering the adjoining case of three items and assume that* $\Omega=5$.

j	σ_j	v_j
1	2	65
2	3	80
3	1	30

Solution:

Step 1. Formulation: Let m_j is the number of units of item j, then the problem becomes

Maximise $(v_1m_1+v_2m_2+\cdots+v_nm_n)$

subject to $\sigma_1m_1+\sigma_2m_2+\cdots+\sigma_nm_n\le\Omega$

$m_j(j=1,2,\ldots,n)$ non-negative integers.

The DP model is constructed as follows:

1. *Stage i* is represented by item i, $i=1,2,\ldots,n$.
2. *State* y_i at stage i is the total weight assigned to stages $i,i+1,\ldots,n$; $y_1=\Omega$ and $y_i=0,1,\ldots,\Omega$ for $i=2,3,\ldots,n$.
3. *Alternative* m_i at stage i is the number of units of item i. The value of m_i may be as small as zero or as large as $[\Omega/\sigma_i]$, where $[x]$ is the largest integer included in Ω/σ_i.

Let $f_i(y_i)$ = optimal value of stages $i, i+1, \ldots, n$, given the state y_i.

The *backward* recursive equation is given as

$$f_n(y_n) = \max_{\substack{m_n=0,1,\ldots,\tau \\ y_n=0,1,\ldots,\Omega \\ \tau=[y_n/\sigma_n]}} \{v_n m_n\} \quad \Big| \quad f_i(y_i) = \max_{\substack{m_i=0,1,\ldots,\tau_i \\ y_i=0,1,\ldots,\Omega \\ \tau_i=[y_i/\sigma_i] \\ i=1,2,\ldots,(n-1)}} \{v_i m_i + f_{i+1}(y_i - \sigma_i m_i)\}.$$

The maximum feasible value of m_i is given by $[y_i/\sigma_i]$.

Step 2. For the given data, stage computations are performed in a table form as follows.

$n=3$ $\qquad f_3^*(y_3) = \max_{m_3} \{30 m_3\}$

y_3 \ m_3	max $\{m_3\} = \left[\frac{5}{1}\right] = 5$						Optimal solution	
	0	1	2	3	4	5	$f_3^*(y_3)$	m_3^*
	$v_3 m_3 = 0$	30	60	90	120	150		
0	0						0	0
1	0	30					30	1
2	0	30	60				60	2
3	0	30	60	90			90	3
4	0	30	60	90	120		120	4
5	0	30	60	90	120	150	150	5

$n=2$ $\qquad f_2^*(y_2) = \max_{m_2} \{80 m_2 + f_3^*(y_2 - 3m_2)\}$; $\max_{m_2} = [5/3] = 1$.

y_2 \ m_2	$80m_2 + f_3(y_2 - 3m_2)$		Optimal solution	
	0	1	$f_2^*(y_2)$	m_2^*
	$v_2 m_2 = 0$	80		
0	0 + 0 = 0		0	0
1	0 + 30 = 30		30	0
2	0 + 60 = 60		60	0
3	0 + 90 = 90	80 + 0 = 80	90	0
4	0 + 120 = 120	80 + 30 = 110	120	0
5	0 + 150 = 150	80 + 60 = 140	150	0

$n=1$ $\qquad f_1^*(y_1)=\max_{m_1}\left\{65m_1+f_2^*(y_1-2m_1)\right\};\ \max m_1=\left[\frac{5}{2}\right]=2.$

m_1 / y_1	$80m_2+f_3(y_2-3m_2)$			Optimal solution	
	0	1	2	$f_1^*(y_1)$	m_1^*
	$v_1m_1=0$	65	130		
0	0 + 0 = 0			0	0
1	0 + 30 = 30			30	0
2	0 + 60 = 60	65 + 0 = 65		60	1
3	0 + 90 = 90	65 + 30 = 95		90	1
4	0 + 120 = 120	65 + 60 = 125	130 + 0 = 130	120	2
5	0 + 150 = 150	65 + 90 = 155	130 + 30 = 160	160	2

Given: $y_1=\Omega=5$, the associated optimal solution is $\left(m_1^*,m_2^*,m_3^*\right)=(2,0,1)$, with a total value of 160.

Example 13.4.4 (Network problem). *A salesman is planning a business tour from Mumbai to Kolkata in the course of which he proposed to cover one city from each of the company's different marketing zones on route. As he has limited time at his disposal, he has to complete his tour in the shortest possible time. The following network shows the number of days time involved for covering any of the various intermediate cities (time includes travels as well as working time). Determine the optimum tour plan.*

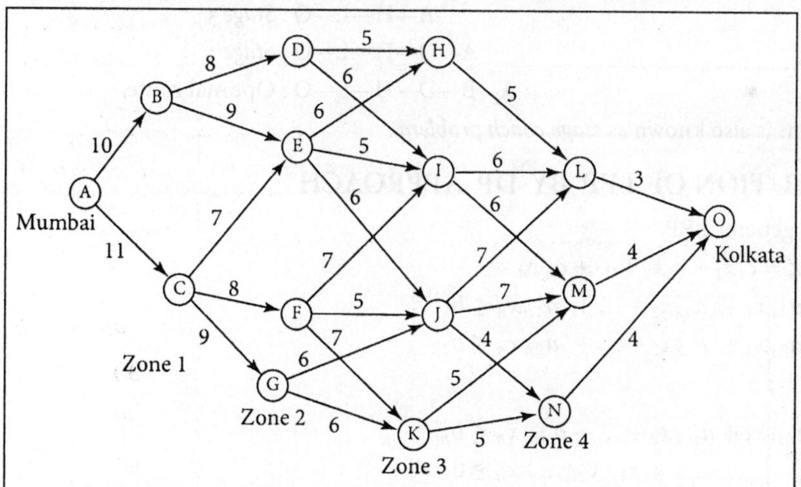

Solution: Starting from A, the cities for various marketing zones may be considered as distinct *stages*.

Stage 1: B or C; *Stage* 2: D, E, F or G; *Stage* 3: H, I, J or K; *Stage* 4: L, M or N; *Stage* 5: Best route to O.

Stage 1. At this stage it is not known whether B lies on the overall shortest route; but if it does, the shortest route from A to B is AB: $\left.\begin{array}{l}\text{A to B} = 10\\ \text{A to C} = 11\end{array}\right\}$ the only routes.

Stage 2. Again, it is not known whether *D* lies on the overall shortest route; but if it does, the only route from A is ABD = 10 + 8 = 18.

Similarly, ABE = 10 + 9 = 19; ACE = 11 + 7 = 18;
ACF = 11 + 8 = 19; ACG = 11 + 9 = 20.

From the above, shortest routes are (from A): A to D = 18; A to E = 18;
A to F = 19; A to G = 20.

Stage 3. Following the similar argument: ADH = 23; AEH = 24; ADI = 24; AEI = 23; AFI = 26;
AEJ = 24; AFJ = 24; AGJ = 26; AFK = 26; AGK = 26.

From the above, shortest routes are (from A): A to H = 23; A to I = 23;
A to J = 24; A to K =26.

Stage 4. Proceeding in the same way: AHL = 28; AIL = 29; AJL = 31; AIM = 29;
AJM = 31; AKM = 31; AJN = 28; AKN = 31.

The shortest routes from A are: A to L = 28; A to M = 29;
A to N = 28.

Final stage. There are three alternatives to reach O from *Stage* 4, viz., LO, MO and NO. Using the optimal times at 4th stage: ALO = 28 + 3 = 31; AMO = 29 + 4 = 33; ANO = 28 + 4 = 32.

Thus, the shortest time from A to O = 31. Now, we retrace the steps backwards along the network to identify the intermediate cities along the shortest route: A—O : Final
A—L—O : *Stage* 4
A—H—L—O : *Stage* 3
A—D—H—L—O : *Stage* 2
A—B—D—H—L—O : Optimal route.

The problem is also known as *stage coach problem.*

13.5 SOLUTION OF LPP BY DP APPROACH

Consider the general LPP.

Maximise $Z = c_1x_1 + c_2x_2 + \cdots + c_nx_n$

$$\text{subject to } a_{11}x_1 + a_{12}x_2 + \ldots + a_{1n}x_n \le b_1$$
$$a_{21}x_1 + a_{22}x_2 + \ldots + a_{2n}x_n \le b_2$$
$$\vdots \qquad\qquad \vdots$$
$$a_{m1}x_1 + a_{m2}x_2 + \ldots + a_{mn}x_n \le b_m$$
$$x_1,\ x_2,\ \ldots,\ x_n \ge 0.$$

This problem can be formulated as a DP model as follows.

Let the general LPP be considered as a multi-stage problem with each activity $j (j = 1,2,\ldots,n)$ as individual stage. Then this is a n-stage problem and decision variables are $x_j \ge 0$ at stage j $(j = 1,2,\ldots,n)$. Now the problem requires the allocation of available resources to the activities. Each constraint represents the limitations on different resources and $b_1, b_2, \ldots, b_m$ are amounts of resources.

Suppose, the amount of resource to the allocated to stage j be $\left(\beta_{1j}, \beta_{2j}, \ldots, \beta_{mj}\right)$ of the resources $1,2,\ldots,m$ and $f_j\left(\beta_{1j}, \beta_{2j}, \ldots, \beta_{mj}\right)$ be the optimum value of the objective function for stage j.

Using backward computational procedure, i.e., the procedure when we optimise last stage first, we get the following *recursive equations*:

$$f_n(\beta_{1n}, \beta_{2n}, \ldots, \beta_{mn}) = \max_{\substack{0 \le a_{in}x_n \le \beta_{in} \\ i=1,2,\ldots,m}} \{c_n x_n\}$$

and $$f_j(\beta_{1j}, \beta_{2j}, \ldots, \beta_{mj}) = \max_{\substack{0 \le a_{ij}x_j \le \beta_{ij} \\ i=1,2,\ldots,m}} \begin{cases} c_j x_j + f_{j+1}(\beta_{1j} - a_{1j}x_j, \ldots, \beta_{mj} - a_{mj}x_j) \\ \text{for } j = 1,2,\ldots,n-1 \end{cases}$$

where $0 \le \beta_{ij} \le b_i;\ i = 1,2,\ldots,m;\ j = 1,2,\ldots,n.$

Example 13.5.1. *Solve the following* LPP *using* DP *technique.*

Maximise $Z = 10x_1 + 30x_2$

subject to $3x_1 + 6x_2 \le 168$

$12x_2 \le 240$

$x_1, x_2 \ge 0$

Solution: The number of decision variables in the given problem is equal to 2. So, there will be two stages. Since backward recursion is used to solve the problem, *Stage* 2 is to be considered first. The sets of states of different stages are:

Stage j	Decision variable	Set of states
2	x_2	(b_{12}, b_{22})
1	x_1	(b_{11}, b_{21})

Recursive function for *Stage* 2: $f_2(b_{12}, b_{22}) = \max_{\substack{0 \le 6x_2 \le b_{12} \\ 0 \le 12x_2 \le b_{22}}} \{30x_2\}.$

To maintain feasibility, x_2 should be minimum of $b_{12}/6$ and $b_{22}/12$ the above objective function is modified as $f_2(b_{12}, b_{22}) = 30 \min\left(\frac{b_{12}}{6}, \frac{b_{22}}{12}\right)$; $x_2^* = \min\left(\frac{b_{12}}{6}, \frac{b_{22}}{12}\right)$.

Recursive function for *Stage* 1: $f_1(b_{11}, b_{21}) = \max_{0 \le 3x_1 \le b_{11}} \{10x_1 + f_2(b_{11} - 3x_1, b_{21})\}$

$$= \max_{0 \le 3x_1 \le b_{11}} \left\{10x_1 + 30 \min\left(\frac{b_{11} - 3x_1}{6}, \frac{b_{21}}{12}\right)\right\}.$$

The *Stage* 1 is the last in the series of backward recursion. Therefore, $b_{11} = 168$, $b_{21} = 240$.

Next to determine the upper limit for x_1^*, we have

$$f_1\left(\frac{x_1}{b_{11}}, b_{21}\right) = \max\left[f_1\left(\frac{x_1}{168}, 240\right)\right] = \max\left[10x_1 + 30 \min\left(\frac{168 - 3x_1}{6}, \frac{240}{12}\right)\right].$$

Now, to which in the ranges of x_1 is defined; $\frac{160 - x_1}{6}$ can be as high as 20 or as low as 0. So equate it to 20 as well as zero and solve for x_1: $\frac{168 - x_1}{6} = 20 \Rightarrow x_1 = 16$

$= 0 \Rightarrow \quad = 56.$

$\therefore 0 \le x_1 \le 16$ and $16 \le x_1 \le 56.$

$$\text{Now } f_1\left(\frac{x_1}{b_{11}}, b_{21}\right) = \max\begin{bmatrix} 10x_1 + 30\min\left(\dfrac{168-3x_1}{6}, 20\right), & 0 \le x_1 \le 16 \\ 10x_1 + 30\min\left(\dfrac{168-3x_1}{6}, 20\right), & 16 \le x_1 \le 56. \end{bmatrix}$$

$$\Rightarrow f_1\left(\frac{x_1}{168}, 240\right) = \max\begin{bmatrix} 10x_1 + 30\times 20, & 0 \le x_1 \le 16 \\ 10x_1 + 30\cdot\dfrac{168-3x_1}{6}, & 16 \le x_1 \le 56 \end{bmatrix}$$

$$= \max\begin{bmatrix} 10x_1 + 600, & 0 \le x_1 \le 16 \\ 10x_1 - 15x_1 + 840, & 16 \le x_1 \le 56 \end{bmatrix}$$

To maximise each of the above cases, put $x_1 = 16$: $f_1\left(\dfrac{x_1}{168}, 250\right) = \max(760, 760) = 760.$

Therefore, $x_1^* = 16$ and $f_1\left(\dfrac{x_1}{168}, 240\right) = 760.$

For the value of x_2^*, we have $b_{12} = b_{11} - 3x_1 = 168 - 3\times 16 = 120$; $b_{22} = b_{21} - 0 = 240$.

Required optimal solution: $x_1^* = 16$, $x_2^* = 20$, $Z_{\max} = 760$.

Example 13.5.2. *Solve the following* LPP *by* DP *approach.*

Maximise $Z = 2x_1 + 5x_2$

subject to $2x_1 + x_2 \le 43$

$2x_2 \le 46$

$x_1, x_2 \ge 0.$

Solution: Since there are two constraints (resources), the state must be represented by a pair (u_j, v_j), $j = 1, 2$. The problem has two decision variables, so the problem has two stages.

Let $f_j(u_j, v_j)$ = optimum variable of objective function for stage $j = 1, 2$; given (u_j, v_j).

Using backward procedure, we have $f_2(u_2, v_2) = \max\limits_{\substack{0\le x_2\le u_2\\0\le 2x_2\le v_2}} \{5x_2\} = 5\max\limits_{\substack{0\le x_2\le u_2\\0\le x_2\le v_2/2}}\{x_2\}.$

Since $\max\{x_2\}$ with $0 \le x_2 \le u_2$, $0 \le x_2 \le v_2/2$ is the minimum of $(u_2, v_2/2)$, we have $f_2(u_2, v_2) = 5\min\{u_2, v_2/2\}$ and $x_2^* = \min\{u_2, v_2/2\}$.

Now, $f_1(u_1, v_1) = \max\limits_{0\le 2x_1\le u_1}\{2x_1 + f_2(u_1 - 2x_1, v_1)\} = \max\limits_{0\le 2x_1\mu\le u_1}\{2x_1 + 5\min(u_1 - 2x_1, v_1/2)\}.$

Since it is a two-stage problem, at the first stage $u_1 = 43$, $v_1 = 46$.

$$f_1(u_1, v_1) = f_1(43, 46) = \max_{0\le x_1\le 21.5}\left[2x_1 + 5\min\left(43 - 2x_1, \frac{46}{2}\right)\right]$$

$$= \max\begin{bmatrix} 2x_1 + 5\times 23, & 0 \le x_1 \le 10 \\ 2x_1 + 5(43 - 2x_1), & 10 \le x_1 \le 21.5 \end{bmatrix}$$

$$= \max\begin{bmatrix} 2\times 10 + 115, & 0 \le x_1 \le 10 \\ 215 - 8x_1, & 10 \le x_1 \le 21.5 \end{bmatrix}$$

$$= 135.$$

$f_1(u_1, v_1) = 135$, which is obtained for $x_1^* = 10$.

Now $x_2^* = \min\left\{u_2, \frac{v_2}{2}\right\} = \min\left\{u_1 - 2x_1, \frac{v_1}{2}\right\} = \min\left\{43 - 20, \frac{46}{2}\right\} = \min\{23, 23\} = 23.$

Required optimal solution: $x_1^* = 10, x_2^* = 23, Z_{\max} = 135.$

Example 13.5.3. *Solve the following LPP by DP technique.*

$$\begin{aligned} &\textit{Maximize } Z = 50x_1 + 100x_2 \\ &\textit{subject to } 10x_1 + 4x_2 \le 2500 \\ &\qquad 4x_1 + 10x_2 \le 2000 \\ &\qquad x_1 + \tfrac{3}{2}x_2 \le 450 \\ &\qquad x_1, x_2 \ge 0. \end{aligned}$$

Solution: The problem involves two decision variables and three constraints (resources). Therefore, the states of the equivalent DPP are $b_1 = 2500$, $b_2 = 2000$, $b_3 = 450$.

Stage 1. $f_1(b_1, b_2, b_3) = \max\limits_{0 \le x_1 \le b} [50x_1]$, where maximum is to be taken over $0 \le 10x_1 \le 2500$

$$0 \le 4x_1 \le 2000$$
$$0 \le x_1 \le 450.$$

The maximum of b that x_1 can assume is $\min\left(\frac{2500}{10}, \frac{2000}{4}, 450\right) = 250.$

$$f_1(2500, 2000, 450) = \max_{0 \le x_1 \le 250} [50x_1] = 50 \min\left[\frac{2500 - 5x_2}{10}, \frac{2000 - 10x_2}{4}, \frac{450 - \frac{3}{2}x_2}{1}\right].$$

Stage 2. $f_2(b_1, b_2, b_3) = \max\limits_{0 \le x_2 \le b} [100x_2 + 50x_1].$

$$f_2(2500, 2000, 450) = \max_{0 \le x_2 \le b}\left[100x_2 + 50 \min\left(\frac{2500 - 5x_2}{10}, \frac{2000 - 10x_2}{4}, 450 - \frac{3}{2}x_2\right)\right].$$

Now, the minimum value of b that can x_2 assume $= \min\left(\frac{2500}{5}, \frac{2000}{10}, \frac{450}{3/2}\right) = 200.$

$$\therefore f_2(2500, 2000, 450) = \max_{0 \le x_2 \le 200}\left[100x_2 + 50 \min\left(\frac{2500 - 5x_2}{10}, \frac{2000 - 10x_2}{4}, 450 - \frac{3}{2}x_2\right)\right], \text{ where}$$

$$\min\left(\frac{2500 - 5x_2}{10}, \frac{2000 - 10x_2}{4}, 450 - \frac{3}{2}x_2\right) = \begin{cases} \dfrac{2500 - 5x_2}{10}, & 0 \le x_2 \le 125 \\ \dfrac{2000 - 10x_2}{4}, & 125 < x_2 \le 200. \end{cases}$$

$$\therefore f_2(2500, 2000, 450) = \max\begin{cases} 75x_2 + 12500, & 0 \le x_2 \le 125 \\ 25000 - 25x_2, & 125 \le x_2 \le 200 \end{cases}$$
$$= 21875 \text{ at } x_2 = 125.$$

$$\therefore x_2^* = 125, x_1^* = \min\left[\frac{2500 - 5x_2^*}{10}, \frac{2000 - 10x_2^*}{4}, 450 - \frac{3}{2}x_2^*\right] = 187.5 \text{ and } Z_{\max} = 21875.$$

Required optimal solution: $x_1^* = 187.5, x_2^* = 125, Z_{\max} = 21875.$

13.6 PROBABILISTIC DP

Probabilistic DP differing from deterministic DP is that the state at the next stage is not completely determined by the state and policy decision at the current stage. Here, there is a probability distribution for what the next stage will be. This probability distribution still is completely determined by the state and policy decision at the current stage. The resulting basic structure for the probabilistic DP is described diagrammatically in the following figure.

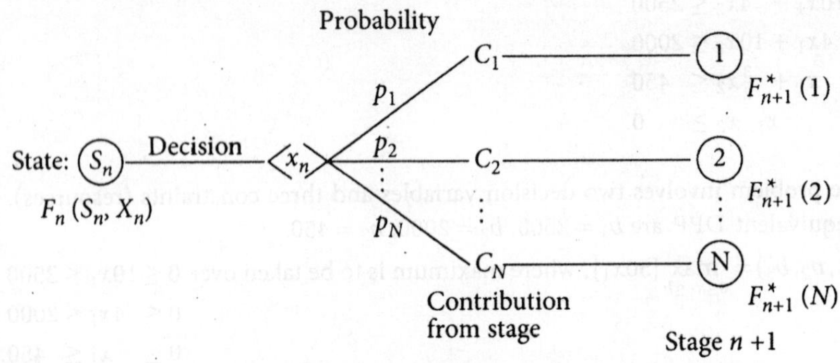

Fig. The basic structrue of probabilistic dynamic programming

Here, N denotes the number of states at stage $n+1$; $(p_1, p_2, \ldots, p_N)$ is the probability distribution of what the state will be, given the state S_n and decision x_n at stage n; and c_i is the resulting contribution to the objective function from stage n if the state turns out to be state i.

Because of the probabilistic structure, the relationship between $F_n(S_n, x_n)$ and the $F^*_{n+1}(S_{n+1})$ necessarily is somewhat more complicated than deterministic model. The precise form of this relationship depends upon the form of the overall objective function. To illustrate, suppose that the objective is to minimise the expected sum of the contributions from the individual stages. In this case, $F_n(S_n, x_n)$ would represent the minimum expected sum from stage n onward, given that the state and policy decision at stage n are S_n and x_n respectively.

Therefore, $F_n(S_n, x_n) = \sum_{i=1}^{N} p_i \left[C_i + F^*_{n+1}(i)\right]$ with $F^*_{n+1}(S_{n+1}) = \min_{x_{n+1}} F_{n+1}(S_{n+1}, x_{n+1})$, where the minimum is taken over the *feasible values* of x_{n+1}.

Example 13.6.1. *An enterprising young statistician believes that he has to develop a system for winning a popular game. His colleagues do not believe that this is possible, so they make a large bet with him that, starting with three chips, he will not have five chips after three plays of the game. Each play of the game involves betting any desired number of available chips and then either winning or losing this number of chips. The statistician believes that his system will give him a probability of 2/3 of winning a given play of the game.*

Assuming the statistician is correct, determine his optimal policy regarding how many chips to bet (if any) at each of the three plays of the game. The decision at each play should take into account the results of earlier plays. The objective is to maximise the probability of winning his bet with his colleagues. [Las Vegas game]

Solution: The basic structure for the problem.

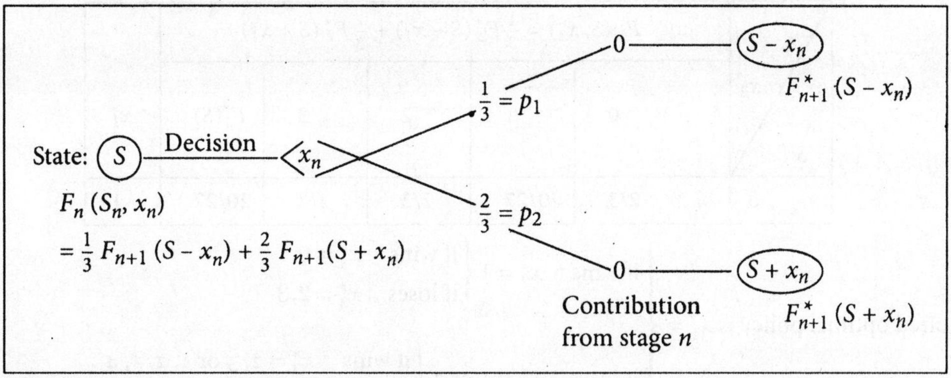

The above figure leads to the following computational results.

Recursive relationship: $F_n^*(S) = \max\limits_{\substack{x_n = 0,1,2,\ldots,S \\ n=1,2,3}} \left\{ \frac{1}{3} F^*_{n+1}(S - x_n) + \frac{2}{3} F^*_{n+1}(S + x_n) \right\}.$

$n = 3:$

S	$F_3^*(S)$	x_3^*
0	0	—
1	0	—
2	0	—
3	2/3	2 or more
4	2/3	1 or more
≥ 5	1	0 or $\leq$ 5.5

$n = 2$

x_2 / S	$F_2(S, x_2) = \frac{1}{3} F_3^*(S - x_2) + \frac{2}{3} F_3^*(S + x_3)$					$F_2^*(S)$	x_2^*
	0	1	2	3	4		
0	0					0	—
1	0	0				0	—
2	0	4/9	4/9			4/9	1, 2
3	2/3	4/9	2/3	2/3		2/3	0, 2, 3
4	2/3	8/9	2/3	2/3	2/3	8/9	1
≥ 5	1					1	0 or $\leq$ 5.5

$n = 1$

S \ x_2	$F_1(S, x_1) = \frac{1}{3} F_2^*(S - x_1) + \frac{2}{3} F_2^*(S + x_1)$					
	0	1	2	3	$F_1^*(S)$	x_1^*
3	2/3	20/27	2/3	2/3	20/27	1

$$\text{Required optimal policy is } x_1^* = \begin{cases} \text{if wins} \quad x_2^* = 1 \begin{cases} \text{if wins} & x_3^* = 0 \\ \text{if loses} & x_3^* = 2, 3 \end{cases} \\ \text{if loses} \quad x_2^* = 1 \text{ or } 2 \begin{cases} \text{if wins} & x_3^* = 2, 3 \text{ or } 1, 2, 3, 4 \\ \text{if loses} & \text{bet is lost.} \end{cases} \end{cases}$$

This policy gives the statistician a probability of 20/27 of winning his bet with his colleagues.

13.7 CONCLUSIONS

DP is a very useful technique for making a sequence of *interrelated decisions.* It requires formulating an appropriate *recursive relationship* for each individual problem. However, it provides a great combination of decisions, particularly for large problems. For example, if a problem has 10 stages and 10 possible decisions at each stage, then exhaustive enumeration must be considered up to 10^{10} combinations, whereas DP need makes no more than 10^3 calculations (10 for each state at each stage).

13.8 EXERCISE 13

1. Solve the following problem by DP.

   $$\text{Minimise } \sum_{i=1}^{10} x_i^2$$

   $$\text{subject to } \prod_{i=1}^{10} x_i = 8$$

   $$x_i > 0.$$

   [CU(MSc App) 1986, MBA 2001]

2. Formulate the following problem as a DPP and find the optimal solution.
   Maximise $Z = (x_1 + 2)^2 + x_2 x_3 + (x_4 - 5)^2$, subject to $x_1 + x_2 + x_3 + x_4 \leq 5$; x_1, x_2, x_3, x_4 are non-negative integers.

3. Formulate dynamic recursive equation for the problem $\min_{\substack{\sigma_i \\ i=1,2,\ldots,n}} \{\max[k(\sigma_1), k(\sigma_2), \ldots, k(\sigma_n)]\}$

   $$\text{subject to } \sum_{i=1}^{n} \sigma_i = c$$

   $$\sigma_i \geq 0.$$

   Then solve assuming that $n = 3, c = 10$ and $k(\sigma_1) = \sigma_1 + 5$

   $$k(\sigma_2) = 5\sigma_2 + 3$$

   $$k(\sigma_3) = \sigma_3 - 2.$$

4. Solve the following problem using DP.

$$\text{Minimise } Z = \sum_{j=1}^{n} y_j^2$$

$$\text{subject to } \prod_{j=1}^{n} y_j = k$$

$$y_j \geq 0 \ \forall \ j.$$

5. Explain the following in the context of DP: (a) Bellman's principle of optimality (b) State (c) Stage (d) Forward and backward algorithms.
6. Differentiate between the deterministic and probabilistic DP models. Explain how you can apply probabilistic DP technique in multistage inventory management.
7. A student of OR has five days at his disposal to revise the subject before examination. The course is divided into four sections. He decided to devote a whole day to the study of some sections so that he may study a section for one day, two days, three days, etc. or not at all. The expected grade points he will get for different alternative arrangements are as follows.

Study days	Course sections I	II	III	IV
0	1	1	0	0
1	2	1	0	1
2	2	2	1	2
3	3	3	2	2
4	4	3	3	3
5	4	4	3	4

How should he distribute the available days to the different sections of the course so that he maximises his grade point average? [MSc(BESU) 1996, MCA 1997]

8. Use DP to find the value of Maximise $Z = y_1 y_2 y_3$ subject to $y_1 + y_2 + y_3 = 5$, $y_1, y_2, y_3 \geq 0$. [MBA(June) 2003]

9. Production is to be planned for a four-period horizon. There is no initial inventory, and the final inventory is to be zero. No shortage is allowed. Production and inventory costs have given in the following table.

Period (t)	Demand (D_t)	Set-up cost (S_t) (in ₹)	Unit production cost C_t (in ₹)	Unit holding cost per period (H_t) (in ₹)
1	20	30	3	2
2	30	40	3	1
3	40	30	4	1
4	30	50	4	1

(a) Formulate the above as a DP model and establish the recurrence relation to be used for solving the problem.

(b) Obtain the optimal production quantity in each period of the planning horizon. Also compute the total cost of the optimal plan. [MCA 2001, IAS(Main) 1998]

10. Explain the basic idea involved in solving an LPP by DP approach.

11. Solving the following LPP by DP method:

(a) Maximise $Z = 2x_1 + 4x_2$

subject to $2x_1 + 3x_2 \le 48$

$x_1 + 3x_2 \le 42$

$x_1 + x_2 \le 21$

$x_1, x_2 \ge 0.$

[BIT(BE) 1984, BESU(MTech ME) 2001]

(b) Maximise $Z = x_1 + 9x_2$

subject to $2x_1 + x_2 \le 25$

$x_2 \le 11$

$x_1, x_2 \ge 0.$

[DU(MSc Maths) 1974, BESU(MSc Maths) 2010]

(c) Maximise $Z = 8x_1 + 7x_2$

subject to $2x_1 + x_2 \le 8$

$5x_1 + 2x_2 \le 15$

$x_1, x_2 \ge 0.$

[MBA 2001, IISc(Indl. Mang) 1977]

(d) Maximise $Z = 4x_1 + 14x_2$

subject to $2x_1 + 7x_2 \le 21$

$7x_1 + 2x_2 \le 21$

$x_1, x_2 \ge 0.$

(e) Maximise $Z = 3x_1 + 4x_2$

subject to $2x_1 + x_2 \le 40$

$2x_1 + 5x_2 \le 180$

$x_1, x_2 \ge 0.$

12. The network given below gives different routes for reaching City B from City A passing through a number of other cities. The lengths of the individual routes are shown on the arrows. It is required to determine the shortest route from A to B. Formulate the problem as a DP model. Also define the stages, states and return function and finally obtain the optimal solution.

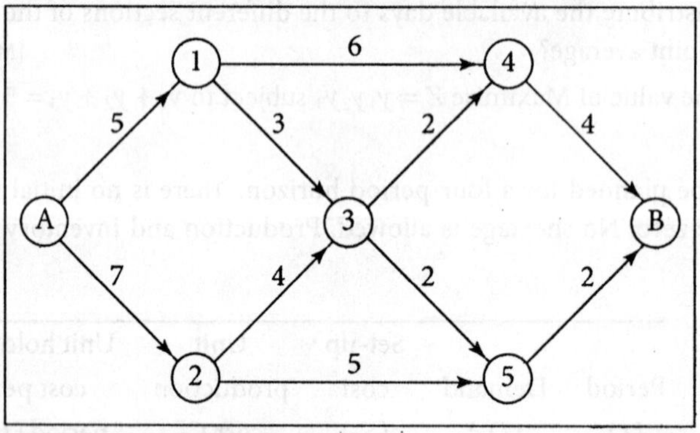

13. Consider the *Cargo-loading* problem defined in Ex. 13.4.3. Assume the following case of three items.

Find the optimal solution in each of the following cases (a) $\Omega = 3$ (b) $\Omega = 4$.

j	σ_j	v_j
1	2	65
2	3	80
3	1	30

14. Consider the transportation problem with m sources and n destinations. Let $a_i (i = 1,2,\ldots,m)$ be the amount available at source i and $b_j (j = 1,2,\ldots,n)$ be the amount demanded at destination j. If the cost of transporting x_{ij} units from source i to destination j is $C_{ij}\left(x_{ij}\right)$. Formulate the problem as a DP model.

15. A 4-tonne vessel is loaded with one or more of the three items. The adjoining table gives the unit weight W_i in tonnes and the unit revenue in thousand of rupees r_i for item i. How should the vessel be loaded to maximise the total return.

Item i	W_i	r_i
1	2	31
2	3	47
3	1	44

ANSWERS

1. $x_i^* = 0.8, i = 1,2,\ldots,10$. Minimum value = 6.4.
2. $\left(x_1^*, x_2^*, x_3^*, x_4^*\right) = (5,0,0,0)$. $Z_{\max} = 74$.
3. $\left(\sigma_1^*, \sigma_2^*, \sigma_3^*\right) = \left(\frac{13}{11}, \frac{7}{11}, \frac{90}{11}\right)$.
4. $y_j^* = b^{1/n}, j = 1,2,\ldots,n$. $Z_{\min} = n \cdot b^{1/n}$.
7. No. of ways = 12. Maximum grade point average = 6.
8. $y_i^* = 5/3, i = 1,2,3$. $Z_{\max} = 125/27$.
11. (b) $x_1^* = 7, x_2^* = 11, Z_{\max} = 106$.
    (c) $x_1^* = 0, x_2^* = 7\frac{1}{2}, Z_{\max} = 52\frac{1}{2}$.
    (d) $x_1^* = 0, x_2^* = 3, Z_{\max} = 42$.
    (e) $x_1^* = 5/2, x_2^* = 35, Z_{\max} = 147\frac{1}{2}$.
12. Optimum route: $A \to 1 \to 3 \to 5 \to B$. Total distance = 12.
13. (a) $\left(m_1^*, m_2^*, m_3^*\right) = (1,0,1)$. Total value = 95. (b) $\left(m_1^*, m_2^*, m_3^*\right) = (2,0,0)$. Total value = 130.
15. 2 units of item 1 only. ₹62000.

Chapter 14

An Introduction to Information Theory

14.1 INTRODUCTION

Information Theory (IT) is a new branch of probability theory with extensive potential applications to communication systems. It was originated by scientists, while studying the statistical structure of electrical communication equipment. IT has its origin in the twentieth century itself, when Hartley tried to develop a quantitative measure of information to assess the capacities of the telecommunication systems. It is only during the last three decades or so, however, that a theory of information has been developed and its concepts have found widespread use outside the telecommunication engineering.

Mathematical theory of communication was principally originated by Claude Shannon in 1948. It plays an important role in modern communication theory, which formulate a communication system as a stochastic or random process.

Communication processes are concerned with the flow of some sort of information in some network. The process by which one mind affects another mind is called a *communication process.* This may be any means by which information is conveyed from a transmitter to a receiver. The information is usually conveyed by means of letters, newspaper, books, human voice (as in telephone, radio, TV), etc.

The various components of the process through which some information is transmitted from a given source to the receiver form a *communication system.* The simplest communication system is given in the following figure.

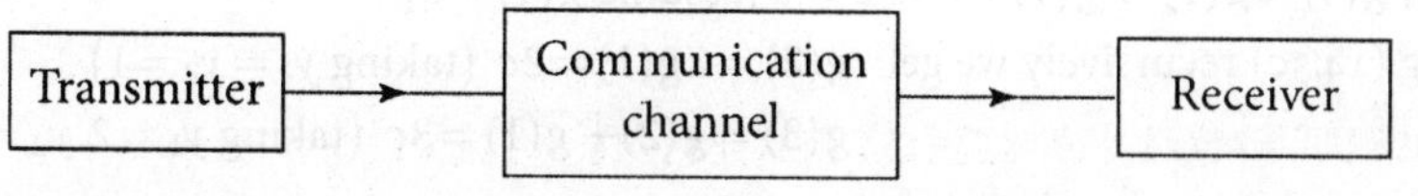

In general, there are some disturbances in communication channel that results in distortion of the original information and the system is said to be noisy, e.g., unwanted noise in radio, television, errors in newspaper-printing, etc. In electrical model a transformer is used to improve its efficiency. Similarly, in IT a device called *encoder* is used to improve the efficiency of the channel and at the receiver terminal a decoder used to transform the encoded message into the original form acceptable to the receiver. Therefore, the general structure used in IT is given by the following figure.

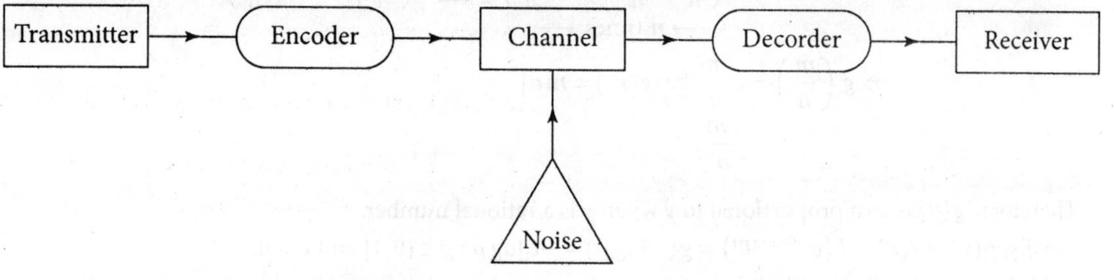

14.2 AXIOMS OF INFORMATION

Let the probability of occurrence of an event A is p and I be the information associated with A.

Axiom 1. $I = I(p)$ is a function of $p \in (0, 1]$, i.e., the information depends only on p.

Axiom 2. $I(p)$ is monotonically decreasing continuous function of p in $(0, 1]$, that is, $I(p_1) \geq I(p_2)$ for all $0 < p_1 < p_2 \leq 1$.

Axiom 3. No information is conveyed by an event, which is sure to occur, i.e., $I(1) = 0$.

Axiom 4. For two independent events A and B with probability of occurrence p_1 and p_2 the information content of the message that both have occurred is equal to the information of the message dealing with only A plus that of the message dealing with only B.

$$I(p_1 p_2) = I(p_1) + I(p_2) \text{ for all } 0 < p_1, p_2 < 1.$$

14.3 MATHEMATICAL EXPRESSION OF INFORMATION

The function $I(p)$ satisfying *Axiom* 1 to *Axiom* 4 can be expressed in a mathematical form as $I(p) = -c \log p : 0 < p \leq 1$ and $c > 0$ is an arbitrary constant.

Deduction. Introduce the transformation: $y_1 = -\log p_1$ and $y_2 = -\log p_2$. (14.3a)

$$\left.\begin{aligned} \text{Then, } I(p_1) &= I(e^{-y_1}) = g(y_1) \\ I(p_2) &= I(e^{-y_2}) = g(y_2) \end{aligned}\right\}. \tag{14.3b}$$

From *Axiom* 4, $I(p_1 p_2) = I(p_1) + I(p_2)$

$$g(y_1 + y_2) = g(y_1) + g(y_2),\ y_1, y_2 \geq 0. \tag{14.3c}$$

Since y_1, y_2 are defined as a monotonically decreasing function of p_1, p_2 it follows from *Axiom* 2 that $g(y_1)$, $g(y_2)$ are monotonically increasing functions of y_1, y_2 so that $g(y_1) < g(y_2) : 0 \leq y_1 < y_2$. (14.3d)

Put $y_1 = y_2 = 0$ in (14.3c): $g(0) = 2g(0)$.

Again, from *Axiom* 3, $g(0) = I(1) = 0$.

From (14.3d), $g(0) < g(1) \Rightarrow g(1) > 0 \Rightarrow c > 0$ [assume $g(1) = c$].

Next applying (14.3c) recursively we get: $g(2) = 2g(1) = 2c$ (taking $y_1 = y_2 = 1$)

$$g(3) = g(2) + g(1) = 3c \text{ (taking } y_1 = 2, y_2 = 1)$$

$$\vdots$$

$$g(n) = nc, \text{ where } n \text{ is an integer and } c > 0.$$

Hence, $g(y)$ is proportional to y, where y is a positive integer. Now consider the case, when $y = m/n$ is a rational number; m, n being non-negative integers and $n \neq 0$.

$$g(m) = g\Big(\underbrace{\frac{m}{n} + \frac{m}{n} + \cdots + \frac{m}{n}}_{n \text{ times}}\Big) = \sum g\left(\frac{m}{n}\right) = ng\left(\frac{m}{n}\right)$$

$$\Rightarrow g\left(\frac{m}{n}\right) = c\frac{m}{n} \quad [\because g(m) = mc]$$

$$= \frac{cm}{n}.$$

Therefore, $g(y)$ is also proportional to y when y is a rational number.

Finally, $g(y) = I(p) = I(e^{-(-\log p)}) = g(-\log p) = -c\log p : p \in (0, 1]$ and $c > 0$.

$\therefore$ $I(p) = -c\log p : 0 < p \leq 1$ and $c > 0$ is an arbitrary constant.

14.4 UNITS OF INFORMATION

Consider a simple case of selection between two events E_1 and E_2 with equal probabilities. For example, E_1, E_2 may be the head and tail in the throwing of an unbiased coin. Probability of selection of any one of two events E_1 and E_2 is equal to 1/2. Therefore, amount of information associated with the selection of one out of two equiprobable events is given by $1 = -c\log\frac{1}{2} \Rightarrow c = \frac{1}{\log 2}$.

Therefore, $I(p) = -\log_2 p$. Hence, when the logarithmic base is taken to be 2, the unit of information corresponding to the selection of one out of two equiprobable cases is called *one bit.*

When the logarithmic base is taken as 10, that is one out of ten equiprobable cases, the unit of information is known as *hartley* as it is suggested by Hartley in 1928.

Again, when natural logarithmic base is used, the unit of information is called *Nat.*

Note that when we consider the selection of one out of $2^2, 2^3, 2^4, \ldots, 2^N$ equally likely choices, by successively partitioning a selection into two equally likely selections, we come to the conclusion that the amounts of information associated with the previous selection schemes are 2, 3, 4, ..., N bits.

14.5 MEASURE OF INFORMATION

Let there be n events $\{x_1, x_2, \ldots, x_n\}$ with respective probabilities $\{p_1, p_2, \ldots, p_n\}$ such that $p(x_i) = p_i$ for $i = 1, 2, \ldots, n$, $p_i \geq 0$ and $\sum_{i=1}^{n} p_i = 1$. Then, the measure of information, also called *entropy* or uncertainty of the probability distribution $P=\{p_1,p_2,\ldots,p_n\}$ is the mathematical expectation of the information $I(p_i)$ and is given by

$$H_n(P)=H_n(p_1,p_2,\ldots,p_n)=\sum_{i=1}^{n}p_iI(p_i)=-c\sum_{i=1}^{n}p_i\log p_i,$$

where $H_n(p_1,p_2,\ldots,p_n)\geq 0$ if $p_i=1$ for some i and $p_j=0$ for all $j\neq i$.

In 1948, Claude Shannon suggested the form of entropy or uncertainty by the expression

$$S_n(P)=S_n(p_1,p_2,\ldots,p_n)=-\sum_{i=1}^{n}p_i\log p_i$$

and accordingly it is known as *Shannon's form of entropy.* This form has an extensive potential applications in every branches of science, technology and communication systems.

14.6 SOME IMPORTANT PROPERTIES OF SHANNON'S ENTROPY

(P1) $S_n(p_1,p_2,\ldots,p_n)$ is symmetric. It does not change if $p_1,p_2,\ldots,p_n$ are reordered among themselves. This property is useful since the labelling of the outcomes should not affect the measure of information.

(P2) Both p_i and $\log p_i$ are continuous function of $p_i\in(0,1]$ for $i=1,2,\ldots,n$. When $p_i=0$ $(p_i\log p_i)$ is not defined. But $\lim_{p_i\to 0}p_i\log p_i=\lim_{p_i\to 0}\frac{\log p_i}{1/p_i}=\lim_{p_i\to 0}(-p_i)=0$.

However, if we define $0\log 0\triangleq 0$, then $(p_i\log p_i)$ becomes continuous at $p_i=0$. Hence, $S_n(p_1,p_2,\ldots,p_n)$ is a continuous function for all permissible probability distribution.

(P3) The entropy does not change by the inclusion of an impossible event.

$$S_{n+1}(p_1,p_2,\ldots,p_n,0)=-\sum_{i=1}^{n}p_i\log p_i-0\log 0=\sum_{i=1}^{n}p_i\log p_i=S_n(p_1,p_2,\ldots,p_n).$$

(P4) Let $\phi(p)=-p\log p, \phi'(p)=-(1+\log p), \phi''(p)=-\frac{1}{p}<0$. Therefore, $\phi(p)$ is a concave function in p. Since the sum of a concave function is a concave function, it follows that

$$S_n(p_1,p_2,\ldots,p_n)=-\sum_{i=1}^{n}p_i\log p_i$$

is a concave function of $(p_1,p_2,\ldots,p_n)$.

(P5) Let us now maximise $S_n(p_1,p_2,\ldots,p_n)=-\sum_{i=1}^{n}p_i\log p_i$ subject to condition $\sum_{i=1}^{n}p_i=1$ by Lagrange's method.

$$\mathscr{L}(p_1,p_2,\ldots,p_n,\lambda)=-\sum_{i=1}^{n}p_i\log p_i-\lambda\left(\sum_{i=1}^{n}p_i-1\right).$$

Now, $\frac{\partial\mathscr{L}}{\partial p_i}=0,\ i=1,2,\ldots,n$ gives $-(1+\log p_i)-\lambda=0\Rightarrow p_i=e^{-(\lambda+1)}=k$ (say).

From $\sum_{i=1}^{n}p_i=1\Rightarrow k=\frac{1}{n}$, which gives $p_1=p_2=\cdots=p_n=\frac{1}{n}$. (14.6a)

Again, $\left(\frac{\partial^2 \mathcal{L}}{\partial p_i^2} - \lambda \frac{\partial^2 \mathcal{L}}{\partial p_i \partial p_j}\right) = H$, the second order Hessian matrix $= \begin{pmatrix} -\frac{1}{p_1} & 0 & 0 & \cdots & 0 \\ 0 & -\frac{1}{p_2} & 0 & \cdots & 0 \\ \vdots & & \vdots & & \\ 0 & 0 & 0 & \cdots & -\frac{1}{p_n} \end{pmatrix}$

which is always negative definite. Therefore, the value obtained for $p_1, p_2, \ldots, p_n$ in (14.6a) determine a maximum value, which again due to the concavity property is the global maximum value.

Hence, the maximum value of $S_n(p_1, p_2, \ldots, p_n)$ attained for the *uniform distribution*

$$U = \Big\{\underbrace{\frac{1}{n}, \frac{1}{n}, \ldots, \frac{1}{n}}_{\longrightarrow n \text{ times} \longleftarrow}\Big\}. \tag{14.6b}$$

Therefore, entropy $S_n(p_1, p_2, \ldots, p_n)$ should be maximum when all outcomes are equally likely and the maximum value is given by

$$(S_n)_{\max} = -\sum_{n \text{ times}} \frac{1}{n} \log \frac{1}{n} = \log n. \tag{14.6c}$$

(P6) Let $P = \left\{ p_1, p_2, \ldots, p_n \middle| p_i \geq 0, \sum_{i=1}^{n} p_i = 1,\ i = 1, 2, \ldots, n \right\}$

and $Q = \left\{ q_1, q_2, \ldots, q_n \middle| q_j \geq 0, \sum_{j=1}^{n} q_i = 1,\ j = 1, 2, \ldots, n \right\}$

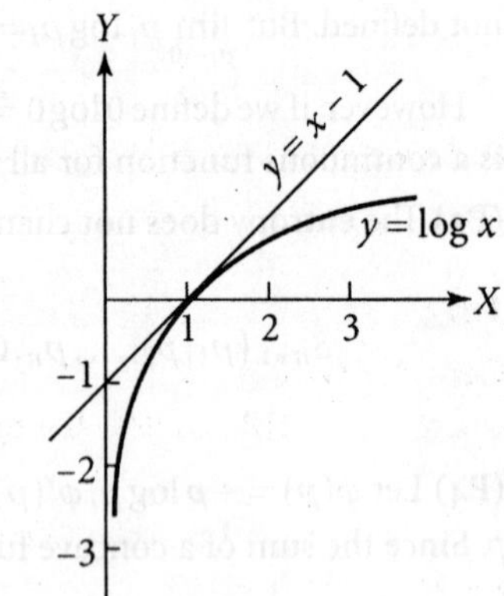

are two probability distributions. Then

$$S_n(p_1, p_2, \ldots, p_n) \leq -\sum_{i=1}^{n} p_i \log q_i, \tag{14.6d}$$

only equality holds iff $p_i = q_i$ for all $i = 1, 2, \ldots, n$.

We know the inequality $\log x \leq x - 1$, only equality holds if $x = 1$.

Put $x_i = \frac{q_i}{p_i}$: $\log \frac{q_i}{p_i} \leq \frac{q_i}{p_i} - 1$ only equality holds if $q_i = p_i$

$$\Rightarrow p_i \log q_i - p_i \log p_i \leq q_i - p_i$$

$$\Rightarrow -\sum_{i=1}^{n} p_i \log p_i \leq -\sum_{i=1}^{n} p_i \log q_i \text{ only equality holds if } p_i = q_i$$

$$\Rightarrow S_n(p_1, p_2, \ldots, p_n) \leq -\sum_{i=1}^{n} p_i \log q_i.$$

In particular, if $q_i = \frac{1}{n}\ \forall\ i = 1, 2, \ldots, n$, then $S_n(p_1, p_2, \ldots, p_n) \leq -\sum_{i=1}^{n} p_i \log\left(\frac{1}{n}\right) = \log n$, only equality holds if $p_i = q_i = 1/n$.

(P7) From definition

$$S_{n-1}(p_1+p_2, p_3, p_4, \ldots, p_n) = -(p_1+p_2)\log(p_1+p_2) - \sum_{i=3}^{n} p_i \log p_i$$

$$= (p_1+p_2)\log(p_1+p_2) + p_1\log p_1 + p_2 \log p_2 - \sum_{i=1}^{n} p_i \log p_i$$

$$= (p_1+p_2)\left[\left(-\frac{p_1}{p_1+p_2}\right)\log\frac{p_1}{p_1+p_2} - \frac{p_2}{p_1+p_2}\log\frac{p_2}{p_1+p_2}\right] + S_n(p_1, p_2, \ldots, p_n)$$

$$= (p_1+p_2) S_2\left(\frac{p_1}{p_1+p_2}, \frac{p_2}{p_1+p_2}\right) + S_n(p_1, p_2, \ldots, p_n).$$

$$\therefore S_n(p_1, p_2, \ldots, p_n) \geq S_{n-1}(p_1+p_2, p_3, p_4, \ldots, p_n). \tag{14.6e}$$

(14.6e) indicates that if two outcomes are combined the entropy is reduced. We need two stages to find $S_n(p_1, p_2, \ldots, p_n)$. In the first stage, we get $S_{n-1}(p_1+p_2, p_3, p_4, \ldots, p_n)$ and in the second stage, we have a probability (p_1+p_2) divided into two parts p_1 and p_2, which gives the probability distribution

$$\left\{\frac{p_1}{p_1+p_2}, \frac{p_2}{p_1+p_2}\right\}$$

and a weight (p_1+p_2) to give the expression $(p_1+p_2) S_2\left(\frac{p_1}{p_1+p_2}, \frac{p_2}{p_1+p_2}\right)$. This property is known as the *branching property.*

14.7 JOINT AND CONDITIONAL ENTROPIES

Consider two sets of messages in a communication channel $X = \{x_1, x_2, \ldots, x_n\}$ and $Y = \{y_1, y_2, \ldots, y_m\}$, where $x_i (i = 1, 2, \ldots, n)$ is the message sent (*channel inputs*) and $y_j (j = 1, 2, \ldots, m)$ is the message received (*channel outputs*).

$p_{ij} = p(x_i, y_j)$ denotes the probability of joint events of message sent and message received (x_i, y_j), $i = 1, 2, \ldots, n$, $j = 1, 2, \ldots, m$ through the communication channel.

$$p_{i0} = p(x_i) = \sum_{j=1}^{m} p_{ij} \text{ and } p_{0j} = p(y_j) = \sum_{i=1}^{n} p_{ij}$$

are respectively the marginal probabilities of message sent and message received through the channel.

The marginal entropies of X and Y are given by

$$H(X) = -\sum_{i=1}^{n} p_{i0} \log p_{i0} = -\sum_{i=1}^{n}\left\{\sum_{j=1}^{m} p_{ij}\right\}\log p_{i0} \tag{14.7a}$$

$$H(Y) = -\sum_{j=1}^{m} p_{0j} \log p_{0j} = -\sum_{j=1}^{m}\left\{\sum_{i=1}^{n} p_{ij}\right\}\log p_{0j}. \tag{14.7b}$$

The joint entropy of X and Y is given by $H(X, Y) = -\sum_{i=1}^{n}\sum_{j=1}^{m} p_{ij} \log p_{ij}$. (14.7c)

Adding (14.7a) and (14.7b), $H(X)+H(Y)=-\sum_{i=1}^{n}\left\{\sum_{j=1}^{m}p_{ij}\right\}\log p_{i0}-\sum_{j=1}^{m}\left\{\sum_{i=1}^{n}p_{ij}\right\}\log p_{0j}$

$$=-\sum_{i=1}^{n}\sum_{j=1}^{m}p_{ij}\log\left(p_{i0}p_{0j}\right)=-\sum_{i=1}^{n}\sum_{j=1}^{m}p_{ij}\log q_{ij}, \quad (14.7d)$$

where $q_{ij}=p_{i0}p_{0j}$.

Now, $\sum_{i=1}^{n}\sum_{j=1}^{m}q_{ij}=\sum_{i=1}^{n}p_{i0}\sum_{j=1}^{m}p_{0j}=1$.

Again, by using *Property* 6 of Sec. 14.6, we have

$$-\sum_{i=1}^{n}\sum_{j=1}^{m}p_{ij}\log p_{ij}\le-\sum_{i=1}^{n}\sum_{j=1}^{m}p_{ij}\log q_{ij}, \quad \text{only equality, if } p_{ij}=q_{ij}$$

$$\Rightarrow H(X,Y)\le H(X)+H(Y), \qquad \text{only equality, if } p_{ij}=q_{ij}=p_{i0}p_{0j},$$

that is when X and Y are independent.

We use the notation $p_{j/i}=\dfrac{p\left(x_i,y_j\right)}{p(x_i)}=\dfrac{p_{ij}}{p_{i0}}$ and define the conditional entropy of Y given $X=x_i$ as

$$H(Y/X=x_i)=-\sum_{j=1}^{m}p_{j/i}\log p_{j/i} \quad (14.7e)$$

and the average conditional entropy of Y given X as a weighted average of $H(Y/X=x_i)$ as

$$H(Y/X)=\sum_{i=1}^{n}p_{i0}H(Y/X=x_i)=-\sum_{i=1}^{n}\sum_{j=1}^{m}p_{i0}p_{j/i}\log p_{j/i}=-\sum_{i=1}^{n}\sum_{j=1}^{m}p_{ij}\log p_{j/i}. \quad (14.7f)$$

Similarly, $H(X/Y)=-\sum_{i=1}^{n}\sum_{j=1}^{m}p_{ij}\log p_{i/j}$. (14.7g)

14.8 SOME USEFUL IMPORTANT RESULTS

Result 1. $H(X/Y)=H(X)+H(Y/X)$.

Proof. $H(X)+H(Y/X)=-\sum_{i=1}^{n}p_{i0}\log p_{i0}-\sum_{i=1}^{n}\sum_{j=1}^{m}p_{ij}\log p_{j/i}=-\sum_{i=1}^{n}\sum_{j=1}^{m}p_{ij}\log p_{i0}-\sum_{i=1}^{n}\sum_{j=1}^{m}p_{ij}\log p_{j/i}$

$$=-\sum_{i=1}^{n}\sum_{j=1}^{m}p_{ij}\log\left\{p_{i0}p_{j/i}\right\}=-\sum_{i=1}^{n}\sum_{j=1}^{m}p_{ij}\log p_{ij}=H(X).$$

The implication of the result is: if X and Y are observed but only the observation on X reveals, the remaining uncertainty about Y is $H(Y/X)$.

Similarly, $H(X,Y)=H(Y)+H(X/Y)$.

Result 2. $H(Y/X)\le H(Y)$, only equality holds if X and Y are independent.

Proof. From **Result 1**, $H(X,Y)=H(X)+H(Y/X)$. (14.8a)

Also, we have $H(X,Y)\le H(X)+H(Y)$, only equality holds when X and Y are independent. (14.8b)

Combining (14.8a) and (14.8b) $H(X)+H(Y/X)\le H(X)+H(Y)\Rightarrow H(Y/X)\le H(Y)$, only equality holds when X and Y are independent.

This particular result indicates that revelation of the observations on X cannot increase the uncertainty about Y.

Result 3. The quantities $H(X)-H(X/Y)$ is defined to be the information conveyed by Y about X and $H(Y)-H(Y/X)$ be the information conveyed by X about Y and they are respectively denoted by $I_c(X/Y)$ and $I_c(Y/X)$ so that $I_c(X/Y)=H(X)-H(X/Y)=-\sum_{i=1}^{n}\sum_{j=1}^{m}p_{ij}\log\left\{\frac{p_{i0}}{p_{i/j}}\right\}$

$$I_c(Y/X)=H(Y)-H(Y/X)=-\sum_{i=1}^{n}\sum_{j=1}^{m}p_{ij}\log\left\{\frac{p_{0j}}{p_{j/i}}\right\}.$$

We see that (i) $I_c(X/Y)=H(X)-H(X/Y)=H(X)-\{H(X,Y)-H(Y)\}=H(Y)-H(Y/X)=I_c(Y/X)$.

(ii) Since $H(X/Y)-H(X)\leq 0\Rightarrow H(X)-H(X/Y)\geq 0\Rightarrow I_C(X/Y)=I_c(Y/X)\geq 0$, only equality holds if X and Y are independent.

14.9 PROBLEMS

Example 14.9.1. *Show that the entropy of the following probability distribution is* $[2-2^{-(n-2)}]$ *bits*

$$P(X=x_i)=p_i=\begin{cases}\frac{1}{2^i} & \text{for } i=1,2,\ldots,n-1\\ \frac{1}{2^{n-1}} & \text{for } i=n.\end{cases}$$

Solution: $H_n(p_1,p_2,\ldots,p_n)=-\sum_{i=1}^{n-1}p_i\log_2 p_i-p_n\log_2 p_n=-\sum_{i=1}^{n-1}2^{-i}\log_2 2^{-i}-\frac{1}{2^{n-1}}\log_2 2^{-(n-1)}$

$$=\sum_{i=1}^{n-1}\frac{i}{2^i}+\frac{n-1}{2^{n-1}}=\frac{1}{2}+\frac{2}{2^2}+\frac{3}{2^3}+\cdots+\frac{n-1}{2^{n-1}}+\frac{n-1}{2^{n-1}}.$$

$$\therefore H_n-\frac{1}{2}H_n=\frac{1}{2}+\frac{1}{2^2}+\frac{1}{2^3}+\cdots+\frac{1}{2^{n-1}}-\frac{n-1}{2^n}$$

$$\Rightarrow\frac{1}{2}H_n=\frac{1}{2}\frac{1-\frac{1}{2^{n-1}}}{1-\frac{1}{2}}-\frac{n-1}{2^n}=1-\frac{1}{2^{n-1}}-\frac{n-1}{2^n}$$

$$\Rightarrow H_n(p_1,p_2,\ldots,p_n)=2-\left(\frac{1}{2}\right)^{n-2}=[2-2^{-(n-2)}]\text{ bits.}$$

Example 14.9.2. *A single unbiased die is tossed once. If the face of the die is* $\{1,2,3,4\}$ *a coin is tossed once, but if the face is* $\{5,6\}$ *the coin is tossed twice. Find the information conveyed about the face of the die by the number of heads obtained.*

Solution: X is the r.v. associated with the face of the die and Y associated with the number of heads obtained. Then we have to find $I_c(X/Y)$, which is the same as $I_c(Y/X)$.

$p(x_1)=P(X=x_1)=$ probability that the face of the die is $\{1,2,3 \text{ or } 4\}=\frac{4}{6}=\frac{2}{3}$.

$p(x_2)=P(X=x_2)=$ probability that the face of the die is $\{5 \text{ or } 6\}=\frac{2}{6}=\frac{1}{3}$.

$Y=\{y_0=$ no head, $y_1=$ one head, $y_2=$ two heads$\}$.

Then from the given information, $p(y_0/x_1)=\frac{1}{2},\ p(y_1/x_1)=\frac{1}{2},\ p(y_2/x_2)=0,$

$p(y_0/x_2)=\frac{1}{4},\ p(y_1/x_2)=\frac{1}{2},\ p(y_2/x_2)=\frac{1}{4}.$

$$p(y_0)=\sum_{i=1}^{2} p(y_0/x_i)\,p(x_i)=\frac{1}{2}\times\frac{2}{3}+\frac{1}{4}\times\frac{1}{3}=\frac{5}{12}$$

$$p(y_1)=\sum_{i=1}^{2} p(y_1/x_i)\,p(x_i)=\frac{1}{2}\times\frac{2}{3}+\frac{1}{2}\times\frac{1}{3}=\frac{1}{2}$$

$$p(y_2)=\sum_{i=1}^{2} p(y_2/x_i)\,p(x_i)=\frac{1}{4}\times\frac{1}{3}=\frac{1}{12}.$$

$$H(Y)=-\sum_{j=0}^{2} p(y_j)\log_2 p(y_j)=\left(-\frac{5}{12}\log_2\frac{5}{12}-\frac{1}{12}\log_2\frac{1}{12}-\frac{1}{2}\log_2\frac{1}{2}\right)\text{ bits}$$

$$H(Y/X)=\sum_{i=1}^{2} p(x_i)H(Y/X=x_i)$$

$$H(Y/x_1)=-\sum_{j=0}^{2} p(y_j/x_1)\log_2 p(y_j/x_1)=-\frac{1}{2}\log_2\frac{1}{2}-\frac{1}{2}\log_2\frac{1}{2}=1\text{ bit}$$

$$H(Y/x_2)=-\sum_{j=0}^{2} p(y_j/x_2)\log_2 p(y_j/x_2)=-\frac{1}{4}\log_2\frac{1}{4}-\frac{1}{2}\log_2\frac{1}{2}-\frac{1}{4}\log_2\frac{1}{4}=\frac{3}{2}\text{ bit}$$

$$H(Y/X)=p(x_1)H(Y/x_1)+p(x_2)H(Y/x_2)=\frac{2}{3}\times 1+\frac{1}{3}\times\frac{3}{2}=\frac{7}{6}.$$

$$\therefore\ \boxed{I_c(X/Y)=I_c(Y/X)=\frac{1}{2}-\frac{5}{12}\log_2\frac{5}{12}-\frac{1}{12}\log_2\frac{1}{12}-\frac{7}{6}\text{ bits.}}$$

Example 14.9.3. *Each of the signals $\{A_1,A_2,\ldots,A_n\}$ has equal probability of being transmitted over a communication channel.*

(i) *In the absence of noise in the channel the signal A_i has probability one for receiving the symbol $\{a_1,a_2,\ldots,a_n\}$ for $i=1,2,\ldots,n$.*

(ii) *In the presence of noise in the channel A_i has the probability p of being received symbol a_i $(i=1,2,\ldots,n)$ and equal probability of being received any other symbol.*

What is the information $\{A_1,A_2,\ldots,A_n\}$ conveyed by receiving one of the symbols $\{a_1,a_2,\ldots,a_n\}$ for both cases (i) and (ii) in the communication channel.

Solution: Case 1. *In absence of noise.* Given, $P(a_i/A_j)=\begin{cases}1, & \text{for } i=j\\ 0, & \text{otherwise}\end{cases}$ where $i,j=1,2,\ldots,n$.

Also given, $P(a_1)=P(a_2)=\cdots=P(a_n)=1/n$ as communication channel is equiprobable.

We have to find $I_c(A/a)=I_c(a/A)=H(a)-H(a/A)$.

Now $H(a) = -\sum_{i=1}^{n} P(a_i)\log P(a_i) = -\sum_{i=1}^{n} \frac{1}{n}\log\frac{1}{n} = \log n$

$$H(a/A) = -\sum_{i=1}^{n}\sum_{j=1}^{n} P\left(A_i, a_j\right)\log P\left(a_j/A_i\right)$$

$$= 0 \left[\because P\left(A_i, a_j\right) = P(A_i)\,P\left(a_j/A_i\right) = 0\right].$$

$\therefore \boxed{I_c(A/a) = \log n}$.

Case 2. *In presence of noise.*

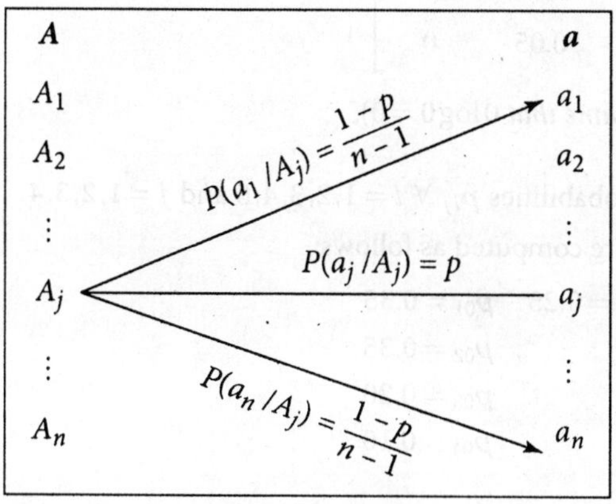

$H(a) = \log n$ [from Case 1]

$$H(a/A) = -\sum_{i=1}^{n}\sum_{j=1}^{n} P\left(A_i, a_j\right)\log P\left(a_j/A_i\right)$$

$$= -\sum_{i=1}^{n} P(A_i)\sum_{j=1}^{n} P\left(a_j/A_i\right)\log P\left(a_j/A_i\right)$$

$$= -\sum_{j\neq i}\frac{1-p}{n-1}\log\frac{1-p}{n-1} - p\log p$$

$$= -(1-p)\log\frac{1-p}{n-1} - p\log p.$$

$\therefore \boxed{I_c(A/a) = \log n + (1-p)\log\frac{1-p}{n-1} + p\log p}$.

Example 14.9.4. *During summer it rains about once in every five day's, the weather being fair rest of the time. Every night* AIR *predicts the next days weather. Suppose, prediction about rain is wrong about half the times while prediction about fair weather is correct nine times out of ten. How much information about the weather is conveyed on the average by the prediction?*

Solution: $X = \{x_1 = \text{rain},\ x_2 = \text{fair}\}$ associated with predicted weather.

$Y = \{y_1 = \text{rain},\ y_2 = \text{fair}\}$ associated with actual weather.

We have to find $I_c(Y/X)$.

From given information $p(y_1) = \frac{1}{5}$ $\quad p(y_2) = \frac{4}{5}$

$p(y_1/x_1) = \frac{1}{2}$ $\quad p(y_2/x_1) = \frac{1}{2}$

$p(y_1/x_2) = \frac{1}{10}$ $\quad p(y_2/x_2) = \frac{9}{10}$

$$p(y_1) = p(y_1/x_1)\,p(x_1) + p(y_1/x_2)\,p(x_2) \Rightarrow 5p(x_1) + p(x_2) - 2 = 0 \quad \text{(i)}$$

$$p(y_2) = p(y_2/x_1)\,p(x_1) + p(y_2/x_2)\,p(x_2) \Rightarrow 5p(x_1) + 9p(x_2) - 8 = 0 \quad \text{(ii)}$$

Solving (i) and (ii), $p(x_1) = \frac{1}{4}$; $p(x_2) = \frac{3}{4}$.

$$H(Y) = -p(y_1)\log p(y_1) - p(y_2)\log p(y_2) = -\frac{1}{5}\log\frac{1}{5} - \frac{4}{5}\log\frac{4}{5}$$

$$H(Y/x_1) = -p(y_1/x_1)\log p(y_1/x_1) - p(y_2/x_1)\log p(y_2/x_1) = -\frac{1}{2}\log\frac{1}{2} - \frac{1}{2}\log\frac{1}{2}$$

$$H(Y/x_2) = -\frac{1}{10}\log\frac{1}{10} - \frac{9}{10}\log\frac{9}{10}$$

$$H(Y/X) = -\frac{1}{4} - \frac{3}{40}\log\frac{1}{10} - \frac{27}{40}\log\frac{9}{10}.$$

$$\boxed{I_c(Y/X) = -\frac{1}{5}\log\frac{1}{5} - \frac{4}{5}\log\frac{4}{5} - \frac{1}{4} + \frac{3}{40}\log\frac{1}{10} + \frac{27}{40}\log\frac{9}{10}}.$$

Example 14.9.5. *A transmitter has the alphabet consisting of five letters* $\{x_1, x_2, x_3, x_4, x_5\}$ *and the receiver has the alphabet of four letters* $\{y_1, y_2, y_3, y_4\}$. *The joint probability for the communication are given below.*

$$\begin{array}{c} \\ x_1 \\ x_2 \\ x_3 \\ x_4 \\ x_5 \end{array}\begin{array}{c} \begin{array}{cccc} y_1 & y_2 & y_3 & y_4 \end{array} \\ \begin{bmatrix} 0.25 & 0 & 0 & 0 \\ 0.10 & 0.30 & 0 & 0 \\ 0 & 0.05 & 0.10 & 0 \\ 0 & 0 & 0.05 & 0.10 \\ 0 & 0 & 0.05 & 0 \end{bmatrix} \end{array}$$

Determine different entropies for the channel in bits (assume that $0\log 0 \triangleq 0$*).*

Solution: The channel is described here by the joint probabilities $p_{ij}\ \forall\ i = 1,2,3,4,5$ and $j = 1,2,3,4$.

The various conditional and marginal probabilities are computed as follows:

$$p_{10} = 0.25+0+0+0 = 0.25 \qquad p_{01} = 0.35$$
$$p_{20} = 0.40 \qquad p_{02} = 0.35$$
$$p_{30} = 0.15 \qquad p_{03} = 0.20$$
$$p_{40} = 0.15 \qquad p_{04} = 0.10$$
$$p_{50} = 0.05$$

The conditional probabilities are given in the following channel matrix (using $p_{j/i} = p_{ij}/p_{i0}$)

$$\begin{pmatrix} 1 & 0 & 0 & 0 \\ 1/4 & 3/4 & 0 & 0 \\ 0 & 1/3 & 2/3 & 0 \\ 0 & 0 & 1/3 & 2/3 \\ 0 & 0 & 1 & 0 \end{pmatrix}$$

Let us now calculate various entropies associated with the channel in *bits* as follows:

$$H(X) = -\sum_{i=1}^{5} p_{i0}\log_2 p_{i0} = 2.066$$

$$H(Y) = -\sum_{j=1}^{4} p_{0j}\log_2 p_{0j} = 1.856$$

$$H(Y/X) = -\sum_{i=1}^{5}\sum_{j=1}^{4} p_{ij}\log_2 p_{j/i} = 0.60$$

$$H(X/Y) = H(X) + H(Y/X) - H(Y) = 0.07$$
$$H(X,Y) = H(X) + H(Y/X) = 1.926$$
$$I_c(X/Y) = I_c(Y/X) = H(Y) - H(Y/X) = 1.256.$$

14.10 TYPES OF CHANNEL

(a) *Channel matrix.* A convenient way of describing a channel in information system is to arrange the output conditional probabilities in the form of a matrix.

$$\begin{array}{cc} & \text{Output} \\ & \begin{array}{ccccc} y_1 & y_2 & \cdots & y_s \end{array} \\ \text{Input} \begin{array}{c} x_1 \\ x_2 \\ \vdots \\ x_r \end{array} & \begin{bmatrix} p_{1/1} & p_{2/1} & \cdots & p_{s/1} \\ p_{1/2} & p_{2/2} & \cdots & p_{s/2} \\ \vdots & \vdots & \cdots & \vdots \\ p_{1/r} & p_{2/r} & \cdots & p_{s/r} \end{bmatrix} \end{array}$$

where $p_{j/i} = P\left(y_j/x_i\right)$, $i = 1,2,\ldots,r$ and $j = 1,2,\ldots,s$. Each row of the channel matrix corresponds to an input of a channel and each column corresponds to output. Note that in every channel matrix the sum of terms in every row must be equal to one, that is, $\sum_{j=1}^{s} p_{j/i} = 1$ for $i = 1,2,\ldots,r$.

(b) *Binary symmetric channel* (BSC). A binary symmetric channel has just two input symbols ($x_1 = 0, x_2 = 1$) and two output symbols ($y_1 = 0, y_2 = 1$) and is symmetric in the sense that $P(y_1/x_1) = P(y_2/x_2) = \bar{p}$ and $P(y_1/x_2) = P(y_2/x_1) = p$, where $\bar{p} = 1 - p$, p being the probability of error in transmission through communication channel.

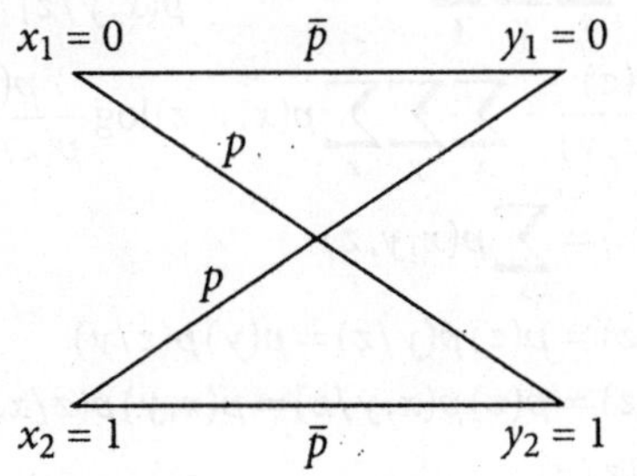

Channel diagram

$$\begin{bmatrix} \bar{p} & p \\ p & \bar{p} \end{bmatrix}$$

Channel matrix of BSC

(c) *Noiseless channel.* A channel described by a channel matrix in information system having one and only one non-zero element in each column is called a *noiseless channel.*

For example, (i) A BSC with $p = 0$ or 1 is a noiseless channel.

(ii) $\begin{pmatrix} 1/2 & 1/2 & 0 & 0 & 0 & 0 \\ 0 & 0 & 3/5 & 5/10 & 1/10 & 0 \\ 0 & 0 & 0 & 0 & 0 & 1 \end{pmatrix}$ is a noiseless channel.

(d) *Discrete memoryless channel* (DMC). The DMC is an object in information system that accepts at every unit of time one of the r inputs and responses one of the s outputs. The channel is discrete as there are only a finite number of input-output symbols and also it is memoryless because the current output depend only on the current input and does not depend on any other previous inputs. DMC is governed by a $(r \times s)$ matrix having transition probabilities as given by: $P\left(y_j/x_i\right) = p_{j/i}$, $i = 1,2,\ldots,r$

$j = 1,2,\ldots,s$

such that (i) $p_{j/i} \geq 0 \; \forall \; i$ and j (ii) $\sum_{j=1}^{s} p_{j/i} = 1$.

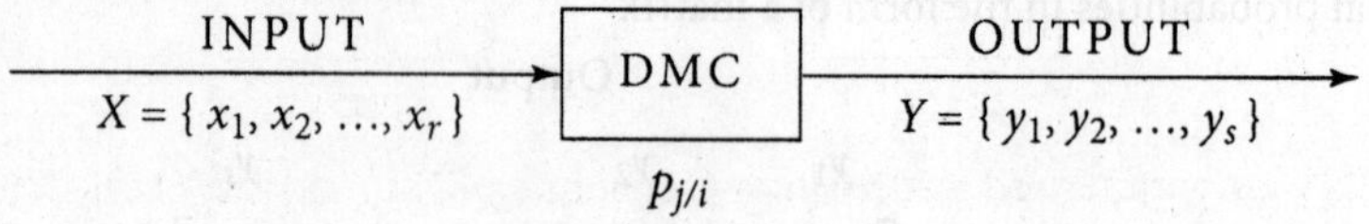

Diagram of DMC

Therefore, corresponding to a DMC there is a pair of r.v. X the *input to* and Y the *output from* the channel. Conversely, given a pair of r.v. X and Y there exists a DMC and an input distribution X and output distribution Y.

Some Results Related to DMC

Result 1. $I_c(X, Y/Z) \geq I_c(Y/Z)$ only equality holds when $p(z/x, y) = p(z/y)$.

Proof. We have already mentioned earlier that $I_c(Y/Z)$ represents the information conveyed by Z about X and here it is equivalently defined as $I_c(Y/Z) = -\sum_y \sum_z p(y,z) \log \frac{p(y)}{p(y/z)}$.

Likewise, $I_c(X, Y/Z) = -\sum_x \sum_y \sum_z p(x,y,z) \log \frac{p(x,y)}{p(x,y/z)}$.

Now

$$I_c(Y/Z) - I(X, Y/Z) = -\sum_y \sum_z p(y,z) \log \frac{p(y)}{p(y/z)} + \sum_x \sum_y \sum_z p(x,y,z) \log \frac{p(x,y)}{p(x,y/z)}$$

$$= -\sum_x \sum_y \sum_z p(x,y,z) \log \frac{p(z)}{p(z/y)} + \sum_x \sum_y \sum_z p(x,y,z) \log \frac{p(y)}{p(z/x,y)}$$

$$\left[\because p(y,z) = \sum_x p(x,y,z) \right.$$
$$p(y,z) = p(z)\,p(y/z) = p(y)\,p(z/y)$$
$$\left. p(x,y,z) = p(z)\,p(x,y/z) = p(x,y)\,p(z/x,y) \right]$$

$$= +\sum_x \sum_y \sum_z p(x,y,z) \log \frac{p(z/y)}{p(z/x,y)} \quad (14.10a)$$

$$= E\left[\log\left(\frac{p(Z/Y)}{p(Z/X,Y)}\right)\right], \text{ where } E(X) = \text{expectation of } X$$

$$\leq \log\left\{E\left(\frac{p(Z/Y)}{p(Z/X,Y)}\right)\right\} \text{ [by Jensen's inequality of expectation]}$$

$$= \log\left(\sum_x \sum_y \sum_z \frac{p(x,y,z)\,p(z/y)\,p(x,y)}{p(x,y,z)}\right) = \log\left(\sum_x \sum_y p(x,y) \sum_z p(z/y)\right)$$

$$= \log\left(\sum_x \sum_y p(x,y)\right) \quad \left[\because \sum_z p(z/y) = 1\right]$$

$$= \log 1 = 0.$$

$\therefore$ $I_c(X, Y/Z) \geq I_c(Y/Z)$, only equality holds when $p(z/x, y) = p(z/y)$, from (14.10a).

Implication of Result 1.

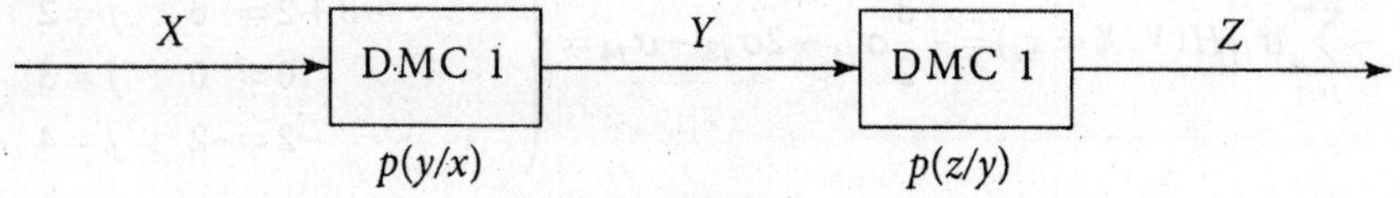

Suppose, DMC 1 is characterised by transition probability $p(y/x)$ and that of DMC 2 $p(z/y)$. If $p(z/x,y) = p(z/y)$, that is when $I_c(X.Y/Z) = I_c(Y/Z)$, the r.v. triplet (X, Y, Z) is said to form a *Markov chain* from information theoretic point of view and there exists a pair of discrete memoryless channel.

Result 2. If (X, Y, Z) forms Markov chain, then (Z, Y, X) also forms a Markov chain.

Proof. Since (X, Y, Z) forms a Markov chain, $p(z/x,y) = p(z/y)$. To prove that (Z, Y, X) also forms a Markov chain, we have to show that $p(x/y,z) = p(x/y)$.

Now, $p(x/y,z) = \dfrac{p(x,y,z)}{p(y,z)} = \dfrac{p(x,y,z)}{p(y)p(z/y)} = \dfrac{p(x,y,z)}{p(y)p(z/x,y)} = \dfrac{P(x,y,z)p(x,y)}{p(y)p(x,y,z)} = \dfrac{p(x,y)}{p(y)} = p(x/y)$.

Result 3. If (X, Y, Z) is a Markov chain. Then $I_c(X/Z) \leq I_c(X/Y)$ and $I_c(X/Z) \leq I_c(Y/Z)$.

Proof. Since (X, Y, Z) forms a Markov chain, we have $I_c(X, Y/Z) = I_c(Y/Z)$. (14.10b)

Also, we have from **Result 1**, $I_c(X, Y/Z) \geq I_c(X/Z) \Rightarrow I_c(X/Z) \leq I_c(Y/Z)$. (14.10c)

By **Result 2**, (Z, Y, X) also forms a Markov chain.

$\therefore\ I_c(Z/X) \leq I_c(Y/X) \Rightarrow I_c(X/Z) \leq I_c(X/Y)\ [\because\ I_c(X/Y) = I_c(Y/X)]$. (14.10d)

Combining (14.10c) and (14.10d), we get $I_c(X/Z) \leq I_c(X/Y)$ and $I_c(X/Z) \leq I_c(Y/Z)$.

Result 3 states that information conveyed by Z about X is less than the information conveyed by Y about X as well as Z about Y. This suggests that DMC behaves like a link information. This means that if DMC is deterministic, that is, if Y is a function of X and Z is a function of Y, then the series of DMC provides a kind of data processing configuration.

(e) *Channel capacity.* Let the channel be described by the input $X = \{x_1, x_2, \ldots, x_m\}$ and output $Y = \{y_1, y_2, \ldots, y_n\}$ and the channel matrix $(p_{j/i})$. Then we know that information processed by the channel is $I_c(X/Y) = H(X) - H(X/Y)$ or, $I_c(Y/X) = H(Y) - H(Y/X)$.

The channel capacity η_c of a channel is a number defined by $\eta_c = \max_{p_{i0}} I_c(X/Y)$ or $\max_{p_{0j}} I(Y/X)$.

Let P be a non-singular square matrix and σ_{ji} is the (j, i)th element of P^{-1}. Then the channel capacity is given by $\eta_c = \log_2 \sum_{j=1}^{n} 2^{-\sum_{i=1}^{m} \sigma_{ji} H(Y/X=x_i)}$.

Example 14.10.1. *Find the capacity of the memoryless channel by the channel matrix* $P = \begin{pmatrix} 1/2 & 1/4 & 1/4 & 0 \\ 1/4 & 1/4 & 1/4 & 1/4 \\ 0 & 0 & 1 & 0 \\ 1/2 & 0 & 0 & 1/2 \end{pmatrix}$.

Solution: Here, $\det(P) = \frac{1}{16}$ and $P^{-1} = \begin{pmatrix} 2 & -2 & 0 & 1 \\ 0 & 4 & -1 & -2 \\ 0 & 0 & 1 & 0 \\ -2 & 2 & 0 & 1 \end{pmatrix}$; $\eta_c = \log_2 \sum_{j=1}^{4} 2^{-\sum_{i=1}^{4} \sigma_{ji} H(Y/X=x_i)}$.

Now $H(Y/X = x_i) = -\sum p_{j/i} \log p_{j/i}$

$H(Y/X = x_i) = -\frac{1}{2}\log\frac{1}{2} - 2\left(\frac{1}{4}\log\frac{1}{4}\right) = \frac{3}{2}$

$H(Y/X = x_2) = 2$

$H(Y/X = x_3) = 0$

$H(Y/X = x_4) = 1.$

$$-\sum_{i=1}^{4}\sigma_{ij}H(Y/X=x_i)=-\frac{3}{2}\sigma_{j1}-2\sigma_{j2}-\sigma_{j4}=\begin{cases}-\frac{3}{2}\times 2+4-1=\ \ 0\ :\ j=1\\ -8+2=-6\ :\ j=2\\ 0=\ \ 0\ :\ j=3\\ -2=-2\ :\ j=4\end{cases}$$

$$\therefore \sum_{j=1}^{4}2^{-\sum_{i=1}^{4}\sigma_{ji}H(Y/X=x_i)}=2^0+2^{-6}+2^0+2^{-2}=\frac{145}{2^6}.$$

$\therefore\ \eta_c=\log_2\frac{145}{2^6}=1.176$ bits per symbol.

14.11 AXIOMS OF UNCERTAINTY AND ITS MATHEMATICAL DERIVATION

Suppose, $X=\{x_1,x_2,\ldots,x_m\}$ is a discrete r.v. having probability distribution

$$P=\left\{p_1,p_2,\ldots,p_m : p_i\geq 0\ \forall\ i=1,2,\ldots,m,\sum_{i=1}^{m}p_i=1\right\}.$$

$I(p_i)$ is the corresponding information associated with x_i, $i=1,2,\ldots,m$. Then we have already defined

$$H_m(p_1,p_2,\ldots,p_m)=H(X)=\sum_{i=1}^{m}p_iI(p_i)$$

is the uncertainty associated with X, which is also known as *entropy* of the probability distribution P of r.v. X in information system.

Now, let us assume that $P(X=x_i)=p_i=1/m\ \forall\ i=1,2,\ldots,m$.

Then $H(X)=H_m(1/m,1/m,\ldots,1/m)=f(m)$ (say). $f(m)$ represents the uncertainty of uniform distribution. With this definition of $f(m)$ we state the following *axioms of uncertainty.*

Axiom 1. $f(m)$ is a monotonically increasing function of m so that for $m<m', f(m)<f(m')\ \forall\ m,m'=1,2,\ldots$.

Axiom 2. For two independent discrete r.v. $X=\{x_1,x_2,\ldots,x_m\}$ and $Y=\{y_1,y_2,\ldots,y_l\}$ with $P(X=x_i)=1/m\ \forall\ i=1,2,\ldots,m$ and $P\left(Y=y_j\right)=1/l\ \forall\ j=1,2,\ldots,l$.

$$P\left(X=x_i,Y=y_j\right)=P(X=x_i)P\left(Y=y_j\right)=1/ml.$$

Then, *Axiom* 2 of uncertainty states that $f(ml)=f(m)+f(l)$.

Axiom 3. Let $X=\{x_1,x_2,\ldots,x_m\}$ with probability distribution

$$P=\left\{p_1,p_2,\ldots,p_m : p_i\geq 0, i=1,2,\ldots,m,\sum_{i=1}^{m}p_i=1\right\}$$

form two groups $\{x_1,x_2,\ldots,x_r\}$ forming *Group* A and $\{x_{r+1},x_{r+1},\ldots,x_m\}$ forming another *Group* B such that

$$P(X=x_i : x_i\in Group\ \text{A})=\frac{p_i}{\sum_{k=1}^{r}p_k}\quad\Bigg|\quad P(X=x_i : x_i\in Group\ \text{B})=\frac{p_i}{\sum_{k=r+1}^{m}p_k}.$$

$$P(X\in Group\ \text{A})+P(X\in Group\ \text{B})=\sum_{k=1}^{r}p_k+\sum_{k=r+1}^{m}p_k=\sum_{i=1}^{r}p_i=1.$$

$$\text{Uncertainty associated with } \textit{Group} \text{ A and } \textit{Group} \text{ B} = H_2\left(\sum_{k=1}^{r} p_k, \sum_{k=r+1}^{m} p_k\right).$$

$$\text{Uncertainty associated with } \textit{Group} \text{ A only} = H_r\left(\frac{p_1}{\sum_{k=1}^{r} p_k}, \frac{p_2}{\sum_{k=1}^{r} p_k}, \ldots, \frac{p_r}{\sum_{k=1}^{r} p_k}\right).$$

$$\text{Uncertainty associated with } \textit{Group} \text{ B only} = H_{m-r}\left(\frac{p_{r+1}}{\sum_{k=r+1}^{m} p_k}, \frac{p_{r+2}}{\sum_{k=r+1}^{m} p_k}, \ldots, \frac{p_m}{\sum_{k=r+1}^{m} p_k}\right).$$

$$\begin{aligned}\therefore H_m(p_1, p_2, \ldots, p_m) = H(X) &= H_2\left(\sum_{k=1}^{m} p_k, \sum_{k=r+1}^{m} p_k\right)\\ &+ \left(\sum_{k=1}^{r} p_k\right) H_r\left(\frac{p_1}{\sum_{k=1}^{m} p_k}, \frac{p_2}{\sum_{k=1}^{m} p_k}, \ldots, \frac{p_r}{\sum_{k=1}^{m} p_k}\right)\\ &+ \left(\sum_{k=1}^{m} p_k\right) H_{m-r}\left(\frac{p_{r+1}}{\sum_{k=r+1}^{m} p_k}, \frac{p_{r+2}}{\sum_{k=r+1}^{m} p_k}, \ldots, \frac{p_m}{\sum_{k=r+1}^{m} p_k}\right).\end{aligned}$$

Axiom 3 given above is known as *group axiom*.

Axiom 4. $H_2(p, 1-p)$ is a continuous function of p. By this we shall mean that a small change in probable value will correspond to a small change in the value of uncertainty.

Mathematical Derivation

The uncertainty $H_m(p_1, p_2, \ldots, p_m)$ satisfying the above axioms can be mathematically expressed by

$$H_m(p_1, p_2, \ldots, p_m) = -c\sum_{i=1}^{m} p_i \log p_i,$$

where $c > 0$ is an arbitrary constant and logarithmic base is a number greater than unity.

The mathematical derivation consists of four steps.

Step 1. First we establish the result $f(m^{\mu}) = \mu f(m)$ by mathematical induction. For $\mu = 1$, the result is true. Let the result is true for a particular μ so that $f(m^{\mu}) = \mu f(m)$.

Now $f(m^{\mu+1}) = f(m^{\mu} \cdot m) = f(m^{\mu}) + f(m)$ [by *Axiom* 2]

$$= \mu f(m) + f(m) = (\mu+1) f(m).$$

Hence, the result is true for all positive integer μ by mathematical induction.

Step 2. Here, we show that $f(m) = c\log m$, where $c > 0$ is an arbitrary constant and $m = 1, 2, \ldots$.

$$f(1) = f(1 \cdot 1) = f(1) + f(1) \text{ [by } \textit{Axiom } 2\text{]}$$

$\Rightarrow f(1) = 0$, so for $m = 1$ the result is true.

Suppose, $m > 1$ and m is a positive integer. If r is an arbitrary positive number, then there exists a positive number v such that

$$m^v \le 2^r \le m^{v+1} \Rightarrow f(m^v) \le f(2^r) \le f\left(m^{v+1}\right) \text{ [by } \textit{Axiom } 1]$$

$$\Rightarrow \frac{v}{r} \le \frac{f(2)}{f(m)} \le \frac{v+1}{r}. \tag{14.11a}$$

Again, $v \log m \le r \log 2 \le (v+1) \log m \Rightarrow \dfrac{v}{r} \le \dfrac{\log 2}{\log m} \le \dfrac{v+1}{r}$. (14.11b)

From (14.11a) and (14.11b), since both $\dfrac{f(2)}{f(m)}$ and $\dfrac{\log 2}{\log m}$ lies between $\dfrac{v}{r}$ and $\dfrac{v+1}{r}$ and as r is an arbitrary positive number, we get

$$\frac{f(2)}{f(m)} = \frac{\log 2}{\log m} \Rightarrow f(m) = c \log m, \text{ where } c = \frac{f(2)}{\log 2} > 0.$$

Step 3. Let p = r/s be a rational number and consider $H_s(1/s, 1/s, \ldots, 1/s) = f(s)$. Let first r numbers of equal probable values form a group and remaining $(s-r)$ numbers form another group so that by *Axiom* 3

$$H_s\left(\frac{1}{s}, \frac{1}{s}, \ldots, \frac{1}{s}\right) = H_2\left(\frac{r}{s}, 1-\frac{r}{s}\right) + \frac{r}{s} H_r\left(\frac{1}{s}, \frac{1}{s}, \ldots, \frac{1}{s}\right) + \left(1-\frac{r}{s}\right) H_{s-r}\left(\frac{1}{s}, \frac{1}{s}, \ldots, \frac{1}{s}\right).$$

$$\begin{aligned}
\Rightarrow f(s) &= H_2(p, 1-p) + p f(r) + (1-p) f(s-r) \\
\Rightarrow H_2(p, 1-p) &= f(s) - p f(r) - (1-p) f(s-r) \\
&= c[\log s - p \log r - (1-p)\log(s-r)] \text{ [from } \textit{Step } 2] \\
&= c[(1-p)\log s + p \log s - p \log r - (1-p)\log(s-r)] \\
&= -c\left[(1-p)\log\frac{s-r}{s} + p \log\frac{r}{s}\right] = -c[p \log p + (1-p)\log(1-p)].
\end{aligned}$$

Therefore, when p is a rational number, $H_2(p, 1-p) = -c[p \log p + (1-p)\log(1-p)]$. Hence, $H_2(p, 1-p) = -c[p \log p + (1-p)\log p]$ holds for any p by *Axiom* 4.

Step 4. Finally, we show that $H_m(p_1, p_2, \ldots, p_m) = -c \sum_{i=1}^{n} p_i \log p_i$ by mathematical induction.

The result already holds for $m = 1, 2$. Assume that it holds for particular m. Then

$$\begin{aligned}
H_{m+1}(p_1, p_2, \ldots, p_m, p_{m+1}) &= H_2\{(p_1, p_2, \ldots, p_m)\ p_{m+1}\} \\
&\quad + (p_1 + p_2, \cdots + p_m)\, H_m\left(\frac{p_1}{\sum_{i=1}^{m} p_i}, \frac{p_2}{\sum_{i=1}^{m} p_i}, \ldots, \frac{p_m}{\sum_{i=1}^{m} p_i}\right) + p_{m+1} H_1(1) \\
&= -c\left[(p_1 + p_2 + \cdots + p_m)\log(p_1 + p_2 + \cdots + p_m) + p_{m+1}\log p_{m+1}\right] \\
&\quad + (p_1 + p_2 + \cdots + p_m)\left[-c \sum_{i=1}^{m}\left(\frac{p_i}{\sum_{i=1}^{m} p_i}\right)\log\left(\frac{p_i}{\sum_{i=1}^{m} p_i}\right)\right] + 0 \\
&= -c \sum_{i=1}^{m+1} p_i \log p_i.
\end{aligned}$$

Therefore, by mathematical induction, $H_m(p_1, p_2, \ldots, p_m) = -c\sum_{i=1}^{m} p_i \log p_i$.

14.12 MEASURE OF UNCERTAINTY FOR CONTINUOUS VARIATE

Let the r.v. is a continuous variate with density function $f(x)$ over the interval $[a, b]$. Consider the partition of the interval $[a, b]$ by a set of points $x_0, x_1, \ldots, x_n$, where $a = x_0$ and $b = x_n$.

$$\Delta x_i = x_i - x_{i-1},\ i = 1, 2, \ldots, n. \tag{14.12a}$$

An approximation to p_i is given by $f(x_i)\Delta x_i$ so that

$$-\sum_{i=1}^{n} p_i \log p_i \cong -\sum_{i=1}^{n} f(x_i)(\Delta x_i)\log(f(x_i)\Delta x_i) = -\sum_{i=1}^{n} f(x_i)\Delta x_i \log f(x_i) - \sum_{i=1}^{n} f(x_i)\Delta x_i \log \Delta x_i.$$

If we take all partition interval lengths to be equal, $h = \Delta x_i = \dfrac{b-a}{n}$, we get

$$-\sum_{i=1}^{n} p_i \log p_i \simeq -\sum_{i=1}^{n} f(x_i)\log f(x_i)\Delta x_i - \log h \sum_{i=1}^{n} f(x_i)\Delta x_i. \tag{14.12b}$$

The right-hand side of (14.12b) can be approximated by

$$\text{RHS} \cong -\int_a^b f(x)\log f(x)\,dx - \log h \int_a^b f(x)\,dx = -\int_a^b f(x)\log f(x)\,dx - \log h, \tag{14.12c}$$

since $\int_a^b f(x)\,dx = 1$.

Similarly, if $\{q_1, q_2, \ldots, q_n\}$ is the probability distribution corresponding to the density function $g(x)$ we can approximate

$$-\sum_{i=1}^{n} q_i \log q_i \text{ by } -\int_a^b g(x)\log(g(x))\,dx - \log h. \tag{14.12d}$$

Now in (14.12c) and (14.12d) $-\log h \to \infty$ as $h \to 0$. To get rid of this troublesome term, we take the difference of both sides of these equations and thus find that

$$\left(-\sum_{i=1}^{n} p_i \log p_i\right) - \left(-\sum_{i=1}^{n} q_i \log q_i\right)$$

can be replaced approximately by

$$\left(-\int_a^b f(x)\log f(x)\,dx\right) - \left(-\int_a^b g(x)\log g(x)\,dx\right). \tag{14.12e}$$

The above discussion suggests, but does not prove, that we should consider

$$-\int_a^b f(x)\log f(x)\,dx \tag{14.12f}$$

to be a measure of uncertainty or entropy for the continuous variate distribution with probability density function $f(x)$. However, we have to be careful because the above discussion is not rigorous.

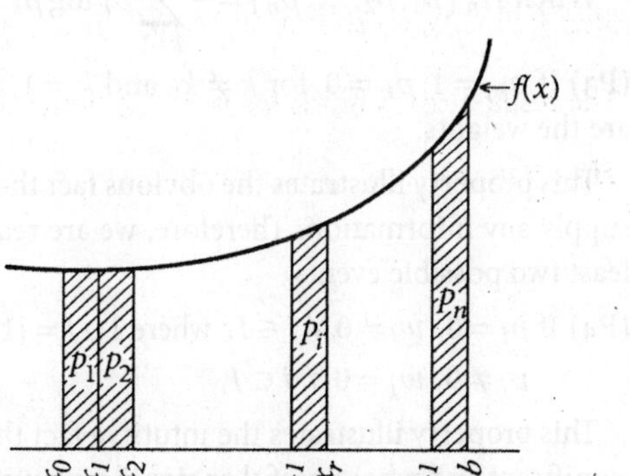

Fig. Approximation of $-\sum_{i=1}^{n} p_i \log p_i$ by $\int_b^a f(x)\log f(x)\,dx$

14.13 WEIGHTED ENTROPY

We have seen that Shannon's entropy is a measure both of the uncertainty and of the information supplied by a probabilistic experiment. Underlying the importance of Shannon's entropy, it is necessary to notice at the same time that this formula gives us the measure of information as a function of the probabilities with which various events occur only. But there exist many fields dealing with random events, where it is necessary to take into account both these probabilities and some qualitative characteristics of event.

Consider a probabilistic experiment, whose corresponding probability space has finite number of elementary events $E_1, E_2, \ldots, E_n$ with the objective probabilities of these events given respectively by the numbers $p_k \geq 0, k = 1, 2, \ldots, n, \sum_{k=1}^{n} p_k = 1$. The different elementary events E_k depend more or less relevantly upon the experimenter's goal or upon some qualitative characteristic of the system taken into consideration, i.e., they have different objective or subjective weights. The weight of an event may be either independent of or dependent on its objective probability.

In order to distinguish the events $E_1, E_2, \ldots, E_n$ of a good directed experiment according to their importance w.r.t. a given qualitative characteristic of the system taken into consideration, we shall ascribe to each event E_k a non-negative number $w_k \geq 0$ directly proportional to its importance or significance. We shall call w_k, the weight of the elementary event E_k.

Definition. We define the weighted entropy by the expression

$$I_n(w_1, w_2, \ldots, w_n; p_1, p_2, \ldots, p_n) = -\sum_{k=1}^{n} w_k p_k \log p_k.$$

Let us notice some *properties of weighted entropy.*

(P1) We have always $I_n(w_1, w_2, \ldots, w_n; p_1, p_2, \ldots, p_n) \geq 0$.

(P2) If $w_1 = w_2 = \cdots = w_n = w$, then

$$I_n(w_1, w_2, \ldots, w_n; p_1, p_2, \ldots, p_n) = -w \sum_{k=1}^{n} p_k \log p_k = w H_n(p_1, p_2, \ldots, p_n).$$

When $H_n(p_1, p_2, \ldots, p_n) = -\sum_{k=1}^{n} p_k \log p_k = S_n(p_1, p_2, \ldots, p_n)$ is the Shannon's entropy.

(P3) If $p_{k_0} = 1, p_k = 0$, for $k \neq k_0$ and $k = 1, 2, \ldots, n$, then $I_n(w_1, w_2, \ldots, w_n; p_1, p_2, \ldots, p_n) = 0$ whatever are the weights.

This property illustrates the obvious fact that an experiment of which only one event is possible does not supply any information. Therefore, we are really interested only in the probabilistic experiment having at least two possible events.

(P4) If $p_i = 0,\ w_i \neq 0\ \forall\ i \in I$, where $I \cup J = \{1, 2, \ldots, n\}, I \cap J = \phi$, then $I_n(w_1, w_2, \ldots, w_n; p_1, p_2, \ldots, p_n) = 0$.
$p_j \neq 0,\ w_j = 0\ \forall\ j \in J$,

This property illustrates the intutitve fact that an experiment, whose possible events are useless or non-significant and whose useful or significant events are impossible, supplies a total information equal to zero, even if the corresponding Shannon's entropy $S_n(p_1, p_2, \ldots, p_n)$ is different from zero, provided that the set J has at least two elements. In particular, when all events have zero weights, we get $I_n = 0$, even if S_n is not null, i.e., if there exists $0 < p_k < 1$.

(P5) We have $I_{n+1}(w_1, w_2, \ldots, w_n w_{n+1}; p_1, p_2, \ldots, p_n) = I_n(w_1, w_2, \ldots, w_n; p_1, p_2, \ldots, p_n)$ whatever the weights $w_1, w_2, \ldots, w_n, w_{n+1}$ and the complete system of probabilities.

(P6) For every non-negative real number λ, we have

$$I_n(\lambda w_1, \lambda w_2, \ldots, \lambda w_n; p_1, p_2, \ldots, p_n) = \lambda I_n(w_1, w_2, w_n; p_1, p_2, \ldots, p_n).$$

So far we have not imposed any restriction on the weights ascribed to the elementary events of the probabilistic experiment (except that they are non-negative real numbers). Let us suppose that the weight of the union of two incompatible events is the mean value of the respective event's weight, i.e.,

$$W(E \cap F) = \frac{P(E)W(E) + P(F)W(F)}{P(E) + P(F)}$$

for any incompatible events E, F, where $W(E)$ is the weight of the event E and $P(E)$ is the probability of the same event E.

14.14 GENERAL CONCLUSION

In recent years unifying idea and extremal principle embracing a broad spectrum of subjects are becoming more and more important in modern science. IT has penetrated into almost all human endeavour providing enormous impetus for mathematical modelling of a diverse area of application in a wide range subjects like Physics, Chemistry, Biology, Psychology, Economics to mention a few. The word entropy is a much over used word in ordinary parlance suggesting a transformation from order to disorder. Although it originated in the literature on thermodynamics, its usage has penetrated almost all disciplines, mainly because of its association with the concept of information as envisaged by Claude Shannon (1948) in the mathematical theory of communication. His objective was to measure the amount sent, amount of information received and the amount of information lost. Shannon's discovery of a measure of entropy comes in connection with communication theory and very soon his concept of entropy has a pervasive influence on several other disciplines. This particular chapter provides the reader only a fundamental concept of information and entropy and their some uses in real life.

Multiple Choice Questions

Below each question four alternatives are given. Only one of the alternatives or more than one of the alternatives is/are correct. Credit will be given only on identification of all the correct options in a question. No credit will be given if any incorrect option is marked as correct answer. No partial credit is allowed.

1. Let S be a finite subset of a vector space V. Then
   (a) S generates V and S is linearly independent.
   (b) S is a maximal linearly independent.
   (c) S is a minimal generating set of V.
   (d) Every element of V cannot be expressed as a linear combination of elements of S.
2. If A and B are two matrices of same order, then
   (a) $\text{rank}\,(A+B) \leq \text{rank}\,(A) + \text{rank}\,(B)$
   (b) $\text{rank}\,(AB) \leq \min\{\text{rank}\,(A), \text{rank}\,(B)\}$.
   (c) $\text{rank}\,(AB\text{-}I) \leq \text{rank}\,(A\text{-}I) + \text{rank}\,(B\text{-}I)$.
   (d) $\text{rank}\,(A^T A) \neq \text{rank}\,(A)$.
3. Let $A = (a_{ij})$ be a square matrix of order n. Suppose, $\lambda_i, i = 1,2,\ldots,n$ be the eigenvalues not necessarily distinct of A. Then
   (a) $|A| \neq \prod_{i=1}^{n} \lambda_i$.
   (b) $\sum_{i=1}^{n} \lambda_i = \sum_{i=1}^{n} a_{ii}$.
   (c) The similar matrices may or may not have the same trace.
   (d) If X is an eigenvector of A corresponding to eigenvalue λ_1, then X is not an eigenvector of A^n corresponding to the eigenvalue λ_1^n.
4. Which of the following statements is/are true?
   (a) A complex number α is a root of the minimal polynomial of a matrix A if α is an eigenvalue of A.
   (b) The minimal polynomial of a diagonal matrix A is $\sum_{i=1}^{n}(\lambda - d_i)$, where $d_i (i = 1,2,\ldots,n)$ are distinct diagonal elements of A.
   (c) The constant term in the minimal polynomial of A is non-zero, iff A is non-singular.
   (d) The minimal polynomial of A divides the characteristic polynomial of A.

5. Let $f(n)=\begin{vmatrix} n & n+1 & n+2 \\ {}^{n}P_{n} & {}^{n+1}P_{n+1} & {}^{n+2}P_{n+2} \\ {}^{n}C_{n} & {}^{n+1}C_{n+1} & {}^{n+2}C_{n+2} \end{vmatrix}$, where the symbols have their usual meanings. Then $f(n)$ is divisible by (a) n^2+n+1 (b) $(n+1)!$ (c) $n!$ (d) $\frac{n+1}{2}!$

6. Which of the following statements is/are true?
   (a) In an LP model replacing $\leq$ or $\geq$ by = in the constraints can improve the value of the objective function.
   (b) In a two-dimensional LP solution, the objective function can assume the same value at two distinct extreme points.
   (c) In an LP model the feasible solution space can be affected, where redundant constraints are deleted.
   (d) A two-dimensional space with two equality constraints can include at most one feasible point provided that the resulting two lines do not coincide (i.e., the two equations are independent).

7. Consider an LPP: Optimise $Z=\boldsymbol{cx}$
   subject to $A\boldsymbol{x}\ (\leq, \geq)\ \boldsymbol{b}$
   $\boldsymbol{x}\geq \boldsymbol{0}$
   (a) The objective function represents hyperplane.
   (b) The constraints with signs $\leq$ or $\geq$ are the half spaces produced by the hyperplanes.
   (c) If $\boldsymbol{x}_B$ be the set of feasible solutions (if it exists), then it is a closed convex set.
   (d) The hyperplane has no extreme point and hence they are not a convex set.

8. Which of the following statements is/are true?
   (a) If $V(F)$ be a finite dimensional vector space of dimension n, then any set of n linearly independent vectors in V forms a basis of V.
   (b) If the vectors $(1,-1,2)$, $(0,k,3)$ and $(-1,2,3)$ are linearly dependent, then $k=\frac{5}{3}$.
   (c) The set of all non-zero polynomials in x of degree ≤ 2 a vector space.
   (d) The set of all polynomials in x of degree ≤ 2 a vector space.

9. In R^3, let $\boldsymbol{\alpha}=(1,2,1)$, $\boldsymbol{\beta}=(3,1,5)$ and $\boldsymbol{\gamma}=(3,-4,7)$. Let $L(S)$ and $L(T)$ the subspace spanned by $S=\{\boldsymbol{\alpha},\boldsymbol{\beta}\}$ and $T=\{\boldsymbol{\alpha},\boldsymbol{\beta},\boldsymbol{\gamma}\}$ respectively, then (a) $L(S)\subseteq L(T)$, (b) $L(T)\subseteq L(S)$, (c) $L(T)=L(S)$, (d) None.

10. For the matrix $A=\begin{pmatrix} 1 & 0 & 0 \\ 1 & 0 & 1 \\ 0 & 1 & 0 \end{pmatrix}$,
   (a) Characteristic equation of A is $\lambda^3-2\lambda^2-\lambda+1=0$.
   (b) For every integer $n\geq 3$, $A^{n-2}+A^2-I=A^n$.
   (c) One of the eigenvalues is unity.
   (d) All the diagonal elements of A^{50} is one.

11. In R^3, $\boldsymbol{\alpha}_1=(1,-3,2)$, $\boldsymbol{\alpha}_2=(2,4,1)$, $\boldsymbol{\alpha}_3=(3,1,3)$, $\boldsymbol{\alpha}_4=(1,1,1)$.
   (a) $\{\boldsymbol{\alpha}_1,\boldsymbol{\alpha}_2,\boldsymbol{\alpha}_3\}$ forms a basis (b) $\{\boldsymbol{\alpha}_1,\boldsymbol{\alpha}_2,\boldsymbol{\alpha}_4\}$ forms a basis
   (c) $\{\boldsymbol{\alpha}_1,\boldsymbol{\alpha}_3,\boldsymbol{\alpha}_4\}$ does not form a basis (d) $\{\boldsymbol{\alpha}_2,\boldsymbol{\alpha}_3,\boldsymbol{\alpha}_4\}$ does not form a basis.

12. Which of the following statements is/are true?
    (a) The solution of a homogeneous system $AX = 0$ in n unknowns forms a subspace of vector space $V_n(F)$.
    (b) If $X(A)$ be the solution space of the system $AX = 0$, then rank (A) + rank $X(A) > n$.
    (c) The set of n vectors $\{\boldsymbol{a}_1, \boldsymbol{a}_2, \ldots, \boldsymbol{a}_n\}$ in R^n, where $\boldsymbol{a}_i = (a_{i1}, a_{i2}, \ldots, a_{in})$, $i = 1, 2, \ldots, n$ is linearly independent if and only if $\det\left(a_{ij}\right) = 0$.
    (d) If $(\boldsymbol{a}_1, \boldsymbol{a}_2, \ldots, \boldsymbol{a}_n)$ be a basis of $V_n(F)$ and $B = \left(\boldsymbol{\beta}_1, \boldsymbol{\beta}_2, \ldots, \boldsymbol{\beta}_{n+1}\right)$ be any set of $(n+1)$ vectors in $V_n(F)$, then B is linearly dependent in $V_n(F)$.
13. Let A be a $p \times n$ matrix and B be a $q \times n$ matrix. Define
    System 1. $A\boldsymbol{x} < 0$, $B\boldsymbol{x} = 0$ for some $\boldsymbol{x} \in R^n$.
    System 2. $A^T\boldsymbol{u} + B^T\boldsymbol{v} = \boldsymbol{0}$ for some non-zero $(\boldsymbol{u}, \boldsymbol{v})$ with $\boldsymbol{u} \geq \boldsymbol{0}$.
    (a) If *System* 1 has a solution, then *System* 2 has no solution.
    (b) If *System* 1 has no solution, then *System* 2 has a solution.
    (c) Both *System* 1 and *System* 2 have solutions.
    (d) If B has full rank, then exactly one of the systems has a solution.
14. Let $S_1 = \{\boldsymbol{x} : x_2 \geq e^{-x_1}\}$ and $S_2 = \{\boldsymbol{x} : x_2 \leq -e^{-x_1}\}$.
    (a) S_1 and S_2 are not disjoint.
    (b) S_1 and S_2 are disjoint convex sets.
    (c) A hyperplane always separates S_1 and S_2.
    (d) There exist two non-zero vectors $\boldsymbol{p}_1$ and $\boldsymbol{p}_2$ such that $\boldsymbol{p}_1\boldsymbol{s}_1 + \boldsymbol{p}_2\boldsymbol{s}_2 \geq 0$ for all $\boldsymbol{s}_1 \in S_1$ and $\boldsymbol{s}_2 \in S_2$.
15. Consider the LPP.
    Minimise $Z = x_1 + x_2$
    $$\begin{aligned} \text{subject to } 5x_1 + 9x_2 &\leq 45 \\ x_1 + x_2 &\geq 2 \\ x_2 &\geq 4 \\ x_1, x_2 &\geq 0. \end{aligned}$$
    (a) The LPP admits a unique feasible solution.
    (b) The LPP has an infinite number of feasible solutions.
    (c) There are alternative optimal solutions.
    (d) The origin coincides with the boundary line $x_1 + x_2 = 2$ of the feasible region.
16. Consider the LPP.
    Maximize $Z = 3x_1 + 4x_2$
    $$\begin{aligned} \text{subject to } x_1 - x_2 &\geq 0 \\ -x_1 + 3x_2 &\leq 3 \\ x_1, x_2 &\geq 0. \end{aligned}$$
    (a) The feasible region is a closed polygon.
    (b) The profit line is moved indefinitely from the origin parallel to itself.
    (c) There is a finite maximum value of Z within the feasible region.
    (d) There are alternative optimal solutions.

17. Consider the LPP.

Maximize $Z = x_1 + x_2$

subject to $x_1 - x_2 \geq 0$

$2x_1 - x_2 \leq -2$

$x_1, x_2 \geq 0.$

The problem has (a) an unbounded solution (b) one optimal solution (c) more than one optimal solution (d) no feasible solution.

18. Consider the system of equations: $x_1 + 2x_3 = 1$

$x_2 + x_3 = 4.$

(a) $\left(0, \frac{7}{2}, \frac{1}{2}\right)$ is the only basic feasible solution of the system.

(b) $(-7, 0, 4)$ is one of the degenerate basic solutions of the system.

(c) $(1, 4, 0)$ is one of the non-degenerate basic solutions.

(d) $(1, 0, 3)$ is a basic feasible solution of the system.

19. Which of the following statements is/are true?

(a) In an LP with m constraints, a simplex iteration mav include more than m positive basic variables.

(b) In the simplex method, the optimality conditions for the maximisation and minimisation problems are different.

(c) In the simplex method, the feasibility conditions for the maximisation and minimisation problems are different.

(d) In a simplex iteration, the pivot element can be zero or negative.

20. In R^2, define $X = \left\{(x_1, x_2) \mid x_2 - 3 \geq x_1^2, x_1, x_2 \geq 0\right\}$, $Y = \left\{(y_1, y_2) \mid y_2^2 \geq 4y_1\right\}$, $Z = \{(z_1, z_2) \mid z_1 z_2 \leq 4\}$ and $T = \{(t_1, t_2) \mid |t_1| \leq 1, |t_2| \leq 1\}$.

(a) X is not a convex set.

(b) Y and Z are convex sets.

(c) Y is convex but Z is non-convex.

(d) Extreme points of T are $(1, 1), (-1, 1), (-1, -1), (1, -1)$.

21. An intermediate tableau of an LPP by simplex method is given in an incomplete form.

(a) The row giving $(z_j - c_j)$ is $(7, 0, 4, 10, 0, 0)$.

(b) This gives the optimal solution table of the problem.

(c) y_4 is the entering vector in case the above table is not the optimal table.

(d) y_5 is the departing vector.

		c_j	3	5	4	0	0	0
c_B	x_B	b	y_1	y_2	y_3	y_4	y_5	y_6
5	y_2	9	2	1	0	2	0	0
0	y_5	9	3	0	4	3	1	0
0	y_6	14	4	0	5	1	0	0
		$z_j - c_j$						

22. The first tableau of an LPP by simplex method is given below (for a maximisation primal problem) in an incomplete form.

		c_j							
c_B	x_B	b	y_1	y_2	y_3	y_4	y_5	y_6	y_7
0	y_5	20	−4	6	5	−4	1	0	0
0	y_6	10	3	−2	4	1	0	1	0
0	y_7	20	8	−3	3	2	0	0	1
		$z_j - c_j$	−4	−1	−3	−5	0	0	0

(a) The objective row c_j of the incomplete table (4, 1, 3, 5, 0, 0, 0).

(b) One of the constraints of the problem is $4x_1 - 6x_2 - 5x_3 + 4x_4 \geq -20$.

(c) The dual objective function of the problem is min $W = -20v_1 + 10v_2 + 20v_3$.

(d) One of the constraints of the dual problem is $-5v_1 + v_2 + 3v_3 \geq 3$.

23. Which of the following statements is/are true?

(a) An unrestricted primal variable will have the effect of yielding an equality dual constraint.

(b) If the number of primal variables is much smaller than the number of constraints, it is more efficient to obtain the solution of the primal by solving its dual.

(c) When the primal problem is non-optimal, the dual problem is automatically infeasible.

(d) If the primal is infeasible, the dual always has unbounded optimum.

24. Consider the LPP.

Maximum $Z = 5x_1 + 2x_2 + 3x_3$

subject to $x_1 + 2x_2 + 2x_3 \leq b_1$

$x_1 - 5x_2 - 6x_3 \leq b_2$

$x_1, x_2, x_3 \geq 0.$

The following table in an incomplete form gives the optimal solution of the above problem.

		c_j	5	2	3	0	0
c_B	x_B	b	y_1	y_2	y_3	y_4	y_5
5	y_1	30	1	α	2	1	0
0	y_5	10	0	β	−8	−1	1
		$z_j - c_j$	0	γ	7	δ	0

The values of: (a) $\alpha = 23, \quad \beta = 5, \quad \gamma = -10, \quad \delta = 5$

(b) $\alpha = -10, \quad \beta = 5, \quad \gamma = 23, \quad \delta = 5$

(c) $\alpha = 5, \quad \beta = -10, \quad \gamma = 23, \quad \delta = 5$

(d) $\alpha = 5, \quad \beta = -10, \quad \gamma = 5, \quad \delta = 23.$

25. Consider the following LP in standard form.

Maximize $Z = 4x_1 + 14x_2$

subject to $2x_1 + 7x_2 + x_3 = 21$

$7x_1 + 2x_2 + x_4 = 21$

$x_1, x_2, x_3, x_4 \geq 0.$

Each of the following cases provides an inverse matrix and its corresponding basic variables for the LP above:

$$A_1 : (x_2, x_4); \begin{pmatrix} \frac{1}{7} & 0 \\ -\frac{2}{7} & 1 \end{pmatrix}; \qquad A_2 : (x_2, x_3); \begin{pmatrix} 0 & \frac{1}{2} \\ 1 & -\frac{7}{2} \end{pmatrix};$$

$$A_3 : (x_2, x_1); \begin{pmatrix} \frac{7}{45} & \frac{2}{45} \\ -\frac{2}{45} & \frac{7}{45} \end{pmatrix}; \qquad A_4 : (x_1, x_4); \begin{pmatrix} \frac{1}{2} & 0 \\ -\frac{7}{2} & 1 \end{pmatrix}.$$

(a) Both A_1 and A_2 are feasible solutions. (b) A_1 is feasible but A_2 is not a feasible solution.
(c) A_3 is not a feasible solution. (d) A_4 is a feasible solution.

26. Which of the following statements is/are true?
(a) In dual-simplex method, the LP starting solution must be optimal and infeasible.
(b) In the dual-simplex method, if none of the constraint coefficients associated with the leaving variable equation are negative, the LPP has no feasible solution.
(c) The addition of a new activity can improve the objective value.
(d) If we change both the right-hand side of the constraints and the coefficients of the objective function, we can destroy both optimality and feasibility of the solution.

27. Consider the primal LPP.
Maximise $Z = 3x_1 + x_2 + 2x_2 - x_4$
subject to $2x_1 - x_2 + 3x_3 + x_4 = 1$
$x_1 + x_2 - x_3 + x_4 = 3$
$x_1, x_2 \geq 0$; x_3, x_4 are unrestricted.
(a) The objective function of the dual problem is: minimise $W = v_1 + 3v_2 - v_3$.
(b) One of the constraints of the dual problem is: $3v_1 - v_2 \leq 20$.
(c) The number of equality constraints of the dual are three.
(d) All the dual variables are unrestricted.

28. If $(\boldsymbol{x}, \boldsymbol{x}_s)$ and $(\boldsymbol{v}, \boldsymbol{v}_s)$ be feasible solutions to the primal and the associated dual problem, then
(a) Both $(\boldsymbol{x}, \boldsymbol{x}_s)$ and $(\boldsymbol{v}, \boldsymbol{v}_s)$ are optimal solutions provided the conditions of complementary slackness holds.
(b) Both $(\boldsymbol{x}, \boldsymbol{x}_s)$ and $(\boldsymbol{v}, \boldsymbol{v}_s)$ are optimal without satisfying the conditions of complementary slackness conditions.
(c) $(\boldsymbol{x}, \boldsymbol{x}_s)$ is optimal but $(\boldsymbol{v}, \boldsymbol{v}_s)$ is non-optimal.
(d) $(\boldsymbol{v}, \boldsymbol{v}_s)$ is optimal but $(\boldsymbol{x}, \boldsymbol{x}_s)$ is non-optimal.

29. Which of the following statements is/are true?
(a) The set-up cost in an inventory situation is independent of the size of the order quantity.
(b) It is permissible to incur both holding and shortage costs in the same inventory model.
(c) The optimum order quantity decreases with the increase in the shortage cost.
(d) As the holding cost increases, the optimum order quantity also increases.

30. If in an inventory model demand is constant over time with instantaneous replenishment and no shortages, k be the set-up cost incurred every time an order is placed, H, the holding cost per unit inventory per unit time and β is the rate of demand occurring per unit time, then Wilson's economy lot size is given by

(a) $\dfrac{2k\beta}{h}$ (b) $\sqrt{\dfrac{2k\beta}{h}}$ (c) $\sqrt{\dfrac{2k}{\beta}+h}$ (d) $\sqrt{\dfrac{2k}{h}+\dfrac{\beta}{k}}$.

31. The daily demand for a commodity is approximately 100 units. Every time an order is placed, a fixed cost of ₹100 is incurred. The daily holding cost per unit inventory is ₹0.02. Then

(a) Economy lot size = 100 units (b) Economy lot size = 1000 units

(c) Optimum cycle length = 10 days (d) Reorder point = 2 days, if the lead time is 12 days.

32. Which of the following statements is/are true?

(a) In queueing theory, if the arrivals occur according to the Poisson distribution, the inter-arrival time is exponential.

(b) Under the Poisson assumption, two arrivals can occur during a very small time interval.

(c) The arrival rate in the Poisson distribution equals the mean of the exponential inter-arrival time.

(d) An arriving customer may balk if he expects a long waiting time.

33. Consider the queueing situation with one server in which arrival occurs at the rate $\lambda = 3$ per hour and service is performed at the rate of $\mu = 8$ per hour. The probabilities p_n of n customers in the system are computed for the situation as given in the following table.

n	0	1	2	3	4	5	6	7	≥8
p_n	0.625	0.234	0.088	0.033	0.012	0.005	0.002	0.001	0

Which of the following measures is/are true?

(a) Expected number in the system = 0.6 customers.

(b) Expected waiting time in the system = 0.2 hour.

(c) Expected waiting time in the queue = 0.075 hour.

(d) Expected number in the queue = 0.225 customers.

34. In $(M/M/1):(GD/\infty/\infty)$ queueing model arrivals and departures are Poisson with rates λ and μ.

(a) Steady-state probabilities p_n of n customers follows a geometric distribution.

(b) If $\rho = \dfrac{\lambda}{\mu}$ the convergence of $\sum_{n=0}^{\infty} \rho^n$ is ensured because $\rho > 1$.

(c) Expected number in the system $L_s = \dfrac{\rho}{\rho - 1}$.

(d) Expected number in the queue $L_q = L_s + \dfrac{\lambda}{\mu}$.

35. In a car-wash service facility, information gathered indicates that cars arrive for service according to a Poisson distribution with mean 5 per hour. The time for washing and cleaning of each car varies but is found to be followed an exponential distribution with mean 10 minutes per car. The facility cannot handle more than one car at a time.

(a) To analyse this situation the results of $(M/M/1):(GD/\infty/\infty)$ are appropriate.

(b) Parking spaces available for number of cars that arrive at the facility = 4 cars.

(c) The percentage of time the facility is idle = 17% (approximately).

(d) A car is expected to wait = 2 hours.

36. Which of the following statements is/are true in the context of queueing theory.

36. Which of the following statements is/are true in the context of queueing theory.
   (a) If the time between successive arrivals is exponential, the time between the occurrences of every third arrival is also exponential.
   (b) A knowledge of the steady-state probabilities of the number of customers in the system can be used to determine all the basic measures of performance in queueing situation, regardless of the types of the distributions describing the arrivals and departures.
   (c) The output of a Poisson queueing model (number of departures) is also Poisson.
   (d) The distribution of waiting time is independent of the service discipline used in selecting the waiting customers for service.

37. A company uses 10000 units per year of an item. The purchase price is ₹1 per item, ordering cost ₹25 per order and carrying cost per year is 12% of the inventory level. The EOQ is equal to
   (a) 2080 units (b) 2083 units (c) 2085 units (d) 2087 units.

38. Assume that the contract specifies merely some total demand D, to be satisfied during some long time period T, with the proviso that the output will be shipped to the customer uniformly between production run. If c_3 is the set-up cost per production run, c_1 holding cost per unit for one time unit, then the total cost TC(q) attains its minimum when the value of the quantity produced at each run q is given by
   (a) $q=\sqrt{\dfrac{2c_3D}{c_1T}}$ (b) $q=\sqrt{\dfrac{2c_1D}{c_3T}}$ (c) $q=\sqrt{\dfrac{c_3D}{T}+c_1}$ (d) $q=\sqrt{\dfrac{c_3D}{c_1T}}$.

39. Consider the following data:
Assume an ordering cost of ₹5 and holding cost of 10%. The EOQ (q) and total variable cost (C) of items are:

Item(s)	Annual demand	Unit price (₹)
A	800 units	0.02
B	400 units	1.00
C	392 units	8.00
D	13800 units	0.20

   (a) $q_A=2000, C_A=4$ (b) $q_B=205, C_B=20$
   (c) $q_C=75, C_C=55$ (d) $q_D=2627, C_D=54.5.$

40. For the *Problem* 39 above, number of orders per year (i.e., EOQ frequency) n is given by
   (a) $n_A=0.3$ (b) $n_B=2$ (c) $n_C=5.2$ (d) $n_D=5.6.$

41–42. Based on the following statement:

Consider Birth-Death process, where the probability of a birth occurring in a small time interval Δt is considered as $\lambda_n\Delta t+O(\Delta t)$ and death occurring in Δt is considered as $\mu_n\Delta t+O(\Delta t)$, when the system is in state E_n. If the system is in E_n at time t, then it will remain in E_n at time $t+\Delta t$ provided there is no birth and no death or one birth and one death and in E_{n-1} and had a birth or in E_{n+1} and had a death. Let arrival rate λ_n and service rate μ_n depending on n. Then

41. (a) Steady state probability $p_n=p_0\prod_{i=0}^{n-1}\dfrac{\lambda_i}{\mu_i},\ n\geq 1.$
   (b) Steady state probability $p_n=p_0\prod_{i=0}^{n-1}\dfrac{\lambda_i}{\mu_{i+1}},\ n\geq 1.$
   (c) $p_0=1/S$
   (d) $p_0=S$, where $S=1+\dfrac{\lambda_0}{\mu_1}+\dfrac{\lambda_0\lambda_1}{\mu_1\mu_2}+\cdots+\infty$, a convergent series.

42. (a) If $\lambda_n = \lambda, \mu_n = \mu$ for all n, $p_n = \rho^n(1-\rho)$, where $\rho = \dfrac{\lambda}{\mu} < 1, n > 0$.

(b) If $\lambda_n = \dfrac{\lambda}{n+1}, \mu_n = \mu$ for all n, $S = e^{\rho}$, where $\rho = \dfrac{\lambda}{\mu}$.

(c) If $\lambda_n = \lambda, \mu_n = n\mu$ for all n, $p_n = \dfrac{e^{-\rho}\rho^n}{n!}$, where $\rho = \dfrac{\lambda}{\mu}$.

(d) If $\lambda_n = \dfrac{\lambda}{n+1}, \mu_n = \mu$ for all n, p_n follows exponential distribution.

43. Let $X(t)$ be the number of customers in $(M/M/1):(GD/\infty/\infty)$ queueing system with arrival rate $\lambda > 0$ and service rate $\mu > 0$. The process $X(t)$ is a

(a) Poisson process with birth rate $\lambda - \mu$.

(b) Pure birth process with birth rate $\lambda - \mu$.

(c) Birth and death process with birth rate λ and death rate μ.

(d) Birth and death process with birth rate $1/\lambda$ and death rate $1/\mu$.

44. At any iteration of the usual simplex method if there is at least one basic variable in the basis at zero level and all $z_j - c_j \geq 0$ the current solution is

(a) infeasible (b) unbounded (c) non-degenerate (d) degenerate.

45. If for feasible solution $\boldsymbol{x_B}$, the problem Minimise $Z = \boldsymbol{cx}$ subject to $A\boldsymbol{x} = \boldsymbol{b}, \boldsymbol{x} \geq \boldsymbol{0}, z_j - c_j \leq 0$ for all j, then $\boldsymbol{x_B}$ is

(a) an optimal solution (b) a non-optimal solution

(c) an only basic feasible solution (d) none of these.

46. Which of the following statements is/are true in the context of game theory?

(a) Every two-person zero-sum game can be represented by a pair of primal dual LP.

(b) If two-person zero-sum game is stable, neither player can improve his expected payoff by changing his minimax (maximin) strategies.

(c) In a two-person zero-sum game, if the optimal solution requires one player to use a pure strategy, the other player must do the same.

(d) The addition of a constant to all the elements of a payoff matrix in a two-person zero-sum game can affect only the value of the game, not the optimal mix of strategies.

47. A mixed strategy game in Game theory can be solved by

(a) Matrix method (b) Graphical method (c) Algebraic method (d) All of the above.

48. Given two games (G1) and (G2):

(G1): Player A (rows) vs Player B (columns)

	Player B		
(G1): Player A	1	q	6
	p	5	10
	6	2	3

(G2): Player B (rows) vs Player A (columns)

	Player A		
(G2): Player B	2	4	5
	10	7	q
	4	p	6

The range of values of p and q that will render the entry (2, 2) a saddle point of the games (G1) and (G2) are:

(a) G1: $p \geq 5, q \leq 2$ (b) G2: $p \leq 7, q \geq 7$ (c) G1: $p \geq 5, q \leq 5$ (d) G2: $p \geq 7, q \geq 7$.

49. In a game of matching coins, player A wins ₹2 if there are two heads, wins nothing if there are two tails and loses ₹1, when there are one head and one tail.

(a) the payoff matrix of above game problem is as below: Player B

Player A	2	−1
	−1	0

(b) best strategy for player A: (3, 1)

(c) best strategy for player B: (1, 4)

(d) value of game player A: ₹$\left(-\frac{1}{4}\right)$

50. Let x_1, x_2, x_3 and y_1, y_2, y_3, y_4 be the probabilities with which player A and player B select their pure strategies of the following rectangular game and V be the value of the game.

Player B

		y_1	y_2	y_3	y_4
Player A	x_1	5	7	4	10
	x_2	4	3	7	9
	x_3	1	2	5	6

(a) One of the constraints of the primal problem is $y_1 + 2y_2 + 5y_3 + 6y_4 \geq V$.

(b) One of the constraints of its associated dual is $5x_1 + 4x_2 + x_3 \leq V$.

(c) Both the relations $y_1 + y_2 + y_3 + y_3 = 1$ and $x_1 + x_2 + x_3 = 1$ are true.

(d) If we consider the game from player B's point of view then player A is always trying to minimise V.

51. If the following game has a saddle point, Player B

Player A	18	β	36
	α	54	99
	63	27	36

then (a) $54 < \alpha < 60$ (b) $18 < \beta < 54$ (c) $54 < \beta < 60$ (d) $18 < \alpha < 54$.

52. Consider two games:

G1: (B columns, A rows)

A	a	0
	0	b

G2: (A_1 columns, A_2 rows)

A_2	a	$-b$
	$-c$	d

(a) Optimal strategies in G1 are: $A\left(\frac{b}{a+b}, \frac{a}{a+b}\right)$.

(b) Value of the game of G1 $= \frac{a}{a+b}$.

(c) Optimal strategies in G2 are: $A_1\left(\frac{b+d}{E}, \frac{a+c}{E}\right)$, $A_2\left(\frac{c+d}{E}, \frac{a+b}{E}\right)$.

(d) Value of the game of G2 $= \frac{ad+bc}{E}$, where $E = a+b+c+d$.

53. Which of the following statements is/are true?

(a) The different criteria for making decision under risk always yield the same optimum choice.

(b) In decision-trees, no more than two alternative courses of action can emanate from a decision point node.

(c) In decision-trees, it is necessary to know in advance all the probabilities of the chance events and all the monetary evaluations of the different alternatives.

(d) In decisions under uncertainty, the Laplace criterion is the least conservative while the minimax criterion is the most conservative.

54. Consider the system of equations: $\sigma_1 x_1 + \sigma_2 x_2 + \sigma_3 x_3 + \sigma_4 x_4 = \sigma_5$, where $\sigma_1 = \begin{pmatrix}1\\2\\3\end{pmatrix}$, $\sigma_2 = \begin{pmatrix}0\\2\\1\end{pmatrix}$,

$\sigma_3 = \begin{pmatrix}1\\4\\2\end{pmatrix}$, $\sigma_4 = \begin{pmatrix}2\\0\\0\end{pmatrix}$, $\sigma_5 = \begin{pmatrix}3\\4\\2\end{pmatrix}$.

Indicate which of the following combinations forms/form a basic:

(a) $(\sigma_1, \sigma_2, \sigma_3)$ (b) $(\sigma_1, \sigma_2, \sigma_4)$ (c) $(\sigma_2, \sigma_3, \sigma_4)$ (d) $(\sigma_1, \sigma_3, \sigma_4)$.

55. During a very small time interval h, at most one arrival can occur. The probability of an arrival occurring is directly proportional to h with the proportionality constant equal to 2. Then
   (a) The average time between two successive arrival = 0.5 time unit.
   (b) $p_0(0.5)$ = probability of no arrivals occurs during 0.5 time unit = 0.3679.
   (c) $P(t \geq 3) = 0.0024$.
   (d) $P(t \leq 2) = 0.9817$.

56. Which of the statements is/are true?
   (a) The critical path of a project network represents the minimum duration needed to complete the network.
   (b) A critical path need not constitute a connected chain of activities between the start and the terminal nodes.
   (c) A network may include more than one critical path.
   (d) If a network has more than one critical path, the duration of different paths may not be equal.

57. Consider the (4×2) game: B

A		B_1	B_2
	A_1	2	4
	A_2	2	3
	A_3	3	2
	A_4	−2	6

(a) The game has a saddle point. (b) The game cannot be solved by graphical method.

(c) A's optimal strategies are $\left(\frac{1}{3}, 0, \frac{2}{3}, 0\right)$. (d) The value of the game $v = \frac{4}{3}$.

58. Which of the following statements is/are true in the context of PERT network?
   (a) The computation of the critical path in PERT is basically different from that in CPM.
   (b) In a PERT network, there is always a 50 : 50 chance that a critical activity will be completed by its earliest (or latest) completion time.
   (c) A non-critical activity can be scheduled anywhere between its earliest start and latest completion.
   (d) The use of the normal distribution to compute the probabilities of events in PERT becomes more accurate with the increase in the number of activities leading from the start point to the event under consideration.

59. Consider a pure IPP:
Maximize $Z = 5x_1 + 7x_2$
subject to $-2x_1 + 3x_2 \leq 6$
$6x_1 + x_2 \leq 30$
$x_1, x_2 \geq 0$ and integer.
The following table represents optimal feasible non-integer solution:

		c_j	5	7	0	0
C_B	x_B	b	x_1	x_2	x_3	x_4
7	x_2	$\frac{24}{5}$	0	1	$\frac{3}{10}$	$\frac{1}{10}$
5	x_1	$\frac{21}{5}$	1	0	$-\frac{1}{20}$	$\frac{3}{20}$
		$z_j - c_j$	0	0	$\frac{37}{20}$	$\frac{29}{20}$

(a) According to Gomory's cutting plane method select x_2 to find cutting plane.
(b) Select x_1 to find the cutting plane.
(c) By using x_2 the cutting plane constraint is $\frac{3}{10}x_3 + \frac{1}{10}x_4 - \frac{4}{5} \geq 0$.
(d) Using constraint (c) to find optimal integer solution dual-simplex method is most appropriate.

60. Which of the following statements is/are true?
(a) If a constant value is added to every cost element c_{ij} in the transportation tableau, the optimal values of the variables x_{ij} will change.
(b) A balanced transportation model may not have any feasible solution.
(c) Every basic solution in the assignment problem is necessarily degenerate.
(d) The assignment problem cannot be solved by the transportation technique.

61. With reference to the figure:

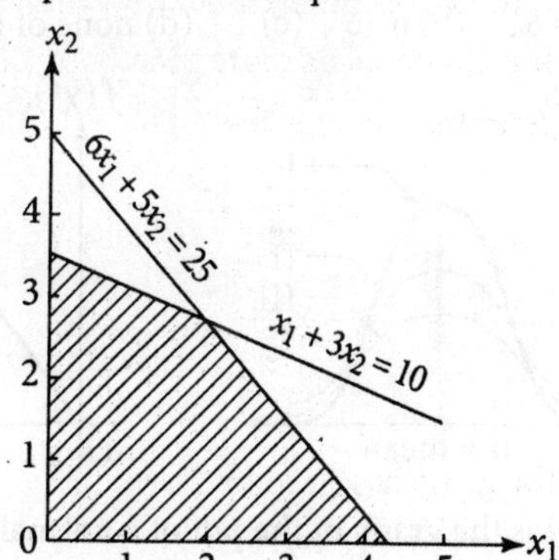

(a) The constraints of the problem are: $6x_1 + 5x_2 \leq 25$, $x_1 + 3x_2 \geq 10$, $x_1, x_2 \geq 0$.
(b) The constraints of the problem are: $6x_1 + 5x_2 \leq 25$, $x_1 + 3x_2 \leq 10$, $x_1, x_2 \geq 0$.
(c) The non-integer optimal solution: $x_1^* = \frac{25}{13}$, $x_2^* = \frac{35}{13}$.
(d) To find integer solution by branch and bounds technique we construct two branches $x_2 \leq 2$ and $x_2 \geq 3$.

62. Which of the following statements is/are true?
(a) The construction of fractional cut does not require the slack variables to be integer.
(b) In the application of cutting plane methods, it is necessary to retain all the generated cuts in the simplex tableau until the optimum integer is reached.
(c) In the branch and bound procedure, the branching step effectively removes continuous parts of the feasible space.
(d) A bound obtained by the branch and bound procedure may not necessarily be associated with a feasible point of the integer problem.

63. Which of the followings is/are not true for a distribution function $\phi(x)$
(a) $\phi(\infty) = 1$ (b) $\lim_{x \to -\infty} \phi(x) = 0$ (c) $\phi(x)$ is a strictly increasing function (d) $0 \leq \phi(x) \leq 1$.

64. If $f(x)=1-\frac{x}{2}, 0\le x\le 2$ is a pdf of an r.v. X, then $P(|X-1|<2)$ is

(a) -1 (b) 1 (c) 0 (d) $\frac{1}{3}$.

65. If $F(x)=\begin{cases}0, & -\infty<x<4\\ \frac{x-4}{2}, & 4\le x<6\\ 1, & 6\le x\le\infty\end{cases}$

be the distribution function of a uniform r.v., then its pdf on [4, 6] is

(a) $\frac{1}{3}$ (b) $\frac{1}{6}$ (c) $\frac{1}{4}$ (d) $\frac{1}{2}$.

66. If X has exponential distribution with parameter $\lambda=2$, then its pdf is

(a) $f(x)=e^{-2x}, x>0$ (b) $f(x)=2e^{-2x}, x\in(-\infty,\infty)$

(c) $f(x)=2e^{-2x}, x>0$ (d) $f(x)=2e^{-x}, x>0$.

67. If X is a normal variate with mean -2 and variance 25, then which one of the following is standard normal variate?

(a) $\frac{X-2}{5}$ (b) $\frac{X+2}{25}$ (c) $\frac{X-25}{2}$ (d) $\frac{X+2}{5}$.

68. If X and Y are two independent χ^2 variates with degrees of freedom (dof) 3 and 4 then their sum $X+Y$ is:

(a) χ^2 variate with dof 12 (b) Normal variate

(c) Gamma variate (d) χ^2 variate with dof 7.

69. For a χ^2 variate if $P(0<\chi^2<3)=0.64$, then $P(-1<\chi^2<3)$ is:

(a) 0.64 (b) 0.36 (c) 1 (d) none of these.

70.

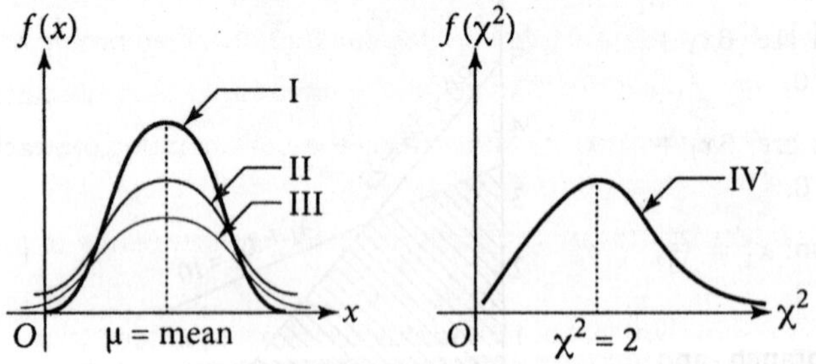

(a) I is the graph of the pdf of a normal variate, when SD $(\sigma)=0.5$.

(b) II is the graph of the pdf of a normal variate, when SD $(\sigma)=1.5$.

(c) III is the graph of the pdf of a normal variate, when SD $(\sigma)=2$.

(d) IV is the χ^2-curve for dof $n=4$.

71. Dijkstra's algorithm is used

(a) To find maximum flow in a network

(b) To scan all vertices of a graph

(c) To find the shortest path from a specified vertex to another

(d) None.

72. In Dijkstra's algorithm for a diagram if the edge AB is directed from A to B only, then we take weight on the edge BA.

(a) 0 (b) ∞ (c) $-$(weight on the directed edge AB) (d) None.

73. Minimum spanning tree is found by

(a) Dijkstra's algorithm (b) Ford's algorithm (c) Floyad's algorithm (d) Kruskal's algorithm.

74. Minimum spanning tree in a graph

(a) More than one (b) Unique

(c) Unique obtained by Kruskal's algorithm (d) Unique obtained by Ford's algorithm.

75. Using Dijkstra's algorithm the shortest path from the vertex a to f in the adjoining graph.

(a) $a-b-c-d-e-f$

(b) $a-c-b-d-e-f$

(c) $a-c-b-e-d-f$

(d) $a-e-b-c-d-f$.

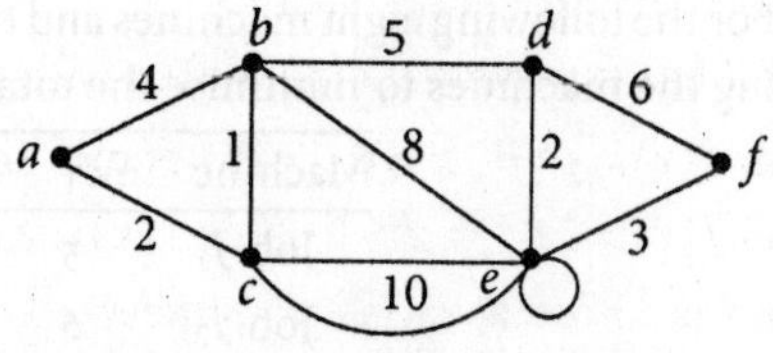

76. Using Kruskal's algorithm a minimal spanning tree weight of the adjoining network.

(a) Minimum weight = 52

(b) Minimum weight = 50

(c) Minimum weight = 10

(d) None of these.

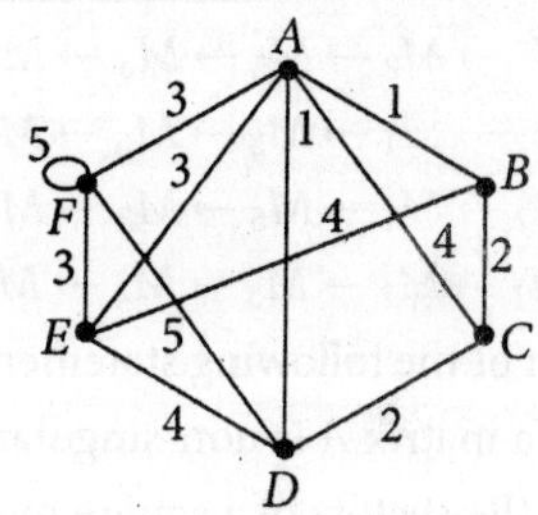

77. Which of the following statements is/are true?

(a) In dynamic programming models, the number of stages equals the number of subproblems.

(b) In dynamic programming it is usually more difficult to define the stage rather than the states.

(c) Recursive computations in dynamic programming require using the information from each of the previously considered stages in the current stage's calculations.

(d) The principle of optimality guarantees that future decisions are made independently of previously made decisions.

78. Which of the following represents/represent dynamic programming recursive equation?

(a) $f_0(x_0)=0,\ f_j(x_j)=\max\limits_{c_j(k_j)\le x_j}\{R_j(k_j)+f_{j+1}(x_j-c_j(k_j))\},\ j=1,2,\ldots$

(b) $f_0(x_0)=0,\ f_j(x_j)=\max\limits_{c_j(k_j)\le x_j}\{R_j(k_j)+f_{j-1}(x_j-c_j(k_j))\},\ j=1,2,\ldots$

(c) $f_0(x_0)=0,\ f_j(x_j)=\max\limits_{c_j(k_j)\le x_j}\{R_{j+1}(k_j)+f_j(x_j-c_j(k_j))\},\ j=1,2,\ldots$

(d) $f_0(x_0)=0,\ f_j(x_j)=\max\limits_{c_j(k_j)\le x_j}\{R_{j-1}(k_j)+f_j(x_j-c_j(k_j))\},\ j=1,2,\ldots$

79. The main unifying idea in dynamic programming problem (DPP) is

(a) Kuhn-Tucker conditions of optimality (b) Fritz-John saddle points conditions

(c) Bellman principle of optimality (d) Karmarkar principle of optimality.

80. The dynamic programming approach is applicable to

(a) Probabilistic inventory models (b) Queueing models

(c) Shortest path problem (d) Reliability improvement problem.

81. Let there be n jobs $\langle J_1, J_2, \ldots, J_n \rangle$ to be processed by m machines $\langle M_1, M_2, \ldots, M_m \rangle$ in the order $M_1 M_2 \ldots M_{m-1} M_m$. Then for finding the optimal sequence the following conditions hold good.
   (a) The minimum time on machine $M_1 \geq$ maximum time on $\langle M_2, M_3, \ldots, M_{m-1} \rangle$
   (b) The maximum time on machine $M_1 \geq$ maximum time on $\langle M_1, M_3, \ldots, M_{m-1} \rangle$
   (c) The minimum time on machine $M_m \geq$ maximum time on $\langle M_2, M_3, \ldots, M_{m-1} \rangle$
   (d) The maximum time on machine $M_m \geq$ minimum time on $\langle M_2, M_3, \ldots, M_{m-1} \rangle$.

82. For the following eight machines and two jobs sequencing problem, the optimal sequence of scheduling the machines to minimise the total elapsed time is

Machine	M_1	M_2	M_3	M_4	M_5	M_6	M_7	M_8
Job J_1	5	4	22	16	15	11	9	4
Job J_2	6	10	12	8	20	7	2	21

   (a) $M_1 \rightarrow M_2 \rightarrow M_5 \rightarrow M_3 \rightarrow M_4 \rightarrow M_8 \rightarrow M_6 \rightarrow M_7$
   (b) $M_2 \rightarrow M_1 \rightarrow M_3 \rightarrow M_5 \rightarrow M_8 \rightarrow M_4 \rightarrow M_7 \rightarrow M_6$
   (c) $M_2 \rightarrow M_1 \rightarrow M_5 \rightarrow M_3 \rightarrow M_4 \rightarrow M_6 \rightarrow M_8 \rightarrow M_7$
   (d) $M_1 \rightarrow M_2 \rightarrow M_3 \rightarrow M_4 \rightarrow M_5 \rightarrow M_6 \rightarrow M_7 \rightarrow M_8$.

83. Which of the following statements is/are true?
   (a) If a matrix A is non-singular, its vectors must be independent.
   (b) If the vectors of a square matrix A are independent its determinant must equal to zero.
   (c) In the system $AX = b$, if A is singular and b is a dependent vector, the system will have infinity of solutions.
   (d) A systems of m independent linear equations with n unknowns will always have an infinite number of solutions, when $m > n$.

84. The following is the optimal table of a certain maximisation LPP.

	c_j		3	5	4	0	0	0
c_B	x_B	b	x_1	x_2	x_3	x_4	x_5	x_6
5	x_2	$\frac{50}{41}$	0	1	0	$\frac{15}{41}$	$\frac{8}{41}$	$-\frac{10}{41}$
4	x_3	$\frac{62}{41}$	0	0	1	$-\frac{6}{41}$	$\frac{5}{41}$	$\frac{4}{41}$
3	x_1	$\frac{89}{41}$	1	0	0	$-\frac{2}{41}$	$-\frac{12}{41}$	$\frac{15}{41}$
	$z_j - c_j$		0	0	0	$\frac{45}{41}$	$\frac{24}{41}$	$\frac{11}{41}$

The ranges of c_3, c_4 for which the above current optimal solution remains optimal are:

(a) $\frac{5}{4} \leq c_3 < \infty, -\infty < c_4 \leq \frac{45}{4}$ (b) $\frac{5}{4} \leq c_3 \leq \frac{23}{2}, -\infty < c_4 \leq \frac{45}{4}$

(c) $\frac{5}{4} \leq c_3 < 11, 5 < c_4 < \infty$ (d) $11 \leq c_3 < \infty, -\infty < c_4 \leq 11$.

85. Consider the following table which represents an optimal solution to some LPP.

		c_j	2	4	1	3	2	0	0	0
c_B	x_B	b	x_1	x_2	x_3	x_4	x_5	x_6	x_7	x_8
2	x_1	3	1	0	0	-1	0	$\frac{1}{2}$	$\frac{1}{5}$	-1
4	x_2	1	0	1	0	2	1	-1	0	$\frac{1}{2}$
1	x_3	7	0	0	1	-1	-2	5	$-\frac{3}{10}$	2
	$z_j - c_j$		0	0	0	2	0	2	$\frac{1}{10}$	2

If the additional constraint $2x_1 + 3x_2 - x_3 + 2x_4 + 4x_5 \leq k$ is annexed to the system, then

(a) For $k = 5$ the current optimal solution remains optimal.
(b) For $k = 1$ the current optimal solution remains optimal.
(c) For $k = 5$ optimality condition violates.
(d) For $k = 1$ optimality condition violates.

86. Given a general LPP,

Maximize $Z = \boldsymbol{cx}$

subject to $A\boldsymbol{x} = \boldsymbol{b}$

$\boldsymbol{x} \geq \boldsymbol{0}$.

(a) Any discrete change in cost vector $\boldsymbol{c}$ will violate the condition of optimality.
(b) Any discrete change in cost vector $\boldsymbol{c}$ will violate the condition of feasibility.
(c) Any discrete change in cost vector $\boldsymbol{b}$ changes the feasibility condition.
(d) Any discrete change in cost vector $\boldsymbol{b}$ changes the optimality condition.

87. Consider the following figures:

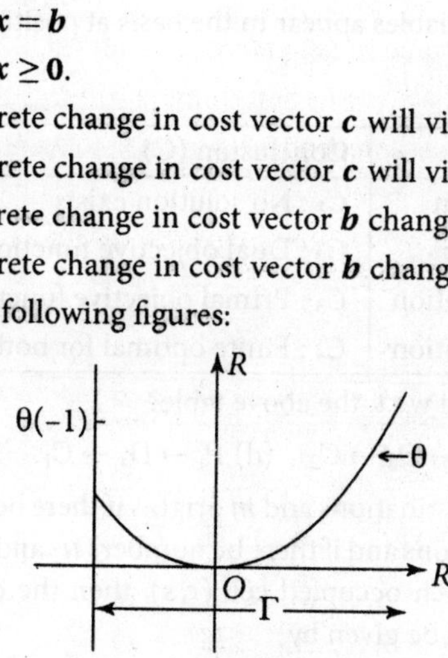

Fig. 1

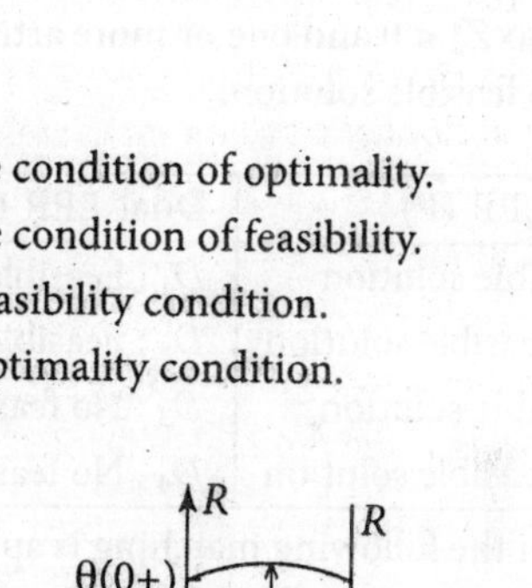

Fig. 2

(a) Fig. 1 indicates that θ is a convex function on $\Gamma = [-1, \infty)$.
(b) Fig. 2 indicates that θ is a convex function on $\Gamma = [0, 1]$.
(c) Fig. 1 indicates that θ is a convex function on $\Gamma = [-1, \infty]$.
(d) Fig. 2 indicates that θ is a concave function on $\Gamma = [0, 1]$.

88. The necessary and sufficient condition for the existence and non-degeneracy of all possible basic feasible solutions of $A\boldsymbol{x} = \boldsymbol{b}, \boldsymbol{x} \geq \boldsymbol{0}$, where A is the $m \times n$ coefficient matrix is:

(a) the linear dependence of every set of m columns of the augmented matrix $[A, b]$
(b) the linear independence of every set of m columns of the augmented matrix $[A, b]$
(c) the linear dependence of every set of m columns of the coefficient matrix A

(d) the linear independence of every set of m columns of the coefficient matrix A.

89. Which of the following conclusion is false:

(a) If the set X represents all the points on the surface of a sphere in R^3, then the whole sphere is its convex hull.

(b) A square is the convex polyhedron generated by the four vertices in R^2.

(c) A point as well as the line segment is the simplex in one dimension.

(d) If the set S represents the three vertices of a triangle in R^2, then the whole triangle is its convex hull.

90. Consider a maximisation LPP. To solve the problem by two-phase simplex method, in phase 1 usually we construct a new objective function Z^*

(a) if $\max Z^* = 0$ and all artificial variables disappear from the basis, then we get a basic feasible solution.

(b) if $\max Z^* = 0$ and one or more artificial variables appear in the basis at zero level, then we have also a basic feasible solution.

(c) if $\max Z^* < 0$ and one or more artificial variables appear in the basis at positive level, then also we have a basic feasible solution.

(d) if $\max Z^* < 0$ and one or more artificial variables appear in the basis at positive level, then there is no feasible solution.

91.

Primal LPP (P)	Dual LPP (D)	Conclusion (C)
P_1 : Feasible solution	D_1 : Feasible solution	C_1 : No solution exists
P_2 : No feasible solution	D_2 : Feasible solution	C_2 : Dual objective function unbounded
P_3 : Feasible solution	D_3 : No feasible solution	C_3 : Primal objective function unbounded
P_4 : No feasible solution	D_4 : No feasible solution	C_4 : Finite optimal for both exists

Which of the following matching is appropriate w.r.t. the above table?

(a) $P_1 \to D_1 \to C_4$ (b) $P_2 \to D_2 \to C_3$ (c) $P_3 \to D_3 \to C_2$ (d) $P_4 \to D_4 \to C_1$.

92. In a balanced transportation problem with n destinations and m origins if there be a feasible solution having $(m+n-1)$ independent positive allocations and if there be numbers u_i and v_j $(i = 1,2,\ldots,m;$ $j = 1,2,\ldots,n)$ satisfying $c_{rs} = u_r + v_s$ for each occupied cell (r,s), then the cell evaluation Δ_{ij} corresponding to the unoccupied cell (i,j) will be given by

(a) $\Delta_{ij} = c_{ij} + (u_i + v_j)$ (b) $\Delta_{ij} = c_{ij} - (u_i + v_j)$ (c) $\Delta_{ij} = c_{ij} - u_i + v_j$ (d) $\Delta_{ij} = c_{ij} + u_i + v_j$.

93. By selecting the correct option from (92), choose the appropriate alternatives from the following:

(a) If $\Delta_{ij} > 0$, then the solution of transportation problem is optimal and unique.

(b) $\Delta_{ij} < 0$, then the solution is not optimal.

(c) If all $\Delta_{ij} > 0$ with at least one $\Delta_{ij} = 0$, then the solution is optimal but not unique.

(d) If $\Delta_{ij} < 0$, then we are to seek a new basic feasible solution.

94. It is required to find the optimal replacement time of a certain type of equipment. The initial cost of the equipment is C. Salvage value and repair cost are given by $S(t)$ and $R(t)$ respectively. The cost of capital is β per cent and T is the time period of the replacement cycle. If k is the present value of the cycle, then optimal value of T is given by

(a) $R(t)+S(t)=\frac{dS(t)}{dt}+\frac{\beta k}{(1-e^{-\beta t})}$, (b) $R(t)+rS(t)=\frac{dS(t)}{dt}+\frac{\beta k}{(1-e^{-\beta t})}$,

(c) $rR(t)+S(t)=\frac{dS(t)}{dt}+\frac{\beta k}{(1-e^{-\beta t})}$, (d) $\frac{R(t)+S(t)}{r}=\frac{dS(t)}{dt}+\frac{\beta k}{(1-e^{-\beta t})}$.

95. The cost of a new machine is ₹5000. The maintenance cost during the nth year is given by $M_n =$ ₹$500(n-1)$, where $n = 1,2,3,\ldots$. If the discount rate per year is 0.05, then most economical time to replace the machine by a new one is

(a) At the end of 5th year (b) At the beginning of 5th year
(c) At the end of 4th year (d) At the beginning of 4th year.

96. In a two-person zero-sum game:

(a) Each player has finite number of strategies to use.

(b) Each specific strategy results in a payoff.

(c) Total payoff to the two players at the end of each play is zero.

(d) Not only two players are involved.

97. Consider the game G with the following payoff:

		Player B	
		B_1	B_2
Player A	A_1	2	6
	A_2	−2	λ

(a) G is not determinable unless λ is prescribed.

(b) G is strictly determinable, whatever λ may be.

(c) The value of the game is 2.

(d) The value of the game cannot be determined unless λ is prescribed.

98. On an average, 6 customers reach a telephone booth every hour to make calls. Then the probability that exactly 4 customers will reach in 30-minute period, assuming that arrivals follow Poisson distribution is

(a) 0.4 (b) 0.6 (c) 0.7 (d) 0.5.

99. Let $f(r)$ be the pdf of a continuous quantities r, C_S the shortage cost, C_H the holding cost per unit of quantity per unit of time, then the optimum level of inventory S_0, which minimises the total expected cost satisfies the condition:

(a) $F(S_0)=\frac{C_S}{C_H+C_S}$ (b) $F(S_0)=\frac{C_H}{C_H+C_S}$ (c) $F(S_0)=\frac{C_H+C_S}{C_H-C_S}$ (d) $F(S_0)=\frac{C_H-C_S}{C_H+C_S}$,

where $F(x)=\int_0^x f(r)\,dr$.

100.

Column I	*Column* II
C_1 : Deciding the quantities of the three products to be produced per week by the company.	D_1 : Queuing model.
C_2 : Opening another reservation counter at the railway station.	D_2 : Inventory model.
C_3 : Deciding the optimal lot size of a product for placing order by a trading company.	D_3 : Replacement model.
C_4 : Deciding the recruitment policy of salesman in a state on the expansion of business.	D_4 : Allocation model.

An appropriate OR model, suggested by *Column* I with *Column* II is:

(a) $C_1 \to D_1,\ C_2 \to D_2,\ C_3 \to D_3,\ C_4 \to D_4$ (b) $C_1 \to D_4,\ C_2 \to D_1,\ C_3 \to D_3,\ C_4 \to D_2$

(c) $C_1 \to D_4,\ C_2 \to D_1,\ C_3 \to D_2,\ C_4 \to D_3$ (d) $C_1 \to D_1,\ C_2 \to D_4,\ C_3 \to D_2,\ C_4 \to D_3$.

Answers of Multiple Choice Questions

Q.	Answers	Q.	Answers	Q.	Answers	Q.	Answers
1.	● ● ● (d)	26.	● ● ● ●	51.	(a) ● (c) (d)	76.	(a) (b) ● (d)
2.	● (b) ● (d)	27.	(a) (b) (c) ●	52.	● (b) ● (d)	77.	● (b) (c) ●
3.	(a) ● (c) (d)	28.	● (b) (c) (d)	53.	(a) (b) ● ●	78.	(a) ● (c) (d)
4.	● (b) ● ●	29.	● ● (c) (d)	54.	● ● (c) ●	79.	(a) (b) ● (d)
5.	● (b) ● (d)	30.	(a) ● (c) (d)	55.	● ● ● ●	80.	● (b) ● ●
6.	(a) ● (c) ●	31.	(a) ● ● ●	56.	● (b) ● (d)	81.	● (b) ● (d)
7.	● ● ● (d)	32.	● (b) (c) ●	57.	(a) (b) ● (d)	82.	(a) (b) ● (d)
8.	● (b) (c) ●	33.	● ● ● ●	58.	(a) ● (c) ●	83.	● (b) ● (d)
9.	● ● ● (d)	34.	● (b) (c) (d)	59.	● (b) ● ●	84.	(a) ● (c) (d)
10.	(a) ● ● ●	35.	● ● ● (d)	60.	(a) (b) ● (d)	85.	● (b) (c) ●
11.	(a) ● (c) (d)	36.	(a) ● ● (d)	61.	(a) ● ● ●	86.	● (b) ● (d)
12.	● (b) (c) ●	37.	(a) ● (c) (d)	62.	(a) (b) ● (d)	87.	● (b) (c) ●
13.	● ● (c) ●	38.	● (b) (c) (d)	63.	(a) (b) ● (d)	88.	(a) ● (c) (d)
14.	(a) ● ● ●	39.	● (b) (c) ●	64.	(a) ● (c) (d)	89.	(a) (b) ● (d)
15.	(a) ● ● ●	40.	(a) ● (c) (d)	65.	(a) (b) (c) ●	90.	● ● (c) ●
16.	(a) ● (c) (d)	41.	(a) ● ● (d)	66.	(a) (b) ● (d)	91.	● (b) (c) ●
17.	(a) (b) (c) ●	42.	● ● ● (d)	67.	(a) (b) (c) ●	92.	(a) (b) ● (d)
18.	(a) (b) ● (d)	43.	(a) (b) ● (d)	68.	(a) (b) (c) ●	93.	● ● ● ●
19.	(a) ● (c) (d)	44.	(a) (b) (c) ●	69.	● (b) (c) (d)	94.	(a) ● (c) (d)
20.	(a) (b) (c) ●	45.	● (b) (c) (d)	70.	● (b) ● ●	95.	● (b) (c) (d)
21.	(a) (b) (c) ●	46.	● ● (c) ●	71.	(a) (b) ● (d)	96.	● ● ● (d)
22.	● ● (c) (d)	47.	(a) ● ● (d)	72.	(a) ● (c) (d)	97.	(a) ● ● (d)
23.	● ● ● (d)	48.	(a) ● ● (d)	73.	(a) (b) (c) ●	98.	(a) (b) (c) ●
24.	(a) (b) ● (d)	49.	● (b) (c) ●	74.	● (b) (c) (d)	99.	● (b) (c) (d)
25.	● (b) ● (d)	50.	(a) (b) ● (d)	75.	(a) ● (c) (d)	100.	(a) (b) ● (d)

Index

Some exciting gifts are up for grabs with this book!!

A FIRST COURSE ON OPERATIONS RESEARCH AND INFORMATION THEORY

Dr Sanat Kumar Mazumder

FREE Gifts Rs. 1000/-

Dear Readers

By now you must have gone through this book in the entirety. So we invite your assessment on this title with absolute impartiality and candid observations. After all, we publishers blindly depend on your benchmarking. Friends, please fill up the open spaces below with CAPITAL LETTERS. You may add some extra sheets of paper if the space provided is not sufficient for you.

i. What are the important topics of your syllabus which are not adequately covered in this book?

ii. In which chapters and on what topics the treatment of the subject-matter by the author is not satisfactory and why?

iii. Have you come across the typos, factual inaccuracies, inconsistencies, and other forms of mistakes in the book? If yes, then please specify the mistakes and page numbers.

iv. Name top three books on the same subject, which, in your consideration, are better than this book. Could you provide some reasons?

Your 1st Preference: ....

Your 2nd Preference: ....

Your 3rd Preference: ....

v. Any suggestion to improve the quality of illustrations, diagrams, etc.?

vi. How did you like the cover design? Any suggestion on colours?

vii. Suggestions for further improvement of production-standard:

viii. Who recommended you this book:

☐ Teacher ☐ Friend ☐ Parents ☐ Bookseller ☐ Librarian

ix. Name of the person who has recommended:

Designation: ....

Address: ....

Phone No.: ....

e-mail: ....

x. Name and address of the bookseller from whom you have purchased this book:

....

....

....

xi. Name and address of the library where you would like to find the book:

....

....

xii. Name and address of your institution (Please mention the University or Board):

....

....

xiii. Your name, e-mail, and complete postal address:

....

....

....

xiv. A few other titles published by us that you would like to read:

....

....

The best assessment will be rewarded half-yearly. The award will be in the form of our publications, as decided by the Editorial and Marketing Operations Division, amounting to Rs. 1000/- (Rupees one thousand) only.

....

Please mail the filled up coupon at your earliest to :

Editorial & Marketing Operations Division

NEW CENTRAL BOOK AGENCY (P) Ltd

8/1 Chintamoni Das Lane, Kolkata 700 009

West Bengal, INDIA

Phone + Fax: 033 + 2241 8411, 2241 8573, 2241 9094

e-mail: ncbapvtltd@eth.net, ncba@cal2.vsnl.net.in

Website: www.centralgroup.com